D1757077

Throughout

Art and Culture Emerging with Ubiquitous Computing

edited by Ulrik Ekman
foreword by Matthew Fuller

The MIT Press
Cambridge, Massachusetts
London, England

MIT Press books may be purchased at special quantity discounts for business or sales promotional use. For information, please email special_sales@mitpress.mit.edu or write to Special Sales Department, The MIT Press, 55 Hayward Street, Cambridge, MA 02142.

This book was set in Stone Sans and Stone Serif by Toppan Best-set Premedia Limited, Hong Kong. Printed and bound in the United States of America.

Library of Congress Cataloging-in-Publication Data

Throughout : art and culture emerging with ubiquitous computing / edited by Ulrik Ekman ; foreword by Matthew Fuller.
p. cm.
Includes bibliographical references and index.
ISBN 978-0-262-01750-3 (hardcover : alk. paper) 1. Information technology—Social aspects. 2. Computers and civilization. 3. Technology and the arts. I. Ekman, Ulrik, editor of compilation.
T58.5.T499 2012
303.48'34—dc23
2011048776

10 9 8 7 6 5 4 3 2 1

Le groupe humain se comporte dans la nature comme un organisme vivant; de même que l'animal ou la plante, pour qui les produits naturels ne sont pas immediatement assimilables, mais exigent le jeu d'organes qui en préparent les éléments, le groupe humaine assimilé son milieu à travers un rideau d'objets. . . . L'étude de cette enveloppe artificielle est la Technologie, les lois de son développement relèvent de l'économie technique. En soi, l'enveloppe technique de l'homme ne possède pas d'énergie, elle fixe la tendance créatrice.

—André Leroi-Gourhan, *Évolution et techniques: Milieu et techniques*

The real perfecting of machines, which we can say raises the level of technicality, has nothing to do with an increase in automatism but, on the contrary, relates to the fact that the functioning of the machine conceals a certain margin of indetermination. . . . The machine with superior technicality is an open machine.

—Gilbert Simondon, *On the Mode of Existence of Technical Objects*

Contents

Foreword

Matthew Fuller

Computers Require Hinges

What does a world enfolded into computational processes feel like, look like? How does it work? These questions concern many, and for one inquiry into such a world it might be appropriate to turn to a text from early in the history of computing. In 1851, a modest proposal was delivered to the public by Alfred Smee, a renowned surgeon and Fellow of the Royal Society. Smee's plan was for a remarkable device for the computing and evaluation of English-language statements, which built on his research into Galvanism (chemical and biological forms of electromagnetism) and that he named "electrobiological language." It was to combine a logical ordering of the structure of language with an understanding of the human body's nervous activity.

In the plan for Smee's Relational Machine (figure F.1), each word in the English language was to be assigned a number or a letter according to kind and ordered according to a geometrical hierarchy, with the act of thinking consisting of soberly comparing the relations between these symbols. Smee noted that although the work may be done algebraically, a machine is preferable because "each cypher may be best represented by any contrivance, the parts of which continually divide by a hinge joint into two portions." The proposal aimed to create conditions in which language might become exact, reducible to compressed statements in cipher, where "the entire words of the English language were arranged in their mutual relations" (Smee 1851, 25).[1]

Given that a number of Smee's example statements are conspicuously racialized, it is notable that this system was not solely to be a matter of conforming consciousness to a higher order, but one in which statements could be arranged by different creeds or sets of belief materialized in their own sets of geometrical articulation (Smee 1851, 49). The Differential Machine, a variant form of the project, was to provide a means of exemplifying the laws of logical judgment, but with a twist. At the same time as promulgating a plurality of reason, Smee also proposed an "artificial system of reasoning," the correct use of which would guarantee that "no form of sophistry or quibble can be successfully employed" (1851, 38), the machine being useful in this way for

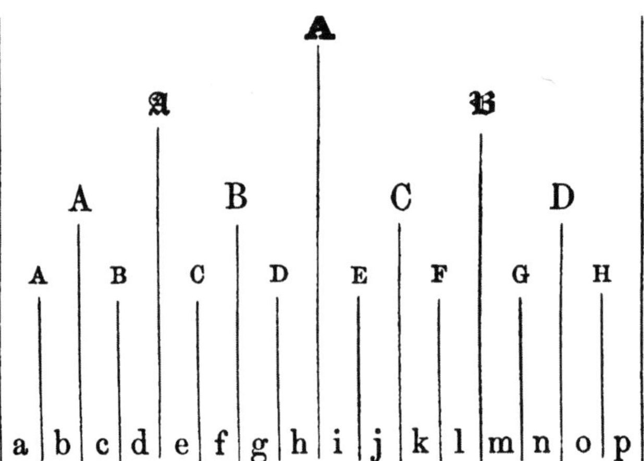

Figure F.1
Alfred Smee's Relational Machine.
Source: From Smee 1851, 41.

the settling of civil and criminal trials according to logical principle and adherence to the correctly phrased law.

Although contemporaneous to Charles Babbage's long attempts to produce mechanical calculation machines, this linguistic computer had no planned level of automation. Its hand-powered machinic form, the precise design of which remains obscure, did produce, however, certain problems that placed it in direct relation to the city in which it was envisaged, as Smee noted: "When the vast extent of a machine sufficiently large to include all words and sequences is considered, we at once observe the absolute impossibility of forming one for practical purposes, inasmuch as it would cover an area exceeding probably all London, and the very attempt to move its respective parts upon each other, would inevitably cause its own destruction" (1851, 43).

In the present day, thanks to miniaturization, the logical equivalent of such a device can fit into a semiconductor. For Smee, thought was a process of ease and efficiency, but the brain, being of God's work, would never be improved upon by mere artfulness. Thanks to the living complexity of language and the material culture of his time, upon which the whole thing hinged, the Differential Machine and the Relational Machine were sadly unfeasible. Although Smee's project was not conceptually unrelated to earlier projects proposed by others, such as Gottfried Leibniz, for the rationalization and logical machining of language or in the present day to certain tendencies in artificial intelligence, it is perhaps the first of such schemes to perform a collapse of the scales of logic, language, and space. As such, it is one that makes an ideal precursor to the fields of ubiquitous or pervasive computing, urban computing, augmented reality, and mixed reality, which alongside locative media are the currents that in their variegation, resonances, and splits form a context for this volume.

Smee's map is far larger than the territory in spatial terms, but it is linguistically substantially more compressed, and here there is another convergence with the subject of this book. Small pockets of space, an icon, or a patch of street opens up into multifarious imaginings, access to vast networks, or the collective mumblings and inanities of hundreds of fellow citizens—arrangements with enormous and unprecedented capacity for dynamics of interrelation and the condensation and expansion of such relations. And here Smee's anticipation of the self-destructive impossibilities of his machine are instructive. Language, standing in for culture more generally, is in excess of machining. Machines, also part of culture, produce worlds beyond the capacity of the simply human scale. Somewhere in the interplay between the forces that cannot be circumscribed by the particularities of the one or the other and riddled with influences from other scales is computational culture. As mentioned, Smee's system has resonances with other attempts to systematize the whole of language or the interpretation of movement to set out laws and taxonomies—to establish underlying architectures for thought, language, culture. Quite a number of these attempts have arisen as research projects in computing; others with more specialized usages are widespread. Another approach is possible however, one based around the recognition of patterns or patching; the recognition of the unstability of systems and of multiplicitous forces acting with, among, and against each other with different effects; and the recognition of objects, knowledge, and events at each scale. Again, many obscure and rather more familiar computational systems take such a stance. Among them, this book puts in place something of such a lively patchwork approach toward the assemblage of a cultural recognition of the prospects of ubiquitous computing (ubicomp).

As such, this foreword, responding to the diversity and energy of approaches here, does not attempt to provide a summary overview of the book, something its editor achieves more insightfully in the introduction. What I aim to do here is to circulate a few responses, little relational machines in their own way, that travel among the various sections and contributions assembled here in order to draw out some resonances and questions. These responses, together with the grouping of texts along thematic lines in the book's sections, aim to develop, as one might in a database, different *views* onto the materials assembled here to recognize certain aspects of the ways in which these texts speak to each other and to the contemporary problematics of art and culture emerging with ubicomp.

Early Ubiquity

To begin rather abruptly then, it would perhaps be relatively easy to write off the preliminary work in ubiquitous computing as the result of the site of its genesis.

Xerox fluffed the opportunity to capitalize on its brilliant early development of windowing systems and in the end saw the interface devices and concepts largely developed at its Palo Alto Research Center (PARC) providing the inspiration for the Macintosh (another such source being the product design of Dieter Rams–era Braun) and subsequently, so the story goes, for Windows. For the researchers at PARC, on the opposite coast to Xerox's corporate head office and far more substantially plugged into research at nearby Stanford and local professional networks than was the company that hosted them, the capacity to experiment was both imperative and possible. The idea of promoting a third generation of computing, first the mainframe, with many users time-sharing one computer, then the personal computer (PC), with one user to one computer, and then many computers time-sharing one user or flows of users shared in the progressive narratives of liberation that these earlier generations, in particular the PC, had been prone to. In such a context, ubicomp might be assumed simply to be the human-factors imaginary of an office equipment company dreaming of a computational update to its competitors' products. The early image of what ubicomp might be is suggested in an early popularizing text, which gives us the image of computers refigured as Post-it notes, whiteboards, employee name tags, and locationally aware telephone forwarding systems (Weiser 1991). You might say they were the hardware equivalent of apps, but, perhaps more interesting, the model also shifts computing from being a monolinear process to being a multidimensional process.

A notable contemporary competitor was virtual reality (VR). VR (except in much of the science fiction of the time, which generally networked it—in another, rather more charred liberation narrative—as a collective hallucination) was an outgrowth of the PC, but one paradigmatically concerned with the rate at which polygons can be thrown at an eyeball. That is, it incorporated the human perceptual mechanism into a classic problem of computing in relation to time. How much processing power and how much resolution does it require to induce a user to sense a three-dimensional world without experiencing perceptual conversion problems? Such a question once implied a supposed future convergence point of all media, especially those locked into the ocular socket. Now (as if this particular point in time when I write has anything substantial to itself as assayer of futures and pasts) VR is a rather specialist technology with uses in occupational therapy and scientific imaging. It hit something of a brick wall through its combination of computational complexity with an adherence to aesthetic realism. Realism has a complicated and troubled history in the arts, and its particular manifestation in VR tends to be governed by a technical adherence to perspective as a symbolic form—that is to say, by stepping right into the visual high tech of the Renaissance (Panofsky 1993). In some respects, this step can be seen as quite an historical advance on computing's perennial fascination with a pop Platonic or, at best, Kantian understanding of beauty as the conceptual horizon for aesthetics. Given this, ubicomp's scattered and, one might say, even fragmented image of computing with multiple devices provides a promising step toward other forms of aesthetic drive.

Mark Weiser's image of a fragmented, partial form of computing is one that decreases the staging of computing, proposing one that is peripheral, intuitive, and nonostentatious. His modest advocacy of ethnography in the first flush of its integration within corporate information technology speaks of a welcoming idealism, though one that kept the sociologists, cognitive scientists, and others at the opposite end of the building separate from the computer scientists. At PARC, ideas from the humanities and social sciences were used as means of deriving new perspectives in computer science rather than as part of a fully fledged commitment to interdisciplinarity. The root humanism of ubicomp at this phase was one that de-emphasized the foregrounding of computers to make their manifestations freer and "unobtrusive" (Weiser 1993b), a term that perhaps describes more fully than *ubiquity* the quality Weiser sought. To write ubicomp off, then, as a branch of futurism for stationers is potentially rather preemptive.

Preemption of another sort might be rather more germane to the topic, however. Although the sites of the foundational devices and texts of ubicomp may be many and dispersed away from a terminal, they are by and large gathered round a person or what passes for a person—namely, patterns of events in software, in sensors, that are read as behaviors signifying intentions or conditions. And here is one crucial distinction between many of the contributions to this book and the earlier formulations of ubicomp: an awareness that a reliance on pattern recognition and the prediction of future behaviors on the basis of recorded traces of habits is something requiring critical attention. Such awareness is something that partially differentiates early work in ubicomp from some of its other competitors—for instance, the intelligent agent, proposed by Nicholas Negroponte, among others, and the models of intimate computing or personal dynamic media, promulgated by Alan Kay and collaborators (Kay and Goldberg 1977), which aimed, by other means, to make the computer more personal.

Among the aspects of culture that this book probes are the specificities of the particular scales at which such attention might operate. Mark Hansen's arguments for an aesthetics at the scale of microsensation imply, as he notes, forms of interrelation, which may be disjunctive with those of longer durations, such as those of media systems, but these forms afford fragmentary connections to wider networks, themselves of different kinds and pacings, modes of address, valorization, and recognition. Such systems may also be manifest in economic, political, and computational terms at multiple scales and produce further disjoint entities such as data sets and customer and user profiles, tracking and inducing value, plugging flickers of affect into share-price indexes or fits of the giggles. In addition to such disjunctions, there are strange loops between different schema by which multiple scales and temporalizations of perception are interrelated. As Stamatia Portanova has suggested in relation to dance's cadences, numberings, and rhythm, calculational forms themselves move in and out of conscious perception, involving several different layers of sensation, coordination, planning, and other modes of thought at different levels of abstraction, not precluding the transcendental because abstractions are woven in at multiple scales and moments of the dance (2009, 245). Such work suggests that the autonomy of the neural may be partial and momentary, not absolute. Katherine Hayles develops in her chapter here an argument for understanding such processes in terms of a refiguring of information and thus continues some of the crucial work done in her book *How We Became Posthuman* (1999). Such an approach is inherently multiscalar, recognizing different sites at which information is generated, ingested, informed—each site in different perspectival modes and contexts and at different states of an interpretative process. Differing in kind, timing, mechanism, and spatialization but articulable as variegated yet coherent processes, each scale bears relation in turn to different forms of intellection, abstraction, and physicality. The question running among various texts in this book and giving one of several inflections to the title is how integrated or not these scales and systematizations may be.

To return to what is parsed as a person: many ubicomp devices do not take records of their usage. Others do or can be hooked up to do so in great detail. Certain of these devices are also saturated in connections to networks of other devices, databases, and recording. They might ostensibly be very good and proper, as in instruments that record someone's vital signs and prompt any necessary medical measures. Other mechanisms might enable the discovery or analysis of other kinds of unrecognized phenomena. In other cases, however, in the making recordings of events and the "personalizing" of interactions with populations of users on the basis of predictions based on such records, a risk is run of preempting the future on the basis of the past. Smee recognized this risk in the closing chapter of his proposal. It was ultimately deemed impossible to restrain the development of language to the axiomatic workings of a machine simply because there can be what he nicely calls "quibbles" of interpretation or use—in other words, because language changes over time and in context. Political interpretations of such things, filtered through different means of formulating the questions (as issues of privacy, surveillance, control, and so on), ally themselves to interpretations that are also aesthetic in nature. One question to ask of such things is how, in a system that hones in on the personal on the basis of recorded habits, may the new arise? A further question is how best to recognize the cultural valence of models and predictions, abstract operators, as active in themselves.

Among such abstract operators, a characteristic of certain strands of contemporary aesthetics is their development as open systems. Such systems maintain relatively coherent sets of behaviors despite their constitution by changing sets of different entities or energies flowing in and out of them and by those that are readily able to conjoin or interoperate with others. Choosing the right pinch points, the precise means of articulating these movements; establishing the anatomy of linkages, constraints, and derivations between movements and the ways they are attended to; and, in turn, tracing or inventing means by which such pinch points can themselves be handled by distributed agency become crucial to an aesthetics of such systems. But a description of such artfulness can equally be applied to contemporary forms of control, making the recognition of patterns and the choice of patterns to invent or attend to becomes a crucial ethical as well as aesthetic task.

Calm

Following this ethicoaesthetic conjuncture, it is not clear if the founders of ubiquitous computing imagined their project in relation to art. But one aspect of contemporary computing that seems to attract dissensus in this volume is the optimal amount of arousal to be generated in users. Ubicomp was originally envisaged as an enabling, "calm" (Weiser and Brown 1995, 1996), pleasant, and effective way of getting things done. In commentary on more recent manifestations, which are proliferating in terms of nomenclature into differing tendencies in pervasive computing, physical computing, tangible media, locative media, and so on, we are reminded that "there are powerful informatics underlying the apparent simplicity of the experience, but they never breach the surface of awareness: things Just Work" (Greenfield 2006, 1).

For anyone versed in the sociology or philosophy of technology, things never "just work," not on their own. As Smee's machines show, things barely even exist without cascades of operations on and around them in order to stabilize and modify their operations. As Kristin Veel notes in her chapter, following Paul Valéry in a formulation shared by Roberto Simanowski, art, by contrast, calls attention to itself or, perhaps further, takes part in the arranging of attention, occluding its peripheries. There is a great deal of sleight of hand, of behind-the-scenes number crunching or prop lifting, in maintaining the theater of operations with apparent smoothness. It may be the case that certain layers in art systems are submerged beneath the levels of particular kinds of aesthetic interpretation or operation. It is in part the particular repertoire of calling attention to itself that defines the art concerned. But attention itself is mutable, mobile, and fallible; particular attunements to certain qualities of tone, tension, pace—the range of expressive capacities of various elements in a composition that are induced, encouraged, entrained, provoked, or perhaps not quite reached—characterize much of what is valuable in art, but which we yet have to learn to work with in computing.

At times, there is a direct contradiction between calm smartness and art. Calmness is a quality that may be desirable in vehicle satellite-navigation devices or expert systems for surgeons, but even in these cases whether technology is "commanded"

(Weiser and Brown 1996) or "dwelt" with (Weiser and Brown 1995), it may be arrived at only during a sweet spot when all other factors are conducive. Using such technologies, at least in the affective mode prescribed, requires that one not be faced with hemorrhaging patients on the operating table or vehicles stacked with screaming offspring or maddening delivery schedules. That is to say, as many of the contributors of this volume aver, calmness is an emergent property of the interactions of multiple scales of entity and process, not something that can be technically delivered as an item on a checklist of features. Calm may indeed be something generated by users in spite of the technical features of the devices with which they operate. Calm is the state of moral people tranquilly going about their allotted business, but it is also the state of sleep of the crew of a BP oil rig who "inhibited" alarms designed to register malfunctioning equipment (Pilkington 2010a, 2010b).[2] The twist of the artwork's "opening out," in Lev Vygotsky's (1971) terms, into the unexpected is perhaps more appropriate.

In a strange echo of such a capacity, Noortje Marres's (2009) study of the use of technology such as green smart meters to monitor domestic energy consumption in "green living experiments" is used to show how the system of energy controls to monitor and change habits in relation to climate damage is currently "undoable," unfeasible rather than reversible, at the level of the individual or household. It is tricky, even improper, to be calm about the nature of energy supplies and the convolutions that the artifacts that use them put users through in the overdeveloped world. But even with wall-to-wall informatic carpeting that runs from fridges to kettles to meters to blogs, finding means of recognizing and effectively working on their entanglements is more difficult. If ecological interwovenness is often beneath and beyond our abilities to perceive and ostensibly beyond our capacities to "do," a raging calmness is thus a common result. Another option, as Marres advises, is to start experimenting with things.[3]

Such experiments may do well to start by reworking the preconditions of usefulness or implicit desiderata in computing. Humanist approaches to computing abjure what is often perceptively called "data fetishism," which tends to valorize the qualities of the artificial, the nonintimate, the alienated and manipulable in favor of the truthful supported subject. An "evil" or sophistic approach to contemporary media might see this fetishism as precisely a point where media become interesting, with overt artificiality providing the grounds to escape from what is presented as a natural fait accompli (Fuller and Goffey 2010). Nevertheless, one suggested response to information overload in this vein is wise: to demand more. As an example of how access to information should be, how it should feel, Mark Weiser suggests that it bears comparison to a refreshing walk in the woods, an ecological situation absolutely laden with information, but perhaps not as much as is immediately demanding of a contemporary office worker (1991, 104). For others, different relations run through woods, perhaps, as Weiser (1996) notes on this motif in a later text, the traces of recently passing animals. Alternately, as the historian of commons Peter Linebaugh asks, "Are the woods beautiful or horrible? . . . The answer depends on whether you were a baron or a commoner" (2008, 27).[4] Regardless of the starkness of his contrast, it is an illustrative one that chimes with considerations of the ethical dimensions of systems.

Perhaps it makes a certain sense not merely to demand and create more information and data, but also to demand access to the structures and powers by which information is connected to processes that create the opposite of calm or, more accurately, that see the presence or absence of calm as something open to speculation—that turn a liability, a likelihood, or a debt into property and a trait into a risk. As ready examples of ubicomp, sensors in building information systems are in turn often linked to regulations, insurance policies, international standards, landscapes of smoothly interlocking or ill-fitting and grating machining, much of which is kept highly peripheral to consciousness. According to which databases or systems one consults, locations are linked to administrative regions, health policies, transport mechanisms, systems that channel and produce certain kinds of expressivity of their parts. The recent pseudo-scandals around climate science, derived from hacked emails and documents concerning in part where certain sensors were sited or claimed to be sited, illustrate to a staggeringly verbose extent how much the nuance and precision of the kinds of media systems under discussion here are interlocked with wider systems of evaluation, recording, contestation, and manipulation. Showing your working seems increasingly imperative (see Rusell 2010). To make such things appear calm by reducing their degree of interrogability is unhelpful in this regard. Experiments with the nature of contemporary media—as exemplified in projects such as *Google Will Eat Itself* by UBERMORGEN, Paulo de Cirio, and Alessandro Ludovico, discussed by Inke Arns in this book—provide a means of opening up such dynamics, making them recurse in interestingly tricky, revelatory, and discombobulating ways.

Ubiquity Distributions

Christiane Paul notes the dark irony in the term *ubiquity* in a world where, like the figurations of the woods mentioned earlier, access to clean drinking water is effectively a privilege of the accident of birth. The saturation of computing in spaces around individuals and in workplaces, homes, roads, hospitals, cities, and elsewhere is wildly uneven in its global distribution. Certain parts of the world are making major subventions in terms of lifetimes (through the poisoning of workers by production chemicals and overwork and the violent treatment of trade unionists), ecological despoliation (through metals poisoning), and chronic low-intensity conflict (through the mining of Coltan, used in many mobile devices, which funds the civil war in Congo)[5] in order that these computing systems are rolled out. What makes possible the massive proliferation of integrated circuits, sensors, antennae, and networks in certain parts of the planetary landscape? One answer points to the inventive development of small-scale operating systems suitable for embedding in chips that is coming from academic operating-system research and FLOSS[6] in particular; another answer involves the improvement in battery technologies—both answers suggesting that the subject be addressed in another mode of technological history (Weiser 1993a). Yet another answer, however, is the price of labor—the massive and perhaps temporary cheapening of it in manufacturing in global terms—and the lackadaisical attitude to primary materials such as metals generated by many contemporary systems of ownership and consumption.

Such disparity will draw readers to question not simply the equitability of the systems that arrange such distributions, but also the traits of technologies, their uses, and the assemblages they form. Under the literal and conceptual violence of neoliberalism, markets have been imposed, in Michel Foucault's (2008) term, as the means of veridiction for the value of things. Markets of various kinds act as a means of computing an assumed correct value for a thing, which, alongside digitization, means that the vast disjunctive, barely interlocking systems of equivalences put in place and invented in various kinds of capitalism operate at a certain scale as a form of computational process. Questions can be thrown at them that are location based, personalized, and time sensitive and that tend to produce an answer in a set of languages that is highly interoperable: money. At other times, markets will make decisions autonomously and at yet others become articulate through forms of subjectivication such as "positive thinking" (Ehrenreich 2009). Numerous patches and work-arounds such as local-economy trading schemes, gangs, corruption, education, calculational systems, governments, illicit and licit flows of information, nations, cultures, systems of mutual aid, revolutions of various kinds, and many other measures have been found necessary to keep this computer from crashing or burning out its hardware and are in turn ameliorated and eroded by it. Like ubicomp, capitalisms, too, are unequally distributed. Other means for the computation of value in terms other than monetary are constantly being generated. Needless to say, some of these means are far in excess of mere common-or-garden capitalism (faced with, let's say, running a design studio or a small holding, with its straightforward emphasis on keeping things ticking over and enjoyable, often uselessly so). But alongside and interwoven with computational and networked digital media, more than one "environmental" system of calculation, slipping in and out of direct perception, and the multiple interfaces between them are to be reckoned with.

Expanded Minds and Inventive Commons

One of the important discussions running through this book is how ubicomp environments may contribute to software-sorted societies as a form of iniquitous computing.

As the human geographer Stephen Graham has noted, "Code-based technologised environments continuously and invisibly classify, standardise, and demarcate rights, privileges, inclusions, exclusions, mobilities and normative social judgements across vast, distanciated, domains" (2005, 568). Sorting occurs in terms of access to infrastructures, spaces, networks, and allocation for special measures, or what Graham calls "life-chances." Heath Bunting (2010), working with art as a domain in which to register such processes, has produced a substantial volume of maps and diagrams of such gating systems in his Status Project. Enormous concatenations of Boolean yeses and noes chart biographies and their inverses, untaken or untakable paths through life, and the formalisms that enfold them. The events and blockages mapped by Bunting happen in very fine-grained or long-drawn-out real-time states.

As space becomes increasingly coupled with software, often lacking any kind of public scrutiny, it is increasingly reforged by processes equivalent to the much-mooted abandonment of "net neutrality" on the Internet. That is, network organizations provide access to certain sites or services at differential rates or qualities according to alliances, cartels, or systems of paybacks, leaving those without access to such systems with slower and more decrepit functionality. However, software sorting is not simply a form of enclosure but also produces new kinds of spatial relation—for example, the world of logistics, long abstracted and improved by the techniques of operations research. Thus, rather than being seen as a second layer, something that might sit on top of society and order it, software and computational processes more generally are more adequately recognized as a fundamental part of culture and the social. Indeed, both the technical and the cultural are fundamentally mixed and always unevenly require new forms of ideation and understanding to articulate them. Things become more like software, more algorithmic, and computationality in turn mutates in different ways as it comes into combination with other kinds of material, numerous kinds of processes of thinking and sensing of different kinds of understanding, creating, sorting, and deleting. This process should not be understood as it is in the celebrations of some recent branches of media studies in which the grammar of "copy–paste" becomes a glib paradigm for repetitive effusion about new literacies, but rather it should be understood as more fundamental and multifaceted, with the proliferation of layerings of systems. The impact of computational culture on cities, buildings, and space drives innumerable kinds of change.

The kinds of technologies that this book presents are often ambivalently described as "disruptive," presenting new entrepreneurial or other possibilities while shaking out older compositions (Christensen 1997). There may be more than one set of finely looped contradictions at work in the rhetoric regarding the production of the new, couched as this rhetoric often is in terms of being a discreet enabler of a modest but comfortable, creative, but regularly expressed Western lifestyle committed to securing itself against the instabilities that it in turn plays a part in generating. The question

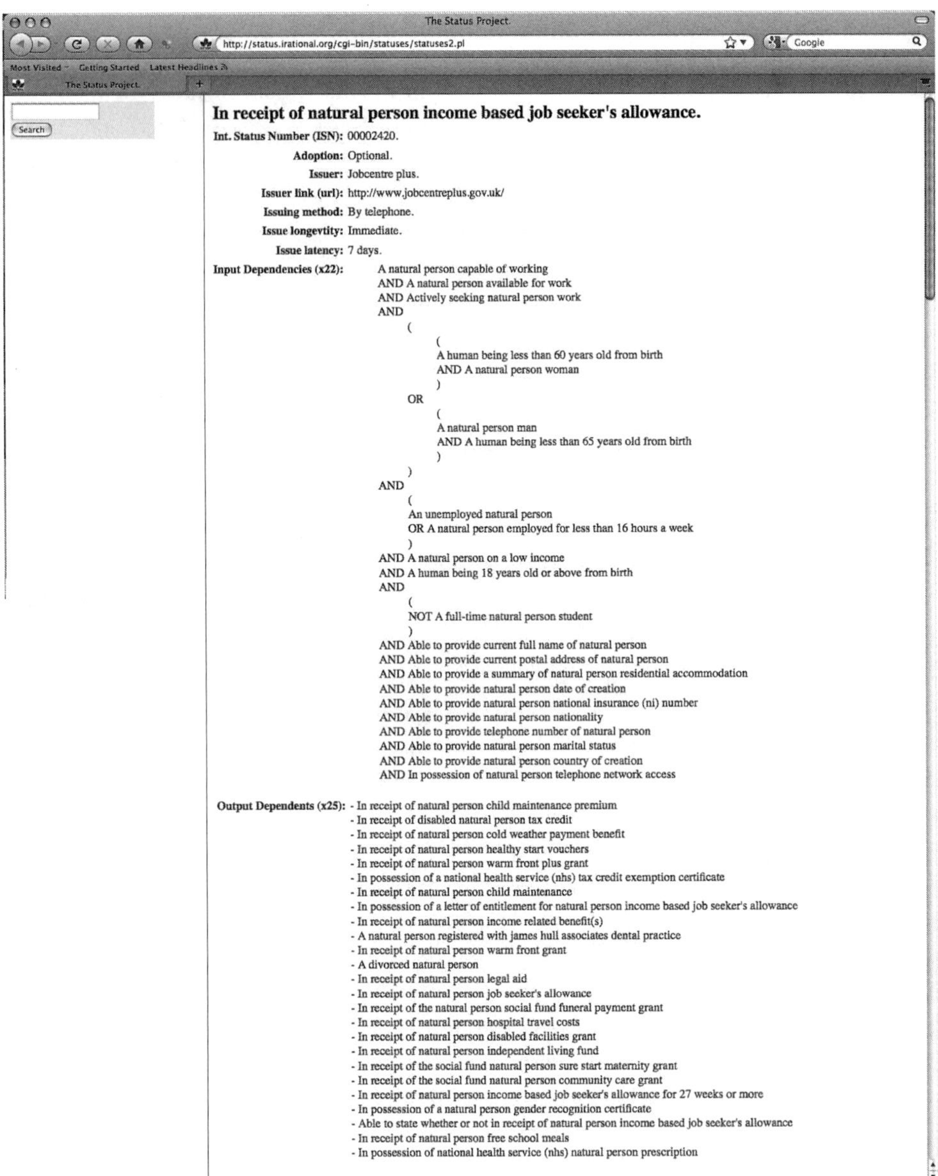

The Status Project.

http://status.irational.org/cgi-bin/statuses/statuses2.pl

Most Visited · Getting Started · Latest Headlines

The Status Project.

Search

In receipt of natural person income based job seeker's allowance.

Int. Status Number (ISN): 00002420.
Adoption: Optional.
Issuer: Jobcentre plus.
Issuer link (url): http://www.jobcentreplus.gov.uk/
Issuing method: By telephone.
Issue longevtity: Immediate.
Issue latency: 7 days.

Input Dependencies (x22):

A natural person capable of working
AND A natural person available for work
AND Actively seeking natural person work
AND
(
(
A human being less than 60 years old from birth
AND A natural person woman
)
OR
(
A natural person man
AND A human being less than 65 years old from birth
)
)
AND
(
An unemployed natural person
OR A natural person employed for less than 16 hours a week
)
AND A natural person on a low income
AND A human being 18 years old or above from birth
AND
(
NOT A full-time natural person student
)
AND Able to provide current full name of natural person
AND Able to provide current postal address of natural person
AND Able to provide a summary of natural person residential accommodation
AND Able to provide natural person date of creation
AND Able to provide natural person national insurance (ni) number
AND Able to provide natural person nationality
AND Able to provide telephone number of natural person
AND Able to provide natural person marital status
AND Able to provide natural person country of creation
AND In possession of natural person telephone network access

Output Dependents (x25):

- In receipt of natural person child maintenance premium
- In receipt of disabled natural person tax credit
- In receipt of natural person cold weather payment benefit
- In receipt of natural person healthy start vouchers
- In receipt of natural person warm front plus grant
- In possession of a national health service (nhs) tax credit exemption certificate
- In receipt of natural person child maintenance
- In possession of a letter of entitlement for natural person income based job seeker's allowance
- In receipt of natural person income related benefit(s)
- A natural person registered with james hull associates dental practice
- In receipt of natural person warm front grant
- A divorced natural person
- In receipt of natural person legal aid
- In receipt of natural person job seeker's allowance
- In receipt of the natural person social fund funeral payment grant
- In receipt of natural person hospital travel costs
- In receipt of natural person disabled facilities grant
- In receipt of natural person independent living fund
- In receipt of the social fund natural person sure start maternity grant
- In receipt of the social fund natural person community care grant
- In receipt of natural person income based job seeker's allowance for 27 weeks or more
- In possession of a natural person gender recognition certificate
- Able to state whether or not in receipt of natural person income based job seeker's allowance
- In receipt of natural person free school meals
- In possession of national health service (nhs) natural person prescription

Figure F.2

A page from *The Status Project*.

Source: Heath Bunting, *The Status Project*, 2005-onward, http://status.irational.org.

of instability and even of disruption tends to mitigate against simple patterning or the readily formalizable, so understanding the ramifications of disruptions is something carried out very well by the fine-tunings and sensitivities exemplified in the explicitly cultural. The shift to an emphasis on a computational nature undergirding contemporary social formations is recognizable, for instance, in the ideas of swarming.

Also working on a means of understanding the implications of such technologies through models attuned to nonlinear processes, Bernard Stiegler recalls Andre Leroi-Gourhan's formulation of a "third memory"—that which is formed in objects, language, "mnemotechnics"—as something belonging to the species, but that also becomes part of a milieu of individuation. Here, a multiscalar interrelation of parts that is understood in connection to Gilbert Simondon's theories of the genesis of technical forms —a mapping of the process of becoming of things in morphologic, energetic, and conceptual terms—is traced across to language, systems of recording and circulating, and means for ideas and information to persist. The stakes, as Stiegler rightly assesses, are high. The systems by which memory, understanding, and possible mutualities are achieved fold into the determination of the genesis of the cultures of which they are part. And importantly, although the species whose work is under discussion here is understood to be experiencing many kinds of coevolution with technology, among which it emerges, being able to differentiate among *techné* and to develop critical analyses of such processes becomes a significant and more complex problem.

This question of the genesis of culture is approached from a different angle by Malcolm McCullough, for whom ubicomp implies a notion of the commons. But this commons is developing in ways that are different and sometimes supplementary to those that have hitherto been founded. Commons are collective processes of sustenance and differentiation rather than, like Smee's hinged concatenation of statements, simply those processes that may be codified in advance by lawyers, although they may certainly articulate themselves through legal codes, licenses, and other means.[7] For ubiquitous information, the classical lament that the commons is inherently subject to tragedy and abuse is pertinent, but not the whole story. Commons may be invented, fought over, negotiated, and reinvented. It is partly the tussle of figuring things out that makes them commons, demanding arrangements be made rather than leaving them to fiat.

The question of the public domain that arises at numerous times in this volume can be pertinently rethought according to some secondary consequences of the extended mind thesis in which, for Andy Clark and others, "portions of the external world thus often function as an extra-neural memory store" (Clark 2000, 141). The question of the commons, when taken as an active rather than passive resource, suggests that such a tendency should not be limited to questions of memory but can also be reflected on as what Ed Hutchins calls "cognitive ecologies" (2008, p. 2011), in which what the archeologists Lambros Malafouris and Colin Renfrew call "ontological coalitions" (2010, 4) between different states of matter—organized as machines, minds, ambiences, objects, producing complex states of mentation and sensation as bodies—interact with the rest of world. But the question of the commons also means, as a number of authors suggest here, that media systems and devices are also inherently more collective than they might be imagined (especially in a world that is in parts tending to experiment with walled gardens as a backlash against what can thusly be recast as the abundant but passé phase of open experimentation on the Web).

Commonality as such, then, is also constituted by the nonpersonal and the prepersonal, meaning that the astute emphasis here on ambience and atmospheres, as discussed by Torben Sangild and Ulrik Schmidt, can be crucial in determining the pleasure, inclusiveness, and viability as well as, indeed, the nature of the computational commons and its discontents and thus also in developing the modes of memory, experience, and genesis this commons undergoes and affords.

Multithreading Realities

Just as conviviality—collective movements of differentiation—emerges as a form of extended mind, there is also a sense in which ubiquitous computing has become a crucial locus for various kinds of understanding and work to meet each other, driven by the possibilities of a field that is as yet undetermined, in which classical lines and trajectories of politics, conflict, and invention are being drawn and redrawn in a way that yields the necessity of sustained thought and urgent experiment and yet that is also manifest in grand schemes, vast scales of investment, the clenching and flexing of regimes of ownership and control ranging from the apportioning of the electromagnetic spectrum to the arrangement of standards.

What is taken as ubicomp here is rather different from what was given in some of the original prognoses of the field: mobile phones, surveillance cameras, finite-state machines running as antishoplifting devices and automatic doors, radio-frequency identification technologies, as well as additional paradigms of layering, tactility, and augmentation. Mobile phones, for example, appear in this book in multiple guises: as sites for the development of art projects and films; as, in Lev Manovich's astute analysis, key platforms for the economization and invention of experience (that are attractive rather than invisible) (see also Weiser 1994); but also as loci for the intensification and sorting of kinds of interaction. These kinds of ubicomp may in turn be supplemented by the numerous kinds of enthusiasm seen in recent years for more hands-on engagement with electronics and the production of custom gadgets stirred by the proliferation of free and open-source software and an accompanying cycle of interests in hacking, the abundant availability of information and plans via the Web, and the development of new rapid prototyping tools as exemplified in fablabs and hacklabs. As the sites of computing spread and change, they are arranged in correspondence with other tendencies, including, as authors here clearly mark, the gearing of societies toward consumption rather than toward knowledgeable engagements with production.

The city has often been understood as a mechanism for allowing the incommensurable to exist side by side with multithreading realities. This is one of the motifs of the great nineteenth-century novels mentioned here by Michael Bull: the moral scandal of cocooning, of distanciation, has never failed to be revived, whether it is achieved by a railway seat and a cheap Balzac or Dickens novel or by the back seat of a bus and an MP3 player (see Williams 1973 and Moretti 1998). The proximity and differentiation of spatialities, thoughts, manufacture, reading, indifference, rage, and autonomy—of all the subtle movements of contraband and ostentation, the play of the visible—that provide the psychosocial matrices of the novel couple with the means of bringing all these currents into untold or numbingly repetitive conjunction, out in the open, folded into pockets, held between bodies, running in circuits. The twenty-first century sees cities emerge with populations of thirty million and more humans and billions of devices. In such an environment, one can expect rather interesting kinds of conjunction: What are the spatial equivalents of spam, malware, and insistent pop-ups in a pervasive-computing environment?

Waves

One of the questions asked in this book concerns the way in which different aesthetic modes and medial forms come into composition with ubiquitous computing. Indeed, the form of conjunction itself is crucial here as the differing kinds of attention to layering and conjoining of mixed and augmented realities attest. The amphetamine humor of science fiction, in both its up and its down phases, appears as an important register in the work of a number of writers. Alongside it is another current, heading toward what Philip Agre called a "critical technical practice," a primary goal of which is "to cultivate awareness of the assumptions that lie implicit in inherited technical practice" (1997, 105). As may come as a relief to some and a source of perplexity to others, this book has not emerged directly out of labs and has not been written by technical developers as sets of reports and proposals. The discussion of technicity here is predominantly mediated by its handling of art and other cultural currents, which means at times that the loops back to explicit discussion of computation, software, and so on can be interestingly convoluted. Several authors here suggest that art objects tend to draw attention to themselves rather than arrange themselves as the peripherals of attention. It may be that technical objects also do so, but that a sufficient means has yet to be established to recognize the "selves" that might be attended to. The peripheral attention to and repertoire of small social promptings emphasized in ubicomp is one way by which such things might occur, but we can also see several suggestions in this book for ways in which the technocultural can come to be known in new ways.

In pursuit of such knowledge, the turn to affect via phenomenology and other experientially geared means that are perhaps less inertially attracted to the scale of the cogito is well represented here; the book provides one of a recent wave of attempts to engage with what had previously been regarded as "low-level" functions in culture. A renewed and almost parallel engagement with objects and material culture provides another such shift of emphasis within social and cultural theory and has its precursors in many forms—including the decidedly sensual material worlds of Neoconcretist art and consequent currents that form a countervalently nontechnicized yet highly medial proliferation of energies, capacities, and attention. At the same time as the object gains new kinds of attention as a category, other fields, architecture in particular, are moving away from a too easy stability to work with dynamic interrelations of forces and materials (see Hensel, Menges, and Winstock 2010). The art is in finding the specific scales of composition that align conjunctions of powers, tensions, and virtualities. Once such conjunctions have been found that seem to work or that prise open something new, the temptation, however, is to assume that they are the determining factors in a more widespread set of conditions. It is often useful to keep such "ultimate" or decisive levels in circulation, to multiply them rather than either to ignore or to fall for them. In this vein, other levels emerge. As mentioned in Ulrik Ekman's introduction, attending to ubiquitous computing occurs here on the brink of what may be another such tilting of emphasis—that is, to the technical, something quite palpable in a number of the articles here. Numerous projects discussed in the book combine cultural intelligences and sensitivities operating at multiple scales with sustained exploratory and inventive engagements of technical materials that in turn produce and condition the cultural.

A figure who was not averse to the generation of such entities, the cybernetician Gordon Pask, argued that all phenomena can be understood as the interaction of waves acting upon waves. In such a sense, fields such as ambience or atmosphere are foundational. Electronic circuits, for Pask, were simply a special case, a means of making waves somewhat linear by channeling them along a more conductive medium, that of wires and components.[8] Art has sociologically been described as a set of intermeshing fields, but perhaps it can also be understood (and here I defer to Ekman's considerations of Simondon in the introduction) in terms of those fields that are technical, emotional, symbolic, variously abstract, each with its own discreet and shifting apparatus, organization, looseness, and forms of becoming. As a dynamic expression of material capacities that is inherently predicated on interference, waves do not rely on hinges and hierarchies for their capacity to generate effects or to be understood.

Art projects intercept and produce such waves, stabilize momentary vortices and ripples among them, and in turn induce further processes of subjectivication.

Machines of Movement upon Movement

As another form of attention to movement, cultural theory often derives its force from reexamining the well known, the commonplace or settled, and finding that it is not so well known, that it is idiosyncratic, troubling, growing, divisible. A too easy adherence to the known is nonempirical, suffocating. Phenomenology proposed such an attentive approach be applied to the human sensorium. Like any particular approach, the phenomenological approach also tends to generate its own blind spots, in this case composed of wider assemblages of sensorial, material, and intellectual force unconstrained by a primary relation to the human sensorium as seat of interpretation. (Art that is, for instance, pop, ecological, or otherwise perverse tends to fall outside of its purview, requiring further concatenations of understanding that are not simply sensational.) What is suggestive in this context is that although phenomenological concerns form a significant and well-worked set of ideations for the understanding of the experience of computational cultures, they also contribute to a wider range of ideas, building on the work of Gilles Deleuze and others, anticipating a more open range of experiential, knowing, and sensual dimensions of relationality operating at multiple scales, not only those of the transcendental, but of the other kinds of "ambient" as well. Not only does computing itself, as an expanded field, become more irregular and generative, an object of dissensus, a space in which claims, inventions, and experiments can be made that are different from those based on the paradigmatic concerns for efficiency, rationalization, and problem solving, but also the domain of reflexive experiential analysis grows multiple kinds of entity to inhabit. I am not arguing here for a flatness and generality of kinds of intelligence, but rather recognizing the multiplication and differentiation of intelligence and noting the migration of automatisms and seriality into the fleshier parts of circuits.[9]

Smee anticipated and rather looked forward to the implications of his machines in such terms, stating how they might handle a person: "Thus if we use the word John, it may be necessary in some cases to show that John is of a certain family, and that he is a citizen, a Londoner, a white, a European, a man, an animal, an organized being" (1851, 23).

In database-driven culture, any of these characteristics, taken as classes, predicates, or categories, can be considered the core aspect, with the proper name "John" or the individual being that is tagged by that name being simply a component of such stuff. In such a context, what Katherine Hayles refers to here as "behavior inferences" becomes a massive state of figuring out as much as of sorting. Although there is no census, it seems likely that the vast majority of ubiquitous computing refers, as Anne

Galloway indicates, simply to itself, consisting of networks of sensors, actuators, finite-state machines, maintaining homeostatic levels, feeding and tracking information from one integrated circuit to another. The human subject may come late in the chain, if at all. This domain is generally prosaic, unexceptional, bearing no trace of a notable creative gesture and existing as a media ecology of billions of parts. Indeed, we might find that the tantalizing freak effects among interlocking waves (in Pask's sense) registering in what is understood as culture should not be a means of drawing attention away from the landscape that, as John Johnston describes here, is building itself in "smart cities," logistics depots, hospitals, battlefields, and many other disconnected or aggregatable and inventive ways, nor should these effects draw attention away from that which is fading from the possibility of becoming among the fields gathered and accentuated in such spaces and their specific scales of operation.[10] Rather, they should serve as an invitation to a culture that is predicated on the circuit bending of experience and realities and that takes the computational as part of its core.

Smee imagined that his machine would established a kind of motion requiring a "whole series of movements to move upon other movements," a relational machine, the like of which he was unacquainted with among the abundance of machines of the metropolis of his time. Such a machine is a delight, a menace, myriad things, perhaps a metropolis in itself. This book presents its readers with the challenge to take part in thinking about such machines and about the layered, mixed, and conjunctive kinds of relations they offer. It crucially also offers us a treasure trove of differential machines equipped to handle not just the parsing of quibbles, but also, as art and culture enter into composition with ubicomp, the processes capable of marking and making significant difference.

Notes

1. For those eager to follow up on Smee's work, an extensive catalog of equipment and materials was published in the back of his book (Smee 1851) as an advertisement for a firm of "philosophical instrument makers."

2. The numerous levels of malfunction and anticipated malfunction are notable here.

3. See the work of the group Ambient TV, in particular the project *Function Creep* (http://www.ambienttv.net/content/?q=functioncreep, accessed 6 December 2010), for some iterative discussions on how such experiments might take place. See also Luksch and Patel 2010.

4. The conjunction of scales between owner and commoner has ramifications that are interestingly articulated by computing. Notable in this regard is that it is only with the introduction of systematic use of satellite imagery that the despoliation of the Amazon, 60–70 percent of which is for meat ranching, became apparent in real time, prompting and to some degree facilitating opportunities to enforce regulations on deforestation. See Souza, 2006.

5. As explored in some notable projects by artists and others; see the information about Harwood, Yokokoji, Wright's *Tantalum Memorial* (2008) at http://yoha.co.uk/tantalum.

6. The acronym FLOSS stands for "Free Libre and Open-Source Software." An example of such an operating system is Minix, initially developed by Andy Tannenbaum at the Vrije Universiteit in Amsterdam for teaching purposes and released under the Berkeley Software Distribution license.

7. For a strategic proposal for the commons that readily recognizes their need to be invented as much as recognized as natural and that crucially integrates an infrastructure for circulating technical innovation, see Winstanley [1651] 2010. This text is also online in several places.

8. For an account of Pask's life and work, see Pickering 2010.

9. The complexity of such conditions is notable in particular in the first of Masaki Fujihata's long-term Field Works of performances, investigations, and installation series. The 1992–1994 project *Impressing Velocity [Mt. Fuji]* consisted of a team of people climbing Mount Fuji. Each walker was equipped with a backpack containing a Global Positioning System–linked laptop that recorded their ascent up the mountain. The speed or slowness of their movement up this uneven and culturally potent surface from many different angles rephrased Katsushika Hokusai's famous series of prints of views of Mount Fuji. Instead of producing a series of multiple views, though, Fujihata's team generated an aggregate, visualized record of the mountain, logged and experienced in terms of time and the difficulty of ascension, which, given the whole when mapped together from the interaction of all these parts, provides perhaps a form of what might be called a "quantitative impressionism."

10. The stories of that which is slowly or abruptly evaporated by the heat of particular becomings is suggested by Katherine Hayles in her discussion of Philip K. Dick's novel *Ubik* and are gathered in a certain way as narratives themselves in Sigiszmund Krzhizhanovsky's stories, in particular "The Bookmark" (2009). Such work calls for an attentiveness to a melancholy of technics and to the generative movements and becomings that are beyond affirmation of the coordination and timings of what becomes recognizable as a thing, a movement, a work, a device; it also calls for an attentiveness to sense to what is fading, falling away, uninterpreted, or deleted.

References

Agre, Philip. 1997. *Computation and Human Experience.* Cambridge, UK: Cambridge University Press.

Bunting, Heath. n.d. "The Status Project." Available at http://status.irational.org. Accessed 6 December 2010.

Christensen, Clayton. 1997. *The Innovator's Dilemma: When New Technologies Cause Great Firms to Fail.* Cambridge, MA: Harvard Business School Press.

Clark, Andy. 2000. *An Introduction to the Philosophy of Cognitive Science.* Oxford, UK: Oxford University Press.

Ehrenreich, Barbara. 2009. *Smile or Die: How Positive Thinking Fooled America and the World.* London: Granta.

Foucault, Michel. 2008. *The Birth of Biopolitics: Lectures at the College de France 1978–1979.* Translated by Graham Burchell. London: Palgrave Macmillan.

Fuller, Matthew, and Andrew Goffey. 2010. "Towards an Evil Media Studies." In *The Spam Book,* edited by Jussi Parikka and Tony Sampson, 141–159. Cresskill, NJ: Hampton Press.

Graham, Stephen. 2005. "Software-Sorted Geographies." *Progress in Human Geography* 29 (5): 562–580.

Greenfield, Adam. 2006. *Everyware: The Dawning Age of Ubiquitous Computing.* Berkeley, CA: Peachpit Press.

Hensel, Michael, Achim Menges, and Michael Winstock. 2010. *Emergent Technologies in Design: Towards a Biological Paradigm for Architecture.* London: Routledge.

Hutchins, Edwin. 2008. "The Role of Cultural Practices in the Emergence of Modern Human Intelligence." *Philosophical Transactions of the Royal Society B* 363:2011–2019.

Kay, Alan, and Adele Goldberg. 1977. "Personal Dynamic Media." *ACM Computer* 10 (3): 31–41.

Krzhizhanovsky, Sigizmund. 2009. "The Bookmark." In *Memories of the Future,* translated by Joanne Turnbull and Nikolai Formozov, 15–51. New York: New York Review of Books.

Linebaugh, Peter. 2008. *The Magna Carta Manifesto: Liberties and Commons for All.* Berkeley and Los Angeles: University of California Press.

Luksch, Manu, and Mukul Patel, eds. 2010. *Ambient Information Systems.* London: Ambient.

Malafouris, Lambros, and Colin Renfrew. 2010. "Introduction." In *The Cognitive Life of Things: Recasting the Boundaries of the Mind,* edited by Lambros Malafouris and Colin Renfrew, 1–12. Cambridge, UK: McDonald Institute Monographs.

Marres, Noortje. 2009. "Testing Powers of Engagement: Green Living Experiments, the Ontological Turn, and the Undoability of Involvement." *European Journal of Social Theory* 12 (1): 117–133.

Moretti, Franco. 1998. *Atlas of the European Novel 1800–1900.* London.

Panofsky, Erwin. 1993. *Perspective as Symbolic Form.* Translated by Christopher S. Wood. New York: Zone Books.

Pickering, Andrew. 2010. *The Cybernetic Brain: Memories of Another Future.* Chicago: University of Chicago Press.

Pilkington, Ed. 2010a. "BP Rig's Alarms Were Switched Off to Help Workers Sleep." *The Guardian,* 24 July.

Pilkington, Ed. 2010b. "Revealed: The Safety Breaches on Stricken Well." *The Guardian,* 24 July.

Portanova, Stamatia. 2009. "The 'Minor' Arithmetic of Rhythm: Imagining Digital Technologies for Dance." In *Deleuze and Performance*, edited by Laura Cull, 240–260. Edinburgh: Edinburgh University Press.

Rusell, Muir. 2010. *The Independent Climate Change E-mails Review*. Available at http://www.cce-review.org. Accessed 6 December 2010.

Smee, Alfred. 1851. *The Process of Thought Adapted to Language Together with a Description of the Relational and Differential Machines*. London: Longman, Brown, Green and Longmans.

Souza, Carlos M., Jr. 2006. "Mapping Land Use of Tropical Regions from Space." *Proceedings of the National Academy of Sciences* 103 (39): 14261–14262.

Vygotsky, Lev. 1971. *Psychology of Art*. Cambridge, MA: MIT Press.

Weiser, Mark. 1996. "Open House." Interactive Telecommunications Program Review 2.0, March 1996. Available at http://www.ubiq.com/hypertext/weiser/WeiserPapers.html. Accessed 6 December 2010.

Weiser, Mark. 1994. "The World Is Not a Desktop." *ACM Interactions* 1 (1): 7–8.

Weiser, Mark. 1993a. "Some Computer Science Issues in Ubiquitous Computing." *Communications of the ACM* 36 (7): 75–84.

Weiser, Mark. 1993b. "Ubiquitous Computing.'" *IEEE Computer* 26 (10): 71–72.

Weiser, Mark. 1991. "The Computer for the 21st Century." *Scientific American* 265 (3): 94–104.

Weiser, Mark, and John Seely Brown. 1996. "The Coming Age of Calm Technology." Available at http://nano.xerox.com/hypertext/weiser/acmfuture2endnote.htm. Accessed 6 December 2010.

Weiser, Mark, and John Seely Brown. 1995. "Designing Calm Technology." Available at http://sandbox.xerox.com/hypertext/weiser/calmtech/calmtech.htm. Accessed 6 December 2010.

Williams, Raymond. 1973. *The Country and the City*. Oxford, UK: Oxford University Press.

Winstanley, Gerrard. [1651] 2010. "The Law of Freedom in a Platform, or True Magistracy Restored." In *The Complete Works of Gerrard Winstanley*, edited by Thomas N. Corns, Ann Hughes, and David Loewenstein, 278–404. Oxford, UK: Oxford University Press.

Acknowledgments

This book circles around the problem of always already having gotten mixed up with ubiquitous computing—becoming aware without being aware of it. It is about being moved by that problem as an event—only to discover that its other affectivity preceded any kinesthetic self-affectation one would be tempted to call one's own. The writings in its many pages will thus have been worthwhile if here and there, now and then, you mesh with and become carried along in the text with a metastability, a disparation in the multiplicitous relations between a peripherally operative human context awareness and some differently technical process on the horizon—not least because this meshing might grant an interactivity beyond any given design, whether yours or that of any system, and so approximate a contact, a primordial tactility, a different getting in touch among the partakers of two types of distributive, open machines. This process would irritate established communicational protocols, provide kinds of perturbation without any given sense or sensible message. In that case, this book would have contributed by way of considerable indirection to an ambience whose sonics put gentle pressure on "my" hearing before it is "mine." So a force field of microsensation-hither organization will have had a me pass on even though I did not see it arrive or leave until afterward, if it became visible at all.

This book has been developing for five years, concurrently with the gradual coming into prominence of ubiquitous and pervasive computing and their accompanying cultural developments. It could not have developed without support from a great many parties, of whom I can mention only a regrettably small fraction. I remain indebted to Siv Colding Ekman, Rune Colding Ekman, Aske Colding Ekman, and Janne Colding Ekman, whose openly live capaciousness paved the way for all my joys and frustrations as editor. My colleagues at the University of Copenhagen have not ceased to provide inspiration and valuable feedback, and I thank in particular Arild Fetveit for sharing a greatly rewarding and productive type of research network collaboration, Frederik Tygstrup for having me think and for running a doctoral school that continues to make our research environment something that makes a difference, Anders Michelsen for boosting studies and sharing Gilbert Simondon while laughing with me on the mobile phone, and Marianne Ping Huang for grounding both me and two consecutive research networks institutionally.

I also thank the Danish Research Council for the Humanities, a section of the Danish Agency for Science, Technology, and Innovation, for the funding it provided in 2007–2008 for the national research network "Digital Art and Culture in the Age of Pervasive Computing," whose events and participants have been the main driving force behind this volume. Without the active participation from the more than forty Danish researchers, notably from Copenhagen, Odense, and Aarhus, this publication would not have seen the light of day.

Thanks are also due to the visiting international scholars, many of whom contributed to this book and whose work was essential to make this network so productive: John Johnston, Mark B. N. Hansen, N. Katherine Hayles, Lev Manovich, Joseph Auner, Dieter Daniels, Georgina Born, and Bernadette Wegenstein. I thank all the contributors to this volume for making a difference, for their generosity, and for their forbearance and patience with respect to seeing realized a publication of this scope.

The NordForsk Research Board widened and strengthened the research network activity and training in this field by funding for 2009–2012 the Nordic network "The Culture of Ubiquitous Information," whose more than 140 participants from Finland, Norway, Sweden, and Denmark are currently at work to deepen the insights in the research field proper to this book.

Finally, my thanks go to Annie Barva for her work as a truly excellent copy editor, and to Douglas Sery and Katie Helke in their capacity as ever-competent and helpful in-house editors at the MIT Press.

Introduction

Ulrik Ekman

> Where the sea meets the land, life has blossomed into a myriad of unique forms in the turbulence of water, sand, and wind. At another seashore between the land of atoms and the sea of bits, we are now facing the challenge of reconciling our dual citizenships in the physical and digital worlds. Our visual and auditory sense organs are steeped in the sea of digital information, but our bodies remain imprisoned in the physical world. Windows to the digital world are confined to flat, square screens and pixels, or "painted bits." Unfortunately, one cannot feel and confirm the virtual existence of this digital information through one's hands and body.
>
> —Hiroshi Ishii, "Tangible Bits"

> There is disparation when two twin sets that cannot be entirely superimposed, such as the left retinal image and the right retinal image, are grasped together as a system, allowing for the formation of a single set of a higher degree which integrates their elements thanks to a new dimension.
>
> —Gilbert Simondon, *L'individu et sa genèse physico-biologique*

I

Were the relation between technics and human culture today so that atoms and bits were always already grasped as a single set of a higher degree and so that the virtual existence of information technology continued through human embodiment much as we felt our individual and sociocultural existence through its layers and events of digital information, this rather weighty volume would hardly be needed, and most of its contents would present matters taken for granted. Because this technology–body relationship remains an as yet impossible invention, one might say that two very general problems of proximity, at the very least, are somehow at the heart of a great many chapters contributing to this publication. Current developments of ubiquitous and pervasive computing are now very much at work in distal terms to attempt to attend to human culture as such and to its inhabitants in their anthropic character (no matter how many difficulties doing so presents), but they do not manage to remark upon that *from* which they attend—notably, their indeterminate openness to a type of energetic dynamics that would permit of technical self-organization. A considerable part of global human culture today pays attention, consciously or not, to the unfolding of ubiquitous and pervasive computing, very often in modes of learning enough to live with them, but less often in modes of invention that come to influence their operationality. However, in this we tend not to remark upon that which will prove to be nearer to us—the proximal here not just in the sense of the *anthropos* as such, but rather in the sense of *how* it is that we exist as humans with technics, generally as well as more specifically speaking with respect to ubiquitous and pervasive computing. Self-organization of ubiquitous computing (ubicomp) and human existence with pervasive technics remain too close, or one might say that they are matters of a certain tacit dimension, as Michael Polanyi would have called it:

> [I]n an act of tacit knowing we *attend from* something for attending *to* something else; namely, *from* the first term *to* the second term of the tacit relation. In many ways the first term of this relation will prove to be nearer to us, the second further away from us. Using the language of anatomy, we may call the first term *proximal*, and the second term *distal*. It is the proximal term, then, of which we have a knowledge that we may not be able to tell. (1966, 10)

In the broadest sense, then, this book is motivated by a double epistemological delimitation of the proximate—at the edge of which both a different cultural technics and a different technical culture are to be articulated in their coevolution. Insofar as the chapters further such articulations, ubicomp cultures and modes of existing with ubicomp technics will become considerably less tacit, only then to be relegated later on to another kind of murmuring memory where other technical tendencies reside, perhaps to be concretized in and as environments or milieus affording another climate.

Bits and atoms were never altogether divorced in this context, however, just as ubicomp and our cultural forms of life are less than disparate at this point in time. In fact, once one does try to invert attention, one comes into contact with a surprising number and variety of tacit developments ongoing today in many places. In contemporary visual culture, which perhaps still enjoys a certain hegemony, the major technical currents no doubt contribute to existing screen cultures of the digital TV, home videos, movie theater projections, high-resolution advertising, and the displays (now considerably wider than they were ten years ago) for stationary (personal) computers. At the same time, though, digital visual culture approaches ubiquity via a quite complex technocultural variability and dispersion—that is, by having its technical and cultural phenomena become at once larger, smaller, four-dimensional, mobile, and more ambient. When you encounter the large-scale integrated light-emitting diode (LED) displays literally covering the facades of Electrabel's power station in Drogenbos, Belgium, the Aspire Tower in Qatar, and the National Library in Belarus, they are quite likely to impress you with another sense of a technically living urban and architectural culture. Similarly, when you sit in the train to Tokyo, in the car to Copenhagen, or at home in New York, you might well notice the incorporation of small-tech items and their miniature screens in our everyday culture.[1] Such experiences might include encounters with the woman in the train engaged in a mobile novel, the children in the backseat watching a movie, the driver tapping the screen of his Global Positioning System (GPS) device, or the husband putting aside his Blackberry when coming home to greet the kids but finding them preoccupied with their Nintendo PlayStations. Not entirely unlike the architectural projects mentioned at the beginning of the paragraph, certain media-art installations at museum exhibitions and LED sculptures such as James Clar's *3D Display Cube* and the NOVA system from ETH Zürich break with the traditional two-dimensional notion of screens and displays so as to operate with displays in three spatial dimensions that change over time and call upon the spectators' bodily and circumferential or invasive movement. The dramatic increase in the cultural use of laptops, notebooks, pads, personal digital assistants (PDAs), and not least more than six billion mobile phones have brought along a new kind of mobile small-screen culture to the point where messages and e-books may be read everywhere or photographs, motion graphics, Web pages, ads, TV, videos, and movies may be watched on the phone and on the go.

This trend already suggests some of the ongoing dynamics of a well-nigh omnipresent visual digital culture, but the visuality of a ubicomp culture, if any, is perhaps still a rather open question. It is not yet clear to what extent Mark Weiser's original idea of ubiquitous computing as a matter of "calm" embeddedness will or should hold (Weiser and Brown 1995, 1996) or to what extent the current developments will or should adhere to a notion such as Donald Norman's (1998) "invisible computing." Hence, ubicomp visuality is perhaps best thought of as what is now brought forth by the production, installation, and everyday use of ambient video; that is, one might very well approach ambient video as one interesting borderline strategy for the actualization of the visuality of ubicomp culture. Paradoxically, ambient video indicates that ubicomp visuality is best seen without being seen. That is, it is best designed when it manages to play in and as the background of our everyday lives, being around for us so as to permit intermittent but gratifying attention, typically on a wall (in public spaces, at work, or at home), and in its images drawing upon a predominant repetition of the same versus a miniscule amount of the slow and small-scale variation of some artificially "natural" scenery (landscapes, fireplaces, materialities, textures, colorations, light and shadows, and so on).

However, nothing yet prohibits this development from going in the opposite direction or from moving toward some middle variations. Thus, at least initially one would have to take into account also an intensification of visual imaging along with solicitation of a hyperattentiveness to the very presence of what is projected or shown. This intensification is no doubt lurking in the attractiveness of the Blu-Ray movie format and resolution and in the gratifying and viscerally visual experience many people have when bringing home their first high-definition multimedia interface (HDMI) television (often larger than thirty-two inches). Another good example of such intensification is the kind of upscaling of computational imaging infrastructures that Lev Manovich (2005) indicates when describing the combination in grid computing of telepresence, interactive visualization, and science collaboration over superfast, optical networks using distributed computing resources (between Tokyo and California). In that case, one would be contemplating interactions with telepresences on a wall-size display with something like a 78,797 × 31,565 pixel resolution—enough, as Manovich recalls, to produce ubiquity effects in the form of haptic vision and impressions of physical proximity:

> I feel that this new level of resolution indeed changes things: the people on the other side of the globe are very much present in our space; and this creates a new level of attentiveness and focus for me. I feel that, in fact, they are even more present than the audience in the auditorium where I am sitting, since I see them large and in amazing detail. Indeed, normally we expect to see this level of detail only when looking at objects that are quite close to us, while objects further away appear to us less sharp and with less detail. Therefore, 4K teleconferencing plays a trick on our brains, sending signals that tell the brain that the objects on the screen are physically closer than the people and objects physically present nearby. (2005)

A very similar ambivalence characterizes the widening of effects from the post-9/11 development of surveillance, which hovers indeterminately between the visible and the invisible, the explicit notification and the kinds of embeddedness that escape human awareness (Levin, Frohne, and Weibel 2002; Lyon 2006, 2007). Ubiquitous and pervasive computing depend for their operationality on the deployment, maintenance, and further expansion of the kinds of hardware technics and software systems involved and so unquestionably contribute to the emergence of "soft" and "flexible" control societies (Deleuze 1995) with remarkably complex assemblages of closed-circuit television, Webcams, security video cameras, sensor networks and actuators, digital profiling and behavioral-recognition programs, as well as biometrics and digital identity systems. As the inclusion of sensor networks and actuators in this list already indicates, we already live with ubiquitous and pervasive computing not only in our visual culture, but considerably beyond it.

One's sense of ubicomp culture thus cannot but extend to other kinds of registration—such as the sounds of the city and our means of transport or the very auditory ambience of networked societies and publics. Many of us now take for granted and no longer question how it is that MP3 players, notably in the form of mobile phones and iPods, seem to cover contemporary urban sprawls with a highly personalized digital auditory culture that has seen everyday practices of sensory and aesthetic cocooning extend themselves very widely.[2] Errors, malfunctioning, and alerts aside, we also for the most part overhear the multitudes of digital auditory signals from all manner of stand-alone, portable, or networked devices that accompany our daily lives as an ambient soundscape—from an operating system starting up to a microwave or a PDA going to sleep. However, we still do tend to notice an auditory ubicomp culture when we enter an interactive auditory environment such as media artist David Rokeby's early installation project *Very Nervous System* with its twenty algorithms for musical "personalities" (Anthes 2006); when we enter a dance club whose cameras, infrared sensors, and floor sensors afford a socially interactive flow of music and bodily movement; or when we listen at a dance performance in which the dancers' body movements trigger sounds due to the interaction with worn sensors that register muscle contractions (Morales-Manzanares, Morales, Dannenberg, and Berger 2001; Ulyate and Bianciardi 2002).

The claim on being pervasive or ubiquitous may well appear most convincing, in quantitative sociological terms, for the area of communication. Information and communication technology (ICT) was already a massively present phenomenon before the millennial turn, during the broader sociocultural engagement with the Internet after 1993 and during the rise of new media in the second half of the 1990s, notably in terms of a broad use of email messages. This trend has only been strengthened via the dual development of Web 2.0 versions of social media (Facebook alone counting more than half a billion users at this time) and via that roll-out of variants of wireless networks and cell spaces that allowed mobile phone communications to become the kind of seemingly omnipresent technical and social formation that we live with today, globally speaking, although significant regional divides remain as regards affordability and sheer access. In a great many Western, Southeast Asian, South American, and African network societies, others rather immediately notice the brand and model of one's mobile phone, and the status of this device today as an object of desire is perhaps something worthy of a quite detailed Bourdieuean analysis of distinction. However, we do tend to take mobile phones and mobile communication (via calls, Short Message Service, and Multimedia Messaging Service) for granted, now mostly on a three-gigahertz basis, with four-gigahertz capability emerging unevenly, and this process has happened with a speed and a degree of acceptance that might otherwise cause some surprise. Both the speed and the acceptance are interesting matters for further reflection, not least as regards alternative public spheres, flash-mob phenomena, and the formation of loose but influential kinds of mobile "social" chains, such as those at play in the violent social uprisings in the suburbs of France in 2005, in "the safran revolution" in Burma in 2007, in Barack Obama's use of the Internet and (mobile) social media during the U.S. presidential election in 2008, and in "the Twitter revolution" associated with the election in Iran in 2009. But the ubiquity effects of mobile communications also tend to mask the fact that all too little research has so far been undertaken in this area. Hence, we are still quite far from understanding in comparative analytical terms how it is that pervasive mobile ICT for the young woman commuting in Japan is something technosocially and practically very different from pervasive mobile ICT for the teenage boy on the way home from school in Finland. For instance, how is it that many Japanese mobile phones are more akin to a relatively powerful laptop, whereas the vast majority of European and North American mobiles remain sophisticated but much simpler computational units aimed in the main at auditory and texted telecommunication (even if the smartphones are now beginning to reverse some of this difference)? Does this comparison attest to a culturally shared notion of developing an increasingly strong wired *and* wireless technological infrastructure for ubiquitous and pervasive computing, but a cultural difference as regards the pursuit of clearly identifiable individual systems *or* environmentally embedded ones, respectively?

We do observe mobiles interrupting work meetings, classes, art performances, or physical face-to-face conversations, just as we remark in passing upon individuals either talking very loudly on the phone while on the train or adopting quite intimate and affective discursive registers while talking on the mobile in public places. However, such observations amount only to marginal comments bespeaking the fact that we are obviously still in the midst of a rather massive change and reorientation of social and individual norms for communicational practice, just as we still await more and more thorough fieldwork in research that may delineate the various current remakings or dissolutions of distinctions between public and private spheres, distance and intimacy, presentation and secrecy.[3]

You probably seldom consider this anymore, but the touch screens at the library, at the airport or railway station, and on your smartphone, iPad, or Kindle are already small-scale harbingers of the changes in interaction design now under way in order to concretize parts of ubiquitous and pervasive computing, such as the dozens of small test-bed inventions in tangible computing that have already seen the light of day via the work of Hiroshi Ishii and his colleagues in the MIT Tangible Media Group.[4] Something similar might well be said of the vibrations of your mobile phone; of the smart textiles now appearing in coats, outdoor clothing, and sports accessories as one kind of actualization of wearable computing; as well as of the buildings to whose intelligent management of doors, lighting, air, heating, windows, and flexible walls you hardly pay attention. Many interaction designers are still at work on Web pages, Internet services, advertising, social media, and well-established forms of (online) games, but a slowly increasing number of others are involved in front-end development and research outside this line of work. Therefore, we have already been interacting enough beyond command lines, menus, desktops, and traditional graphical user interfaces (GUIs) to have realized that another set of models is operative. As a consequence, influential multivolume handbooks in human–computer interaction now include lengthy sections not only on methodology, usability, evaluation, Web design, learning and "edutainment," but also on the kinds of multimodal and kinesthetic interaction designs at stake in virtual, augmented, and mixed-reality environments (Jacko 2007;

Jacko and Sears 2003). This trend is recognizable, but in the strict and narrow sense it is far from mature and not much more than ten years old, and it is marked, much like its sister disciplines contributing to a ubicomp culture, by an unresolved series of questions respecting the ethicopolitical desirability, technical feasibility, and functional robustness pertaining to various kinds and degrees of embeddedness versus explicit unfolding of interaction designs. This (in)visibility or (un)calmness undoubtedly explains in part why you may have slowed your strides across Trafalgar Square in London in 2008 for at least two kinds of reasons. First, it might be due to your feeling affirmatively invited into media artist Rafael Lozano-Hemmer's large installation *Under Scan* (2008) at the square by the elegant technical and embodied interactive play with the movement of individuals' shadows and a great many prerecorded video portraits (figures I.1 and I.2). Then it might be because you began to think as the shadow play of the installation broke off in order to illuminate and visualize the embedded grids and control mechanisms at stake in its surveillance and tracking systems operating on this public square.[5]

When you visit Lozano-Hemmer's *SubTitled Public* (2005–) installation, you see people not wanting to enter its black box or making a fast escape just after entering it, but you also see others remaining to move around inside in order to explore the projections of verbs that continuously follow each individual as "public subtitles," perhaps even pushing their exploration to the point of enjoying a playful exchange of "subtitles" by touching another person. If you were present at one of the earlier installations of David Rokeby's *Very Nervous System* (1986–1990), you might have observed a blind boy jumping back as if hitting a physically erected wall when he tried to enter the unmarked interactive auditory environment of the installation. This reaction did not occur just because the boy's senses of hearing and touch were operative, however acutely. It happened also because Rokeby's performative interactions involved contact with sonic blocks seemingly alive so they fostered an affective and sensorimotor event in which hearing was first another protosensory touch, an auditory spacing with a vibrant force of tactility to whose impression the boy could only be responsive.

In a pervasive game such as *SuperFly* by the Swedish company It's Alive Mobile, you are not only preoccupied with the goal of becoming a virtual celebrity, with all its concerns relating to performative self-presentation, but also immersed in the flow of the game because play appears to command presence and thus responds by granting a sense and sensation of presence. When you enter into pervasive gaming with Blast Theory's *Uncle Roy All Around You*, doing so means engaging with a largely post-GUI setting relying on wearable, mobile, or embedded software and hardware for its provision of a virtual and "natural" physical environment that does not just *facilitate* the game but is technologically prepared so as to be continuously *responsive* to mobile, location-oriented gameplay. You stay involved on a performative basis largely

Figure I.1
A young woman and an *Under Scan* video portrait exchanging greetings in the streets of Leicester, UK (2006).
Source: Photograph courtesy of Rafael Lozano-Hemmer.

Figure I.2
A laying bare of the surveillance and tracking grids in *Under Scan* (2008), Trafalgar Square, London.
Source: Photograph courtesy of Rafael Lozano-Hemmer.

because the game manages to engage you in an ongoing mixed-reality (re)organization of time and space. (See figure I.3.)

In other words, whether you are running on a virtual plane or moving through city streets and buildings, the gameplay has you swallowed by the seeming presence of playing. You are in the flow, as Mihály Csíkszentmihályi (1990) would say, and this means keeping on playing live, playing with liveness—that is, prolonging a sense and sensation of presence and presencing.[6]

Some of us have participated (less playfully) in meetings at work that took place in rooms that were aware of the people (tele)present to the extent that digital projections were adjusted accordingly, just as calendar arrangements were made more easily. Such rooms did much in terms of illustrating why the development of systemic context awareness is a chief goal for ubiquitous and pervasive computing, just as the ensuing errors and misunderstandings did much to make clear that an approximation of interacting with human context awareness still remains a formidable technical challenge—for instance, in terms of going from awareness of physical location and movement to

Figure I.3
Pervasive augmented-reality gaming with Third Echelon.
Source: Photograph courtesy of Earthmine/Layar.

awareness of intention, action, affect, passion, emotion, and semantics. Others among us are either part of one of many groups among elderly people on the rise in many Western countries or part of one of the research teams comprising computer scientists, physicians, nurses, information and media scientists, industrial designers, engineers, and ethnographers dedicated to qualitative analysis of such groups of the elderly. In both cases, there would then be a shared experience pertaining to the current development of smart homes (Streitz, Kameas, and Mavrommati 2007), coupled with the development of pervasive health care (Boye and Spure Nielsen 2003; "Centre for Pervasive Healthcare" 2009; Dourish et al. 2007; Orwat et al. 2008). This research is not so much a bodily matter of pervasiveness qua the introduction of aids for prosthetics, computationally augmented implants, or assistance in organ transplants. Rather, it is a question of designing, developing, and evaluating the usage of context-aware pervasive computer technologies (e.g., communication devices for assistance or emergencies, sensor-based surveillance of the home, wireless technics for acute medicine, better equipment for the disabled, preventive maintenance of equipment) for health care anywhere and at any time, not least to permit individuals and their families a much more active role in their own health care.

If this example of ubicomp is only marginally recognizable to you, you are far more likely to have become acquainted with the navigationally aware GPS system in your car (including its capacity for leading you astray or making you forget to watch the real environment around you). Perhaps you were one of the participants in one of

Blast Theory's interactive media-art projects in the United Kingdom, Japan, and Germany for locative mixed-reality gaming, such as *Can You See Me Now?* (2003) or the sequel *Day of the Figurines* (2006). Whether these locative-media projects took place in Preston, Tokyo, or Berlin, they drew upon the Internet, wireless connections, GPS and geographic information system (GIS) technology, and handheld devices to provide a wide array of participants with a socially shared experience in which their everyday urban settings and cultures became a mixed reality that was virtually and physically mobile but constantly aware of the context at stake. You might even have followed the development of augmented-reality browsing and augmented advertising as it appears in the work of a company such as Earthmine/Layar (figures I.4 and I.5), in which case you were probably a bit astounded at the sensitivity to your whereabouts, interests, and the contextual particulars demonstrated by these devices and applications.[7]

It goes for the majority of us that we have become blind to or only vaguely cognizant of being citizens in the kind of network societies that Manuel Castell's magnum opus *The Rise of the Network Society* (1996) began to lay bare, not least as regards the cultural assimilation of their Internet dimensions. An increasing number of us have also become rather familiar with the use in our daily lives of some subset of the massive development of wireless devices and their overlapping networks (including wireless personal area network [WPAN], wireless local area network [WLAN], and wireless metropolitan access network [WMAN] or WiMax variants). Today we are thus much closer to considering ourselves confident, especially if we are part of the younger

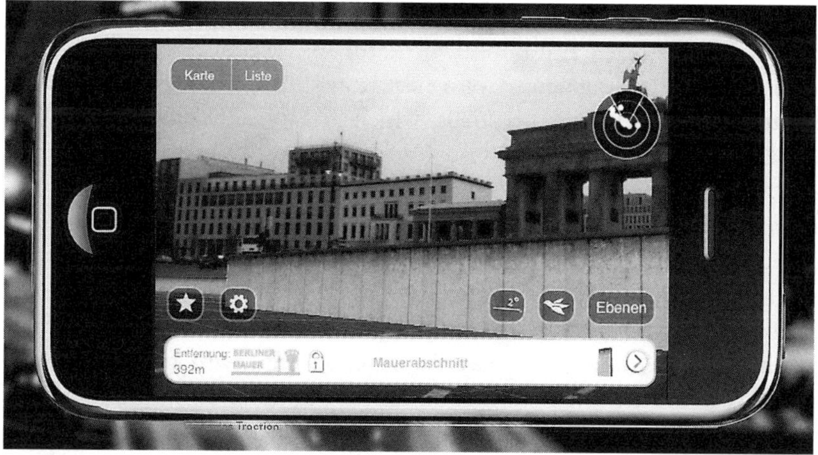

Figure I.4
Historical augmented-reality context awareness in Berlin.
Source: Photograph courtesy of Earthmine/Layar.

Figure I.5
Locative and context-aware augmented-reality advertising for the *Prince of Persia* game.
Source: Photograph courtesy of Earthmine/Layar.

generations, in our chosen roles as members of the several kinds of dynamically changing and mobile networked publics described and analyzed by Mizuko Ito (2007a, 2009, 2010) and others. Hence, we cannot but have noted the expanding and deeply intensifying development of the inherent logic of networked information societies, including the kind of "physical turn" that out-of-the-box ubiquitous or pervasive computing draws upon for part of its reach and impact. If that is so, we probably nod in agreement with Manovich's (2006) diagnosis of a historical shift from the 1990s, which were oriented toward virtuality, to the 2000s, which are arguably preoccupied with physical space filled with electronic and visual information.

Nonetheless, even if this broad development seems to confirm Mark Weiser's somewhat earlier emphasis on the pursuit not so much of a virtual reality in the relation between technics and culture, but of a distinctly "embodied virtuality,"[8] we still tend to stop short (much as in a first encounter with an augmented-reality browser, as mentioned earlier) when trying to recognize a "poetics of augmented space" or when trying to articulate its implications. We may also agree strongly with an effort such as Paul Dourish's linkage of an existential phenomenology of the body with a sociology of the lifeworld in order to provide the basis for the development of a new framework for the design and evaluation of context-aware ubicomp technologies, but that agreement does not necessarily mean that we can provide a detailed and commonsensical description of the modes of embodied interaction in a ubicomp culture that we are likely to be living with at home, in public, at work or that we live with in our leisure time today or will be living with at the end of the current decade. Likewise, if you have had to explain to somebody what a "mixed reality" is and what its cultural ramifications are likely to be, you will probably have met with certain difficulties—on both sides of the exchange. In large part, these difficulties stem from the fact that you are dealing with quite complex emergent phenomena. Moreover, even if we momentarily manage to put in parenthesis the most massive ontological and/or metaphysical presuppositions linked to the use of a term such as *mixed reality*, we still come into contact with a remarkable ambiguity.

On the one hand, the articulation of what inheres in a "mixed reality" might envelop you in a rather posthuman discourse, or it might begin to concretize this discourse quite a bit more literally. The latter might take place via your adoption of the use of smart textiles, wearable computing units such as hearing aids and augmented-reality glasses, or artifactual body sensoria that attend to your individual informational profile and to the fluxes of energy in your temperature, skin, muscles, balance, or other biometric signaletic materials, not to mention via your incorporation of combinations of intelligent prosthetic limbs and implants. In effect, such a concretization would begin to gesture toward a preunderstanding of "mixed reality" as something involving humans in a much closer contact with technics, even to the liminal point that they enter into a literally technical life form (or entropy or inertness), whether this process is a matter of an involution or an externalization of a memory of bare singular life.

On the other hand, much of the discourse concerning "mixed realities"—in new media studies, human–computer interaction studies, computer science, and engineering, for example—guides one toward a preconception of ubicomp technics entering into "mixed realities" by moving such technics much closer to the human, perhaps so as to mix with desirable characteristics. The presumption that intelligence is a human trait might well be the reason why these disciplines can be seen to pursue such goals for ubicomp as "intelligent" services and agents; "smart" devices, homes, and environments; and the harnessing of "swarm intelligence" so as to provide models for inherently innovative ad hoc networking (typically drawing upon studies of flocking behavior, theories of emergence, dynamic systems theory, or variants of complexity theory).

Although the "intelligence" of ubicomp mixed realities (human and otherwise) is still very loosely defined, it still indicates the metaphorics at play for the very concrete and already actualized development of ubiquitous and pervasive computing under the rubric of "things that think."[9] Quite likely, you know of this effort to embed computation into both the environment and everyday objects less because it has produced solid results with respect to sensor networks, ambient information displays, and biometrics, but rather because it has also led to the radio-frequency identification (RFID) technology that is now a pervasive and ubiquitous matter in much the same sense as mobile phones (in terms of sheer numbers, massive distribution, and stationary as well as mobile connectivity) and especially in the sense that it constitutes mixed realities in the unobtrusive, peripheral way that Weiser alludes to with his notion of calm embeddedness. The billions of RFID tags you find today in stores, transportation systems, logistics and product tracking, libraries, schools and universities, museums, hospitals, animal identification systems, and human implants admittedly undertake very little individualized, abstractly reflective thinking in each case, but synergy and the law of the big number provide them with another kind of serious interest as an object of study, not least with respect to the syntheses of individual and social profilings, the political economy of ubicomp databases, privacy, and information rights in mixed realities.[10]

Mixed-reality developments remain ambiguous as regards their ontogenetic relationality of human culture and technics, and their tendential vacillations have not hardened into a dualism or a binary opposition, nor is it easy to pinpoint one or more kinds of dialectics at work. However, the latter do afford a glimpse of the kind of embeddedness, miniaturization, and complexly dynamic connectivism that is evidently very influential now more than fifteen years after Weiser's original work. In that respect, Weiser and his colleagues at the Palo Alto Research Center went to work on assemblies of tabs, pads, and boards—or ubicomp entities on the scale of inches (such as wearables), feet (handhelds), and yards (interactive displays and smartboards). Today, these things would be considered ubicomp culture on the macroscale, whereas much interesting research and development today has begun to focus on the potentials of a microscaling that would include what moves from nanometers (dust) through micrometers (skin) to millimeters (clay), usually drawing upon networked Micro Electro-Mechanical Systems (MEMS) to generate computational artifacts in arbitrary three-dimensional shapes, including those resembling a number of well-known physical surfaces, fabrics, objects, and tools already used in our everyday cultures (Poslad 2009). This notion of mixed reality obviously reaches far into a theater of production for artifactually "natural" environments and things, just as it signals certain departures from prevalent modern notions of computation and the computer as a universal machine.

It is not predictable at this point in time where this trend will lead, but it nonetheless seems as if we are already considerably closer to the actual concretization of what Castells projected as a mere vision in the early 1990s. In *The Rise of the Network Society* (1996), he took a perceptible ongoing shift from decentralized, stand-alone mainframes and microcomputers to various Internet units to be the start of a more pervasive computing system. On that view, the logical progression from an early Internet paradigm would be to a system where that networking logic becomes applicable in every realm of daily activity, in every location, and in every context. Thus, Castells envisaged a system where billions of miniature, ubiquitous intercommunicating devices would be spread worldwide like pigment in the wall paint. Both "things that think" and "dust" MEMS seem to move in such a direction, but perhaps Neil Gershenfeld's remarks concerning "fungible computation" are just as evocative of mixed-reality things to come in ubicomp cultures:

> We are developing fungible computation—computation as a raw material that can be poured, sprayed or unrolled, that can be applied where you want it in the quantities you need. For example, you have a display and you need a little more screen space, or you have a server and you run out of resources. Today, you can add another display or another server, but that's about the granularity that's possible. So the research is looking at how you can make millimeter- or submillimeter-size [computers] and put them in various form factors, such as paint or wallpaper, and then build programming models so the little devices organize locally and globally. So that display becomes wallpaper you unroll, and if you want more display, you add more wallpaper. If your server needs more resources, you open the top and pour in more server. We are pushing the frontiers of fabrication, process integration, packaging, communications and, most importantly, programming models. (in Anthes 2006)

II

As should be evident from these initial remarks, the cultural movements and events of the epoch emerging with the unfolding and embedding of modes and variants of ubicomp across a great many regions of the world (notably in Southeast Asia, Europe, and the United States) are still a matter of a history of the present. In that sense, this coemergence of culture and technics does not yet belong to a well-defined period or to a field with clearly drawn contours. Rather, it still remains the somewhat undecidable matter of a dynamic eventuality and a space whose structurations and formations are perhaps in the main to come. As such, this coemergence seems to put quite some emphasis on issues of anticipation and new inventions, which perhaps is the reason why a number of researchers hesitate for a moment today in considering whether ubicomp culture exists for real or remains but an inspired vision. Nonetheless, as also attested to by the many valuable and thought-provoking contributions to this volume, which must by necessity partake of and add to the developments investigated, and by the quite remarkable myriad actual developments in this aspect of technical cultures during the period after Mark Weiser's early work,[11] ubicomp is already in more ways than one what André Leroi-Gourhan (1943) would have called a "technical fact." That is, if universal technical dynamics exist as tendencies, operating independently of the human or ethnic groupings that are nevertheless the only forms through which they are concretized, ubicomp as a dynamical tendency has already begun specific and differentiated concretization in several groups—for example, in the inclinations toward total media in Chinese culture, an overtly personalized and pervasive mobile technoculture in Japan, and a more infrastructural project in European culture. Insofar as we participate in this tendency in one or more ways, ubicomp is already our artificial envelope, our interposed membrane, or that curtain of objects through which we try to assimilate the exterior milieu (Leroi-Gourhan 1945). In other words, ubicomp is already a movement within the interior milieu (of individuals and their memories, their social cultures, and their past as well as of current technics with their databases and rather capacious storage devices) that is in the process of gaining a foothold in the exterior milieu (animals, vegetation, landscape, locations, spaces, geography, climate). As such, ubicomp is already a mode of survival by other means, more or less inhuman.

This technical tendency is concretized along with and within a certain history of technics and culture, specifically after World War II. In the broad sense, ubicomp culture no longer primarily refers to the first of the three waves of cybernetics outlined by Katherine Hayles in *How We Became Posthuman* (1999, 50–130)—that is, the 1945–1960 period drawing upon homeostasis as a central concept—except that its key notion of information is still very much with us because Claude Shannon and Warren Weaver's (1949) mathematical theory of communication is hardly less in force today. It would also seem as if the second period (1960–1980), centrally involved with reflexivity as a key concept, is largely a matter of the past. It might even seem as if we are now in several respects beyond or at the outer edges of the third period (from 1980 onward) emphasizing virtuality. However, this assessment moves things quite a bit too fast because a number of important efforts from both of the first two periods are still with us and quite decisively so. Perhaps the early notions of reflexivity—such as Heinz von Foerster's (1984) work on observing systems—have indeed been displaced, but we still live with vast bodies of cultural research and technics that draw upon self-organization as a paradigm: witness the continued influence today of second-generation cybernetics, late systems theory, autopoiesis, and versions of more or less radical social constructivism, for instance. Likewise, the hypostatizings of virtual reality, from the mid-1960s through the 1990s, with its transcendental ideal of simulation and its alleged "escape from the meat," perhaps seem ghostly relics today.[12] But virtuality today remains the paradigm for the development of ubicomp culture, albeit now accompanied by certain important modifications and competing approaches. A physical turn after the new millennium slowly but surely seems to permit a greater unfolding of embodied virtuality under the aegis of a pursuit of a mixed reality, including augmented reality as well as augmented virtuality, a real environment as well as a virtual environment.

Even if virtuality is with us as a paradigm, however, it is not yet entirely clear how to navigate among approaches to virtuality as different as, say, Paul Milgram and Fumio Kishino's (1994) technical notion of the virtuality continuum, hyper- or postphenomenological notions in work by Giorgio Agamben or Jacques Garelli of a pre-personal reservoir of manifold potentialities for more or less bare life forms

(Agamben 1998; Agamben and Heller-Roazen 1999, 177–242; Garelli 1991), or a Deleuzian transcendental empiricism affirming virtuality as an idea of multiplicitous differentiations/differenciations that is real as potential but not as actual (Deleuze 1993, 208–221).

It might well be that the common denominator here is that the idea of ubicomp solicits, in a quite transdisciplinary manner, a very thorough technocultural augmentation—an expansion, widening, or delimitation that goes so far as to stage new reality effects ("ubiquity effects"). Hayles's rehistoricization of cybernetics was and still is quite acute in that respect: virtuality qua "ubiquity" concerns a "computational universe" for and with contemporary network societies, whether this universe be thought of along the lines of an all-encompassing continuum, an irreducible (negative) theological reserve of dissemination-granting phenomena, a plane of pure immanence whose singularities open onto dynamic differential syntheses, or something else again. No doubt, both "ubiquity" and "pervasiveness" call for ongoing deconstruction and reconstruction of their ontological and metaphysical remainders (i.e., their penchant for altogether abstract idealizations or excessively essential or substantial extensions, or both). However, certain other traits of a contemporary diagnosis are perhaps just as interesting: we seem to be situated historically and paradigmatically between 1985 and 1995 still, between paradigms of reflexivity and virtuality—no matter that both have undergone quite some revision. This ground remains fertile today probably because it involves a return of the transcendental/empirical divide, with a difference. In other words, ubicomp culture appears at one and the same time to call for a new mode of cybernetic and human self-organization capable of a wider, more complex, and more smoothly and finely differentiated relationality with the other[13] as well as for a new mode of machinic and sociocultural heterogenesis capable of a wider range of individual emergences and differential syntheses, including technical systems, subjectivity effects, and social formations.[14]

Surely at this point, we have approached but little of a culture of living with open machines in which they would generate and operate as a computational universe. There is today, however, a remarkable tendency to pursue out-of-the-box computing, to live with and within an expansion of information-intensive environments or milieus. The latter do develop along with a culture of living with mixed realities, which begins to demonstrate that we will now continue to operate with the concretization of embodied as well as more abstract virtualities, thus providing at least some kind of counterweight to Hayles's convincing earlier critique of a strong tendency in information science to favor a posthuman ideal of transcendental disembodiment.

The recent work by Paul Dourish (2001) furnishes one good example of such a counterweight as it draws upon the thought of the phenomenological lifeworld (from Edmund Husserl through Alfred Schütz) so as to revisit *in* our existing everyday culture the historical traces of the interactions and interaction designs with which we now live in a ubicomp culture—from the electric through the symbolic, textual, and graphic to the explorations of embodied interaction with tangible and social computing during the past fifteen years. However, more abstract virtualities remain with us as well because virtual reality is still an active research field, because the major part of the gaming industry still favors virtuality qua immersive three-dimensional worlds of a certain illusionist realism, because phenomena such as *Second Life* still demonstrate a considerable cultural pull, and because a concretization of ubicomp culture may very well be assimilated in large part by developments of abstract platform services such as those we see emerging today under the rubric of "cloud computing."

Insofar as projects such as those mentioned earlier undertake actualizations of virtuality and gradually bring forth an everyday culture of living with the mixed realities of information-intensive milieus, they begin to indicate that ad hoc dynamic exchanges among technical and human types of context awareness present both a daunting task (for humans and machines alike) and a source of surprise (welcome or not). Perhaps it is still too early to say whether and how ubicomp as technical tendency will be concretized as a new set of overtly unfolded modes of living with pervasive computational technics or, rather, as a more calm technical culture[15] with a higher degree of embeddedness of context-aware computational units. However, embedded components already vastly outstrip the number of stand-alone and in-the-box computers in our world today. Thus, the varied specialization, the sheer number, the ad hoc networking, and the increasing mobility of computational units have in any case already begun to problematize the notion of the modern computer as a universal machine, and it is an open question what will emerge from this inclination toward a dynamics of multiplicitous singularization.

III

The focus and special merit of this book is to enter into an altogether contemporary field of research in order to make a certain difference while the cultural and technical developments at stake are still ongoing and emergent. Hence, this book engages in a history of the present, specifically as regards the traits of contemporary culture, ICT, and media that are in the process of fast-paced innovative change, both generally speaking over several decades and more particularly with respect to ubicomp and pervasive computing during the past two decades, about which cultural theorists do not yet agree, and regarding which the engineers, the computer scientists, the software developers, and the interaction designers have not achieved a first consensus (not to mention an established array of standards). Culturally speaking, this publication appears in the wake of studies of network and information societies, new media, and media art during the past decade and a half. It inscribes itself in a context in which we have in fact witnessed a number of conferences concerning the technical development of ubiquitous and pervasive computing, many of which have resulted in the publication of conference proceedings, and these conferences now continue on a regular basis.[16] Likewise, the interested reader will today be able to find a few state-of-the-art handbooks and at least two dozen books treating of special issues in hardware engineering as well as software and middleware design for pervasive and ubiquitous computing.[17] However, even though some other kinds of conferences have been held (in Yokohama, New York, Weimar, London, and Copenhagen), mostly by culture and art organizations as well as by universities, the field of research is more than anything characterized by the delay and underdevelopment of organized and more substantially developed approaches from the perspectives of cultural studies or from the human and social sciences broadly speaking. At least two interesting monographs have appeared, though; the studies done by Malcolm McCullough (2004) and Adam Greenfield (2006) provide a quite detailed account of what is at stake culturally and architecturally in the emergence of ubiquitous and pervasive computing, each drawing in its own way on a sound, vocal skepticism so as to point to a first set of critical evaluations. Nonetheless, this volume is the first to present a relatively comprehensive anthology that engages in an explicit treatment of a considerable subset of the sociocultural, ethicopolitical, media-specific, aesthetic, and philosophical aspects and implications of the contemporary development of ubiquitous computing.

The thirty-four chapters in this book therefore proceed toward a timely and, it is hoped, quite thought-provoking mapping of a number of the recent developments in those forms of cultural life, sociality, interaction, design, media art, and aesthetics that are now emerging with ubicomp. This mapping takes place in a situation that seems to solicit at least two broad kinds of gradual paradigm shifts in cultural approaches. If we are now past the first intense waves of research treating the rise of the Internet and Net culture, new media, e-communication, and media art, it appears that the further maturation of studies in this field of information culture implicitly continues to call upon distinctions between the technical inside and the cultural outside of computers, the abstract virtuality and the actual embodiment of information. It is too early to tell where a perceived shift drawing upon these distinctions will lead. Very likely, though, at least two broad efforts will necessarily continue to inform each other in the exploration of the relation between technics and culture, both now hinging on a notion of ubiquity.

We have already seen the first results of the recent call from a number of scholars to begin considering "software studies" as one very salient path toward outlining a new field or discipline that would expand and deepen computer literacy and so meet the ubiquity of computing via a more broadly shared sociocultural competence in coding and interaction design. This initiative should be sufficient to indicate the import of viewing and practically approaching software not primarily as a privileged and rather invisible cultural practice behind a certain pervasive coding and tagging of our environment and life form, but rather as something we would want to see distributed to the point of becoming a user-driven mode of expression and innovation available to a great many inhabitants of information and network societies. This broadly conceived effort will concern the ways in which the cultural practice and study of "new media" and "media art" can and should bracket the concrete products and the contents of media platforms so as to be brought further *into* the media themselves (as Marshall McLuhan already called for) in order to understand how their forms and operations contribute to the shaping of culture. The solicitation of software studies seems to promise one very productive and interesting path insofar as it may become an interdisciplinary approach in the human and social sciences to software as a technical artifact that has its own cultural history, sociology, and art criticism. It remains to be seen how formalistic software studies will have to be, just as it is not yet clear how close to software engineering, computer science, and computing in itself this effort will have to move. In any case, it involves a call to bring culture and cultural studies *into* computing and seems to bespeak an understanding of ubiquity as a question of the relation between, on the one hand, a pervasive presence of software processes and sources in media and, on the other, an extended computer literacy in mediation, especially in the areas of programming and source code.

The other effort will, in a manner of speaking, proceed on an inverse course, inspired at once by the original vision concerning ubiquity issuing from Mark Weiser and a number of associated researchers as well as by a host of existing disciplines in the human and social sciences. This effort will involve a renewed investigation of where we are today with respect to Weiser's rather resolute call for a distinctly human-centered third epoch of post–personal computer, post-desktop, post-GUI computing. That is, it concerns a development that brings computing *out* into the physical world, repositioning it in the environmental background, allegedly on our terms and within the everyday culture of work, leisure, and the home, notably in such ways that computers get out of the way rather than insistently demanding that attention be paid to their autonomy and specific modes of operation. It would also involve a renewed encounter with the question of how to think, work, and live with "embodied virtuality" today—that is, the question of where we are today with the process of drawing computers *out* of the box so that the "virtuality" of information is brought into the real environment, embedded and integrated more or less (in)visibly in the rather rich and complex context of our lived and living embodiment, perhaps on the hither side of our awareness. As Weiser sensed very early, this out-of-the-box physical turn of computing toward integration in a context of live embodiment (machinic and human) demands the articulation of an incredibly intelligent, intimate, and robust knowledge of our life forms and everyday culture. This turn can therefore proceed only by drawing on a vast set of interdisciplinary resources in the human and social sciences as well as in other natural sciences. It remains to be seen how far the current involvement of anthropologists, sociologists, psychologists, cognitive scientists, neurobiologists, and medical specialists in computing will move information processing toward a strong delimitation of the *anthropos* and toward a mix with others and the other. In any case, ubicomp involves a call to bring computing very far *out* into both culture and cultural studies (in the broadest sense).

The chapters here confirm—as does the book's constellation of researchers from computer science, human–computer interaction studies, media studies, science and technology studies, sociology, and the arts and humanities—that this book responds largely to questions raised by this second kind of effort. Thus, it investigates not least the philosophical, sociocultural, aesthetic, and artistic implications of a computing that is well on the way toward operating infinitely close to human culture and our life form—one interesting paradox being that the closer and more intimate this human-centered computing becomes, in its abstract top-down programming and in its concrete bottom-up embodiments, the more it raises the question of the in- or ahuman, the question of our inexistence.

The contributors to this book, counting almost forty researchers from across the globe, do not have an explicitly shared methodology, just as the reader will not find obvious agreement with respect to the major research issues dealt with. They all do agree, however, that the broad field of mutually (de)constitutive relationality between contemporary culture and ubicomp needs to see considerably more cultural theoretical work and that this work must necessarily happen as an unfolding of exchanges in transdisciplinary fashion. The contributors agree that ubiquitous and pervasive computing exists as a recognizable and potentially very important developmental trend that is now well on its way to making its cultural implications felt. However, this agreement comes supplemented with at least two major reservations. First, if cultural modalities in contemporary network societies have already changed enough to warrant the recognition that in a number of ways we *are already* living in a ubicomp epoch and world, then it is also the case that ubicomp largely remains to come: in technical terms, a fully developed, robust, pervasively distributed, innovatively ad hoc networked, relatively intelligent, and context-aware ubiquitous computing in and of mixed realities operating with a set of recognized paradigms for interaction design and multimodal exchanges has yet to emerge. Second, the contributors are divided in their critical evaluations of this emergence but agree that it is still not possible to decide the kinds and degrees of embeddedness and overt unfolding, respectively, that will come to prevail, although at this point it appears to incline asymmetrically toward more embeddedness and thus toward a "calm" ubicomp.

When setting to work on their chapters, the authors also agreed that out-of-the-box computing should be granted a relatively but not absolutely privileged focus in this particular book. Hence, the chapters operate on the shared assumption that the field of inquiry involves in particular a ubicomp that resides with a third epoch of computing (after the mainframe and the personal computer), one preoccupied with the question whether and how computing is, should be, or can be moving on from existing primarily as distinctly recognizable units so as to be multiplicitously and pervasively integrated into our living and working environments and perhaps altogether invisibly embedded in our lifeworld and life form. The contributors thus share a working definition of ubiquitous computing as a sociocultural *and* technical thrust to integrate and/or embed computing pervasively, to have information processing thoroughly integrated with or embedded into everyday objects and activities, including those pertaining to human bodies and their parts.

In other words, the chapters share the largely silent initial hypothesis that if an individual is living with ubicomp, then this "living with" does not concern or only marginally concerns engaging consciously with a single device or application for some definite purpose. Rather, it concerns engaging with multiple computational devices and systems simultaneously during more or less ordinary activities, without necessarily being aware of doing so. This is also to say that the models and practical implementations of ubicomp investigated here largely adhere to something like Weiser's vision of myriad small, inexpensive, robust, networked information-processing devices, perhaps mobile but certainly distributed at all scales throughout everyday life and culture, most often turned toward distinctly mundane, commonsensical, and commonplace ends.

IV

This volume is structured in seven parts, each motivated by a core problematic, and these seven major research issues constituted the original invitation to the contributors. Thus, they all agree on the questions as a relevant series of problem statements for this research field, just as they have signaled that these seven broadly defined issues provide not a complete or an altogether comprehensive, but certainly a productive if provisional and initial delimitation such as befits a first, partly exploratory publication in a field. The seven parts of the book can be read independently, as can the individual chapters, but the reader will find that the chapters contain numerous cross-pollinating references internal to the book and that the parts give rise to certain kinds of internal resonance. Moreover, the book parts proceed, generally speaking, toward immanence, or it might be said that they undertake an "abstraction downward," much like the paragraphs in the first section of this introduction. In broad strokes, then, the thirty-four chapters contribute to seven parts that move through questions concerning the visual sense and sensation of living with an ubicomp culture (part I), the auditory impressions made upon us in an ubicomp culture and the sense we might try to make of these impressions (part II), the continuities and changes one observes in communications in an ubicomp epoch and world (part III), the general trends and concrete specificities of interaction designs for ubiquity and concomitant changes in our notions of interactivity (part IV), the ways in which we become moved by ubicomp-experience engineerings and designs of a live character (part V), manifestations of the context awareness of ubicomp and their exchanges with our being contextually aware in the world (part VI), and approaches to those literal and more metaphorical or discursive claims made on a pervasiveness and ubiquity that are to justify the use of the terms *augmented reality*, *real environment*, and *mixed reality* (part VII). The contributors can be read as responding to the following series of suggestive questions, articulated more fully:

- How are your sense and sensation of a culture and an art installed thoroughly, as artifactual augmentations and augmented virtualities in and as objects, in and as environments?
  - In what ways do contemporary information art and its abstractly virtual and embodied aesthetics perhaps exceed or come before sense making in their deployment of augmentation, mixing, and ubiquity effects? If the thorough reach and the tendential embeddedness of ubicomp culture hint at a privileging of sensation over sense, how are the field and dynamics of the sensations evolving from interaction with new media events and installation spacings to be approached? More specifically, what is the status in this context of the synaesthetic relations or more or less singularly anesthetic breaks among such phenomena as
    - The visuality of surveillance and tracking as well as the expanded cinematics of locative media?
    - The auditory culture of technologically informed attunement, ambience, soundscapes, and atmospheres?
    - The increased import in mixed realities of the sense of touch, haptics, and primordial tactility?
    - The sensation of corporeal movement, suspension, exposition, or danger—for example, the performative and receptive roles played today by kinesthesia, proprioception, and interoception when one is living on with embedded networks of sensors and actuators?
- If everyday cultural practices in contemporary network societies indicate that an ubicomp culture includes communicating "everyware" everywhere, what would then constitute an appraisal of the social and personalized pervasiveness today of mixed-reality communications? How can one describe, analyze, and critically evaluate events and spaces of communication—at once situated and mobile, plugged in and wireless, tangible and withdrawn, filled with lacunae and distributed everywhere? What are the implications of new forms of medial distribution for cultural communication, convergent as well as irreducibly medium specific, in texts and literature, photography and digital images, film and video, music, radio, vague haptic signals, physical vibrations,

and force feedback? What is the technocultural impact on social communication patterns when one considers new backbones for networked communication at high speed as well as myriad embedded and often tiny, wireless communication units or macroscale devices such as PDAs, mobile phones, iPods, new handheld and very large screen surfaces implemented everywhere?

• Given that there is not yet one or more recognized interaction paradigms for a ubicomp culture but nonetheless multiple performative interaction designs making themselves felt thoroughly in real time and in three dimensions, how are these designs as well as our very notion of interactivity to be approached, engaged with, grasped, and evaluated? Where are we today with regard to the disappearance of the visible computer and the rise of the intuitively appealing interaction design in mixed realities? Are we approaching the actualization of that ideal of an immanent invisibility that Mark Weiser and others proposed for projects in "calm" computing, so that ubicomp cultures already operate with interaction designs and interfaces characterized by their visual invariance (Gibson 1984), their proximity to a situated and lived experience (*Erlebnis*), their partaking of a tacit dimension (Polanyi), their vague and unobtrusive peripheral reach (John Seely Brown), their compiling (Simon), their horizontality (Gadamer), and their being ready to hand (Heidegger)? In that case, how do you approach not only the complex technical integration and embeddedness at stake, but also its more or less unknowable experience engineering—that is, its implications in terms of an increasingly affective and haptic dimension of embodied interaction, a discretization of sensation and perception, and a delimitation of conscious awareness?

• To what extent and how, then, are humans being corporeally and virtually moved in a live fashion today by ubicomp-experience engineering toward passion, affect, emotion, and action or being bypassed by it? How can our existing approaches—for instance, in cultural studies, media studies, and technology studies—accommodate the kinds of liveness and performativity at play in this movement? What paths are to be followed in response to the management of value and power or ethics and politics inherent in the potential and actual delimitations of human awareness by such engineerings of movement and liveness? In what ways are new life forms, new modes of social emergence, new modes of self-presentation and self-affectation developing alongside such engineering of live dynamics, and how will they be approachable in experience on the hither side of the movement? Alternatively, how are movements of anthropic liveness affecting us (in)organically in ubicomp cultures—in extended, borderline, or implanted ways that might prove productive of a more or less (post) human or (in)human lifeworld?

• Are we to live with an embedded context awareness throughout—an awareness that is perhaps less or more than just human? What is one to make of the reach and consequences of the multiplicitous distribution and networking of embedded computa-

tional units in ubiquitous or pervasive computing? If one encounters today a certain rise in ecotechnics, in the sense of an extensive set of mutual implications between an embedded ecology of technics and an informed technics of ecology, how does one approach and assess the context-sensitive interplay among humans and the seemingly intelligent ecosystems of machines at stake? If one meets, for the most part without being aware of it, hosts of new technocultural assemblages, in the sense of historically contingent and scalable collections of heterogeneous machinic and culturalizing components (each in its manner defined by relations of exteriority or its plugging out and in to other components), how then does one address issues of thorough technical embeddedness and the potential or real delimitations of an embodied human life and its kinds of awareness? In short, to what extent does the implementation of ubiquitous context awareness make it difficult or even impossible to distinguish between a more or less commonsensical lifeworld and a more or less invisible technosphere of contextual sensitivity? More specifically, what would "context" mean or be if at least minimally explicit tags, markers, and traces were not inserted, for humans and technics alike, more or less indeterminately, more or less purposefully?
• How pervasive, ubiquitous, and tangible are the information technologies in the culture of today and in what literal or metaphorical discursive senses? Do they indeed constitute one or more genuinely mixed realities? Do they change reality throughout in virtually simulacral and augmentationally artifactual ways, or do they at most impinge periodically and locally on our notions of reality, or are they, all hyperbole aside, deployable and interpretable in meaningful or commonsensical ways through and through? In what ways are questions concerning the theoretical or practical breaks and relations between virtuality and actuality, virtual environment and real environment, to be met with respect to any such "mixed" reality (for example, in terms of strict demarcations, overlays, augmented virtuality, augmented reality, and/or remixes involving analog–digital as well as digital–analog conversions)? How do we encounter mixed realities as a problematic in the concrete spaces and events in which our lives are lived today as a matter of everyday culture? What are mixed realities as information-intensive environments, what are their kinds of thingness and their bodily dimensions, and what do their mixes imply for contacts among human sociocultural or individual self-organization and otherness?

In part I, entitled "Sense and Sensations 1: Image," four authors begin to investigate and explicate what a ubicomp culture amounts to in terms of its visuality, if any, and as a matter of the sense and sensations of images. Mark Hansen's chapter, "Ubiquitous Sensation: Toward an Atmospheric, Collective, and Microtemporal Model of Media," delineates the sensory impact of ubicomp as a question of an expansion of the visible to include the imperceptible: a new correlation of media and sensation that occurs beneath the temporal frame definitive of both image and conscious perception. Hansen approaches the invisibility of ubicomp as the invocation of a microsensational address by the image in its technical expansion to include a periphery of imperceptible but objectively sensory informational flows. In a rereading of Weiser's vision and of key texts in the phenomenological tradition as well as in an encounter with Olafur Eliasson's media-art environment *Your Color Memory* (2004), he thus indicates how one may further develop an existential postphenomenology of the body that may meet peripheral ubicomp visuality as what impacts the sensing brain microtemporally in the form of an imaging at a level beneath the threshold of conscious attention and awareness. In "The Ubiquity of Photography," Arild Fetveit retraces the development of photographic practices that has taken place during the medial migration to a digital support and the use of software for image making and image editing. Fetveit sees in this migration less a demise of photography than a continuous development of photography as a medium toward its present ubiquity, which includes not only the introduction of a malleability of the image that potentially expands its area of operation and its distribution, but also an adjustment of its ontology so as to make it more contingently performative while its medium of storage and its medium of display are kept separate. In a ubicomp culture, photographic images are thus what can migrate performatively to be visualized anywhere at any time; they are an ability to originate, multiply, and distribute malleable visualizations through networked societies so as to imbricate the photo-graphic in the very fabric of our everyday lives. Mette Sandbye continues the reconsideration of the photographic image in "The Family Photo Album as Transformed Social Space in the Age of 'Web 2.0'" by rehistoricizing the status of the family photo album in a ubicomp culture. Sandbye argues that the decisive shift took place due to a broad increase in computer literacy and with the advent of social media in a Web 2.0 sense. The family album has thus become an instantaneous and speedy performance of sociality, memory, identity, and history in increasingly mobile and dynamic ways. In detailed analyses of album presentations via Flickr, MySpace, 23hq, Fotolog, Facebook, and Picasa in particular, Sandbye's chapter addresses the family album as part of a photographic media ecology to be understood at one and the same time as social practice, networked media, and technology and as material image objects. In "Calm Imaging: The Conquest of Overload and the Conditions of Attention," Kristin Veel explores the link between ubicomp and "calmness" by analyzing a subset of those imagings that do not address our conscious and focused attention but rather operate smoothly in the background, including various modalities of surveillance and their ethicopolitical implications. Veel reconsiders the viability of a wish to counter information overload as an argument for calm and invisible technological imaging in order to call for a closer scrutiny of what is now a less noticeable set of effects on human engagement with the world because overload situations are dealt with prior to reaching our awareness. Such scrutiny can arguably be undertaken better via the use of a more fine-grained notion of attention, one that would provide a model for understanding how we can be affected by what goes on at the visual and visualizing margin of calm computing in software-sorted societies. Thus, in a number of visual case studies Veel develops and deploys with resources in cognitive psychology and neuroscience a certain lexicon of attention, including at least the three levels of theme, context, and margin, to be viewed as a fluctuating field in constant transformation.

Part II, "Sense and Sensations 2: Sounds," comprises four chapters engaging with the auditory dimensions of an emergent ubicomp culture. It opens with Joseph Auner's "Losing Your Voice: Sampled Speech and Song from the Uncanny to the Unremarkable," which undertakes an extended treatment of the ubiquity of recorded voices, human and posthuman, in our musical soundscape and in our everyday lives. Auner provides a varied array of analyses of the remixes and mashups not least in instrumental hip-hop that tend to decontextualize and recontextualize (our) voices, occasionally in uncanny ways but most often in the unremarkable fashion characteristic of a ubicomp culture now emerging. Moreover, this chapter affords a series of insights respecting the use of artificial-speech software and various kinds of samplings as well as their glitchy dislocation in murmurs and stutterings that may well have us doubt whether there is someone in or behind the voice. Michael Bull expands on the aesthetic nature of the influence on our private and public urban experience of such pervasive mobile communication technologies as the iPod. In "The End of *Flânerie*: iPods, Aesthetics, and Urban Experience," Bull thus investigates everyday urban experience under the rubric of audiovisual aestheticization of the city, with sound as the key factor. Specifically, this chapter moves through results from an empirically grounded and qualitative case-based analysis involving more than one thousand iPod users worldwide toward a critique of *flânerie* for being an inadequate concept with respect to grasping the ways in which citizens create mostly privatized and privatizing auditory bubbles as they move through the city. In "Virtual Space and Atmosphere in Electronic Music," Torben Sangild begins to roll out the implications of virtual space and atmosphere as two key concepts for understanding electronic music as being everywhere today. Sangild's text hence paves the way for a more finely differentiated understanding of the spatiality of ambient sounds and mobile devices in ubicomp auditory culture, not only in terms of the virtual spatiality of electronic music itself, but also in terms of the various blendings of this spatiality with real, dynamic spatializations in individual and social listening situations. Here an aesthetics of mixed spatiality in a ubicomp culture is approached via the experience of a musical atmosphere: a blending of the sonic atmosphere of the virtual space with the general atmosphere of the listening space, the former usually predominating. Ulrik Schmidt brings further detail to such a reconsideration of aesthetic atmospheres by pursuing an interpretation of the notion of "ambience" in both quasi-objective and quasi-subjective registers. Schmidt's endeavor in "Ambience and Ubiquity" is to reread ambience at once as a feeling or mood and as a tuning of spaces and things in their formal and material properties, only then to go on having us reconsider a great many variants of ambience in contemporary ubicomp culture and its ambient informatics. In general, this chapter would open into a different approach to the broad cultural and technological development of ambient intelligence by identifying and discussing some of the key questions of the aesthetics this intelligence presupposes: What formal and material properties produce ambient effects, and what characterizes the aesthetic experience of such properties?

Part III treats of ubiquitous ICT with respect to its communicational traits. Roberto Simanowski puts special emphasis on the aesthetic ambiguity hidden in cultural and communicational projects involving ubicomp: invisibility and calmness are logically contradicted by artworks insofar as they aim to call attention to themselves as interventions in the everyday life environment. In "Text as Event: Calm Technology and Invisible Information as Subject of Digital Arts," readers will find an attempt to revisit the aesthetics of the textual communication of digital art in such a way that they may critically reconsider whether text has declined in the digital condition to the point of losing its cultural authority or whether it has rather become eventual in a postalphabetic fashion. Simanowski thus invites us to consider textual communications in the mixed-reality spaces of a ubicomp culture, such as Julius Popp's installation *Bit.Falls* (2006), as events of presencing that shift attention to the more or less asemantic surface of text (the very materiality and appearance of information as text). Larissa Hjorth's "The Novelty of Being Mobile: A Case Study of Mobile Novels and the Politics of the Personal" considers the mobile phone, one of the most pervasive technologies of the twenty-first century, as a heralding of the importance of place as well as a personalization or portabilization of ubicomp. It provides a more detailed analysis of ubiquitous mobile media as they currently appear in Tokyo, specifically with respect to the personalization techniques at stake—both top-down, industry-driven variants and bottom-up variants driven through participatory user practices. Here special focus is granted to an investigation of mobile novels as exemplary media products behind the part of the success of mobile media due to the growth of subversive user activity. Mitchell Whitelaw enters into an extensive and occasionally critical dialog with Hans Ulrich Gumbrecht's recent work in order to propose that we recognize a "presence aesthetics" in contemporary media art, specifically one that permits us to realize that media technologies can elicit moments of intensified being-in-the-world in spite of the conventional view of these technologies as distancing that world from us. In "Transmateriality: Presence Aesthetics and the Media Arts," Whitelaw gives the reader first a theoretical elaboration of this argument and then a more practically concrete illustration of media-art projects as instances of transmaterial ubiquity presencing. He suggests a definition of transmateriality as a view of media and computational communication as always and everywhere material but constantly propagating or transducing patterns through specific instantiations.

In turn, Hans Ulrich Gumbrecht provides an alternative perspective in "Infinite Availability—about Hypercommunication (and Old Age)" by reconsidering that considerable increase in our opportunities to communicate due to ubiquitous technical devices whose effects tend toward neutralizing the consequences of physical and temporal distance. Here Gumbrecht willingly acknowledges the innovative aspect of these devices' ubiquity but at the same time adopts a strategy of withdrawal, trying to know as little about them as possible. He indicates in a variety of ways how epiphanies of presencing outside hypercommunication (less thinly spread out, more embodied, physically near, and as locally shared intellectual events or more individually moving events) continue to give form, drama, and flavor to his everyday life in this epoch.

Bo Kampmann Walther opens part IV, "Interaction Designs," with his theoretical and analytical exploration of the consequences of moving from a traditional ludological concept of computer games to an extended one pertaining to pervasive games. In "Reflections on the Philosophy of Pervasive Gaming—with Special Emphasis on Rules, Gameplay, and Virtuality," one thus finds definitions of the rules and the gameplay proper to pervasive gaming, but not least a reconsideration of Gilles Deleuze's concept of virtuality as appropriate for further work on the discontinuous relation between virtual play and actual gaming as the modus operandi of pervasive games. The reader may also appreciate Walther's concrete piecemeal illustrations of the growth in the design of game systems using ubicomp techniques to afford a certain play with mixed realities, such as projects undertaken by Blast Theory and others. In "Trying to Be Calm: Ubiquity, Cognitivism, and Embodiment," Simon Penny grants a historical and theoretical perspective on the challenges confronting interaction design in the process where discourses and technics remain marked by at least a decade of virtuality and at least a decade of ubicomp. Penny specifically pinpoints the ongoing paradigm shift toward embodied and performative cognitive approaches as something that must be further pursued if interaction designs for a ubicomp culture are to take care of currently unresolved issues. Proceeding through a number of cases, he distinguishes between two types of technics, both of which tend to be subsumed under ubicomp and have distinct relations to the social—in other words, one type that is industrial, embedded, effectively invisible, and accessed by experts, and one that is a consumer commodity and thus quite visible and demanding of attention while affording sophisticated data-gathering capabilities to paying customers. This distinction allows for a first set of critical evaluations of the desirability of interaction designs for a more or perhaps less calm ubicomp environment as well as its degrees of perturbing our skilled embodied practices. My own chapter, "Of Intangible Speed: 'Ubiquity' as Transduction in Interactivity," provides an introductory contextualization of ubicomp developments with respect to cybernetics in order to begin rethinking the notion of interactivity as a matter of what has taken place in interactions and interaction designs after the rise of network societies, new media, and media art in the 1990s. In an extensive analysis of media artist David Rokeby's early work *Very Nervous System* as an exemplary precursor of current interactivity in a ubicomp epoch and world, I propose to think of ubiquitous interactivity in Simondonean ontogenetic relational terms as a movement of becoming with a speed on or at the other side of human sensation and its current curtain of technics. In particular, such interactivity may involve a mediation of another energy, another technical tendency—that is, a transduction of human interactants in their individual, social, and technical life forms. Lev Manovich's "Interaction as a Designed Experience" charts the shift in ICT design from 1998 to 2007, emphasizing that interaction is increasingly treated as an event in the sense of being a carefully orchestrated experience. Manovich provides examples of such a new experiential interface design by analyzing in more detail Apple OS X, the LG Chocolate mobile phone, and the iPhone. Such analyses lead toward supporting his more general claim that we see today a trend of aestheticization of information tools, tightly coupled with the democratization of design, the rise of branding, global economical competition, and specifically the pervasive distribution of computers, all of which have led to a replacement of design formulas such as "form follows function" with such formulas as "form follows emotion."

If living with ubicomp moves you, this "being moved" is the field of study for the four contributions to part V, "Being Moved Live." The collaborative work by Jay David Bolter, Blair MacIntyre, Michael Nitsche, and Kathryn Farley presented in "Liveness, Presence, and Performance in Contemporary Digital Media" proceeds to supplement existing digital-media theories with a much needed performative dimension. This supplement allows not only for approaches to the liveness and event-specific presence effects of digital media (social media in particular), but also for the dynamics of mixed realities and their types of augmentation. The research group behind this chapter provides the reader with a set of engaging explorations of actual mixings of the physical dimensions of our world and *Second Life*, with special focus on mixed avatar presentations. Susan Kozel expands such performative studies of "being moved live" by reflecting on ubicomp from the perspectives of phenomenology, dance, and the choreographic practices that include large responsive systems as well as intimate devices in clothing and on skin. In "Sinews of Ubiquity: A Corporeal Ethics for Ubiquitous Computing," Kozel draws on both human kinesthetic awareness and a being in relation with the corporeally tactile or palpable aspects of the infrastructure of ubiquity as she fleshes out an ethics attending to that invisibility and that oblivion that inhere in Weiser's "calm" computing. In a manner of speaking, Kozel's contribution is itself a sensate and moving performance that assigns embodied values during its many selections in ubiquity, each time asking, *What can we, should we, do we notice? What can we, should we, do we overlook and perhaps forget?* Anne Galloway initiates in "Affective Politics in Urban Computing and Locative Media" a set of political reflections by revisiting the very mixed and often overtly critical kinds of reception of ubiquitous and pervasive computing in the early 1990s and again after 2000 as actualization of the research paradigm began in earnest. She lays bare the quite crucial concerns with what appears to be a totalizing vision of technological penetration of everyday life and an expansion of surveillance that makes of the disciplinary panopticon a rather weak model. However, the main impetus behind this chapter is the investigation of whether and how new agendas in urban computing and locative-media research and practice have emerged to present a utopian countervision, which Galloway seems to affirm both by indicating a move from a "power over" in disciplinary society to a "power to" in control society and by depicting the several ways in which collaborative, participatory, and creative action works as a driving force behind a contemporary affective politics of urban computing and locative media. In "Machinic Sutures: From Eighteenth-Century Physiognomy to Twenty-First-Century Makeover," Bernadette Wegenstein presents a historically rich series of analyses of the performative influence of augmented realities, here under the aegis of those cosmetic gazes that have humans experience their own and others' bodies as incomplete projects awaiting the intervention of technologies of enhancement. She identifies in ubicomp and augmented realities a furthering of "machinic sutures" qua the performative operation through which supposedly prior and pure aspects of selfhood (my true self, how I desire to be, my singular body) have been introjected or incorporated in subject formations. Exemplary analyses—from the nineteenth-century ideological categories apparent in Sir Francis Galton's composites and Cesare Lombroso's albums of criminals to twenty-first-century imagery and concretization of bodily makeovers—seem to confirm Wegenstein's thesis that ubicomp technics of augmentation are not altogether different in effect from earlier machinic sutures that bonded virtual images with their potential to become actualized, allegedly as a matter of attaining an elevation of virtue.

At the onset of part VI, "Context Awareness," Inke Arns undertakes a reconsideration of systemic and political-economical context awareness today in view of Deleuze's short text on control societies, diagnosing their "supple molds" in terms of transparency qua invisibilities eluding direct perception, immateriality qua connections among materialities, the performativity of code as law, and the contribution of all three to smooth or haptic close-range spaces. Arns acknowledges in "Feeding the Serpent Its Own Tail: Counterforces to Tactile Enclosure in the Age of Transparency" both the thoroughly extensive mobile reach and the invisibility of smooth and haptic molds in order to indicate how emerging forms of resistance must by necessity participate in the very activity being denounced. The reader thus encounters here a variety of counterforces to tactile enclosure, such as Net activism, software art, reverse coding, hacking, and engineering tools for resisting network domination, each of which pursues its own kind of immanent performative critiques. In "Contexts as Moving Targets: Locative Media Art and the Shifting Ground of Context Awareness" Christiane Paul outlines the contours of a weighty and differentiated treatment of the current status of context awareness in ubicomp projects that make use of mobile devices; she does so with respect to context awareness as both a matter of human, embodied, subjective, phenomenological experience and a matter of the "awareness" of embedded technological systems qua their reading of their physical environments and human inhabitants in these environments. Special emphasis is here granted to how locative media-art projects, one of the most active and fast-growing areas in the field of digital arts, enable forms of social interaction that include embodied relationality, creation of meaning, and expansion of individual autonomy and agency. Paul offers a veritable catalog of such projects and their different categories, including site-specific and translocal variants (e.g., leaving marks on the surroundings, submitting or retrieving site-specific information, reconfiguring maps) as well as projects involving systemic awareness in reactive architectures, embedded surveillance, and sensors for environmental monitoring. The environment as explored by locative media art is also the object of study for Söke Dinkla's "Intimacy and Self-Organization in Hybrid Public Spheres," which delineates the ways in which ubicomp leads to a growing division of public space into distinct fragments and to a telescoping of public and private spaces into each other. Dinkla's treatment of these developments focuses less on the tendential intensification of media intimacy characteristic of the use of mobile phones and handheld computers, separating perception from the specific time and place in which one moves, than on locative arts working toward entanglement of both communication networks and geographical spaces. Dinkla is particularly interested in investigating a substantial series of concrete projects (including the work of Hacktic Netwerk, Jochen Roller & Martin Nachbar, Blast Theory, M + M) and identifying any avant-garde potential, more or less utopian, for the creation of alternate public spheres that would develop radical democracy in postindustrial societies. Dietmar Offenhuber approaches this part's problematic from the perspective of a designer of ambient displays and dedicates his chapter, "Kuleshov's Display—on Contextual Invisibility," to the presentation of six experimental and suggestive strategies for incorporating context in such design as it is now being done in projects in architecture, public art, and interaction design. Offenhuber thus begins to address a major design challenge stemming from Weiser's call for invisibility, embeddedness, and context awareness—namely, that displays, not least very large-scale ones, usually do not tend to blend into their surroundings to achieve contextual invisibility, nor do they share the contextual qualities found in personalized ubicomp devices. Ambient displays as envisioned by Offenhuber and others thus become of interest insofar as they lose interest; that is, they may afford the human and technical processing of large amounts of information in the periphery, but their design must be unobtrusive, the expressive range of their states limited, and the information they offer implicitly encoded into the physical properties of the display itself. Offenhuber's strategies are perhaps of special interest due to their attempt to map out a certain performativity for ambient displays that would have context awareness become an emergent feature of the ongoing and situative interaction with such displays. Malcolm McCullough critically explores context awareness qua the enactment of and interaction with informational markups of urbanity, and so "Inscribing the Ambient Commons" begins to raise questions regarding the new middle ground that has emerged between official and criminal genres of signing because new forms of digital tagging have also created new roles for the rights to mark up the city, some of which turn curatorial and some of which explore the remarkable range of cultural critique. In addition, substantial parts of McCullough's contribution go toward reactualizing the potential for overlays of contextual marking to orient us to a shared urban environmental awareness (an ambient commons) and to give rise to site-sensitive social productions of information rather than information overload, anxiety, or sheer pollution.

Part VII, the final section, encompasses eight chapters that reflect in quite different ways on the relation of the human individual or sociality with ubiquitous i-technics in an environment or world that includes mixed realities. It is at this point far from clear how one would want to think and approach practically the spaces and spatiality of a ubicomp world and its mixed realities, and here Gernot Böhme might well be said to provide a first set of pointers in his treatment of the distinction between space as a medium of representation (as found in mathematics, for example, not least when serving as a medium for representing relationships within manifold objects) and the space of bodily presence (as found in Immanuel Kant and phenomenologies after Husserl, for example, including one's existential being-there in a space of actions, a space of moods, and a space of perception). In "The Space of Bodily Presence and Space as a Medium of Representation," Böhme provides readers with the quite suggestive argument that these two kinds of space can perhaps best be thought together not via a fundamental connection (e.g., approaching the mathematical as founded in bodily or lived space), but rather via a notion of singular interweavings across the gap. Böhme illustrates this relationship by discussing two exemplary forms of such overlappings or overlayings that remain of obvious import for this book's research field—namely, intuitive space and virtual spaces. Jacob Wamberg goes on in "Toward a (Re)Constructed Endosemiotics? Art, Magic, and Augmented Reality" to undertake a further analysis and evaluation of overlays as a promise of improvements and enhancements, here with respect to the broad notion of augmented spaces presented by Manovich. Wamberg's wager, in semiotic terms, is that augmented reality can be placed in a utopian genealogy insofar as it reawakens the index as a primal sign of communication and thereby also reactualizes certain layers of communication in nature. Here Wamberg seeks in particular to investigate initiatives such as the Canadian *whisper[s]* project and the work of Eduardo Kac with a view to the question whether augmented reality fulfills certain repressed desires of art and what role art and aesthetics can play (being subsumed, being made superfluous, taking on an active or critical role).

Bernard Stiegler presents two complementary texts in this publication, "Teleologics of the Snail, or the Errancies of the Equipped Self in a WiMax Network" and "The Indexing of Things," which begin to rethink the character and status of immanent subjective existentiality and objecthood, respectively, in the mixed realities of a ubicomp culture. In the former, Stiegler makes a call for a psychosocial and technical pharmacological "therapy" that may lead to a radical rethinking of teleology in the era of the WiMax networks and quasi-ubiquitous connectivity—in other words, that may lead to a new teleologic capable of taking care of an organology also for the current telecommunicational connections of all objects, bodies, and souls. In the latter chapter, Stiegler engages in an immanent critique of the Internet of Things, exploring the current concretization of these connections (new modes of Internet addressing), their technical objects (RFIDs), and their indexicality (with respect to the milieu or environment). This critique traces not only the gradual and processual production of a new technogeographically associated milieu that threatens an industrial technologization of human-associated milieus, but also the remaining potential in this technologization for approaching "things" and "objects" differently. For Stiegler, they should be approached not just as hypomnesic objects qua artifacts of memory, but also, immanently prior to this approach, as hyperobjects qua transitional gifts that may go beyond short-circuiting intersubjective relationships to intensify them and generate the framework for a new process of psychic and collective individuation. N. Katherine Hayles is at one with Stiegler as regards addressing the questions posed by the Internet of Things (RFIDs) and the implications for relation between humans and environments, including mixes with more or less ubiquitous out-of-the-box computational entities. Her chapter, "Radio-Frequency Identification: Human Agency and Meaning in Information-Intensive Environments," inquires into the role and status of the human, given a situation in which subjects must be epistemologically concerned with the perception of objects that are no longer passive and inert but animated with agency and communicational powers and in which at the same time human autonomy may seem threatened on a constitutive ontological plane. Hayles makes a substantial effort here to account quite precisely and with numerous illustrations for the technical, military, economical, and ethicopolitical stakes in the debates surrounding the development of mixed realities involving an Internet of Things. In the hope of having parenthesized certain coercive and exploitative aspects, she undertakes this project in order to shed a number of misconceptions (about cognition in particular) and thus to prepare the ground for an approach to RFID that sees it as life enhancing and to afford a more processual, relational, and accurate view of embodied human action and construction of meaning.

Tom Cohen can be said to insert a hinge or a turning point in part VII because he and then John Johnston and Timothy Lenoir present contributions that approach mixed realities with ubicomp by questioning any call for a return to human centeredness. Cohen questions this return as a ritual reassertion of anthropic sovereignty, first by deconstructing the ideality of "ubiquity" as a human fable in need of a notion of the posthuman that is not just a wounded humanism and then by exploring any alternatives to be found in the (small) part of Bernard Stiegler's work treating of nanomutations. Here Cohen somewhat emphasizes the ways in which Stiegler makes of nanotechnology a figure of what stands at the limit of the unthinkable—that is, where a human's perceptual and cognitive settings stand to be reconfigured by the promise of the virtual to transform transindividuation itself (Stiegler's adaption of Simondon). In "Digital Gaia," John Johnston's exposition of increasingly large control systems as grown and trained rather than coded and engineered intentionally displaces the anthropological cultural premises for the debate over mixed ubicomp realities with ever so many "intelligent" objects, laying bare one of the key research questions hardly treated elsewhere: How far have we come today with respect to the development of *biologically* inspired computing and *evolutionary* programming? Johnston's rereading of the novels of Vernor Vinge as the imaginary of ubicomp thus has the merit of beginning to foreground the kinds of complex, quasi-organic, and inorganically animate network dynamics and emergences silently presupposed or marginalized in most accounts of mixed realities with ubiquitous or pervasive computing. Timothy Lenoir brings this publication to a close by giving the reader a rich set of critical reflections on where we are today with respect to both the fear and the (non)realization of Vinge's famous speculative scenario of "the technological singularity," which predicts the construction of superhuman intelligent machines and a rapid transition to a nonhuman-dominated world. Lenoir expertly revisits the fields of artificial intelligence, advanced robotics, and cultural theory's predominant treatments of the posthuman as ideologically discursive or narrative formations rather than as material systems and technological processes, thus facilitating an understanding of any crossing over to an era of the posthuman in a postbiological sense. Hence, Lenoir can be said to move us toward the end of this book by opening it to a further questioning to come, respecting whether and how the mixes of quasi-ubiquitous technocultural artifacts in the widest sense might best be considered as coevolving with their human host–parasites, companion species dependent on but also powerfully shaping us through a coevolutionary spiral.

V

An introduction to a first publication concerning a research field in emergence can perhaps best end on an opening note. In that sense, this last section constitutes, as does the book in its entirety, a call for further critical engagement with ubicomp culture as not just a fact of life, but also as an emergent development with some cultural, technical, anthropological, social, economical, juridical, political, ethical, and aesthetic implications, not least as regards its takes on a certain normativity for our forms of life. In issuing such a call, I do not mean to signal that "critique" of ubicomp culture has to rely directly on a Kantian heritage of a reflective examination of the validity and limits of a human capacity or of a set of philosophical claims. Critique can well be extended to some systematic inquiry into the conditions and consequences of the existing concepts, theories, disciplines, and approaches to ubicomp culture in an attempt to understand their limitations and validity. It can also very well involve extensions of efforts to (re)evaluate or (re)politicize certain local or delimited manifestations of social problems related to ubicomp culture by situating them in current historical and cultural contexts—that is, by implicating oneself in the process of collecting and analyzing data only to relativize the value or the power of the findings because "meaning" in this context can be seen as unstable due to the rapid transformation in conventions, habits, social structures, media, and technics. In all likelihood, critiques will thus demonstrate quite some interest in the *processes* that give rise to ubiquity effects; these processes can be observable linguistic or symbolic ones but may also well be a matter of immanent and real ones of felt embodied synthesis, social organizings, or tracings of technical production.

Numerous issues obviously await such critical consideration here, but for reasons of brevity I restrict myself to a short initiation of work on four issues: the self-avowed delimitation of ubiquitous and pervasive computing by the hardware engineers, software developers, and interaction designers; the tendential lack in cultural studies, the humanities, and the social sciences to undertake a corresponding delimitation of "ubiquity" and "pervasiveness" as idealities and philosophical tropes; the potentially exaggerated fear of technical embeddedness in cultural studies as well as the potentially underestimated need in technical research and development for culturally informed variants of constructive criticism; and the lack of a more finely differentiated conceptual apparatus in cultural studies that would be capable of engaging with technical, medial, embodied, and relational aspects of a mixed reality.

Embeddedness

Because Weiser's original ideas and ideals for ubicomp have been widely adopted by technical developers and cultural theorists alike, they should be revisited today with respect to the implications of an embedded ubicomp, notably in terms of relations between human and technical context awareness. Pointing toward a human-centered computing with a "calm" context awareness is obviously a move that is culturally and technically far from innocent or value free, and it is still unclear today where technical developments and cultural approaches will end up going. Here it might initially be of interest to pursue a double course, at once parenthesizing some of the potentially exaggerated fear of technical embeddedness evident in cultural studies *and* opening up technical research and development for more culturally informed variants of constructive criticism, because these variants continue to risk being underestimated in spite of laudable moves toward transdisciplinary research teams in this particular field.

"Embeddedness" is in and of itself nothing new (figure I.6). We recognize it easily enough in conventional notions of enfolding so as to provide support or reinforcement, in the recursive nesting of some element in the middle of a similar or different element, or simply in our everyday practices of embedding various media into a text document or a Web page so as to form a compound file. "Embedded systems" have likewise been a staple of computer science for quite a long time and denote devices

Figure I.6

Becoming aware of embeddedness and systemic context awareness in Rafael Lozano-Hemmer's *Under Scan*, Leicester, UK (2006).

Source: Photograph courtesy of Rafael Lozano-Hemmer.

and associated applications designed to do some specific task rather than aiming at being a general and multipurpose computer. Such devices can be standalone, but they very often consist of small, computerized parts within some much larger device that serves a more general purpose—for example, the elements of the graphics cards in personal computers or the elements in the display systems in many cars. Some embedded systems have real-time performance constraints (safety, usability), but others may have very low constraints or none, thus allowing systems hardware to be simplified and cost effective. The program instructions written for embedded systems are usually stored in read-only memory or Flash memory chips (firmware), and the programs run with limited hardware resources, such as very little memory and a small or nonexistent keyboard and screen.

Generally speaking, then, Weiser's focus on embedded systems would in and of itself not be all that groundbreaking or thought provoking but would rather lead one toward a closer examination of the applications and devices intimately related to some particular physical process. This examination would notably involve topics such as the relevant mechanisms, sensors, actuators, and feedback systems; the necessary analog and digital circuits, power amplifiers, signal processing, operational amplifiers, and multiplexing; the channels of input and output, conversion from analog to digital and vice versa, and the use of latching, serial, or parallel interfaces; the modes of signal processing and ways to condition signals; and in particular the real-time programming at stake for the firmware.

One can, however, begin to recognize already in this examination an entire series of implicit and quite remarkable displacements that characterize the development of ubicomp technics and culture, some of which were noted earlier. The very act of placing embeddedness center stage already implies a shift of focus away from the ideal formalization of a general computer to the actual operation of particular devices and their applications as well as a shift from an abstract purposiveness to more concrete purposes intimately linked with the ongoing processes in various places in the physical world. This pragmatic or performative orientation toward emphasizing more strictly bottom-up approaches, real-time computing, and mixed realities involving the dynamics and active processes in the physical world is actually quite momentous, given the emphasis in much of traditional computer science on strictly formal or mathematical abstraction of the virtual, elegant general solutions not necessarily oriented toward events in real time and top-down approaches. Embeddedness in ongoing processes in shifting places also implies displacements both toward a more or less relentless distribution and implementation of computational units in the physical world and toward the granting of a strong primacy to movement and mobility.

Moreover, the embeddedness of so many specific devices and applications bespeaks a displacement toward the quite concrete "law of the big number" in computing.

Ubicomp is not only the distributive and dynamically moving myriad of computational entities and humans in mixed reality, but also the emergence effects of encounters among multiplicities of devices, applications, users, and ways of being put into use. No doubt, this is the reason why complexity theory and notions of synergetics, emergence, biological life formations, the dynamics of animated adaptation and evolution, as well as swarm intelligence and flocking are enjoying quite a vogue as research paradigms, along with inquiry into generalizable principles that govern the self-organized production of new macroscopic structures irrespective of the nature of the microscopic individual parts involved.

All the elements in this series of displacements are certainly necessary but nevertheless not sufficient to delineate the most innovative, difficult, and perhaps disturbing triple move in Weiser's vision of ubicomp: (1) the insistence that "embeddedness" be understood as part of a decidedly human-centered computing; (2) that doing justice to this human orientation means developing a certain advanced humanoid "context awareness" in computing; and (3) that this context awareness should be "calm" and so entail an unobtrusive embeddedness akin to the disappearance of computing elements into invisibility and unrecognizability for any average human "us."

The first move is being received with a quite strong interest in the fields of computer science, social science, and the humanities alike, although in computer science more generally it is still a "mere" supplement. One should note, however, that the emphasis on a human-centered computing is something that prevents any strict or hyperbolic understanding of embeddedness, as if computation and computational units were really or altogether folded in on themselves in monadic and autonomous fashion. This was never the case because at the very least on the circuit level, openings and relations of electricity, signals, and input/output feedback have always remained on the infrastructural plane. With the focus on human-centered computing, embeddedness is actually understood in a new and far less strictly embedded sense, which introduces the need and call for a "context awareness" that goes extraordinarily far in the direction of opening computational devices and applications to themselves, other devices and applications, as well as the entire environment and all manner of human users.

In computer science as well as in the existing transdisciplinary initiatives, the second move has very quickly turned out to be one of the most interesting and fertile fields of research for ubicomp and pervasive computing, although the questions concerning the semantics of "context awareness" and the ways of pursuing it as a defined set of goals in computing and sociocultural human practice are still far from being resolved, not least with respect to the kind and degree of human centering. Generally speaking, context-aware systems not only are regarded as a necessary and enabling technology for ubicomp but are equally much at stake in ambient intelligence projects, mobile computing, wearable computing, and the design of innovative user interfaces, just as they are beginning to be felt in the Internet in the form of personal profiling and hybrid search engines.

When ubicomp becomes a topic of more decidedly heated debate, it is often in relation to the third move, very likely due to associations of "calm embeddedness" with some version of a Big Brother syndrome or at least the problems adhering to what many perceive to be a blockage of conscious enlightenment (or a minimum disclosure of information), practical access and rights to act, ethical responsibility, and an embodied sensate and aesthetic involvement—over and above signal force, blind affectedness, and stress. One can understand the critical overheating because it is not exactly becalming to consider the implementation of embedded, invisible, and hidden interaction designs as well as context-aware, adaptive, and intelligent or cognitive networks and systems that are not subject to your recognition, not subject to your delimitation (as regards their reach, distribution, and cross-referencing), not subject to your desire or need to change them or to your sense of a right to delete their storage of your personal information. As Weiser was already aware, the vagueness or strict indiscernibility of an information-intensive and embedded ubicomp would make it difficult, if not impossible, to figure out what controls what, what is connected to what, where the information flows, how it is (mis)used, what has crashed (or functions "correctly" but certainly not as an improvement), and what the consequences are for any given action or kind of responsiveness vis-à-vis an ineluctable mixed reality.

All of these issues critically need to be addressed further, but at the same time computational embeddedness is here to stay, just as it will in all likelihood increase in the future—witness the ratio of the implementation of around two hundred million processors in computers to the implementation of around eight billion processors in embedded systems. For the time being, we can view the movement toward embeddedness in our environment and lifeworld as a remarkably useful phenomenon with respect to getting us to think about and discuss in a reasonable way the kind of world and ecotechnics we already are and perhaps should be designing for—not least as regards climate, energy, change, mobility, disclosure, access, information rights, responsibility, and modalities of affectedness and affectivity involved.

In addition to an ongoing discussion of this issue (What should be embedded, how much, how, where, and when, involving whom, and how does one address the question of [non]embedded sovereignty?), we need a further examination of the distinction between humans and computers now that we are well into living with a more human-centered computing and its "context-aware" systems. What does it mean for a system to be "context aware" and allegedly in a more or less intelligent, human-oriented way? One might begin to define "context-aware" systems via the discourse of computer science, which generally refers to the idea (and empirical fact) that computers can both sense and react to their environment. "Context" was thus early on often defined very broadly as "any information that can be used to characterize the situation of entities" (Dey 2001, 3). However, in terms of theoretical models as well as practical development, the definition has been rather more restrictive and specific. Once both devices and users were brought squarely into the picture as "entities," "context" initially tended to be reduced to a matter of static location, and only in a next stage was a processual and more mobile and a shifting human-user approach adopted, even though researchers and developers were quite conscious of the reduction; the article by Bill Schilit, Norman Adams, and Roy Want (1995) that coined the term *context awareness* as early as 1994 was a great deal more complex. This reductionism in any case led to the later proposal of more dynamic and sophisticated context models (Bolchini, Carlo A. Curino, Elisa Quintarelli, et al. 2007).

More specifically, context-aware systems operate with a view to information on two axes and with at least three categories on each axis. On an axis relating to the physical environment, "awareness" encompasses information processing with respect to (1) physical conditions, such as pressure, noise, and light; (2) infrastructural conditions, such as surrounding resources for task performance, computation, and communication; and (3) locative conditions, such as absolute position, relative position, and co-location. Along a human-factors axis, "awareness" implies an operationality drawing upon at least three categories relating to the user environment: (1) the user's social environment, such as the user's co-location with others, social interaction, and group dynamics; (2) the user's tasks, such as spontaneous activity, tasks engaged, and general goals; and (3) the individual user, such as knowledge of habits, emotional state, and biophysical condition (Schmidt, Beigl, and Gellersen 1999).

In terms of moving toward making good on operating with such awareness in real-time, three-dimensional practice, the technical research-and-development efforts and their accompanying cultural practices have already gone through at least three phases, after which one can observe increased distribution and mobility, more autonomous multisensory context awareness, and higher levels of abstraction and dynamics of application development. To begin with, in a phase of indirect awareness, when context was in the main perceived as a question of the location of devices and users, it was almost entirely determined at the infrastructural level and then signaled to relevant devices, and one can see the remainders of a static, wired, and relatively distributed network paradigm in this approach. The very large majority of projects in installation media art still operates according to this type of scheme.

Context began to be understood in more strictly distributed, mobile, and embedded ways once advances (in size, cost, and complexity) in the technics of sensors and dynamic wireless networks permitted direct awareness—in other words, permitted that very small embeddable and mobile devices had a built-in awareness, obtaining and analyzing context autonomously. Quite specifically, direct awareness could be embedded in mobile devices on the basis of advances in the form of new, small sensors drawing upon piezo materials, very-large-scale-integration video, optical gyros, and MEMS (Gellersen, Schmidt, and Beigl 2002). Certain innovative and artistic explorations of wearable computing and smart environments have begun to exploit such direct awareness at least in part—one good example being New York–based artist-architects Diller & Scofidio's *Blur Building* (2002) with its coupling of everything from physical water-control systems to scanners and servers to sensor networks and wearable "brain-coats" (Ekman 2009).

In a third phase, another level of abstraction was enabled once such devices began to exchange contextual information with other devices and servers (raising new questions concerning the real-time handling of the context of contexts) and to operate with a multisensor awareness beyond powerful single position sensors and cameras (the trend leading to ever smaller sensor packages that increasingly integrate *in* the sensor hardware capacities for context feature extraction). This phase saw the arrival of more complex modules for application layers (something that is today also becoming more directly user driven—with new applications for mobile phones, for example).

The general need for augmented context awareness has been widely accepted, and the definition of what constitutes "context" has by now been quite widely discussed in this field of research. Some consensus has thus been reached that context-aware systems are concerned with the acquisition of context (e.g., using sensors to perceive a situation), the abstraction and understanding of context (e.g., matching a perceived sensory stimulus to a context), and application behaviors based on recognized contexts (e.g., triggering actions based on contextual understanding). With the arrival of more complex models, the general issue that faces the ubiquitous- and pervasive-computing community is now less what is meant by context awareness than how to reach another level of abstraction in and from context in order to actualize more of the potential of ubiquitous and pervasive computing. Today this challenge is posed by having to move toward the enabling of a next generation of more decidedly "smart" applications and devices, which are aware of their context, are capable of verifying and validating that context, and can operate proactively in that context.

One should note that even this far along into the process of technical and cultural development the human-factors axis remains by far the underdeveloped and more difficult one. The developers and users of ubicomp have so far tended to grant a certain primacy to the physical environment and a rather empirical notion of "context." This focus still in the main ignores or parenthesizes the human users and their context awareness. In the first place, it has certainly kept to decisions made in early cybernetics to marginalize or altogether exclude the exploration of "context" as a matter of meaning—that is, any approaches to "context" stemming from linguistics, discourse analysis, hermeneutics, semantics, semiotics, or the early alternative cybernetic theories trying to work integrally with aspects of context. This bracketing is, however, not unilateral and also seems to be changing over time as research interests now begin to accrue to the role of human awareness, meaningful embodied action and response, and language in ubicomp. Hence, it is of some interest to keep on tracing this development, not just as regards the emergence of coherent connections of words or the examination of the parts of a written or spoken statement that precede or follow a specific word or passage so as to influence or throw light on its meaning, but also much more generally as regards new and mixed-reality approaches to signal and information, force and signification, and semantic webs in and as the (in)human lifeworld. In the second place, although context-aware systems are already quite advanced as regards human-user profiling on biophysical, perceptual, and habitual-action planes, how to have context-aware systems try to make relatively well-informed or even intelligent assumptions about users' current situations is still a challenging and open issue, to put it mildly. We still await, then, an *in actu* and proactive demonstration of controlling systems that incorporate and operate farther along with well-interpreted human intention, individually and socially.

Nonetheless, the discussions can become rather sharply and critically pointed and oppositional, as perhaps they should when treating of the emergence of dynamic and multiplicitous systems of specialized artifacts augmented with context awareness and deeply embedded in personal and private everyday life. After all, who and what owns, has the right to, directs the use of, and designs the aesthetics of those compositional mixes of awareness information deriving from your health-care system components, your pacemaker, your hearing aid, your biometric identity system, your emotive gesture-recognition system (facial expressions, posture, types of movement), your smart coffee cup, your smart watch, your wearable-comp clothes, your augmented-reality glasses, your intelligent briefcase, your smartphone, your laptop, your electronic pads, your iPods, your mixed-reality desk, your wastebasket, and the walls and rooms of your responsive architecture (Bullivant 2006, 2007; Oosterhuis, Xia, and Jap 2007)? However, the critical edge can, I think, very well be tempered all along by an historically attuned acknowledgment that there are very many dimensions and phenomena in our technocultural life form that we are quite willing to live with "calmly" for a great many reasons. For instance, in contrast to the debates of the early twentieth century, we now only rarely engage in very "uncalm" discussions regarding the question of whether electricity, electrical systems, and all manner of electrical devices should be embedded in our houses or society at large, rather unobtrusively, although we have not stopped debating other forms of energy, alternative inventions, or usage economies and still do want to know how we obtain or change more detailed and updated information, if that is what is needed.

Even if embeddedness and context awareness will remain factors to live with in ubicomp culture in the foreseeable future—with, we hope, quite harmless, accessible, and overtly optional types of embeddedness as well as more well-developed human, social, and aesthetic sides of context awareness—the notion of "calm" computing will not cease to demand critical attention. This attention will arguably be directed at the degrees and modes of disclosure, overt interfacing, and optional affectedness and will necessarily come from the most calm, handy, well-informed, and knowledgeable technicians, too (e.g., the people whose everyday culture consists in part in being intimately involved in taking care of unforeseen consequences, malfunctions, and crashes). Such critical attention may also very well take the form of discussions regarding whether there is something wrong with the human values and aesthetics that certain technics seem to presuppose in being installed to the point of simply enveloping us in our daily practices and perceptual modalities.

Perhaps ubicomp technics cannot be altogether withdrawn, discrete, invisible, or indiscernible—emerging in and of "our" living culture—but must involve at the very least a certain atmosphere, an ambience, and an affectivity quite close to "us." Along that line of thought, the contextuality and ecology of ubicomp technics and culture appear to be part and parcel of what calls us to engage critically with an experience economy, an event culture, and a progressive aestheticization in contemporaneity of everyday culture that is perhaps still at a distance from articulate experience rationalities (Schulze 1992). It may thus well be that ubicomp culture is not primarily a question of leading calm lives, but rather (also) a question of emboldening the human side of context-aware invention and play. Ubicomp research projects may very well be a matter of offering devices and systems that, once in the hands of so many human users, will afford a different discovery and development of the environment and lifeworld as well as its inhabitants and will invite our renewed making of inferences, thus involving a nonhabitual learning and doing that are perhaps less calm than playful, provocative, exciting, or in any case hospitably open to the emergence of the other.

Mixed Reality

Many of the chapters in this book repeatedly engage with the notion that "mixed realities" make up the wider context for cultures living on with ubicomp technics. They do so, however, in quite different ways, in part because they do not necessarily agree on the definition and in part because the transdisciplinary research ongoing in this field today has not yet proceeded to a point where a sufficiently differentiated conceptual apparatus has been developed, nor do we yet have syntheses or consensus formations across such apparati. It might be useful to note in passing and before the reader delves into the chapters (those in part VII in particular) that we are still at a stage where agreement is lacking with respect to the question of how real mixed reality is; where technical and anthropological cultural notions are hardly in a dialog; and where technical, medial, embodied, and existentially relational aspects of mixed reality remain thought and approached in rather separate fashions. This section thus forms what can be called an initial exercise in translation.

The texts in this book do seem to agree that mixed realities are real—not in substantial or essential ontological senses or in metaphysical senses, but rather in the sense that they are the kinds of inscriptions in or constructions by finite systems and equally finite human beings and their milieus that afford concrete "ubiquity effects" or promise to alter our *notions* of reality. However, for the most part, the texts here abide by a kind of ontotheological silence that we also know quite well from a major part of the tradition at stake in modern Western thought. Mixed realities in a ubicomp culture tend to be understood here either silently or more vocally as notions of reality subject to erasure and deconstruction with respect to their very ideality so that they become other mixes or real concretizations of mixes whose momentary assembly in order to construct an ontology holds only until affirmation of another assembly appears.

These concerns are almost always marginal in this volume, however important to revisit they may be. However, many of the contributors do employ approaches on a decidedly epistemological plane, frequently drawing upon existing notions. The still hegemonic technical notions of mixed reality arrived almost simultaneously with Weiser's head-on confrontation in the early 1990s with then-prevalent notions of virtual reality in order to call for the development of an embodied virtuality that would draw computers out of their electronic shells so as to enhance and be mixed invisibly with the physical world. Paul Milgram and Fumio Kishino's (1994) definition of mixed reality appeared in the mid-1990s and today remains the standard technical reference, no matter its specific focus on displays, when one contemplates a merging of real and virtual worlds (figure I.7). Perhaps this notion is especially valuable due to its resolute focus first on a virtuality continuum as the major contemporary research paradigm to be actualized and second on no less than four key aspects comprising mixed reality: the real environment, augmented reality, augmented virtuality, and the virtual environment.

Milgram and Kishino's work is thus inclusive and differentiated enough to be of general use in the technical field and beyond, just as one might revisit it today to observe that the two outer edges may well end up being put in parenthesis. That is, a purely virtual environment of an immersive and simulative kind is only one course to follow, as is the kind of inversion of this environment that Weiser had in mind

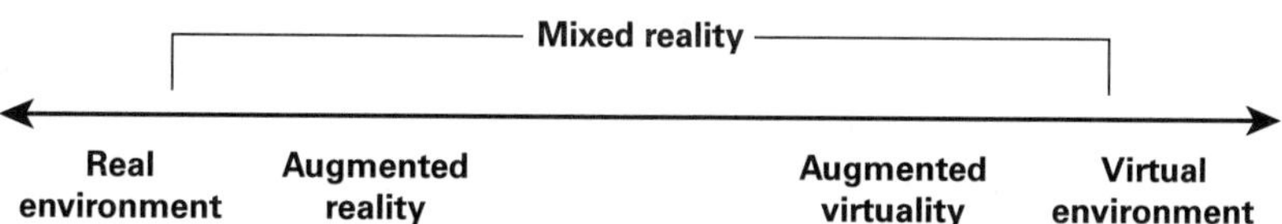

Figure I.7
Visualization of Milgram and Kishino's (1994) notion of mixed reality.

when pointing to a rather strictly embedded embodiment of virtuality. As a matter of fact, although these factors remain core constitutive factors in mixed-reality development, much today seems to indicate that a very large part of inventive trends will be investing in the more in-between notions of augmentation (augmented reality and augmented virtuality), although so far no consensus has been achieved regarding how to pursue these notions. In the technical research literature, though, one definition of augmented-reality systems has now been deployed enough that one can say that it enjoys a certain general acceptance, and it can in part be extended to augmented-virtuality systems. Ronald Azuma (1997) defines an augmented-reality system as one that (1) combines the real and the virtual, (2) is interactive in real time, and (3) is registered in three dimensions.

The coming into focus of notions of augmented reality and augmented virtuality does much to explain how it is that mixed realities tend to be reduced to these types of reality and virtuality as far as media studies in the past decade are concerned. In that respect, a valuable and relatively recent article by Manovich is quite representative in its manner of charting the historical shift in the 2000s to a preoccupation with physical spaces filled with electronic and visual information. Manovich's (2006) symptomatic tracing of contemporaneity via projects by Cardiff, Liebeskind, Venturi, Lozano-Hemmer, Spuybroek, and Kolhaas's Prada store in New York takes place in order to elaborate for media studies the key notion of "augmented space," which is achieved by "overlaying" virtual information over a user's visual field. Manovich thus thinks of augmentation mainly as augmented-reality mediation and is only secondarily interested in the real environment. Manovich's notion implies a reduction of augmented virtuality and the virtual environment in this context, just as it remains mainly a formal matter of mediatory "overlays." These overlays are above all a question of visual mediations rather than of visual experiences, not to mention multimodal, embodied, bodily live, and living experiences. Hence, this diagnostically timely, pragmatically useful, and richly exemplified media-theoretical text is at one with a number of others in this field because its mode of approach via overlays silences any treatment of a mixing of realities, just as it focuses quite sharply on humans as competent users of digital visual media.

Almost the opposite is true of cultural theoretical studies such as Mark Hansen's (2006) recent rethinking of mixed reality as the key question for interfaces with digital media. The very opening of this book, deeply invested in fleshing out a new existential phenomenology of the body vis-à-vis contemporary media art and culture, signals quite clearly not only that virtual reality in the narrower, technical, and digitally media-specific sense cannot and should not be considered different in kind from the rest of experience, but also that the question of mixed reality is uncircumventable or, in Hansen's own words, that "[a]ll reality is mixed reality" (2006, 5). If one subscribes to Brian Massumi's (2002) notion of "the superiority of the analog," as does Hansen, then the body forms the primary agent of the analog processing that creates reality out of the transformative fusion or mixing of realms. That is, the body here figures, with a certain echo of a Deleuzian transcendental empiricism, as the sensor of change and the transducer of the outside or the virtual continuum.

Hansen insists on pursuing this argument across the epistemological and practical dimensions of augmentation to arrive at a notion of a mixed reality with obvious ontological implications. Although the thought of Maurice Merleau-Ponty and Gilles Deleuze play important roles in this pursuit, Hansen characteristically takes as his point of departure the work of more or less exemplary artist-engineers. Hence, the term *mixed reality* is borrowed from Monika Fleischmann and Wolfgang Strauss, whose projects, along with earlier ones by Myron Krueger, have led Hansen to envision mixed reality as a fluid interpenetration of realms just as the virtual here denotes a "space full of information" that can be "activated, revealed, reorganized and recombined, added to and transformed as the user navigates . . . real space" (Hansen 2006, 2). For Hansen, then, mixed reality qua functional and fluid crossings between virtual and physical realms is necessarily the issue at stake today, and rather than having the human lose his or her body to technology, the body qua embodied motor activity now plays the central role in the interface to the virtual as interactive media projects increasingly support multisensory mechanisms, movement responsiveness, and extensions of humans' space for play and action in a wider, increasingly real, and mobile context.

Although Hansen's kind of work does not provide the technical and digital-media insights that Weiser, Dourish, or Manovich's work does, it enters much farther into a type of cultural theoretical studies that will open up a ubicomp culture and mixed realities to the human and social sciences, not least as regards a treatment of the relationality of technical mixed realities with human embodiment. In quite a few places, Hansen's work, in this respect not unlike Bernard Stiegler's, indicates that this relationality is to be approached also beyond the practical and functional interface level—that is, as a matter of an ontological difference. This approach has not been entirely worked out at this point, but because both Hansen and Stiegler are also avid readers of Gilbert Simondon and Deleuze, one nonetheless can say relatively safely that any pursuit of such a notion of mixed reality must necessarily include a rather difficult encounter between current postphenomenological thought and transcendental empiricism, now long after Deleuze's rather vocal departure from any egological phenomenological line of work. In one way or the other, this encounter with respect to mixed reality will hinge upon the way in which one is to read and work with a few very important concepts in Simondon and inherited by Deleuze: "transduction," "disparation," "metastability," and the "preindividual."

If one thinks of the preindividual as an impersonal and perhaps prevital virtual field of singularities, then it may well lend itself to a radicalization of any existential phenomenology of the body, notably by being approached via a notion of individuation. Along this path, the preindividual would pose as a "reservoir" of singularities that a being taps into in order to integrate intensive differences from a vaster dimension. However well this notion of a reservoir of singularities will suit the work on a postphenomenology, it will also threaten to reintroduce a subjectivity, a holistic notion of being, and a principled Kantian heritage that might not live that well along with the thought of Simondon or of Deleuze—because for both of these philosophers an individual cannot be assumed but remains an effect or an outcome of individuation processes operating with multiple, external relations. Even if one goes so far as to insist that the preindividual cannot be derived, induced, or deduced from an individual order—that is, if one poses the preindividual as a savage proto-ontic domain and as not-being—the preindividual will still name the infraphenomenal source of the givenness of phenomena. Once the preindividual is conceived of as originary (a creative reservoir of phenomena, an unlimited source of givenness), one is on the way to turning a relative, ontogenetic difference into a static, ontological one and to letting a subjectivity-oriented notion of individuation steer the reading of "transduction," "disparation," and "metastability." Thus, if one wishes to think mixed reality as a matter of transduction along this axis, this view would undoubtedly have the merit of further developing a pragmatic and functional approach to a lived experience of live embodiment. However, it would also tend reductively toward becoming a question of *my* or *our* differently organized but very human embodiment, rather statically given alongside with more or less disparate others in a condition of metastability.

The interested reader might consider, as an alternative, that mixed reality might be thought, as in Simondon, by emphasizing a dynamic, relational ontology (Toscano 2005). That is, one might affirm here an ontogenetic relationality of transduction—one that reciprocally generates and defines at once a multiplicity of preindividual fields and contingent events of information. On that path, mixing of realities is what is ongoing transductively between preindividual fields (qua determinable energetic and material conditions) and events (qua informative modulations that individuate a field by resolving in part the field's determinable potential). This description begins to pinpoint the way in which Simondon would think of the virtuality continuum as a question of being in "metastability" by conceiving of a systemic condition "that contains latent potentials and harbors a certain incompatibility with itself, an incompatibility due at once to forces in tension as well as to the impossibility of interaction between terms of extremely disparate dimensions" (1992, 300).

Human embodiments and ubicomp systems may form dynamics of another mixed reality insofar as they are already in metastable equilibrium—in other words, insofar as they contain preindividual potentials belonging to heterogeneous dimensions, and then this false equilibrium is broken, which leads toward concrete actualization of virtuality. Thus, Simondon defines virtuality qua preindividual being as affected by "disparation," by the tension between incompatible and as yet unrelated dimensions or potentials in being. One might be interested, then, in seeing fleshed out beyond any general organology of technical life how mixed realities go on actualizing various kinds of communication among disparates. In that sense, Deleuze is still running ahead of our thought of mixed realities as a problematic field:

> Gilbert Simondon has shown recently that individuation presupposes a prior metastable state—in other words, the existence of a "disparateness" such as at least two orders of magnitude or two scales of heterogeneous reality between which potentials are distributed. Such a pre-individual state nevertheless does not lack singularities: the distinctive or singular points are defined by the existence and distribution of potentials. An "objective" problematic field thus appears, determined by the distance between two heterogeneous orders. Individuation emerges like the act of solving such a problem, or—what amounts to the same thing—like the actualisation of a potential and establishing of communication between disparates. (1993, 246)

Technics

In cultural studies and even in science and technology studies, demonizations of technology still abound, as do castings of technology in the role of the Other, often coupled with variants of technological determinism. Because one also finds a very considerable set of discourses subscribing to a more or less utopian liberalism respecting technology qua human mastery, all too much work appears compromised by a rather traditional, reductive, and sterile opposition. It is thus rather refreshing to find an extensive transdisciplinarity alive and kicking in the field concerned with ubicomp culture, which begins to take this opposition apart in favor of a different distribution of notions as to the almost sidereal order and (de)constitutive ontogenetic relationality of human life and technics. One strand of this distribution, which should also go some way toward halting inclinations toward infinite negative or positive idealization (ontological and/or metaphysical) of ubiquitous computing, can be found in one or several of the self-avowed delimitations of ubiquitous and pervasive computing made by the hardware engineers, software developers, and interaction designers currently involved in its development.

For instance, demarcations of the finitude of ubiquitous computing become explicit and quite interesting when researchers and developers actively involved in human–computer interaction remark on the scarcity of a continued critical debate concerning the ethics of ubicomp and begin to construct teams involving a variety of users and professionals from other disciplines *alongside* development groups in a transdisciplinary and open-ended fashion. This change in convention is already traceable in Dourish's work. It is also making itself felt in Adam Greenfield's (2008) suggestion of five ethical principles for ubicomp: that ubicomp systems should be developed to be harmless in case of failure, conservative of time, conservative of face, self-disclosing, and deniable.

One might well consider in the same vein that the recognitions of unresolved computer science issues that are common to most centers at work on ubiquitous and pervasive computing include, among other things, sensing and collecting meaningful data on "human" activities; model building for real-world human activity; application of software-agent technology; appropriate unobtrusive interfaces; security, privacy, and trust; human factors and social impact; dynamic communications networks (Steventon and Wright 2006, 12). Perhaps the recognition of finitude and the pressures making themselves felt on the developers' side are humble assessments made in response to concrete, technical limitations met in actual current developments, as in the following list by Jon Crowcroft:

- We do not even know the fundamental limits of multi-hop, multiparty radio systems. This is a matter for both theory and practice.
- Hierarchy is an insufficient mechanism to manage the scale and heterogeneity of these new processing elements and communications links and their multifaceted relationships.
- We are only just starting to learn a little about real-world human and device mobility. This is a matter for models as well as real-world data.
- We have no detailed or realistic models for the collective failure modes.
- We do not have a methodology to design or understand systems of loosely integrated agents.
- We are dealing in mixed reality where there are both sensors and actuators. We are not used to modeling the state of the external physical world at the same time as programs.
- We do not have appropriate models of or design patterns for ownership.
- We do not commonly consider energy consumption in these systems, yet many are dependent on batteries, and we are under pressure to accommodate such considerations strongly in designs. (2008, 3833–3834)

Ubiquity

Insofar as treatments have been undertaken in the disciplines of cultural studies, the humanities, and the social sciences, one notes a very frequent appropriation of the terms *ubiquitous computing* and *pervasive computing* without any further critical or deconstructive work being done as regards the need to move through or around the implications of *ubiquity* and *pervasiveness.*[18] One guiding assumption for this book has been that "ubiquity" and "pervasiveness" as idealities and philosophical tropes must be delimited, even as they demonstrate some traditional capacity to survive. The book's main title should hence be read as if in scare quotes or as if a movement of enclosure is on the way inside out of the very ideas of "ubiquity" and "pervasiveness." In other words, the remainders and implications of ontotheological and sovereign ideological notions of "ubiquity" and "pervasiveness" must be questioned reasonably so as to be put under critical erasure in one or more ways (Derrida 2005). This book is nothing if not oriented toward an unconditional critique of the idea that ubicomp is, should be, or may be "ubiquitous"; that pervasive computing is, should be, or may be "pervasive"; or that the discourses, practices, and inventions involved extend, penetrate, and invade "throughout," are always already at stake "all over," are inside "everything" "everywhere," and "at any time," or constitute and deconstitute "all" modes of individuation or subject formation. Rather, ubiquity and ubicomp, pervasiveness and pervasive computing, as well as current individuations living on with these types of computing partake of infinite finitude, and even though it may turn out to be almost impossible to bring such idealizations and their normative side effects to closure, we should not cease to question them with reasonableness. I have thus been very interested to find that a number of the contributions in this book go on addressing this issue, not least in the last part. Nonetheless, I think cultural studies and its sister disciplines are still too silent with respect to this subject, and because this silence does not appear to me a way of working through, I welcome further articulations of this problematic in other contexts, to the point of realizing that ubicomp culture is perhaps most interesting when and where its psychic, social, and technical modalities of invention break down—that is, at the points in finitude opening onto preindividual metastability, onto intensely difficult problems, onto impossible inventions of the other.

Notes

1. Byron Hawk, David Rieder, and Ollie Oviedo's anthology *Small Tech: The Culture of Digital Tools* (2008) provides an interesting treatment of the rise of small tech and its sociocultural implications.

2. Michael Bull's (2007) work on iPod culture does much to describe and analyze these sociocultural tendencies. See also Bull's contribution to this volume (chapter 6). Moreover, I am here referring to Mizuko Ito's (2007b) use of the descriptive terms *cocooning, camping,* and *footprinting* when analyzing the everyday individual and social practices of networked publics.

3. Important and quite interesting initial research has obviously already been undertaken here, and one hopes to see it undergo further elaboration (Brewer and Dourish 2008; Bull 2008; Castells 2007; Goggin and Hjorth 2009; Hjorth 2008; Ito, Matsuda, Okabe 2005; Ling 2008; Wajcman, Bittman, Johnstone, et al. 2008).

4. See the Tangible Media Group Web page at http://tangible.media.mit.edu.

5. For more on information on Lozano-Hemmer's *Under Scan* see http://www.lozano-hemmer.com/under_scan.php (accessed 5 January 2012).

6. I am indebted to Bo Kampmann Walther's (forthcoming) reflections on pervasive gaming; Alexander Galloway's (2006) more general treatment of gaming; Mary Flanagan's (2009) remarks on critical locative play; Paul Dourish's (2006) approach to embodied interactions in ubicomp contexts that alter notions of space and place; and Markus Montola, Jaakko Stenros, and Anikka Waern's (2009) treatment of the theory and design of pervasive games.

7. See also Lenoir's treatment in this volume (chapter 33).

8. Weiser had in mind the process of drawing computers out of their electronic shells so as to have the "virtuality" of computer-readable data and "all the different ways in which it can be altered, processed and analyzed . . . brought into the physical world" (1991).

9. For more on "things that think," see the Web page http://ttt.media.mit.edu/vision/vision.html. I cannot help thinking that it would be more adequate to affirm the biological metaphorics at stake: much seems to oscillate between a bios and an autobios, and so the phrase *things that live* might be a better approximation in spite of the loss of alliteration.

10. See also Stiegler and Hayles's very interesting treatments in this volume (chapters 28, 29, and 30).

11. As the references given earlier already indicate, the treatment of ubicomp culture in this text assumes as a familiar heritage the more influential texts by Mark Weiser and his colleagues (see Weiser 1993, 1994, 1997a, 1997b, 1999a, 1999b, 2001; Weiser, Gold, and Brown 1999). The past decade and a half has not been at a standstill, so several interesting reconsiderations of Weiser's vision and the status of contemporary technocultural developments are now available (see, e.g., Bell and Dourish 2007; Hargraves 2007).

12. The reference here is broadly discursive to the research field but also more specific to part of the early work by William Gibson (1984), Jaron Lanier and Frank Biocca (1992), and I. E. Sutherland (1965).

13. Three indications should begin to give an idea of the reach of this call in this field of research. Hayles's work toward a more seamless integration of humans and machines is one important case in point—that is, her notion of constructing a "posthuman" subjectivity that remains finite and embodied and that lives with technics in a material world of great complexity (see Hayles 1999, 5; 2002, 2005a, 2005b). Mark Hansen's latest work displays a certain convergence with this notion, rethinking Merleau-Ponty's existential phenomenology of the body along with insights from contemporary cognitive science and interactions with new media art in order to delineate and affirm the expanded scope accorded to a holistically embodied human agency that can exist only in conjunction with technics (2006, 2–3, 20). Stiegler's quite extensive work on technics and time, from *The Fault of Epimetheus* on, can perhaps only be read as part of a continued effort to develop "a general organology" with a view to a human history that consists in a series of potentials, tensions, displacements, and inventions among three large organizational formations: the body with its physiological organization; artificial organs (technics, objects, tools, instruments, works of art); and social organizations (see Stiegler 1998, 2009, 2011).

14. I obviously have in mind the legacy from Gilles Deleuze and not least Deleuze and Félix Guattari. Although we wait for a more sustained and convincing study of Deleuze, Guattari, and the open machines, it will have to suffice for now to point to the tangential kinds of work done so far (De Landa 2002, 2006; Galloway 2004; Galloway and Thacker 2007; Massumi 2002).

15. I am alluding here to Weiser's call for ubicomp as both calm and embedded (Weiser and Brown 1995, 1996).

16. The ubicomp conferences have been held annually under the aegis of the Association for Computing Machines since around the turn of the twenty-first century, the latest publication of proceedings appearing during the past few years (Helal et al. 2009). Likewise, via the Institute of Electrical and Electronics Engineers (IEEE), among other organizations, conferences concerned with pervasive and grid computing have been organized regularly in the same period (*Advances in Grid and Pervasive Computing* 2011IEEE Computer Society and University of Texas 2010; *Pervasive Computing* 2010).

17. The sources are obviously too numerous to be listed here, but perhaps it will suffice to point to the major work in three volumes edited by Judith Symonds (2010), not least because it manages to treat of a number of important cultural issues at stake in a way that most other comparable works do not.

18. Interesting exceptions exist; see Tom Cohen's contribution to this volume (chapter 31), for example.

References

Advances in Grid and Pervasive Computing: 6th International Conference, GPC 2011, Oulu, Finland, May 11–13, 2011, Proceedings. 2011. New York: Springer.

Agamben, Giorgio. 1998. *Homo Sacer: Sovereign Power and Bare Life.* Translated by Daniel Heller-Roazen. Stanford, CA: Stanford University Press.

Agamben, Giorgio. 1999. *Potentialities: Collected Essays in Philosophy.* Edited and translated with an introduction by Daniel Heller-Roazen. Stanford, CA: Stanford University Press.

Anthes, Gary. 2006. "Bits to Atoms (and Atoms to Bits): Interview with Neil Gershenfeld." *Computerworld.* Available at http://www.computerworld.com/s/article/110043/Bits_to_Atoms_and_Atoms_to_Bits_. Accessed 4 April 2011.

Azuma, Ronald T. 1997. "A Survey of Augmented Reality." *Presence: Teleoperators and Virtual Environments* 6 (4): 355–385.

Bell, Genevieve, and Paul Dourish. 2007. "Yesterday's Tomorrows: Notes on Ubiquitous Computing's Dominant Vision." *Personal and Ubiquitous Computing* 11 (2): 133–143.

Bolchini, Cristiana, Carlo A. Curino, Elisa Quintarelli, et al. 2007. "A Data-Oriented Survey of Context Models." *SIGMOD Rec.* 36 (4): 19–26.

Boye, Niels, and Jeppe Spure Nielsen. 2003. "Pervasive Healthcare: Et Visionært Bud På Fremtidig Anvendelse Af Teknologi Inden for Sundhedsområdet." Århus-regionens IT-råd. Available at http://2093.rh.dk/it/Sundheds_IT.pdf. Accessed January 5, 2012.

Brewer, Johanna, and Paul Dourish. 2008. "Storied Spaces: Cultural Accounts of Mobility, Technology, and Environmental Knowing." *International Journal of Human–Computer Studies* 66 (12): 963–976.

Bull, Michael. 2007. *Sound Moves: iPod Culture and Urban Experience*. London: Routledge.

Bull, Michael. 2004. *Sounds of the City: Mobile Technologies and Urban Experiences*. London: Routledge.

Bullivant, Lucy. 2007. *4DSocial: Interactive Design Environments*. Chichester, UK: Wiley.

Bullivant, Lucy. 2006. *Responsive Environments: Architecture, Art, and Design*. New York: V & A.

Castells, Manuel. 2007. *Mobile Communication and Society: A Global Perspective*. A project of the Annenberg Research Network on International Communication. Cambridge, MA: MIT Press.

Castells, Manuel. 1996. *The Rise of the Network Society*. Cambridge, MA: Blackwell.

"Centre for Pervasive Healthcare." 2009. Available at http://www.pervasivehealthcare.dk. Accessed 5 January 2012.

Crowcroft, Jon. 2008. "Engineering Global Ubiquitous Systems." *Philosophical Transactions of the Royal Society A* 366:3833–3834.

Csíkszentmihályi, Mihály. 1990. *Flow: The Psychology of Optimal Experience*. New York: Harper & Row.

De Landa, Manuel. 2006. *A New Philosophy of Society: Assemblage Theory and Social Complexity*. London: Continuum.

De Landa, Manuel. 2002. *Intensive Science and Virtual Philosophy*. New York: Continuum.

Deleuze, Gilles. 1995. "Postscript on Control Societies." In *Negotiations, 1972–1990*, translated by Martin Joughin, 177–182. New York: Columbia University Press.

Deleuze, Gilles. 1993. *Difference and Repetition*. Translated by Paul Patton. New York: Columbia University Press.

Derrida, Jacques. 2005. *Rogues: Two Essays on Reason*. Translated by Pascale-Anne Brault and Michael Naas. Stanford, CA: Stanford University Press.

Dey, Anind K. 2001. "Understanding and Using Context." *Personal and Ubiquitous Computing Journal* 5 (1): 4–7.

Dourish, Paul. 2006. "Re-Space-Ing Place: 'Place' and 'Space' Ten Years On." Available at http://www.dourish.com/publications/2006/cscw2006-space.pdf. Accessed 5 January 2012.

Dourish, Paul. 2001. *Where the Action Is: The Foundations of Embodied Interaction*. Cambridge, MA: MIT Press.

Dourish, Paul, Ken Anderson, and Dawn Nafus. 2007. "Cultural Issues in HCI–Cultural Mobilities: Diversity and Agency in Urban Computing." *Lecture Notes in Computer Science* 4663 (0): 100–114.

Ekman, Ulrik. 2009. "Irreducible Vagueness: Mixed Worlding in Diller & Scofidio's Blur Building." *Postmodern Culture* 19 (2).

Flanagan, Mary. 2009. *Critical Play: Radical Game Design*. Cambridge, MA: MIT Press.

Galloway, Alexander R. 2006. *Gaming: Essays on Algorithmic Culture*. Minneapolis: University of Minnesota Press.

Galloway, Alexander R. 2004. *Protocol: How Control Exists after Decentralization*. Cambridge, MA: MIT Press.

Galloway, Alexander R., and Eugene Thacker. 2007. *The Exploit: A Theory of Networks*. Minneapolis: University of Minnesota Press.

Garelli, Jacques. 1991. *Rythmes et mondes : au revers de l'identité et de l'altérité*. Grenoble: Ed. Jérôme Millon.

Gellersen, Hans W., Albrecht Schmidt, and Michael Beigl. 2002. "Multi-Sensor Context-Awareness in Mobile Devices and Smart Artifacts." *Mobile Networks and Applications* 7 (5): 341–351.

Gibson, William. 1984. *Neuromancer*. New York: Ace Books.

Goggin, Gerard, and Larissa Hjorth, eds. 2009. *Mobile Technologies: From Telecommunications to Media*. New York: Routledge.

Greenfield, Adam. 2008. "Some Guidelines for the Ethical Development of Ubiquitous Computing." *Philosophical Transactions of the Royal Society A* 366:3823–3831.

Greenfield, Adam. 2006. *Everyware: The Dawning Age of Ubiquitous Computing*. Berkeley, CA: New Riders.

Hansen, Mark B. N. 2006. *Bodies in Code: Interfaces with Digital Media*. New York: Routledge.

Hargraves, Ian. 2007. "Ubicomp: Fifteen Years On." *Knowledge, Technology, & Policy* 20 (1): 3–10.

Hawk, Byron, David M. Rieder, and Ollie Oviedo, eds. 2008. *Small Tech: The Culture of Digital Tools*. Minneapolis: University of Minnesota Press.

Hayles, N. Katherine. 2005a. "Computing the Human." *Theory Culture Society* 22 (1): 131–151.

Hayles, N. Katherine. 2005b. *My Mother Was a Computer: Digital Subjects and Literary Texts*. Chicago: University of Chicago Press.

Hayles, N. Katherine. 2002. "Flesh and Metal: Reconfiguring the Mindbody in Virtual Environments." *Configurations* 10:297–320.

Hayles, N. Katherine. 1999. *How We Became Posthuman*. Chicago: University of Chicago Press.

Helal, Abdelsalam A., ed.. 2009. *Ubicomp '09: Proceedings of the 11th International Conference on Ubiquitous Computing: September 30–October 3, 2009, Orlando, Florida, USA*. New York: Association for Computing Machinery.

Hjorth, Larissa. 2008. *Mobile Media in the Asia Pacific Gender and the Art of Being Mobile*. New York: Routledge.

Institute of Electrical and Electronics Engineers (IEEE) Computer Society and University of Texas at Arlington. 2010. *2010 IEEE International Conference on Pervasive Computing and Communications: (Percom 2010), Mannheim, Germany, 29 March–2 April, 2010.* Piscataway, NJ: IEEE.

Ishii, Hiroshi. 2008. "Tangible Bits: Beyond Pixels." In *Proceedings of the Second International Conference on Tangible and Embedded Interaction*, xv–xxv. New York: ACM.

Ito, Mizuko. 2010. *Hanging Out, Messing Around, and Geeking Out: Kids Living and Learning with New Media.* Cambridge, MA: MIT Press.

Ito, Mizuko. 2009. *Engineering Play: A Cultural History of Children's Software.* Cambridge, MA: MIT Press.

Ito, Mizuko. 2007a. "Introduction—Networked Publics." Available at http://www.itofisher.com/mito/ito.netpublics.pdf. Accessed 28 July 2009.

Ito, Mizuko. 2007b. "Portable Objects in Three Global Cities: The Personalization of Urban Places". Available at http://www.itofisher.com/mito/portableobjects.pdf. Accessed 28 July 2009.

Ito, Mizuko, Misa Matsuda, and Daisuke Okabe. 2005. *Personal, Portable, Pedestrian: Mobile Phones in Japanese Life.* Cambridge, MA: MIT Press.

Jacko, Julie A., ed. 2007. *Human–Computer Interaction. Part III. HCI Intelligent Multimodal Interaction Environments: 12th International Conference, HCI International 2007, Beijing, China, July 22–27, 2007: Proceedings.* Berlin: Springer.

Jacko, Julie A., and Andrew Sears. 2003. *The Human–Computer Interaction Handbook: Fundamentals, Evolving Technologies, and Emerging Applications.* Mahwah, NJ: Lawrence Erlbaum Associates.

Lanier, Jaron, and Frank Biocca. 1992. "An Insider's View of the Future of Virtual Reality." *Journal of Communication* 42 (4): 150–172.

Leroi-Gourhan, André. 1945. *Évolution et techniques: Milieu et techniques.* Paris: Albin Michel.

Leroi-Gourhan, André. 1943. *Évolution et techniques: L'homme et la matière.* Paris: Albin Michel.

Levin, Thomas Y., Ursula Frohne, and Peter Weibel, eds. 2002. *CTRL-Space: Rhetorics of Surveillance from Bentham to Big Brother.* Cambridge, MA: MIT Press.

Ling, Richard Seyler. 2008. *New Tech, New Ties: How Mobile Communication Is Reshaping Social Cohesion.* Cambridge, MA: MIT Press.

Lyon, David. 2007. *Surveillance Studies: An Overview.* Cambridge, UK: Polity.

Lyon, David. 2006. *Theorizing Surveillance: The Panopticon and Beyond.* Cullompton, UK: Willan.

Manovich, Lev. 2006. "The Poetics of Augmented Space." *Visual Communication* 5: 219–240.

Manovich, Lev. 2005. "Scale Effects." Available at http://www.manovich.net/DOCS/scale_effects.doc. Accessed 10 April 2011.

Massumi, Brian. 2002. *Parables for the Virtual: Movement, Affect, Sensation.* Durham, NC: Duke University Press.

McCullough, Malcolm. 2004. *Digital Ground: Architecture, Pervasive Computing, and Environmental Knowing.* Cambridge, MA: MIT Press.

Milgram, Paul, and Fumio Kishino. 1994. "Taxonomy of Mixed Reality Visual Displays." *IEICE Transactions on Information and Systems* E77-D12:1321–1329.

Montola, Markus, Jaakko Stenros, and Annika Waern. *Pervasive Games: Theory and Design.* Burlington, MA: Morgan Kaufmann, 2009.

Morales-Manzanares, Roberto, Eduardo F. Morales, Roger Dannenberg, and Jonathan Berger. 2001. "SICIB: An Interactive Music Composition System Using Body Movements." *Computer Music Journal* 25 (2): 25–36.

Norman, Donald A. 1998. *The Invisible Computer: Why Good Products Can Fail, the Personal Computer Is So Complex, and Information Appliances Are the Solution.* Cambridge, MA: MIT Press.

Oosterhuis, Kas, Xin Xia, and Sam E. Jap. 2007. Ia #1. Rotterdam: Episode, 2007.

Orwat, Carsten, Andreas Graefe, and Timm Faulwasser. 2008. "Towards Pervasive Computing in Health Care—a Literature Review." *BMC Medical Informatics and Decision Making* 8 (1): 26.

Pervasive Computing: 8th International Conference, Pervasive 2010, Helsinki, Finland, May 17–20, 2010. Proceedings. 2010. New York: Springer.

Polanyi, Michael. 1966. *The Tacit Dimension.* Terry Lectures. Garden City, NY: Doubleday.

Poslad, Stefan. 2009. *Ubiquitous Computing: Smart Devices, Environments, and Interactions.* Chichester, UK: Wiley.

Schilit, Bill N., Norman Adams, and Roy Want. 1995. "Context-Aware Computing Applications." In *Workshop on Mobile Computing Systems and Applications: Proceedings, December 8–9, 1994, Santa Cruz, California,* edited by Luis-Felipe Cabrera, et al., 85–90. Los Alamitos, CA: IEEE Computer Society Press.

Schmidt, Albrecht, Michael Beigl, and Hans-W. Gellersen. 1999. "There Is More to Context Than Location." *Computer & Graphics* 23 (6): 893–901.

Schulze, Gerhard. 1992. *Die Erlebnisgesellschaft: Kultursoziologie der Gegenwart.* Frankfurt am Main: Campus.

Shannon, Claude Elwood, and Warren Weaver. 1949. *The Mathematical Theory of Communication.* Urbana: University of Illinois Press.

Simondon, Gilbert. 1992. "The Genesis of the Individual." In *Incorporations,* edited by Jonathan Crary and Sanford Kwinter, 296–319. New York: Zone.

Simondon, Gilbert. 1964. *L'individu et sa genèse physico-biologique.* Paris: Presses universitaires de France.

Steventon, Alan, and Steve Wright. 2006. *Intelligent Spaces: The Application of Pervasive ICT*. London: Springer.

Stiegler, Bernard. 1998. *Technics and Time*. Vol. 1: *The Fault of Epimetheus*. Translated by Richard Beardsworth and George Collins. Stanford, CA: Stanford University Press.

Stiegler, Bernard. *Technics and Time. Disorientation*. Vol 2. Translated by Stephen Barker. Stanford, CA: Stanford University Press, 2009.

Stiegler, Bernard. *Technics and Time*. Vol. 3. *Cinematic Time and the Question of Malaise*. Translated by Stephen Barker. Stanford, CA: Stanford University Press, 2011.

Streitz, Norbert A., Achilles Kameas, and Irene Mavrommati, eds. 2007. *The Disappearing Computer: Interaction Design, Systems Infrastructures, and Applications for Smart Environments*. Berlin: Springer.

Sutherland, I. E. 1965. "The Ultimate Display." In *Proceedings of IFIP 65*, vol. 2, edited by Wayne Alexander Kalenich, 506–508. Washington, DC: Spartan Books.

Symonds, Judith, ed. 2010. *Ubiquitous and Pervasive Computing: Concepts, Methodologies, Tools, and Applications*. 3 vols. Hershey, PA: Information Science Reference.

Toscano, Alberto. 2005. *The Theatre of Production: Philosophy and Individuation between Kant and Deleuze*. New York: Palgrave Macmillan.

Ulyate, Ryan, and David Bianciardi. 2002. "The Interactive Dance Club: Avoiding Chaos in a Multi-Participant Environment." *Computer Music Journal* 26 (3): 40–49.

Von Foerster, Heinz. 1984. *Observing Systems*. Systems Inquiry Series. 2nd ed. Seaside, CA: Intersystems.

Wajcman, Judy, Michael Bittman, Lynne Johnstone, et al. 2008. "The Impact of the Mobile Phone on Work/Life Balance." Available at http://www.oii.ox.ac.uk/downloads/index.cfm?File=research/Report_on_Mobiles_and_Work_Life_Balance.pdf. Accessed 5 January 2012.

Walther, Bo Kampmann. 2011."Reflections on the Philosophy of Pervasive Gaming—with Special Emphasis on Rules, Gameplay, and Virtuality." *Fibreculture* 19: 126–143. Special issue on interaction designs for ubicomp cultures, edited by Ulrik Ekman.

Weiser, Mark. 2001. "Whatever Happened to the Next-Generation Internet?" *Communications of the ACM* 00044.00009:61–70.

Weiser, Mark. 1999a. "How Computers Will Be Used Differently in the Next Twenty Years." In *1999 IEEE Symposium on Security and Privacy, 9–12 May, 1999, Oakland, California, USA*. IEEE Computer Society, online publication. 234–235.

Weiser, Mark. 1999b. "The Spirit of the Engineering Quest." *Technology in Society* 21 (4): 355–361.

Weiser, Mark. 1997a. "It's Everywhere. It's Invisible. It's Ubicomp." *Training & Development* 51 (5): 34–35.

Weiser, Mark. 1997b. "Software Engineering That Matters to People." In *Proceedings of the 1997 International Conference on Software Engineering*, 538. New York: City: ACM Press.

Weiser, Mark. 1994. "The World Is Not a Desktop." *interactions* 1 (1): 7–8.

Weiser, Mark. 1993. "Some Computer Science Issues in Computing." *Communications of the ACM* 36 (7): 75–84.

Weiser, Mark. 1991. "The Computer for the 21st Century." *Scientific American* 265 (3): 94–104.

Weiser, Mark, and John Seely Brown. 1996. "The Coming Age of Calm Technology." Available at http://nano.xerox.com/hypertext/weiser/acmfuture2endnote.htm. Accessed 15 August 2010.

Weiser, Mark, and John Seely Brown. 1995. "Designing Calm Technology." Available at http://sandbox.xerox.com/hypertext/weiser/calmtech/calmtech.htm. Accessed 14 August 2010.

Weiser, Mark, Rich Gold, and John Seely Brown. 1999. "The Origins of Ubiquitous Computing Research at PARC in the Late 1980s." *IBM Systems Journal* 38 (4): 693–696.

I Sense and Sensations 1: Image

1 Ubiquitous Sensation: Toward an Atmospheric, Collective, and Microtemporal Model of Media

Mark B. N. Hansen

Machines that fit the human environment, instead of forcing humans to enter theirs, will make using a computer as refreshing as taking a walk in the woods.
—Mark Weiser, "The Computer for the 21st Century"

Technics and Sensation

The desire to expand human sensory capacities has long informed the development of technology. From the telescope to the photographic camera to contemporary machine vision and infrared systems, technologies for expanding vision have made formerly imperceptible domains of sensation accessible to human experience. Referring to photography (and only subsequently to cinema), Walter Benjamin (2008) quite aptly characterized this process as the opening up of an "optical unconscious."

The invocation of Benjamin serves as a reminder of the fundamental historical dimension informing the correlation of sensation with technics: with each technical "liberation" of some formerly invisible area of the sensory world, the operation and meaning of sensation change in some crucial way. What Benjamin teaches us is how sensation gets repeatedly transformed in ways that necessarily tighten the circuit binding human perception with its technical supplementation.

It is noteworthy that, for all of Benjamin's interest in tactile experience, his thematization of the historical correlation of sensation and technics privileges the domain of the visual. As I have argued in *New Philosophy for New Media* (2004), this privileging has largely determined the theorization of the technical supplementation of sensation from photography (and its precursors) to the digital computer. As exemplified by Jonathan Crary's archaeology of technical spectatorship, Rosalind Krauss's attention to optical devices as sources of art production, Paul Virilio's explorations of machine vision systems and real-time optics, and Lev Manovich's embedding of new media procedures within cinematic culture, developments of Benjamin's insight have continued to invest the visual as the privileged sensory domain for technics's impact on sensation.

Although this privileging of the visual certainly instances a valuation that has been central not simply in Western art history, but in Western thinking as such, as Hans Jonas (2001) has compellingly demonstrated, it has, to my mind, gone hand in hand with another valuation central to Western history—namely, the correlation between media and human perceptual ratios. From the cave paintings of the Upper Paleolithic period to contemporary social-media networks for sharing photographs (Flickr) and videos (YouTube), the perennial role played by media has been to give durable, external support to private, fleeting human experiences. With no more than a bit of competition and incursion from the domain of the aural, the history of this media supplementation of human experience has played itself out on the terrain of the visual. From this process, we can, I think, safely conclude that media history in the West has coincided largely with the history of visual images and modes of image making.

Indeed, if we take the "visual" to designate the fundamental correlation of sensation with human perceptual ratios, we can readily include the other sensory modalities—touch, perhaps taste, and, above all, hearing—as part of, if not the visual itself, at least an expanded visual aesthetic, by which I mean a conceptualization of sensation as bound up with humanly perceptible images. As the example of sound cinema demonstrates, notwithstanding experimental practices that counter its dominant apparatus, the aural is subordinated to a visual logic of narration or presentation. This shows, or so I want to suggest, that the aural is indexed to a model of sensation whose prototype is the visual image.

If modern media history appears to witness the assimilation of all sensory streams into a single media model—a model in which all potentiality for playing one sensory mode against another is from the outset subordinated to the capture and storage of experience in humanly accessible form—recent developments promise a return of sensory heterogeneity. Informing such a return is the displacement of a spatial conceptualization of the image in favor of a temporal one. It is just such a displacement that is at stake in the computational revolution we are currently living through.

To elucidate the significance of this displacement, let me simply and briefly invoke two correlated sites of contemporary cultural practice. Artist Warren Neidich (2003), in his effort to articulate an aesthetics rooted in the operation of neural plasticity, develops an account of image/art production in terms of "ergonomics." By "ergonomics," Neidich means the tuning of sensory material to the requirements of the nervous system. The development of digital technology prompts Neidich to contrast two kinds of "ergonomics": visual and cognitive. Even as he admits that we currently live in a period of transition in which both models of ergonomics are in operation, Neidich couples the projected passage to cognitive ergonomics with a liberation of temporality—specifically, a liberation of microtemporal processes of neural imaging—from its (their) subordination to the spatial/visual image:

> Visual and cognitive ergonomics are distinguished in a number of ways. Visual ergonomics developed first and is tethered to early forms of representation such as painting, sculpture, and drawing. It is primarily concerned with the representation of static space. It delineates a process through which natural space is coded to be represented as space on a canvas, and it describes a historical process by which that space becomes palpable and haptic. . . . Visual ergonomics is linked to traditional forms and materials of representation like painting; but because certain ideas of space and its representation discovered in, say, landscape painting, were carried over to photography and later cinema, it also has some relevance to them. Cognitive ergonomics is a later phenomenon and is involved in delineating dynamic processes. Whereas visual ergonomics was involved in defining space, cognitive ergonomics is involved in describing temporality. . . . [In contrast to visual ergonomics, cognitive ergonomics] is much more pertinent to recent digital and internet art. In this regard it is involved in determining the process through which information on a computer screen is obtained, and for that it relies on knowledge of how cognitive systems operate. . . . Cognitive ergonomics, as its name implies, takes into account the whole brain and conceptual system, as is necessary when organizing technologies that interface with the entire body and being. (2003, 23–24)

In his development of the specifically temporal dimension of cognitive ergonomics and the aesthetics of digital media, Neidich draws on neuroscientific research into the problem of temporal binding. What this research has shown is that visual and motor cognition arises through the synchronization of microtemporally asynchronous quasi-autonomous processes. In the field of the visual cortex, for example, as the work of Semir Zeki (1999) and his colleagues has demonstrated, distinct processes for recognition of color, motion, orientation, and location—each with its own specific timeframe—are bound by the sheer fact of their overlapping within a single microtemporal window. Because there is no need for any supplementary "agent" of binding according to his account, Zeki considers these processes to be distinct "microconsciousnesses" that form the basis for our higher-order experiences of seamless, integrated visual sensation.

As a mediator in the process of temporal binding, the aesthetics of cognitive ergonomics thus operates at the microtemporal level, which is to say that it concerns itself with how these quasi-autonomous microconsciousnesses combine to generate macrosensations. According to Neidich, the aim of an aesthetics attuned to this microtemporal domain of sensation, is to target and engineer the development of the brain's secondary repertoire at this microtemporal level. "Could we conjecture then that binding and the process of reentry which allows it to happen is more than just a neurobiological process binding different areas of the brain, but is also a process that operates in the world of networked relations?" (2003, 29). Neidich's gambit—one that I fully endorse—is that the creation of certain types of images and (I would add) media environments can promote certain patterns for the assembly of macrosensations out of the microtemporal operations of cognitive and visual processing. I maintain with Neidich that "aesthetics is constantly reassembling the partialities that make up the perception of physical objects and their relations. . . . These partialities are linked together by processes analogous to those we saw at work in the brain. Processes analogous to reentry tie these fragments together into wholes. . . . [Only] those relations with an ergonomically consistent temporality will be inscribed into the secondary repertoire" (2003, 29–30). What Neidich's work foregrounds is the necessity for contemporary media theory to engage the temporal dimension of sensation beyond the restrictive frame imposed by the model of sensory assimilation we have inherited from modern media history.

A second and altogether complementary plea for a temporal theory of media comes by way of philosopher Maurizio Lazzarato's neo-Bergsonist (and post-Deleuzian) account of video as a "machine to crystallize time." Conceptualizing video as the first technology that corresponds to a generalized decoding of the flows of images, a decoding whose genesis is traced in Henri Bergson's *Matter and Memory* ([1911] 1988), Lazzarato contrasts video and cinema as two distinct machinic mediations of perception (2007, 93–94). At the heart of this contrast is the difference between recording and modulation: whereas cinema, the paradigm of recording media, operates by capturing light as impression on a surface (and thus by imposing its spatial organization, the form of the frame, on infinitesimal modulations of light), video "modulates the flows of electromagnetic waves. Video images are contractions and dilations, 'vibrations and tremors' of light, rather than 'tracings,' reproductions of reality. The video camera's take is a crystallization of time-matter" (2007, 111). With the introduction of video, exemplary of "electronic and digital technologies," we have at our disposal for the *very first time in history* a machine that operates *like* we do:

> The technologies of time [by which is meant, above all, video] imitate the various syntheses (conservation, passage and splitting-arising [*dédoublement-surgissement*]) of time, and . . . through these functions of contraction–relaxation they work on the conditions of production of affective force. As in Bergson, the "matter" contracted by these technologies consists of the various temporal stratifications of memory. . . . [T]he term "imitation" . . . indicate[s] that electronic and digital technologies operate like the *material and spiritual syntheses* in Bergson: *they crystallize time*. Video and digital technologies can thus be grasped as technologies that imitate perception, memory and intellectual work. (Lazzarato 2007, 110, emphasis in original)

What remains crucial for this determination of video as marking a certain break in the history of machinic perception is the way it imitates the specifically *temporal* operation of "intellectual work." In contrast to cinema, which, in line with Bergson's critique in *Creative Evolution* ([1896] 1998), can grasp time only as the product of a mechanical activity proceeding according to an external and predetermined form of image, video directly engages the flux of the real, of time matter, prior to its contraction into the image or, better, *in the very process of such contraction*. If video (and electronic and digital technologies more generally) can help us appreciate the temporal basis of Bergson's theory of the production of images, as Lazzarato argues, the reason can only be that it expands our access to the power of time. As a media technology that imitates and intensifies the operation of the brain's temporal syntheses, video literally explodes the optical image. What appears beneath the shards of this exploded image is the dynamic and constructive, microtemporal process of imaging or modulation that directly engages and synthesizes (contracts–dilates) time matter itself, without the assistance of the form of the image and prior to the operation of macroconscious perception.

These two examples together attest to a certain imbrication of microtemporal neural processes with microtemporal modulation of digital technologies. For both Neidich and Lazzarato, with differing emphases to be sure, there is a necessity to correlate the technical mediation of sensation with the cognitive operation of the sensing brain and to do so at a level that breaks with what I characterized earlier as the assimilatory form of media we have inherited from modern media history. By way of provisional conclusion and in preparation for the discussion of the sensory impact of ubiquitous computing (ubicomp) to come in this chapter, let me suggest that this microtemporal correlation of technical mediation and cognitive operation marks the end of the historical dialectic of sensation and technics as this dialectic was conceptualized by Walter Benjamin (and his successors) through the figure of the optical unconscious. In the context of the twin—and, to my mind, conceptually and practically correlated—revolutions of neuroscience and computation, the dialectic of the progressive, technically enabled expansion of the visible world has reached its end point. In its place is a new correlation of media and sensation that occurs beneath the temporal frame definitive of both image and conscious perception.

Ubiquitous Computing and the Autonomy of the Peripheral

In the eyes of its progenitors, ubicomp designates the next phase in the evolution of computation following the personal computer (PC). "The important waves of technological change," write Mark Weiser and John Seely Brown in "The Coming Age of Calm Technology,"

> are those that fundamentally alter the place of technology in our lives. What matters is not technology itself, but its relationship to us. In the past fifty years of computation there have been two great trends in this relationship: the mainframe relationship, and the PC relationship. Today the internet is carrying us through an era of widespread *distributed computing* towards the relationship of *ubiquitous computing*, characterized by deeply embedding computation in the world. Ubiquitous computing will require a new approach to fitting technology to our lives, an approach we call "calm technology." (1997, 1)

Central to this account of a third, post-PC phase of computation is a massive transformation in how humans relate to computers: rather than the one person–one computer relation definitive of the PC era, the third wave of ubicomp "has many computers serving each person everywhere in the world" (Weiser 1996). In line with Weiser's prophetic vision of computation's coming to realize its inmost potential, this transformation is presented as a corrective to the social aberration of personal computing, where again the issue at stake is how computers relate to their human users: "My colleagues and I at PARC," Weiser writes in "The Computer for the 21st Century," "think that the idea of a 'personal' computer itself is misplaced, and that the vision of laptop machines, dynabooks and 'knowledge navigators' is only a transitional step toward achieving the real potential of information technology" (1991, 78).

Closely related to this position is Weiser's distancing of ubiquitous computing from "present-day trends," including mobile computing, screen-centered multimedia, and especially virtual reality.[1] Because each preserves and indeed enhances the atomistic correlation of single user and single computer, these trends run directly counter to the aim informing ubicomp: to enhance the user's intercourse with *the world that already exists*. In place of virtual reality, Weiser proposes the notion of "embodied virtuality," which references "the process of drawing computers out of their electronic shells": rather than simulating the world inside the computer, embodied virtuality means bringing "the 'virtuality' of computer readable data—all the different ways in which it can be altered, processed and analyzed . . . into the physical world" (1991, 98). Such a move is crucial to the seamless and transparent connections that Weiser and his colleagues envision as computers are "push[ed] into the background" and individuals are made "more aware of the people on the other ends of their computer links" (Weiser 1991, 104).

Perhaps the most significant characteristic differentiating ubiquitous computing from the PC and from PC-based Internet and distributed computing is its invisibility. Weiser and his colleagues return to this point repeatedly. PCs, they insist, "cannot truly make computing an integral, invisible part of the way people live their lives." That is why it is imperative "to conceive a new way of thinking about computers in the world . . . that takes into account the natural human environment and allows the computers themselves to vanish into the background" (Weiser 1991, 94). Invisibility comprises the very crux of the vision of calm computing: "Just as a good, well-balanced hammer 'disappears' in the hands of a carpenter and allows him or her to concentrate on the big picture, we hope that computers can participate in a similar magic disappearing act" (Weiser, Gold, and Brown 1999, 695). Weiser and his colleagues speak of embedded computers "so unobtrusive we will not even notice our increased ability for informed action" (Weiser 1996); they envision a world where machines "take care of our unconscious details" (Weiser 1996); and they insist on the multiscalar dimensions of ubiquitous-computing networks, which importantly include connection at the "microscopic" scale (Weiser and Brown 1997, 4). For them, the catchwords of the third computational revolution are not *intelligent* and *agent*, but rather *invisible*, *calm*, and *connection* (Weiser 1996).

In his vision of invisible ubiquity, Weiser emphasizes the psychological and social over the technical: "Such a disappearance [of computers into the background] is a fundamental consequence not of technology, but of human psychology. Whenever people learn something sufficiently well, they cease to be aware of it. When you look at a street sign, for example, you absorb its information without consciously performing the act of reading. . . . [W]hen things disappear . . . we are freed to use them without thinking and so to focus beyond them on new goals" (1991, 94). In line with this reality of human life, the goal of the ubicomp designer must be to render computers invisible so that attention can be focused on action rather than connection.

It is important not to forget that this goal can be realized only because of the *actual* invisibility of contemporary computers:

> Most of the computers that participate in embodied virtuality will be *invisible in fact* as well as in metaphor. Already computers in light switches, thermostats, stereos, and ovens help to activate the world. These machines and more will be interconnected in a ubiquitous network. . . . Hundreds of computers in a room could seem intimidating at first, just as hundreds of volts coursing through wires in the walls did at one time. But like the wires in the walls, these hundreds of computers will come to be invisible to common awareness. People will simply use them unconsciously to accomplish everyday tasks. (Weiser 1991, 98)

Far from being a trivial "necessary condition" for the implementation of computational ubiquity, this *invisibility-in-fact* of contemporary computers is, I suggest, absolutely central to our reckoning of the sensory and experiential impact of ubiquitous computing.

One crucial reason for this centrality concerns what we might call the "sensory address" of ubicomp: unlike the PC (even in the transitional phase of networked and distributed computing), which frames information for focused sensory assimilation, ubiquitous computational environments solicit a far broader range of sensory contact from their users. Weiser and Brown engage this expanded sensory address through the concept of the "periphery," which in their vision is key to the successful development of calm technology. The periphery designates "what we are attuned to without attending to explicitly," and its inclusion in the circuit linking human user and computational system vastly expands the range of our attunement to the environment: "by placing things in the periphery," Weiser and Brown claim, "we are able to attune to many more things than we could if everything had to be at the center. Things in the periphery are attuned to by the large portion of our brains devoted to peripheral (sensory) processing" (1997, 9).

Yet even as the address to the peripheral expands the sensory solicitation of ubiquitous computational systems, Weiser and Brown are quick to insist on its dialectical coupling to the center. Calm technology is defined in terms of the movement back and forth between periphery and center, which means in the end that the enfranchisement of the periphery of attention serves the expansion of cognitive agency and its power to act: "by recentering something formerly in the periphery we take control of it. Peripherally we may become aware that something is not quite right, as when awkward sentences leave a reader tired and discomforted without [her] knowing why. By moving sentence construction from periphery to center we are empowered to act, either by finding better literature or [by] accepting the source of the unease and continuing. Without centering[,] the periphery might be a source of frantic following of fashion; with centering[,] the periphery is a fundamental enabler of calm through increased awareness and power" (Weiser and Brown 1997, 9). It is as if, in relation to the task of designing computational systems, the periphery cannot carry a value in itself but is important and can serve to expand human sense capacities only because of its payoff for centered awareness and self-present action.

In concluding my discussion of ubiquitous computing, I suggest that this functional (if not indeed downright instrumental) approach to sensory expansion misses what is truly revolutionary about ubicomp, which should be understood as a phase not simply in the development of computation, but more specifically in the evolving imbrication of technics and sensation. What the constitutive and defining invisibility of ubiquitous computing actually foregrounds is the centrality of microtemporal and by definition *imperceptible* informational flows at the very heart of contemporary sensory experience. Unlike the peripheral attunement theorized by Weiser and Brown, this microtemporal and imperceptible dimension of ubiquitous computational environments *can never be brought into the sphere of direct, conscious attention and awareness*; rather, it impacts sensory experience *unconsciously, imperceptibly—in short, at a level beneath the threshold of attention and awareness*. It impacts sensory experience, that is, by impacting the sensing brain microtemporally, at the level of the autonomous subprocesses or microconsciousnesses that, as we saw in section I, compose the infrastructure of seamless and integrated macroconscious experience.

Natalie Jeremijenko's artwork *Dangling String* (1995, which Weiser and Brown offer as an example of calm technology (and which was created during Jeremijenko's tenure at Xerox PARC), gestures toward this fundamental shift in the reality of sensory experience precisely by foregrounding the autonomy of the peripheral. *Dangling String* is just what its title suggests it is: an eight-foot piece of plastic string hanging from a small electric motor mounted in the ceiling and connected via an Ethernet cable to the Internet. The motor is programmed so that each bit of information flowing through the network causes it to perform a tiny twitch; accordingly, when the network is quiet, the string twitches every few seconds, and when the network is busy, the string whirls madly and emits the muffled, hollow noise of its own vibrations. In the work's installation at Xerox PARC, it was placed (as intended) in an unused corner of a hallway, adjacent to offices from which it could be seen and heard without being obtrusive.[2]

Given its predominantly peripheral functioning, *Dangling String* would seem to present an imperfect exemplar of the oscillation characteristic of calm technology.

Reversing the trajectory from periphery to center that marks Weiser and Brown's description, *Dangling String* initially attracts focal attention but then subsequently fades into the periphery: "At first," note Weiser and Brown, *Dangling String* "creates a new center of attention just by being unique. But this center soon becomes peripheral as the gentle waving of the string moves easily to the background. That the string can be both seen and heard helps by increasing the clues for peripheral attunement" (1997, 8). Weiser and Brown appear to recognize the work's bias toward the peripheral, which they correlate with its presence within the actual world: "The dangling string increases our peripheral reach to the formerly inaccessible network traffic. While screen displays of traffic are common, their symbols require interpretation and attention, and do not peripheralize well. The string, in part because it is actually in the physical world, has a better impedance match with our brain's peripheral nerve centers" (1997, 8). Yet by emphasizing how the work can be "fun and useful" and by comparing it favorably with screen-based but otherwise kindred data visualizations of network traffic, Weiser and Brown impose on the work the value of cognitive payoff that informs their functionalist approach.

It is, I suggest, precisely the autonomy of the peripheral that renders *Dangling String* exemplary of the more profound sensory revolution I wish to correlate with ubiquitous and, we can add, augmented-reality computing.[3] To appreciate this point, let us dwell for a moment on something Weiser and Brown effectively ignore: namely, that what is "communicated" by the dangling string's vibrations is neither solely nor primarily the sensory experience it directly affords, but rather the underlying patterns of Internet network traffic that it translates into sensory form. To be even more precise, what *Dangling String* affords is a sensory interface onto a "world," which is to say, onto a realm of microtemporal operations from which perception and sensory awareness are ordinarily excluded. In this sense, what the comparison with other screen-based visualizations highlights is the striking singularity of *Dangling String*: in stark contrast to a visualization such as John Klima's *Ecosystem* (2002), which uses flocking birds to track stock-market fluctuations and can be said to succeed to the extent that it offers a focalized perceptual—and, indeed, virtual—analog to the imperceptible,[4] what supports the aesthetic experience of microtemporal data flux in *Dangling String* is precisely the unwavering commitment to the peripheral that it requires of its experiencers. Put another way, the work doesn't tell us much about data traffic when it is engaged through focal awareness; all it can really tell us is that there is a little traffic or that there is a lot of traffic. By contrast, as users grow accustomed to the peripheral presence of *Dangling String*, they develop what can only be characterized as an *affective* connection to it. As users become free to *not attend focally to the work* and begin to sense it at the margins of awareness, their mode of sensing shifts from the macroperceptual level—What is it telling me about the traffic volume?—to the microperceptual level; at the latter level, microtemporal recognitions of motion, orientation, sound, and so on sustain an ongoing microaffective connection that never reaches the level of a conscious, focal perception. Wouldn't we accordingly need to conclude that this microaffective connection materializes the microtemporal flow of Internet traffic in the form of embodied microsensation? And because we cannot thematize or focalize the latter without transforming it fundamentally —that is, without transforming it into a unified or synthetic macroperception— wouldn't we need to accept that such microsensation enjoys autonomy from consciousness? Precisely this irreducibility of sensation is at stake in the autonomy of the peripheral.

Depresencing

It is only by focusing on the temporal specificity of ubiquitous computing that we can appreciate its revolutionary impact on our sensory interchange with the world. To do so, we must put pressure on the claims advanced in the name of ubicomp, which have more or less exclusively tended to emphasize the computer's disappearance into the environment and the resulting, allegedly transparent focus on unencumbered human interaction. Far more significant than the simple fact of the computer's disappearance, however, is the fundamental shift in mode of address that accompanies the proliferation of ubicomp into our contemporary lifeworld: put bluntly, within ubiquitous computational environments, computers address us at the level of microsensation, which is to say at a microtemporal level *that is by definition invisible to perceptual consciousness*. For this reason, we must conclude that *ubicomp marks a qualitative shift in the economy of sensation* and not just a new configuration of computer-mediated human interaction. To be even more precise, ubicomp calls microsensation into service as the predominate mode of human envelopment in the world at the same time as it exemplifies the irreducible technical basis for such envelopment: *ubicomp environments, precisely because they offer information peripherally—which is also to say, in a time frame beneath the threshold of conscious perception—catalyze sensation according to a protocol that is not wholly biotic but is crucially and irreducibly technical*. We might say then that ubicomp environments catalyze a form of sensation that obeys two masters at once: the neural logic of sensory fusion *and* the technical logic of computational processing. Accordingly, although proponents of ubicomp may take pains to design environments where computers are made to disappear, this disappearance takes place on top, as it were, of a more fundamental infrastructural disappearance: the plunge into the autonomy of the peripheral where sensing brains interface directly with microtemporal information, outside of the perceptual relation dominated by vision and the macroscale time consciousness that this relation exemplifies.

If ubicomp comprises a sensory revolution that marks the endpoint of a certain trajectory in the dialectic of technics and sensation (as I suggested earlier), our effort to grasp its significance requires us to correlate it with a new paradigm of media. For just as ubiquitous computing introduces flexibility in the coupling of human and computer, so too does it abandon an object-centered model of media in favor of an environmental one. No longer a delimited temporal object that we engage with focally through an interface such as a screen, media become an environment that we experience simply by being and acting in space and time—which is to say, without in most cases explicitly being aware of it, without taking it as the intentional object or target of our time consciousness. To anticipate a bit here, we can say that ubicomp signals a fundamental modification in our interface with technics: no longer object centered, resolutely personal, individually framed, and of the order of conscious perception, the technical mediation of sensation in ubicomp environments is atmospheric, impersonal, collectively accessible, and microtemporal in its sensory address.[5]

In the remainder of this chapter and by way of explicating this thesis, I unpack exactly what is at stake in ubicomp understood as catalyst for a revolution in the function of media and in the coupling of sensation and technics. This unpacking requires a fundamental intervention into the phenomenology of time consciousness that I ultimately want to put forth as a media-theoretical deepening rather than critical repudiation of phenomenology. As we have now seen, ubicomp media environments solicit a mode of sensation that is molecular and diffuse—which is to say, a sensibility comprising precisely those microsensory processes that are at stake in the autonomy of the peripheral. On this ground, "ubiquitous sensibility" contrasts starkly with phenomenological sensibility: whereas time consciousness synthesizes time in order to create temporal unities that provide contents for conscious experience, microsensory processes operate at a fine-grained temporal scale that cuts against the grain of phenomenological experience and must accordingly be considered to be nonconscious. The promise of ubicomp environments is directly tied to this last fact, for if the sensory—or microsensory—dimension of contemporary technics evades the grasp of consciousness (and thus of phenomenology in its traditional forms), we can "experience" it only indirectly by means of the enactive possibilities that "smart" environments afford.

The sensory revolution ushered in by ubicomp converges with a transformation in the focus of phenomenology—from perception to sensation—that, I want to emphasize, has always already been under way *within* phenomenology, from Edmund Husserl onward. Although the dominant thread of Husserlian phenomenology is certainly the analysis of perception and perceptual consciousness, Husserl's ultimate legacy to us may turn out to be his detailed attention to the fine structure of sensation and its imbrication with the problematic of temporality. Recent commentaries on Husserl, especially the work of French philosopher Renaud Barbaras (2006), not only have suggested as much but have correlated this displacement at the heart of Husserl's work with the trajectory of Maurice Merleau-Ponty's philosophy (from the phenomenology of perception to the ontology of the sensible that is *The Visible and the Invisible* [1969]) as well as with the significance of the redemptive project of Jan Patocka (to carry through on Husserl's initial formulation of a phenomenology of world manifestation). We can add to these references Emmanuel Levinas (1981, 1998) and Michel Henry (2008), both of whom have in their own ways pinpointed sensation as an anchoring point for a critical transformation of Husserlian phenomenology, along with certain poststructuralists, most notably Gilles Deleuze (1993), who have rejected phenomenology in the name of what its philosophical commitments (to common sense and recognition) bracket out—namely, "transcendental sensibility." What all of these varied and perhaps in part incompatible interventions share is a sense that the egocentric or Cartesian basis of phenomenology must be abandoned in favor of some affirmation of the embeddedness of the mind–body within the world. With specific respect to my argument here, this affirmation asserts that sensibility precedes perception and involves a directedness to the sensory world as such rather than to specific objects uniquely available to (or constituted by) consciousness.

My focus on the sensory impact of ubicomp aims precisely to correlate this internal transformation of phenomenology with the material/technical transformation of our contemporary lifeworld. To state this focus in the form of a thesis: ubicomp environments carry out in practice—and indeed expand—the upsurge of the sensible that now comprises the necessary focus of contemporary phenomenological (or post-phenomenological) analysis. In line with such a thesis, the de-marginalization of the peripheral—and the correlative de-marginalization of microtemporal neural processing—might well be understood as a discrete stage in the progressive displacement of perception by sensation. Indeed, we might even think of this stage as a kind of litmus test demonstrating the necessity for such a displacement: to the extent that the microtemporal resists conscious presentation, it can be accessed only through the medium of subperceptual sensation.

Ubiquitous computing makes the microtemporal sensuous. In doing so, it puts into contact the technical (micro)temporality of computation and the neural (micro)temporality of the mind–body. As a result of this connection, two further displacements ensue: on one hand, of the visual by the sensory as such and, on the other, of subject-centered (perceptual) agency by the agency of the environment. Both of these displacements concern the imbrication of technics and sensation and therefore speak directly to my general argument in this chapter. Indeed, both correlate more or less immediately with the findings of recent neuroscientific research on sensation and specifically on the visual cortex that I described in section I. This research, with its focus on the microsensory processes that underlie the perception of images (or, we might now want to say, appearances), suggests a reconfiguration of the "image" and its role in experience: rather than treating the image as an object in the world, we must henceforth consider it as the entire process through which thinking happens and hence as a sensory operation that is in some sense amodal or even simply *beneath* the differentiation of the senses. To this idea must be added the notion that sensation, far from constituting its own matter (whether in the form of an object or otherwise), *takes place within and as part of the world*: rather than attributing the role of time constitution to time consciousness, as does the classical Husserlian account, we must rather ascribe the power of temporalizing—what Husserl's student Eugen Fink calls "depresencing" (*Entgegenwärtigung*)—to the world itself. And, following this ascription, we must seek to elucidate how the phenomenon of time consciousness emerges on the basis of a more primitive, microsensory *reception* of worldly temporalizing. Consciousness, far from being its own agent and producing contents that are cut off from the world, responds to the world's microsensory solicitation, and it is from such responding that the self-affection constitutive of time consciousness is born.

Considered together, contemporary neuroscientific research into the temporality of imaging and (post)phenomenological developments of Husserl's work inform an account of the irreducible technicity of sensation that differs in crucial ways from the deconstructive paradigm for the technical contamination of thinking. This paradigm, initially formulated in Jacques Derrida's (1973, 1976) early work on Husserl, Heidegger, and Freud and later developed into a full-fledged philosophy of technics by Bernard Stiegler (2009, chapters 29 and 30 in this volume), takes root from the motif of "retentional finitude." Because living memory is finite and imperfect, it must rely on external, nonliving, *technical* memory supplements, which, from writing up to the latest forms of archive (e.g., Internet databases), cannot simply be dismissed as merely secondary but must rather be seen to *inhere within* or *contaminate* the inmost intimacy of living thought. Although a full account is beyond the scope of my discussion here, I want to make two observations that will foreground the shortcomings of this paradigm in the face of contemporary technical developments (ubicomp in particular, but also smart phones, social media, and the Internet). First, the deconstructive paradigm identifies media with memory and by doing so both imposes a higher-order frame of reference (consciousness, thought, etc.) and lends weight overwhelmingly to the past and its continuity with the present at the expense of all concern with the future. Second, this paradigm identifies media with the form of the object and by doing so effectively institutes a content model of thinking, which, moreover, it passes off as originary.

Although these identifications may remain largely benign or even invisible so long as the purpose of technics is to store previous experience (one need only think of the technology of writing), they become pernicious in the face of today's massive technical distribution of cognition beyond the brain. Given these latter developments—developments at whose center lies pervasive computing—the deconstructive paradigm cannot but appear antiquated, a quaint remnant of a world that has now passed us by, for the fact of the matter is clear: in our world today, technics does not remain indexed to human consciousness and its constitutive time frame(s) but operates at scales well outside of what humans can perceive. This distinction, again, is precisely why we must turn from perception to sensation in our effort to think the contemporary correlation of technics and life.

Beyond the Object

Because developments such as ubicomp address us at the pre-perceptual level of sensation, they not only expose the necessity for a postdeconstructive phenomenology but in the process link the limitations of the deconstructive paradigm to its enabling critical assimilation of a certain phenomenological heritage. Situated in this historical context, the deconstructive model fails to the precise extent that it preserves the object-centered, perception-focused, egological approach facilitated by the traditional (Husserlian) phenomenological reduction.[6] Despite its important and persuasive demonstration that the phenomenological cogito (or time consciousness) cannot function without the assistance of technologies that broach its intimacy, this paradigm does nothing to question the more general egological framework imposed by classical phenomenology.

This limitation finds perfect exemplification in the central figure of Stiegler's philosophy: the technical temporal object. Updating Husserl's analysis, Stiegler argues powerfully that the advent of technical recording in the nineteenth century secured the possibility for excavating the structure of time consciousness: specifically, the fact that consciousness can experience (hear or see) the same exact temporal object more than once gives it the possibility to account for the role of (secondary) memory in the creation of new present experiences (which Stiegler somewhat misleadingly calls "primary retention"). What makes the second (or *n*th) experience of the same temporal object different from that or those preceding it is the memory of previous experiences that consciousness brings to bear on it.

In Stiegler's updating, the technical temporal object—phonographic and cinematographic recording—takes the place of the Husserlian melody as objectal support for the flux of time in consciousness.[7] In the process, what was simply a heuristic for exposing the fine structure of time consciousness gets transformed into a cultural industrial technology: in contrast to Husserl, who urged voluntary recourse to the melody as a method for accessing the ineffable flux of time consciousness, Stiegler insists that contemporary consciousness, in order to experience itself as being affected by time, has no option but to rely on industrial temporal objects. From a vehicle for exposing the intimacy of time consciousness, the (technical) temporal object has now become the central external support for the very production of time consciousness. The cost of this dependence on industrialized (recorded or "tertiary") memories is time consciousness's susceptibility to co-optation by the culture industries. That is why Stiegler, at what are perhaps his bleakest moments, paints a picture of purely passive consciousnesses in the collective thrall of the standardized fluxes of television programs and other audiovisual temporal objects.

Despite Stiegler's astute grasp of a certain effect of televisual culture, his model remains emphatically partial. Bluntly put, it addresses the impact of technics exclusively through the figure of perceptual consciousness: technics matters only insofar as it supports and constrains the production of new contents of consciousness.[8] With regard to the distinction between perception and sensation that has guided my argument here, the significance of this limitation should be clear: by instituting the object as a privileged perceptual figure, Stiegler's model effectively leaves aside the entirety of technics's subperceptual, sensory impact on embodied human life; because microtemporal sensation cannot take the form of an object constituted by perceptual consciousness, it simply falls by the wayside. At the very least, this conclusion reveals just how little Stiegler's model—together with the deconstructive paradigm it exemplifies—suits the contemporary phase of our technogenesis.

It is precisely this bias toward object perception and the more general egological framework it requires that is put into question and finally overcome by the methodological transformation that, I suggest, is currently reconfiguring the field of phenomenology and that takes root in the displacement of perceptual consciousness in favor of subrepresentational, impersonal, microtemporal sensation. Insofar as it lends practical motivation to this displacement, the ubicomp revolution goes hand in hand with the fundamental reenvisioning of the phenomenological project after its own deconstruction. Not surprisingly, this reenvisioning proximately concerns the most fundamental motif of the phenomenological project: temporality. And it takes root in Husserl's own failure to reconcile—indeed, in the patent impossibility of reconciling—two aspects of his research: on one hand, his radical insight into the necessity for a nontemporal, nonegological *absolute* foundation of temporalization; and, on the other, his enduring methodological privileging of consciousness that, so it would seem, marks the phenomenological project at its deepest level.

In the late manuscripts on time (the *C-Manuscripts* from 1929 to 1934), the symptom of this failure goes by the name of the "living present" (*lebendige Gegenwart*). What remains constant across Husserl's various characterizations of the living present is the necessity to fuse two dimensions of the absolute flow of temporalization—namely, the "standing" and the "streaming." Husserl addresses this necessity differently in different manuscript groupings: in some places, he introduces a nonegological dimension of *hyle* ("matter" or "stuff" in Ancient Greek) that stands against the egological as co-constitutive of temporalization; at other places, he seeks to resolve the paradox of the standing, streaming nature of temporal flux without abandoning the framework of the egological. In the former case, the "standing" dimension is identified with the nonegological hyletic impression, and the "streaming" dimension with the egological response to this impression; in the latter case, it is the ego that both stands and streams: it repeats machinically as a purely formal *nunc stans* ("standing I or now"), and it streams away as the intentional modification of the pure impression. In both versions of the "living present," however, Husserl fails to give a coherent account of the absolute foundation of temporalization; both accounts, that is, gesture toward a hyletic, worldly or material, foundation of temporalization only to reimpose the framework of the ego and, with it, a certain priority of the present.

This critique of Husserl's mature thinking on temporality has been advanced most forcefully and most constructively by Husserl's final assistant and the putative heir to his project, Eugen Fink. In his own development of Husserl's work on temporalization and time consciousness, Fink opposes to Husserl's figure of the living present (*lebendige Gegenwart*) the operation of "depresencing" (*Entgegenwärtigung*). Convinced that Husserl's fatal error was to have begun with time *consciousness* rather than with the more fundamental worldly temporalization within whose horizon time consciousness is made possible and emerges, Fink argues that the true problem of the phenomenological analysis of time is explaining how time is constituted independently of any presencing *in* time. "Horizon-forming depresentings [or depresencings] are not any kind of intentional experience, not any kind of act that in some way first carries off some objective something, so that now presentification would be the countermove against this carrying off. Rather depresencings are a way in which original temporality itself comes about as temporal process—temporalizes [*eine Zeitigungsweise der ursprünglichen Zeitlichkeit selbst*]" (Fink 1966, 24). Depresencing must thus be differentiated categorically from the living present: it is not the flow of time itself (that is, the standing–streaming living present), but rather that which makes such flow possible: "The flow of time is just presencing [*Gegenwärtigen*]; it takes place in time. Depresencing temporalizes time [*zeitigt die Zeit*, brings it about as temporal], depresencings are not in time" (Fink quoted in Bruzina 2004, 235).

By drawing a categorical distinction between presencing and depresencing and, in effect, by differentiating two separate time series or levels of temporalization, Fink succeeds precisely where Husserl fails. Whereas Husserl merely asserted the need to view the fundamental time-constituting structures as nontemporal without being able to give a coherent account of these structures, Fink manages to ground the presencing of consciousness within a more fundamental giving of time—within depresencing. What allows Fink to do this is his (Heidegger-inspired) methodological conviction that phenomenology in its mature form must begin with the *pregivenness* of the world. The analysis of time, accordingly, must begin from *world* time—the time that encompasses both transcendence and immanence—and must, moreover, reject the traditional approach (constitution via thematic objects) in favor of a focus on its own horizonality. When Fink asserts that "time-constitution is horizon-constitution, *not object-constitution*" (quoted in Bruzina 2004, 207), he means to suggest precisely that Husserl's most fundamental problematic *is* the constitution of the world as a dynamic, pregiven process.

Without doing justice to the complexity of Fink's intervention, let me single out two aspects of his account of "world time as depresencing" that directly concern my argument here. First, Fink asserts the need to found time's pregivenness not on the flow of contents through consciousness, but rather on the horizonality (or, more precisely, the "swinging") of depresencing itself. Ronald Bruzina perfectly captures the significance of this assertion in his definitive commentary on Fink's phenomenology of time: "Depresencings are antecedent to protentions and retentions. Past and future are not stretches to be 'cashed in' [i.e., 'cashed in' in terms of determinate content or objects]. If for Husserl protention and retention have to do with the transformation of *contents* as seen in their passage from the present, for Fink depresencings as horizonal are the condition of possibility for *presenting* itself, for '*presencing*,' for bringing something to presence [*Gegenwärtigung*]" (2004, 236, emphasis in original).[9] Stated even more emphatically: time does not pass because the present becomes past and anticipates the future or because the impression is inseparable from retentions and protentions; quite to the contrary, the very possibility for the present to be present itself, for a moment to become present or to presence, stems from a more fundamental, originary passing of time: depresencing.

Presencing and depresencing, notwithstanding their lexical affinity, characterize what are at bottom categorically different levels—one on this side of being and time, the other on their hither side. Again, Bruzina clarifies this differentiation in terms of the content–horizon distinction: "The protentional and retentional horizons do not gain their operative value *from presencing*, as if the latter is achieved first and depresencing is then a modification of it. . . . One may characterize in that way the *content* that is 'held' retentionally or protentionally, but the horizons of depresencing themselves are quite another thing. Far from being the negative derivative from the centering hold-in-presence of an object that perception effects, they are intrinsic to the total possibility of the 'hold' in the now precisely as dynamic and flowing, rather than as frozen and static" (2004, 239). It is as if the thickness of time reverberates in two directions or, better, on two distinct planes: when related to the experience of an ego, retentional–protentional thickness qualifies the *contents* of consciousness; by contrast, when related to world time, it qualifies the horizonality or swinging of depresencing *independently of any subjective activity*. In stark contrast to Husserl, who, as I have noted, never ceased his efforts to reconcile absolute time constitution with egological experience, Fink offers the fundamental point that these two reverberations are not equal: depresencing conditions presencing; world time conditions egological time consciousness.

This conclusion immediately broaches the second aspect of Fink's work that is relevant for my purposes here: the "I-antecedency" of depresencing. "Time-constitution proper," writes Fink in altogether unequivocal terms, "is I-less. . . . [T]he I is only possible in a horizon of time, is a being that is constituted as identical in time-horizons" (quoted in Bruzina 2004, 239).

V—Impersonal Sensation

Let us pause here to take stock of just how far we've come. If the I (including time consciousness) and the object (including the temporal object) come "after" or on this side of the constitution of time, then an approach such as Stiegler's can do no more than capture the impact of technics on the constitution of subjects and objects within time; it simply cannot address the impact of technics on time. By contrast, the wager of *my* argument is that technics *does* impact time at the level of its absolute constitution—which is to say, prior to any experience in time—and that this impact paradoxically holds far greater significance for our experience than the fact that media proximately mediate our intratemporal lives. We might even say that technics's impact on experience is predominately indirect: technics impacts embodied experience—impacts the very emergence of such experience—precisely because and insofar as it impacts or supports worldly depresencing.

To unpack this logic of indirection, we need first to take cognizance of the irreducible sensory dimension of depresencing, its categorical antecedence to the ego notwithstanding. The crucial point to grasp here is that embodied human beings, quite independently of their subjective singularity, compose part of the world: they are an element in worldly (or, we might say, "objective") depresencing. (I borrow this particular valence of the term *objective* from Czech phenomenologist Jan Patocka, for whom the subject is both a subjective interiority subtracted from the world's manifestation *and*, more primordially, an *objective* aspect of that manifestation; it is crucial that we appreciate the singularity of this usage: the objectivity at issue here precedes the constitution of innerworldly objects.) How, we need to ask, are we able to sense depresencing *objectively*, to sense an *objective* aspect of that depresencing, "prior to" and independently of any subjectively constituted phenomenological experience?

Although Jean-Paul Sartre's distinction of consciousness and ego remains constrained by its fidelity to the Husserlian concept of intentionality, it points us in the right direction. For the early Sartre of *The Transcendence of the Ego* (2004), consciousness is equivalent to the qualitative experience it is having at any given moment in time. There simply is no need for a further unifying agent and thus no reason to postulate an ego at all: "There is no I on the unreflected level. When I run after a tram, when I look at the time, when I become absorbed in the contemplation of a portrait, there is no I. There is a consciousness of the *tram-needing-to-be-caught*, etc.

and a non-positional consciousness of consciousness. In fact, I am then plunged into the world of objects, it is they which constitute the unity of my consciousnesses" (2004, 13, emphasis in original).

Advancing the strong and unmistakably counterintuitive claim that Husserl's phenomenology itself has no need for a transcendental and subjective principle of unification," Sartre's analysis seems to confirm the priority of absolute consciousness over any egological subjective experience: "The World did not create the me, the me did not create the World, they are two objects for the absolute, impersonal consciousness, and it is through that consciousness that they are linked back together. This absolute consciousness, when it is purified of the I, is no longer in any way a *subject*, nor is it a collection of representations; it is quite simply a precondition and an absolute source of existence" (2004, 51, emphasis in original).

What makes Sartre's position so suggestive is his insistence on the impersonality of absolute consciousness. At the same time, his particular conceptualization of impersonality effectively prevents him from engaging with the fundamental problematic of time constitution. For Sartre, that is, the impersonality of consciousness entails its absolute spontaneity: "transcendental consciousness is an impersonal spontaneity. It determines itself to exist at every instant, without us being able to conceive of anything *before* it. Thus every instant of our conscious lives reveals to us a creation *ex nihilo*. Not a new *arrangement* but a new existence" (2004, 46, emphasis in original). Although certainly correct where constituted consciousness is concerned, Sartre's position leaves the mystery of time's flowing—precisely what Fink names in the most radical way with his concept of depresencing—not only unsolved but fundamentally unaddressed.

In seeking to capitalize on this motif of impersonality and, specifically, to bring it to bear on our account of time, we should perhaps take seriously the possibility of a continuity that has a physical or worldly basis rather than a subjective, mental one. Just such a *physical* continuity is at issue in Fink's depresencing: well in advance of the unified experience of the self-conscious subject that has literally dictated the trajectory of post-Cartesian modern philosophy, there is an originary sensory continuity that is presubjective, worldly, and "objective" (in Patocka's sense). Precisely because and to the extent that worldly depresencing is necessarily physical or material, it entails an *"objective" sensory dimension*, and it does so, significantly, whether this dimension ever gets actually experienced by embodied, sensing mind–bodies or not.

Understood in this context, impersonality qualifies a kind of sensibility that is more physical than psychological, and the issue we must now address is how embodied human mind–bodies can enjoy such impersonal sensation. How can we experience the world and time from the standpoint of our own irreducible worldliness, *as physicomaterial elements of the world itself?* How close can human mind–bodies, those most complex physicopsychological mixtures, actually come to direct experience of worldly depresencing? And how, finally, can technics be deployed to enhance this possibility for direct physicomaterial sensation?

To begin answering these questions, let me turn to a recent media-art environment that, in my opinion, successfully broaches the domain of the microsensory and that, for this reason, captures the promise of ubicomp as a new stage in the history of technics and sensation. Olafur Eliasson's *Your colour memory* (2004) is an immersive panoramic color installation designed to catalyze the experience of afterimages and thereby to generate an experiential "reflection" on color sensation. The work cycles through changes of color at thirty-second intervals and generates the production of afterimages as a function of time spent in the installation. Consider Eliasson's own characterization of the installation:

> *Your colour memory* investigates aspects of color perception, one of which is afterimages and their temporal relationship with their sources. If we enter a room saturated in red light, our eyes, as a reaction, produce so much green—with a delay of approximately 10–15 seconds—that the red appears much less intense; it is almost erased. If the color of the room were to change from red to colorless, a clear green afterimage would appear on our retinas. In *Your colour memory*, the color fades from one to the next in a sequence of 30 seconds. In that ½ minute the single color slowly appears, ripens, and subsequently fades into another color. If the room is blue when you enter, after about 10 seconds you will begin to produce an orange afterimage; if the installation fades from blue to yellow, the subsequent movement of afterimages in your eye will be from orange to purple. The retinal fade-out occurs with a delay of about 10–15 seconds in relationship to the actual change of color in the room. There are, in other words, two color curves at work: one pertaining to the work itself, one being created belatedly in your eyes. One could argue that another curve finally appears, namely the curve of colors perceived by the brain, which is an average of the two preceding curves. . . . If I were to enter the color-saturated room some time after you, my experience of the color would differ substantially from yours, as you would already be enrolled in a sequence of wall colors and afterimages that determine your present experience. I, on the other hand, may not yet have produced afterimages that color my perception to the same degree—so to speak. Our perception of the room, therefore, depends on the amount of time we spend immersed in the changing colors and on what use the room is to us. (Eliasson 2006, 77–78)

Two aspects of the work cry out for immediate attention. First, the temporal structure of the experiences solicited by the work perfectly mimics the temporal structure of time consciousness according to Husserl's specifications: just as retentional sedimentation impacts the production of new presents, so too does retinal sedimentation modulate the continuous presencing of color. And yet what is at stake in the two cases could not be more different: whereas, for Husserl, temporalization follows the dictates of consciousness, within Eliasson's sensory environment, temporalization emerges directly from the brain's initial response to the materiality of the world (light). Second, and stemming directly from this difference, the work productively exploits and complicates the divide between the physical and the psychological. Whereas the science of color perception, informed by technical incursions beginning in the nineteenth century, postulates a categorical distinction between the physical wavelength of light and the qualitative perception of color, Eliasson seeks to occupy the space between these two distinct phenomena, to give his viewers access to an inchoate sensory domain where the transfer from the physical to the qualitative is somehow still in process.

What allows Eliasson to do this is, I suggest, precisely the microsensory dimension associated with the neural processing of vision. In relation to the resulting macrosensations (distinct color perceptions), the microsensations at issue here compose a domain of "virtual" activity, with no conscious experiential correlate, where the divide between the physical (wavelength of light) and the mental (qualitative perception) has not yet been effectuated. At this microtemporal level of "experience," sensation is predominately a function of worldly depresencing, which is to say that it occurs "in" the embodied brain, but in it specifically *as a part of the world* or, perhaps better still, *prior to any division between mind and matter*. Whatever sensation is involved here occurs not in relation to a present that passes and thus to a subject separated out from the world, but rather as a function of the ongoing depresencing of the world itself, of the continuous replacement of one color with another, coupled with the entirety of worldly processes (quantity of external light, density of traffic in the room, etc.) that further "color" that world. The specific qualitative experiences catalyzed by *Your colour memory*—delays in reaction, afterimages, and so on—are testimonials to this primordial domain of sense: literally presentifications of absent microsensations, these experiences have a status somewhere between the microconsciousness of neural processing and constituted time consciousness, between purely impersonal, *quasi-direct* registering of light by the brain and personal qualitative experiences of color perception.

Without perhaps affording any *direct* sensory experience of the brute physical materiality of light, *Your colour memory* catalyzes a fundamentally different experience than what is at issue in Husserl's analysis of time consciousness, even in the form it takes following Sartre's reworking. The microsensory domain of neural processing lies on the very cusp of the brutely physical: it is the mind–body's very first layer of response to the primal materiality (primal impressionality) of depresencing. For this reason, it enjoys a more radical impersonality than what Sartre attributes to the myriad consciousnesses of intentional experience: *this* impersonality stems less from the simple lack of any egoic dimension than from the sheer materiality of the brain's resonance with the world. Microconscious neural processing is impersonal precisely because it *is* physical and material: it is the brain in the process of modulating the *pure hyle*, "before" any division between the egoic and the nonegoic (hyletic). It is the brain participating in the process of depresencing.

For similar reasons, *Your colour memory* is a technification of experience that is at odds with the technical supplementation of time consciousness at issue in Stiegler's updating of Husserl. Far from impacting the constitution of temporal objects that mirror consciousness's self-experience of its own existence in time, Eliasson's use of digital technics mediates the flux of microsensation as it emerges from and operates in the space opened by the complex interplay between the physical impressionality of light and the qualitative experience of color. What is at stake in *Your colour memory* is accordingly an experience directed against the "entertainment industry's commodification of the experience economy" and the "Disneyfication of the experiencing of art" (Eliasson 2006, 83). Expanding on these claims, art historian Jonathan Crary astutely identifies the performative dimension at issue in Eliasson's environment: more than a mere demonstration, *Your colour memory* exposes a sensory dimension normally concealed in contemporary image consumption. According to Crary,

> It's important to emphasize that Eliasson has no interest in some demonstration piece that informs us about the fascinating peculiarities of color vision. If afterimages preoccupy him, it is, in part, as a strategy of challenging and displacing perceptual habits imposed by dominant features of contemporary technological culture. Quite simply, to vividly experience one's own afterimages is, at least temporarily, to cease to be a mere consumer of radiant images or energy from screens, monitors, pages, and other sources that clutter our lives. It is to recognize one's self as a generator of luminous phenomena. (2006, 22)

The issue is, however, not just that our afterimages comprise counterimages to the "radiant images" of contemporary capitalist culture; they attest, rather, to an entirely other sensory life than that which informs the cultural industrial capture of the time of consciousness. What we learn from Eliasson's installation—and learn through, indeed, *as* experience—is precisely that beneath the level at which our personal consciousness is targeted (whether for hypersynchronization or for expansion), there operates an impersonal nexus of microsensory processes that sustain our sensory envelopment within the physicomaterial world. Our afterimages, with the complex temporalities they involve, are ciphers of this envelopment: they comprise direct emergences from the microsensory response of our embodied brains to contact with physical wavelengths of light.

Your colour memory, notwithstanding its distinctly and intentionally low-tech quality, exemplifies the potential for technics to modulate our impersonal microsensory "experience." Eliasson's installation points toward the affordances of ubiquitous computational environments without itself being one. In particular, it consecrates a mode of sensation that materializes what we might call our originary "environmental condition": our direct contact with the world that "precedes" any division of mind and matter and that continues surreptitiously, imperceptibly, to inform "our" sensory experience, as it were, "before" it becomes ours. It thus contributes to a new understanding of the function of media, one that breaks with the longstanding determination (a determination culminating in the deconstructive paradigm discussed earlier) of technical media as memory supplement. In Eliasson's environment, as in ubicomp environments more generally, media does not function to store personal experience so much as it operates to secure access to and facilitate sensory experience of a domain of temporal commonality—the depresencing of the world—that happens independently of the vicissitudes of consciousness. By participating in this process, we literally join the common movement of the world and hence experience in a direct sensory mode the fundamental openness of the future.

If *Your colour memory* gives a new specificity to the autonomy of the peripheral—a specificity that, I suggest, characterizes ubicomp environments more generally—that is because it emphatically demonstrates, again through and *as* experience, that sensing happens first and foremost in the medium of the physical and without conscious awareness. As our most basic response to the depresencing of the world, sensing is by definition proximately ecstatic, out of sync, and out of scale with conscious experience. And that, precisely, is why ubiquitous sensation is proximately and autonomously peripheral.

Notes

1. "Perhaps most diametrically opposed to our vision is the notion of 'virtual reality,' which attempts to make a world inside the computer. Users don special goggles that project an artificial scene on their eyes; they wear gloves or even body suits that sense their motions and gestures so that they can move about and manipulate virtual objects. Although it may have its purpose in allowing people to explore realms otherwise inaccessible—the insides of cells, the surfaces of distant planets, the information web of complex databases—virtual reality is only a map, not a territory. It excludes desks, offices, other people not wearing goggles and body suits, weather, grass, trees, walks, chance encounters and in general the infinite richness of the universe. Virtual reality focuses an enormous apparatus on simulating the world rather than on invisibly enhancing the world that already exists" (Weiser 1991, 78).

2. My description of *Dangling String* is based on that given in Weiser and Brown 1997, 15–16.

3. In his characterization of "augmented reality," Ronald Azuma foregrounds the possibility of opening human contact with information via channels other than those of habitual perception and sensory awareness: "What is Augmented Reality good for? Basically, applications of this technology use the virtual objects to aid the user's understanding of his environment. For example, a group at UNC scanned a fetus inside a womb with an ultrasonic sensor, then overlayed a three-dimensional model of the fetus on top of the mother's womb. The goal is to give the doctor 'X-ray vision,' enabling him to 'see inside' the womb. Instructions for building or repairing complex equipment might be easier to understand if they were available not in the form of manuals with text and 2D pictures, but as 3D drawings superimposed upon the machinery itself, telling the mechanic what to do and where to do it. Groups at Boeing and Columbia are exploring these types of applications. *Fundamentally, Augmented Reality is about augmentation of human perception: supplying information not ordinarily detectable by human senses*" (n.d., emphasis added).

4. For a description of *Ecosystem*, see http://www.cityarts.com/lmno/ecosystm.html.

5. Weiser, Gold, and Brown assess the transformation effectuated by ubicomp: "In the end, ubicomp created a new field of computer science, one that speculated on a physical world richly and invisibly interwoven with sensors, actuators, displays, and computational elements, embedded seamlessly in the everyday objects of our lives and connected through a continuous network. What is truly startling is how quickly we are finding this new form of computation manifesting itself around us" (1999, 694).

6. In reality, this figure of the traditional Husserlian phenomenological reduction is nothing more than a simplification and artificial stabilization of one perhaps dominant strand of Husserl's thinking. To get a full sense of what is at stake here, we would have to follow the myriad permutations of the *epoche* across Husserl's career and in the work of his more important students and disciples. Suffice it to say here that there are many (or at least several) Husserls, which is to say that against this traditional picture there is a Husserl who correlates the reduction with the encounter with the *hyle* prior to the advent of perceptual consciousness.

7. Husserl offers in his 1905 lectures on time consciousness, *On the Phenomenology of Internal Time Consciousness* (1991), the melody as the example par excellence of a temporal object. A temporal object is defined as an object that does not simply exist in time, but that has time as its content. A finite temporal structure with a beginning and an end, the melody forms a perfect surrogate to "objectify" the ineffable flux of time consciousness. It is by analyzing the retentions of just-past sounds as well as expectations of sounds just to come that we acquire insight into the complex structure of time consciousness.

8. Technics thus instances what I have elsewhere called "technesis": the putting-into-writing of technology (Hansen 2000).

9. My understanding of the significance of Fink's departures from Husserl owes much to Bruzina's meticulous reconstruction of Fink's work from his scant published texts and unpublished notes.

References

Azuma, Ronald. n.d. "Registration Errors in Augmented Reality." Available at http://www.cs.unc.edu/~azuma/azuma_AR.html. Accessed 7 February 2011.

Barbaras, Renaud. 2006. *Desire and Distance: Introduction to a Phenomenology of Perception.* Stanford, CA: Stanford University Press.

Benjamin, Walter. 2008. "Little History of Photography." In *The Work of Art in the Age of Its Technological Reproducibility and Other Writings on Media*, by Walter Benjamin, edited by Michael William Jennings, Brigid Doherty, and Thomas Y. Levin, translated by Edmund F. N. Jephcott, Rodney Livingstone, and Howard Eiland, 274–298. Cambridge, MA: Belknap Press of Harvard University Press.

Bergson, Henry. [1911] 1998. *Creative Evolution.* New York: Dover.

Bergson, Henry. [1896] 1988. *Matter and Memory.* Translated by N. M. Paul and W. S. Palmer. Brooklyn, NY: Zone.

Bruzina, Ronald. 2004. *Edmund Husserl & Eugen Fink: Beginnings and Ends in Phenomenology, 1928–1938*. Yale Studies in Hermeneutics. New Haven, CT: Yale University Press.

Crary, Jonathan. 2006. "Illuminations of the Unforeseen." In *Olafur Eliasson: Your Colour Memory*, 22. Glenside, PA: Arcadia University Art Gallery.

Deleuze, Gilles. 1993. *Difference and Repetition*. New York: Columbia University Press.

Derrida, Jacques. 1976. *Of Grammatology*. Baltimore: Johns Hopkins University Press.

Derrida, Jacques. 1973. *Speech and Phenomena, and Other Essays on Husserl's Theory of Signs*. Northwestern University Studies in Phenomenology and Existential Philosophy. Evanston, IL: Northwestern University Press.

Eliasson, Olafur. 2006. "Some Ideas about Color." In *Olafur Eliasson: Your Colour Memory*, 77–78. Glenside, PA: Arcadia University Art Gallery.

Fink, Eugen. 1966. "Vergegenwärtigung und Bild: Beiträge zur Phänomenologie der Unwirklichkeit." In *Studien zur Phänomenologie, 1930–1939*, 74–78. The Haag: Nijhoff.

Hansen, Mark B. N. 2000. *Embodying Technesis: Technology beyond Writing*. Ann Arbor: University of Michigan Press.

Henry, Michel. 2008. "Hyletic Phenomenology and Material Phenomenology." In *Material Phenomenology*, 7–42. New York: Fordham University Press.

Husserl, Edmund. 1991. *On the Phenomenology of the Consciousness of Internal Time (1893–1917)*, translated by John Barnett Brough, edited by Rudolf Bernet. Vol. 4 of *Collected Works*. The Hague: Nijhoff.

Jonas, Hans. 2001. "The Nobility of Sight: A Study in the Phenomenology of the Senses." In *The Phenomenon of Life: Toward a Philosophical Biology*, 135–156. Evanston, IL: Northwestern University Press.

Lazzarato, Maurizio. 2007. "Machines to Crystallize Time: Bergson." *Theory, Culture & Society* 26 (6): 93–122.

Levinas, Emmanuel. 1998. "Intentionality and Sensation." In *Discovering Existence with Husserl*, 135–152. Evanston, IL: Northwestern University Press.

Levinas, Emmanuel. 1981. *Otherwise Than Being: Or, Beyond Essence*. The Hague: Nijhoff.

Merleau-Ponty, Maurice. 1969. *The Visible and the Invisible*. Evanston, IL: Northwestern University Press.

Neidich, Warren. 2003. "Visual and Cognitive Ergonomics: Formulating a Model through Which Neurobiology and Aesthetics Are Linked." Available at http://www.warrenneidich.com/wp-content/uploads/2010/01/warren_neidich_visual_cognitive_ergonomics.pdf. Accessed 15 April 2011.

Sartre, Jean-Paul. 2004. *The Transcendence of the Ego: A Sketch for a Phenomenological Description*. London: Routledge.

Stiegler, Bernard. 2009. *Technics and Time*. Vol. 2: *Disorientation*. Stanford, CA: Stanford University Press.

Weiser, Mark. 1996. "Open House." *ITP Review* 2. Available at http://www.itp.tsoa.nyu.edu/~review. Accessed 7 February 2011.

Weiser, Mark. 1991. "The Computer for the 21st Century." *Scientific American* 265 (3): 94–104.

Weiser, Mark, and John Seely Brown. 1997. "The Coming Age of Calm Technology." In *Beyond Calculation: The Next Fifty Years of Computing*, 75–86. New York: Springer; available at http://www.johnseelybrown.com/calmtech.pdf, 1–17. Accessed 25 January 2012.

Weiser, Mark, Rich Gold, and John Seely Brown 1999. "The Origins of Ubiquitous Computing Research at PARC in the Late 1980s." *IBM Systems Journal* 38 (4): 693–696.

Zeki, Semir. 1999. *Inner Vision: An Exploration of Art and the Brain*. Oxford, UK: Oxford University Press.

2 The Ubiquity of Photography

Arild Fetveit

The advent of software such as Photoshop in 1990 was at the time seen as instigating a crisis that even had the potential to bring about the death of photography as a medium. Digital alteration was perceived as undermining and depleting the very quality that distinguishes photographs from other pictures—namely, its causal connection to its motive, by which photography, in Charles Saunders Peirce's words, "is physically forced to correspond point by point to nature" (1955, 106). This physical connection was taken to be undermined by software that could make it impossible to judge from the pictures whether the physical connection was in place or partially corrupted.

A second momentous encounter between digital technology and photography came with the migration of photography from the chemical support that grounded its invention as a medium to the digital support implemented in the early years of the new millennium.

The fallout of photography's crisis, its double encounter with digital technology, has not been the demise and death of the medium, however. On the contrary, photography has never been as vital to human affairs and as ubiquitous as it is today. How can this be? Has the advent of digital alteration and distribution, rather than causing the demise of photography, in some ways prepared for photography's present ubiquity?

This double encounter—which has supplied photographic practices with powerful alteration software and secured photography's migration to a digital support—has left photography with momentous changes to its technological makeup and set the stage for further developments to take place in a dynamics between technology and use, software creation and emergent practices. The future trajectory of these interconnected developments of technologies and practices of production and reception will speak to how photography as a medium will continue to evolve.

Here I argue that the two encounters—the advent of digital-alteration technologies and the migration to a digital platform—have occasioned two distinct but related adjustments to our notion of what photography *is*, to its ontology. I explore these adjustments to the ontology of photography by assessing a series of connections between the operational logic of the computer and the logic of the medium of photography. This series of connections not only contributes to adjusting our notions about what photography is but also provides explanations for the current vitality of the photographic medium. As part of the argument, I discuss computer scientist Mark Weiser's vision for a third wave of computing and recent interventions addressing the ontology of photographical images.[1] I focus mainly on what I have called the "second encounter," digital storage and distribution, but before coming to that, I briefly sketch how I envision key consequences of the first encounter, the advent of digital-alteration tools.

As I have pointed out elsewhere, digital alteration does not represent the demise of visible evidence but ensures a shift in emphasis from a technologically grounded to a more institutionally grounded trust (Fetveit 1999). If the alteration techniques have not undermined photography, though people have become more alert to alteration, can the case possibly be made that the alteration techniques in some ways support the present surge in photographic imagery? As Lev Manovich has noted, a hyphen is pressing itself into the word *photography* today in our increasingly hybrid image culture. "'Photographic' today is really photo-GRAPHIC," he says, "the photo providing only an initial layer for the overall graphical mix" (2006, 27). A thriving image development is taking place where the photographic image has become sampled, remixed, and mutable. But a photographic aesthetic "look" remains a key reference point in this wider image culture. The development of graphical image production in computer games, for instance, increasingly adopts the aesthetic of the effects-driven movies they tend to pair with. Thus, what we can call "the photographic" thrives both within and beyond the realms of photography itself.

This more malleable photographic culture also relates to what Donna Haraway has called "the translation of the world into a problem of coding" (1991, 164). In the wake of this translation appears an increased manipulability of the body of photography and the human body alike, which in part explains how photographic alteration practices to this day tend to revolve around the human body. Thus, the emergent outcome of this first encounter—the advent of alteration software—is an adjustment to the ontology of photography whereby photography emerges as more contingent and malleable, just as the human body appears more malleable in the wake of contemporary body-alteration technologies. This increased malleability affords new uses of photographic images, thereby potentially expanding their areas of operation and adding to their ubiquity.

If this description represents a provisional account for the fallout of the first encounter, what bearings has the second encounter—the migration of photography to a digital platform—had on photography's present ubiquity? And in what ways might it adjust the ontology of photography?

Ontology in Question

The invention of automated recording of visual and auditive data—by means of photography, moving images, and sound recording—allowed paintings, sculptures, musical concerts, as well as other objects and events to be mediated in revolutionary ways. It ensured that those who could not travel to the Museo del Prado in Madrid to see *Las Meninas* by Diego Velázquez (1656) or to Egypt to see the pyramids or to La Scala in Milano to hear Maria Callas or to Paris to see Notre-Dame Cathedral now could "experience" them by means of media, which in Marshall McLuhan's (1994) vocabulary represent an extension of the human sensory apparatus—in particular, the senses of seeing and hearing. Among the consequences of the mechanical means of reproduction, as Walter Benjamin puts it, is that the "cathedral leaves its locale to be received in the studio of a lover of art" (1992, 221). Digitalization takes this to a new level. Its retooling of analog media seems to bring us the cathedral with an unprecedented speed. But does this retooling also change what is brought? How do the computer's characteristics come to define the ways in which the cathedral can be received, or, more generally, how does the computer set the framework for the medial logic by which cultural artifacts such as photography may become accessible?

Addressing the extensive digitalization of photographic collections, Elisabeth Edwards and Janice Hart remind us that "a photograph is a three-dimensional thing, not only a two-dimensional image. As such, photographs exist materially in the world, as chemical deposits on paper, as images mounted on a multitude of differently seized, shaped, colored and decorated cards, as subject to additions to their surface" (2004, 1). This statement briefly sums up the major elements that are lost in digitalizing analog photographs, though the material aesthetics of various photographs can be more fully described.[2] Though extraphotographic material, often valuable for understanding the context and history of a photograph, seems increasingly to be included in digitalization processes, the material object itself, of course, is not carried over in the digital format other than in the form of digital representations. Now, these questions about what to include when photographic collections are digitalized illustrates how these practices also involve decisions about what the photographic object is.

But the question of what constitutes the photographic object contains an even more radical question relating to the fundamental logic of the computer as we know it. What is the original of the photographic image: the negative film or the positive print? Where there is a choice, the negative film is often taken to be the original and is thereby the one that merits protection and digitalization. In the case of art, however, a positive copy printed on a special paper in a certain size, perhaps also signed and given a special presentation in a selected frame, tends to be the original. For photographs, the object's ontological uncertainty is not merely a challenge to archiving or an abstract philosophical question. It might also have tangible, practical, and institutional consequences in the art world.

Photography—as Performative Art

Seydou Keïta from Mali produced some beautiful photographs of life on Africa's western coast in the 1950s and 1960s. When the interest for photographic art practically exploded in the 1990s—fueled by a complex cocktail in which the cultural stir about digital alteration must be factored in—art galleries also looked to the past for interesting works to present. Thus, the Gagosian Gallery came to show a selection of Keïta's photographs in 1997, first in Los Angeles and then in New York. For the shows, new 20-by-24-inch and 48-by-60-inch prints were made from the negatives. What the audience could see was, according to an article by Michael Rips in the *New York Times*, "mural-size black-and-white portraits in which the intricate designs of tribal costumes were set against backdrops of arabesque and floral cloths, the subjects disappearing into dense patterning that suggested Vuillard" (2006). Many prints were sold the first night for up to $16,000 each. However, Keïta had made his own prints from the negatives in the 1950s and 1960s. The original prints were small, 5 by 7 inches, with minimal contrast, and they looked modest compared to the stunning prints offered by Gagosian. As Rips puts it, in Keïta's prints "the contrast and density of the blacks and whites were minimal, the light modest, and the patterns on the costumes barely visible" (2006). Could the credibility of the Gagosian's prints, even if they were also signed, risk being undermined by prints that appeared as the early, true originals?

This potential problem did not deter the Sean Kelly Gallery in New York from launching another version of Keïta photographs in 2006. They hired the photographic printer Charles Griffin, who also had been working for Cindy Sherman and Hiroshi Sugimoto, to do the prints. According to Griffin, "printers are influenced by the preference wealthy collectors have for highly graphic images," a problem he says he was reminded of when seeing the Gagosian show. Thus, when he later made prints from Mr. Keïta's negatives, he says he made several changes, including the decision to "give more emphasis to the ground between the blacks and whites" (quoted in Rips 2006). Griffin's statements at the time of the opening of the show at Sean Kelly Gallery makes the excellent performance of these prints the selling point rather than their authenticity by means of their closeness to the artist and the time and place they were taken. Keïta's photographs are implicitly presented as a productive arena in which a great printer may excel. This point is apparent in the discrepancy between the rich potentials inherent in his negatives, the modest prints Keïta himself produced, as well as the exaggerated contrasts in the prints presented by Gagosian.

The case embodies a tension between two conflicting models of photography operating in the art world: one privileging the original first prints signed by the photographer shortly after the picture is taken, another more performative model putting emphasis on creative performance in printing and thereby opening up the way for interesting versions.

As part of the emergent adjustment to the ontology of photography deriving from digital storage and distribution, I believe we can expect photography to be pushed slightly in a performative direction whereby it becomes somewhat more like a performative art.[3] Against this background, it can be claimed that the new versions of Keïta's photographs produced by Gagosian and Sean Kelley are somewhat comparable to competing contemporary realizations of a play by William Shakespeare or a song by Cole Porter. Thus, the new prints can be seen to offer timely versions of Keïta's work that are more compelling than previous prints. In general, according to the logic of the performative arts, something is composed—whether it be a drama, a song, or a photographic negative—and must also be realized in order to become fully available and possibly also realized again to keep up with changing sensibilities.[4]

To underscore the importance of the printing process and to claim that this performative dimension is vital to artistic creation in photography are far from new. The American photographer Ansel Adams is famous for his performances in the dark room. Adams actually also compared the negative to a musical score and the printing process to a performance. For one of his most famous pictures, *Moonrise, Hernandez, New Mexico* ([1941] 1972), he first made a straight print to plan his "performance." The dramatic quality of the finished print was the result of careful burning and dodging during printing, a process in which the photographer used a paper card to let more or less light pass through certain areas of the negative onto the printing paper (see Ansel Adams Gallery 2009).

Art historian and media theorist Boris Groys takes a strong position on photography as performative art:

> [L]ooking at digital images we are also confronted every time with a new event of visualization of invisible data. . . . A digital image, to be seen, should not be merely exhibited but staged, performed. Here the image begins to function analogously to a piece of music, whose score, as is generally known, is not identical to the musical piece—the score itself being silent. For music to resound, it has to be performed. Thus one can say that digitalization turns the visual arts into a performing art. But to perform something is to interpret it, to betray it, to distort it. Every performance is an interpretation and every interpretation is a betrayal, a misuse. (2008, 84)

Continuing his argument, Groys proposes that "the curator becomes now not only the exhibitor but the performer of the image" (84). I sympathize with the tenor of this diagnosis, which in principle fits well with the making of the new Keïta prints for the Gagosian and Sean Kelly shows. However, I also believe that Groys may be ahead of current developments in his strong claim for performing "digital images" like music.[5]

The structural divide between composition and realization, negative and positive copy, can also be located in the fundamental divide between storage and presentation in the computer. This divide has important consequences for the development of photography as medium on a digital platform, not only for its ontology, but also for its representational capacities and the possible toll they take in losses of information.

Storage, Display, and Weiser's Third Wave

As I have suggested in an article on media convergence (Fetveit 2007), the computer ensures a radical divide between medium of storage and medium of display.[6] I illustrated the divide by noting how a traditional painting such as Velasquez's *Las Meninas* (1656) is both displayed and stored by the singular painting hanging in the Museo del Prado in Madrid. Likewise, the daguerreotype, which is a positive and unique picture, also knows no separation between medium of storage and medium of display. The negative-positive process, however, made public by Fox Talbot in 1839 introduces a separation that construes the negative as the privileged medium of storage for photography, whereas the positive print comes to take care of the display function, albeit the use of positive prints in a storage function—in family albums and elsewhere—should not be underestimated (see Sandbye, chapter 3 in this volume).

Now, as it happens, a basic structural logic informing Weiser's vision of a third wave in computing, after mainframes (shared by a number of people) and the personal computers that dominate today, echoes the divide between medium of storage and medium of display. In fact, we can also claim that such a distinction characterizes the computer's operational logic in general. In his account of how the future of ubiquitous computing may play out, Mark Weiser says: "Carrying a project to a different office for discussion is as simple as gathering up its tabs; the associated programs and files can be called up on any terminal" (1991, 96). This description evokes computing as being based precisely on a separate storage and display function, allowing anything to be "called up" and displayed whenever we want it to. In his vision for ubiquitous computing, Weiser expands the separation between storage and display characteristics of a single computer to depict the interconnectedness and ubiquity of computers, allowing us to call up any data at any time without carrying any physical computer around. When we are working on a project, relevant data files migrate seamlessly across spaces, where we work, at our homes, and wherever we want them available.

Weiser's vision remains to be realized, but it has informed major developments in computing. The present surge in cloud computing, which places an increasing amount of data "in the cloud," on servers accessible throughout the Internet, allows files to be "called up on any terminal." But this realization of Weiser's vision is not supported by the interlinked and ubiquitous minicomputers he envisioned. It is based on server parks and Internet distribution, and display is taking place predominantly on personal computers, leaving questions open about what form a possible third wave of computing might take.

Photography's migration from a chemical support to a digital support may actually strengthen the medial logic premised on a divide between storage and display already inherent in the negative-positive process. This strengthening has consequences for photographic practice as well as for what photography is. Photographs are now increasingly digitally stored—in some cases because they originally were analog photographs scanned and stored for preservation and access purposes and in even more cases simply because they stem from a camera with digital support. If we open the black box of the concept "medial support" here, we are reminded that it is a complex entity in that the storage medium and the display medium may be quite separate, and the transition between storage medium and display medium may be cumbersome or may be swift and easy. The ease with which digital technology allows photographs to be called forth from storage to display—just as Benjamin's cathedral or Weiser's projects—goes a long way toward explaining why photographs now tend to be digitally stored. What consequences more precisely does the computer's medial logic as concerns its separation of storage and display have for the photograph?

When Photography Adopts the Computer's Medial Logic

First, the computational separation between storage and display, now adopted for digital photographs, is, as we have seen, not something entirely new to photography. It can be seen as a radicalization of a separation already inherent in the negative-positive process made public by Fox Talbot. We can even turn the tables and say that the medial logic of Fox Talbot's negative–positive process prefigures the one adopted for computers. No matter how these similarities are conceptualized, however, it remains that the digital construal of the divide between storage and display has important consequences, including adjustments to the ontology of photography as a medium.

In its digitally stored form, the photograph is ready to be called forth and materialized on available surfaces, whether it be the screens we use on various devices, paper fed into a printer, or more ambitious forms of display such as a T-shirt, a pair of sneakers, a doll, humans moving in an exhibition space, or architectural surfaces. The medial setup potentially allows for more migratory options and for more flexible forms of display. As Groys puts it, these images have "an ability to originate, to multiply, and to distribute themselves through the open fields of contemporary means of communication, such as the Internet or cell-phone networks, immediately and anonymously, without any curatorial control" (2008, 82).

The digital-image file has only a virtual existence as image, a potentiality, and must be actualized to be seen. Once the actualization ends—for example, because we shift to actualizing another image on our screen—the existence as actualized image ceases. In its actualizations, the image will manifest itself differently according to the screen, the paper, or other surface on which it is actualized. British philosopher and art theorist Peter Osborne seems largely in agreement with what I am suggesting here as he notes that "it is in its potential for an infinite multiplication of visualizations that the distinctiveness of the digital image lies" (2010, 60). Thus, the screen "lends" materiality to images during the time they are activated. This principles affords actualization games by which photographs or, for that matter, video images may migrate across a wide set of surfaces, acquiring shifting materialities under way. When Rafael Lozano-Hemmer's installation *Under Scan* (2004) was shown in Trafalgar Square in London in November 2008, its video images of people projected onto the street enlisted viewers to interact with them at times by laying themselves down on the street to replace the materiality of the street with that of their own bodies, which had now become screens for photographic display ("Tate Intermedia" 2008).

Although the image can adopt material qualities from where it is displayed, it also carries material qualities irrespective of how it is actualized, which will follow it in its various manifestations. They are the result of complex dynamics between the surfaces photographed, the light used, the atmosphere at a location, and so on, but they can also be construed through various forms of filters and effects, either used at the time of exposure or, which is as likely for recent photographs, as part of a postproduction process.

In some ways, as we have seen, digitalization entails a reduction of complexity for the medial materiality of photography in that a rich set of paper forms, chemical processes, and techniques disappear. The loss of medial complexity has spawned two reactions. Inside the digital realm, photographic software has been equipped with numerous filters and effects that emulate lost processes and formats such as sepia, solarization, black and white with variable graininess, and so on. Outside of the digital realm—and partly in active negation of and response to digitalization—a host of older techniques have been reactivated by photographers who cherish the unique qualities of the various chemically based techniques. This double effort to restore materialities lost with the migration of photography to a digital platform also relates to more general current sentiments, where the body, materiality, and presence are activated as a response to a digital realm often conceived to be disembodied and virtual.

The Metamedium and the Photographic

Reduction of medial complexity is also associated with another connection imbricating the photographic with the computational, beyond the medial logic of storage and display. This connection comes to the fore if we ask: By what medial means can the computer portray and reproduce other media such as sculptures, paintings, drawings, daguerreotypes, and other photographs?

Alan Kay was among the pioneers who sought to develop the computer as a media machine, a "metamedium"—a machine that can handle all previous media and lay the foundations for creating new media. The medial logic whereby the computer can handle all these media is through the modalities of numbers, letters, sound, and still and moving images.[7] This means that when it handles all previous media, it does so by reducing them to these modalities. Thus, the medium of sculpture is handled through three-dimensional graphics or preferably through a photographic representation that also conveys the sculpture's material surface qualities in a realistic manner. The still and moving images that in part afford the computer its status as a metamedium capable of handling all other media are largely photographic, suggesting a deep connection between the computer and the photographic medium.

However, the metamedium function based on digital photography takes a considerable toll when daguerreotypes and a host of other chemically based manifestations of photography are displayed. This is why photography scholars, film theorists, and practitioners have been concerned with a loss of materiality. But something peculiar has happened with the recent change photography has gone through. Photography has approached the computer by adopting the same material practices: the replacement of chemically based storage with digital storage has in effect transformed photographic cameras into specially designed minicomputers with lenses. This transformation, of course, has radical consequences for the loss of the information in question. The difference in material practices has more or less disappeared, and with that disappearance the loss of information has also in principle ceased.

These close relations between the medial logic of the computer and that of photography provide important cues as to why the present ubiquity of computing—largely supported by a ubiquity of personal computers—in many ways seem part and parcel of the ubiquity of photography. Now, how this intimate relation will play itself out in a projected third wave of computing—involving embedded, invisible, and partly undetectable entities—remains to be seen.

Photography, Ubiquity, and Weiser's Third Wave

I have discussed how the present ubiquity of photography is closely connected to the ubiquity of computers and to the intimate integration of the medium of photography with the computer. I have also touched on Weiser's vision for a third wave in computing, after the mainframe and the present wave of personal computing. I refrain here from predicting to what extent and how such a third wave might materialize itself, but it is interesting to note that the situation emerging at present seems to effect what

Weiser was urging in the early 1990s in many ways, through personal computers that multiply and become smaller and more user friendly as well as through an increasing amount of data "in the cloud."

A key hindrance for the realization of Weiser's vision, possibly also for cloud computing, is the issue of security. Weiser was also alert to this problem but did not in principle see it as different from security issues in ordinary life. However, he may have underestimated how security concerns and the urge for freedom may hold people back from implementing the changes that will realize the third wave. Worries about security make people restrict access to their Wi-Fi networks. Security issues are also vital for decisions to place data "in the cloud." Will the data be there to tomorrow? Will someone sift though them, as gmail users may fear is happening to their accounts? (See Kirkpatrick 2008.)

Moreover, the recent frenzy in downloading music and films has created more or less legal archives, and with aggressive copyright holders urging convictions to contain the practice, many may feel safer storing data on a personal hard drive rather than in the cloud.

Photography has an ambiguous position here. The photographic practice of everyday life is largely a public practice, where images are immersed in the fabric of social relations to friends, family, and prospective others. Thus, among our files that have moved effortlessly into the cloud, photographic files figure prominently. They inhabit Flickr, Facebook, Picasa, MySpace, YouTube, and a host of other sites, from which they can be immediately called up and showed through an online computer. Thus, digital photography has in a sense been a forerunner in realizing cloud computing and some of the effects Weiser envisioned as part of the third wave. However, among our photographic files we may also find personal items, souvenirs of intimate moments that we do not want to see made public. For some, such materials can end careers when publicized. Photographic material may therefore also make us hesitate before transferring all our data to the cloud. In addition, there are concerns about the increased surveillance and control that the used-to-be "free" Internet increasingly seems subjected to (Galloway 2004). In assessing the issue of how far we have come toward ubicomp, it may also be interesting to revisit Weiser's notion of "calm computing." Weiser said, "The most profound technologies are those that disappear. They weave themselves into the fabric of everyday life until they are indistinguishable from it" (1991, 94).

I think we can safely say that smartphones, which are in effect small portable computers, *have* woven "themselves into the fabric of everyday life . . . [and become] indistinguishable from it." So how did that happen? In his 2007 Tate Lecture, Lev Manovich addresses "information as an aesthetic event." "Contrary to ten years ago," he says, "today the designers no longer try to make the interfaces invisible. Instead, the *interaction is treated as an event*. . . . [U]sing personal information devices is now conceived as a carefully orchestrated *experience*, rather than only a means to an end" (2007, 2). He claims that an "aesthetization of interfaces"—as opposed to the attempt to make interfaces invisible—started around 1996. The reason for these changes, Manovich claims, was predominantly that these objects now sought to conquer our leisure life and become consumer objects:

> As these machines came to be redefined as consumer objects to be used in all areas of people's lives, their aesthetics were altered accordingly. The associations with work and office culture and the emphasis on efficiency and functionality came to be replaced by new references and criteria. They include being friendly, playful, pleasurable, expressive, fashionable, signifying cultural identity, aesthetically pleasing, and designed for emotional satisfaction. Accordingly, the modernist design formula "form follows function" came to be replaced by new formulas such as "form follows emotion." (2007, ibid.)

From a number of rather theatrical products foregrounding fancy colors and design details, such as the LG Chocolate mobile phone, offering "a unique . . . interactive narrative which can be called a real Gesamtkunstwerk" (Manovich 2007, 4), a more calm approach to design, Manovich argues, broke through after the turn of the millennium, especially in the design of Apple products:

> Titanium and Aluminum PowerBooks (2001, 2003), iPod and iPod shuffle (2001, 2005), Mac Mini (2005), the accompanying power cables, earphones, and so on—adopted very different minimal aesthetics. In this aesthetics the technological object seems to want to disappear, fade into the background, and become ambient—rather than actively attracting attention to itself and its technological magic, like the original iMACs. Whether consciously or not, these Apple designs communicate, or rather foretell, the new identity of personal IT [information technology] . . . the actual practical disappearance of technological objects as such as they become fully integrated into other objects, surfaces, spaces. ... This is the stage of ubiquitous computing in which a technological fetish is dissolved into the overall fabric of material existence. (2007, 6)

What is emerging here may be the actual ways in which ubiquitous computing is integrated into our lives by way of attractive yet calm, ambient environments supported by pleasant but unobtrusive designs creating environments for working and for living. This same development is also taking place in applications handling photographs, such as Apple's iPhoto and Google's Picasa. They seem to be increasingly object oriented, slipping us right into our photographic collections, undisturbed by complex technologies. This is also a way in which the technologies are woven "into the fabric of everyday life until they are indistinguishable from it."

Concluding Remarks

Martin Hand notes that "many people now live in a culture of 24/7 instant messaging, iPods and mp3's, streamed content, blogs, ubiquitous digital images, and Facebook" (2008, 1). In effect, we live in many ways somewhat like Weiner envisioned we would in what he called the "third wave of computing," although these effects are created by means of personal computers that have become intimately integrated with our lives. Photographical images are in the forefront when it comes to migrating into "the cloud," which allows them to be called up at any computer, as Weiser projected our "projects" would. The intimate connections between the operational logic of computing and the logic of photography seems in part to ground the present ubiquity of photography.

When it comes to the two encounters, digital alteration and distribution, and their specific bearings on the adjusted ontology of photography, I suggested briefly in the beginning of this chapter that photography has become more contingent and malleable. This shift has also allowed photography to enter into hybrid relations and to fuse with other image types, a situation Osborne may well be considering when he says that "the photographic is not best understood as a particular art; it is currently the dominant form of the image in general" (2010, 62).

In the wake of the second encounter, the migration to a digital platform, I have suggested that in the years to come we will see a photographic medium brought somewhat in the direction of the work ontology of the performative arts, where new realizations in tune with contemporary sensibilities may demonstrate the power of a composition. But until the art world can renew its notion of originality, which seems increasingly maladapted to current photographic developments, performative efforts may still be met with considerable resistance.

Notes

1. The most important of these recent interventions, providing new vitality to questions about what photography as well as film are, comes from film theorist D. N. Rodowick in his provocative intervention *The Virtual Life of Film* (2007); from the German art historian Boris Groys's book *Art Power* (2008); from digital-media theorist Lev Manovich (2006, 2007); as well as from the new journal *Philosophy of Photography*, to which especially the British philosopher Peter Osborne (2010) has contributed a productive piece.

2. Rodowick (2007) makes an intuitively suggestive but somewhat underdeveloped case for various losses related to the digitalization of film, one of them being duration. Many filmmakers seem to agree that digital postproduction, even digital screening, yields quite satisfactory results, whereas shooting digitally cannot achieve the magic touch that film stock at its best can yield.

3. Michael Rips (2006) also argues that there is an emergent performative tendency within art photography, though he phrases his argument in different terms.

4. Neither the Gagosian Gallery nor the Sean Kelly Gallery works with the Keïta photographs anymore. I am not sure whether this decision is due only to the problematic lawsuits his estate became mired in following his success or if it also reflects a more conservative approach toward

the making of new editions of older photographs, and therefore a backlash for the conception of photography as a more performative art.

5. There are also other problems relating to Groys's account. First, I believe Osborne is right in reminding us that although image files may be digital, the images themselves, presented to our eyes, are not (2010, 63). Second, Groys construes the "digital image," by which I assume he means digital-image file, as "a copy" and goes on to suggest that "the event of its visualization is an original event, because the digital copy is a copy that has no visible original" (2008, 84). I believe, however, that digital-image files have default display modes that complicate the notion that they have "no visible original." Moreover, when a visualization can be an original event, it is hardly because the visuals originate from a digital file, but rather because an artist or a curator deliberately has orchestrated the visualization as such an event.

6. Both Rodowick and Osborne introduce somewhat similar distinctions. Rodowick talks about the photographic image as "ever more available to the creative intentions of information processing made possible by the separation of inputs and outputs" (2007, 125). The distinction between medium of storage and medium of display is in Rodowick's vocabulary replaced by a distinction between "inputs" and "outputs," where he notes that digital photo production allows a greater "separation" between the two where "information processing" or alteration can take place. Osborne distinguishes between the "event of capture" and the "event of visualization" (2010, 60), which may seem much like the distinction Rodowick makes, though clearer in its focus on the actual processes in question. Rodowick argues that this separation compromises indexicality, but I believe that Osborne is basically right when he claims that the digitalization of "the act of photographic capture . . . *retains* both the causal and deictic aspects of photographic indexicality" (2010, 63, emphasis in original). However, our trust in such an indexicality may be undermined by the multitude of altered photographs (see Fetveit 1999).

7. The latter are most of the time photographically based, but they can also be modeled on graphics or drawing, as maps presented by the computer mostly are. However, the computer is, through its processing and calculation abilities and a flood of specialized software, perfectly able to break down and blur distinctions between various forms of imagery. This is well illustrated by Google Earth in its partial merger of map and photography as well as by films with superheroes that routinely involve smooth mergers of animation and live-action film on a medial level in order to blur the boundary between the possible and the impossible in its representation of reality.

References

Ansel Adams Gallery. 2009. "Ansel Anecdotes: Perspectives on Moonrise." Available at http://www.anseladams.com/Articles.asp?ID=145. Accessed 20 January 2012.

Benjamin, Walter. 1992. "The Work of Art in the Age of Mechanical Reproduction." In *Illuminations: Essays and Reflections*, translated by Harry Zohn, 217–251. London: Fontana.

Edwards, Elisabeth, and Janice Hart. 2004. "Introduction: Photographs as Objects." In *Photographs Objects Histories: On the Materiality of Images*, edited by Elisabeth Edwards and Janice Hart, 1–15. London: Routledge.

Fetveit, Arild. 2007. "Convergence by Means of Globalized Remediation." *Northern Lights* 5: 57–74. Available at http://www.scribd.com/doc/18797519/Northern-Lights-Film-and-Media-Studies-Yearbook-Volume-5-Issue-1. Accessed 20 January 2012.

Fetveit, Arild. 1999. "Reality TV in the Digital Era: A Paradox in Visual Culture?" *Media, Culture, and Society* 21: 787–804.

Galloway, Alexander. 2004. *Protocol: How Control Exists after Decentralization.* Cambridge, MA: MIT Press.

Groys, Boris. 2008. *Art Power.* Cambridge, MA: MIT Press.

Hand, Martin. 2008. *Making Digital Cultures: Access, Interactivity, and Authenticity.* Hampshire, UK: Ashgate.

Haraway, Donna. 1991. "A Cyborg Manifesto: Science, Technology, and Socialist-Feminism in the Late Twentieth Century." In *Simians, Cyborgs and Women: The Reinvention of Nature,* 149–181. New York: Routledge.

Kirkpatrick, Marshall. 2008. "Do You Trust Google to Resist Data Mining across Services?" *Read-WriteWeb* 20 (April). Available at http://www.readwriteweb.com/archives/do_you_trust_google_to_resist_data_mining_across_services.php. Accessed 20 January 2012.

Manovich, Lev. 2007. "Information as an Aesthetic Event." Lecture given at the Tate, London. Available at http://www.manovich.net/DOCS/TATE_lecture.doc. Accessed 20 January 2012.

Manovich, Lev. 2006. "Image Future." *Animation* 1 (1): 25–44.

McLuhan, Marshall. 1994. *Understanding Media: The Extensions of Man.* Cambridge, MA: MIT Press.

Osborne, Peter. 2010. "Infinite Exchange: The Social Ontology of the Photographic Image." *Philosophy of Photography* 1 (1): 59–68.

Peirce, Charles S. 1955. "Logic as Semiotic: The Theory of Signs." In *Philosophical Writings of Peirce,* edited by Justus Buchler, 98–115. New York: Dover.

Rips, Michael. 2006. "Who Owns Seydou Keïta?" *New York Times,* January 22. Available at http://www.nytimes.com/2006/01/22/arts/22rips.html. Accessed 20 January 2012.

Rodowick, D. N. 2007. *The Virtual Life of Film.* Cambridge, MA: Harvard University Press.

"Tate Intermedia Art: Under Scan." 2008. Tate Online. Available at http://www.tate.org.uk/intermediaart/underscan.htm. Accessed 20 January 2012.

Weiser, Mark. 1991. "The Computer for the 21st Century." *Scientific American* 265 (3): 94–104. Also available at http://www.ubiq.com/hypertext/weiser/SciAmDraft3.html. Accessed 20 January 2012.

3 The Family Photo Album as Transformed Social Space in the Age of "Web 2.0"

Mette Sandbye

Figure 3.1
From private album with analogue single photographs, Denmark, 1940s.

1974. I produce my first family photo album (figure 3.2). The album cover is made of a soft, orange plastic material, and all the photographs in it are in color. They are taken by a child, but apart from that the album looks very much like any other family photo album since the beginning of the genre with the Kodak revolution in the late nineteenth century or at least since the more general and public spread of the practice in the 1930s. The album includes photographs of memorable events, rituals, birthdays, holidays, and so on. It chronicles the life of a postindustrial, nuclear, middle-class family, binding its members to each other, offering a sense of roots and history, and in the end adding to an existential awareness of "living in time."

1989. It is the 150th anniversary of the birth of photography, and at the same time it is the beginning of the "digital age." When photography was officially invented in 1839, the painter Paul Delaroche—according to a widespread public

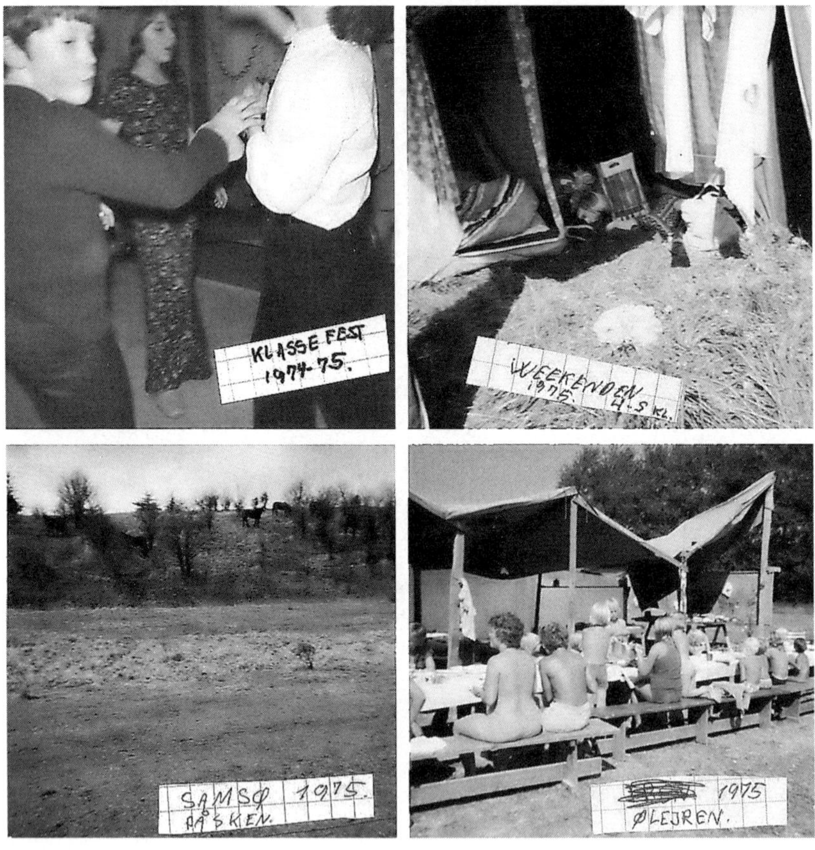

Figure 3.2
From the author's own first photo album, 1974–1975.

myth—exclaimed, "From today painting is dead!" Many commentators on the 150th anniversary stressed, "From today photography is dead!" meaning that the transition from traditional silver-based analog technology to the more immaterial digital technology had forever transformed the medium. But, curiously, the practice and tradition of the family album continued almost unchanged. Yes, you could erase the unpopular Uncle Henry from the Christmas photograph, but you didn't. He *was* there, and he was placed in the album with all the other photographs of rituals, celebrations, vacations, and so on, existentially embalming the family's life and history forever.

2009. I spend three weeks on vacation in India with my husband and three children. All family members carry cameras, both traditional digital cameras and those included in mobile phones. We regularly upload photos to our family Web site at the local Internet café so that our family back home in Denmark can follow our experiences. We provide text as well, and our family members at home subsequently add little comments. Although the album has a Web address that is not too obvious, but difficult to trace, it occasionally happens that perfect strangers also engage with the photos, mostly with technical comments such as, "Great light, how did you manage to get all these details in the photograph?" or "I also went to Aswem Beach, super chill-out place!" My daughters put their photographs on their MySpace and Facebook sites so that their friends in Denmark as well as in Chicago (where we lived the previous year and where they went to school) can see them dressed in Indian sarongs on a beach in Goa.

This is just a brief—personal and idiosyncratic—collagelike sketch of the most recent historical development of the family photo album. Family photography is one of the most widespread practices since the invention of photography, but between 1974 and 2009 something radically changed: we entered the age of ubiquitous computing. I would thus argue that this shift did not, as many critics convincingly suggested, happen in 1989 with the advent of the digital technology. It happened only a few years ago with the so-called Web 2.0, the extended computer literacy among ordinary people, especially children and teenagers, as well as the spread of broadband Internet connections and the whole convergence culture that it implicates. The major differences between my own 1974 physical album and my daughters' 2009 Internet albums are of course the immaterial digital nature and, most important, the immensely increased speed between the act of taking the image and the act of making it visually accessible for friends and family. But as I am writing these words, I admit that to a certain extent they are already outdated because the rapidity with which new media, media platforms, and other technological improvements are introduced on the global commercial market has increased drastically. In 2001, the first mobile phone camera was put on the market, but the technology did not take on until 2004, the same year that Flickr was invented. Today, Facebook contains more than one billion photographs, with 700 million added every month. Photography is converging not only with the Internet, but also with mobile phones. In 2004, 246 million camera phones were sold worldwide—nearly four times the sales of digital cameras. And mobile phone commercials increasingly highlight the camera. Whereas "analog photography" was directed at a *future* audience, pictures taken by camera phones can be seen immediately by people at a distance using mobiles with Multimedia Messaging Service (MMS). In the United Kingdom, where around one in two mobiles are camera phones, "448,962,359 MMS picture messages were sent in 2007, the equivalent of 19 million traditional (24 exposure) rolls of camera film."[1] The affordances of digital photography potentially make photographic images both instantaneous and mobile. Everyday amateur photography will increasingly be regarded as a performative practice connected to "presence" instead of as the storing of memories for eternity, which is how it has hitherto been conceptualized. All this indicates that digital photography is a complex technological network in the *making* rather than a single fixed technology. We need to rethink photography, and now is the moment to do it. The newness of digital photography relates not only to the digitalization of images, but to media convergence, ubiquitous and pervasive computing, and new performances of sociality, memory, history, and identity.

We must now take into consideration both the digital spread of photographs via various Internet sites and the way we take, meet, and handle these images in a much more mobile and dynamic way. For instance, the general proliferation of the iPhone has changed the very situation where we perceive our own and other people's family photographs. Surrounded by bundles of wireless networks, we can now access our photographs much more dynamically at the beach, on our way to school or office, in the night life only few seconds after they were taken, and so on. Ubiquitous computing and the photographic practices related to it indicate that technologies cannot be separated from embodied practices, from *doings*. This changed way of perceiving images and other sorts of digital information of course has already changed and will continue to change the way we take photographs. Nevertheless, regarding the family album we have not yet really reached "the third epoch of computing" or the real ubiquitous and pervasive "Web 3.0" that editor Ulrik Ekman addresses in his introduction to this book. But the fact that the philosophical implications of ubiquitous computing that are investigated in various contexts throughout this book are already appearing and are being conceptualized can open up reflection on the need to formulate a whole new media ecology for the understanding of photography. To develop such a new media ecology, photography must be understood as *at the same time* a social practice, a networked technology, a material object, and an image.

Web 2.0 Albums—and Before

Most writing and analysis within the history of photography are done on art and documentary photography. Much less has been written on family photography, despite the fact that it is the most widespread genre. By tradition, the practice of making family photographs has been theoretically explained in two rather oppositional ways: either as a ritual, conventional, unimaginative practice where people pose themselves to "show off" as nice, well-off, bourgeois, and "ordinary" families (Bourdieu 1965, 1990) or as a more emotional, phenomenological practice linking the viewer to "what was" (Barthes 1980, 1981). Related to the last interpretation is André Bazin's famous phenomenological article from 1945, "The Ontology of the Photographic Image" ([1945] 1980), in which he connects the proliferation of the photo album with its ability to satisfy our "mummy complex"—that is, the desire to embalm time.

Opposed to these two versions (the sociological and the phenomenological–ontological), contemporary digital practices as they are performed via photo blogs, mobile phone photography, Facebook, and MySpace have been described as "MeMedia" (Petersen 2008); that is, this narcissistic and performative practice is related to—mostly young people's—play with identity, gender roles, poses from Hollywood culture, and so on. However—and this point is a main argument of this text—maybe the photo album adheres to all of these definitions at the same time, and maybe it is only with the advent of Web 2.0 that we can fully realize the content, depth, and the potential of family photography, including what was taken before Web 2.0. One can argue that ubiquitous and pervasive computing has increased the use of photography as an integrated part of daily life and has turned the practice of doing photography into a much more embodied and even haptic social practice.

I realize that we are just starting to see how the digital production, perception, and use of photography will develop in new and really ubiquitous ways that we cannot dream of even today and that this development in the near future will have important implications for our very understanding of the thing or phenomenon we call "photography." But as classifications such as Jay David Bolter's "remediation" have demonstrated, the conceptualization of a new medium is often based on previous ones. Thus, the digital photo album is to a large extent still constructed and perceived like the traditional analog precursor. Simultaneously, as new media inventions or practices remediate older forms, they can also shed light back in time to older practices. My argument in this chapter is that the new use of photography we experience with Web 2.0 and with ubiquitous computing can actually highlight aspects of the medium that was always already there: the conception of photography as a primarily social, participatory, performative, and cultural phenomenon. The family photo album is about social exchange and sharing, and it is an act of love and belonging. More philosophically put, it might change our concepts of what authenticity and identity mean in relation to photography.[2]

To fully grasp this argument, it is important to address the *use* and *reception* of photography to a much larger extent than has been done previously. It is significant that *The Photography Reader* opens with the following sentence: "What is a photograph?" (Wells 2003, 1). Instead of asking what *is* photography, the key question of photographic theory since the invention of the medium, ubiquitous computing within daily life compels us to ask what we *do with* photography.[3] People do things with images, and because of ubiquitous computing we have witnessed an enormous growth in the social and publicly accessible exchange of images. In the age of analog photography—that is, before the 1990s—private snapshots were preserved in silent albums, to be looked at only from time to time. Today people take photographs all the time; they often show their album publicly to a global, large audience; and they edit the album on a daily basis at Web sites such as Flickr, MySpace, 23hq, Fotolog, Facebook, and the one I concentrate on here, Picasa. What are the social implications of this augmented communication and presentation of private snapshots? What are people actually photographing and putting in their public, digital albums? Can we still talk about an affective preservation of memories and of "what was there"?

I argue that the album is at the same time both about people performing a representation of "now" and "presence" *and* about embalming time—"rescuing it simply from its proper corruption," as Bazin put it ([1945] 1980, 242). The photo blog is a technological extension of the family photo album, but it also differs radically from it. The digital photo album is privileging the self-expression of the amateur as well as the immediate and—through ubiquitous computing—almost embodied sharing of information by amateurs with other amateurs. It transmits a sense of disposability and immediacy that we have never experienced previously in the history of photography. And as I have already suggested, these aspects—together with the change from a private to a much more public practice—will affect the use of photography even more in the near future. But instead of declaring "from today photography is dead!" I prefer to focus more narrowly on the digital family photo album as an actual move toward "real ubiquity" that at the same time points back in time and hints at changes in the future.

The Analytical "Take"

The study of contemporary uses of family photography—from material albums to photo blogs—poses a challenge to aesthetic theory and analytical practice. In photography history and theory, there has been much focus on emphasizing photography as an art form and as a language of semiotic signs. But what about all the vernacular forms of photography that do not necessarily fit into aesthetic theory and history? Fields such as visual studies and visual anthropology have recently offered new ways to challenge the theory and the historiography of photography. But the material discussed in these cases either is historic (with the distance to the material that this historical take gives, as with *carte-de-visite* albums, for example) or comes from other, non-Western cultures (as in most of the material discussed within visual anthropology). Not much has been written about the digital photo album yet and certainly not about photography as a social practice enhanced by ubiquitous computing.

Family photography is so important for most of us, so emotionally loaded, so widespread, but at the same time it is generally regarded as a conventional, unimportant, rigid, ritualistic, and deeply conservative genre, almost not worth spending a moment of one's academic time studying. Instead of asking whether photographs are real, however, as has been a crucial point of discussion since the invention of the medium, we need to ask how they create and communicate our understanding of the real.

Although there have been academic studies of family photography, various histories of photography as well as academic and curatorial institutions have had problems deciding what to do with this kind of private, vernacular imagery. One of the more recent general overviews of the state of photographic theory is James Elkins's collected volume *Photography Theory* (2007). In this book, the main theoretical foci are (still) the questions of indexicality, time, referentiality, and so on—that is, in general, the question of what *is* photography. During the roundtable discussion included in the book, Diarmuid Costello laconically states: "Whenever we begin to talk about photography outside the art historical frame of reference, it's as if the conversation just dies. We don't know what to say, or how to proceed. We talk about aerial photography, PET scanning, all the uses that photography has, but when such examples come up, beyond acknowledging their existence, no one really seems to know what to do with them. There's no take on it" (Baetens, Costello, Elkins, et al. 2007, 199).

Mary Warner Marien's *Photography: A Cultural History* (2002) was written as a correction to the traditional aesthetic, modernist history—for instance, represented by Beaumont Newhall's *History of Photography* ([1949] 1982). Toward the end of her 530-page book, she includes a 15-page chapter with the title "Family Pictures." She almost exclusively writes off the genre with this single statement:

> In addition, throughout the twentieth century, families accumulated extensive collections of images, the majority taken with simple camera and increasingly reliable film. The content of family photographs was dominated by celebratory occasions, such as weddings, birthdays, and vacations. Few families resolutely set out to record the look of everyday life, such as messy kitchens and unmade beds. Fewer still made visual records of emotionally trying times, or used the camera for psychological self-study or therapy. (2002, 445)

Although the book is called "a cultural history," Marien simply does not know what to write about all these "extensive collections of images," so for the rest of the chapter she moves on to talk about artists inspired by the genre.

With the advent of digital photography and later Web 2.0, analog photography and the photo album have been regarded with a sense of a dying technology. There have recently been a number of museum shows and books that most often present a more or less randomly collected and uncontextualized sample of just nice old amateur shots—with a nostalgic feeling.[4] One book example is Thomas Walther's *Other Pictures: Anonymous Photographs from the Thomas Walther Collection* (2000), made in conjunction with a 2000 exhibition of snapshots from the 1910s to the 1960s at the Metropolitan Museum of Art in New York. The presentation of vernacular images, mostly family photographs, is meant to represent a specifically innocent, maybe even true material and at the same time a material with inherent surreal or poetic qualities. Thomas Walther writes in his afterword: "They [the photos] document a profound innocence, tremendous pride and a unique sense of humor in American society. There is no faking, no strain, no theory here, only the simplicity and directness of capturing moments of life" (2000, n.p.)

Family photography is of course related to the index, to the referent, to time—the main themes of Elkins's book, but neither his book nor all these museum catalogs offer adequate resources to encircle the experience of the photo album and certainly not of the Internet album.

Flickr and the Ephemeral Everyday

There are at least two distinct digital photo-sharing practices these days: the traditional family album and sites where social-networking software is combined with new uses of photography and text. Flickr, Fotolog, MySpace, Facebook, and Google's Picasa Web Album are some of the most popular free photo-sharing sites on the Web. Facebook and MySpace are centered more on text, and the uploaded photographs play a minor role. But the photographs nevertheless play an important role in the identity construction produced on the individual profiles. Flickr, however, is primarily photo based, although text plays a major role. It is also extremely collaborative, compared to more "traditional" Web site albums, such as Picasa.

Susan Murray has described sites such as Flickr this way:

> On these sites, photography has become less about the special or rarefied moments of domestic/family living (for such things as holidays, gatherings, baby photos) and more about an immediate, rather fleeting display of one's discovery of the small and mundane (such as bottles, cupcakes, trees, debris, and architectural elements). In this way, photography is no longer just the embalmer of time that André Bazin (1967, 14) once spoken of, but rather a more alive, immediate, and often transitory, practice/form. (2008, 151)

According to Søren Mørk Petersen, Flickr is really about articulating an aesthetic of the everyday and the ephemeral. Like Murray, he stresses the presence character of the images and the photo sharing at Flickr. His fieldwork demonstrates how people take photographs with their mobile phones and upload them directly in order to get a quick and "fresh" comment by other "Flickrs" and that this element—closely related to pervasive computing within everyday life—is Flickr's primary function. It thereby contradicts Barthes's and Bazin's phenomenological connection of photography to death: "When it registers the banal and mundane aspects of everyday life and not least when it is shared, it becomes a practice closer to life than death," says Petersen. "The practice of mob logging, everyday photography and photo sharing express a desire to retain the experience and sensation of presence and the affective character of everydayness. Uploading becomes a practice that can negotiate the different sensations of presence and the present" (2008, 146, 154).

Picasa as the New Album Site

However, the Web 2.0 practice that comes closest to the traditional photo album is the activity on sites such as Picasa.[5] Picasa was launched in June 2006 by Google, which offers each user an easily accessible design and one gigabyte of server space for free. The site is flooded with family photo albums, so let us just consider a typical sample. Picasa offers the possibility to add a little text beneath each picture, which is not very different from a physical album. People usually add no text or very short, descriptive or anchoring texts such as "Vacation, Lake Michigan, Anna and Jamie, summer 2008." The most distinct difference between a Picasa album and a material one is the amount of images that most people upload and the (hyper)structuring of them, which is at the same time vertical and horizontal: when opening the individual Picasa album, you see a horizontal line of images, but each image represents a depth or a vertical structure with its own headline ("Vacation Images," "Images from Paul's Barbecue," "Bruce and Penny's Wedding," etc.), linking each image to a folder of images under the same thematic headline.

Let's look at Helen's album (figure 3.3). She has three image folders under the following headlines: "Wilson Merge Hotdog Party 2008," "Family cookout and boating trip," "Vacation photos 2008." Apart from the hotdog party, which is documented in 36 photos, each of the other folders contains more than 200 photos. Helen's family apparently consists of a couple with two smaller boys. Other family members, probably grandparents, are also present in some of the images. The 209 photos in "Family cookout and boating trip" seem to stem from one or maybe two different occasions (swimming pool cookout and a boating trip).

Half of the images are taken at the swimming pool, mostly the boys playing in the pool. It gives the presentation a filmic character, where each photo differs very little from the previous and each photograph is shot with a very small interval. Then follows a sequence of 27 photos, where an older man—probably grandfather—lights some kind of firework standing on the ground. The lighting, the development of light and smoke, and finally the firework going out are documented and presented as film frames. The rest of the images are—also almost identical—images of the two boys dressed in life jackets on the boating trip. The "Hotdog Party" folder differs a little from the rest because the 36 photos are taken in some kind of office, probably where

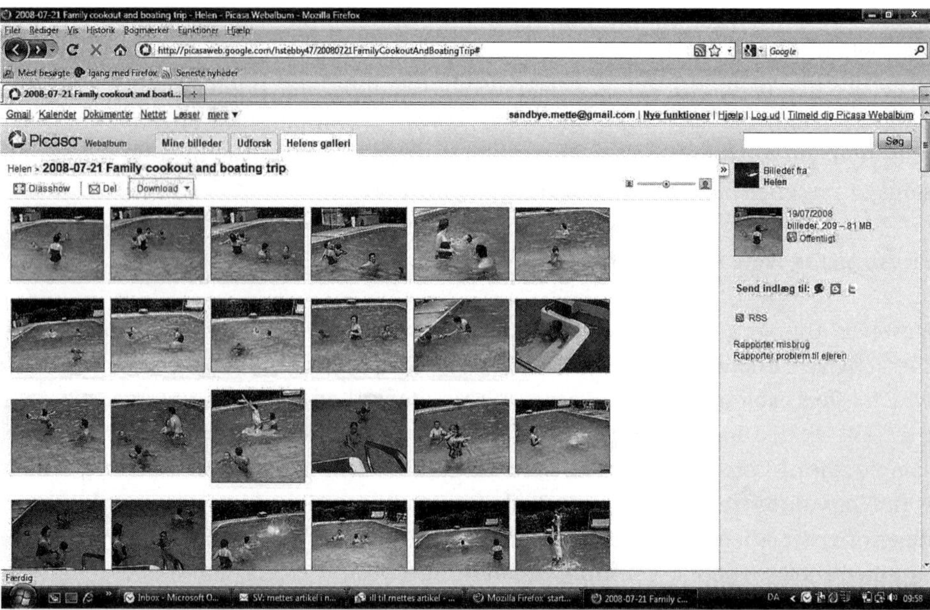

Figure 3.3
From Helen's digital family photo album at Picasa (from https://picasaweb.google.com/hstebby47/20080721FamilyCookoutAndBoatingTrip, last visited January 2012).

Helen works and where the employees are having a party. Most of the photos are unposed snapshots of people (mostly photographed from the back) approaching a table with food or of people eating. Over a sequence of 9 photos, fused with an understated humor, a man is icing a pink cake. In the final image, two women are admiring the result by clapping their hands together in front of the slightly blushing clerk.

The situations that these images document are very similar to what one normally sees in a family album—party, picnic, vacation—but the almost absurd amount of similar images and their filmic representation add a feeling of newness, presence, and immediacy to the album that we do not find in the material album, and these images—many badly composed and showing merely "nothing"—carry some of the same qualities that Murray and Petersen find in the Flickr images: the everydayness, the mundane, the presence. The images seem to function as an immediate framing of the fleeting moments in everyday life. The amount of very similar and not very well-composed images actually increases the photographs' personal affect. These images link each family member affectively to a larger context of family members, thus creating a feeling of "belonging." Each situation's referentiality is rather augmented by the repetition of the almost identical images of the family members or mundane situations. The photographs' "we were there" character is thus emphasized all the more.

It is not so important where "we" actually "were," but this endlessly repeated presence of each family member in front of the eyes of the beholder—probably another family member—almost leaves the photograph as mere phenomenological affect and thus points to the philosophical integration of computing within everyday life.

The album was made publicly accessible (an option at Picasa), so who is meant to see those images? Primarily Helen's family members and her working colleagues, people with whom she wants to connect and to share emotions and affect, maybe even love, by reinstalling a kind of documentary, filmic presence of these situations.

The combination of the phenomenological existential "I was there" and "it happened" associated with photography as well as the sense of filmic presence and "it *is* happening" that characterizes most of the Picasa albums can also be exemplified by thirty-two-year-old Dennis's album (figure 3.4). One of his thirteen image folders is called "Parachute" and contains a filmic documentation composed of more than 113 images of Dennis's apparently first parachute jump.

In that sense, these Internet albums represent an alternative to the modernist, formalistic ways of presenting the individual amateur snapshots as "poetic miracles," as many museums have done—for example, the exhibition from the Thomas Walther collection mentioned earlier. If one were to present Dennis's parachute folder in such

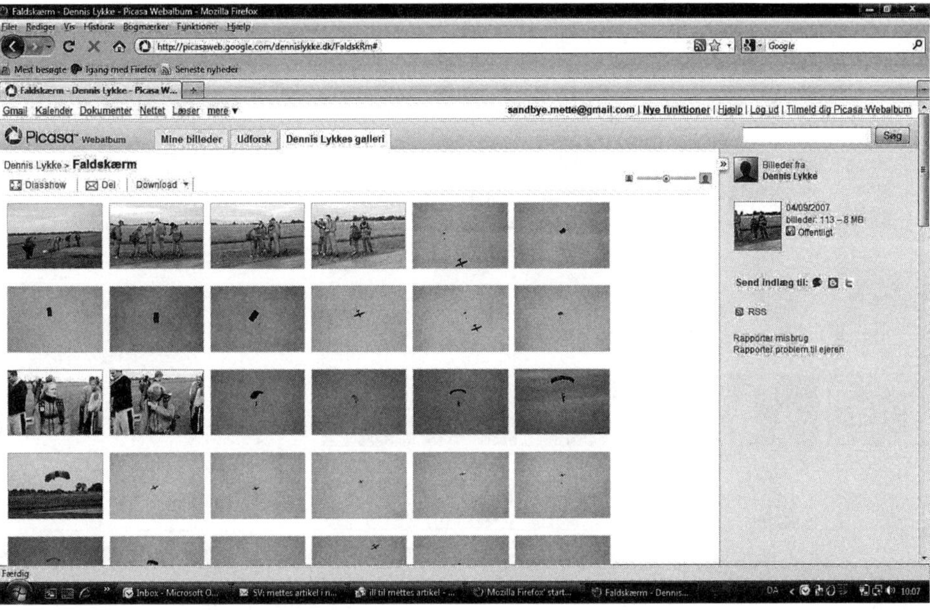

Figure 3.4

From Dennis's digital family photo album at Picasa (from http://picasaweb.google.com/dennislykke.dk/FaldskRm#, last visited June 2009).

a context, it would make no sense to emphasize only one image with a specific "poetic" composition. This folder is about something else; it is about composing his own extensive, still-image presentation, about documenting this special event in his life, and about making it publicly accessible immediately after it took place.

The Philippine woman "beautyconscious11," apparently living in Switzerland, presents portraits of her two teenage daughters and a son with various collage techniques, sandwiching their portraits with magazine covers, so as to make her children appear as if they are on the cover of *Fashion*, *Teengirl*, and *Family&Friends* or in a Valentine's card (figure 3.5).

Her children might find these collages slightly embarrassing, and the collages are certainly not realistic, but they can be considered an act of affection and connection between a mother and her three almost grown-up children. The Picasa sites do not include a written family history, but if we can judge from the pictures, it seems that this family is divided between Switzerland and the Philippines, which makes this "act of connecting" even more important for its maker, based in Switzerland. Many of the photo collages carry imprints such as a photo of the mother and one of the daughters: "My love will find you . . . even when you lose yourself in the oddest place." Both

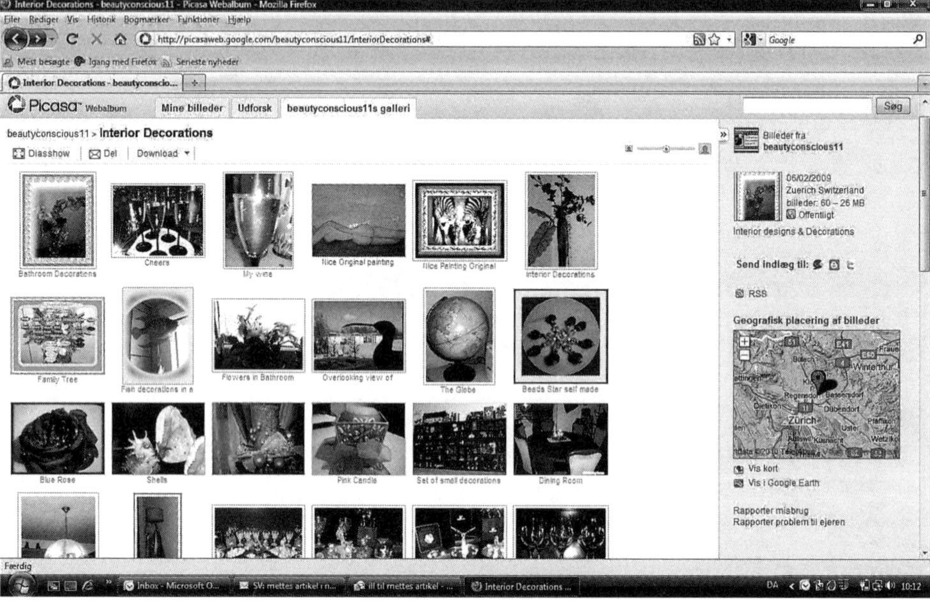

Figure 3.5

Picasa user beauyconscious11 presents her interior decorations (from http://picasaweb.google.com/beautyconscious11/InteriorDecorations#, last visited January 2012).

the imitation of poses seen, for instance, in fashion magazines or on romantic posters and these proverbial phrases imitate mass culture, but the whole is done in a playful, performative, and rather touching tongue-in-cheek way.

The word *amateur* originates from the Greek word *amas*, meaning "love." These amateur photo collages are made as such "acts of love" from the mother to her children. Another of beautyconscious11's folders is called "Interior decorations" and presents stills of home decorations of flowers, candle lights, shells, food arrangements, and Christmas decorations. On Picasa and other Web albums sites, the viewer will find many similar examples of people—mostly women—presenting their hobby or special skills in knitting, poetry writing, gardening, and so on. Such presentation is actually a Web 2.0 practice that is directly connected to album practices from the early years of photography. In *Women's Albums and Photography in Victorian England: Ladies, Mothers, and Flirts* (2007), Patrizia di Bello shows the extent of the photo album's immersion in nineteenth-century culture and illustrates some of the ways it was used to construct different models of femininity.[6] This kind of creative scrapbook character on which the whole idea of the photo album is based has been overlooked by the history of photography and is certainly excluded in museum displays and books, where the individual image is most often isolated from the album context. Hence, the "beautyconscious11" album is another example of a Web 2.0 practice that might make us realize important aspects of older kinds of photography.

Photography's Own History

As mentioned in the beginning of this chapter, there has recently been a tremendous interest in collecting, selling, exhibiting, and publishing vernacular snapshots. A critique of the presentation of this kind of material has also appeared within a modernistic, formalistic, poetic framing that does not present the material in its own right but rather misinterprets it.[7]

The examples of Picasa albums given here represent the most common uses of the digital Internet album. Such albums at Picasa (and elsewhere on the Internet) are in themselves a presentation of vernacular photography that offers a huge amount of material to be studied by academics involved with visual studies, visual anthropology, and cultural studies. I argue that by studying this kind of material, we might encounter aspects of photography that are much more social—aspects that we can bring into play when studying and presenting older albums.

On several occasions, the photography scholar Geoffrey Batchen has asked: "How can photography be restored to its own history?" (2001, 57). By admitting these rather chaotic Picasa family photo albums into the history of photography and by studying the way vernacular photography is used at Flickr and other such photo sites, we might develop a more thorough understanding of photography as simultaneously an aesthetic medium, a historical document, and an emotional, existential, dynamic social practice. In these briefly analyzed album samples, photography is used and represented as presence maker, family genealogy, identity construction, self-therapy, mourning work, social act of "reaching out," and a great deal more. Faced with these simultaneous and very varied practices, we are forced to reevaluate the theoretical classification of the album done in the 1960s and 1970s by scholars such as Bourdieu and Barthes as well as the museum practice mentioned earlier. These digital-album practices might appear radically new and changed, but this newness is most often on a mere technical level. Rather, the Web 2.0 uses of vernacular images point back in time and should make us realize compelling aspects of this kind of material already present but not fully grasped by scholars, historians, and museum institutions.

In the near future, more and more private snapshots will be made public and become a more and more common part of pervasive and ubiquitous computing. The new digital media is a constitutive part of our daily life, and it is a commonly felt experience in a mediatized society. From TV's reality shows to the train station's surveillance cameras, ubiquitous-camera recordings of everyday life have become a common determining factor in the construction of the modern self. Digital ubiquitous technology has also radically changed the use of family snapshot photography and the social role of the photo album, and that use will change even more when we enter "Web 3.0." The Picasa and Flickr albums can be regarded as a personal, creative, and performative counterweight to the objectifying and stereotyping of identity that individuals experience in public life and therefore an augmented part of reality that is worth a closer study.

Notes

1. From http://www.text.it/mediacentre/press_release_list.cfm?thePublicationID=2C4FB155-15C5-F4C0-99FCB4EAAED7A798.

2. For instance, Christopher Pinney's (1997) studies of Indian studio photography, where a heavy amount of staging and image manipulation such as hand coloring is perceived as authentification tools, have implications for our traditional Western conceptual connection between concepts such as authenticity, truth, indexicality, and nonmanipulation.

3. Larissa Hjorth's contribution to this anthology (chapter 10) points in the same direction. Her chapter addresses the social aspects of new media that she discusses as "participatory media." By focusing on the "the growth of the subversive user," particularly in Asian metropoles, she underlines that ubiquity is far from homogeneous in its global dissemination.

4. To name just a few: Snapshots: The Photography of Everyday Life (San Francisco Museum of Modern Art, 1998); Other Pictures (Metropolitan Museum of Art, 2000); Close to Home: An American Album (J. Paul Getty Museum, Los Angeles, 2004); Snapshots: From the Box Brownie to the Camera Phone (Museum of Photographic Arts, San Diego, 2005); and The Art of the

American Snapshot (National Gallery of Art, Washington, DC, 2007). See also Frizot and Veigy 2006; and Skrein 2004.

5. See http://picasa.google.com.

6. Not unlike Larissa Hjorth's argument about the "subversive" possibilities of new media and the new kinds of digital user-created content literature among Asian women in this anthology.

7. See for instance, Batchen 2008, a review of the photography exhibition Impressed by Light: British Photographs from Paper Negatives, 1840–1860, at the Metropolitan Museum of Art, and Zuromskis 2008.

References

Baetens, Jan, Diarmuid Costello, James Elkins, Jonathan Friday, Margaret Iverson, Sabine Kriebel, Margaret Olin, Graham Smith, and Joel Snyder. 2007. "The Art Seminar." In *Photography Theory*, edited by James Elkins, 129–204. London: Routledge.

Barthes, Roland. 1981. *Camera Lucida: Reflections on Photography*. Translated by Richard Howard. New York: Hill and Wang.

Barthes, Roland. 1980. *La chambre claire: Note sur la photographie*. Paris: Gallimard.

Batchen, Geoffrey. 2001. "Vernacular Photographies." In *Each Wild Idea: Writing, Photography, History*, 56–81. Cambridge, MA: MIT Press.

Bazin, André. [1945] 1980. "The Ontology of the Photographic Image." Translated by Hugh Gray. In *Classic Essays on Photography*, edited by Alan Trachtenberg, 237–244. New Haven, CT: Leete's Island Books.

Bourdieu, Pierre, with Luc Boltanski, Robert Castel, Jean-Claude Chamboredon, and Dominique Schnapper. 1990. *Photography: A Middle-Brow Art*. Translated by Shaun Whiteside. Stanford, CA: Stanford University Press.

———. 1965. *Un art moyen: Essai sur les usages sociaux de la photographie*. Paris: Minuit.

Di Bello, Patrizia. 2007. *Women's Albums and Photography in Victorian England: Ladies, Mothers, and Flirts*. Farnham, UK: Ashgate.

Elkins, James, ed. 2007. *Photography Theory*. London: Routledge.

Frizot, Michel, and Cédric de Veigy. 2006. *Photos trouvées*. London: Phaidon.

Marien, Mary Warner. 2002. *Photography: A Cultural History*. New York: Harry N. Abrams.

Murray, Susan. 2008. "Digital Images, Photo-Sharing, and Our Shifting Notions of Everyday Aesthetics." *Journal of Visual Culture* 7:147–163.

Newhall, Beaumont. [1949] 1982. *History of Photography: From 1839 to the Present*. 5th ed. New York: Bulfinch Press.

Petersen, Søren Mørk. 2008. "Common Banality: The Affective Character of Photo Sharing, Everyday Life and Produsage Cultures." Ph.D. diss., IT University, Copenhagen.

Pinney, Christopher. 1997. *Camera Indica: The Social Life of Indian Photography*. London: Reaktion Books.

Skrein, Christian. 2004. *Snapshots: The Eye of the Century*. Ostfildern-Ruit, Germany: Hatje Cantz.

Walther, Thomas. 2000. *Other Pictures: Anonymous Photographs from the Thomas Walther Collection*. New York: Twin Palm.

Wells, Liz. 2003. "General Introduction." In *The Photography Reader*, edited by Liz Wells, 1–9. London: Routledge.

4 Calm Imaging: The Conquest of Overload and the Conditions of Attention

Kristin Veel

Just as water, gas and electricity are brought into our houses from afar to satisfy our needs in response to a minimal effort, so we shall be supplied with visual or auditory images, which will appear and disappear at a simple movement of the hand, hardly more than a sign. Just as we are accustomed, if not enslaved, to the various forms of energy that pour into our homes, we shall find it perfectly natural to receive the ultrarapid variations or oscillations that our sense organs gather in and integrate to form all we know. I do not know whether a philosopher has ever dreamed of a company engaged in the home delivery of Sensory Reality.

—Paul Valéry, "The Conquest of Ubiquity"

In "The Conquest of Ubiquity," Paul Valéry envisions the reception of art for the future. He captures the Janus-faced quality of technologies developed to make human life more comfortable by likening the imagined future of home-delivered sensory stimuli to energy that satisfies "our needs in response to a minimal effort" and to which we become "accustomed, if not enslaved" ([1928/1934] 1964, 226). This subtle oscillation between service and control is the pivotal point of this chapter—not in regards to the science-fiction scenario Valéry presented in 1928, but as way of approaching the very real implications of ubiquitous computing[1] for imaging in the twenty-first century.

In his seminal writings on ubiquitous computing from the 1990s, Mark Weiser (1991, 1993, 1994) presents the idea of technologies that become so integrated in the daily meshwork of our lives that they no longer draw attention to themselves as technologies: "The most profound technologies are those that disappear. They weave themselves into the fabric of everyday life until they are indistinguishable from it" (1991). It is this conception of invisible technology that he develops into the notion of *calm technology* (Weiser and Brown 1996). Several contributors to this volume allude to this concept, and the ability of technology to operate unnoticed seems indeed to be at the heart of envisaging the implications of ubiquitous computing. Technological "calmness" seems a necessity when imagining an everyday world in which technology pervades our bodies and environments and is embedded in even the most ordinary experiences—from the motion-detecting lights that switch on when you enter the public toilets to the cat flap that reads the chip in your pet's neck and keeps unwanted cats out of your house. If such a world is to function smoothly, it seems that technology *has to* become invisible; it *has to* function without drawing attention to itself; otherwise, the cognitive load would simply be overpowering. And yet the main argument of this chapter is that the nature of the link between ubiquitous computing and calmness as well as the ethical implications of this link (captured in the sliding of Valéry's sentence from calmness to control) are issues worth considering with great carefulness. As Mike Featherstone highlights in a 2009 issue of *Theory, Culture, & Society* on ubiquitous media, we are not only dealing with benign and friendly wireless environments; ubiquitous media also offers greater possibilities for surveillance and recording (2009, 4). In this chapter, I explore the link between ubiquitous computing and calmness—its aim, area of operation, and wider implications—focusing in particular on the images that are not addressing our conscious, focused attention, but that operate smoothly in the background as what may be termed *calm imaging*. Examples can be found in the digital identity systems used by the police, intelligence services, public institutions, workplaces, and marketing industry, but, as we shall see, the implications of such systems are perhaps most eloquently articulated, explored, and challenged in artworks such as *Sorting Daemon* (2003) by David Rokeby and *The Heart Library Project* (2009) by George Khut.

Home Delivery of Sensory Overload

One of the most widespread arguments for the necessity of technology that does not draw attention to itself is to counter information overload. The term *information overload* has its roots in the context of computer-mediated communications and has since the 1970s prospered in particular in information sciences, business sciences, and marketing (Edmunds and Morris 2000). Today the term has become so common used that it has lost almost any conceptual rigor. However, because the relation between information overload and ubiquitous computing is such an intricate part of the argument for envisioning ubiquitous computing as calm, it is worth exploring a little more closely. The correlation features heavily in Weiser's texts: "Most important, ubiquitous computers will help overcome the problem of information overload. There is more information available at our fingertips during a walk in the woods than in any computer system, yet people find a walk among trees relaxing and computers frustrating. Machines that fit the human environment, instead of forcing humans to enter theirs, will make using a computer as refreshing as taking a walk in the woods" (1991).

Weiser's solution to the overload situation that computers can create is to make them blend into our environment in a way that allows the processing to function in what he terms "the periphery" of our attention (Weiser and Brown 1996). He thus suggests that the conditions of overload created by information and communication technology does not have to be different from other situations of potential cognitive overload, which we can handle easily. We are thus reminded that although at present the term *overload* is intimately linked with the experience of a contemporary society pervaded by information and communication technology, the discourse of overload has a history that stretches well beyond the current situation. Pointing to the conditions of overload in the period 1550–1750,[2] historian Daniel Rosenberg deals with the difficulty of outlining a history of information overload, arguing that we need to ask "how and why a phenomenon so patently old can periodically and convincingly be re-experienced as a fundamental symptom of the new" (2003, 9). This observation is interesting because it articulates more concisely the relativity of the concept of overload, which, Weiser seems to imply, has as much to do with the unfamiliarity of the sensory and cognitive inputs that need to be processed as it has to do with their volume and intensity. The accounts of the modern metropolis from the late nineteenth century on bear remarkable resemblances to accounts of late-twentieth-century encounters with technologically wired environments in which our current conception of overload was born. At the turn of the twentieth century, Georg Simmel famously described the sensory overload of the modern metropolis thus:

> The psychological basis of the metropolitan type of individuality consists in the *intensification of nervous stimulation* that results from the swift and uninterrupted change of outer and inner stimuli. Man is a differentiating creature. His mind is stimulated by the difference between a momentary impression and the one which preceded it. Lasting impressions, impressions which differ only slightly from one another, impressions which take a regular and habitual course and show regular and habitual contrasts—all these use up, so to speak, less consciousness than does the rapid crowding of changing images, the sharp discontinuity in the grasp of a single glance, and the unexpectedness of onrushing impressions. These are the psychological conditions which the metropolis creates. ([1903] 2005, 25)

Simmel emphasized precisely the contrast between the experience of "habitual" impressions and the experience of "unexpected" impressions, arguing that the latter demands the most resources for our consciousness. This contrast underpins not only Rosenberg's point on the experience of information overload as closely related to how accustomed we are to incoming stimuli, but also the point Weiser makes about the wood as a well-known and relaxing environment and the computer as frustrating. According to this comparison, ubiquitous calm computing, which is designed to blend into our environment and not draw attention to itself, simply smoothens the frustrating period of adaptation when we learn to interpret a new set of impulses. The hope is that when the possibility of potential overload is dealt with before it reaches our attention, humans will not have to adapt to the technology in the way Simmel observed that the urban dweller in the early part of the twentieth century had to develop "an organ protecting him against the threatening currents and discrepancies of his external environment which would uproot him" ([1903] 2005, 25). It seems logical that the more calm and invisible the technology is designed to be, the less noticeable the effects on human engagement with the world are likely to be. However, this comparison does not mean that there are no such effects; rather, it calls for a closer scrutiny of the nature of the apparently seamless link between human beings and technology that deals with overload situations *before* they reach our awareness.

Let us take the example of facial-recognition software, which is used in security systems and involves identifying a person by comparing selected facial features from a digital image with a facial database. The system Smartgate, for instance, has been adopted at a number of Australian airports.[3] It takes an image of a traveler's face and matches it with a digitized image stored in the traveler's ePassport. If the match is successful, the traveler is cleared through customs and immigration control. The technique obviously allows for fast processing of the increasing number of travelers in a globalized world. However, it is also likely to have a significant impact on traveling patterns and on what has been termed "software-sorted societies" (Wood and Graham 2006). David Murakami Wood and Stephen Graham pinpoint precisely the calmness of these types[4] of automated systems of surveillance and social sorting that control the "spaces of flows" (Castells 1996) of modern societies: "Crucially, these techniques of prioritization and inhibition are often so invisible and automated that neither the losers nor the beneficiaries are even aware that they are in operation within the complex sociotechnologies that increasingly constitute the ordinary and taken-for-granted environments of contemporary societies" (2006, 188).

In the case of software sorting, we are thus seeing an example of calm surveillance technologies, which are undeniably countering the risk of overload inherent in border control, but which have a huge impact on people's lives and the structures of our societies. Although the situation of overload is both created and countered on the system side and therefore, in principle, never has to be brought to our attention, the process affects us significantly.

The images involved in such digital identity systems are most often not taken by humans and not received by humans. They can be understood as examples of *calm imaging*. The Canadian artist David Rokeby explores this type of imaging in several of his surveillance pieces—for instance, *Sorting Daemon* (2003) (figure 4.1),[5] which works explicitly with software sorting. In this piece, a camera pans, tilts, and zooms through the street outside the gallery, searching for moving things that might be people, which it removes from the background, analyzes and sorts according to color (in particular skin and clothing), and places in an evolving collage projected in an adjacent room. *Sorting Daemon* thus deals with a situation of potential overload (the amount of people passing by a gallery) by dividing them into entities that can be rearranged according to arbitrary rules. This means that on the left side flesh-colored patches are sorted by color (from olive on the left to pink on the right) and size (from

Figure 4.1
David Rokeby, *Sorting Daemon* (2003). Permission kindly granted by the artist.

largest on the bottom to smallest on the top), and on the right side the other colored patches are sorted by color (horizontally) and intensity (vertically). The tangled and varicolored world outside is thus organized and systematized into something rule based and controlled. However, the piece also plays ingeniously with notions of overload insofar as the evolving collage may pose a new constraint on the capacity of the viewer's attention due to the unfamiliarity of the evolving pattern, which can appear more difficult to decode than the recognizable outline of a human body. Besides highlighting how overload is a result not only of the amount of input, but also of the recognizability of input, the arbitrariness of the output turns the overload-reducing aim of calm technologies into an absurd mechanism with an eerie feel of control. The evolving collage is simultaneously teasingly simple in its color sorting and yet raises immensely complex implications precisely due to its arbitrariness (for instance, the simple but disturbing performance of sorting human flesh according to skin tones).

Sorting Daemon thus explores and challenges the seamless integration of technology and environment that can be found in a number of recent artworks by Rokeby and others.[6] It points to the sensation that something to which we perhaps ought to be paying attention is glossed over in the aim to reduce complexity and implement ubiquitous computing as smoothly as possible, and it seems to suggest that other complexities are arising in the wake of this reduction. Images emerge and are received calmly as a matter of computational exchanges, but in the process they acquire new potentialities, qualities, and risks that might deserve our attention. To further explore these calm dynamics, we need a closer consideration of "where," so to speak, our interaction with technology (which Weiser situates in the periphery of our attention) takes place.

Between Calm and Controlling

In this volume, Mark Hansen (chapter 1) points out that the unique thing about ubiquitous computing is that much of what is happening takes place below the threshold of conscious attention and awareness. This means that the oscillation of calm technologies between the center and periphery of our attention, which Weiser envisions, is simply not possible because the interaction is taking place at a precognitive level. The concept to which we constantly return when trying to understand our interaction with calm technologies and the images they generate is *attention*.[7] As Jonathan Crary (1990, 2001) has emphasized, the concept of attention has a deeply historical character. Although conceptualizations of attention may be found throughout the history of philosophy, it was in particular the challenges to the perceptual apparatus (the conditions of overload) following from the social, economic, technological, and artistic developments in the modern industrial city in the second half of the nineteenth century that fostered a critical interest in attention. In particular, new industrial modes of production raised the need for increased understanding of human attention and inattention with respect to the performance of repetitive actions in factories. The late nineteenth and twentieth centuries were dominated by two distinct approaches to the study of attention—the empirical-psychological approach[8] and the philosophical-phenomenological approach,[9] respectively. Both of these approaches have in recent years been increasingly influenced by the findings of neuroscience, and attempts to bridge the two have been taken.

In *The Sphere of Attention: Context and Margin* (2006), Sven Arvidson aims to develop a phenomenological approach to attention based on the theory of Edmund Husserl, Jean-Paul Sartre, Maurice Merleau-Ponty, and Aron Gurwitsch, while supporting his argument with laboratory results from cognitive psychologists and neuroscientists. Starting with a framework provided by Gurwitsch, Arvidson argues that attention should be regarded as a sphere with three levels of attention, which he terms *theme*, *context*, and *margin* and which should be viewed as a fluctuating field in constant transformation. Arvidson gives the example of the visual perception of a coffee cup in a café, which involves a focal attention to the cup (as the theme), a contextual attention to the café counter on which it is placed and to the server withdrawing from the counter, and a marginal attention to the facts that time is passing and previous events are related to current ones, that I am standing rather than sitting, and that there the ambient conversations and noises from the coffee-making machines

(2003, 101). Over the past few decades, experiments within the cognitive sciences have taken considerable interest in stimuli outside the focus of attention. However, it is only recently that the discourse and vocabulary within psychology as well as philosophy has shifted from the dominant "spotlight" metaphor that fosters a way of thinking of attention in binary oppositions such as illuminated/unilluminated, focal attention/inattention, and, indeed, center/periphery (Weiser 1991) to a conception of attention as a subtle gradation with many nuances, allowing for different levels and types of attention to be present simultaneously. Arvidson's tripartite model seems particularly apt at capturing this multilevel quality of attention. What is of particular interest for us here is his substitution of the term *unconscious* with *margin of attention* because he finds the negation inherent in *unconscious* to be maldescriptive: "The margin has depth and is a genuine dimension in our lives—an ongoing presence in attending life. Just as everything in the unconscious can never be made conscious, but nonetheless some of its content may be active in my ongoing life, everything in the margin can never be made thematic, but nonetheless some of its content may be active in my ongoing life" (2006, 181).

Replacing the term *unconscious* with *margin of attention* does not imply that we are aware of the whole sphere of attention all the time or that events cannot occur below the threshold of our awareness. However, Arvidson's conception of attention as a sphere (rather than as a binary opposition between conscious and unconscious) makes it easier to imagine the nature of our interaction with calm technology, and it provides a model for understanding how we can be affected by what goes on in the margin even if we are not aware of it, which seems to be at the heart of the discomfort with ubiquitous, calm computing that we have seen in the criticisms of software-sorted societies and in Rokeby's *Sorting Daemon*.[10]

Barbara Maria Stafford explores further the nature of this discomfort in *Echo Objects: The Cognitive Work of Images*:

> The convergence of advanced information technology with cognitive science is, I fear, sidelining the effortful and deliberative aspects of thinking. One fall-out of the merger between automaticity and high-speed processing is that the making of cognitive meaning—emerging from acts of connecting of which we are aware—tends to get lost. The contribution of focused attention gets drowned in the expanding imaging technologies dedicated to ferreting out what we are thinking and in experimental regimes interested in direct brain interventions. Unlike the artworks of Alimpiev, Goldsworthy, Cutler-Shaw, or Gursky—which incite the perceiver to discover relations between herself and aspects of the environment predicated on what a person is functionally able to process—the new paradigm of massive automatic data collection, instantaneous interpretation, and simultaneous archiving bypasses both human comprehension and volition. (2007, 191)

Stafford here creates a distinction between how some artworks encourage the viewer to explore the relation between herself and the environment and how technology's ability to process large amounts of data drowns out this human ability. This distinction not only implies that the dependency of neuroscientific research on information technology influences the view of human cognition but also suggests a process leading to a marginalization of the part of human cognition that does not function through more or less automated stimuli–response processes but consciously focuses outward on the world (in what Arvidson would call "thematic attention"). It implies the fear that when technology processes data quickly and seamlessly, performing collective, interpretative, and archival functions and allowing us to manage the amount of data we have to cope with in the modern world, deliberate thinking that could have arisen does not get the chance to evolve.[11] Not only are we saved a great deal of unimaginative, effortful work, but we also risk losing touch with the deliberative aspects of thinking because technology makes the decision about what should be thematic and what should be at the margin of our attention for us. Stafford poses the question polemically: "We are so caught up in the alternate reality spun by mass media—not multi-, but individually tailored media designed to interlock with specific brain functions—that the question becomes what impels us to resist insinuating forces that shape how we think?" (2007, 203). Although such fears may seem overly suspicious, it is nonetheless the prospect of acquiring further understanding of such "insinuating forces" that fuels the interest in attention studies within marketing and advertising research, which undoubtedly has a strong interest in countering information overload and making sure that a particular image is picked up by the consumer. What has been termed *neuromarketing*[12] may thus serve as an example of imaging that aims to control rather than to calm. To an even more explicit extent than facial-recognition systems, neuromarketing strategies highlight how difficult it is to determine when calmness capsizes in control and thus to pinpoint ethical concerns that need to be raised also when it comes to apparently benign ubiquitous calm computing.

Advertising and marketing research has had a long-term engagement with attention research in the cognitive sciences. More than thirty years have passed since recordings of electrical activity in the brain were first used to evaluate viewer responses to television commercials, and since the end of the 1990s brain scans, heart rate, respiratory rate, and galvanic skin response have increasingly been used to better understand consumer decisions and what may affect them. Marketing and advertising people in particular have heralded neuromarketing as paving the way for reaching consumers on affective and preconscious levels. Whereas calm technology (as Weiser describes it) aims to reduce overload and to allow our attention to focus on things other than the technology, strategies such as neuromarketing aim at refining those "insinuating forces that shape how we think" and in this way actively control rather than service the margin of our attention.

In a world saturated with visual overload (think of the billboard bombardment in Times Square in New York City or Akihabara electric town in Tokyo), there seems to be two possible marketing strategies. One continues the way of thinking about images that we saw in the example of digital identity systems, where the data that need to be processed are software sorted. This is what we see in Amazon's personalized recommendations or YouTube's referrals to "related videos," both examples of software sorting based on previous behavior. Another marketing approach to overload works from the assumption that visual impressions alone are not the most effective way of reaching the consumer in a contemporary world where most of us have developed what Simmel referred to as a "protective organ." Images appear to leave a bigger imprint when combined with impressions from senses other than the visual—for instance, scent, touch, and sound, which create an emotional response. This is what is at stake when the aroma of honeydew melon is distributed through the ventilation system in Samsung's flagship store in New York, when Bang & Olufsen's remote controls contain redundant blocks of aluminum to increase the weight and seem more robust, or huge resources are assigned to make the crunch of Kellogg's cornflakes stand out from that of other cornflake brands (Lindström 2008). Thus, we may talk about sensory branding as a very active and effective addition to visual impressions that does not reside in the thematic sphere of our attention, but that actively engages with the margin of our attention and thereby affects our impressions of an image or a brand.

What we can now begin to see, from the attempt I have made in this chapter to explore the implications of the link between ubiquitous computing and calmness, is the ways in which imaging is influenced as a result of these developments and how Valéry's vision is in fact taking an even more radical shape. It is not only the "simple movement of the hand" that makes the visual and auditory images appear and disappear, but also bodily functions even more at the margin of our attention that are engaging with the technology and evoking images. This idea is perhaps most clearly articulated in *The Heart Library Project* (2009) by the Australian artist George Khut (figure 4.2), which playfully engages with the issues dealt with in this chapter. Whereas neuromarketing research aims to measure responses to sensory stimuli displayed to the test subject through heart-rate monitoring or brain imaging, *The Heart Library Project* reverses the process and displays images generated by the interaction between the human heart rate and a computer projecting images. Its biofeedback system thus bears resemblance to digital identity systems, which feature images that remain on the system side, but it makes the human body an intricate part of the system in a more radical way than Rokeby's *Sorting Daemon* and generates images that are the product of a relation between technology and what normally goes on at the margin of our attention—that is, our heart rate.

In *The Heart Library Project*, visitors are invited to rest on their backs and place their hands onto a pair of wireless heart-rate sensors, which measure changes in heart rate that can be influenced by breathing and stress/relaxation responses. These changes are collected by a sensor, analyzed, and translated into color and sound patterns by a

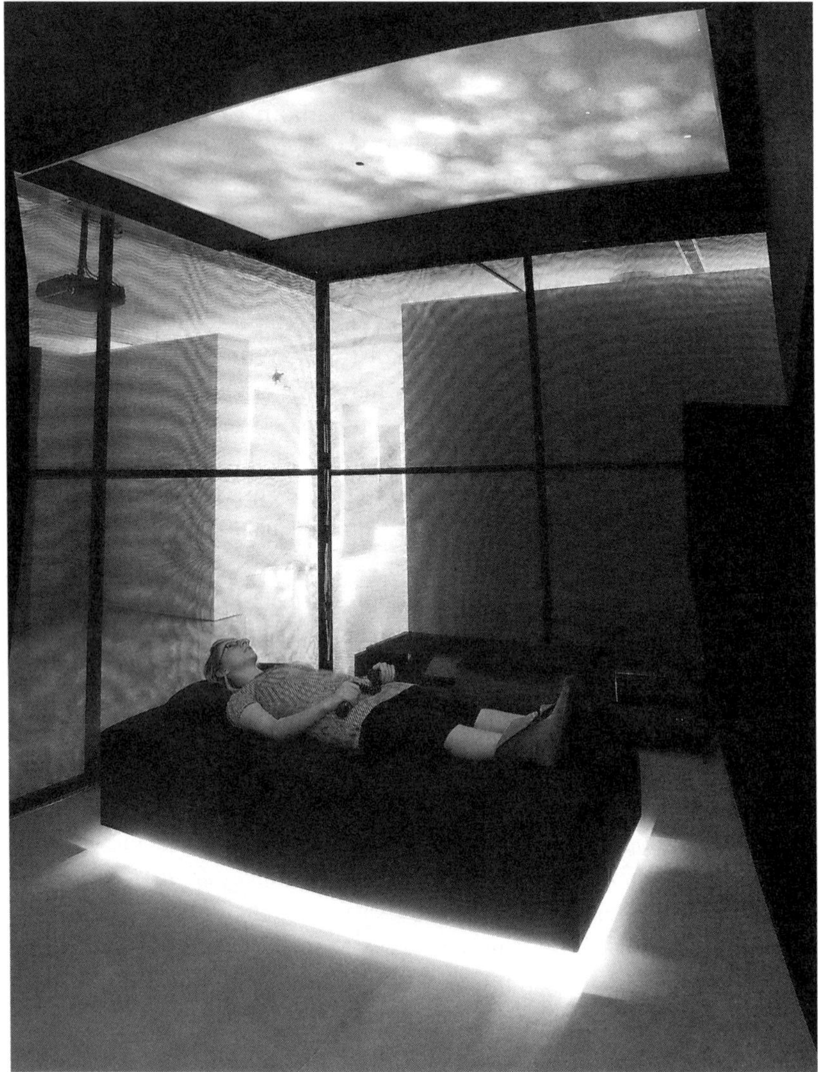

Figure 4.2
George Poonkhin Khut, with David Morris-Oliveros, *The Heart Library Project* (2009). Permission kindly granted by the artist.

computer. The colors are projected on the ceiling above the participant, which features a mirrorlike projection of the participant immersed in water. The water gradually becomes obscured by colored spots that change in response to changes in the participant's heart rhythm. The documentation of the piece explains the visualization: "Cooler colours, soft, muted sounds, objects falling away or down for *decreasing* heart rates; and warmer colours, crackly/tingly sounds, and objects moving forwards or floating upwards for *increasing* heart rates."[13] The participant is invited to try to influence the patterns through a change of breathing patterns and mental and emotional focus, which will produce a heart-rate variation. *The Heart Library Project* can thus be said to explore the impact of human volition on the feedback loop between technology and the human being. Hereby attention is visualized as a spectrum of colors and sounds in the sense that the artwork directs our attention toward our own heartbeat and transforms it into sound and visual patterns playfully projected onto the reflection of her body. As in *Sorting Daemon*, the piece, rather than calming the overload, makes the participant conscious of a complexity to which she was not paying attention previously. *The Heart Library Project* creates a keen awareness of the interaction between the heartbeat and the computer entering into a symbiosis, which leaves the participant an engaged yet also strangely immobilized observer, thus offering an intriguing comment on the effect of *calm imaging* on the status of the image. Even though there is a correspondence between the participant's heartbeat and the image, there is also software sorting going on over which she has no control, and insofar as her heartbeat and breathing are such fundamental parts of being human, they can be affected voluntarily only in minor ways without causing her physical discomfort. The level of interaction is thus limited and may in fact capsize in a feeling of detachment from her own body.[14] The camera, which records the image of the body, is placed over the heart, which means that the participant is not able to make eye contact with her own reflection. It thus remains a *calm image*, born and evolving in the fluctuating field between the margin of her attention (her heart rate) and the computer analysis and rendition of color codes, intricately interweaving the human being and the imaging technology in a way that blurs the boundaries between the observer and the observed, the controlling and the controlled, and leaves the participant simultaneously challenged, entertained, overloaded, and calmed.

Notes

1. By the term *ubiquitous computing*, I refer to computing that no longer operates as a stable entity located in a specific place but has become a context-aware part of our everyday environments. As Ulrik Ekman states in the introduction to this volume, ubiquitous computing is "a sociocultural *and* technical thrust to integrate and/or embed computing pervasively, to have information processing thoroughly integrated with or embedded into everyday objects and activities, including those pertaining to human bodies and their parts."

2. After the invention of the printing press, Europe faced a vast increase in the production, circulation, and dissemination of scientific and scholarly texts (Rosenberg 2003).

3. For information on Smartgate, see http://www.customs.gov.au/site/page5552.asp. Facial-recognition software is a thriving business, and the providers and purposes are multiple; see, for instance, information on the system used in the United Kingdom at http://www.omniperception.com, on the system used in Japan at http://www.ayonix.com, and on the system used in Israel at http://www.ex-sight.com.

4. Other examples are road pricing, call-center queuing systems, and Web site prioritization of customers.

5. For information on *Sorting Daemon*, see http://homepage.mac.com/davidrokeby/sorting.html.

6. See, for instance, information on Rafael Lozano-Hemmer's *Subtitled Public* (2005), in his Shadow Box series, at http://www.lozano-hemmer.com/projects.php, and on Adam Harvey's work on makeup patterns that confuse facial-recognition software at http://ahprojects.com/blog/c/itp.

7. As Susan Kozel notes in chapter 19 in this volume, "Ubiquity implies selection: What to notice? What to overlook?"

8. Key thinkers taking the empirical-psychological approach include Gustav Theodor Fechner, Wilhelm Wundt, Carl Stumpf, Theodor Lipps, Théodule Ribot, F. H. Bradley, and, to some degree, William James. They share the aim of approaching attention from an objective third-person perspective. The heirs of this tradition can be found in particular in cognitive psychology and neurobiology (Steinbock 2004).

9. In the phenomenological tradition, Edmund Husserl, Max Scheler, Maurice Merleau-Ponty, Jean-Paul Sartre, and Aron Gurwitsch address attention from first-person (subjective) and second-person (intersubjective) perspectives.

10. The conception of attention as a sphere may also further enhance the understanding of the term *technological unconscious* (Clough 2000; Thrift 2004; Thrift and French 2002), which Nigel Thrift has used to describe knowledge that has coevolved between humans and the environment and that takes place below the threshold of consciousness. See also the chapters by Ulrik Schmidt and Dietmar Offenhuber on ambience and ambient design in this volume (chapters 8 and 25).

11. Interestingly, Crary has raised concerns about a different aspect of attention, which he sees pressured by the ability of digital technology to control attention: "What once might have been called reverie now most often takes places aligned with preset rhythms, images, speeds, and circuits that reinforce the irrelevance and dereliction of whatever is not compatible with their formats" (2001, 78). If attention is in some way controlled, then it leaves as little room for free association as it does for deliberative aspects of thinking.

12. Although some neuroscientists distance themselves from the more commercial usage of the term *neuromarketing*, arguing that there is a long way from observing what happens in people's brains while they are making decisions to being able to identify a "buy button," the academic

field of neuromarketing can in general terms be defined as "the application of neuroscientific methods to analyze and understand human behaviour in relation to markets and marketing exchanges" (Lee, Broderick, and Chamberlain 2007, 200); the field of neuroeconomics is closely related (Murphy, Illes, and Reiner 2008; Wilson, Gaines, and Hill 2008).

13. For information on *The Heart Library Project*, see http://files.georgekhut.com/texts/heartlibrarystv-programme-20090707.pdf.

14. Many have described the experience of *The Heart Library Project* as an "out-of-body experience"; see http://georgekhut.com/blog.

References

Arvidson, P. Sven. 2006. *The Sphere of Attention: Context and Margin*. Dordrecht, Netherlands: Springer.

Arvidson, P. Sven. 2003. "A Lexicon of Attention: From Cognitive Science to Phenomenology." *Phenomenology and the Cognitive Sciences* 2 (2): 99–132.

Castells, Manuel. 1996. *The Rise of the Network Society*. Oxford, UK: Blackwell.

Clough, Patricia Ticineto. 2000. *Autoaffection: Unconscious Thought in the Age of Teletechnology*. Minneapolis: University of Minnesota Press.

Crary, Jonathan. 2001. *Suspensions of Perception: Attention, Spectacle, and Modern Culture*. Cambridge, MA: MIT Press.

Crary, Jonathan. 1990. *Techniques of the Observer: On Vision and Modernity in the Nineteenth Century*. Cambridge, MA: MIT Press.

Edmunds, Angela, and Anne Morris. 2000. "The Problem of Information Overload in Business Organisations: A Review of the Literature." *International Journal of Information Management* 20: 17–28.

Featherstone, Mike. 2009. "Ubiquitous Media: An Introduction." *Theory, Culture, & Society* 26 (2–3): 1–22.

Lee, Nick, Amanda J. Broderick, and Laura Chamberlain. 2007. "What Is 'Neuromarketing'? A Discussion and Agenda for Future Research." *International Journal of Psychophysiology* 63 (2) (2007): 199–204.

Lindström, Martin. 2008. *BuyOlogy: Truth and Lies about Why We Buy*. New York: Doubleday, 2008.

Murphy, Emily R., Judy Illes, and Peter B. Reiner. 2008. "Neuroethics of Neuromarketing." *Journal of Consumer Behaviour* 7 (4–5): 293–302.

Rosenberg, Daniel. 2003. "Early Modern Information Overload." *Journal of the History of Ideas* 64 (1): 1–9.

Simmel, Georg. [1903] 2005. "The Metropolis and Mental Life." In *The Urban Sociology Reader*, edited by Jan Lin and Christopher Mele, 23–31. London: Routledge.

Stafford, Barbara Maria. 2007. *Echo Objects: The Cognitive Work of Images*. Chicago: University of Chicago Press.

Steinbock, Anthony. 2004. "Introduction to This Special Issue." *Continental Philosophy Review* 37 (1): 1–3.

Thrift, Nigel. 2004. "Remembering the Technological Unconscious by Foregrounding Knowledges of Position." *Environment and Planning D: Society and Space* 22 (1): 175–190.

Thrift, Nigel, and Shaun French. 2002. "The Automatic Production of Space." *Transactions of the Institute of British Geographers* 27 (3): 309–335.

Valéry, Paul. [1928/1934] 1964. "The Conquest of Ubiquity." In *Aesthetics*, vol. 13 of *The Collected Works of Paul Valéry*, translated by Ralph Manheim, 225–228. New York: Pantheon.

Weiser, Mark. 1994. "The World Is Not a Desktop." *Interactions* 1 (1): 7–8.

Weiser, Mark. 1993. "Ubiquitous Computing." *Nikeei Electronics* (6 December): 137–43.

Weiser, Mark. 1991. "The Computer for the 21st Century." *Scientific American* 265 (3): 94–104. Available at http://www.ubiq.com/hypertext/weiser/SciAmDraft3.html. Accessed July 31, 2009.

Weiser, Mark, and John Seely Brown. 1996. "The Coming Age of Calm Technology." Available at http://nano.xerox.com/hypertext/weiser/acmfuture2endnote.htm. Accessed July 31, 2009.

Wilson, R. Mark, Jeannie Gaines, and Ronald Paul Hill. 2008. "Neuromarketing and Consumer Free Will." *Journal of Consumer Affairs* 42 (3): 389–410.

Wood, David Murakami, and Stephen Graham. 2006. "Permeable Boundaries in the Software-Sorted Society." In *Mobile Technologies of the City*, edited by Mimi Sheller and John Urry, 177–191. London: Routledge.

II Sense and Sensations 2: Sound

5 Losing Your Voice: Sampled Speech and Song from the Uncanny to the Unremarkable

Joseph Auner

The 2008 Pixar film *Wall-e* depicts our world seven hundred years in the future, piled with mountains of debris and totally devoid of human life. The title character, Wall-e, is essentially a walking trash compactor, the last of his kind still functioning. He spends his days converting rubbish into cubes that he stacks up in tall towers, interrupting his work only to collect objects that catch his interest. For the first forty minutes of the film, the only human voices we hear are from recorded advertisements that are still playing even though there are no humans left to hear them and from Wall-e's most cherished possession, a VHS video of the musical *Hello Dolly*. Wall-e has only limited vocal capacities, but he is equipped with a built-in recording device that allows him to capture and play back short samples of songs from the video. He uses these borrowed voices to express his feelings and to keep himself company as he goes about his solitary existence, accompanied only by his pet cockroach.

Wall-e does eventually meet and fall in love with another robot, Eve, traveling with her to the vast spaceship where all the humans have gone. Together they liberate the humans from their dependence on all the technologies that have turned them into obese, full-time consumers who communicate only via video screens and headsets. It is not surprising that audiences embraced the second half of the film with its happy ending marked by the return of the humans to recolonize Earth. But it is remarkable to me that the same audiences were willing to accept the first part, a literally posthuman world in which only recordings survive.

That the film succeeds in getting us to contemplate the ruins of our civilization so calmly and with only mild nostalgia can be attributed in part, I would argue, to the ubiquity of recorded voices throughout our musical soundscape and in our everyday lives. It seems as if new objects are gaining the capacity of speech every day; voices call out to us from smartphones, greeting cards, and automated supermarket checkouts. In many cases, the recorded voices we hear on telephones, the radio, and MP3s are still firmly attached to the people, contexts, and bodies that produced them. But voices are more and more coming loose from their origins and circulating independently without the knowledge or consent of the person who spoke or sang. Remixes and mashups re- and decontextualize the voices of the famous and the unknown; a widely viewed YouTube series, "Auto-Tune the News," turns broadcasters and politicians into "unintentional" singers. Even the control over our own voices is increasingly tenuous, as shown by the "posthumous partnership" *Ray Sings, Basie Swings* (2007), in which an old vocal track by Ray Charles is paired with a newly recorded accompaniment, and by Hillary Clinton's complaint in the closing days of the 2008 US presidential election that her voice had been commandeered for an onslaught of anti-Obama "robo-calls."

Music that makes use of borrowed or stolen recorded voices can be found in many different styles and traditions of popular and concert music, but it is in hip-hop production that sampled voices have been the most pervasive. Although any instrumental or natural sounds one can imagine have been used in loops and layers, recorded voices have proven to be of particular interest to producers such as Madlib, DJ Shadow, RZA, and Fatboy Slim as well as to various related offshoots of sample-based music by the Boards of Canada, the Books, Girl Talk, and many others. For example, the song "America's Most Blunted" from the 2004 release *Madvillainy* by the MC MF Doom and the producer MadLib opens with a chaotic collage of samples of instruments, noises, and voices from advertisements, educational records, and even Steve Reich's 1966 tape piece *Come Out*. In this track, MF Doom eventually makes an appearance as an ostensibly live and "authentic" voice as opposed to all the recorded sounds. But in most of the examples of the genre known as "instrumental hip-hop" I discuss, there are no actual vocalists, only samples of speech and song.

Software for creating and manipulating voices, from the sophisticated systems at the Institut de recherche et coordination acoustique/musique to free "voice-changer" applications, have fulfilled the centuries-old desire for automata that can speak or sing, going back to devices such as Wolfgang von Kempelen's 1791 design for a *vox humana* that used a keyboard to control mouth-shaped resonators (Pompino-Marschall 2005, 150). Jonathan Sterne has written of the rise of recording technologies as shifting the locus of sound reproduction from such machines based on the mouth to machines such as the gramophone based on the tympanic membrane of the ear. In so doing, according to Sterne, a development was launched that made it possible to regard the voice as a sound like any other, just another source of vibration (2003, 73–81). Indeed, the new sampling technologies and the convergence of digital media have made possible a far more ambitious *vox humana* than von Kempelen could have imagined, one that allows producers to play with any noise or sound that has ever been recorded. That producers are still so drawn to the voice is thus also a striking fact meriting further attention.

Of course, with the exceptions of live broadcasts and music that uses artificial-speech software, every voice we hear through a loudspeaker is a recorded voice and subject to what Mark Katz has identified as an extensive range of "phonograph effects"

(2004, 8–47). But my focus here is on pieces that point to the most general phonograph effect—namely, that we are listening to a recording. This mediated, artificial quality of the voice is often a product of the dislocation of the sample to a new context and of manipulations that alter the original's temporal continuity. The producer Prefuse 73 has made a specialty of creating new works by chopping up and recombining parts of several pieces. His song "Nuno" from the 2001 release *Vocal Studies and Uprock Narratives* is constructed from small slices of the vocal track from "One Love" by the rapper NAS off the 1994 release *Illmatic*. This track is layered with several vocal samples from other songs, including by the rhythm and blues singer Erykah Badu. We might think at first that "Nuno" is just a conventional rap track, but with the glitchy slices and obsessive stuttering it soon becomes clear we are hearing something else entirely. To sketch out what this "something else" might be is the purpose of this chapter.

The way in which such vocal technologies, to paraphrase Mark Weiser (1991), are so woven into the fabric of everyday life that they are indistinguishable from it, suggests that it is in the sphere of the voice that the idea of ubiquitous computing has been the most fully realized. For Weiser, ubiquitous computing involves the movement of computers into the background of our experience, thus making us more aware of the "people on the other ends of [our] computer links." In his and John Seely Brown's view, technologies become "calm" when they recede into the "periphery" of our attention, where they can inform us "without overburdening," thus making it possible to "attune to many more things than we could if everything had to be at the center" (Weiser and Brown 1996). But it is not so simple when it is the voice—that most demanding of sounds and the ultimate sign of human subjectivity and individuality—that is now moved to the periphery, where it can provide stimulus without overburdening us with the need to respond. And if we are not quite yet living in Wall-e's world, when we hear a voice, we increasingly have to question whether there actually is someone on the other end of the line.

Some vocal samples that I discuss are staged to produce a sense of strangeness and disorientation long associated with the recorded voice, a sense notable even in the critical vocabulary developed to describe it: *uncanny, simulacral, schizophonic, acousmatic* (Abbate 2001; Chion 1994; Connor 2001; Reynolds 2006). We can hear musicians intensifying the sense of attraction/repulsion produced by the *unheimlich* (uncanny) recorded voice in the metallic, machinelike voices distorted by vocoders and autotuners that have colonized significant segments of rhythm and blues, rock, and dance music (Auner 2003; Dickinson 2001; Weheliye 2002). Yet still stranger are the many examples of music in which the remarkable act of speaking through borrowed voices is presented as absolutely unremarkable. If the experience of recorded voices as uncanny, as "dead" or disembodied, depends on the belief that these voices were once connected with bodies of flesh and blood, the demystified, disenchanted voices that increasingly surround us—and that perhaps are already emerging from us—are treated as if they had never been alive.

Voices Unmoored

Vocal samples obviously have different meanings for different listeners in different contexts. Thomas Edison's belief that recording would make immortal the speech of the powerful is no doubt frequently realized (Kittler 1999, 21). When Prefuse 73 samples the NAS track off what is widely regarded as one of the greatest hip-hop albums, he clearly intends the reference to be recognized, to establish his own place in a lineage, and to define a community of listeners (Katz 2004, 123–124; Rose 1994, 89; Sterne 2003, 350–351). We can hear this mode of listening vividly staged in DJ Food and DK's remix of the DJ Shadow song "Right Thing" in their 2007 release *Now, Listen Again*. The original piece is interwoven with other DJ Shadow samples and remixes as well as with a host of borrowed voices lecturing us on how to listen; as one voice observes, "The source of that sound is perfectly familiar to everyone."

Of course, the insistence of those recorded voices of authority that we recognize the samples points to the fact that most listeners will not. And as such mediated music circulates through manifold spaces from the iPod to the dance club, the new meanings that accrue to all these unmoored sounds recall Jacques Attali's pessimistic analysis of the repetitive world of mass production, with "the death of the original, the triumph of the copy, and the forgetting of the represented foundation" (1996, 89). MF Doom's "America's Most Blunted" with its sample of Reich's *Come Out*, demonstrates how recorded voices can now travel far beyond their original contexts and audiences, radically accelerating the normal processes of forgetting. Thus, we hear a recording of Daniel Hamm, one of six black teenagers arrested and convicted for the murder of a white shop owner in the 1964 Harlem riots, turned into a piece of *musique concrète* by Reich, which was remixed more than thirty years later by the Japanese DJ Ken Ishii on *Reich Remixed* (1999), eventually landing on MF Doom's "America's Most Blunted," where it is likely to be sampled and reused again. And although some MF Doom fans in online discussion groups indicated an awareness of Reich, I have not come across any reference by such fans that reconnects Daniel Hamm back to his own voice.

In contrast to the world before recording when one's own voice was never farther from one than an echo, the broad circulation of all forms of digital information radically destabilizes notions of intended audience and author-determined meaning. And although there are many pieces where samples are chosen to make a specific point or reference, there are probably just as many cases where samples are chosen purely on musical features with no regard for the original meaning. For example, the producer Blockhead describes finding a vocal sample on a 1964 LP from India: "Obviously I don't speak an Indian [language], so I have no idea what she's saying, but it resembles an African stringed instrument and Mickey Mouse at the same time. It works with the track because it's got this lighthearted feel to it. The sample itself is kind of fun" (quoted in Weiss 2006, 38). Such a mode of listening is not surprising in an environment where we are likely to hear music not in a club or concert performance, but in our cars, over loudspeakers in public places, and through our iPod headphones, where the voices in the piece will merge with other voices around us. That such voices may be recorded or live is probably most often besides the point. Michael Bull has discussed how people listening to their iPods can have a filmic experience of their environment. One of his informants describes the sense that the people and things around him are "inanimate and not fully connected. . . . When I look at the people around me, they appear to be two dimensional and without significance" (chapter 6 in this volume).

Séance

In the early days of recording, listeners could respond to the recorded voice as somehow still real; thus, scholars have discussed the "crooner" phenomenon with Rudy Vallee and others as depending on the closely microphoned voice that produced a feeling of physical proximity and thus the potential for romantic intimacy (McCracken 1999, 372–378; Smith 2008, 81–86). The unsettling and uncanny potential that comes from the realization that there is no body actually attached to those voices whispering in our ears is a central theme in writings by Carolyn Abbate, Jonathan Sterne, Steven Connor, Simon Reynolds, Friedrich Kittler, and others, who have described recordings in terms of "resonant tombs," "zombies," and "grave robbing." Jeffrey Sconce's *Haunted Media* (2000) traces the long history of spirits inhabiting media from the telephone to the television; there is a thriving subculture on the Internet concerning paranormal "EVP," electronic voice phenomena.

Tracing a development from eighteenth-century automata to the advent of recording technology, Carolyn Abbate focuses more generally on the uncanny aspects of musical performance in her book *In Search of Opera* (2001). She explores the ways that music can turn the human into an instrument or automaton; in her most extreme formulation, she writes, "Perhaps it is the musical works that are alive, and we who are dead" (xiv). A recurring theme in Abbate's study is the head of Orpheus continuing to sing after it is severed. The notion of music animating a disembodied voice is specifically thematized in many musical pieces using vocal samples, such as DJ Shadow's "Building Steam with a Grain of Salt" on *Entroducing* (1996). Like a ventriloquist's dummy, the sampled voice of a pretentious drum instructor is made to acknowledge unwittingly the producer who is pulling the strings: "I would like to continue to let what is inside of me, which is—which comes from all the music that I hear—you would like for that to come out. It's not really me that is coming—the music is coming through me."

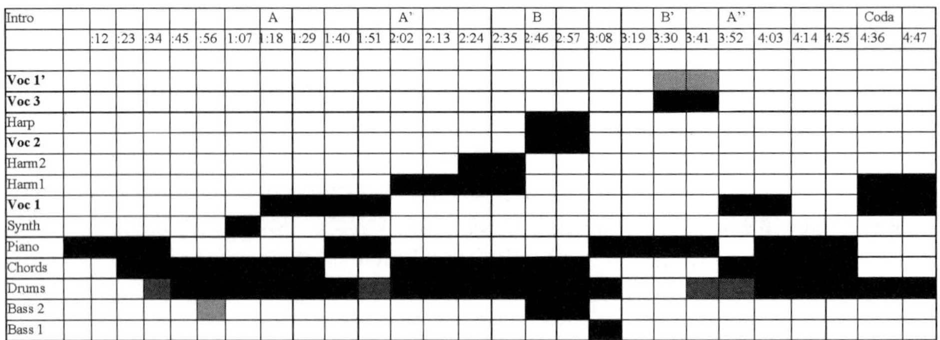

Figure 5.1
Diagram of samples in Blockhead's "Sunday Séance," from *Music by Cavelight* (Ninja Tune, 2004). Gray boxes indicate partial loops.

Some producers exploit the uncanny and supernatural potential of recorded voices for expressive effects, as in the track "Sunday Séance" on the 2004 release *Music by Cavelight* by the producer Blockhead. "Sunday Séance," as the diagram in figure 5.1 shows, is built on short samples that are looped and layered in various combination to build up a piece lasting just less than five minutes. The foundation of the piece is a four-measure piano loop based on the opening measures of Keith Jarret's *Köln Concert* (1974) slowed down and lowered in pitch. The unsettling atmosphere of the piece is established right at the outset with the altered piano loop, still clearly a piano but sounding somehow lifeless and decayed. As "Sunday Séance" progresses, additional loops of very different sounds are introduced, including drums, bass, various synthesizers, harmonica, harp, and most prominently three different vocal samples. Vocal samples play a major role in much of Blockhead's music; as in this piece, he frequently speeds up or slows down the samples to make them fit the tempo and key rather than using software that makes it possible to adjust tempo and pitch independently.

The séance of the title is literally referenced in the first sample through the spirit-summoning text, "Can you hear me call your name?" But the vocal samples are also modified to reinforce the strange mood, as if to evoke the paranormal voices on tape that have been part of the history of recorded sound from the beginning. And the voices are *unheimlich* on multiple levels. The first voice is difficult to place in terms of age or gender—Is it a child's voice, a woman's voice, a boy soprano, or something else? (The sample is taken from recording by a 1970s progressive-rock group with a female lead singer). The third vocal sample is the most natural on one level because the pitch is unchanged and we can identify the gender, but it is reversed so that we cannot understand what she is trying to say. The use of backward voices for supernatural effects has its own history, including the recorded voice of the demon in the 1973 film *The Exorcist.*

Voice Activated

But the voices in "Sunday Séance," along with their expressive function in evoking the supernatural, also point to the important formal role played by vocal samples in this repertoire as a particularly effective solution to the compositional challenges of composing in a style with limited melodic and harmonic motion. When producers work with an MC they can count on the lyrics and music of the rapping to shape the overall song, but in the absence of a vocalist, they have to face the challenge of sustaining the listener's interest. As the Blockhead diagram shows (figure 5.1), one way of doing this is by constantly changing the number and combination of layers; indeed, he never repeats the same combination for more than two cycles of the basic loop. The other main technique to maintain interest is to introduce strikingly new timbres as the piece progresses—such as the harmonica and the harp.

As many producers have apparently realized, the most striking timbre is the voice. In "Sunday Séance," all the key moments in the song are marked by the appearance of a vocal sample. Blockhead and many producers working in this style use the sudden appearance of recorded voices to create moments of climax, arrival, transition, or other formal functions. In the case of "Sunday Séance," the placement of the vocal samples serves to impose a more traditional song structure on the succession of loops. At the same time, Blockhead's manipulation of the vocal samples also responds to the compositional challenge of introducing the voice in a genre that often strives for ambient effects and immersive listening (see the essays by Torben Sangild and Ulrik Schmidt in this volume, chapters 7 and 8). By altering the voices, as Blockhead almost always does, he signals to the listener that there is no living singer demanding their attention, thus allowing the vocal layer to move in and out of the periphery of the listener's attention, comparable to the other instrumental layers.

In their compositional treatment of recorded voices, these producers are consciously or unconsciously exploiting aspects of what Mark Hansen has characterized as embodied perception (2004, 11); they in effect use the samples as sonic stimuli to manipulate our listening bodies and minds. Recent writings on speech and music cognition demonstrate—no doubt unsurprisingly—that voices provoke a whole range of emotional and affective responses in listeners. The 2005 publication *Wired for Speech*, for example, provides an overview of research showing that voices are a special category of sound received by the ear and processed by the brain independently from other acoustic phenomena. The authors cite studies showing that "one-day old infants respond differently to speechlike sounds than they do to any other sounds" (Nass and Brave 2005, 1–2). It is again no surprise that the brain would have evolved to be specially attuned to vocal timbre, thus allowing us to extract a vast array of information from the voice to identify and differentiate people along all the axes of gender, age, geographic origin, social status, health, and nuances of psychological state, personality, and intent.

But it may be more surprising that this research shows that listeners similarly interpret even the most distorted and obviously artificial voices as bearing social and emotional information. With relevance to the powerful expressive impact of songs such as Radiohead's "Fitter Happier" that use intentionally primitive speech software, Clifford Nass and Scott Brave note: "Users respond to even the most monotone synthetic voice as if it were manifesting extremely low arousal and neutral valence" (2005, 95; see also Auner 2003). Indeed, the focus of *Wired for Speech* is the development of guidelines for software and hardware engineers who are designing voice interfaces for automated phone services, the Internet, automobiles, and so on. The goal is to predict an artificial voice's effect on a target audience, or, as the authors put it: "How will a voice-activated brain that associates voice with social relationships react when confronted with technologies that talk and listen?" (Nass and Brave 2005, 4).

The matter-of-fact way in which the authors of *Wired for Speech* discuss the voice points in turn to manifold ways in which the disembodied, recorded voice is becoming increasingly less uncanny. Although there are pieces such as "Sunday Séance" that present vocal samples as strange and unsettling, even stranger and more unsettling is how normal and unremarkable it is becoming to hear and accept voices that have only distant relationships to the bodies that produced them. As already noted regarding the Prefuse 73 and DJ Food excerpts, many other pieces also use vocal samples with little sense of the uncanny or unusual. Torben Sangild writes in similar terms of a piece by the Boards of Canada: "There is a also a sense of the unreal and dreamlike and even of a disturbing, claustrophobic mood. At the same time, the uncanniness is not dramatic" (chapter 7 in this volume).

It is as if, rather than positing a living voice that is now dead, many works of vocal sampling treat recorded voices as never having been alive, simply as sounds to be manipulated in the periphery of our awareness. The notable absence in most cases of any indication of the source of the sample can be explained in part by the problem of clearing rights, but the enforced anonymity also underscores the way the voices retain much of their expressive and emotional impact even without the assumption that a human was or is attached to them. This phenomenon might be compared to what Bernadette Wegenstein has described in visual culture as the "obsolescence of the face," marked by the transformation of what has been regarded as "the most representative signifier of human appearance" into just another autonomous body part (2006, 80).

In the essay "The Decomposing Voice of Postmodern Music" (2001), Steven Connor writes of the advent of digital technology with its unlimited storage and retrieval capacity as creating a new stage in the "sonorous economy. " In contrast to earlier phases where the introduction of a new recording technology caused products of earlier media to degrade and be disposed of, digital recording turns voices into "a kind of nondegradable debris" that just keeps piling up (475–476). The image of producers sifting through mountains of debris is vividly demonstrated in the 2002 hip-hop documentary *Scratch* directed by Doug Pray in a scene that shows DJ Shadow in the basement of a record store surrounded by teetering towers of vinyl LPs piled up in every inch of space. It is noteworthy that he acknowledges that he, too, is part of the same "sonorous economy": "If you are making records, you're adding to this pile whether you want to admit it or not. Ten years down the line you'll be in here." DJ Shadow's self-reflexive remark about how his own music will eventually join the accumulation points to Connor's most radical claim—namely, that our relation to voices around us and to our own voices has also been transformed by this piling of vocal debris: "If every transmitted sound is, in principle, also a recorded sound, then the very living presence of the voice becomes a kind of detritus" (2001, 476). Of course, it is just this sense of the voice that is enacted in *Wall-e* as Wall-e scavenges voices from the landfill and communicates by means of his record and playback buttons. And that this scenario in which we encounter our own voice among the detritus is not some science-fiction prophecy is underscored by Bernard Steigler's comments on the objectifying process of encountering his texts, image, and voice through his personal digital assistant, "where I can meet up with myself and gaze as into a mirror" (chapter 29 in this volume).

The Posthuman Voice

Such an understanding of the living voice as a potential recording points in turn to the degree to which ideas of the posthuman are shaping our conceptions of our own voices and our selves. As discussed by N. Katherine Hayles (1999) and others, the posthuman is a way of thinking that views the mind and body in terms of metaphors of software and hardware, that sees the body as prosthesis, and that interprets consciousness and all other bodily functions as interacting cybernetic systems. The book *Wired for Speech*, as should be clear, is a profoundly posthuman project, signaled in the title and in passages such as the following: "Over the course of 200,000 years of evolution, humans have become voice-activated with brains that are wired to equate voices with people and to act quickly on that identification" (Nass and Brave 2005, 1–2).

We can also see posthuman ways of thinking more literally in the techniques that producers and engineers use for working with the recorded voice. The software program Recycle, which was created for making loops out of samples, illustrates the level of control that is available as well as the way in which the voice is now subject through

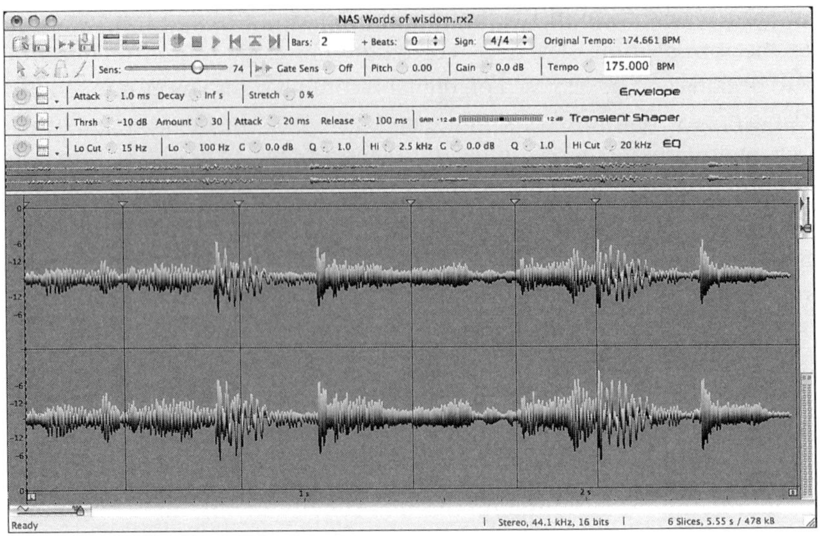

Figure 5.2
Sample from the rapper NAS's "One Love," from *Illmatic* (Columbia Records, 1994). Screenshot from Recycle.

graphic representation to the microtemporal level of control discussed by Hansen in his contribution to this volume (chapter 1). Figure 5.2 shows a segment from "One Love" by NAS, the same sample used in the Prefuse 73 track discussed earlier. Recycle—the program is named as if to refer to what Connor calls "nondegradable debris"—makes it possible to independently modify the tempo or pitch and to chop up the sample into any number of slices. These slices can then be manipulated separately, adjusting pitch or other features. Once a loop is created, it can be imported into other programs, such as Reason, and then further manipulated, reordered, and processed in countless ways. One can then trigger the slices of the vocal sample with a keyboard or any other device. It is striking that what might seem the bizarre act of playing someone's voice by pressing levers—clearly monstrous for the gaping mouths of Von Kempelen's *vox humana*—passes by unnoticed.

And yet even when we are listening to recordings of ostensibly live performers, in many cases the voices have been subjected to extensive modifications and assembled from fragments. Sound engineers' shoptalk provides striking evidence of the voice as literally mixed reality and embodied virtuality. Under the subtitle "Turning Geese into Song Birds," an article from the November 2006 issue of *Electronic Musician* states: "With sufficient effort you can seemingly cure a bad sense of pitch and worse sense of rhythm. You can modify a singer's vocal timbre, enhance his or her breathing technique and turn one singer into as many as you need" (Yelton 2006, 60).

Many such articles exhibit a way of listening to the voice not as some sort of organic whole, but as a conglomeration of noises. One engineer writes, for example, "Besides esses, sometimes you get palate sounds from the singer and other anomalies, like clicks or plosive pops, which can mar an otherwise good take." Particularly striking is his description of the problem of breath sounds in vocal editing: "Although it is tempting to just remove them all, doing so can sound unnatural in many musical situations. Breaths are a really important part of a vocal performance. . . . I've had people go out and record breaths sometimes, if I don't have the right one'" (Levine 2006, 56, 48).

Whereas it used to be the case that the reliance on such vocal enhancements would have been something singers would have kept private, the wide use of autotuned vocals in popular music illustrates how attractive the cyborg persona has become. It also is not surprising that there is a market for software that enables producers to avoid working with live singers completely, such as Sony's Ilona: Universal Female Vocal Toolkit. An article about the program in the magazine *Remix* starts out, "Are you less than confident in the female vocalists you've been working with? Or are you a Paxil-popping agoraphobic afraid to test out the vocal talent pool in your area? Sony Media Software's 'Ilona!' may be of some service" ("Trapped in a Box" 2004, 15). A similar program called Pocket Diva provides, for $29.95, the "royalty-free" voice of a woman singing thousands of single pitches and melodic fragments as well as words and phrases such as "love," "my vision," and "come to me." The attraction of such a voice, made for the periphery and safe from the threat of ever overburdening us, might be understood by anyone who has made a phone call hoping to get the answering machine rather than a real person.

Such a product—part of the software for the modern *vox humana*—might be seen as marking the final stage in the technological dehumanization of music. The ability to speak through multiple borrowed voices seems to grant engineers and producers a kind of power connected with the long history of invisible speech as a sign of divine authority, from the burning bush to the omniscient narrator in film (Abbate 2001, 148). Producers are able to preserve their authorship, the "composer's voice," and, like ventriloquists, to speak through the vocal samples to their listeners while remaining behind the scene. The way in which producers play with our embodied reactions to voices and other sounds raises many issues of gender, race, and class, of course. In the case of the many white DJs, there are countless examples of racial impersonation and minstrelsy—often very much foregrounded and made part of the meaning of the piece. And such ramifications of sampling go far beyond only representations in the works, as, for example, when in concert performances Moby used a live singer to perform the loops originally taken from Alan Lomax's field recordings. The practice of having live musicians take on the role of samplers is increasingly common as producers avoid dealing with copyright issues by re-recording samples in the studio.

Abbate cites Stanley Cavell's view of what ultimately makes automata terrible—namely, the fear that we will discover that we, too, are simply machines, "that we could look down to find our own chests covered by brass plates, ripped open to expose an elegant clockwork within" (2001, 195). From this perspective, we can see the evocation of the uncanny in works using vocal samples such as "Sunday Séance" as an attempt to head off such a realization by summoning up the supernatural and the dead to stabilize our sense of being alive and thus in turn to stabilize the category of the human. The whole notion that there is something problematic about the recorded voice can be seen as representing a kind of nostalgia for all sorts of stabilities that are now called into question.

Similarly, a device such as Kempelen's *vox humana* assumes that there will be a real person operating the keyboard. But if digital technology has made possible the ultimate *vox humana* rather than consolidating power for those operating the machine, there is a remarkable attenuation of authorship and identity associated with sample-based music. It is as if the more voices you borrow, the more you lose your own. In live performances, as Sangild discusses (chapter 7), unlike the diva or virtuoso who commands center stage, electronic musicians tend to stay out of the spotlight. In this repertoire, which leads to posthuman modes of listening where every sound is a potential sample and every voice a potential recorded voice, it is striking that many of these producers seem to view identity as a similar kind of patchwork of multiple personae. Indeed, it is more common than not for producers to release music under multiple names and in very different styles for different audiences (Taylor 2001, 136–144). Thus, in addition to Prefuse 73, Guillermo Scott Herren has produced music under the names "Savath and Savalas," "Piano Overlord," and "Delorasa and Assorda." MF Doom—the rapper Daniel Dumile, who always wears a metal mask in performance—goes by "Mad Villain," "Viktor Vaughn," "Venomous Villain," and "King Geedorah"—all names from Marvel Comics and Godzilla movies. I would regard as another manifestation of the posthuman how little anxiety, loss, and uncertainty appear to accompany this destabilization of identity among these producers; on the contrary, many are astonishingly productive in all of their many personae. By losing our one, "true" voice, we may be gaining the potential to speak through other voices.

Those who write about the liberating potential of the posthuman see such decentering as holding open the possibilities of new models of collective or multiple identities, precisely those forms of rhizomatic subjectivities that flourish on the Internet and digital media (Plant 1997, 136–137). For Hayles, an awareness of the increasingly animate environment in which humans are not the only ones who can "interpret information and create meaning" frees us to "imagine how a world rich in embodied contextual processes might be fashioned to enhance the distributed cognitive systems that surround us and that we ourselves are" (chapter 31 in this volume). Indeed, it seems that there is something surprisingly restorative and calming about surrounding ourselves by all these ubiquitous technologized voices, just as it is for Wall-e. This effect is illustrated by many songs by the Books, a duo that works extensively with vocal samples. Their song "Be Good to Them Always" from the 2005 release *Lost and Safe* assembles a range of everyday and historical voices that provide all the lyrics. At the start of the piece, we can hear the band members singing over and dominating the samples, but as the piece progresses, the balance shifts so that the live voices move to the periphery, part of a virtual chorus accompanying the samples, as if to illustrate the line in the text that speaks of "a mixed consort of soft instruments." The calm dissolution of the famous and unknown voices from different places and times into a collage of fragments produces very little drama and no great sense of mystery or strangeness. Rather, the piece makes the process of losing our voices into the vast archive of recorded sound seem hardly worth noting.

References

Abbate, Carolyn. 2001. *In Search of Opera*. Princeton, NJ: Princeton University Press.

Attali, Jacques. 1996. *Noise: The Political Economy of Music*. Translated by Brian Massumi. Minneapolis: University of Minnesota Press.

Auner, Joseph. 2003. "'Sing It for Me': Posthuman Ventriloquism in Recent Popular Music." *Journal of the Royal Musical Association* 128 (1): 98–122.

Chion, Michel. 1994. *Audio-Vision: Sound on Screen*. Translated by Claudia Gorbman. New York: Columbia University Press.

Connor, Steven. 2001. "The Decomposing Voice of Postmodern Music." *New Literary History* 32 (3): 467–483.

Dickinson, Kay. 2001. "'Believe?' Vocoders, Digitalized Female Identity, and Camp." *Popular Music* 20 (3): 333–347.

Hansen, Mark. 2004. *New Philosophy for New Media*. Cambridge, MA: MIT Press.

Hayles, N. Katherine. 1999. *How We Became Posthuman: Virtual Bodies in Cybernetics, Literature, and Informatics*. Chicago: University of Chicago Press.

Katz, Mark. 2004. *Capturing Sound: How Technology Has Changed Music*. Berkeley and Los Angeles: University of California Press.

Kittler, Friedrich. 1999. *Gramophone, Film, Typewriter*. Translated by Geoffrey Winthrop-Young and Michael Wutz. Stanford, CA: Stanford University Press.

Levine, Mark. 2006. "Vocal Magic." *Electronic Musician* 7 (July): 42–57.

McCracken, Allison. 1999. "'God's Gift to Us Girls': Crooning, Gender, and the Re-Creation of American Popular Song, 1928–1933." *American Music* 17 (4): 365–395.

Nass, Clifford, and Scott Brave. 2005. *Wired for Speech: How Voice Activates and Advances the Human–Computer Relationship*. Cambridge, MA: MIT Press.

Plant, Sadie. 1997. *Zeros and Ones: Digital Women and the New Technoculture*. New York: Doubleday.

Pompino-Marschall, Bernd. 2005. "Kempelen et al. Remarks on the History of Articulatory-Acoustic Modelling." *ZAS Papers in Linguistics* 40:145–159.

Reynolds, Simon. 2006. "Haunted Audio." *The Wire* 273:26–33.

Rose, Tricia. 1994. *Black Noise: Rap Music and Black Culture in Contemporary America*. Hanover, CT: Wesleyan University Press.

Sconce, Jeffrey. 2000. *Haunted Media: Electronic Presence from Telegraphy to Television*. Durham, NC: Duke University Press.

Smith, Jacob. 2008. *Vocal Tracks: Performance and Sound Media*. Berkeley and Los Angeles: University of California Press.

Sterne, Jonathan. 2003. *The Audible Past: Cultural Origins of Sound Reproduction*. Durham, NC: Duke University Press.

Taylor, Timothy D. 2001. *Strange Sounds: Music, Technology, and Culture*. New York: Routledge.

"Trapped in a Box." 2004. *Remix* 4 (May): 15.

Wegenstein, Bernadette. 2006. *Getting under the Skin: The Body and Media Theory*. Cambridge, MA: MIT Press.

Weheliye, Alexander G. 2002. "Feenin': Posthuman Voices in Contemporary Black Pop." *Social Text* 20 (2): 21–47.

Weiser, Mark. 1991. "The Computer for the 21st Century." *Scientific American* 265 (3): 94–104.

Weiser, Mark, and John Seely Brown. 1996. "The Coming Age of Calm Technology." Available at http://nano.xerox.com/hypertext/weiser/acmfuture2endnote.htm. Accessed August 15, 2009.

Weiss, David. 2006. "Cheap Tricks." *Remix* 5 (February): 34–38.

Yelton, Gary. 2006. "Adventures in Vocal Processing: Turning Geese into Song Birds." *Electronic Musician* 7 (November): 45–61.

Discography

Blockhead. *Music by Cavelight*. Ninja Tune, 2004.

The Books. *Lost and Safe*. Tomlab, 2005.

DJ Food and DK. *Now, Listen Again*. Ninja Tune, 2007.

DJ Shadow. *Entroducing.* Fontana Island, 1996.

Jarret, Keith. *Köln Concert.* ECM, 1974.

Madvillain. *Madvillainy.* Stones Throw, 2004.

NAS. *Illmatic.* Columbia Records, 1994.

Pray, Doug, director. *Scratch* (documentary). Palm Pictures, 2002.

Prefuse 73. *Vocal Studies and Uprock Narratives.* Warp Records, 2001.

Ray Sings, Basie Swings. Concord Records, 2007.

Reich Remixed. Nonesuch, 1999.

6 The End of *Flânerie:* iPods, Aesthetics, and Urban Experience

Michael Bull

The use of mobile communication technologies has become integral to our cultural and urban universe—a technology-mediated universe in which an increasing amount of our experience is channeled through a wide array of consumer technologies saturating both public and private spaces (McCarthy 2001). The impact that these technologies have on the fabric of everyday urban life is complex and multifaceted both structurally and individually. This chapter focuses primarily on the aesthetic nature of this influence by examining the use of the first consumer cultural icon of the twenty-first century—the Apple iPod.

The aesthetic construction of urban experience has frequently been viewed through a visually based epistemology in which the figure of the flaneur looms large. The flaneur is thought to re-create the cinematic nature of experience transposed onto the street. The habitual consumption of film and television is thought to feed into how city dwellers might re-create their daily experience in the city street (Morse 1998). In contrast to this primarily visual understanding of urban experience, I investigate the nature of an *audiovisual* aestheticization of the city undertaken by iPod users and in doing so place sound at the heart of everyday aesthetics. I examine and question the nature of the urban aesthetic through the supplementing of vision by sound.

The use of MP3 technologies has become commonplace in the city, with more than 50 percent of the citizens of the industrialized West possessing the ability to create their own privatized and privatizing auditory bubbles as they habitually move through the city.[1] My analysis draws upon primary data collected from more than one thousand iPod users worldwide.[2] It questions the relevance of contemporary understandings of the flaneur as an explanatory tool for the aesthetic practices of iPod users and simultaneously dismisses alternative critiques of *flânerie* based on a range of premises, which attribute the modern nature of cities, their architecture, and how we move through it as symbolizing the end of *flânerie* (Young 2006). In effect, both views are wrong. I critique both the proponents of *flânerie* and their critics—replacing them with an empirically grounded analysis that furthers our understanding of contemporary forms of mobile, technologically mediated forms of urban aesthetics. To be clear, I am not stating that no such thing as *flânerie* exists in contemporary urban culture; forms of *flânerie* might exist in the appropriation of artistic databases or in the appropriation of dominant landmarks and their attendant artistic installations.[3] Rather, I am claiming that it is not a useful concept through which to understand the daily experience of millions of iPod users.

Flânerie and iPod Use

Technology has come to the aid of the senses, enhancing and diminishing them, reconfiguring them and empowering them. It was Walter Benjamin (1973) who first alerted us to the transformative power of film on human cognition as, indeed, it was his writings that reintroduced the concept of the flaneur into mainstream cultural and urban studies. The placing of earphones over (or in) the ears, an intrinsic element of iPod use, transforms the historical adage that the ears are the most democratic of the senses, democratic precisely because of their passivity in the face of the auditory. The science-fiction writer William Gibson captured in his description of the first mobile auditory technology the intensity of this auditory "privatization": "The Sony Walkman has done more to change human perception than any virtual reality gadget. I can't remember any technological experience since that was quite so wonderful as being able to take music and move it through landscapes and architecture" (1993, 49). iPod users differ from Walkman users in the users' ability to carry around their whole musical collection with them in the form of dedicated playlists or through the random workings of the machine's shuffle capacity. It is in this ability to micromanage the relationship between mediated audition, space, place, and cognition that a more "listening" self develops to distinguish iPod users from Walkman users (Bull 2007).

Linearism as a mode of urban appropriation is representative of the dominance of the visual in urban and cultural studies (Amin and Thrift 2002; Friedberg 1993; Jenks 1995a; Tester 1994; Tonkiss 2005). The flaneur in this literature is understood as a rootless, displaced subject who places herself in the shoes of the "other"—imagining what the world would be like from the position of the other. *Flânerie* is an act of alienated integration representing a quest to understand the other, albeit in imaginary terms, and is "characterized by its very receptive disposition, a mode of embracing rather than of excluding external impulses" (Gleber 1999, 26). Benjamin also understood the flaneur as representing the image of the outsider, yet in contemporary rhetoric the term *flânerie* has become universalized—we all become flaneurs in a sanitized image of urban relations in which *flânerie* is an integral part of the "tourist" gaze (Urry 2000). Integral to an understanding of contemporary *flânerie* is that the city is understood in some sense as "filmic," that our media experience in the home is reproduced in our apprehension of the urban street: "As a social and textual construct of mobile visuality, *flânerie* can be historically situated as an urban phenomenon linked in gradual ways to the new aesthetic of reception found in 'movie-going.' . . . [A]n increased centrality of the mobile gaze [is] a fundamental feature of everyday life" (Friedberg 1993, 3).

The visual aesthetic embodied in the contemporary gaze is asserted in terms of its empirical veracity and as a conceptual tool through which to understand the nature of our appropriation of the city: "The *flâneur*, though grounded in everyday life, is an analytical form, a narrative device, an attitude towards knowledge and its social context. It is an image of movement through the social space of modernity" (Jenks 1995b, 146).

In its aesthetic appropriation of urban space, flaneurism is understood as both pleasurable and inconsequential: "The technology of aesthetic spacing makes the eye into the primary aperture through which the pleasures the crowded space has to offer can be taken in. . . . The beauty of 'aesthetic control'—the unclouded beauty, beauty unspoiled by the fear of danger, guilty conscience or apprehension of shame—is its inconsequentiality" (Bauman 1993, 168).

The city thus becomes a stimulating, enticing, and rich force—a place of difference in which the subject's emotional and cognitive engagement with it is characterized by intensity. The flaneur becomes representative of the person for whom movement and aesthetics are fused. This aesthetic colonization of urban space becomes an integral part of an urban tale whereby experience is synonymous with technological experience. This technological structure to experience is both pervasive and increasingly taken for granted in wide areas of daily life. The age of mechanical reproduction is the age of mediation—from the birth of the telegraph to the most recent developments of ubiquitous computing articulated in the present volume—wherein mediated experience is quickly becoming "second nature" to many. This pervasiveness is simultaneously empowering and dependent for contemporary consumers inasmuch as they tend to be operationalized only through communication technologies (Bull 2000, 2007). For the iPod user, the aesthetic re-creation of her environment is invariably associated with intense, privatized music reception. The use of earpieces placed directly into the ears connects the user with her environment, integrating and assimilating her into the world, yet in a transcendent manner whereby her everyday experience is transformed through the medium of sound. In doing so, urban space undergoes a reenchantment precisely through the sonic sounds of the culture industry (Horkheimer and Adorno 1973). In chapter 7 of this volume, Torben Sangild discusses the atmospheric nature of sonic places and the way in which they interact with the experiencing subject. iPod users implicitly deny the "objective" nature of any soundworld by re-creating it as their own. In creating a hermetically sealed mobile bubble of sound whose characteristics might be represented in terms of a saturation of the users' soundworld, both immediate and intense, iPod users appear on the face of it useful candidates for contemporary flaneurism inasmuch as the aestheticizing potential of this "totalizing" technology permits them to aesthetically re-create their environment at will. Indeed, early accounts of Walkman use often drew upon notions of *flânerie* to explain the technology's aestheticizing potential (Chambers 1994; Hosokawa 1984). Mobile forms of audiovisual experience were thus welded seamlessly to previous accounts of the visually experienced city, reducing the audiovisual to the visual. However, the privatized audiovisual re-creation of urban experience is diametrically opposed to *flânerie*. The audiovisual dimension of experience demands a different explanation than the merely visual.

The Filmic City

iPod users often describe the city in filmic terms, yet this visual aesthetic is not a form of *flânerie*. The world experienced as a movie script in which the user takes command is a common description of iPod users. The world and the users' experience within it gain significance through their enveloping and privatized soundworld. iPod users invariably prefer to listen to their music loud, providing them with an overwhelming sense of presence while simultaneously blocking out any sound from the environment that might sully the heightened and empowering pleasure of use.

> The world looks friendlier, happier, and sunnier when I walk down the street with my iPod on. It feels as if I'm in a movie at times. Like my life has a soundtrack now. It also takes away some of the noise of the streets, so that everything around me becomes calmer somewhat. It detaches me from my environment, like I'm an invisible, floating observer. (Berklee)
>
> I find when listening to some music choices I feel like I'm not really there. Like I'm watching everything around me happening in a movie. I start to feel the environment in the sense of the mood of the song and can find that I can start to love a street that I usually hate, or feel scared for no reason. (Susan)
>
> I'll pick music that complements the weather, and that can alter the outlook on the world around me. I can take joy in otherwise gloomy, rainy, dank weather by putting on something wonderfully gloomy and dank, something I love to hear. It's a fine synergy of the visual and auditory environments. It makes me feel like I'm walking through my own movie, with my own soundtrack. The people around me look like extras on the set. I see myself in the third person. (Angie)

The conditioning of the filmic in the creation of a personalized audiovisual aesthetic is prominent in these accounts of iPod use, so it is useful to interpret the dynamic of aesthetic appropriation in some detail. For the most part, users claim that the aesthetic principle tends to be dependent on the use of their iPods. Users will pick playlists or fast forward to music tracks that suit either their mood or their surroundings. In Berklee's account, the environment is transformed by the music played; indeed, the environment becomes a function of individualized sound. The listener becomes an auditory spectator. Yet, as in Susan's account, the iPod user is also dependent on the music in order to re-create specific moods or images within his urban experience. Angie picks music that will enhance the environment—that suits her mood. It is important to recognize the cognitive strategies being employed here. The world is being aesthetically reproduced in conformity to the user's mood or the mood of the music listened to. iPod users aim to create a privatized sound world that is in harmony with their mood, orientation, and surroundings, enabling them to recapitalize urban experience through a process more akin to solipsistic aestheticization. Rather than reaching out to understand or see the "otherness" of the city as "otherness," they aim to create habitually an aesthetically pleasing urban world for themselves in their own image. This is an intensely pleasurable world; indeed, Benjamin himself described the visually orientated flaneur in terms of the intoxification of urban experience. Yet the visual might be conceived of in terms of a level of discontinuity—distractions, the opening and shutting of the eyes—leading urban theorists to articulate the modern city in terms of the experience of *Erlebnis.* The audiovisual experience of the urban is more readily understood, however, through the continuity of experience through which the subject attempts to integrate experience into a unified whole—the experience of *Erfahrung.* Joseph Auner discusses the reception of the mechanized voice in terms of the posthuman or fragmentary nature of experience (chapter 5 in this volume), whereas iPod users appear to be more concerned with the integrating and centering of their experience. Theirs is a strategy of bringing the world in line with their cognitive predispositions—indeed, doing so is an act of mimicry. This aesthetic appropriation of urban space is one cognitive strategy operationalized as they attempt to create a seamless web of mediated and privatized experience in their everyday movement through the city, enhancing virtually any chosen experience in any geographical location at will. Aesthetic enhancement is a central strategy taken by iPod users as they bring the city into themselves as a habitable presence. It would be a mistake, however, to understand this appropriation merely in terms of the audiovisual. All media reorient the senses; indeed, the history of the media is one of sensory enhancement and deprivation. iPod users often report, for example, a diminishing of their sense of touch as they weave through the crowded city, which makes this movement more pleasurable. Use might equally become dysfunctional for users if the environment they move through is too loud—meaning that they can hear the sounds of the underground train, for example, or that they are subject to too much interruption by others. The seamlessness of experience is paramount to iPod users.

Derealized Others

If urban spaces are aestheticized in relation to the users' cognition and music, then what of other people? The city as a place of otherness is one of its defining features (Sennett 1990). How then do iPod users interpret the existence of others?

For some reason, Talking Heads seems to work best for this. Like, I will look at an old woman with a cane, and imagine her singing one lyric. Then move on to a hip-hop style teenage boy, and have him sing the next line. My imagination really can take off. It sometimes makes me laugh and smile to myself—especially if a particularly amusing line comes up. It really does transform my surroundings—I sort of feel like I'm in my own music video. (Karen)

It removes an external layer. I see people and things as inanimate or not-fully-connected. It seems that I have an external connection they lack. It's quite odd, actually. . . . Yes. With the iPod and news talk radio files, I am having an interactive session with the anchor. When I look at the people around me, they appear to be two dimensional and without significance. (Mark)

On my walk to work, I'm leaving downtown and walking across a river into a neighbourhood of small shops and restaurants, so it's quite pleasant. The music helps me feel like I'm leaving dreary downtown and going someplace happy. On my way home, it transforms my path from "the path home" into "the path to whatever I'm going to be doing." Sometimes I'll use it to ignore homeless people, because they're always asking for change, and I carry none. (John)

City life is invariably about surfaces—the superficial reading and the transitory clues involved in our observations of others, hence the overriding dominance of the visual in urban culture. Connectivity—if it occurs—is largely virtual for iPod users. The "personalization" of the user's soundworld imbues the street and others with its own atmosphere in which the world appears intimate and endowed with significance. Karen gives roles out to others while listening to the Talking Heads—the world mimics and moves to the rhythm of the music. Other users refer to the absent-derealized nature of the other as they view them through their own soundworld. For other users, the bright-hued colors of the city enacted through iPod use permit them to neutralize the messy, grimy side of the city that confronts them. Hence, the other is made into the image of the iPod user or neutralized to make the city a habitable space.

Although derealization is a dominant motif of iPod use, it would be a mistake to hypostasize the totality of separation. Not all urban space is devoid of interest or narrative for users. Use might sometimes heighten a user's sense of place—, for instance, in walking by the sea, whereby the physicality and smell of the sea are heightened by the user's chosen music, making her feel—at the very least—more connected to her environment. This connectivity differs from the experience of audiowalks and augmented-reality settings in museums, where users are either focused on the specifics of the activity or are being directed toward certain forms of connectivity, narrative, and histories. I am concerned here more with the mundane everyday life practices of aestheticization. It is important to note that the interface between technologies and use is subject to a series of strategic possibilities based on the user's cognitive orientation, the technology itself, and the place–space within which the activity takes place (Bull 2000).

Cosmopolitanism in the iPod

In early discussions of flaneurism, the flaneur was interpreted as integral to the cosmopolitan city. The cosmopolitan image of city life is at least partially a function of life on the street (Simmel 1997). Through interacting with and being open to experience, the urban citizen contributes to the rich fabric of city life. Yet although many iPod users report enjoying city life, theirs is a mediated experience of the pleasures of the city. They frequently view the city through the products of the culture industry in the form of music, talking books, and the iPod itself:

> I refer to my iPod as my pace maker, it helps me find that place. I almost exclusively Travel to NYC when not in London. I have a dedicated playlist called "NY State of Mind"[;] this includes a lot of New York rap music and NY/ East coast Jazz. Something With N.Y. in the lyrics, but also the sophistication, edge and energy of the place. (Sami)
>
> It makes NY City feel like a happy place—a place where taxi's don't honk. . . . [A]lso, it Always helps adjust my mood—if I'm listening to John Denver, I am happy go lucky—If it is AC/DC, I'm feeling like a New Yorker. (Susie)

In these examples, the meaning of city spaces itself derives from the user's playlist. Cosmopolitanism becomes a fictional reality existing in the often eclectic mix of music contained in the iPod, in the user's music collection itself. For many iPod users, the pleasure of the city comes not from interacting with others, who would "disrupt" and "distract" their energy, but rather from listening to music that might remind them of what it is to live in a city. This mediated cosmopolitanism is encased in the user's iPod.

Although the audiovisual is dominant in iPod use, it is not a form of *flânerie*; rather, iPod users aim to create a privatized soundworld that is in harmony with their mood, orientation, and surroundings, enabling them to respecialize urban experience through a process of solipsistic aestheticization. They aim to create an aesthetically pleasing urban world for themselves as a constituent part of their everyday life. The aesthetic appropriation of urban space becomes one cognitive strategy as they attempt to create a seamless web of mediated and privatized experience in their everyday movement through the city, enhancing virtually any chosen experience in any geographical location at will. They create an illusion of omnipotence through mediated proximity and "connectedness" engendered by the use of their iPod. Susan Kozel asks how we should exist and move through the world, pointing implicitly to a notion of recognition as fundamental to a sense of the "other" (chapter 19 in this volume), and Georgina Born (2011) asks, How can we understand the transformations of auditory media in relation to the modes of experience they afford? Jonathan Sterne has traced the historical technological antecedents to this auditory solipsism (audile technique is based on the listener's *individuation*), arguing that "the auditory field produced through technicized listening becomes a kind of personal space" (2003, 158). iPod users resemble Christopher Lasch's "minimal self" in which the user withdraws into a world small enough to exert total control over it. This is not a technological argument, but rather a cultural one; nor is it an argument that pits direct interaction against mediated interaction, but rather one that poses the question as to how shared space is managed and what might be the consequences of this form of mediated solipsism. Forms of urban reciprocity, urban recognition, are habitually denied within iPod use. The empowerment of the subject implies an incipient crises in the way in which users "recognize" the other (Honneth 1995). Although aestheticization has traditionally been viewed as both pleasurable and inconsequential—the world remains untouched by the aesthetic mode—iPod practices highlight its relational quality, which contains cognitive and moral resonances. iPod users' aestheticizing impulse highlights the users' underlying values and their relation to the "other" and to the spaces passed through.

Nonspaces, Automobiles, Speed, and iPod Use

Alternative critics of contemporary *flânerie* point to the role that automobiles play in the city, in which the city is no longer a walking city, but a driving or transit one. Large areas of the city are given over to transportation systems, relegating the pedestrian to a bit part of city life. The very nature of driving facilitates against *flânerie* because the driver focuses on merely the road ahead, qualitatively devaluing the journey itself to the instrumental task of arriving at one's destination (Young 2006). The speed of modern cities is also thought to destroy the conditions for aimless strolling, a key feature of *flânerie*. At best, all that remains are tourist flaneurs on their "three day itineraries" (White 2001, 27). Added to these adverse urban conditions is the very architectural nature of the modern city. Essential to the health of the flaneur, it is argued, is the city's strangeness and uniqueness. Modern cities, in contrast, are defined by their essential similarity—a bland internationally homogenous architecture—whose coupling with the suburbanization of the city results in the proliferation of nonspaces that work against aestheticization (Auge 1995).

Although dismissing *flânerie* as a largely inappropriate concept through which to understand the aesthetics of the city, at least in the daily experience of iPod users, alternative rejections of *flânerie* based largely on the architectural anonymity of modern cities, their attendant modes of transportation, and the speed of daily life also misunderstand the aesthetics of iPod users.

The creation of modern cities into increasingly privatized and mobile nodules within which citizens move either in their automobiles or on foot with headphones firmly on might be described in terms of urban chill (Bull 2007). The use of communication technologies such as the iPod and car radios warm up the users' space of habitation as they commune with others (through mobile phones) or the products of the culture industry (through their musical narrative encased within their iPods). Urban chill thus resides in the streets we walk through, the buildings we pass by, the modern shopping centers we are inevitably drawn to, the anonymous spaces of airports, train stations, parking lots, and the endless motorways that many of us progressively live in as we shuttle backward and forward in our cars, on public transport, or on foot. Marc Auge (1995) uses in his analysis of urban space the term *nonspace* to describe an urban culture of semiologically denuded spaces—shopping centers, airports, motorways, and the like. He thinks of these invariably architecturally bland spaces as if they had been dropped onto the urban landscape at random. Who can tell one shopping center from another, for example? From this perspective, urban spaces increasingly function as the endless transit zones of urban culture—emblems of the increasingly mobile nature of urban culture.

However, with iPod use, any urban space can become a nonspace. The defining feature of our relationship to urban space is not necessarily how culturally situated that space might be. For iPod users, any urban space might become a "nonspace"; their relationship with this space is not dependent on the anthropological nature of the space itself, but increasingly on the technologically empowered subjective response to that space or, indeed, on the prior negation of that space through the users' cognitive predilections. Just as the placing of earphones over the ears empowers the ear, so the urban subject is free to re-create the city in his or her own image through the power of sound, as the following iPod user indicates very aptly: "When I plug in and turn on, my iPod does a 'ctrl+alt+delete' on my surroundings and allows me to 'be' somewhere else" (Wes).

iPod users resemble the imaginative city dwellers that aesthetically re-create any chosen space at will. Furthermore, the iPod permits users to control and manage their urban experience, reclaiming the time of the commute, whether it is achieved by traveling on foot, on public transport, or by automobile. In the process, time becomes subjectivized, and speed is brought into the user's rhythm. "I view people more like choices when I'm wearing my iPod. Instead of being forced to interact with them, I get to decide. It's almost liberating to realize you don't have to be polite or smile or do anything. I get to move through time and space at my speed [and] my pace" (Andrea).

iPod users equally use their iPods in their automobiles as well as in the street, thus further removing them from those on the street, and although drivers tend to focus on the road while driving, they also engage in a wide range of behaviors while doing so. Drivers habitually listen to their iPod or car radios and use their mobile phones while driving. Many drivers are forced to drive in daily gridlock with others to and from work—prisoners in their cars, often forced out of living in the city by the cost or in search of space and the domestic and privatized life of the suburbs. Automobile habitation provides the driver with his or her own regulated soundscape. Inside the car, the process of placing oneself elsewhere is similar to the strategies other users employ while walking down the street:

> Driving in the countryside of Indiana does not quite take as much concentration as driving through the rush hour traffic in London. I usually set my car on "cruise control" and just keep an eye on the traffic in front of me (which is not too heavy here in Indiana). The songs transform me to all kind of places in my life. . . . And that is what I love about the "shuffle" feature. Whenever a "childhood" song comes on, I "feel" like I am back in my parents' house. Then a track from an Australian band might bring me back to the 2 years I have spent in Sydney. I sometimes don't even remember that I have passed certain "points" on my drive from or to work. This thing is a wonderful "time machine" and is better than any diary. (Jerome)

The nostalgic use of music to place the subject elsewhere is merely one use of the iPod in the car. Drivers tend to reclaim space by privatizing it. The aural space of the automobile becomes a safe, pleasurable, and intimate environment. The structural nature of contemporary cities—with their traffic, global architecture, and swift rhythms—is managed through communication technologies such as the iPod, enabling users to bring under control, at least cognitively, what it means to live in the city. Mediated forms of aestheticization are central to these user strategies.

Sound both colonizes the listener and actively re-creates and reconfigures the spaces of experience. Through the power of a privatized soundworld, the world becomes intimate, known, and possessed. Imagination is mediated by the sounds of the iPod, which become an essential component of the ability to imagine at all. iPod users construct an aesthetic narrative to the city deciphered from the sounds of the culture industry emanating from their iPods. In doing so, they become the center of their world: "The world looks smaller—I am much bigger and more powerful listening to music. The world is generally a better place, or at the very least it is sympathetic to my mood" (Sophie).

The world is brought into line through a privatized yet mediated act of cognition. Yet aestheticization has utopian implications for users. To aestheticize is to transcend the mundane world as it is experienced. Aestheticization remains an active mode of appropriating the urban, transforming that which exists, making it the user's own. In this process of aestheticization, iPod users transform the world in conformity with their predispositions; the world becomes a mimetic fantasy in which its "otherness" in various guises is negated. Space itself becomes technologized; experience becomes real through technological appropriation—or hyper-real precisely through its technologization. iPod users prefer to live in this technologized space whereby experience is brought under control. The twenty-first-century city is the space of the iPod user, not the flaneur.

Notes

1. The majority of these users possess mobile phones with MP3 capability. Jean Baudrillard was ahead of his time in stating that "to each his own bubble; that is the law today" (1993, 39). The predisposition to privatize ones experience while on the move is prefigured by the development of the automobile (Sachs 1992).

2. For details, refer to Bull 2007.

3. See, for instance, Delphine Benezet's (2009) analysis of how visitors understood an historical database of Los Angeles from 1920 to 1986 and Devin Zuber's (2006) analysis of the artworks surrounding Ground Zero.

References

Amin, Ash, and Nigel Thrift. 2002. *Cities: Re-Imagining the Urban.* Cambridge, UK: Polity.

Auge, Marc. 1995. *Non-Places: Introduction to Anthropology of Supermodernity.* Translated by John Howe. London: Verso.

Baudrillard, Jean. 1993. *Symbolic Exchange and Death.* Translated by Iain Hamilton Grant. London: Sage.

Bauman, Zygmunt. 1993. *Postmodern Ethics.* Oxford: Blackwell.

Benezet, Delphine. 2009. "Recombinant Poetics, Urban *Flânerie*, and Experimentation in the Database Narrative Bleeding Through: Layers of Los Angeles 1920–1986." *Convergence: The International Journal of Research into New Media Technologies* 15:55–74.

Benjamin, Walter. 1973. *Illuminations.* Translated by Harry Zohn. London: Penguin.

Born, Georgina. 2011. *Music, Sound, and the Transformation of Public and Private Space.* Cambridge: Cambridge University Press.

Bull, Michael. 2007. *Sound Moves: iPod Culture and Urban Experience.* London: Routledge.

Bull, Michael. 2000. *Sounding Out the City: Personal Stereos and the Management of Everyday Life.* Oxford: Berg.

Chambers, Ian. 1994. *Migrancy, Culture, and Identity.* London: Routledge.

Freidberg, Anne. 1993. *Window Shopping: Cinema and the Postmodern.* Berkeley and Los Angeles: University of California Press.

Gibson, William. 1993. "The Walkman." *Time Out*, October 6.

Gleber, Anne. 1999. *The Art of Taking a Walk: Flânerie, Literature, and Film in Weimar Culture*. Princeton, NJ: Princeton University Press.

Honneth, Axel. 1995. *The Fragmented World of the Social: Essays in Social and Political Philosophy*. Albany: State University of New York Press.

Horkheimer, Max, and Theodor W. Adorno. 1973. *The Dialectic of Enlightenment*. Translated by John Cumming. London: Penguin.

Hosakawa, Sushei. 1984. "The Walkman Effect." *Popular Music* 4:165–180.

Jenks, Chris, ed. 1995a. *Visual Culture*. London: Routledge.

Jenks, Chris. 1995b. "Watching Your Step: The History and Practice of the Flâneur." In *Visual Culture*, edited by Chris Jenks, 142–160. London Routledge.

McCarthy, Anna. 2001. *Ambient Television: Visual Culture and Public Space*. Durham, NC: Duke University Press.

Morse, Margaret. 1998. *Virtualities: Television, Media Art, and Cyberculture*. Bloomington: Indiana University Press.

Sachs, W. 1992. *For Love of the Automobile: Looking Back into the History of Our Desires*. Berkeley: University of California Press.

Sennett, Richard. 1990. *The Conscience of the Eye*. London: Faber.

Simmel, George. 1997. *Simmel on Culture*. London: Sage.

Sterne, Jonathan. 2003. *The Audible Past: Cultural Origins of Sound Reproduction*. Durham, NC: Duke University Press.

Tester, Kieth, ed. 1994. *The Flâneur*. London: Routledge.

Tonkiss, Fran. 2005. *Space, the City, and Social Theory: Social Relations and Urban Forms*. Cambridge, UK: Polity Press.

Urry, John. 2000. *Sociology beyond Societies: Mobilities for the Twenty-First Century*. London: Routledge.

White, Edward. 2001. *The Flâneur—a Stroll through the Paradoxes of Paris*. London: Bloomsbury Books.

Young, Sherman. 2006. "Morphings and Ur-Forms: From *Flâneur* to Driveur." *Scandinavian Journal of Media Arts Culture* 3 (3): 1–9.

Zuber, Devin. 2006. "*Flânerie* at Ground Zero: Aesthetic Countermemories in Lower Manhattan." *American Quarterly* 58 (2): 269–299.

7 Virtual Space and Atmosphere in Electronic Music

Torben Sangild

Music is everywhere. It emanates from radios, stereos, earphones; indoors and outdoors; in public and private spaces. Technological development is constantly taking this diffusion further, allowing music everywhere and allowing individual choices of music through embedded and portable media. In light of this development, two concepts seem to be of increasing importance in understanding our perception of music: virtual space and atmosphere.

Music endows spaces with significant atmospheric qualities; it contributes to the characteristics of spaces and situations, whether it is played at low or high volume, whether we like it or not. It can do that only insofar as it possesses these atmospheric qualities within its own virtual space.

In order to understand the spatiality of ambient sounds and mobile devices, it is necessary to analyze the virtual spatiality of music itself before moving on to the different blendings of this space with real and changing spatialities in individual as well as social listening situations.

The virtual space is understood as the relative spatial organization and the spatial qualities of the sounds as they are produced on a phonograph—that is, a musical track. This concept is of particular importance in understanding electronic music and sound collages. The virtual space has different relations to the listening space—the particular space in which the music is played out—depending on the listening situation. It is *projected out* into the listening space when transmitted through loudspeakers, whereas it is *superimposed* on the surrounding space when listened to through headphones. In both instances, there is the rudimentary element of a "mixed reality" or, rather, a "mixed spatiality" and a "mixed atmosphere," one might say.

The mainstream technological means of sound production and distribution point toward ubiquity and ubiquitous computing in several ways: we are able to carry our music with us everywhere, listening through headphones and plugging our MP3 device into amplifier/loudspeaker systems in private and public places, sharing our preprogrammed playlists with others. New Internet services enable us to access gigantic music repertoires on subscription terms on the fly via mobile phones. The mobility and creative playability of phonographs will probably increase to a point where storage and playing devices can be implemented and designed to be almost invisible sources of atmospheres.

Atmosphere plays an important role in electronic music in general and in ambient electronica in particular, where sounds pervade virtual spaces—virtually transcending the limits of physical laws. Electronic music is liberated from the playing musician and the myths of subjective expression but is nevertheless an essentially corporeal phenomenon.

This chapter examines the interrelations between electronic music, virtual space, and atmosphere, arguing that the experienced musical atmosphere is a blending of the sonic atmosphere of the virtual space with the general atmosphere of the listening space, wherein the former is usually dominant. The electronica soundtrack as a multispatial phenomenon, the electronica concert as immersive ambience, and iPod listening as superimposition of atmospheres are addressed as special instances of atmosphere and space with their own aesthetics of ubiquity and mixed spatiality.

Atmosphere as a General Aesthetic Concept

Atmosphere is related to moods and therefore also to emotions. But it is not a subjective thing. When you enter a room, you also "enter" an atmosphere with certain qualities that affect you more or less. It is possible to register the mood in a certain place without taking part in it. Indeed, it is quite possible to be subjectively melancholic at a party while registering the merry mood of the surrounding people and the space in general. *Atmosphere* is a broader, slightly less affective term than *mood* and relates to spaces in general. It is far from a subjective state of mind, even though it exists only through being perceived by subjects.

The idea of an atmosphere as an objective (or quasi-objective) mood may sound slightly esoteric, but atmosphere is in fact a very concrete phenomenon that we experience every day: the clinical atmosphere at a specific hospital; the merry atmosphere at a specific party; the solemn atmosphere in a specific cathedral. These descriptions are crude, categorical characterizations of complex and singular phenomena. The room you are located in right now has its very own atmosphere that cannot be reduced to one adjective but can be very difficult to describe in words. Indeed, the atmosphere is a gestalt product of every sensuous thing in a space: the light, the smell, the colors, the architecture, and the objects, their material qualities and placements, the people and their behavior—and, of course, the sounds. All these and many more elements take part in the atmosphere in outdoor as well as indoor spaces. Pervasive information technology affords significant extensions of atmospheric design possibilities.

This concept of atmosphere is inspired by German philosopher Gernot Böhme, who has endeavored to delineate an aesthetics of atmospheres. He defines atmosphere as follows:

- "An indefinite, spatially outpoured quality of emotion"[1] (1995, 27).
- "Quasi-objective emotions" (2001, 48).
- "Objectlike emotions, which are randomly cast into a space" (2000, 15).

It is clear that the concept of atmosphere combines emotions, space, and objectivity.[2] Another important characteristic of an atmosphere is that it is not solid or localizable within the space but is rather an inevitable product of that space. Atmospheres are "*quasi*-objective" in that a total distancing is not possible; without a certain amount of sensible investment on behalf of the subject, atmospheres are not accessible. They are thus not things, but rather "half-things" (Böhme 2001, 46) or "in-betweens" (Böhme 2000, 15). In some formulations of the theory, Böhme distinguishes between "ingression" and "discrepancy" in the experience of atmospheres (2001, 46–50). In the ingressive experience, one takes part in the atmosphere and lets it dominate one's subjective mood, whereas in the discrepancy experience the atmosphere is perceived as different from one's subjective mood.

With these thoughts, Böhme has managed to make an important aesthetic concept out of something hitherto so vague and subtle that it has been relegated to everyday language and tacit knowledge. At the same time, there are many problems in Böhme's aesthetics, the most important being the reduction of all aesthetic phenomena to questions of atmosphere: nature, urban culture, design, commercials, and all the arts are essentially or exclusively about atmosphere, according to Böhme (1995, 7–12, 46–48, and 1998, 73). I argue that atmosphere is a useful and pertinent concept to describe only one aspect among many in the understanding of aesthetic phenomena and aesthetic experience.[3]

In addition, how important this aspect is varies. If we look at the arts, some types of artworks are more "atmospheric" than others, meaning that this aspect is more prominent in the aesthetic expression. The atmospheric aspect is more important in an installation by Bill Viola than it is in a conceptual work by Lawrence Weiner; it is far more prominent in Proust than in Aesop's fables, more in films by Andrei Tarkovsky than in films by Luis Buñuel, and more in ambient music than in house music. For music where the atmosphere is a dominating aspect, I use the term *atmospheric music*.

Music and Atmosphere

Sound has a strong impact on the atmosphere of a space. Music in particular, even when played at low volume, affects the atmosphere significantly. Böhme calls music "the fundamental atmospheric art" (2000, 16). This effect is key in most film music, where music, often unnoticed, frames the way we perceive a certain scene and enhances the characters' emotional expression.

Using muzak and György Ligeti's notes for his composition *Atmosphères* as examples, Böhme seems to locate atmospheric music in the background as well as to locate the background *in* music (1998, 71–75). *Music as background* accentuates its abilities to create an atmosphere in a room, getting little or no attention. This is known not only in muzak, but also in older forms of entertainment and dinner music as well as in certain types of sound design and ambient music installations. *The background in music* probably stems from the idea that in traditional music we perceive lead instruments, lead vocals, melody, and other salient elements as a foreground or figure. Behind these foreground elements, we often find an accompaniment or atmospheric layer of music that supports the foreground. Musical "events" happen in the foreground rather than in the background. Ligeti's idea is that if he eliminates the foreground, the conspicuous musical events, the pauses, and the action in favor of the musical background, a flow of textural sound, he will obtain purely atmospheric music. We find here an obvious anticipation of ambient music in which these "background" elements are often all there is.[4]

However, Böhme's idea implies two logical problems that must be solved. First, background music and music as background are two distinct things that must be differentiated, as shown in the previous descriptions of them. Second, to claim that music is essentially atmospheric and that the musical atmosphere is in the background is to say that music is essentially background, which does not make sense. The solution to this problem is to accept aspects of music other than the atmospheric and to differentiate between the atmospheric and atmosphere. The atmosphere of music must include its foreground events, which by definition also have atmospheric qualities. With this in mind, we can nevertheless talk about certain background qualities as *quintessentially* atmospheric and to say that these qualities work primarily as atmospheric qualities rather than as focused events. Textural sonic webs; sustained sounds that float and perhaps change gradually; significant use of reverb; soft and blurred sounds that have no clear borders or sharp edges—these types of musical sound will normally work primarily as atmospheric aesthetic agents. For the same reason, they are prominent in ambient music.

Thus, the atmosphere may be concentrated in the traditional background of music, but a more precise description would arise from regarding the atmosphere as the aspect that reveals itself when one doesn't approach the individual sound objects as distinct entities with clear borders but instead focuses on their "ecstasies"—that is, "ways in which a thing goes out of itself and modifies the sphere of its surroundings" (Böhme 2000, 15). This is the reason why the atmosphere is more obvious in types of music with blurred, vague, and sustained sound objects.[5] Sounds that are abrupt, percussive, clearly located, and profiled will rather be perceived as individual entities or agents that may be in dialog with other elements but have their own borders and identity. Nevertheless, of course, they affect the atmosphere as musical gestalt.

In this chapter, the focus is on electronic music, where musical gestures are separated from playing musicians and become gestures of the musical objects themselves. The dismissal of subject-oriented ideas of expression is a challenge for music discourse in all genres, but it appears most clearly when there simply are no disturbing playing bodies. The *experience* of electronic music, however, is no less bodily than other types of music, despite rumors to the contrary (see Sangild 2002).

Virtual Space in Electronic Music

A specific example might illustrate the virtual space of musical tracks: "Gyroscope" by Boards of Canada.[6] The virtual space of this track actually consists of three separate, interplaying spaces: the moving from left to right of "waves" of percussive beats in the foreground; the all-over dominance of the synthesizer-played-backward sounds; and the muffled and distorted voice of a child counting. Added to these elements are a few noise sounds. Thus, the sound objects do not form one homogenous space. The percussive sounds reverberate in a big virtual space; the synth sounds are without reverb, like a flat panel in the middle; and the voice appears strongly mediated through a bad microphone and at the same time as if stifled under a pillow. This voice, like the synthesizer, is placed at the center of the soundscape. The virtual spaces are incompatible and nevertheless coexist in the stereophonic soundscape. Thus, we have two levels of virtual space: the space of each sound object and the overall spatial collage where the different sound objects are related. The latter, the relative positioning of sound objects, may be called the "sound stage"—an overall three-dimensional virtual space entailing the various sound objects, each of which often has its own virtual spatiality. This spatial arrangement is actually strange, rudimentary, and inconsistent, but we nevertheless accept it when listening.

In some compositions, there is only one consistent virtual space that the sound objects are experienced as sharing. The sound sources may still come from highly different environments, but the sounds are processed in a way that creates the experience of one shared space. This single shared space is actually the ideal of composers such as Trevor Wishart and Denis Smalley—not only in their own compositional practice, but also as a normative standard for electronic music in general that one should rarely and only carefully deviate from (Smalley 1996, 93; Wishart 1996, 147). The most common space in electronic music, especially in electronica, is, however, a heterogeneous space composed of several virtual spaces.

What I call "virtual space" has also been called "perceived acoustic space" (Wishart 1996, 140), "implied space" (Emmerson 1998, 137), "internal space" (Bayle 2007, 243), "musical space," "composed space" and "imagined space" (Smalley 1996, 90–93). I call the space of the musical track a "virtual" space in order to make sure that it is not understood as a metaphorical or allusive space, but rather as an immediate perceptive experience of spaciousness.[7]

I use the term *virtual* in its common and traditional sense: possessing all or many of the sensuous qualities of the real except the ontological status of being real. The virtual is a perceptual rather than an ontological reality. Visual examples of virtual space include mirrors, painterly depth perspective, and photographic as well as filmic space.[8]

This concept of virtuality differs from that of "virtual reality" in that the virtual space is not interactive in the sense that the listener can navigate on individual paths through the space. The listener is fixed in relation to the virtual space. It is not a metaphorical space, for it does not present itself as an imposed image but works directly on the senses. It is just as immediate as an illusion, but it is not an illusion insofar as it is incomplete, and one does not have to believe that it is real.

The virtual spaces of electronic music do not have all the qualities of real spaces and are often arranged as collages of spatial elements. Nevertheless, they have enough auditory spatial qualities to create the experience of space. The most obvious example is the depth of the stereophonic effect in itself, but more important are the spatialities created by reverb, by foreground–background depth, and by the relative location and movement of sound objects.

Virtual space works because even when we listen musically, our sensory apparatus is developed to orient us within an environment. This means that the so-called reduced listening in which we focus only on abstract sonic qualities is almost impossible; there will always be an aspect of identifying or "indicative" perception involved, often in combination with other listening modes.[9] The spatial indicators create quasi-illusions of spaces because we perceive them that way.

The virtual space is never empty. It exists only insofar as sound objects indicate it. The sound objects have properties and indicate not only size and materiality, but also a certain distance, a certain spatial context, a relation to the other sound objects, and, occasionally, a movement within the virtual space, as in the Boards of Canada example given earlier. And, of course, virtual spaces are flexible and can change radically during a piece of music.

The sound objects' virtual material properties define our perception of them. With contemporary technology, it is possible to create virtual sound objects that are close to specific real ones as well as sound objects that have no common physical equivalent and even objects that cannot possibly exist or behave as they do in the physical world. For instance, a very "heavy" virtual object with a sound materiality reminiscent of a huge shipping container can be treated the same way you would treat a light stick, "pounding" it fast against something, almost like a drum roll. An explosion can be immensely slow. A human voice can blend with that of an animal or of a robotic machine. These examples are banal; the point is that we perceive even physical impossibilities indicatively. We thus accordingly perceive even contradictory virtual spaces as spaces.

Atmosphere, Virtual Space, Listening Space

If atmosphere is always connected with space, then the atmosphere of electronic music unfolds itself in virtual space. It is a gestalt affected by all the sounds and their virtual spaces, although some sounds are more atmospheric than others. The atmosphere will often be a composite of different and perhaps even conflicting atmospheric qualities, and it is rarely reducible to one of the crude categories our language offers.

In the Boards of Canada "Gyroscope" example, there are elements of disorientation in both the percussive movement and the ambivalent spatiality of the voice—amplified and muffled at the same time. There is also a sense of the unreal and dreamlike and even of a disturbing, claustrophobic mood. At the same time, the uncanniness is not dramatic—there is a melancholic and slightly cool detachment in the dominating synthesizer, combined with the sense of being not really there. Like a bad dream that is not quite a nightmare, the atmosphere of "Gyroscope" is disturbing in its own discreet way.

The atmosphere of the virtual space is projected out into the listening space, the space in which people listen to the music. It is possible to hear a "pure" version of the virtual space only by wearing headphones; otherwise, this version will blend with the acoustics of the listening space. The meeting of the two spaces is a kind of "mixed spatiality."

The listening space is normally secondary, and its atmosphere is highly affected by the virtual space. But, of course, the atmosphere of the listening space affects the perception of the music and tints the atmosphere. All the elements in the listening space blend with the music and participate in the perceived atmosphere. Individuals may focus almost exclusively on the musical atmosphere (especially if they know the music well), and it is certainly possible to distinguish consciously between the atmospheres of the two spaces—for instance, when trying to match the music to the actual mood or, inversely, when judging a discord between them. A less conscious experience, however, will perceive the gestalt of the two spaces, which is more likely with low background music.

Live Listening Space—Atmosphere and Immersion

"Live" is not the standard mode of listening; it is rather the exception, although within most genres of music there seems to be a discourse considering the live as more authentic. At a typical laptop concert, this ideology of liveness is played down, and it often becomes a question of experiencing a social and atmospheric audiovisual space rather than of witnessing a star's performance.[10]

In a *classical* live performance, the audience is seated on chairs facing the musicians, expected to be quiet and to concentrate on the performance and the details of the music. The performers are introverted and equally concentrated on delivering a perfect and intense version of the musical score. At the typical *rock* music concert, the audience stands and is less disciplined. People are encouraged to sing along, move their bodies, shout, drink, and so on. The focus is on the stage, where the performers are normally extroverted, communicating with the audience.

The typical electronica concert is difficult to define because it is an institutional nomad, being equally at home in clubs, concert halls, venues, outdoor festivals, cinemas, art galleries, museums, shelters, and desolate industrial buildings. However, certain generic features seem to recur as typical. The center of the concert is less the stage or the performer's location than it is for other musical genres. This shift is a consequence of the often minimal or lacking element of performance or "playing," combined with a postsubjective ideology of not focusing on the person behind the music.[11] The composer-musician is often introverted as opposed to the rock musician, and it is almost impossible to figure out what he or she is doing, in contrast to the classical musician. Simon Emmerson laments this lack of "control intimacy," understood as the immediate cause–effect relation between the physical gestures of a musician handling his instrument and the sonic output (2007, 94–95). He treats this lack as a problem for electronic music and suggests ways to regain control intimacy. The frustration of having no control intimacy when watching a laptop composer live is a well-known experience and is justified in light of traditional live expectations. But perhaps this lack can also be seen as a potential for a different approach to the concert situation.

With no control intimacy at an electronica concert, there is actually little reason to gaze at the performing musician unless he or she performs expressively or theatrically. The lack of control intimacy is a special version of the "acousmatic curtain," severing the sound from the visual display of its source. It can be seen as a liberation and thus not just as a deprivation. Emmerson distinguishes between event, stage, arena, and landscape as four inscribed "circles" of a concert (Emmerson 2007, 97–102). They are not clearly defined, but the point is that the center, the event on stage, is partly blurred or erased, and to a certain extent it collapses to become a part of the arena, the audience space. The source of the music becomes less important, and with loudspeakers throughout the venue, the music emanates from everywhere, creating an experience of ubiquity. This type of concert has more atmospheric potential than other types of concert, and the experience of ubiquity is often visually supported by the presence of video projections on walls or screens, either preproduced or partly produced live by the so-called VJs (video jockeys). The typical electronica concert aims at a centerless immersive ambience rather than a division of stage and arena, and the event is more about experiencing this atmosphere than about watching musicians play live.

Mobile Listening and Atmosphere

Listening to music on portable MP3 players is a peculiar instance of musical atmosphere. Here, the atmosphere of the music is not projected out into a listening space; it is normally not shared with anyone, but it is nonetheless *superimposed* on the environment. This superimposition creates an intimacy with the music and at the same time a distance to the surroundings. As Michael Bull has shown in his sociological studies of listeners using their iPod between work and home, both the intimacy and the distance are essential motivations for listening to music while on the move (see chapter 6 in this volume).

The experience of atmospheric superimposition is often compared to watching a movie or a music video (e.g., Bull, chapter 6 in this volume), only here the space is physically real, and the listener actually moves through it and chooses the soundtrack via simple programming. The analogy with a movie involves, of course, the superimposition of a nondiegetic soundtrack upon things, events, landscapes, and people. The main function of a mainstream film soundtrack is to tint the scenes with specific atmospheric qualities, which affect our experience of the film significantly, albeit most of the time unconsciously. In a music video, the music is prominent, with the moving images as a kind of visual accompaniment. The iPod experience is akin to both because the listener can be more or less focused on the music and its atmospheres, on the surroundings, or on her own thoughts.

When we carry a mobile, virtual space with us, the result is a mixed spatiality of a different and more radical kind than when we are listening to music that comes through loudspeakers. The listening space is eliminated, and instead a virtual sound space and sound atmosphere are *projected* on the surrounding space. The sound aspects are virtual, whereas the rest—the space one moves through, the phenomena of the other senses, the whole environmental atmosphere—is "real." Loud and distinct sounds of the surrounding space occasionally enter into the virtual space and blend with the earphone sounds, which is important for orientation in traffic, warnings, social attention, and so on. Sometimes the sounds from the two spaces are confused, especially when the music entails environmental sounds, which can be a quite unsettling experience if sounds such as alarms or shouts come from the surrounding space.

Walking down a main street with mobile music is very different from walking the same distance without music. The heterogeneous, stressful atmosphere of a coincidentally composed crowd of people can be turned into a poetic display of urban loneliness with one soundtrack or into a brutal surge of energy with another. In both instances, the atmosphere aestheticizes the chaotic swarm of strangers. Mobile music listening is a possibility for creating one's own movable territory and, to a certain degree, for designing one's own atmosphere. This is a clear benefit in urban environments with dense crowds of people and loud traffic noise, which are complex and overwhelming and demand a severe filtering or sorting out of sensuous impressions. Here, music listening can create a territorial center, and the aestheticization can calm urban noise stress.

The possible downside to this creation of an individual territory is the solitude in that mobile music listening is normally an internal rather than a social experience. But mobile music listening takes place mostly in situations where one would be "in one's own world" anyway and where incidental communication with strangers is rare—at least in Western culture. Although the mobile sound environment may reduce the number of certain unexpected incidents of social encounters on the move, the dystopia of solipsistic narcissism seems exaggerated. The ethics and safety precautions of mobile listening demands a volume at which one can always be contacted.

Moreover, there are social potentials to mobile listening, not only through splits that allow more than one headphone to connect with the playing device, but also through the option to plug the device into a stereo when visiting others, thus easily sharing one's own music collection with them and reestablishing the interplay between virtual space and listening space.

Perspectives

I have shown how normal, contemporary music listening has moved toward greater and more complex diffusion, ubiquity, and mixed spatiality with electronic music and mobile listening media. This development will probably continue as devices get smaller and easier to seamlessly implement in clothes, other equipment, and architectonic environments. These technologies are being developed and might reach mass markets in the years to come. Music collections become less and less bound to specific places and persons, and utopia seems to be the availability of all music everywhere. At the same time, we can see countermovements of site-specific music, devotion to vinyl records, subculture distributions outside the established channels, and so on. These movements will probably increase as well, pursuing the lost aura of specialties.

There are many possibilities in implementing sound atmospheres in architecture and in creating interactive feedback systems that affect the sounds. Sound is a still very intrusive phenomenon, though, and there is always the danger of annoyance. To be surrounded by ambient music or atmospheric sound design all day long is hardly desirable, but more flexible and advanced possibilities of affecting the atmosphere in certain situations, especially in public spaces, will certainly have a future.

Notes

1. The German word *Gefühle* can be translated as "emotions" or "feelings." The most common translation is "emotions."

2. The dialectical relation between expression and objectivity in art is the topic of Sangild 2009.

3. I am currently working on a semantic model for electronic music in which there are several levels of meaning. Atmosphere is a parameter on the gestural–virtual perceptive level, together with materiality and movement.

4. See Ulrik Schmidt's chapter in this volume (chapter 8) for more on ambience as a centerless, "all-over" aesthetics and a critical discussion on foreground and background.

5. I use the term *sound object* to describe a sound element that is perceived as a unit. I do *not*, however, attach an ideology of "reduced listening" (listening to the sound "in itself" without attempt at identification) to the sound object.

6. From the album *Geogaddi* (Warp Records, Warp101, 2002). I have chosen Boards of Canada as a well-known and somewhat typical example of electronica production.

7. This terminology is in line with that used by Albert Bregman (1990, 456–460) and Eric Clarke (2005, 71, 74, 154, 183–187).

8. Rob Shields provides a thorough discussion of the concept of the virtual (2003, chapters 1–2). I do not use the term *virtual* in Gilles Deleuze's special sense.

9. This distinction refers to a long discussion that has taken place over the past few decades (e.g., Clarke 2005; Emmerson 1998, 136; Smalley 1996, 78–82), confronting the notion of reduced listening, where sounds are only abstract sensuous qualities, with ideas emphasizing the identifying intentionality of perception.

10. Of course, this level of "liveness" varies a great deal and depends on the fame of the composer-musician, the arranging of the space, and the (lack of) performance.

11. There are, of course, many exceptions, such as electronica stars, but even they will often play down their appearance. Aphex Twin, perhaps the most famous of them all, has often played with no lights pointing at him so that he is almost concealed in the venue space.

References

Bayle, Francois. 2007. "Space, and More." *Organised Sound* 12 (3): 241–249.

Böhme, Gernot. 2001. *Aisthetik.* Munich: Wilhelm Fink.

Böhme, Gernot. 2000. "Acoustic Atmospheres." Translated by Norbert Ruebsaat. *Soundscape* 1 (1): 14–18.

Böhme, Gernot. 1998. *Anmutungen: Über das Atmosphärische.* Ostfildern, Germany: Tertium.

Böhme, Gernot. 1995. *Atmosphäre.* Frankfurt am Main: Suhrkamp.

Bregman, Albert S. 1990. *Auditory Scene Analysis: The Perceptual Organization of Sound.* Cambridge, MA: MIT Press.

Clarke, Eric F. 2005. *Ways of Listening.* Oxford: Oxford University Press.

Emmerson, Simon. 2007. *Living Electronic Music.* Hampshire, UK: Ashgate.

Emmerson, Simon. 1998. "Aural Landscape: Musical Space." *Organised Sound* 3 (2): 135–140.

Sangild, Torben. 2009. *Objektiv sensibilitet.* Copenhagen: Multivers.

Sangild, Torben. 2002. "Sensitive Electronics." In *Look at the Music—Seesound,* edited by J. W. Goetz, 20–28. Ystad, Sweden, and Roskilde, Denmark: Ystad Art Musem and Museum of Contemporary Art.

Shields, Rob. 2003. *The Virtual.* London: Routledge.

Smalley, Denis. 1996. "The Listening Imagination: Listening in the Electroacoustic Era." *Contemporary Music Review* 13 (2): 77–107.

Wishart, Trevor. 1996. *On Sonic Art.* Amsterdam: OPA.

8 Ambience and Ubiquity

Ulrik Schmidt

Ambience is often described as a "feeling or mood associated with a particular place, person, or thing."[1] In this sense of the word, ambience has a close affinity with Martin Heidegger's ([1927] 1993) notion of *Stimmung*—"mood" or "attunement"—and, in particular, with the concept of "atmosphere" as analyzed by Gernot Böhme and others. Atmospheres are what Böhme calls "quasi-objective" phenomena, having both an objective and a subjective side. With explicit reference to Heidegger, Böhme thus defines atmosphere as a "tuned space" and as a set of "undefined, spatially distributed moods" (2001, 47). And at the same time, atmospheres have a "thinglike" (*Dinghaftes*) character in the sense that every specific atmosphere is "articulated" by things and relations between things "according to their properties" (Böhme 1995, 33). In other words, atmosphere and hence also ambience in this "atmospheric" sense are basically concerned with the complex and subtle ways different things are related in space and the discreet emotions and affections produced in the experience of such relations.

But ambience may also be understood in a less subjective and anthropomorphic sense.[2] When we talk about *ambient air, ambient light, ambient sound, ambient music, ambient findability, ambient intelligence, ambient infomatics*, and so on, we are not doing so in order to describe a special mood or atmosphere surrounding the phenomena in the way we would do, for instance, when describing an atmosphere or ambience in a restaurant or at a meeting. Rather, we characterize a phenomenon as "ambient" in order to point to a set of specific *formal* and *material* properties that characterize the phenomenon and to the particular way the phenomenon, on account of these properties, is constituted in our experience with a certain "ambient" character. According to this notion, ambience is rather the production of a distinctive ambient *effect* unfolding in the aesthetic experience—that is, the sensation and perception—of a specific situation.[3] Things, persons, or places no longer *have an ambience*; they can *be ambient* by producing ambient effects. This also means that some things, persons, and places—even some surroundings—are more ambient than others.

Ambient aesthetics, as the production and sensoperceptual experience of ambient effects, plays an important, although still quite inconspicuous, role in Western culture—for example, in relation to the aesthetic experience of nature and to the aestheticization of modern urban living from the experience of the metropolis (artificial light, *flânerie*, crowds), transport (driving, flying, freeways, airports), and shopping (arcades, malls, super markets) to the aesthetic aspects of many popular leisure activities and sports (surfing, swimming, sunbathing, attending sporting events). However, since the 1960s, the staging of ambient experiences has become increasingly important within media culture, design, and the arts, often significantly blurring the boundaries between them. Ambience is thus often an important part of the aesthetic experience in contemporary installation art, video, and digital art; in music and sound art; in abstract animation; in architecture, interior design, and urban design and landscape architecture. A similar tendency toward ambient aestheticization is traceable in the design and experience of contemporary media—from the use and design of radio and television (flow, broadcast, zapping, etc.) to new digital media such as computer games, the Internet (scrolling, surfing, hypertext, animated Web pages)—as well as in software design and computer graphics (Mac OS X; Windows Vista)[4] and in human–computer interaction in general. No doubt the emergence of new strategic paradigms for everyday human-centric computing environments such as *ubiquitous computing* (ubicomp) and *ambient intelligence*[5] as well as the digital distribution of information as what has been called "ambient informatics"[6] have strengthened the tendency to move toward an ambient aestheticization of digital media and information tools.

It is not my aim here, though, to discuss the complex historical, aesthetic, and technological developments of and relations between different ambient manifestations in contemporary aesthetic culture. Such a treatment presupposes, according to my view, an understanding of ambient aesthetics, which has not been sufficiently developed yet. Instead, I focus on ambient aesthetics on a more general level by identifying and discussing some of its key features. Such an investigation involves posing the basic questions: What formal and material properties produce ambient effects, and what characterizes the aesthetic experience of such properties?

The Ambient Field

The word *ambience* stems from the Latin word *ambire*, meaning to "go around."[7] Ambience accordingly can be described as the experience that a phenomenon "'goes around" the subject. In this understanding, ambience is the production of a distinctive *effect* characterized by an *intensification of the experience of being surrounded.*[8] But what phenomenal qualities will potentially produce ambient effects? First, in order to intensify the experience of being surrounded, the ambient character of a phenomenon depends on its ability to "place" the subject *in the center* of a given situation, thereby producing the experience that everything is "going around" the subject and nothing else but the subject. The ambient experience is thus characterized by a dissolution of the relation between subject and object. An ambient phenomenon is not experienced as an object or a group of interrelated objects, but rather as a *field*.[9] Whereas objects are experienced as enclosed and impenetrable forms more or less clearly distinguishable from their surroundings, ambient phenomena are experienced as open, formless fields where such distinctions are no longer possible or relevant.

As a field, the ambient phenomenon is essentially *objectless* in the sense that its immanent elements are distributed in such a way that they do not establish local centers or pregnant elements that stand out from the rest. Isolated entities and pregnant differences within the field will potentially constitute a center of attention, and the field will no longer produce the experience of a "personal" surrounding, but rather of an object within a surrounding—that is, of an object within *its own* surrounding. Ambient fields, in contrast, are undifferentiated, dehierarchized, and decentered. The elements are "all over," "all around," and "everywhere" in the field. Hence, there is a close relation between ambience and *ubiquity* in the sense that ambient fields are experienced as "total fields," all over and ubiquitous. Ubiquity is basically characterized by a dissolution of figurativity. Whereas figurativity builds internal hierarchies between different parts within the field—thereby creating potential focal points for the experiencing subject—ubiquity dissolves the tension between more and less important parts, between figure and ground. In order to produce a distinctive surround effect, all separate elements must be experienced as constituting a coherent and consistent whole.[10]

A sphere and an all-encompassing atmospheric matter can thus be seen as basic ambient phenomena. They simply go all around the subject, filling up the space from all sides. As an example—among many in contemporary installation art—of an interest in the sensory effect of such a "pure ubiquity," one can consider the different so-called *Ganzfeld Pieces* (1970–) by American artist James Turrell. Here, the subject is placed in a ubiquity of monochrome light. But ambient fields, despite their essentially ubiquitous qualities, do not necessarily take the form of an all-enclosing (atmo)-sphere in order to produce ambient effects.

This is clear if one considers Turrell's *Skyspaces* (1975–), another important group of his works. In these works, a structural cut in the ceiling of a room creates a space that is open to the sky but at the same time appears somewhat enclosed or framed from the beholder's perspective. The *Skyspaces*, however, are never experienced as objects in the way a painting or a sculpture is. On the contrary, despite being enclosed, they still appear somewhat objectless; they still give the impression of being "everywhere." This quasi-ubiquitous quality of the *Skyspaces*, though, is not so much due to the immanent all-over character of the spaces themselves; monochromatic paintings or minimalist geometric sculptures, for example, are also immanently undifferentiated, but objecthood, the quality of being an object, is nevertheless a fundamental part of their appearance. Rather, what differentiates enclosed ambient phenomena such as Turrell's *Skyspaces* from objects, what makes them intensify the experience of being surrounded, is more than anything else the *dynamic*, *processual*, and *topological* character of the fields. The ambient effect of the framed *Skyspaces* is *predominantly temporal* rather than spatial. This distinction leads to another important aspect of ambience: although the mere vastness of a phenomenon might play an important part in many ambient experiences, spatial ubiquity, in the sense that a phenomenon is actually being "everywhere," is not essential to all ambient situations. The ubiquitous effect of ambient experiences can be primarily spatial, as in the effect of a "total field" (*Ganzfeld*) actually surrounding the viewer. But it can also be primarily temporal, as in the experience of a time–space surrounding, circulating around, the subject. An ambient field may be a river, a car ride, a digital device, a distant soundscape, or a fly on the wall. Ambient aesthetics thus cannot be reduced to a mere question of space and the experience of ubiquity, consistency, and nonfigurativity as spatial characteristics. It must rather be considered as the unfolding of an event, the becoming of a dynamic and consistent spatiotemporal situation.

Ambient Events

Ambient events are not autonomously organized according to principles internal to the form—as opposed to the way a narrative structure, for example, organizes its own immanent time–space. An ambient field does not structure its own time. Rather, it unfolds its effect in *real time*; it surrounds the subject in and with real time. The ambient experience can last for hours or minutes, but it needs a certain duration to establish itself as ambience. If the time–space is too short, it will close in on itself as a distinguished moment and potentially become a focal point, a climax, within a longer span of time.

Immanent elements move about in the field, and the subject moves, actually or virtually, in relation to it (through, across, about, along, toward, etc.).[11] The specific pattern of movement created by each set of dynamic relations is not only an essential part of the ambient experience; it is itself of an ambient character. Thus, qualities such as nonfigurativity, dehierarchization, and ubiquity, which characterize the basic spatial organization of the ambient field, also apply to the temporal structure of the event as an unfolding time–space. Ambience is also nonfigurative and ubiquitous in time in the sense that its dynamic processes are of a *nonteleological* character. A telos eventually invests the experience with meaning from somewhere outside, somewhere *after*, the event. In contrast, the ambient event relates to nothing outside itself as event. Its movements may have a direction, but they have no goal or endpoint; they move about without "knowing" where. Instead, what gives the pattern of movement within the field an ambient character is the continuity of the movement as event. An ambient field varies constantly, but in order for it to maintain its surrounding, its effect, it is never experienced as changing in any essential way. It rather appears as what Gilles Deleuze and Félix Guattari (1988) refer to as *continuous variation*, a situation where nothing "happens," and still everything is new.[12]

The ambient field's ubiquitous, nonfigurative character does not mean that it is uniform in any ontological sense. The field can be hypercomplex and chaotic, consisting of an infinite amount of discrete elements and still be experienced as consistent, undifferentiated, and whole. It can be a "chaosmos" (Deleuze and Guattari 1996, 204–206), a chaotic cosmos or cosmic chaos. Ocean waves, the sound of a howling wind, and the song of birds are chaosmic events in the sense that they produce a continuous and "chaotic" immanent variation but at the same time remain distinctively consistent throughout the entire time–space. What matters is not the existence of different singularities—or the variation between them, for that matter—but the preservation of the nonfigurative, nonteleological, and ubiquitous quality of the field, no matter how complex and divided it may actually be. Instead, what is still important is that no singular element in the event takes the quality of a figure and becomes a center of the subject's attention.

For that reason, *continuity* and *repetition* are the key principles in the spatiotemporal distribution of singularities in the ambient event. They eliminate any figurative properties the elements may have and establish a dehierarchized, ubiquitous whole. This is, for example, the case in ambient music—from the classic pieces by ambient music pioneer Brian Eno and German groups such as Cluster and Tangerine Dream in the 1970s to contemporary electronic musicians such as Aphex Twin, Biosphere, Oval, Robert Rich, and others. Ambient music typically unfolds as a quite complex sonic chaosmos, constantly vibrating in continuous variation. At the same time, however, the music always preserves a strong nonfigurative character, exactly because of the way each element is distributed in continuity and repetition throughout the entire event. Hence, there are no musical "figures" in ambient music; no melodic elements or foregrounded gestalts stand out from the "surrounding" background. The music consists only of fragments of continuous and repetitive sounds and timbres, very often with a strong reverberation to "soften" the individual sounds and "blur" the boundaries between them. When some parts in the field take what first might seem like a quasi-melodic quality, the melody always either has a very "weak" identity (it is always *too* simple, *too* monotonous, *too* unfinished and fragmented) or starts to become a repetition or a discreet variation of itself (a sequence, a curve). Consider as a visual example of a quite similar situation the interactive light installation *Pulse Room* (2006–) by Canadian Mexican media artist Rafael Lozano-Hemmer. Here, one hundred to three hundred clear light bulbs hang from the ceiling in a large grid. While entering the space, the participants are invited to let a sensor detect their individual heartbeats by placing their hands on an interface by the entrance. Each bulb now flickers in its own "individual" tempo according to the registered heart rate of the different visitors. Lozano-Hemmer and the visitors thus create at the same time a representational space of strong poetic qualities and an objective, abstract–concrete ambience. Because of the serial character of the composition, the dynamic space is never experienced as hierarchical or teleological but rather appears as an ambient chaosmos of flickering electric light, constantly varying in repetitive pulsation.

Ambient Experience

No element within the chaosmic field is of particular pregnancy or interest; no part calls for attention more than others, everything is continuous variation: these are the basic characteristics of ambient aesthetics. Ambience therefore challenges the conventional understanding of the aesthetic experience as an attentive, concentrated, and focused experience. But what modes of experience are called for, then, when there no longer is an object or figure to direct attention to, but just a ubiquitous, continuously varying all-over field? How can one describe the ambient experience of ubiquity and continuous variation as an aesthetic experience and still maintain that it has an inattentive, unconcentrated, and unfocused character? In order to approach such questions, I suggest two modes of experience already well known within media theory as especially relevant in describing different aspects of ambient experience: *distraction* and *immersion*.

Distraction is typically understood as the diversion of attention away from its focal center and into the periphery. Walter Benjamin ([1935] 1980) famously distinguished the distractive experience of technologically reproducible artifacts from the concentrated experience of auratic, original artworks. Of special interest here, though, is Benjamin's description of distraction (*Zerstreuung*) as a decentering or "spreading out" of experience, opposed to the German concept of *Sammlung*, meaning both "concentration" and "collection."[13] But distraction, in Benjamin's understanding, refers not only to a spreading out and thereby a dissolution of cognitive concentration—that is, a decentering of experience—but also to a spreading out of the phenomena themselves—that is, a decentering of the experienced structure. Thus, there is, in Benjamin's concept of distraction, a close link between the spreading out of a given structure and the spreading out of the experience of that structure.

Immersion, in contrast, refers to the subject's deep—physical or cognitive—absorption in a phenomenon. It is the experience of being submerged or sucked into an alternative environment that more or less completely replaces the familiar surrounding reality.[14] Distraction and immersion can therefore be and have often been understood as having quite opposite meanings. Where the immersive experience is characterized by intense focus and absorption, distraction is characterized by distance and lack of focus. But, as I argue, immersion is just as central to ambience as distraction is. Distraction and immersion can in fact be seen as two closely related ways of experiencing ambient events.

The German philosopher Bernhard Waldenfels (2004) has indicated, although only implicitly, the existence of such a relationship between distractive and immersive modes of experience. In a discussion of the relationship between attention and distraction, Waldenfels argues that when attention dissolves into distraction, it does so in two different ways, closely related to two different kinds of formal organization. On the one hand, distraction can be what Waldenfels calls "chronic distraction" (*chronischen Zerstreutheit*), related to the experience of an unfocused "chaos." This notion corresponds roughly to Benjamin's understanding of distraction as a spreading out of the perceptual field and the unconcentrated experience of it. On the other hand, distraction can also be a result of "overconcentration" (*Überkonzentration*). And this mode of distraction is not related to an unfocused chaos, but rather to the experience of a "fixed order" (*fixe Ordnung*) (2004, 104).

In his investigation of attention and media culture in the nineteenth and early twentieth centuries, the art historian Jonathan Crary makes a similar point. In aesthetic thought and psychology of that period, Crary argues, attention "always contained within itself the conditions for its own disintegration, it was haunted by the possibility of its own excess" and would inevitably reach a "threshold" at which it would break down. Crary indicates how this disintegration of attention can go in two different directions. The threshold can be either a point where "the perceptual identity of [the] object begins to deteriorate and in some cases . . . disappear altogether" or "a limit at which attention imperceptibly mutates into a state of trance or even autohypnosis" (2001, 47).[15]

Thus, according to Waldenfels and Crary, attention can dissolve in two opposite directions: toward inattention and lack of concentration—that is, Benjaminian distraction—or toward excessive, absorbed, and trancelike overconcentration. The former disintegration of attention into a distractive lack of concentration is linked to the dissolution of the isolated object into an expanded and unfocused chaos. In the latter situation, trancelike overconcentration, the attention directed toward the object becomes "too much"; the focal point becomes too fixed, and the intensification of awareness has reached a point of excess where everything else but the object in focus is blocked out of the perceptual system. Just like the distractive spreading out of attention, overconcentration thus eventually produces a nonfigurative, nondevelopmental, and nonteleological all-over event without any pregnant or isolated elements to which attention can be directed. When the subject is completely concentrated and absorbed in the object, when "everything is figure" and in focus, attention eventually dissolves *into a state of immersion*; it becomes an experience of being surrounded by a ubiquitous, undivided, and consistent whole. And this attention disintegrated into overconcentration becomes a state of immersion exactly because the event of fixation, the sustained awareness, "stays itself" in that it continues and creates a ubiquitous event where "nothing happens." In other words, instead of being essentially opposed modes of experience, lack of concentration and overconcentration or distraction and immersion share many of the same basic properties. And so distraction and immersion can be understood as extreme poles on a graduated continuum of what is basically the same experience: the inattentive experience of being surrounded by a ubiquitous whole.

Backgrounds and Foregrounds

Ambience is often associated with a certain *background* character. This is the case with respect to the basic ideas of both ambient music and ubicomp. The common understanding of ambient music has been highly influenced by the British composer and producer Brian Eno after he introduced the term in the mid-1970s to describe his own "environmental" music. Eno here saw a close relationship between ambience and a certain *discreetness* of the music and what he described as its ability to "completely sink into [the] environment somewhere" (quoted in Tamm 1995, 138). Eno's thoughts on ambient music correspond quite accurately to an important trait in the general notion of ubicomp since Mark Weiser coined the term in 1991 (see Weiser 1991). Hence, ubicomp—much like later concepts and strategies such as "pervasive computing," "ambient intelligence," "everyware," and so on— is basically understood as something that recedes into the *periphery* of attention. "For many of the field's originators," Adam Greenfield has observed, "the whole point of designing ubiquitous systems was that they would be ambient, peripheral, and *not* focally attended to" (2006, 70). A ubicomp network is basically understood as a *calm* technological environment that, as Weiser and John Seely Brown famously described it, "informs but doesn't demand our focus or attention" (1995).

Indeed, it seems reasonable to put an emphasis on the background character in the particular cases of Eno's music and Weiser's idea of ubicomp. However, background character cannot itself explain what is distinctly "ambient" or "ubiquitous" about ambient, aesthetic experience in general.[16] The nonfigurative qualities of the ambient field might share many of its formal characteristics with backgrounds in figure-ground-organized environments, but such formal qualities (lack of focal points, objectlessness) do not necessarily lead to calm stimulation. A decentered, nonfigurative, ubiquitous phenomenon will not necessarily sink discreetly into the periphery of attention. When figure–ground relations are dissolved, they dissolve into nonfigurativity, not into backgrounds. And this process can go in two directions: figurativity can dissolve either into the ground plane or into the figure plane, giving the entire—still essentially nonfigurative—ambient field different degrees of foreground or background character. For example, an ambient, ubiquitous soundscape—as in the extreme noise music by

Japanese sound artist Merzbow—might be so loud and noisy that it masks out all other auditory stimuli and fills up the foreground more or less completely, without losing its distinct ambient and ubiquitous qualities. And the ambient experience, because of its dynamic character, might also change—and do so continuously—from discreetness (periphery, background) to predominance (all over, foreground), and vice versa without losing its ambient characteristics. An ambient field can be a discreet horizon as well as a dense substance vigorously closing in on the subject.

As already indicated, the ambient dissolution of figurativity into backgrounds and foregrounds is closely related to the continuum between distraction and immersion in the sense that ambient fields with a high degree of foreground quality generally appeal to immersive experience, and fields with a strong background character generally appeal to distraction. Furthermore, immersive, foregrounded fields tend to encourage *haptic* perception, where spread-out, backgrounded fields rather appeal to optic—or, in general audiovisual terms, *distant*—perception. Whether an ambient field is experienced as immersive, haptic, and foregrounded or as distractive, distant, and backgrounded can be a matter of mere perspective. The same ambient field—a fireplace or an intelligent digital environment, for example—can thus at one moment be experienced in distraction as an atmospheric background phenomenon, flickering chaotically somewhere in the periphery of attention, and soon after become a focal point for attention—or, rather, a "focal field" because it has no immanent fix point—giving way to a haptic and immersive experience of the fireplace or the digital network as a ubiquitous chaosmos.[17]

In other situations, the field may gradually change from a distractive and distant character to an immersive and haptic character (or vice versa) during the event, as when a repetitive structure—for instance, a repetitive sound, passing cars, or a light flashing repetitively—gradually changes from a slower to a faster pulse (from larger to smaller intervals), literally filling out the empty areas between the discrete elements. For example, the digital device Ambient Orb™ oscillates between distant and haptic qualities in a similar way. Ambient Orb™ is a small, globular glass lamp that shows "ambient information" by gradually changing color according to a graduated set of incoming data (e.g., weather forecasts, market trends).[18] In broad daylight, the light from the device blends discreetly with the incoming daylight and other light sources in the room, creating a discreet background experience. But as the surrounding light becomes darker, the light from the device will start to dominate, and everything in the room will eventually become immersed in a constantly varying monochrome light.

During this process when the ambient event changes from a distractive background to an immersive foreground quality or vice versa, the field never loses its nonfigurative character—for example, by passing a state of figure–ground organization somewhere in between. By becoming figurative, the phenomenon would eventually lose its ambient characteristics. Compared to a figure–ground relationship, the dissolution of such a relationship is something completely different.

Notes

1. "Ambience," *Merriam-Webster Online Dictionary*, available at http://www.merriam-webster.com/dictionary/ambience, accessed 4 January 2012.

2. Böhme (1995, 2001) mentions "character" and "physiognomy" as the most important characteristics of atmospheres.

3. I follow the common distinction made in contemporary psychology between sensation and perception, wherein, as Harvey Richard Schiffman explains, sensation "refers to the initial processes of detecting and encoding environmental energy," but perception "refers to the product of psychological processes in which meaning, relationships, context, judgment, past experience, and memory play a role." However, as Schiffman further observes, it is "difficult, perhaps even impossible, to make a clear separation between sensation and perception. . . . Generally speaking, sensation and perception are unified, inseparable processes" (2001, 2–3).

4. Lev Manovich has described—especially in relation to Apple's popular design of their consumer products—an increased tendency toward what he calls "aestheticization of information tools," where interfaces are designed to give the experience of a "rich, smooth, and consistent sensorial whole" (chapter 17 in this volume). As I argue later, this experience of a rich, smooth, and consistent sensorial whole is basically what characterizes ambient aesthetics.

5. Ubicomp describes the general development from subject-object-based human–computer interaction (mainframe and personal desktop computing) to the creation of a "ubiquitous" digital environment with detached, intercommunicating computer systems potentially integrated "everywhere" in the physical surroundings. Ambient intelligence is a more recent Philips- and MIT-based research concept. Although it, more than ubicomp, emphasizes interactive elements such as the network's context awareness, personalization, and adaptability, it draws in all its central aspects on the general ideas behind ubicomp (Aarts and Encarnação 2006, 2).

6. "Ambient informatics is a state in which information is . . . detached from the Web's creaky armature of pages, sites, feeds and browsers, and set free instead in the wider world to be accessed when, how and where you want it" (Greenfield 2006, 24).

7. According to Leo Spitzer, the term *ambient* was first introduced in Latin translations of Aristotle to render the Greek word *περιέχον*, which Spitzer defines as "that which surrounds, encompass[es]" (1942a, 2). In Aristotelian cosmology, the term was used to describe the surrounding and all-encompassing character of the spheres, the air, and the ether. As Spitzer has thoroughly demonstrated, the word *ambient* has a long history in Western philosophy and literary history, with different meanings. In Newtonian physics, for example, it refers to the "empty" space between solid bodies (ambient medium).

8. A production of surround effects is clearly an essential part of the aesthetic appearance in several modern technological inventions—from panoramas, dioramas, and kaleidoscopes in the

nineteenth century to widescreen television, IMAX cinema, surround sound, and virtual reality in the twentieth century, to name just a few significant examples. A similar interest is noticeable in different areas of visual art and music, from Jackson Pollock's all-over paintings and Gyorgï Ligeti's atmospheric pieces to techno music and visuals in contemporary club culture.

9. The concept "field"—used here to describe an important aesthetic characteristic of ambient space—is basically understood in a way similar to its general use in modern physics (as in electromagnetic fields, vector fields, force fields, quantum fields, chaos fields, etc.) As Albert Einstein's collaborator, the physicist Leopold Infeld explained in 1941, "Changes in space, spreading in time through all of space, are the basic concepts of our descriptions. These basic changes characterize the field. . . . We can look upon an object as upon a portion of space where the field is especially dense. The mechanist says: here is the object localized at this point of space. The field physicist says: field is everywhere, but it diminishes outside this portion so rapidly that my senses are aware of it only in this particular portion of space" (quoted in Spitzer 1942b, 196).

10. As discussed later, the ambient field may be hypercomplex, extremely differentiated, and chaotic and may still potentially be experienced as a coherent and consistent whole.

11. As Brian Massumi has argued, the experience of—relatively rare and always artistically or scientifically controlled—situations where both subject and environment are completely static, such as in the so-called *Ganzfeld* experiments in experimental psychology, is in fact also fundamentally characterized by movement (2002, 144–161).

12. Continuous variation, in Deleuze and Guattari's sense, is linked to the dissolution of figurativity into fluid, vibrating matter. As they explain, continuous variation is a situation where "we witness a transformation of substances and a dissolution of forms, a passage to the limit of flight from contours in favor of fluid forces, flows, air, light, and matter, such that a body . . . does not end at a precise point." This continuous variation "occurs on the plane of a single liberated matter that contains no figures, is deliberately unformed, and retains in expression and in content only those cutting edges, tensors, and tensions. Gestures and things, voices and sound, are caught up in the same 'opera,' swept away by the same shifting effects of stammering, vibrato, tremolo, and overspilling. A synthesizer places all of the parameters in continuous variation, gradually making 'fundamentally heterogeneous elements end up turning into each other in some way.' The moment this conjunction occurs there is a common matter" (1988, 109).

13. The quality of "deconcentration" is more clearly emphasized in the German word for distraction, *Zerstreuung,* which literally points to the spreading out or dissemination itself.

14. Oliver Grau describes immersion as a situation where "the feeling of being *in* the images, produced by the spatially enveloping visual impression, is . . . amplified" (2003, 193, emphasis in original). As Grau also observes, though, immersion is often associated with intense experience and "increasing emotional involvement in what is happening" (13). I use the word *immersion* here in a broader sense, similar to the former of Grau's descriptions, as the experience of (virtually or actually) being placed in and surrounded by a consistent, all-encompassing environment.

15. Among several examples, Crary quotes the German neuropsychologist Kurt Goldstein's observation (from 1943) that "distractibility and abnormal fixation are expressions of the same functional change under different conditions" (2001, 47).

16. In the case of ubicomp and ambient intelligence, it is important to distinguish between, on the one hand, a background character in relation to the technological distribution of a digital network as "invisibly embedded" in our natural surroundings and, on the other hand, background character as a trait in a specific aesthetic experience. When Werner Weber, Jan Rabaey, and Emile Aarts describe ambient intelligence as "characterized by an environment . . . where technology is embedded, hidden in the background" (2005, 1), the specific product (information, activities, etc.) offered to the user by the network is not necessarily experienced as backgrounded at the same time. "The medium is not the message in a digital world," Nicholas Negroponte remarks, with reference to Marshall McLuhan, "it is an embodiment of it. A message might have several embodiments automatically derivable from the same data" (1996, 71). In other words, background character as an aesthetic feature in relation to ubicomp environments depends on *how* the "message" is presented to the user in each sensoperceptual situation.

17. This change from periphery to center of attention, it must be noted, was in fact central to both Eno's ideas of ambient music and Weiser's understanding of ubicomp, despite their shared focus on the background character of the phenomenon. Eno wanted to make music "that could be listened to and yet could be ignored" (a description given on Eno's album *Discreet Music*, EG Records, 1975). And as Weiser and Brown famously observed, "Calm technology engages both the *center* and the *periphery* of our attention, and in fact moves back and forth between the two. . . . A calm technology will move easily from the periphery of our attention, to the center, and back" (1995, emphasis in original).

18. Ambient Orb was developed by Ambient Devices, Inc., a private company with relations to the MIT Media Lab.

References

Aarts, Emile, and José Luis Encarnação. 2006. *True Visions: The Emergence of Ambient Intelligence*. New York: Springer.

Benjamin, Walter. [1935] 1980. "Das Kunstwerk im Zeitalter seiner technischen Reproduzierbarkeit." In *Gesammelte Schriften I*, 471–508. Frankfurt am Main: Suhrkamp.

Böhme, Gernot. 2001. *Aisthetik*. Munich: Vilhelm Fink.

Böhme, Gernot. 1995. *Atmosphäre*. Frankfurt am Main: Suhrkamp.

Crary, Jonathan. 2001. *Suspensions of Perception: Attention, Spectacle, and Modern Culture*. Cambridge, MA: MIT Press.

Deleuze, Gilles, and Félix Guattari. 1996. *What Is Philosophy*? Translated by Hugh Tomlinson and Graham Burchell. New York: Colombia University Press.

Deleuze, Gilles, and Félix Guattari. 1988. *A Thousand Plateaus: Capitalism and Schizophrenia.* Translated by Brian Massumi. London: Athlone.

Grau, Oliver. 2003. *Virtual Art.* Cambridge, MA: MIT Press.

Greenfield, Adam. 2006. *Everyware: The Dawning Age of Ubiquitous Computing.* Berkeley, CA: New Riders.

Heidegger, Martin. [1927] 1993. *Sein und Zeit.* Tübingen, Germany: Max Niemeyer.

Massumi, Brian. 2002. *Parables for the Virtual.* Durham, NC: Duke University Press.

Negroponte, Nicholas. 1996. *Being Digital.* New York: Vintage.

Schiffman, Harvey Richard. 2001. *Sensation and Perception.* New York: Wiley.

Spitzer, Leo. 1942a. "Milieu and Ambiance [Part 1]." *Philosophy and Phenomenological Research* 3 (1) (September): 1–42.

Spitzer, Leo. 1942b. "Milieu and Ambiance [Part 2]." *Philosophy and Phenomenological Research* 3 (2) (December): 169–218.

Tamm, Eric. 1995. *Brian Eno: His Music and the Vertical Color of Sound.* New York: Da Capo Press.

Waldenfels, Bernhard. 2004. *Phänomenologie der Aufmerksamkeit.* Frankfurt am Main: Surhkamp.

Weber, Werner, Jan M. Rabaey, and Emile Aarts. 2005. "Introduction." In *Ambient Intelligence,* edited by Werner Weber, Jan M. Rabaey, and Emile Aarts. New York: Springer: 1–4.

Weiser, Mark. 1991. "The Computer for the 21st Century." *Scientific American* 265 (3): 94–104.

Weiser, Mark, and John Seely Brown. 1995. "Designing Calm Technology." Available at http://www.ubiq.com/hypertext/weiser/calmtech/calmtech.htm. Accessed 4 January 2012.

III Communications

9 Text as Event: Calm Technology and Invisible Information as Subject of Digital Arts

Roberto Simanowski

Calm Technology and Postalphabetic Text

In their essay "Designing Calm Technology" (1995), Mark Weiser and John Seely Brown use an artwork to explain the concepts "ubiquitous computing" and "calm technology." Natalie Jeremijenko's 1995 *Live Wire* (also known as *Dangling String*) consists of an eight-foot-long string attached to a small electric motor that is mounted in the ceiling and connected to a nearby Ethernet cable so that the string twitches proportionally to the amount of traffic on the Internet and consequently whirls in degrees from mildly to madly. *Live Wire* is placed in the office environment of the Xerox Palo Alto Research Center Computer Science Lab and represents calm technology, for it allows "peripheral attunement" and—in contrast to screen displays of network traffic—does not require interpretation and attention.[1] In the artist's words, "*Live Wire* is tacit information, rather than more of the precisely graphed, data fetishism of information rhetoric."[2]

Weiser and Brown conclude their essay with the notion that despite frequent complaints about information overload, "more information could be encalming," stating that "the way to become attuned to more information is to attend to it less" (1995). Mark Hansen, who refers to Weiser and Brown's essay in his contribution to this book (chapter 1), considers Jeremijenko's piece an example of the "sensory revolution" he sees in ubiquitous computing. Although the work does not tell more about data traffic than whether there is little or much, users develop an "*affective* connection" to it, according to Hansen, and, becoming "free to *not attend focally to the work,*" shift their mode of sensing "from the macroperceptual level—What is it telling me about the traffic volume?—to the microperceptual level; at the latter level, microtemporal recognitions of motion, orientation, sound, and so on sustain an ongoing microaffective connection that never reaches the level of a conscious, focal perception" (emphasis in original). It is important to recognize not only that in *Live Wire* information is not simply present in the background, moving to center stage when needed, but also that it has changed its nature through the specific way of presentation. Ubiquitous computing as represented by *Live Wire* or by Roy Want's similarly working *Internet Stock Fountain* (1999), also at the Xerox Palo Alto Research Center,[3] makes not only computers invisible—so that they disappear into the environment—but also information. *Live Wire* does so not only by addressing us, as Hansen points out, at the level of microsensation, "that is by definition invisible to perceptual consciousness" (Hansen, chapter 1 in this volume), but also by rendering information imperceptible. If we decide to attend focally to these works, we still will only find blurred information because they will tell us only whether there is much Internet traffic or whether the value of the Xerox share is increasing or decreasing respectively but will never give out exact measurings of a moment's flux. The text parsed by *Live Wire* and *Internet Stock Fountain* is mapped only as movement.

Neither Weiser and Brown nor Hansen engages in discussing this characteristic of *Live Wire*, which explains why Weiser and Brown are able to offer this work as an example of calm technology—one that enhances the peripheral reach and "increases our knowledge and so our ability to act without increasing information overload" (1995)—without considering the extent to which a work such as *Live Wire* really allows for informed actions. For the same reason, Hansen can celebrate the shift from macroperception to microaffectivity without addressing the ambiguity hidden in *Live Wire* but not invisible to perceptual consciousness: the fact that an artwork logically contradicts the notion of ubiquity and invisibility because by nature its aim is to call attention to itself as an intervention into the everyday life environment.[4] Taking this aspect into account, we should explore the hidden, subconscious symbolic of the way *Live Wire* presents information and wonder what else is at stake in what Hansen calls "revolution in the function of media and in the coupling of sensation and technics" (chapter 1 in this volume). Therefore, I propose, as a supplement to Hansen's discussion of the issue in the context of neurobiology and Edmund Husserl's phenomenology, a more critical approach from a cultural studies perspective linking ubiquitous computing to another noteworthy phenomenon in contemporary culture and media history: "information designed to resists information" (Liu 2004, 179). My starting point is the constant decline of the word in media history.

In his 2001 book *The Language of New Media*, Lev Manovich claims, "The printed word tradition that initially dominated the language of cultural interfaces is becoming less important, while the part played by cinematic elements is becoming progressively stronger. This is consistent with a general trend in modern society toward presenting more and more information in the form of time-based audiovisual moving image sequences, rather than as text" (78). The notion of the decline of the printed-word tradition is in line with the assumption that electronic media, computer, and the Internet undermine the authority and cultural supremacy of the word. Three significant books demonstrate this view: Neil Postman claims in *Amusing Ourselves to Death* (1985) that the inevitable message of the medium television is entertainment and distraction; Barry Sander holds in *A Is for Ox: Violence, Electronic Media, and the Silencing of the Written Word* (1994) that literacy is on the decline because of our fascination with electronic media—television, videos, computer games—which fail to provide the narrative power of true literary sources; and Nadin Mihai entitles his book *The Civilization of Illiteracy* (1997) precisely because it addresses an unfolding civilization in which the language of the Internet, interactive multimedia, and virtual reality have become the new languages of human interaction. Hyperfiction author and theorist Michael Joyce predicted in 1995 that the "post-alphabetic image" will soon "either rob us of the power—or relieve us of the burden—of language" (Joyce 2000, 42), and Jay David Bolter, who investigated in his 1991 book *Writing Space: Computers, Hypertext, and the History of Writing* the new opportunities for the word in digital media, spoke in 1996 of the "breakout of the visual" in the digital world, observing that in multimedia the relationship between word and image is becoming as unstable as in the popular press, where images do not appear subordinate to the word anymore (258).

The claim and complaint that the word no longer obtains the cultural authority it traditionally had been given should remind us of the many predictions we heard in the 1990s about the end of the Gutenberg Galaxy. With the profusion of Web logs (blogs) and millions of tweets sent every day, however, one can argue that the written word has certainly regained territory in digital media. Are those blogs and tweets not a response to the pictorial turn that took place more than half a century ago? Or are they only a glitch in technological history, an interregnum in the immanent hegemony of the postalphabetic image, as Joyce claimed in 1995 with respect to the text-based MOOs (42)? Although it should be mentioned that blogs and tweets also have gone multimedial and that more and more queries on the Internet end up on YouTube, we have to leave the answers to these questions to future debates. In this chapter, I simply wish to explore the role text plays when it becomes an event within digital environments and discuss the reasons and implications of the fact that we have come to live more with the sensation of textuality than with the sense of the text.

To a certain extent, in digital-media text is always an event. As N. Katherine Hayles points out in her essay "The Time of Digital Poetry: From Object to Event," even the seemingly static text on the screen is the result of the computer's processing. However, the reader may not be aware of this "eventilization" of the text (2006, 182) because the processing is invisibly embedded behind the interface. Now, if text starts to move or to react to the reader's action, then the situation changes. In the installation *Overboard* (2004) by John Cayley, a program of carefully designed algorithms allows letters to disappear or to be replaced by other letters, thus undermining the lexical relationship of the word until the original letters are restored.[5] The poem about a man falling overboard during a storm continually drifts in (rising) and out (sinking) of legibility and thus renders visually its own message. Whereas *Overboard* is processed without user input, in Natalie Bookchin's *The Intruder* (1999), which combines several arcadelike game interfaces to tell the short story *La Intrusa* by Jorge Luis Borges,[6] the reader moves forward through the text as a player by shooting, fighting, or catching and being rewarded with a piece of the narrative told in a voice-over.

Text as event inevitably shifts the reader's attention from the content of text to its materiality. Although in *Overboard* and *The Intruder* the way in which the text is presented contributes to its verbal meaning, as is the case in classical concrete poetry, in many other instances the event takes over the text, turning it into the raw material for various transformations into visual objects, sound, or (inter)action. In those examples, words are more or less deprived of their linguistic meaning, which limits or liberates respectively the audience engagement with the text to a joyful play or intriguing fascination. The words have not been replaced by the "postalphabetic image," as Joyce predicted in 1995, but they are turned into "postalphabetic text."[7]

I have illustrated the asemanticization of text in another essay (Simanowski 2010), reading Oswald de Andrade's concept of cultural anthropophagy from 1928 as media anthropophagy in the context of the shift from the "culture of meaning" to the "culture of presence" proposed in the aesthetic discourse at the end of the twentieth century.[8] In this chapter, I discuss further such transformation with respect to Julius Popp's installation *Bit.Fall* (2006), which exemplifies how contemporary art relates to (and opposes) ubicomp and demonstrates how communication in mixed-reality spaces shifts attention to the surface of text (materiality, appearance). I conclude the chapter with thoughts on the audience's voyeuristic approach to text stripped of linguistic value and on the code behind such text.

Impermanent Signifiers

In *Bit.Fall* (2006) by the German artist Julius Popp (figure 9.1) a computer scans news Web pages, pulls keywords (nouns, verbs, and proper names), and writes them as a "waterfall of letters" by means of magnetic vents that enable each of the several water jets to emit individual water drops.[9] The shift in writing—from the invisible processing of words on the Web page to their spectacular processing within the installation—certainly addresses the question of ubiquitous computing and calm technology. Popp himself considers *Bit.Fall* a symbol for the fast change of what is currently valuable and meaningful to us,[10] just as Lutz Koepnick, professor of German, film, and media studies at Washington University in St. Louis, attributes an element of cultural and media critique to this installation, stating that it "foregrounds the utter transience of what we consider news in our world of increasingly global and instantaneous connections" (2006, 69). In a similar way, Popp's former teacher at the Academy of Visual Arts Leipzig, Astrid Klein, considers *Bit.Fall* a critique of technology that addresses the ephemeral and manipulable nature of information.[11]

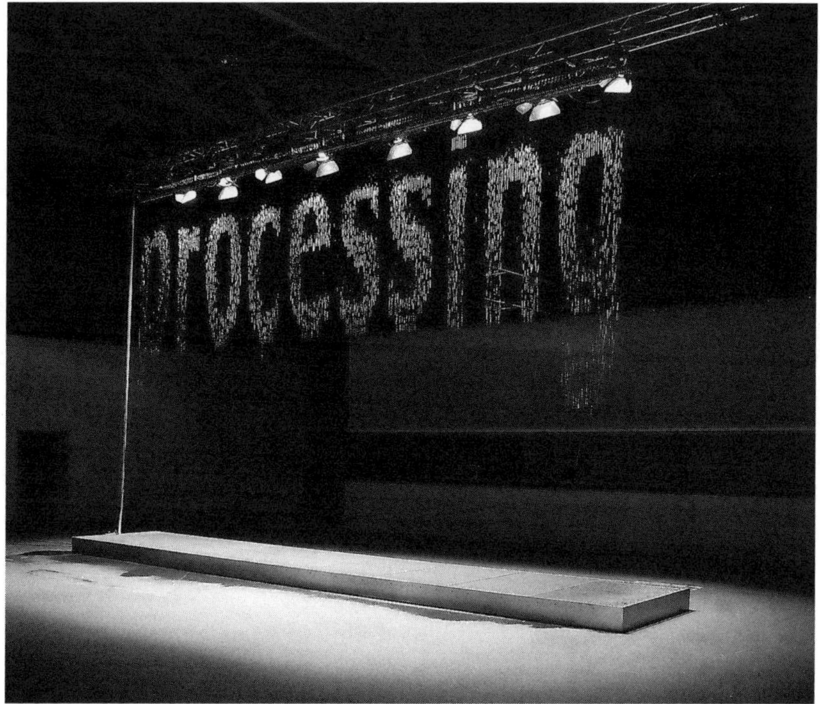

Figure 9.1
Julius Popp, *Bit.Fall* (2006). Permission kindly granted by the artist.

One wonders to what extent the premise of ephemeral information is correct in an age where television and radio programs are no longer broadcasted "away" but instead accessible online for repeated individual perception. This turn of the ephemeral into the permanent started with tape and video recorder and now does not even require any preparation for saving the information needed prior to their broadcast. Digital media and the Internet in particular actually stop the element of transience that had long characterized information and news not presented in printed form. In a way, digital media bestow the quality of script upon any spoken word. It is the specific way information is presented in *Bit.Fall* that reverses this process and gives script the transience of spoken words. Whereas from the cave paintings to contemporary social-media networks, "the perennial role played by media has been to give durable, external support to private, fleeting human experiences," Hansen notes (chapter 1 in this volume), *Bit.Fall* presents the opposite by making information artificially perishable. Although Popp claims thereby to represent a central experience in contemporary culture, he rather, as I will argue here, represents a specific reaction to this experience.

Apart from the accuracy of the work's premise, it should be noted that the technology employed in *Bit.Fall* embodies the logic of flux and manipulation. One wonders about the extent to which this embodiment undermines the critical impetus that the critic, the artist, and the artist's teacher see at work in *Bit.Fall.* It is obvious that critical statements about the transience of text in modern life made within the medium text (as an essay, a novel, or a poem) would hardly be as fascinating as this installation is. Do words written by falling water eclipse ("water down"?) the criticism on culture by the fascination of technology? Does the sensual pleasure of the incessant flood of words and of their medial transience as water droplets inevitably erode the philosophical point of view? A media-archaeological perspective may illustrate the problem and help find an answer.

The technology employed in Popp's installation was invented as early as 1982 by Stephen Pevnick, professor of computer art at the University of Wisconsin. The Graphical Waterfalls®, as Pevnick called his technology in 1990, was first exhibited by the Klein Gallery in 1988 at the International Art Exhibition at Navy Pier in Chicago but was soon used primarily outside the art context, presenting, for example, the word *Jeep* or the image of the Mercedes star at spectacular auto shows. "Graphical Waterfalls provide the ultimate WOW factor," Pevnick states on his Web site.[12] It is the "WOW factor" that makes this writing technology so interesting for entertainment and commercial use.[13]

Popp, who declares he was unaware of Pevnick's work, holds that his technology is different—it is simpler, smaller, cheaper—and is used for a different purpose.[14] He considers technology as a tool, like a brush or a camera, with which one can create completely different content and form. One may wonder, though, whether this technology itself is a message no matter the specific content provided. Is the (political) text in *Bit.Fall* only—to use Marshall McLuhan's phrase from his essay *The Medium Is the Message*—the "juicy piece of meat carried by the burglar to distract the watchdog of the mind" (1964, 32)? Or, phrased in a less imputing manner, does the sustained aesthetic framework inevitably and unintentionally compromise the artwork's announced purpose? The car industry at least does not seem to be concerned at all that the perishability of the signifier this technology renders might be perceived as devaluation of the signified. However, if the content does not change the medium's message, the context may—that is, the appearance of the "WOW factor" in the realm of the art world. Before turning to this issue, we should first explore to what extent *Bit.Fall* in fact undermines the signifier.

At first glance, *Bit.Fall* seems to question the stability of words through the utmost instability of writing material, thus addressing the assurance of meaning itself. Such understanding can be challenged from a deconstructive perspective, which links phonocentrism to logocentrism because of the illusory presence and transparency of the phonetic signifier in contrast to the distorting materiality of the written signifier. Writing with water imitates the temporality of oral language and equally avoids recontextualization (or *diffèrance*) to which the written word is subjected. Popp even artificially intensifies the "phonocentric" nature of the word by accelerating its transience with a dimmed environment and spotlights set up at the top of the construction so that the word disappears in the dark before the water hits the ground. This process not only makes the word's real disappearance invisible but also means that the word remains (though only for a short moment) present in its absence. In a deconstructive reading, such contradiction can be explored as the passage in which *Bit.Fall* undermines the very dichotomy its announced message is based on. However, here it must suffice to note that the words uttered by *Bit.Fall* are not only ephemeral, but also decontextualized and that their "recontextualization" in the random order of their appearance hardly allows a deconstructive reading. In this regard, a second glance reveals that *Bit.Fall* stabilizes rather than undermines the signifier. With regard not to the instability of the writing material, but to its constant reuse—the same "ink" is used again and again to write different words (words as oppositional as *Bush* and *Bin Laden*)—we might say that Popp's installation does contain a certain deconstructive element. However, we doubt that the pragmatic decision of recycling the water justifies reading this reuse as deconstruction and would rather want to point out another aspect of the piece.

Although the materiality of water makes the written text as ephemeral as the spoken word, it does not, despite its transparent material, provide the same transparency—or calm technology—to that matter. In fact, the striking material markings—the "WOW factor" that here ink is fluid not before but after letters have been written—affect the audience's attention and distort their thinking. Rather than (re)considering the meaning of the appearing words, and rather than reflecting "the utter transience of what we consider news," to use Koepnick's words, people will dance beneath this kind of "text rain," walk through it with an umbrella, try getting to the other side without the text/water hitting them, or just enjoy the beauty of words represented by water drops.[15] In contrast to how they treat oral communication, they will not look *through* the signifiers but *at* them. They will do so, however, not in order to discover how the text deconstructs its own rhetoric strategy, but to enjoy the spectacular way of its presentation. *Bit.Fall* does not correct (or undermine) but instead neglects the semiotic value of the text by shifting it into an artifact, like paint and shape in nonfigurative painting, although it is much "cooler" than abstract painting ever could be. Because this neglect occurs in an artistic environment, one can even consider it as being in line with the artist's intention. It fits the message of the ephemeral nature of information if one does not recognize, let alone remember and reflect on, the words presented—as long as this absence of reflection is eventually reflected on.

The term *cooler* may surprise the reader as rather nonacademic language. However, it refers to the theoretical concept of "cool" as developed in Alan Liu's 2004 study *Laws of Cool: Knowledge Work and the Culture of Information*, according to which cool is an ethos of information that is against information, the uselessness of useful information, the use of information to abuse information (185–186). By presenting information out of context and furnishing it with the "WOW factor" of its bizarre materialization, *Bit.Fall* certainly carries out such abuse of information. It does so in contrast to Pevnick's advertisements that stabilize the fluid words through their repetition and contextualization within a clearly defined situation. In the latter advertisements, the fluid words add, because of their specific appearance, the notion of "cool" to the companies the words present but are not cool in Liu's sense precisely for communicating this information. Reading Pevnick's installations against Popp's reveals the different message in the use of the same technology. Whereas in Pevnick's case the signified is stabilized, in Popp's case it is undermined—not by addressing the process of signification, but by ignoring its result.

The "WOW factor" at work in this installation does not necessarily undermine the critical impetus claimed by the artist but actually represents a critical impetus in itself, albeit in a different way than the artist declares—namely, if the ethos of the uselessness of useful information is understood as a critical reaction to the information society with its symptoms of information overload. This shift of attention from the meaning of words to their appearance reads like an ironic response to Weiser and Brown's notion that "the way to become attuned to more information is to attend to it less" (1995). By bringing technology to the fore rather than turning it calm and invisible, by rendering information useless rather than making it visible, *Bit.Fall* contradicts the aim of ubiquitous and calm computing to provide information unobtrusively at the level of microsensation. Against the background of *Bit.Fall* and similar astounding mappings and visualizations of information, and in taking Jeremijenko's remark seriously that *Live Wire* is different from the usual "data fetishism of information rhetoric," we may wonder whether *Live Wire* really supports the agenda of ubiquitous computing or rather represents a playful—and "cool"—relationship to information conceptualized as an event in the center of attraction or an ornament in an otherwise "spectacularly banal office environment."[16] Such perspective on contemporary art is better understood if linked to the preceding and accompanying aesthetic discourse.

Revealing Code

Depriving text of its linguistic value and turning information into an ornament can be situated within the aesthetics of the spectacle that is part of the contemporary "society of the spectacle" and offspring of the "postmodern condition."[17] As is well known, Jean-François Lyotard, in his writing on aesthetics following the description of the erosion of grand narratives in *The Postmodern Condition* (1984), focused on the event and the intensity of the (sublime) moment in the expanse of message and signification. This focus has been described as a shift of attention "from the determination of a general truth or general operating strategy to an interest in 'performativity,'" as Marvin Carlson notes in the context of performance art (1996, 138). With respect to more recent media genres such as film, music videos, and computer games, Andrew Darley similarly notes a "shift away from prior modes of spectator experience based on symbolic concerns (and 'interpretative models') towards recipients who are seeking intensities of direct sensual stimulation." The reader, Darley holds, becomes a sensualist "in pursuit of the ornamental and the decorative, modes of embellishment, the amazing and the breathtaking" (2000, 3, 169).[18]

As far as text in digital media is concerned, I mentioned at the beginning of this chapter the fear (or at least the report and prophecy) of the "breakout of the visual" (Bolter 1996, 258) and the dominance of the "postalphabetic image" (Joyce 2000, 42). The transformation of text from a linguistic artifact to an audiovisual object can also be discussed by means of the concept of the visual as pornographic, as developed in Frederic Jameson's *Signatures of the Visible* (1992). According to Jameson, "the visual is *essentially* pornographic" because "it has its end in rapt, mindless fascination"; pornographic films are therefore "only the potentiation of films in general, which ask us to stare at the world as though it were a naked body" (1). As in McLuhan's dictum that "the medium is the message" and Postman's use of this dictum with respect to television as inevitable medium of amusement, Jameson ascribes a certain quality to the medium of film and questions its critical-utopian potential. For him, film is part of mainstream culture to the extent that it presents a phenomenon as interesting, attractive, and seductive as a naked body at which the spectator is staring with astonishment and affection.

Jameson's concept of the visual has been applied to the role text plays in electronic media. Thus, Janez Strehovec—who picks up Manovich's notion about the cinematic character of the language of new media quoted at the beginning of this chapter—holds that an important part of the textual production in contemporary culture is based on words in motion and that a great amount of it is "presented as naked bodies" (2010, 221).[19] As a case in point, Strehovec refers to Brian Kim Stefans's *The Dreamlife of Letters* (2000), a flash animation of moving letters that ends, quite adequately, with the sentence "Thanks for *watching*" (emphasis added).[20] Like many other examples of kinetic text in digital media and in contrast to earlier text films such as Michael Snow's *So Is This* (1982), *The Dreamlife of Letters*, with its syntax of surprise and shortcuts, owes much to the aesthetic of cinema and music video. Hence, Strehovec notes that text, formerly representing the rather elite medium of literature, is refashioned, appropriated, or "hijacked" as something adequate to the contemporary movie industry and club culture.

A similar observation can also be made concerning *Bit.Fall.* Text appears as a captivating event and physical body to be stared at rather than as a linguistic object to be read and understood. Jameson, describing the visual and musical as the physical and not essentially linguistic elements of text, notes: "The more advanced and rationalized activity"—that is, the engagement with text as a linguistic object—"can also have its dream of the other, and regress to a longing for the more immediately sensory, wishing it could pass altogether over to the visual, or be sublimated into the spiritual body of pure sound" (1992, 2). *Bit.Fall, Live Wire,* and *Internet Stock Fountain* surely carry out such sublimation into the sensory. The text, in its physicality, is stared at in "rapt, mindless fascination," to use Jameson's words (1992, 1).[21]

To be precise, what is stared at is the hidden, unexposed, embedded text: the programming code. The code makes the text—the words pulled from Web sites in *Bit. Fall,* the network traffic data in *Live Wire,* the stock-market numbers in *Internet Stock Fountain*—appear in a particular, fascinating way, and so during this process the code is in fact exhibited itself. However, we do not stare at the code as an alphanumerical equation, but rather as a materialization on the screen or on the scene: the "fluid" letters, the dangling string, and the increasing or decreasing fountain. Staring at the code processing the text or numbers is interreliant with stripping this text of its linguistic value or the numbers of their mathematical nature. Blending McLuhan and Jameson, we can describe the concept in the following way: the pornographic message of digital media is code concealing information. With respect to the issues of ubiquitous computing and calm embeddedness, we can say that the "eventilization" of the text (Hayles 2006, 182), invisibly and permanently taking place within each letter in digital media, is brought to attention by a mode of processing much more sophisticated and spectacular than in regular digital-text production. In this perspective, the pornographic turns into elucidation: making the text illegible makes the code visible.

Such a conclusion can be arrived at with respect to *Bit.Fall* and many other installations employing text as audiovisual objects as well as with respect to other genres of digital art, such as kinetic concrete poetry and mapping art.[22] In fact, the focus on code may, with the application of the title of another seminal text by Jameson (1991), even be considered the inherent "cultural logic" of digital technology. Even though digital technology is primarily invisibly embedded in our lifeworld, we may say that it is this technology's natural (narcissistic) intention to center-stage its own basic material: code work. The shift from the linguistic to the physicality of text, from the expression of ideas to the thrill of technical effects, demonstrates the desire for publicity and recognition. This desire, however, builds completely on discipline (i.e., the skill of virtuoso programming), for it is the faultless code that generates the "perfect body" (or "visual") that we cannot help staring at.

The discipline of coding has its counterpart in perception. As this reading of *Bit. Fall* has shown, the thrill of the technical can, beyond sensual stimulation, also be approached within a hermeneutic model. Although text deprived of its linguistic value no longer utters a specific message, the way such text is presented is surely meaningful. In the end, the pornographic of the medium lies in the eyes of the beholder: staring *at* the materialization of code can always (and finally should) turn into looking *through* it down to its deeper meaning.

Notes

1. As Weiser and Brown further explain, "Technologies encalm as they empower our periphery"; however, "a calm technology will move easily from the periphery of our attention, to the center, and back" (1995).

2. For more on Jeremijenko's work, see http://tech90s.walkerart.org/nj/transcript/nj_04.html.

3. Roy Want's *Internet Stock Fountain* (1999) at Xerox's Palo Alto Research Center indicates by the rate of its water flow whether Xerox shares are up or down.

4. It should be noted that whereas Hansen speaks of *Live Wire* as a work of art in his chapter in this volume (chapter 1), Weiser and Brown refer to it as a "radically new tool" (1995). I thank Luciana Gattass for drawing my attention to this inherent contradiction between ubiquitous computing and art.

5. For more information on *Overboard*, see http://programmatology.shadoof.net/index.php?p=works/overboard/overboard.html.

6. For more information on *The Intruder*, see http://bookchin.net/intruder.

7. Matthew G. Kirschenbaum uses the term *postalphabetic text* to describe David Carson's design style, which "refashions information as an aesthetic event" (1999).

8. For a discussion of mapping art similar to Jeremijenko's *Live Wire* and Want's *Internet Stock Fountain* from an aesthetic and philosophical perspective, see chapter 5 in Simanowski 2011.

9. For a viewing of *Bit.Fall* and more information on it and Julius Popp, see http://youtu.be/ygQHj1W0PPM; http://www.artnet.com/artist/424543553/julius-popp.html; and http://sphericalrobots.org.

10. See http://www.youtube.com/watch?v=AICq53U3dl8.

11. For Astrid Klein's assessment of *Bit.Fall*, see http://netzspannung.org/cat/servlet/CatServlet?cmd=document&subCommand=show&forward=%2fnetzkollektor%2foutput%2fdigital-sparks.project.xml&entryId=342596§ion=context&lang=en.

12. Pevnick's Web site is at http://www.pevnickdesign.com.

13. The Wowlab—a visual design studio specialized in commercials, installations, and multimedia work (see, for example, the work *Light Rain* [2007])—announces the WOW factor right in its name (wowlab.net). As for *Bit.Fall*, Jan Karabasz, former collaborator with Popp, utilizes the *Bit.Fall* installation in the context of the *Rhythmus Berlin* revue at Friedrichstadtpalast,

Berlin (opening night, 2 March 2007) where a 65-foot-wide installation (*Bit.Fall*'s size is 16 by 26) presents images and words representing Berlin. Karabasz's company Elektronische Steuerungen also offers commercial applications of *Bit.Fall*'s technology (see http://www.el-steuerungen.de).

14. Email message from Popp to the author, 18 May 2009.

15. Such forms of connecting with the text in *Bit.Fall* is demonstrated in a video from the Nuit Blanche Festival in 2005, available at http://www.youtube.com/watch?v=vbsAqNlvXE4&feature=related.

16. From http://tech90s.walkerart.org/nj/transcript/nj_04.html. For a detailed discussion of mapping art that distinguishes between its naturalistic and poetic version (providing readable or indecipherable information), see chapter 5 in Simanowski 2011.

17. Guy Debord's phrase "society of the spectacle" from 1967 has been used since then to describe the postmodern time—as, for example, by Jameson (1998, 87).

18. For a critical discussion of the prevalence of excessive decoration in postmodern aesthetics and the shift from contemplative distance to sensual immersion, see Hal Foster's 2002 book *Design and Crime*, which refers to the Austrian architect Adolf Loos, who in his 1910 essay *Ornament and Crime*, confronted the aesthetic hybridity of art nouveau.

19. It should be noted that Jameson's presupposition that the "closest relative" of film is the novel rather than theater or video experimental (1992, 4) helps him make the point regarding a shift away from the cognitive action of reading to the voyeuristic action of staring, at which Strehovec is aiming with his reference to Jameson. Seeing the natural relatives of film in vaudeville and circus with their aesthetics of attraction changes the perspective, though not the account about the signature of the visual (for more on this topic, see Gunning 1999).

20. *The Dreamlife of Letters* can be watched at http://collection.eliterature.org/1/works/stefans__the_dreamlife_of_letters.html.

21. Here and in the following discussion, text is understood in its alphanumeric nature, including numbers.

22. See my discussion of further installations in Simanowski 2010 and of kinetic concrete poetry and mapping art in chapters 2 and 5 in Simanowski 2011.

References

Bolter, Jay David. 1996. "Ekphrasis, Virtual Reality, and the Future of Writing." In *The Future of the Book*, edited by Geoffrey Nunberg, 253–272. Berkeley and Los Angeles: University of California Press.

Bolter, Jay David. 1991. *Writing Space: Computers, Hypertext, and the History of Writing*. New York: Routledge.

Carlson, Marvin. 1996. *Performance: A Critical Introduction*. New York: Routledge.

Darley, Andrew. 2000. *Visual Digital Culture, Surface Play, and Spectacle in New Media Genres*. New York: Routledge.

Foster, Hal. 2002. *Design and Crime (and Other Diatribes)*. New York: Verso.

Gunning, Tom. 1999. "The Cinema of Attractions: Early Film, Its Spectator, and the Avant-Garde." In *Film and Theory: An Anthology*, edited by Robert Stam and Toby Miller, 229–235. Malden, MA: Blackwell.

Hayles, N. Katherine. 2006. "The Time of Digital Poetry: From Object to Event." In *New Media Poetics: Contexts, Technotexts, and Theories*, edited by Adelaide Morris and Thomas Swiss, 181–209. Cambridge, MA: MIT Press.

Jameson, Frederic. 1991. *Postmodernism, or, The Cultural Logic of Late Capitalism*. Durham, NC: Duke University Press Books.

Jameson, Frederic. 1992. *Signatures of the Visible*. New York: Routledge.

Joyce, Michael. 2000. *Othermindedness: The Emergence of Network Culture*. Ann Arbor: University of Michigan Press.

Kirschenbaum, Matthew G. 1999. "The Other End of Print: David Carson, Graphic Design, and the Aesthetics of Media." Available at http://web.mit.edu/comm-forum/papers/kirsch.html. Accessed 15 January 2012.

Koepnick, Lutz. 2006. "[Grid <> Matrix]: Take II." In *[Grid <> Matrix]*, edited by Sabine Eckmann and Lutz Koepnick, 47–75. Washington, DC: Mildred Lane Kemper Art Museum.

Liu, Alan. 2004. *The Laws of Cool: Knowledge Work and the Culture of Information*. Chicago: University of Chicago Press.

Lyotard, Jean-François. 1984. *The Postmodern Condition: A Report on Knowledge*. Translated by Geoff Bennington and Brian Massumi. Minneapolis: University of Minnesota Press.

Manovich, Lev. 2001. *The Language of New Media*. Cambridge, MA: MIT Press.

McLuhan, Marshall. 1964. *Understanding Media: The Extensions of Man*. New York: McGraw-Hill.

Mihai, Nadin. 1997. *The Civilization of Illiteracy*. Dresden: Dresden University Press.

Postman, Neil. 1985. *Amusing Ourselves to Death: Public Discourse in the Age of Show Business*. New York: Viking Penguin.

Sander, Barry. 1994. *A is for Ox: Violence, Electronic Media, and the Silencing of the Written Word*. New York: Pantheon.

Simanowski, Roberto. 2011. *Digital Art and Meaning: Reading Kinetic Poetry, Text Machines, Mapping Art, and Interactive Installations*. Minnesota: University of Minnesota Press.

Simanowski, Roberto. 2010. "Digital Anthropophagy: Refashioning Words as Image, Sound, and Action." *Leonardo* 2: 159–163.

Strehovec, Janez. 2010. "Alphabet on the Move." In *Reading Moving Letters: Digital Literature in Research and Teaching. A Handbook,* edited by Roberto Simanowski, Peter Gendolla, and Jörgen Schäfer, 207–230. Bielefeld, Germany: Transcript.

Weiser, Mark, and John Seely Brown. 1995. "Designing Calm Technology." Available at http://www.ubiq.com/hypertext/weiser/calmtech/calmtech.htm. Accessed 15 January 2012.

10 The Novelty of Being Mobile: A Case Study of Mobile Novels and the Politics of the Personal

Larissa Hjorth

In the rise of networked, ubiquitous, and social media epitomized by Web 2.0 and user-created content (UCC), mobile media has been central in ushering in new types of participation, creativity, and collaboration. The specters of Mark Weiser's (1991) prescient words about the importance of context awareness and embeddedness within the constitution of ubiquitous technologies can be seen in multiple localized forms—as a set of media and communication practices, philosophies, aesthetics, and politics. In each location, ubiquitous computing is taken up in divergent ways.

As this book identifies, ubiquity takes many forms across cultural, aesthetic, and social landscapes. In each context, we see various features of ubiquity getting deployed and embedded subject to the locality. This is particularly the case in one of the most pervasive technologies of the twenty-first century, the mobile phone. Far from being placeless and signaling the demise of geography, the mobile phone heralds the importance of place. Ubiquitous technologies and technics take many forms and require us to locate the phenomenon within specific contexts. One location that has seen personal ubiquitous computing become synonymous with mobile media is Tokyo.

Through the lens of mobile media, we can examine the sociological and cultural dimensions of ubiquitous media. To comprehend fully the phenomenon of mobile media, we must frame it as part of a process of "remediation" (Bolter and Grusin 1999) and convergence of older media; that is, mobile media simultaneously rehearse older forms of intimacy and copresence (Hjorth 2005a; Milne 2001) as they expand and enable new media. Throughout their divergent and rapid uptake across the world, ubiquitous media have become a poignant symbol for contemporary postindustrial models of technology and technics, and personal technologies such as the mobile phone have been key repositories for the rise of ubiquitous media. Personal technologies have also helped foster the emergence of immaterial forms of labor—social, creative, affective, and emotional—such as UCC. Marrying the personal to technology has seen the embedding of ubiquitous media through the process of "personalization," a process that is deployed differently by users than by industry. Moreover, like

Figure 10.1
Tokyo, the ubiquity of mobile phones. Larissa Hjorth 2004.

ubiquitous media, personalization is subject to the forces of the local: in each location, we can see different personalization techniques occurring. In this chapter, I argue that we can understand ubiquitous media through the changing notion of personalization. I discuss ubiquitous media and UCC in a location that has been lauded for its innovation around personal technologies (Ito, Okabe, and Matsuda 2005) and personalization: Tokyo (figure 10.1).

So what do I mean by "personalization"? With the ushering in of ubiquitous media, two dominant tropes of personalization have been incurred—one driven top down from industry, the other driven through user practices such as UCC and user-generated content (UGC, a less active process). Indeed, in an age of "participatory media" (Jenkins 2006), the role of the personal has taken on a new, paradoxical position. This change has led social-networking systems expert Clay Shirky to argue that the "personal" no longer belongs to people, but to technologies. Although some industry-driven approaches and marketing may corroborate such notions, there is an alternative, more insightful route for understanding the rise of ubiquitous, affective technologies—

through the role of UCC. Mobile media epitomize affective technologies (Lasén 2004) by way of their conflation of the personal and the intimate; for many, the mobile phone is *the* most intimate and personal device (Fortunati 2005).[1]

Despite the pervasiveness of industry-driven modes of personalization, the rise of the mobile phone has also included the rise of UCC-driven personalization; the success of mobile media as ubiquitous technology is thus also a history of the growth of the subversive user. In the Asia-Pacific in particular, with "pioneering" locations such as Tokyo and Seoul, twenty-first-century ubiquitous-technology dreams have been transformed into a lived reality—specifically through convergent innovations around mobile media (Hjorth 2009). Through these models of mobile media whereby the mobile phone becomes a multimedia, networked device, we see practices and techniques of UCC begin to reconnect the personal with the political (that is, the user's politics of practice).

I noted one such early example of ubiquitous computing while living in Tokyo in late 1999 and early 2000 with the phenomenal rise of one of the first models of third-generation mobile media—the mobile phone with Internet, Global Positioning System technology, camera, and so on—coming from the dominant service and device provider NTT DoCoMo. In the convergence of various media into the one device, the mobile phone in Japan (called "*keitai*," abbreviated from *denwa keitai*, "mobile phone") represented one of the first mainstream uptakes of context-aware embedded media. DoCoMo's ubiquitous multimedia, plethora of applications, and devices with big screens can be viewed as the precursor to Apple's personalization hyperbolics for the iPhone. Prior to this "walled" version of the Internet proffered by DoCoMo, Internet access via a personal computer or an Internet café in Japan was expensive, but with DoCoMo Japan leapfrogged into twenty-first-century ubiquitous computing via the *keitai*. The dominant ritual of reading hard-copy *manga* (comics) on the long daily public-transport commutes was suddenly replaced by activities such as emailing and net surfing using the *keitai*. This embrace of personal ubiquitous computing via mobile media was due to the significant role *keitai* culture played into what Mizuko Ito, Daisuke Okabe, and Misa Matsuda (2005) call the "personal, pedestrian, and portable" within Japanese everyday life. In particular, the *keitai* highlights the highly significant role that the personal plays both in Japanese tradition (Fujimoto 2005) and in the rise of new media practices (Hjorth 2005b, 2006). This cartography of personalization is specifically marked by the crucial role that young women (*shôjo*) played in the alignment of the personal with the gender politics of UCC.

Indeed, as I have argued elsewhere (Hjorth 2003a, 2003b), one of the dominant symbols of both Japan's and the region's mobile media has been the conspicuous female user. She is representative of emerging cartographies of personalization (through UCC) in the Asia-Pacific that have ensured the success of mainstream ubiquitous media.

One of the first types of UCC to be part of this gendered phenomenon is the *keitai shōsetsu* (mobile novels). The phenomenal rise of *keitai shōsetsu* has to do with the highly significant role played by the *keitai* within Japanese everyday life. For many Japanese, the *keitai* is their main Internet portal, thus rendering the device a tool both for communication and for information and entertainment. In a culture where long train journeys back and from work are the norm, the transformation of the *keitai* into *shōsetsu* is but just one possibility for passing the time. The *keitai shōsetsu* phenomenon began with the founding of one of Japan's most pivotal UCC sites, Maho i-Land (*maho* means "magic"), in 1999. Although *keitai shōsetsu* were initially written by professionals, by 2005 everyday users had begun to be inspired to write and disseminate their own *keitai shōsetsu*.

Predominantly written *by* women *for* women, this mode of new media highlights the significance of remediation (figure 10.2); many of the successful *keitai shōsetsu* (among millions produced yearly) are adapted into older media such as film, *manga*, and anime. This practice can be seen as an extension of earlier gendered tropes of Japanese new media that in the 1980s was dubbed the "anomalous female teenage handwriting" phenomenon (Kinsella 1995). Characterized by *kawaii* (cute) transformations of the Japanese alphabet or by *hiragana*, "women's language/script,"[2] this

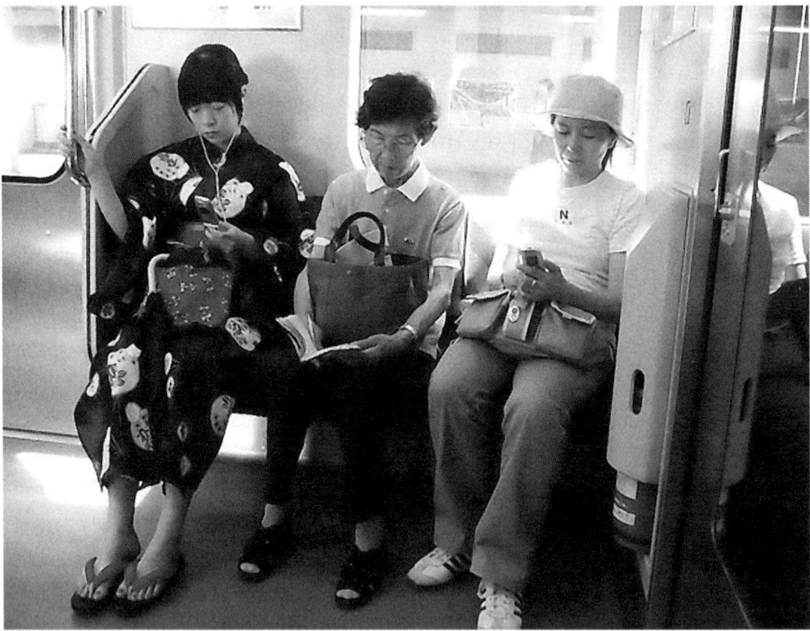

Figure 10.2
Three generations and remediations of personalized media (*keitai* version). Larissa Hjorth 2004.

emerging genre of new media writing soon dominated mobile communication from the pager on, thus heralding what has been called the "high school girl pager revolution," whereby girls' and women's UCC hijacked (through personalization techniques) technologies that industry had aimed at businessmen ("salarymen") (Fujimoto 2005; Matsuda 2005). Moreover, *keitai shōsetsu* can also been seen as an extension of literary traditions evoked by arguably one of the earliest novels in the world, *The Tale of Genji*, written in AD 1000. Drawing on haiku, letters, and love sonnets, "Murasaki Shikibu's" (the pen name of a person thought to be Fujiwara Takako) *The Tale of Genji* deploys hiragana to tell both the men's and the women's versions of the playboy "Genji's" exploits. This tradition of women's writing in Japan, amplified within the genre of *keitai shōsetsu*, was most explicitly highlighted in an updated version of *The Tale of Genji* entitled *Tomorrow's Rainbow* by eighty-six-year-old Buddhist nun Jakucho Setouchi—the "Marguerite Duras of Japan" writing under the pen name of "Purple" (Yourgrau 2009).

By exploring this emerging form of creative, social, affective, and emotional labor typified by *keitai shōsetsu*, this chapter considers how the *keitai* functions in extending the localized and gendered notions of the "personal" (Ito, Okabe, and Matsuda 2005) that, in turn, inform (sociocultural) revisions of "the personal as the political" in an age of ubiquitous media.

The Politics of Ubiquity: Getting Personal

The rise, dissemination, and adaptation of ubiquitous media are characterized by unilateral uptakes. These uptakes are the result of various factors—such as technonationalism and sociocultural nuances—that inform both micro (individual) and macro (cultural) contexts and practices. Hence, to conceptualize ubiquity, we must recognize that it is far from homogeneous in its dissemination globally. Although ubiquitous media might be everywhere or "everyware" (Greenfield 2006), it is through the lens of locality that we can gain insight into the practices and politics of ubiquity. For example, what it means to use ubiquitous computing in Japan—where the *keitai* is pretty much *the* device for everything from emailing to using positioning and social-networking systems to taking pictures—is a completely different embodied experience than it is in the United States, for instance. I argue that these technocultural localities are best understood through the rubric of cartographies of personalization. These cartographies take a specific geoimaginary within the Asia-Pacific.

As the mobile phone has grown from an extension of the landline into a networked multimedia device, it has accompanied and complemented the region's economic, technological, and political transformations since the 1997 Asian economic crisis.[3] In this phenomenon heralding new models of consumption and technocultural lifestyle narratives, the young female mobile-media user has played a central role. It is through the role of personalized micronarratives in the form of UCC, what I have called "imaging communities" (Hjorth 2009), that we can begin to gain insight into new modes of media creativity, literacy, and labor in the twenty-first century. This rise of gendered mobile media can also be read as indicative of the region's broader postindustrial shifts in which gender has colored various types of labor practices.

Indeed, just as female paid employment (predominantly in precarious new media sectors) has increased over this ten-year period (International Labour Organization 2008),[4] so too have the new forms of mobile media and social labor that have accompanied this phenomenon. These parallel and interrelated trends have resulted in the reworking of gender, labor and technology. From social intimacy to UCC, labor has taken on various immaterial and material guises. Labor can be creative, affective, emotional, and social. As Arlie Hochschild (1983, 2000, 2001, 2003) notes, the rise of globalization can be seen through the role of service-care industries whereby women, especially in developing countries, are exploited for their emotional labor. She notes that with the increasing commercialization of human feelings and the intimate, distinctions between work and home have blurred. This phenomenon of commercializing the intimate (or what Lauren Berlant [1998] calls the "publicness of intimacy") is amplified within the ambience and labor of UCC. These new forms of labor and intimacies can be witnessed within localized UCC characterized by camera-phone images and vernacular text messages as well as within new commodity forms such as *keitai shōsetsu*.

Through these UCC practices of gendered mobile media, the Asia-Pacific can be understood as a series of local and transnational geoimaginaries that are marked by personalization. Although the phenomenon of personalization can be seen as a broad global trend across the cultures of lifestyle and mobile media, it is within the Asia-Pacific that we already witnessing particular synergies between gendered intimacy and labor that are almost indivisible from the production and consumption of mobile media. This is a result of the region's shift from comprising a series of newly industrialized countries)—demonstrating increasingly economic and technological power—to comprising a series of localities that amplify ideological prowess with twenty-first-century capital (Arrighi, Hamashita, and Selden 2003; Dirlik 2007; Hjorth 2009). In this transformation of the Asia-Pacific, one can see emerging formations that can only be described as "cartographies of personalization."

Cartographies of personalization are as much geographic and spatial as they are emotional and sociocultural. These topographies are marked by the interior, intimate, and contingent practices that both challenge and reinforce gendered performativity[5] around labor and intimacy. They are a product of the rise of affective technologies such as mobile media in which industry attempts to shift the "personal" away from people and toward technologies (Shirky 2008). Through UCC, however, the personal is reclaimed from technologies and relocated in people. Indeed, as one of the most "personal" and "intimate" devices (Fortunati 2005), the mobile phone affords users a space in which acts of copresent intimacy, emotion, affect, and the haptic can come into play, contesting industry or designers' original intentions. This relationship is highlighted by the fact that the transformation of the mobile phone into a multimedia device has occurred through the burgeoning numbers of subversive users (Hjorth 2003a, 2003b). Many applications are successful simply because users have repurposed their intention.

Like social, networked media, these cartographies are global, but so are they likewise marked by distinctively regional and localized characteristics. Here the notion of the "personal" is significant, with the rise of *keitai* culture (synonymous with "ubiquity" in Japan) marked by three key features—the "personal, [the] portable, and [the] pedestrian" (see Ito, Okabe, and Matsuda 2005). These three P's render new technologies relevant; that is, they transform them into an integral part of the technocultural landscape. Indeed, the role of "personalization" has been crucial in the rise of ubiquitous and affective technologies such as mobile media—playing a significant role in the media localization.

Japanese *keitai* culture is part of broader "personalization" techniques that can be mapped back to the eighteenth century (Fujimoto 2005; Ito, Okabe, and Matsuda 2005) and thus should be contextualized as part of broader shifts within industrialism and postindustrialism. However, within these broader cartographies, localized and temporalized features occur—exasperated at particular key sociocultural and economic periods. One of the key factors that ensured the success of technological ubiquity and the media convergence represented by *keitai* in Japan was the central and defining role that *personalization* played in the uptake of new technologies. And so what does it mean to think about a politics of personalization in an age whereby the "personal" is claimed by technology via industry but movements such as UCC attempt to claim it back for the people? And how does this concept differ or overlap with the 1960s feminist adage "the personal as the political"?

As ubiquitous media spreads, the attendant forms of emerging creativity, collaboration, and community within terrains such as Web 2.0 will undoubtedly transform everyday users and their UCC. One of the key attributes of this personalization phenomenon is what Jean Burgess (2008) calls "vernacular creativity." Here Burgess spearheads the emerging amateur/professional nexus that has been altered by networked social media. Within these new-media social cartographies of UCC, users and their labor—or "playbour" in the case of gaming (Küchlick 2005)—are increasingly becoming coproducers or "produsers" (Bruns 2006).

A key example of UCC "vernacular creativity" is *keitai shōsetsu*. As I argue in this chapter, *keitai shōsetsu* vividly demonstrates the increasing role that personalization plays in the politics of ubiquitous media. Far from renouncing older media, ubiquitous personalized media such as *keitai shōsetsu* are rehearsed and remediated as they converge and diverge—extending and expanding upon the tradition of women's subversive writing through the use of new media in the form of "kitten writing" or *kawaii* cultures. From Hello Kitty customization to *keitai* writing, examining the *kawaii* can give insight into gender practices in Japan (Hjorth 2003a, 2003b). This is most tangible at the intersections between *keitai shōsetsu, kogals* and the *kawaii.*

The Art of Being Mobile: The *Keitai Shōsetsu Kogal* and the *Kawaii*

Tokyo's emerging cartographies of personalization in the form of UCC (Fujimoto 2005; Matsuda 2005; Okada 2005) are most palpable in the rise of the *kogal* (Miller 2005): a new hybrid type of performativity by young women born through the technocultures afforded by the *keitai*. *Kogal*s have been instrumental in the shift from the pager to the personal handy-phone system (a hybrid of the personal digital assistant and mobile phone) to the *keitai* in Japan (Fujimoto 2005; Hjorth 2003a, 2003b; Matsuda 2005; Okada 2005). Beginning in 2000, as the *keitai* phenomenon became increasingly pervasive and synonymous with personal ubicomp, it became apparent that the symbolic and literal meanings associated with the *keitai* were concurrent with a steady increase in the visibility of young women and the new forms of creative and affective labor in which they were involved. This burgeoning of *keitai kogal* new media and emergent new creative industries is most tangible in the case of *keitai shōsetsu*. Behind these images of the successful *keitai* and the specific role of "personalization" within Japanese technologies lies a parallel story—the growth of the active and subversive female user (Hjorth 2005b, 2006). Indeed, the genealogy of the rise of mobile ubiquitous media is tied directly to the subversive, personalization practices of young women by means of UCC rather than the use of industry-driven applications.

The rise of the *keitai* from business tool to social accessory parallels the demise of the national symbol, the "salaryman," and the expanding power of young female users—epitomized by the female high school girl user or the young female consumer, the *shôjo* (Fujimoto 2005).[7] Consumers, in particular young female consumers, have played an integral role in both the growth and adaptation of *keitai* cultures, so much so that the emergence of new tropes of empowered female consumers (or what Axel Bruns [2006] calls "produsers") are indivisible from the *keitai* phenomenon, which, in turn, has been integral within emerging forms of Japanese technoculture.

Like the *keitai, shōsetsu* plays on the significance of the *personal* within Japanese tradition (Fujimoto 2005), a fact that can be evidenced in Japan's successful role in developing "electronic individualism" (Kogawa 1984), from the Sony Walkman to GameBoy. The *keitai shōsetsu* epitomizes the specific role the personal has played in Japan upon both micro (individual) and macro (nationalism) levels (McVeigh 2003). Through the *keitai shōsetsu* and its emerging modes of creative, social, affective, and emotional labor (UCC), we can see the *keitai*'s pivotal role in extending the notion of the "personal" (Ito, Okabe, Matsuda 2005), so much so that I argue that these mobile novels completely revise "the personal as the political" in an age of full-time public intimacy.

The "personal as political," with its feminist overtones from 1960s and 1970s body politics, plays a particular role in *keitai shōsetsu* given that these mobile novels are predominantly written *by* women *for* women. What began as a youth-oriented activity (most *keitai shōsetsu* are both written and read on the long commuting journeys that are part of Tokyo daily life) has more recently become a medium for women of different generations and class. This shift marks a time when the *keitai shōsetsu* becomes more interesting and thus a more compelling study not only for understanding the relationship between new media and older media such as the print novel, but also for gaining insight into Japanese women's practices of storytelling.

Far from eroding Japanese "high" literature (Sullivan 2008), *keitai shōsetsu* invoke the art of haiku poetry (Twitter also arguably draws on such a tradition) and recall the significant role played by a female writer, "Murasaki Shikibu," in the development of the novel through *The Tale of Genji*. In this context, *keitai shōsetsu* highlight not only early models of literature, but also the role female writers have played in the field. Given that women were not allowed to learn the art of *kanji*, the Japanese system of writing, they had to use *hiragana*, an alternate "women's language." *The Tale of Genji* is written in *hiragana*, once the only Japanese alphabet women were allowed to use (when it was invented around AD 800), further reinforcing the development of a female-centered, emotionally charged vernacular. In contemporary *keitai shōsetsu*, we can see *hiragana* and the female, emotionally driven flavor being further intensified, especially through the deployment of emoticons (*emoji*), *kawaii*, and "kitten writing" (a hybridization of *emoji* and *hiragana*) (Kinsella 1995).

Indeed, it is the ambiguous role of *kawaii* culture to evoke multiple forms of performativity able to reinforce and yet transgress gendered stereotypes around technocultures that makes it such a poignant subject for analysis. It is impossible to understand the rise of *keitai* cultures as synonymous with the burgeoning female UCC without comprehending the pivotal role *kawaii* culture has played at both the level of the technonational imagined community and, more important, the level of the imaging community. Through mapping this relationship, we can gain greater acuity in understanding emerging gendered mobile intimacies, labor, and capital. *Kawaii* culture has helped to embed mobile media within forms of localized gendered intimacy and thus provided both the backdrop and the vehicle for the rise of female "produsers."

According to Sharon Kinsella's groundbreaking research, *kawaii* culture arose as a youth subculture in the 1970s as a means of self-expression and rearticulation and as a reaction to the overarching traditions perceived as oppressive. Young adults preferred to stay childlike rather than join the ranks of the corrupt adults (Kinsella 1995). This phenomenon highlighted the way in which "childhood" as a construct is conceived and practiced in locations such as Japan, with its premature adulthood, in contrast to locations such as the West (Ariés 1962; White 1993). In practices such as "kitten writing," youths subverted Japanese cultural concepts by intentionally misspelling words in acts of political neologism (Kinsella 1995).[8]

Kawaii culture draws from the Japanese tradition of gift giving and provides a means to overcome the Japanese proclivity toward shyness in social interactions (Kusahara 2001). The gift-giving genealogy is pertinent in *kawaii*'s translation into mobile telephony, highlighting and facilitating the gift-giving cartography of mobile telephonic social rituals and symbolic exchange (Taylor and Harper 2002). *Kawaii* culture's role in customization articulates a type of social glue to the copresent online space of the *keitai*. It reminds users of the role of subjectivity in technological spaces; at its core, *kawaii* customization domesticates the technology. It transforms the technology into a sociotechnology, bringing the role of the sociocultural to the forefront of the technology. *Kawaii* culture is instrumental in the gendered cartographies of personalization in Japan and can be seen to extend its vernacular creativity in the form of *keitai shōsetsu*. The tendency of customization to be cute—or what Brian McVeigh (2000) calls "technocute" (whereby the cute makes new technology "warm") (figure 10.3)—has taken various guises and turns in the rise of gendered new media in Japan. It has been an important part of women's gaining access and feeling comfortable with the emerging technocultures. The fact that "kitten writing" is now part of the mobile phone industries' gender scripting (i.e., the *keitai* now comes with increasingly varieties of *emoji*) highlights how the UCC feminized practices not only have a long tradition but also have become institutionalized.

Although UCC may provide the everyday user with a voice and models for intimacy, interactivity, and dialog between authors and readers, one of the big problems is that it exploits the user's creative and social labor often without remuneration. However, it seems Japan is providing a different picture for the future of UCC in which media content–distribution companies, such as Maho i-Land, take an active role in encouraging and fostering talent and media literacy programs. For example, Maho i-Land has an annual award for UCC: the winner of the best *keitai shōsetsu* award can win one million yen and a publishing contract, and a runner up can get 500,000 yen and a publishing contract. With its establishment in 1999, Maho i-Land provided avenues for various forms of UCC—poems, images, music, and stories. Its template "Let's Make Novels"—along with unlimited data packages for the *keitai* in 2003—impelled the dramatic rise of writers and readers of *keitai shōsetsu*. By 2007, nearly four million different *keitai shōsetsu* had been printed in hard copy. With one million *keitai shōsetsu* being produced in 2007 and 1.9 billion page views per month, Maho i-Land has become an exemplary case of the popularity of UCC. These data paint a picture of an active UCC scene in which *keitai* cultures are nurturing new talent, but how do they reflect female empowerment through such technologies?

Figure 10.3
Technocute personalization. Larissa Hjorth 2004.

The *keitai shōsetsu* provides an interesting lens to think through new gendered forms of UCC labor. One of the key features of *keitai shōsetsu* is that they tend to follow a diarylike, confessional, autobiographical model—very much reflecting Berlant's (1998) observation of the growing "publicness of intimacy" being forged through the highly personalized and intimate media, the *keitai*. These novels inspire users to become writers and are part of a broader trend toward the professionalization of UCC, particularly through its adaptation and translation into other media such as film. For example, the most popular and famous mobile novel, *Koizara*, written by female *keitai* novelist "Mika," was famously adapted by female director Natsuko Imai into a movie.

Through *keitai* UCC, we can see many examples of female users finding inroads into creative activities. Thanks to UCC-oriented organizations such as Maho i-Land, these users can be empowered on various levels—sharing and collaborating on stories as well as potentially making a career and gaining professional recognition in the form of book publishing or film contracts. Far from a situation in which *keitai shōsetsu* culture is eroding the significance of older, remediated media such as *manga* and film, it is providing new material for and interest in adapting stories by everyday users. The intimate, personal nature of mobile media unquestionably provides a platitude for rehearsing the earlier epistolary traditions of women's fiction, with its literacy devices such as letter writing. To think about ubiquitous networked media is to acknowledge the pivotal role that remediation has played in the practices of UCC new media.

Conclusion

In the rise of participatory, networked, ubiquitous, and social media, we are seeing emerging and yet remediated forms of new media. Through the rubric of UCC practices, we can begin to reconceptualize what these emergent modes of participation, engagement, creativity, and collaboration entail. But within these shifts of media practices, we must ask: What does it mean to be personal and political in an age of ubiquitous media? In other words, what happens to the feminist adage that "the personal as the political"?

In Japan, we can see that creative labor around mobile media—drawing from the history of the first Japanese novels and gendered genres of expression such as *gyaru-emoji* (girl emoticon), kitten writing—has transformed into a multifaceted industry of popular *keitai shōsetsu* and is now being adapted into other media such as film. Women's stories are being heard. Through the personal and intimate frame of the *keitai,* millions of micronarratives are being told to millions of readers. The *keitai shōsetsu* demonstrates its particular role in nurturing the personal as a space for women's literature—a place where personal stories, politics, and communities are founded. These stories take flight across a variety of old and new media—with the *keitai shōsetsu* reinvigorating other media canons such as *manga* and film. Through Web 2.0, social-network media such as 2ch and mixi, community storytelling is taking on new value again, featuring the rise of female directors, creators, and producers. Is this a taste of a future in which traditionally "feminine" social labor has gained some form of value in the market? How will this gendered cartography play out?

As I have demonstrated through the example of *keitai shōsetsu,* the rise of ubiquitous computing through affective technologies has been accompanied by UCC practices—often with subversive results. *Keitai shōsetsu* can be seen as part of the kitten-writing phenomenon that began in Japan in the 1970s—accompanying the birth and rise of personal technologies. Kitten writing has always fused the creative with the emotional and social, playfully merging Japanese alphabets such as hiragana with the logographic in order to personalize a media communication space. In this way, *keitai shōsetsu* extends three traditions—the gendering of *keitai* culture, the gendering of the Japanese language, and the significant role female writers such as Murasaki played in the birth and rise of the novel. For these three reasons and more, it is hard to ignore the role *keitai shōsetsu* has played not only in evoking the personal but also in linking the personal to a political currency in which gender is mobilized as a form of performativity and potential subversion. Thus, through the example of the *keitai shōsetsu* we can revise notions of "the personal as the political" in an age of ubiquitous media.

Notes

1. As sociologist Amparo Lasén has noted, the increasing significance of mobile media is predicated around its role as an "affective" technology in which emotional and affective labor become the dominant currencies. Mobile media is a by-product of the always-on phenomenon whereby work and leisure boundaries are blurred. We are always ready to respond to our mobile phone, always ready to perform particular "feeling rules." Lasén also argues that mobility has always been at the heart of intimacy. This relationship is demonstrated through the various forms of propinquity that have accompanied changing notions of "romance" and "intimacy" (Giddens 1992; Hjorth 2005a; Milne 2001).

2. Invented by a Buddhist priest known as Kûkai (AD 774–835), *hiragana*, as a phonetic version of *kanji*, was taught to women because it was seen as simple in comparison to *kanji*. At this time, women spoke Japanese and wrote *hiragana*, which is why *hiragana* was defined as "women's language."

3. Within models of innovative ubiquitous media, the Asia-Pacific has featured prominently. Beyond techno-orientalist (Morley and Robins 1995; Yoshimi 1999), soft power (Nye 2005, 2007, 2008), and "gross national cool" (McGray 2002) interpretations, the significant role played by ubiquitous media within specific technocultural landscapes in the region can be clearly framed through localized notions of personalization. Since the 1997 financial crisis, locations in the Asia-Pacific region have sought to rebuild and reconceptualize their economies from information and communication technology manufacturing sites into models of twenty-first-century informational societies. The mobile phone, as vehicle for ubiquitous-communication media, has been symbolically and materially integral to this shift.

4. According to the International Labour Organization's 2008 report *Global Employment Trends for Women*, these increases in female employment can be noted in East Asia and the Pacific, whereas South Asia remains relatively unchanged, with an "untapped female potential and sizeable decent work deficit" (21).

5. As Judith Butler (1991) notes, gender is constructed and naturalized through a set of localized regulations and rituals that she defines as performative. Through this revised notion of gender as a set of performances, we can begin to uncover some of the modes of gendered identities—and attendant modes of femininity and masculinity—arising in the transnational interstitials constituting the Asia-Pacific. An important aspect to add to Butler's notion is the pivotal way in which gender is localized within a cultural context. With the rise of postcolonial feminists such as bell hooks, Trinh T. Min-ha, Rey Chow, and Sarah Ahmed, the Western inflection underscoring much of the earlier work in gender studies is now challenged by new regional gender studies and returns of essentialism.

6. As John Whittier Treat (1996) perspicuously notes, the term *shôjo* signifies a sexually neutral, consumption-focused female.

7. Kitten writing can be seen as earlier examples of *emoji* (emoticons) before it was institutionalized by industry as part of built-in *keitai* customization (Hjorth 2003a, 2003b). Under this light, the emergence of kitten writing with personal technologies in the 1970s was no accident; indeed, this emergence highlights that the rise of industry-driven customization has been accompanied by the emergence of UCC personalization. In this way, kitten writing can be read as part of a tradition of female, UCC personalization practices that have sought to align the personal with the interpersonal. *Kawaii* can take various forms: writing, character culture, and animation, to name a few. The *kawaii,* although stereotyped as a young female's preoccupation and thus characterized as "female," is traditionally seen as asexual (Whittier Treat 1996)—that is, as having a gender without sex. Characters like Hello Kitty are emblematic of this asexuality. Like the typical consumer, the *shôjo,* the *kawaii* was a female without agency in a society where the *oyaji* (older man/father) was the national symbol after World War II.

References

Ariés, Philipe. 1962. *Centuries of Childhood: A Social History of Family Life.* Translated by Robert Baldick. New York: Knopf.

Arrighi, Giovanni, Takeshi Hamashita, and Mark Selden, eds. 2003. *The Resurgence of East Asia: 500, 150, and 50 Year Perspectives.* London: Routledge.

Berlant, Lauren. 1998. "Intimacy: A Special Issue." *Critical Inquiry,* special issue edited by Lauren Berlant, 24 (2) (Winter): 281–288.

Bolter, Jay and Richard Grusin. 1999. *Remediation: Understanding New Media.* Cambridge, MA: MIT Press.

Bruns, Axel. 2006. "Introduction." In *Uses of Blogs,* edited by Axel Bruns and Joanne Jacobs, 11–22. New York: Peter Lang.

Burgess, Jean. 2008. "'All Your Chocolate Rain Are Belong to Us'? Viral Video, YouTube, and the Dynamics of Participatory Culture." In *The VideoVortex Reader,* edited by Geert Lovink and Sabine Niederer, 101–110. Amsterdam: Institute of Network Cultures.

Butler, Judith. 1991. *Gender Trouble.* London: Routledge.

Dirlik, Arif. 2007. "Global South: Predicament and Promise." *The Global South* 1 (1) (Winter): 12–23.

Fortunati, Leopoldina. 2005. "Mobile Phones and Fashion in Post-Modernity." *Telekronikk* 3–4:35–48.

Fujimoto, Kenichi. 2005. "The Third-Stage Paradigm: Territory Machine from the Girls' Pager Revolution to Mobile Aesthetics." In *Personal, Portable, Pedestrian: Mobile Phones in Japanese*

Life, edited by Mizuko Ito, Daisuke Okabe, and Misa Matsuda, 77–102. Cambridge, MA: MIT Press.

Giddens, Anthony. 1992. *The Transformation of Intimacy: Sexuality, Love, and Eroticism in Modern Societies*. Cambridge: Polity.

Greenfield, Adam. 2006. *Everyware: The Dawning Age of Ubiquitous Computing*. Berkeley, CA: New Riders.

Hjorth, Larissa. 2009. *Mobile Media in the Asia-Pacific*. London: Routledge.

Hjorth, Larissa. 2006. "Fast-Forwarding Present: The Rise of Personalization and Customization in Mobile Technologies in Japan." *Southern Review* 38 (3): 23–42.

Hjorth, Larissa. 2005a. "Locating Mobility: Practices of Co-Presence and the Persistence of the Postal Metaphor in SMS/MMS Mobile Phone Customization in Melbourne." *Fibreculture* 6. Available at http://six.fibreculturejournal.org/fcj-035-locating-mobility-practices-of-co-presence-and-the-persistence-of-the-postal-metaphor-in-sms-mms-mobile-phone-customization-in-melbourne. Accessed 10 December 2006.

Hjorth, Larissa. 2005b. "Odours of Mobility: Japanese Cute Customization in the Asia-Pacific Region." *Journal of Intercultural Studies* 26:39–55.

Hjorth, Larissa. 2003a. "Kawaii@keitai." In *Japanese Cybercultures*, edited by Nanette Gottlieb and Mark McLelland, 50–59. New York: Routledge.

Hjorth, Larissa. 2003b. "'Pop' and 'Ma': The Landscape of Japanese Commodity Characters and Subjectivity." In *Mobile Cultures: New Media in Queer Asia*, edited by Fran Martin, Audrey Yue, and Chris Berry, 158–179. Durham, NC: Duke University Press.

Hochschild, Arlie R. 2003. *The Commercialization of Intimate Life: Notes from Home and Work*. Berkeley and Los Angeles: University of California Press.

Hochschild, Arlie R. 2001. *The Time Bind: When Work Becomes Home and Home Becomes Work*. New York: Metropolitan/Holt Press.

Hochschild, Arlie R. 2000. "Global Care Chains and Emotional Surplus Value." In *On The Edge: Living with Global Capitalism*, edited by Will Hutton and Anthony Giddens, 130–146. London: Jonathan Cape.

Hochschild, Arlie R. 1983. *The Managed Heart: Commercialization of Human Feeling*. Berkeley and Los Angeles: University of California Press.

International Labour Organization. 2008. *Global Employment Trends for Women*. Available at http://www.ilo.org/global/about-the-ilo/press-and-media-centre/news/WCMS_091102/lang--en/index.htm. Accessed 2 March 2008.

Ito, Mizuko, Daisuke Okabe, and Misa Matsuda, eds. 2005. *Personal, Portable, Pedestrian: Mobile Phones in Japanese Life*. Cambridge, MA: MIT Press.

Jenkins, Henry. 2006a. *Fans, Bloggers, and Gamers: Essays On Participatory Culture.* New York: New York University Press.

Kinsella, Sharon. 1995. "Cuties in Japan." In *Women, Media, and Consumption in Japan,* edited by Lise Skov and Brian Moeran, 220–254. Surrey, UK: Curzon Press.

Kogawa, Tetsuo. 1984. "Beyond Electronic Individualism." *Canadian Journal Of Political And Social Theory/Revue Canadienne De Thetorie Politique Et Sociale,* 8 (3), Fall. Available at http://anarchy.translocal.jp/non-japanese/electro.html. Accessed 20 July 2007.

Kücklich, Julian. 2005. "Precarious Playbour: Modders and the Digital Games Industry." *Fibreculture* 5. Available at http://five.fibreculturejournal.org/fcj-025-precarious-playbour-modders-and-the-digital-games-industry. Accessed 23 July 2008.

Kusahara, Machiko. 2001. "The Art of Creating Subjective Reality: An Analysis of Japanese Digital Pets." *Leonardo* 34 (4): 299–302.

Lasén, Amparo. 2004. "Affective Technologies—Emotions and Mobile Phones." *Receiver* 11. Available at http://ucm.academia.edu/AmparoLasén/Papers/461823/Affective_Technologies._Emotions_and_Mobile_Phones. Accessed 10 June 2005.

Matsuda, Misa. 2005. "Discourses of *Keitai* in Japan." In *Personal, Portable, Pedestrian: Mobile Phones in Japanese Life,* edited by Mizuko Ito, Daisuke Okabe, and Misa Matsuda, 19–40. Cambridge, MA: MIT Press.

McGray, David. 2002. "Japan's Gross National Cool." *Foreign Policy* (May–June): 44–54.

McVeigh, Brian. 2003. *Nationalisms of Japan: Managing and Mystifying Identity.* Oxford: Rowman and Littlefield.

McVeigh, Brian. 2000. "How Hello Kitty Commodifies the Cute, Cool, and Camp: 'Consumutopia' versus 'Control' in Japan." *Journal of Material Culture* 5 (2): 291–312.

Miller, Laura. 2005. "Bad Girl Photography." In *Bad Girls of Japan,* edited by Laura Miller and Jan Bardsley, 127–142. London: Palgrave Macmillan.

Milne, Esther. 2001. "'Don't Send Me Your Saliva': Fantasies of Disembodiment in Email and Epistolary Technologies." In *Politics of a Digital Present: An Inventory of Australian Net Culture, Criticism, and Theory,* edited by Hugh Brown and Geert Lovink, 27–37. Melbourne: Fibreculture.

Morley, David, and Kevin Robins. 1995. *Spaces of Identities: Global Media, Electronic Landscapes, and Cultural Boundaries.* New York: Routledge.

Nye, Joseph. 2008. *The Powers to Lead.* Oxford: Oxford University Press.

Nye, Joseph. 2007. *Power in the Global Information Age.* New York: Taylor & Francis.

Nye, Joseph. 2005. *Soft Power: The Means to Success in World Politics.* New York: Public Affairs.

Okada, Tomoyuki. 2005. "Youth Culture and the Shaping of Japanese Mobile Media: Personalization and the *Keitai* Internet as Multimedia." In *Personal, Portable, Pedestrian: Mobile Phones in

Japanese Life, edited by Mizuko Ito, Daisuke Okabe, and Misa Matsuda, 41–60. Cambridge, MA: MIT Press.

Shirky, Clay. 2008. "Here Comes Everybody." Presented at the Aspen Ideas Festival, 30 June–8 July, Aspen, Colorado. Available at http://www.youtube.com/watch?v=YEHdQiDz1Mc. Accessed 20 December 2008.

Sullivan, Jane. 2008. "Thumbs Down to 'the Nokia Novel.'" *The Age*. February 9.

Taylor, Alex, and Richard Harper. 2002. "Age-Old Practices in the 'New World': A Study of Gift-Giving between Teenage Mobile Phone Users." In *Changing Our World, Changing Ourselves: Proceedings of the SIGCHI Conference on Human Factors in Computing Systems*, 439–446. Minneapolis: ACM.

Weiser, Mark. 1991. "The Computer for the 21st Century." *Scientific American* 265 (3): 94–104.

White, Mary. 1993. *The Material Child: Coming of Age in Japan and America*. New York: Free Press.

Whittier Treat, John. 1996. "Introduction." In *Contemporary Japanese Popular Culture*, edited by John Whittier Treat, 1–16. Honolulu: University of Hawaii Press.

Yourgrau, Barry. 2009. "Thumb Novels: Mobile Phone Fiction." Salon.com. Available at http://www.keitai-shosetsu.com. Accessed 1 January 2012.

Yoshimi, Shunya. 1999. "'Made in Japan': The Cultural Politics of 'Home Electrification' in Postwar Japan." *Media, Culture, and Society* 21:149–171.

11 Transmateriality: Presence Aesthetics and the Media Arts

Mitchell Whitelaw

In Rafael Lozano-Hemmer's *Pulse Room* (2006) is a space filled with hundreds of incandescent light bulbs, hanging in a flickering array. A participant grips a pair of electrodes, causing the closest bulb to pulse in time with her own heartbeat; after a moment, this new pulse moves to join the multitude of the array. The room is full of human pulses, all characteristic double beats, faster and slower, brighter and duller, but palpably reembodied in glass and glowing wire. *Pulse Room* is one example of what I argue is a significant turn within recent media arts emphasizing the materiality of media and computation: a materiality that we are directly implicated in, as this work shows. Through Hans Ulrich Gumbrecht's work, this chapter proposes a "presence aesthetics" in the media arts and argues that media technologies can elicit moments of intensified being-in-the-world despite their more familiar role in distancing that world from us.

After making a specific theoretical argument in its first half, the chapter briefly considers some wider implications of an aesthetics of presence in the media arts. It applies media technologies as concrete, material, and present-with-us rather than as transparent conduits for immaterial, informational content, yet works such as *Pulse Room* also show how patterns can traverse material substrates as the embodied is dynamically reembodied. This is transmateriality: a view of media and computation as always and everywhere material but constantly propagating or transducing patterns through specific instantiations. Extrapolated from examples in the media arts, transmateriality is more or less prospective here, an expansive sketch. It is finally applied, in that spirit, to ubiquitous computing. Transmateriality emphasizes the continuity between computation and material environment—two terms that ubiquitous computing necessarily distinguishes even as it seeks to link them more tightly. Following this turn of presence in the media arts leads, then, to the question of a transmaterial ubiquity.

Presence Culture

In *Production of Presence*, Gumbrecht's project centers on the humanities as an academic discipline dominated by a cluster of concepts he calls "meaning culture":

> "Metaphysics" refers to an attitude, both an everyday attitude and an academic perspective, that gives a higher value to the meaning of phenomena than to their material presence; the word thus points to a worldview that always wants to go "beyond" (or "below") that which is "physical." . . . "Metaphysics" shares [the role of] scapegoat . . . with other concepts and names, such as "hermeneutics," "Cartesian worldview," "subject/object paradigm" and, above all, "interpretation." (2003, xiv)

In this paradigm the exclusive role of the humanities is to interpret the meaning of the world, and meaning here is aligned with concepts such as "essence," "truth," "mind," "spirit," and "the immaterial." The human mind in this paradigm is *in* the world, but not *of* it. Gumbrecht argues that this is a relatively modern state. In presence cultures, by contrast, humans understand themselves as bodies within a material cosmology. Rather than being produced through interpretation and located beyond material things, knowledge in a presence culture is revealed; it occurs in "events of self-unconcealment of the world" or moments of revelation that "just happen" (Gumbrecht 2003, 81). Through Martin Heidegger's notion of Being, Gumbrecht asks us to imagine a knowledge that is "not exclusively conceptual," one prior to or not dependent on interpretation.

For Gumbrecht, the meaning/presence binary is not a simple opposition, and he does not posit one over the other. Instead, the relationship is exclusive but dynamic: Gumbrecht proposes "a relation to the things of the world that could oscillate between presence effects and meaning effects" (2003, xv). "Presence and meaning always appear together . . . and are always in tension. There is no way of making them compatible or of bringing them together in one 'well-balanced' phenomenal structure" (105). "Presence phenomena" become "effects of" presence "because we can only encounter them within a culture that is predominantly a meaning culture. . . . [T]hey are necessarily surrounded by, wrapped into, and perhaps even mediated by clouds and cushions of meaning" (106).

Aesthetic experience plays a significant role here as a source for exemplary instances of presence. For Gumbrecht, aesthetic experiences are "epiphanies" or moments of intensity—fleeting, visceral instants that might be triggered by good food as much as by great art. Interestingly, he writes, "there is nothing edifying in such moments, no message, nothing that we could really learn from them" (2003, 98). What we desire here is "the state of being lost in focused intensity"; we desire it, Gumbrecht suggests, because we are overfed with meaning culture (104). He quotes Jean-Luc Nancy: "There is nothing we find more tiresome today than the production of yet another nuance of meaning, of 'just a little more sense'" (105; see Nancy 1993, 5). The effect of getting lost in this state of intensity is to "prevent us from completely losing a feeling or a remembrance of the physical dimension in our lives"—to remind us of our being "part of the world of things" (Gumbrecht 2003, 116–117). Gumbrecht links this feeling to a state of extreme serenity or composure, of "being in sync with the world," which is not to say in harmony, but with a sense of being in, with, and of the world (117).

Presence Aesthetics and the Media Arts

Telefunken (Rastermusic, 2000) by Noto (Carsten Nicolai) is an audio CD containing thirty short tracks of harsh, synthetic tones; this sound—or rather signal—is intended to be routed to the video input of a standard television set. What results is a startling audiovisual performance enacted by standard consumer media equipment. The television set and the CD player enter a new formation; their former content—well-formed images and the acoustic reproductions—is scoured away by something somehow more intense and immediate. The monochrome flickers of the (cathode ray) screen hint at the materiality of its mechanism; we see disintegrating scanlines, traces of the electron beam playing against the glass. The tracks work methodically through a range of clicks, tones, and pulses, arranged less as elements in a composition than as points of calibration, demonstrations of a gradient of possibilities.

In *Telefunken*, media devices that usually carry meaningful content are redeployed temporarily for presence. The point of intensity that *Telefunken* can induce is the sense of a circuit of materials being with us, and it can strike us, much as Gumbrecht describes being struck by the California sunshine, with "imposed upon relevance" (2003, 103). Of course, the work is equally open to a different reading: we can discuss minimalism, the TV manipulations of Nam Jun Paik, or artistic intervention in mass-media technologies (Moody 2000, para. 4). Such interpretive approaches may be inextricable from the work's immediacy, if presence effects come to us on "clouds and cushions of meaning" (Gumbrecht 2003, 106). Yet if we accept Gumbrecht's formulation, these interpretations do not "bracket" or erase the dimension of presence (108), and I would argue that an aesthetics of presence is central to *Telefunken* and many other works.

One characteristic of "presence culture" is that "legitimate knowledge is typically revealed knowledge. It is knowledge revealed by (the) god(s) or by . . . what one might describe as 'events of self-unconcealment of the world.'" This form of knowledge "presents itself to us . . . without requiring interpretation as its transformation into meaning" (Gumbrecht 2003, 80, 81). Gumbrecht positions this mode of knowledge in a premodern cosmology, but it seems to be echoed in some contemporary practices.

One notable feature of media arts in the past decade has been the appearance of data as a material of choice. I have argued elsewhere (Whitelaw 2009) that this practice often operates against information, where information is a sense of meaningful message or content. Data, as distinct from information, are abstract, blank, meaningless, prior to interpretation. In the work *1:1* (1999), Lisa Jevbratt created software that sampled the entire range of Internet protocol addresses, testing each address to discover Web servers. The resulting data set is, in the artist's words, a "snapshot or portrait of the Web"—a real, if partial, trace of that system at that time (Jevbratt n.d., para. 3). Jevbratt presents the resulting data in images that "have a direct correlation to the reality they are mapping," where every data element corresponds to an image element (Jevbratt 2005, 7). The images are abstract, densely patterned, and visually striking, but again they offer nothing familiar by way of meaning or content. Jevbratt writes: "The images are not realistic representations; they are real, objects for interpretation, not interpretations. They should be experienced, not viewed as dialogue about experience. This . . . allows the image to teach us something about the data by letting the complexity and information in the data itself [*sic*] emerge. It allows us to use our vision to think" (2005, 7).

This practice and others like it seek out what we might call "events of self-unconcealment of data," a form of knowledge more like revelation than like interpretation. Data are often figured as immaterial or ideal, belonging to a separate sphere (as in "cyberspace"); here data are manifest, made present-with-us. Of course, this manifestation is shaped (in-formed) by any number of mediating processes, conventions, and decisions; and here context, interpretation, information, and the meaning pole of the binary inevitably return. So although data art can never render the data themselves, it often pushes toward presence as a mode of experience for the digital, even if only to swing back as new information and meaning emerge.

Music and sound play significant roles here. In Oval's 1994 album *Systemisch* (Mille Plateaux), skipping and stuttering CDs are sampled and assembled into ambient musical textures with a gritty rhythmic punctuation; the sound produced, widely described as the sound of error, is more significantly, I would argue, the sound of a material system. Oval was influential in a proliferation of experimental electronic music in the late 1990s, where glitches, crackles, and other "inframedia" signatures were prominent, and musical "content" was set aside for a feeling-out of audio media as material systems (Whitelaw, 2001). Fused audiovisuals such as *Telefunken* and the work of Australian artists Robin Fox and Andrew Gadow extend this materialization across modalities and with an insular intensity that Ulrik Schmidt (chapter 8 in this volume) characterizes as "haptic." The dynamic visualization of sound and music is a recurring theme in generative art and design; in work such as Robert Hodgin's, audio is algorithmically rematerialized; in projects such as Marius Watz's exhibition Frozen: Sound as Space (2008), this tendency is literalized through digital fabrication.

These examples are a tiny sampling of the presence turn in the media arts over the past decade. The turn spans forms, genres, and modalities and tends to move between music, sound, and the visual arts. Its hallmarks are abstraction and an associated sense of the concrete over the representational: work as object or system rather than as sign or index. It tends toward either minimalism and a heightened attention to a limited sensory field or overwhelming maximalism, an excess that is literally unthinkable. In sound and music, it operates at parallel extremes, from quietness to hyperacuity (as in the Japanese Onkyo scene) to loudness that physically saturates the body and overloads the senses. In general, this field is preoccupied with something like transubstantiation: sound into image, image into sound, anything into anything else, with data as an intermediary. This tendency has been characterized as "XYZ art": a formulaic approach where translation is a clever but ultimately arbitrary performance by the artist (Moody 2007). This critique is valid but seems to be applying an interpretive approach to work that seeks, successfully or not, to manifest or "presence" the flows of digital media and computation in various ways. In the context of an overwhelming excess of media content—Nancy's "sense" (1993, 7)—this practice seems to react, as Gumbrecht does, with a desire for presence.

Presence and Technology

The notion of presence aesthetics in the media arts meets some resistance in Gumbrecht's work, in particular in his ambivalent stance on media technology. "I am trying to neither condemn nor give a mysterious aura to our media environment," he writes in *Production of Presence*. "It has alienated us from the things of the world and their present—but at the same time, it has the potential for bringing back some of the things of the world to us" (2003, 140). Gumbrecht links this alienation with a "Cartesian" desire for omnipresence—the decoupling of experience from the body. But although these tendencies of communications media may serve to drive us back toward a consciousness of and a desire for "presence" (139), for Gumbrecht they themselves seem incapable of providing the experience of presence.

In a more recent paper titled "Aesthetic Experience in Everyday Worlds," technology reappears, however, as Gumbrecht considers how presence-type experiences can manifest themselves outside what he characterizes as the exhausted institution of Art and can perhaps bring about a "re-enchantment of the world." Gumbrecht proposes that "at the intersection between some possibilities offered by contemporary technology with that longing for re-enchantment . . . we have a chance of discovering the potential for a much more dispersed and decentralized map of aesthetic pleasures, and of a much less 'autonomous,' stale and heavy-handed style and gesture of Art" (2006, 315).

However, after warning against any new "program," Gumbrecht seems to square off against the media arts in this article: "For I am not talking of the complicated merits of new art forms like 'video art' or 'digital installations' here but . . . of straightforward pleasures like driving a high-powered car, riding on a speed train, writing with an old fountain pen or, for some of us at least, running a new software program on the computer—pleasures that do certainly not require the institutional status of aesthetic autonomy" (2006, 316).

There is a curious disjunction here between the "complicated merits" of media arts and the "straightforward pleasure" of "running . . . new software." Read in conjunction with the previous quote, this statement suggests that the obstacle here is not the technology itself, but the perceived participation of video and installation art in an institutionally sanctioned "program." In fact, much of the practice outlined earlier fits the more optimistic description of the first quote: it is typically "dispersed and decentralized," operating marginally in an art context but traversing design, electronic music, and performance; it operates both inside and outside galleries, festivals, and universities as well as in a networked environment where it is literally dispersed into the melee of everyday experience and where, in many cases, it is exactly a matter of "running a new software program"—an encounter with a moment of (technological) performance.

The turn to presence in the media arts also makes use of one of the central formal devices Gumbrecht describes in this paper. He argues that in everyday events such as a sports competition or a restaurant meal, we can experience a "frame shift," where the established or authorized context is overtaken momentarily by an intensified aesthetic experience (2006, 311). Gumbrecht commends the dispersed (non-Art) proliferation of these framing moments in Japanese culture, but we can find the same proliferation in the media-art practice considered here. Its myriad translations or transfigurations—what I describe later as *transductions*—trigger such frame shifts. In the same way as a view framed by a bough in a Japanese garden intensifies the existing landscape by drawing our attention to specific relations within it, these translations—such as the manifestation of sound as form in the exhibition Frozen or in Jevbratt's pixel map of Internet addresses—intensify their subject matter by making it available in an altered form. In the process, these transformations, like the Japanese bough, reach outward, suggesting that the aesthetic intensity they present is immanent and ubiquitous rather than (as in the model of Art) exceptional and transcendent. These strategies seem exactly aligned with the utopian project Gumbrecht refers to—an expanded field for aesthetic experience—and with the overarching desire for presence, a moment of connection with the material world.

Materializing Information Technology

If there is a tendency or desire at work here to materialize media technologies, emphasizing their presence-with-us, it runs against a view of media and technoculture that has become dominant in the past few decades. It comes to us in figurative language, as when Nicholas Negroponte describes "the global movement of weightless bits at the speed of light" (1995, 12). George Gilder is more direct, declaring that "the central event of the twentieth century is the overthrow of matter" by way of the computer revolution (1989, 17). Though his language is hyperbolic, Gilder reflects everyday attitudes to digital technologies that bracket their materiality and focus on their informational or mediated content. As N. Katherine Hayles observes, this reification of information is rooted in cybernetics and the quantitative information theory of Claude Shannon and Warren Weaver—an engineering solution whose decontextualization of pattern from substrate has been extrapolated into the paradigm referred to here as "information technology" (1999, 54). Mark Weiser's vision of ubiquitous computing as "embodied virtuality" rethinks the deployment of information technology and tightens its coupling with the physical environment, but it ultimately reflects the same underlying paradigm (1991, 3).

Several critiques of this drive for dematerialization have developed in tandem with it. Simon Penny's 1992 "Virtual Reality as the End of the Enlightenment Project" is one early instance. Felix Stalder wrote in 2000 of the "ideology of immateriality" underpinning the so-called new economy (para. 5). In *How We Became Posthuman* (1999), Hayles asks "how information lost its body," considering this tension in greater detail. She introduces a conceptual pair—inscription and incorporation—that offers a way to think about information as simultaneously abstract and material (198–199).

Matthew Kirschenbaum has more recently borrowed the methods of computational forensics, showing in detail how data are embodied in the computer's hardware. His term *forensic materiality* refers to the material residues or by-products that mark out one digital instantiation as different from another (2008, 9); for example, the instantiations of a single file on two different hard drives will be different due to the drives' material specificities. Yet these files are, for the computers concerned, formally identical. As Kirschenbaum writes, "Computers . . . are material machines dedicated to propagating a behavioral illusion, or call it a working model, of immateriality" (10).

Kirschenbaum turns this insight into a new methodology for studying digital texts, but we can read his analysis more expansively. This illusion of immateriality is instantly familiar to us; it encompasses the paradigm of information technology and most of our interactions with digital media. But what if, following Kirschenbaum, we bracket the informational or immaterial illusion in favor of the material? We might methodically trace every keystroke: a movement, a switch, a change of electrical charge in a semiconductor, then another, in video memory; then a change of state in the picture elements of the screen; then a burst of network traffic, over cables, through routers, under the sea, to a server in a rack somewhere; and so on. It is unsurprising that we abstract these chains away, but if we think instead of media technologies as material from end to end, we can frame them readily as in and of the world, with us, and as capable of striking us with moments of intensity.

Transmateriality

Transmateriality views media and computation as always and everywhere material while maintaining, as Kirschenbaum puts it, the behavioral illusion of immateriality. From this view, concepts such as "data" are functional abstractions for describing the propagation of material patterns through material substrates. But at the same time these material patterns—from optical pulses to hard-disk field polarities, luminous screens, and speakers pushing air—are conditioned by patterns *acting as if they were* symbolic and immaterial. Transmateriality can be elaborated here through another pair of concepts: specificity and transduction.

The digital is premised on generality—the ability to shift (or transduce) a pattern of relations from one instantiation to another such that the pattern is functionally independent of its substrate. The email I send is the same as the one you receive, but only in the sense that its pattern has been accurately propagated across a whole chain of material substrates. As Kirschenbaum points out, computing machinery works hard to support this generality, with the precise engineering of tolerances and thresholds and the active interventions of error correction. Without these mechanisms, a million entropic, material variations would creep in—dust motes, temperature variations, mechanical wear. These variations are potential incursions of specificity into the digital: local accidents, conditions of this or that substrate. "Generality" here is another name for that illusion of immateriality because in fact the digital is always specific, always subject to the local conditions of its instantiation.

Recent media art has seen an outbreak of specificity, where the local manifestation of the digital is emphasized over its functional generality. The audiovisual aesthetics of the glitch are a clear example; from the crackle of Stefan Betke's damaged effects processor (see Betke 1998) to the visual artifacts of Integral Lens's malfunctioning digital camera,[1] artists treasure local, material breakdowns in the industrial paradigm of the digital not only for their aesthetic residues, but also, I would argue, for their immediate demonstration of the materiality of media technologies.

The screen is literally the face of generality in media technology and practice—a homogeneous, uniform, dense, self-effacing substrate. It is notable, then, that a wave of recent practice has expanded this structure, creating physical arrays that can be read as anti- or postscreens. These special-purpose displays not only acknowledge the materiality of their substrate but exploit its specificities. In *Wooden Mirror* (1999),[2] Daniel Rozin creates reactive, low-resolution displays made from wooden tiles; the "pixels" here are mobile physical elements. Whereas Rozin's work mimics the planar, pictorial form of the screen, Troika's *Cloud* (2008),[3] ART+COM's (2008) kinetic array for the BMW Museum,[4] and Robert Henke and Christopher Bauder's *ATOM* (2007) experiment with sculptural, three-dimensional arrays.[5] In all of these cases, specificity and generality interweave; the patterns that play across these arrays—low-resolution imitations of our everyday media experience—are transmaterial, moving across and through, but always in a material substrate.

Transduction, according to its engineering definition, is the conversion of energy from one form to another: a light bulb transduces voltage into light and heat; a loudspeaker transduces fluctuations in voltage into physical vibrations that we perceive as sound. In analog media, transduction is often overt ("put the needle on the record"); in digital media it is less apparent, but no less significant. The keyboard transduces motion into voltage; the screen transforms voltage into light; the printer takes in patterns of voltage and emits patterns of ink on a page. Here I want to extend transduction to talk about the propagating patterns of matter and energy within something such as a computer as well as the patterns between that system and the rest of the world. This interpretation approaches Gilbert Simondon's transduction (1992, 313) but confines itself to technological materials and leaves its wider implications aside for the moment. As Steven Shaviro's reading shows, Simondon's transduction offers a parallel path to medium dependence—here, specificity—and materialized information (2006, para. 6).

If a transmaterial view of computing seems unfamiliar, that is only a matter of historical accident. Mechanical computers, where these patterns are physically perceptible, predate electrical (let alone digital) computers by centuries. Our current computers, however, are more or less closed, black-box systems. Their transductions come as a largely preconfigured bundle or network, a set of familiar relations constructed by mixtures of hard- and software, protocols, standards: generalizing frameworks. Across the media arts and other fields, the computer is currently undergoing a rich and productive decomposition. Hardware hacking, embodied interfaces, homebrew electronics, physical computing: these practices literally and figuratively crack the computer open, hooking it up to new inputs and outputs, extending and expanding its connections with the environment. Tiny, cheap computers such as the Arduino have no screen, no mouse, no keyboard: they present us with nothing but a row of bare input and output connectors. These systems beg the question of what can or should go in and come out of the computer—the question of transduction.

Digital fabrication is part of the same shift: an expansion and extension of the computer's range of transductions—from digital pattern to laser-cutter instructions to a new specificity, a physical form. With fabrication, the specificity of digital media emerges at human scale; the material patterns of computation congeal into objects we can wear, touch, or inhabit. This practice has often presented itself through a narrative of materialization, translating bits into atoms—Marius Watz's "Generator.x 2.0" symposium was subtitled "Beyond the Screen." Not so because, of course, the screen has always been material. Rather than supplanting the screen, then, current digital fabrication demonstrates the same point: the significance of the material substrate. Expanding the range of substrates links computation to new contexts and practices as well as to new sensations.

Ubiquity

If we use the term *information technology* to describe the current dominant technological paradigm, then information technology is to transmateriality as meaning culture is to presence culture. In information technology, information is in but not of the world; material substrates act as its carriers. Transmateriality is a sketch of an alternative view in which both media technologies and their content are present with us. As in Gumbrecht's formulation, transmateriality and information technology undoubtedly mingle, operating simultaneously but always in tension. The turn toward immediacy and material intensity in the media arts is inextricable, for example, from the informational, content-focused paradigm of the Web in which it is documented and disseminated. Like presence, then, transmateriality is not intended as a critical program but is something already in tense coexistence with the status quo.

Nonetheless, a transmaterial approach, at its logical extreme, leads toward the dissolution of the digital as a category. Analyses such as Kirschenbaum's show that the digital is simply the analog, physical world operating within certain limits and thresholds. As the black box of the personal computer is breached, we can see a continuity between the patterns inside the system and those outside it. In the work of Kristoffer Myskja, simple computational logics are embodied in custom electromechanical systems. In *Ouroubos* (2008), Myskja constructs a loop of large solenoid switches, each triggering the next; the performance of the work hinges on the physical specificities of these components—their sound and mechanical slowness—rather than on their nominal logical states.[6] In Thomas Traxler's *The Idea of a Tree* (2008), a solar-powered system fabricates objects from epoxy, dye, and string by turning a spindle.[7] Although the system is informed by digital practices such as visualization, the digital itself is rendered completely obsolete, replaced by an elegant circuit of continuous material relations and energetic flows. To go a step further, consider Tim Knowles's *Tree Drawings* (2005–2006), where the artist attaches pens to a tree's limbs, which make drawings that transduce the tree's specific physical dynamics onto paper.[8]

What can transmateriality tell us about ubiquitous computing? From Weiser's vision on, ubiquitous and pervasive computing has undoubtedly multiplied the transductive aspect of computing, turning the black box outward. Embeddedness—the design of informatic systems to be threaded through the environment at every scale—necessarily addresses material specificities, but, again, it does so largely in order to optimize an informatic function, as in Neil Gershenfeld, Raffi Krikorian, and Danny Cohen's "Internet 0" (2004, 78). If the program of ubiquitous computing is to augment, insert, or interleave computation and media into the lived environment, a transmaterial view tends to weaken any distinction between "computation" and "environment" to the point of meaninglessness. Again, however, this transmaterial view should not be taken as a technological or critical program, but rather as a thought experiment extrapolated from contemporary practice; it is in that prospective sense that this view might apply to ubiquitous media and computation.

Can we think of ubiquitous computing without "information technology?" A ubiquity of heterogeneous specificities—sensors, effectors, and propagating patterns. A reconfigurable network of material flows rather than a communication system. A patchwork of local contexts. The transmaterial view recognizes each instantiation's specificity, its local conditions and constraints as well as its lateral affordances or by-products, and its capacity to be taken as something other. If information technology inherits reified, decontextualized information as in Shannon and Weaver, information in a transmaterial ubiquity more resembles the formulations of British cybernetician Donald MacKay: embedded, context dependent, and locally relevant. Seen from this perspective, Gumbrecht's frame shift is a moment of what MacKay calls "structural information" (1969, 14), a reconfiguration that prompts new relevance; transduction, in the works considered here, is a strategy for inducing or triggering such reconfigurations.

Media art is currently preoccupied with drawing data or live input from anywhere and manifesting it as anything else: seeking out the intensifying moment of the frame shift. As in Gumbrecht's Japanese garden, however, these shifts are momentary and immanent; we experience a (selective) view of a wider outside instead of a reified aesthetic object, and in the process that outside is itself activated, the intensity disperses. This process is literalized in a work such as HeHe's *Nuage Vert* (2008),[9] where electricity consumption is mapped onto a laser-drawn "cloud" drawn on the plume from a power-station smokestack. Power consumption is "presenced" and in the process recast but also literally altered; transduction here forms a distributed loop that not only reframes its source domain but intervenes in it by augmenting or altering its specificity.

In a transmaterial ubiquity, such frame shifts are ever more possible, across every scale and context—local, global, private, public—in modes from the poetic to the prosaic. They are increasingly distributed and decentralized in their creation, supported by open hardware and software platforms (such as Haque Design + Research's Pachube).[10] The promise or the hope is that the result will be a proliferation of diverse moments of intensity, of being struck, of a being-in-the-world that is heightened rather than attenuated by media and computation. Art has a role to play here, at least for the moment; but this project is far wider, and far more than aesthetic experience is at stake.

Notes

1. For more information on Integral Lens's *Broken Camera* (2005), see http://www.flickr.com/photos/integral-lens/sets/72157602986977981, accessed 1 June 2009.

2. For more information on Daniel Rozin's *Wooden Mirror* (1999), see http://www.smoothware.com/danny/woodenmirror.html, accessed May 26, 2009.

3. For more on Troika's *CLOUD* (2008), see http://troika.uk.com/cloud, accessed 26 May 2009.

4. For more information on ART + COM's kinetic sculpture in the BMW Museum," see http://www.artcom.de/en/projects/project/detail/kinetic-sculpture, accessed 1 June 2009.

5. For more information on Robert Henke and Christopher Bauder's *ATOM* (2007), see http://www.monolake.de/concerts/atom.html, accessed 1 June 2009.

6. For more information on Kristoffer Myskja's *Ouroubos* (2008), go to Myskja's Web site at http://www.kristoffermyskja.com, accessed 1 June 2009.

7. For more information on Thomas Traxler's *The Idea of a Tree* (2008), see http://mischertraxler.com/projects_the_idea_of_a_tree_recorder_one.html, accessed 1 June 2009.

8. For more information on Tim Knowles's *Tree Drawings* (2005–2006), see http://www.timknowles.co.uk/Work/TreeDrawings/tabid/265/Default.aspx, accessed 1 June 2009.

9. For more on HeHe's *Nuage Vert* (2008), see http://www.pixelache.ac/nuage-blog, accessed 1 June 2009.

10. For more information on Haque Design + Research's Pachube, see http://pachube.com, accessed 1 June 2009.

References

Betke, Stefan. 1998. "Andrew Duke Interviews Stefan Betke." *Cognition Audioworks* 10. Available at http://cognitionaudioworks.com/pole.htm. Accessed 26 May 2009.

Gershenfeld, Neil, Raffi Krikorian, and Danny Cohen. 2004. "The Internet of Things." *Scientific American* 291 (4): 76–81.

Gilder, George F. 1989. *Microcosm: The Quantum Revolution in Economics and Technology*. New York: Simon and Schuster.

Gumbrecht, Hans Ulrich. 2006. "Aesthetic Experience in Everyday Worlds: Reclaiming an Unredeemed Utopian Motif." *New Literary History* 37 (2): 299–318.

Gumbrecht, Hans Ulrich. 2003. *Production of Presence: What Meaning Cannot Convey*. Stanford, CA: Stanford University Press.

Hayles, N. Katherine. 1999. *How We Became Posthuman*. Chicago: University of Chicago Press.

Jevbratt, Lisa. 2005. "The Infome: The Ontology and Expressions of Code and Protocols." Available at http://jevbratt.com/writing/crash_jevbratt.pdf. Accessed 1 June 2009.

Jevbratt, Lisa. n.d. "*1:1*" (description). Available at http://128.111.69.4/~jevbratt/1_to_1/description.html. Accessed 14 May 2009.

Kirschenbaum, Matthew G. 2008. *Mechanisms: New Media and the Forensic Imagination*. Cambridge, MA: MIT Press.

MacKay, Donald M. 1969. *Information, Mechanism, and Meaning*. Cambridge, MA: MIT Press.

Moody, Tom. 2007. "VVork and XYZ Art." April 30. Available at http://www.digitalmediatree.com/tommoody/?40531. Accessed 30 May 2009.

Moody, Tom. 2000. "THE TROUBLE IS (NOT) WITH YOUR SET." October. Available at http://www.digitalmediatree.com/tommoody/writing/noto. Accessed 14 May 2009.

Nancy, Jean-Luc. 1993. *The Birth to Presence*. Stanford, CA: Stanford University Press.

Negroponte, Nicholas. 1995. *Being Digital*. New York: Knopf.

Penny, Simon. 1992. "Virtual Reality as the End of the Enlightenment Project." Available at http://ace.uci.edu/penny/texts/enlightenment.html. Accessed 30 May 2009.

Shaviro, Steven. 2006. "Simondon on Individuation." *The Pinocchio Theory*, January 16. Available at http://www.shaviro.com/Blog/?p=471. Accessed 4 August 2009.

Simondon, Gilbert. 1992. "The Genesis of the Individual." In *Incorporations: Zone 6*, edited by Jonathan Crary and Sanford Kwinter, 297–319. New York: Zone Books.

Stalder, Felix. 2000. "The Ideology of Immateriality." June 2. Available at http://felix.openflows.com/html/immateriality.html. Accessed 21 May 2009.

Watz, Marius. 2008. "Frozen: Sound as Space." *Generator.x*, July 17. Available at http://www.generatorx.no/20080714/frozen-sound-as-space. Accessed 17 May 2009.

Watz, Marius. 2007. "Generator.x 2.0: Beyond the Screen." *Generator.x*, November 30. Available at http://www.generatorx.no/20071130/generatorx-20-call. Accessed 1 June 2009.

Weiser, Michael. 1991. "The Computer for the 21st Century." *Scientific American* 256 (3): 94–104. Reprinted in *ACM SIGMOBILE Mobile Computing and Communications Review* 3 (3) (1999): 3–11.

Whitelaw, Mitchell. 2009. "Art against Information: Case Studies in Data Practice." *Fibreculture* 11. Available at http://eleven.fibreculturejournal.org/fcj-067-art-against-information-case-studies-in-data-practice. Accessed 14 May 2009.

Whitelaw, Mitchell. 2001. "Inframedia Audio." *Artlink* 21 (3): 49–52.

12 Infinite Availability—about Hypercommunication (and Old Age)

Hans Ulrich Gumbrecht

We have more opportunities to communicate than ever before in the history of *Homo sapiens*. This is the elementary fact that I am referring to with the word *hypercommunication*, and I refrain from saying that hypercommunication is either a very good or a very bad thing. Now, the frequency with which we talk to other persons face to face—that is, in mutual physical presence—has most likely not increased, but it has probably also not dramatically declined during the past decades. If we have more opportunities to communicate than ever before, in the sense of conducting interactions based on the use of natural languages, then this increase is clearly a function of technical devices whose effects neutralize the consequences of physical and sometimes also of temporal distance. Telephone and electronic mail, radio, gramophone, and television are such arrays. Of course, a basic structural difference sets apart, on the one side, telephone and electronic mail as media that allow for exchange and mutual impact and, on the other side, the more "asymmetrical" media such as radio, gramophone, and television, where only persons at the—irreversibly—receiving end have a perception of those individuals who initiate communication without ever getting immediate feedback.

But the most fascinating electronic communication tools are the ones that produce the physical impression of interaction at a distance, although there is but one body involved. Different from the spectators who in the eighteenth century were intrigued by those chess-playing "machines," we know for a fact that there is no employee of our bank or of our airline involved when we use, for example, an automatic teller machine (ATM) or when we check in at the airport by using a screen; nor are we really deceived by the mostly female voices that lend spatial presence to the navigation system in our car. And yet we often act—and we like to act—as if a real person is involved on the other side. Who, quite honestly, has never called that navigation lady "a bitch"? And who has not been pleased or put off at some point by the polite language, the efficiency, and sometimes the design of those airline screens helping us to get ready for the next flight?

My opening sentence, then, presupposed that we are inclined to subsume all these different kinds of technically facilitated "interaction" under the concept of "communication." Many of them—such as the ATM around the corner, the check-in device at the local airport, or the program at the customers service number of your MasterCard—simply replace former institutions and situations of face-to-face interaction. They are never exactly the same as the structures preceding them, but the differences between the real person (formerly) and the electronic function (today) is obviously meant to remain at a level that avoids confusion. I also think that this is the disappointingly banal reason why all these new varieties of technopermeated communication have in the end not inspired theories as earthshaking and grandiose as some of us had originally hoped for (remember with what excitement we once read Jean Baudrillard, Vilém Flusser, and Paul Virilio). We are evidently far from completely controlling, say, the addictive temptations of email. But this is not so terribly different from people's having spent more time than they can afford, for millennia, in pointless face-to-face conversations.

The innovation brought about by those devices, therefore, does not lie in any specific features through which they copy or exceed the possible performance of a human person; it lies in their ubiquity. Without any doubt, the number of cash machines that we can use now, twenty-four hours a day and seven days a week, beats the highest number of bank employees ever hired and paid in order to provide customers with cash. With those touch screens, airlines will spread their welcoming presence more widely throughout the airport buildings than they ever could while they were limited to a coherent segment of space for check in. Through electronic communication, whatever we need seems to be more available than previously. But it is also true that we—those who use ATMs and touch screens—become more available, too, whether we want to be or not.

At my university, I have the enviable privilege of a small office in the middle of the library whose occupant is supposed to remain anonymous. Among other things, this office, different from my other office on campus, where I see students and colleagues, is meant to protect me or, rather, to set me at a distance from the invasiveness of electronic communication (and any other type of communication that I do not actively choose), as the private space of my home does, where I don't do email either. I used to take care of the several hundred email messages that I receive on a normal working day during deliberately limited hours of the morning and of the evening in my official campus office but dedicated the time in the carrel and the working time at home exclusively to reading and writing. What I naively had not taken into account was the strange agency effect of my laptop—the laptop that I had meant to use exclusively as a writing instrument, something like a functionally much improved electronic typewriter. One day, to my surprise, the laptop screen let me know that, thanks to an upgrading of the library buildings to the level of electronically sensitive spaces, it was now making available all the messages in my carrel that I had wanted to reserve for the computer in my other on-campus office, making me thus available to the world during my time in the carrel—very much against my intention. From the perspective of my personal work and my subjective well-being, this excessive availability was vulnerability. I know that universal availability is generally considered to be the main effect and the unconditional value of electronically provided hypercommunication. It has been celebrated as a democratic value, but it is one of those democratic values that Friedrich Nietzsche would have associated with a situation of slavery. Whoever is electronically available must break all democratic rules of politeness to avoid email addiction and email victimage. It is considered rude—and it is therefore difficult—not to communicate. Beside that, availability undoes all hierarchies and social differences. Pretty much every day, I receive some messages in which students tell me that they have a real necessity to talk to me, that they would consider it a great favor and privilege if I set up a meeting with them—and then they continue by letting me know the time and the electronic addresses under which they will be "available." How impossibly old-fashioned is it if I regularly feel that in this type of interaction and under these conditions it should be exclusively my privilege to be "available" or not?

*

Vis-à-vis all these electronic gadgets, vis-à-vis hypercommunication as their effect, and even vis-à-vis the very trendy academic attempts at theorizing them both, I take a position resembling the attitude of those fifteenth-century monks, scribes, and scholars who feared, criticized, and finally even actively rejected the printing press. Although I do not literally believe that electronic communication devices are the devil's work and will have a generally deteriorating effect on culture at large, I quite often give in to the temptation of describing them as agents and symptoms of intellectual decadence, and I try to know as little about them as I can possibly afford. I have learned that my university cannot legally oblige me to change office computers each time that we are given the opportunity to do so, and I relish in the shock that some of my colleagues go through when they realize, for example, that the size of the computer screen in my office is three and a half technological generations behind what they consider to be standard. But I doubt they can explain to me in a really convincing way why it is so much better to have a very large screen.

Nor have I ever believed in that teleological faith according to which we make inventions when we most need them. Of course, this type of thing can happen, at random or as the result of an intense effort, but it clearly is the exception. New technical devices or cultural practices oftentimes—and perhaps even frequently—emerge independently of the collective needs in their environment, and even whether, once invented, they will be broadly assimilated by a society not only hinges upon their practical value but may well be motivated, for example, by their aesthetic appeal. There was no real pragmatic "need" for radio and television, for example, but radio immediately and television after a long period of incubation ended up profoundly transforming more than our sphere of leisure. Once such innovations have become institutionalized, their existence and their presence appear irreversible, and it is in this sense that Niklas Luhmann called them "evolutionary achievements." Such an optimistic-sounding phrase hides the experience that many of the innovations to which we refer with it end up positioning humans in situations of dependence and victimage that greatly reduce their range of agency and efficiency. Ironically enough, some Silicon Valley companies were among the first to realize that they lost billions of dollars year after year and with a sharp increase owing to the addiction that prevented their employees from working with a computer screen without checking its email functions every few minutes.

At any event, the so-called evolutionary achievements are inevitably adding up, and by adding up, they produce the impression of a trajectory that we can then interpret, in a Hegelian mood, as "historically necessary." Nobody will ever be able to prove or to disprove the "historical necessity" of a fact after the fact, and within this unmarked space of uninhibited speculation it has been one of the more exciting hypothesis to say—as, for example, the French paleontologist André Leroi Gourhan did—that civilization, with technology as its core, may have replaced the biological (?) energy that used to propel the evolution of our species and that this happened at a time when the biological evolution of humankind has greatly slowed down and may indeed have come to a standstill.

In this technical, cultural, and intellectual environment, all I have—very modestly—been hoping for during the past ten years (and I am now sixty-three years old) is that certain objects and situations that I grew up with and that therefore belong to my being-in-the-world will not disappear under the pressure of the latest evolutionary achievements. I am also claiming the (moral?) right to be exempted from the obligation of embracing each and every technical innovation—not necessarily because I have profound reasons for my resistance against so much communication, but because its forms and phenomena just hit me too late in life, perhaps only by a few years, for me to assimilate them all in a comfortable way. I know how ridiculous it would be if I pretended that I am trying to slow down and even to stop a historical drift. I just want polite tolerance when I give lectures without using Power Point, and I want a chance to convince my students that it might be an opportunity for them if I do not give in to their regular demand of "using more visuals" in my courses. Theirs, much more than mine, is an everyday world of moving images, so that it might be enriching, for both sides, to be confronted with this difference. At some point, perhaps, I will end up being convinced that the gap between my own communicative style and that of my students has grown to a degree that is seriously problematic. This will be the day for me to change my approach to teaching—or, more likely, to take retirement. But I refuse to make the effort of laboriously adapting myself to an environment that I do not feel comfortable with and that makes me look inept. For example, there are too many potential virtues—and even democratic values—in distance learning to actively fight it. And yet I know that my university will have disappeared the day we are no longer allowed to sit around a table with our (not too many) students. I also know that I would not be very successful and would certainly not look good if I tried to take notes from a lecture or a discussion with a laptop on my knees. And I believe that this is also the case for most colleagues my age who claim unconvincingly to have been early champions of the electronic revolution (I recently saw one of them dropping the laptop from his knees three times in one hour of discussion). What I most fear when I use communication technologies that I have not grown up with is an embarrassing lack of grace in my behavior. In other words: the strongest reason for my anti-electronic attitude is an anticipated aesthetic judgment about myself.

*

A full repertoire exists with figures and configurations that are emblematic of a world that has filled its empty zones with technology-facilitated opportunities to communicate, and these figures and configurations somehow strangely strike me as emblems of solitude and isolation. The most salient among them is the lonesome walker who at first glance seems to speak to himself, often with great emphasis, particular expressivity, and also quite loudly and thus appears to fit perfectly one of the traditional images of the fool as "he who talks to himself." As we all know, the problem here lies in the eye of the beholder, for as soon as we discover around the person's neck or behind her ear the trace of an electronic communication device, she turns from an uncanny figure of foolishness into somebody who is privileged to spend time with a beloved one, say, on her way to work. Now let us assume that the beloved one, in the specific case of the lonesome walker-talker whom we are watching, is her lover. In such a case, the two may well use electronic communication during their working day to allude to moments of erotic intensity that they remember from last night and that they are looking forward to. Such an exchange will draw its specific excitement from establishing a bubble of ecstatic privacy closely surrounded by the most formal and sometimes even most public business relations. I can still remember that late afternoon when I saw, while driving back to our house, that the road was blocked by all the books and furniture that the wife of a colleague had thrown through the window after she had read the daily mail to his two extramarital lovers (who didn't know of each other: one an undergraduate student and one a senior woman colleague) —mail that he by mistake had addressed to his spouse and to the university provost. Possible Freudian interpretations of this particular scenario apart—interpretations, for example, about an "unconscious desire for confession" coming through in such an accident—I believe that it is the danger of contiguity that lends a background of erotic charge to the solitude of electronic communication.

Nothing can be less erotic, by contrast, than those mails and mobile phone calls to spouses or relatives that more than half of the passengers on a normal flight feel the irresistible urge to make in the very first moment—right after touchdown—that they are allowed to do so. This reaction is no different from smokers grabbing their pack of cigarettes as soon as they arrive at one of the few remaining spaces in our world where cigarette smoke is not banned; both are symptoms of addiction. Nobody waiting for us at the airport really needs to know again that our plane has touched down, given that there is a multiplicity of screens in the waiting area that provide the exact same information. Nor do they need to know ten minutes later that we are still waiting for the suitcase at the baggage claim and four minutes later that it is in sight. By the time the arriving passenger embraces his wife, it may feel that he already had arrived "too much," that his body, which he now adds to the already present mind and voice, has no existential place.

To be a bodiless and spaceless medium and thus never to turn into an ecological burden gives an aura of political correctness to electronic communication, at least in the perception of those who aggressively use it—and this surely is a surplus even over the always praised "convenience" of electronic devices. When you ask for hardcopies to be shipped to you by air because your eyes suffer from reading long texts on a screen or because you want to forego the ordeal of printing endless manuscripts, you will often face the threat of a refusal that gives itself the triumphant aura of ecological responsibility, for who would be so selfish as to care more about his or her own remaining eyesight than about the remaining trees? Finally, there is this other aura, the ultimate aura, produced by the line that appears toward the end of some electronic messages: "Sent from my Blackberry." The aristocratic design of this device, the tone conveyed by the four words quoted, the knowledge that his Blackberry is the one body part of President Barack Obama that gives him credibility as being contemporaneous and even futuristic, and other factors may come together in producing an effect of hierarchy in the communication with Blackberry users. Are they perhaps those happy few who let us know that they are graciously available, but that their availability should not be taken advantage of? Whenever I receive a message saying, "Sent from [So-and-So's] Blackberry," I feel that I am at the lower end of a regal message and that, rather than respond, I should wait for subsequent messages—or even orders.

*

Not only do I have so many more opportunities then ever before to communicate, which, if I only managed to control myself, might well be a blessing, these opportunities also make instantly available to me a large portion of those humans whose segments of lifetime overlap with mine, among them many whom I actively care about, such as the two of my four children living in Europe and my only granddaughter. What do I complain about except the victimage that comes from having to be so terribly available myself? My answer is that hypercommunication erodes those contours that used to give form, drama, and flavor to my every day. Here is an example. Whenever I agree to give a reasonably well-paid lecture these days ("reasonably well paid" meaning that the organizers, on whatever grounds, attribute a certain importance to it), I am asked early on to provide a title and a summary of nonnegligible length for the purpose of (mostly electronic) advertising. Almost at the same time, somebody will demand that I make available a manuscript of my lecture to those who, for one reason of the other, will not be able to attend. On the day of the lecture, somebody will want me to sign a form giving my consent to the production of a recording. All of these requests are in part flattering (one feels "in demand") and in part nerve wracking (especially for somebody who for lectures relies on scarce handwritten notes—that is, notes that normally are the very condensed result of a long reflection process). Taken together, however, all these interventions tend to flatten those contours and hard transitions that used to give a specific event character to lectures in the pre-electronic age. Whoever attends a lecture—thus goes the new ideal—should actually be rereading or relistening to an already known text, and whoever chooses not to attend should definitely not lose the chance to read it or to listen to it at a later date. As we are so eager to make our consciousness universally available, we end up spreading thin our physical presence: nothing is ever absolutely new anymore, and nothing is ever irreversibly over.

If hypercommunication levels the excitement coming from the discontinuity implied in any beginning, it also smoothens the pain or the tragedy of ending and separation. Your girlfriend maybe eight hundred (or six thousand) miles away, but—in contrast to when I was young and using a telephone was both very expensive and even more unreliable—there is the consoling privacy of Facebook (if it produces "privacy" at all, I have to ask, admitting that I have never used it). The price to be paid for this palliative effect is that our ideas, our imaginations, and our daydreams are each time less where we are with our bodies. You see people meeting for dinner at gorgeous places on Friday night only to be lured away by a ringing mobile phone or by a message service right after they sit down. And when they arrive at the meeting that they are now coordinating instead of eating dinner or talking to their companion, there minds will again be ahead of their bodies.

With so many "sites" juxtaposed on the Web, we may lose—together with the contours of eventness and with the existential contrasts between presence and absence, private and public—a sense of what matters and what does not. Of course, some sites receive many more "hits" than others, but the hope that electronic sites of all kinds will ever provide the physical and intellectual intensity of a discussion in physical copresence has long vanished. Has anybody ever seen a truly good debate in electronic form, a debate where mutual argumentative resistance turns into mutual inspiration and new ideas? Although it is difficult to explain why electronic discussions produce, at best, spiritual mediocrity, we all know that this is the case—inevitably somehow. Even on my best friend's Web site, I can only be alone, and what I may feel there as even a hint of closeness never transcends the closeness of a tourist or that of a voyeur. Is there anything more pathetic than those tens of thousand (I fear, hundreds of thousand) of blogs that are being written with such self-importance and that will forever remain unread (for good reasons, I want to add)? The elimination of the risk of catching a cold from face-to-face meetings is balanced, at least for me, by the loss of the chance to be moved to tears—not to speak about how the senses of touch, taste, and smell remain unaffected as well.

*

But what do I really want? What is my—practical—ideal? One strong wish that I have is for the continuation of the "philosophical reading group," made up of about thirty faculty and students, that meets at Stanford every Thursday night for a good two or three hours with the aim of discussing, in small segments, just one philosophical book (usually a classic) over a period of ten weeks. Regardless of whether the text chosen for a certain trimester is close to my own working agenda or not, the energy of that reading group has become my intellectual lifeline. But there is no doubt that, for all of its intensity, our philosophical reading group has in recent years lost important participants to an ever-growing number of other workshops whose emergence the electronic gesture of juxtaposition seems to foster.

I also have a much more romantic, archaic, and unrealistic memory of a moment that I loved, a memory that I am obsessed with, a recollection of a world that was never mine and must by now be gone for ever. About fifteen years ago, a former student of mine took me to a small town in Louisiana called New Iberia with the purpose of visiting a former plantation that boasted to be "the home of the first pair of blue jeans." On our way back to the car, I believe, we walked by a bayou where two very old black men stood looking into the water. After a few minutes, one of these two very old black men turned to us to explain, very politely and in a French whose sounds were conjured up from the late seventeenth century, that alligators up to three feet long were very tasty and tender, whereas the flesh of four-foot-long alligators was tough and impossible to eat. Five or six years later I returned to beautiful New Iberia with my family. For the second time in my life, I saw the first pair of blue jeans, and I again walked by the bayou, where, I swear, I again saw those same two very old black men, who seemingly had not aged and who told us, with the very same words of the first time, what they felt my family and I should know about the gastronomic qualities of three- and four-foot-long alligators. No event in my entire life had clearer contours, and no experience is more present in my memory than that double communication with two very old black men at New Iberia, Louisiana.

*

We cannot avoid "having" a body that we occasionally use and whose effects we more frequently bracket, but we are fast losing the ability to "be" a body—that is, the ability to let the body be an enhancing condition of our existence. Nothing by contrast is more Cartesian in the sense of being body free than all the different kinds of electronic communication; nothing is more seamlessly connectable with our consciousness than they are, and nothing is more withdrawn from the dimension of space. This is the reason why electronically based hypercommunication brings to its insuperable completion the process of modernity as the process in which the human subject as pure consciousness has emancipated itself from and triumphed over the human body and all other kinds of *res extensae*. Not that there was much left to be conquered for consciousness, at least in mainstream Western culture, before the first chip was invented and before the first personal computers were sold. But in order to become perfect and, above all, irreversible, the democratically enslaving principle of universal availability needed the reduction of human existence through the computer screen. As contours, discontinuities, and borders tend to vanish within this dimension, we now spend most of our lives in the invariably same position—that is, in front of the eternal computer screen. We are there while we fulfill our professional duties, when we communicate with our beloved ones, and, above all, when the threat arises of being alone, for we have traded the pain of solitude caused by physical absence for the everlasting half-solitude of those who make themselves infinitely available.

Everything melts together; everything is "fusion." But I cannot see any "mixed realities" that would deserve this name in spite of all the talking about it. It may be all my fault—that is, a consequence of my mostly deliberate old-fashionedness—if I insist that a sensual perception will always remain separate from a concept or from a thought. What seems to be new is that most of the time we focus neither on the one nor on the other side of this spectrum, which must be the reason why our new pride is based on the particular type of alertness required in order to manage an existence of complex simultaneities. While I was writing this text, I occasionally checked incoming emails, and, because it was mid-July, I also saw who won today's stage of the Tour de France (it was, to my great American regret, Alberto Contador from Spain). This predominant situation of early-twenty-first-century human realities converges with the impression that the "imperceptibly short" present of the historicist construction of time—that is, the construction of time that emerged in the early nineteenth century and became so dominant that we tended to confuse it with time in and by itself—has now been replaced by an ever-broadening present of simultaneities. In today's electronic present, there is neither anything "from the past" that we need to leave behind nor anything "from the future" that cannot be made present by simulated anticipation.

Some of us old ones feel that this "present of simultaneities" is simply too much and at the same time is not enough presence. If the process of modernity has been largely a process of disenchantment, we have now written "Rational Reenchantment" on our revolutionary banners. But I am fully aware that this rebellion is but another Gray Panther revolution.

IV Interaction Designs

13 Reflections on the Philosophy of Pervasive Gaming—with Special Emphasis on Rules, Gameplay, and Virtuality

Bo Kampmann Walther

The purpose of this chapter is to inspect the theoretical consequences of moving from a traditional, ludological concept of computer games to an extended ludology of pervasive games. In the process of unfolding these consequences, our general understanding of play and games will, we must hope, also be sharpened. Such an assessment should rivet reflections that take seriously the heightened emphasis on physical space as well as the contingency of sociocultural activities in pervasive games. It should further critically investigate the notion of the virtual, as is done in the third section, where I employ Gilles Deleuze's Bergson-inspired claim that the virtual is indeed more "real" than any present actualization as a backdrop against the hypothesis that, rather than invoke a commonsense dichotomy between a tangible reality and the informational bits and bytes of the computer, we should instead focus on the discontinuous relation between virtual play and actualized gaming as the pivotal modus operandi of pervasive games. The noticeable lack of empirical references in this article is not the result of a normative disapproval of the many and very interesting experiments with pervasive technology that flourish these days, but on the contrary it must be regarded as a rather rigid attempt to enlighten the deep axioms and often ambivalent key conceptions underneath the world of digital games.

Rules and Gameplay

In line with economic game theory, we can define games as complex, rule-based interaction systems consisting of three key mechanisms: absolute rules, contingent strategies, and possible interaction patterns. Game rules are absolute in the sense that although the players may question the rationality of the rules at hand, they are nevertheless obliged to obey them—to "play by the rules." Rules are therefore absolute commands (Neumann and Morgenstern 1953) and unquestionable imperatives. They transcend semantic issues, cultural signification, moral agendas, and so on. This requirement does not preclude the fact that game rules are discussed in a cultural or ethical milieu.

In contrast to rules, strategies are contingent, nonabsolute entities because they count as the plans for the execution of turns, choices, and actions in the game. Other strategies than the ones actually carried out might have been outlined and performed. Both in the shape of short-term tactics and as long-term schemes, strategies are contingent. In economic game theory, a strategy is an overall plan for how to act in the assembly of different states that the game may be in (Juul 2006). Game theory studies the affiliations of the rules and the strategic behavior in competitive situations (Smith 2006). Finally, interaction patterns are the moves and choices that become part of the game being played, thus interfering with the game's restrictions and options. As the implementation of game strategies tends to cluster in selected regions of the game's possibility space (in approximation of what is known as the "dominant strategy" in game theory), forming a path through the game space, we may even insinuate that the interaction patterns, taken as a whole, *are* the game itself—especially if we view it from the player's perspective (Holland 1998). This differentiation can be listed even more briefly:

- Rules are commands.
- Strategies are plans for game executions.
- Interactions patterns define the actual path through the game and specify the topography of human–computer (or player-versus-rule) dynamics.

The notion of gameplay involves all three levels of a game, which also explains the difficulty in defining the concept properly. We can refer to the following definition of gameplay as the *ontological* or formal definition. The definition is ontological because it assumes at least the minimal and necessary (axiomatic) existence of some quasi-material, algorithmic entity:

Gameplay: Definition 1. *Gameplay is the actualization of a specific stratification of rules, strategies, and interactions as well as the realization of a certain amalgamation of commands, plans, and paths.*

For a player, successful gameplay means a delicate balance between knowing the rules and mapping one's strategy in accordance with both rules and the possible actions of opponents. Games should be equally challenging and rewarding, hovering between boredom and anxiety, thereby assuring a space of flow through the network of choices. For a computerized game system, successful gameplay implies a balance between fixed rules and the control of player input in variable settings.

A rule, being algorithmic in its core design, consists of a simple, unequivocal sentence—for example, "You are not allowed to use hands while the ball is on the pitch." Hereby, a rule constitutes the game's possibility space by clearly stating limitations (not to use hands) as well as opportunities (the ball is on the pitch). It is always possible to define a game in both negative and positive terms: rules limit actions; they determine the range of choices in the possibility space; they encircle the arenas to be played in, yet they also frame what can be done.

At this point, I am speaking of all games, both traditional games, including sports, and computer games. *Heroes of Might and Magic* rests on rules stored in and processed by a computer. Chess or *Monopoly,* by contrast, relies on rules not accumulated in the database and algorithms of a computer but written down on paper and stored in the players' mind during the play. In a game of soccer, a referee administers such rules ultimately by reference to the *FIFA Handbook.* Implicit rules that are normally considered exterior to the "real" rules (e.g., the clock in chess matches) must be engaged explicitly in digital games. These rules have to be programmed as well. Weather conditions or the general physics of a soccer game are usually taken as "out-of-game" features in the real world. When we simulate a soccer game in a computer, however, the rules of soccer and the general physics (including random variables such as surface granularity, crowds, time of day, etc.) must be built into the rule algorithms and the computer's input–output control.

Rules specify the constitution of the playing "deck" or, more broadly, the playing "field." In games, behavioral patterns inside this field are limited, constrained, and highly codified (Caillois [1958] 2001; Huizinga [1938] 1994; Walther 2003). Rules are guidelines that direct, restrict, and channel behavior in a formalized, closed environment so that artificial and clear conditions inside the "magic circle" of play are created (Salen and Zimmermann 2004). The outside of this circle, reality or nonplay, is essentially irrelevant to gameplay. When a player is confronted with unambiguous rules, his or her strategies (or tactics) might entail best-practice solutions variable to the given rule constraints. Hereafter, interaction patterns map the various player interventions and can hence be viewed as a texture of moves and choices overlain on top of the game's possibility space.

The formal organization of games is a *parameter space.* In this space, the current state of the game counts as a point and ultimately a dimension in the parameter space. A played game has therefore *n* possible state dimensions. In Tic-Tac-Toe, the nine squares constitute the game's parameter space and thus the possibility domain for the arrangement of the board pieces. The rules of the game define the possible edges in the space connecting states, and the total number of discrete points in the parameter space represents the total number of games states. Rules define the possible game, as in the initial framing of the game, whereas a particular game is a path through the state space. This latter particularity consequently rests on a *variability space* upon which one can also measure the system's optimum rate or success probability The crucial factor is that there can be no variability or multiple paths through a game's possibility space without the game's compulsory parameters. (Put slightly differently, there can be no game world without game rules.)

This dialectic between parameter space and actual game path (or variability space) also sheds some light on why games are complex: because there is an uneven relation between the unchanging set of rules and the changing realization of a particular game. This asymmetrical contingency can be termed *game emergence*. It is usually impossible to predetermine the actual moves and outcome of a game only by knowing the set of rules. Also, most games are games of imperfect information (Nash 1997). At the outset, the rules of chess are simple, and yet the wealth of distinct chess-playing tactics is quite enormous. A child can memorize chess rules, but to master all grand openings in the actual game is probably a lifetime achievement.

Play Mode and Game Mode

However, a characteristic feature of many new games with a strong element of "fiction" is that they wish to expand the gaming space, physically and mentally, often by reconfiguring the social landscape into a grid of game objects, game goals, and game worlds, thus obscuring the demarcations between the real and the virtual.

What, then, is most important? Is it the game itself or the social and geographical infrastructure that supports it? Who (or what) has the upper hand? Is it the relational complexities of the characters or other personified "avatars of story" (Ryan 2006), or is it perhaps the fluent vectors of the game world? Here, I explore this tension between the telic game orientation and the presence of a world surrounding the former by drawing upon the recent paradigm of pervasive computing (Walther 2007a, 2007b).[1]

Territorial exploration involves intentional modifications. It is advanced trial and error in a sociosemantic circumstance. You go right. Not interesting. You move to the left. Wait, here's something. You rush straight forward, and the result is immediate action. Such movement requires cognitive mapping and a basic perception of metric coordinates. The elusive coexistence of being present and intentionally moving around for a reason is also known as *rules*. It subsumes three important characteristics of structured, goal-oriented activity: momentum plus direction (vectorization) plus a valorized and quantifiable outcome. Mapping a place through adventurous discovery in order to figure out the story underneath the space and possibly inventing new stories in the same process are all about *playing*. Learning to move and advance in a space filled with discrete norms of orientation—that is, a parametrical space, meaning that you can do this but not that, you can go here but not there—is the art of *gaming*.

Thus, there are two firmly interwoven modes of game epistemology: there is *play space* and there is *game space*. Accordingly, there is *play mode* and *game mode*. We call those games that mix up the tangibility of everyday spaces with the closed information spaces found in digital computers *pervasive games*. Such games may be the next generation in computer games. Make people move around. Don't tie them in front of the screen. Moreover, these games are particularly captivating because they deliberately place the relation between rules and world voyaging, gaming and playing, the parameters of games and the variables of play at the nucleus of the very rule system itself.

In the play mode, one does not want to fall back into reality (although there is always the risk of doing so). In the game mode, it is usually a matter of climbing upward to the next level and not losing sight of structure. Play is about presence, whereas game is about progression (Walther 2003). Play space can be a city, and game space can be the rules and informational network dictating what can and cannot be done during gameplay. Or, to rephrase this in abstract terms, play space can be a fictitious world, with its binding rules, and game space can be the rules and missions within this world: the protagonist's teleology, the endpoint of his trajectory.

Play is also about uncertainty, and herein lies the irreducible element in play that, according to Roger Caillois, makes it inaccessible to mathematics ([1958] 2001, 173). Complete transparency derived from calculation and perfect strategy means the disappearance of player interest together with the pleasurable uncertainty of the outcome.

One notices in play that there is always the inherent but beguiling hazard of being "caught" in reality. Nothing is more distressing for play than the intermission of reality, which at all times jeopardizes play *as* play. Then it's back to normal life—which may be, incidentally, a giant game space in its own right, as McKenzie Wark (2007) suggests (see also Galloway 2006). This intermission is, of course, a structural feature of all play and of all gameplay. It is true of chess and soccer. It is also apparent in *Doom* and *Myst*. Interruption and termination must be avoided at all costs in the continuous pursuit of having fun, but because they are inescapable, they must be built into the very "being" of playing games.

Now, consider pervasive gaming. As a player, I rush down a street in order to amass my next item to be uploaded via my personal digital assistant so that my game buddy at home can keep track of my doings so far. It's 4:00 PM, there is heavy traffic, and I am momentarily barred from reaching the corner with the alacrity I wished for.

We have witnessed a growth in the design of game systems that use ubiquitous-computing techniques to propel forward players to connect objects in the real world with objects of the computational world. *SuperFly* by the Swedish game company It's Alive Mobile is a good example. The player's aim is to become a virtual celebrity. The projects *Can You See Me Now?* (figure 13.1) and *Uncle Roy All around You* (figure 13.2), both created by the UK performance group Blast Theory, use hand-held, digital devices, Global Positioning System tracking, and online agent technology in an attempt to use location and mobility as game features from within the real world. While one player stays at home and moves a virtual character around a representation of a real city, other players speed around the real streets, trying to hunt down the virtual quarry.

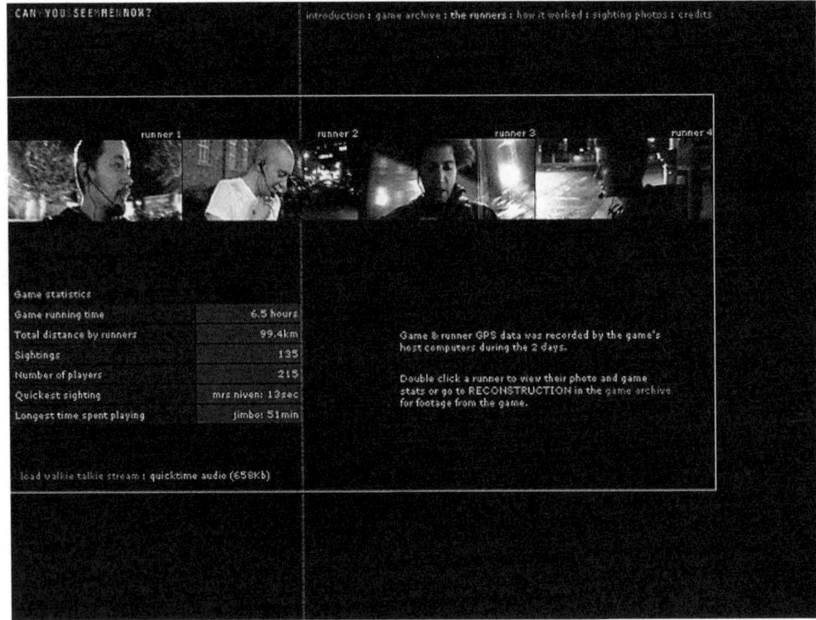

Figure 13.1
Blast Theory, *Can You See Me Now?* (2001–). Permission kindly granted by the artists.

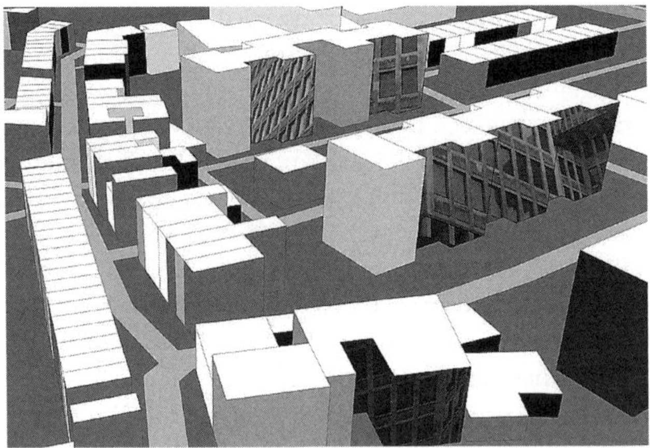

Figure 13.2
Blast Theory, *Uncle Roy All around You* (2003–). Permission kindly granted by the artists.

In chess, there are no strident interruptions between two or more discrete fields. I move my queen independently of physics, be it in the form of weather, traffic jams, or my fellow citizens' occasional bad habits. In a game of soccer, you block your opponent, and he tries to tackle you. However, a nice set of training principles that look for ways to avoid the physicality of blocking is always an option. That is what the refinements of dribble are all about. In pervasive gameplay, mixing play space and game space, "real" problems, like the ones described in my own thought experiment, remain real problems. If not, the aesthetics of producing eloquent game mechanics turns into a matter of ethics. I do not, in the quest of fulfilling the game's teleology, knock down the (real) old lady on the sidewalk just because she is preventing me from targeting a little bit faster the "pac man" farther down the road.

Therefore, we must be careful in judging the fun factor of gameplay. It is not only the city, the social and geographically expanded context in itself, that is the locus of enjoyment in pervasive gameplay. Yes, I can go explore, and, yes, I meet people, and, yes, the site of navigation has become much wider than a trivial board. Nevertheless, the bouncy guarantee of space might indeed become the constraints of the game. Serious gamers do not want to waste their time looking for "interesting" places to explore. They much rather want to understand the structure so as to move forward to reveal new game areas or to climb upward in the hierarchy of levels.

As discussed more fully later, this veiled and all-important prerequisite of playing games, including the pervasive ones, is contained within the notion of "the virtual." Being a conditional *causa sui* of the actualized game and the gameplay that unfolds in the being-present, the virtual explains in its pure form the dual and much overlooked nature of gameplay: the virtual is the "past" of the "now" of gaming because we must always silently remember the enjoyable and playful offspring of a game, and at the same time the virtual drives the articulated though momentarily nonfulfilled target point of gameplay that is the "future."

Why is the virtual a prerequisite of gameplay? Because play is centered in a discovery of open spaces that invite observation through the duration of temporality. One gradually learns how to pilot inside play, and because the completion of more and more successful tasks takes time, corresponding, distinctive forms differentiate the play system into finer grades of subsystems. One inhabits such spaces via certain as-if structures; one assumes a role and lives out characters whether in the form of other players or agents that one can adapt as a player. The gamut of play equalizes a measurement of its geometry: How big is the playing field and where are its borders? And these lengths and widths become in turn the source of gaming's internalization of both geometrical space and discrete progression.

In contrast, play seems to focus on investigations of semantics because the task is not only to measure play space, but furthermore to elaborate on that space's modes of interpretation and means for reinterpretation. We explore a world while playing, but that world's potential meaning and the stories we can invent in that respect also drive us. Play spaces tend to expand, either in structural complexity or in physical extent. This expansion is further reflected in the praxis of play—for instance, when players argue over the exact thresholds of a play domain. Another feature that distinguishes playing from gaming is the notion of presence, as I pointed out earlier. The sensation of presence is obviously tightly interwoven with phenomenological concepts such as "immersion" and "flow." Play commands presence. We have to be there—not only *be* there, but also be *there*. This is the double meaning of Martin Heidegger's "*Dasein*": *da*sein (being *there*) and da*sein* (*being* there). We go with the flow, or, rather, while swallowed by the presence of playing, we are *in* the flow, as Mihály Csíkszentmihályi (1990) claims. A game's success is intimately tied to the organization of space and time. Gamers need to trust this organization. Because a game hinges on a certain finite structure in order to promote infinite realizations of it—the correlation of rules and tactics—the very articulating of presence so important for play must already be presupposed in a game. One already knows in a game that the mission is to *keep on gaming*, which really means, in my vocabulary, to *keep on playing*—that is, to prolong the sensation of presence. The energy can then instead be directed toward elucidation of the game's structure. "How do I get to the next level?" and not "Why do I play?" This *keeping on*, whether done knowingly or unknowingly, is the virtuality of games.

Although one should indisputably respect the ethical boundaries of pervasive games that transport gameplay out in the open—just as one should bear in mind that the metaphysics of fictional worlds often goes beyond the natural laws and moral confines of everyday life—one does not want to hang on too long for the old lady to cross the street. While one is waiting, the question "Why do I play?" might thus threaten to disintegrate the exquisitely balanced halves of gaming (to progress) and playing (to be present).

Thus, we can put forward the second definition of gameplay. In continuance of the first one, we can refer to the following definition as the *epistemological* or player-oriented definition:

Gameplay: Definition 2. *Gameplay is that kind of player activity that intentionally involves the asymmetrical relation between world exploration and level progression.*

In the next section, I further qualify the notions of play mode and game mode by relating them to Deleuze's concept of the virtual.

Virtuality

A prevailing notion of "virtuality" that was especially dominant in the cybertheories and virtual-reality-oriented writings of the 1990s sees it as a kind of spatial and epistemological liberation from Cartesian geometry (Lunenfeld 2000; Ostwald 1997). The kind of space that Renée Descartes had in mind in his *Meditations on the First Philosophy* is organized in accordance with Euclidian mathematics in which space has no resistance, like an ethereal morphology. A typical cybertheory claims that the spatial form of computer representations more willingly obeys the laws of differential topology, which describes spatial singularities. Cartesian space is analog with its emphasis on measurable planes and geometrical continuity, whereas the topological space defined by Henri Poincaré is digital and discontinuous. The effect of the latter is the displacement of spatial orientations (such as up/down and inside/outside) and the possibility of constructing latitudes with infinite dimensions that threaten to adjourn the space as object.

Moreover, the virtual has generally been considered as the apex of a media and artistic evolution. Thus, an important distinction between static images in which the perspective is tied to the observer and virtual-reality environments is the user's command over spatially distributed points of view. Ever since the Italian Renaissance and the theories and works of art by Alberti, Leonardo, and Botticelli, the painted arts have tried to create depth, visual consistency, and smooth continuity. But the idea of artistic creativity in the Renaissance rests on the artist and the way he manipulates an audience's senses. The celebrated trompe l'oeil is a technical culmination of this striving for perfection that can be regarded as a re-form of augmented reality: an illusion within the illusion itself. Later, in photography, the point of view is still linked to physical setting of a camera in concrete space–time. Motion picture and television finally release the perspective into oscillating events in time. Not only do images move around in front of the camera lens, but the camera is itself mobile in relation to the actual viewpoint. Yet this dynamic mode of representing and presenting space–time has a certain limitation in perspective because the photographer completely determines the point of view. It is only with the advent of virtual reality "that the user can have substantial visual control of the scene" (Bolter 1996, 113).

Gilles Deleuze's definition of virtuality and the virtual, which he elaborates in particular in *Bergsonism* (1988), *The Logic of Sense* (1990), and *Difference and Repetition* (1994) is remarkably different from Bolter's conclusion above. Interestingly, he seems to arrive at a classification of the virtual not because of the concept in itself, but rather as a response to a problem with ontological implications posed by structuralism. How can the underlying structures exist if they do not belong to either the mind of a subject or the material world of objects? Deleuze's answer is that these structures, which act as conditional guidelines for present actualizations, represent something that is, ontologically speaking, "in between" subject and object, which is virtuality. How is it possible, Deleuze asks, for something to be a condition of being, to be a catalyst of an actualized presence, while not being discernible or being located in one particular person's mind or otherwise embedded in a material world? The difficulty is to establish the exact existence of such determining structures—in other words, to insist that this ontology is in itself the most comprehensive form of reality and at the same time a detached and left-behind reality. Part of the answer lies in Deleuze's deliberate Kantian design. Similar to Immanuel Kant's notion of space and time as unifying forms imposed by the subject that does not in itself exist *in* space and time, Deleuze holds that pure difference is nonspatiotemporal—reality without actualization, ideality without abstraction.

The reasons why "the virtual" commonly appears obsessively contrary to reality are that we fail to acknowledge virtuality as the "real" condition of actuality and that we one-sidedly prioritize the actual as the being-present over the virtual as pure Being. The virtual is neither nonexistence nor occurrences in the kind of (ontic) ontology we can perceive; rather, it is a real system of differential relations that creates actual spaces, times, and sensations. Deleuze writes in *Bergsonism*: "We have . . . confused Being with being-present. Nevertheless, the present *is not*; rather, it is pure becoming, always outside itself. It *is not*; but it acts. Its proper element is not being but the active or useful. The past, on the other hand, has ceased to act or be useful. But it has not ceased to be. Useless and inactive, impassive, it IS, in the full sense of the word: it is identical with being in itself" (1988, 55).

Can it be that "play" belongs to the virtual and "game" to the actualization of being? And what does that distinction mean in relation to the philosophy of pervasive gaming, which seems to be more attentive toward explorative play than to level-progressive gaming?

Play mode works as the virtual condition for the present activity and the ontological materialization we call "the game." This condition is more than the underpinning algorithms and digital codes; it must also be considered the abstract or even ideal base of games as such. There is a condition, a raison d'être, upon which the materialization of each game depends, and that condition is play. One might argue that play is an ontological praxis, but it is certainly also an ontological condition. New games arise continuously, and old ones cease to be—not just in an inventive sense, but also in a pragmatic sense. Contrary to this constant activity in game time, the inexorable pastime of playing games, "play" has the strange quality of being discontinuous in time: it somehow is there all the time, as a completion of the idea incarnated in a specific game, and at the same time it is not there because it cannot be found in the integral whole of any particular object. The game is the discrete entity that discriminates the conditional past (play) as abstract and fictional. However, as Deleuze states in chapter 4 of *Difference and Repetition*, "Ideas and the Synthesis of Difference," "The virtual is opposed not to the real but to the actual. *The virtual is fully real in so far as it is virtual.* . . . 'Real without being actual, ideal without being abstract'; and symbolic without being fictional. Indeed, the virtual must be defined as strictly a part of the object—as though the object had one part of itself in the virtual into which it plunged as though into an objective dimension" (1994, 208–209, emphasis in original).

Virtuality is not the unreal in a stark contrast to the actual existence of either ideal subjectivity or material objectivity, but rather it is the structure or "embryonic" element that *completes* the actualization more than makes it whole. Following from this distinction, we can say that a game is a discrete, unconnected and actualized entity that belongs to one and the same relational system—the latter being "play" or the Bergsonian pure past. The game is experienced in time as a discontinuous emanation, but play accounts for the process in which we unknowingly move from the virtual domain of ideal singularities that characterize a system to uniquely actualized entities. Whereas games constantly move about and reorganize themselves into discrete actualities with epistemic qualities, the "purity" of play withstands this perpetually passing-by through a strong sense of *simultaneity*. Play, then, completely determines a game but is only a part of the object.

There is of course the danger that "past Play" becomes a secret transcendental teleology of "present Game" or that the virtual-as-Substance turns into a Spinozian metaphysic. In temporal terms, the actual (which I call "game mode") corresponds to *chronos*, the pure present, whereas the *aion*, or the virtual (which I call "play mode"), is the pure past and the condition of chronos. A certain impassivity therefore clings to virtuality as an abstract ontological memory that insists in all actuality and yet can never be said to contribute anything to the concrete instances of our chronological time. We then fall prey to the Spinozian idea that everything that exists is a modification of the one substance.

Do these distinctions imply that games cease to exist the moment they occur and that, by contrast, play is composed of the real substance that endures despite the constant fragility of relational organization? No, insofar as play is the "past" of gaming's "presence," this does not mean that play contributes nothing to actuality and disappears as a tragic but true Being. Rather, the two levels—substance and actualization, playing and gaming, the ontology of the virtual and the epistemology of the present—exist in a continuous state of flux, a nomadic unrest that perpetually reproduces the encounters from moment to moment and from one game state to another. This is especially true in the later writings of Deleuze—the Deleuze who turns to chaos and complexity theory—where the distinction between the virtual and the actual progressively disappears, and we instead get interrelating processes where events reproduce certain patterned organizations.

Taking off from Deleuze, we can pursue the proposed link between the virtual past and the being-present gameplay. I suggest reading the Bergsonian framework not as a metaphysics of time, but as a conceptual scheme of causal conditioning. Figure 13.3 illustrates the double realm of virtuality.

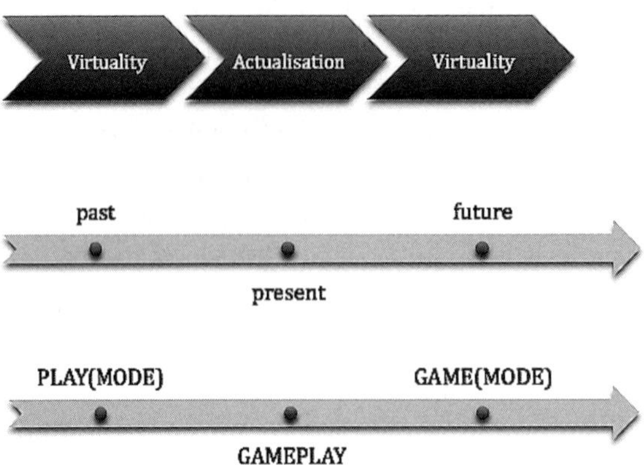

Figure 13.3
Virtuality, temporality, and gameplay.

First, the virtual accounts for the underlying past of the actualized game, resulting in present gameplay as it separates itself from the other of play—that is, reality or nonplay. This is how I described the virtual earlier. However, there is a second and just as important characteristic of virtuality in that it also occupies the teleological domain of games. Here we find the level-oriented progression of gaming, and, in a way, this very modality of the virtual signifies the irrefutable "arrow" of play and games. Traditional videogames as well as novel pervasive games always possess this telic attribute—heading with or without detours for the quantifiable outcome. Furthermore, the two poles of virtuality, both pointing directly toward the now of gameplay, are intimately coupled with the transitionality of games. Dangerously near the edge where a game exactly stops being fun to play, play mode is a feeble confine because of the latent likelihood of stepping out of the magic circle and back into reality. Game mode bears a similar stamp of transitional delicacy due to the all-pervading threat of blocking the unidirectional gameplay, thus freezing the player between two levels and denying him the bliss of advance, the potent omen of triumph.

Concluding Remarks

The Deleuzian outline is a step forward from the overtly hyped understanding of virtuality as the ontologically "unreal." Rather than focus on whether the virtual, in the traditional cybertheoretical sense, dictates an essentially different metaphysics or a whole new set of phenomenological qualities, we should inquire into the imposing forms of play and games as they mutually determine the logic of virtually conditioned actualizations in time and space. This way we do not need to come up with any new metaphysics. Furthermore, this approach emphasizes the virtual as the driving force behind the praxis of play, but nevertheless with real implications. The virtual *is* not play, but it in-forms its being. The virtual *is* not (the) game, but it shapes its imminent horizon. Virtuality becomes a conceptual tool with which to describe both the playful past and the goal-oriented future of gameplay—thus being a kind of synonym for the *what if* and *as if* of the *Homo ludens.*

Gameplay is the actualization of rules, strategies, and interaction patterns as well as a nonequilibrious poise between explorative play and level-oriented gaming. Pervasive gaming, as we have seen, revitalizes exploration as naturalized gameplay, and yet it never completely abandons the telos of the discrete, parametrical, and competitive. The virtual domain, including the past of play and the future of games, is hardly ever questioned as such in gameplay; the conditioning forces always ensure the unsaid framework within which play and games can take place. In this way, the virtuality of games is perhaps not just the logicoformalistic precondition of gameplay as it hovers between the mimicry of play and the teleological desire of progression, but a violently imposing "discrete ideology," as Slavoj Žižek (2008) would say. The constant reterritorialization of the virtual that happens in the course of playing games is thus a "play *within*" the virtual much more than it is a "play *with*" the virtual.

Note

1. I should stress that when I refer to "pervasive gaming," I exclude persistent games (*Everquest, World of Warcraft*) as well as alternate-reality games and massively multiplayer online role-playing games, on the one side, and mobile games, on the other. Thus, pervasive gaming represents a technological paradigm that relies on adaptronics and wearable, mobile, or embedded software and hardware in order to facilitate a "natural" environment for gameplay that ensures the explicitness of computational procedures in a postscreen setting. As a result, pervasive games frequently use Global Positioning System tracking, various types of Wi-Fi, and signal triangulation techniques. In true pervasive gaming, the physical environment must be *prepared* technologically for mobile, location-oriented gameplay.

References

Bolter, Jay David. 1996. "Virtual Reality and the Redefinition of Self." In *Communication and Cyberspace*, edited by Lance Strate, Ron Jacobson, and Stephanie Gibson, 105–119. New York: Hampton Press.

Caillois, Roger. [1958] 2001. *Man, Play, and Games.* Urbana: University of Illinois Press.

Csíkszentmihályi, Mihály. 1990. *Flow: The Psychology of Optimal Experience.* New York: Harper and Row.

Deleuze, Gilles. 1994. *Difference and Repetition*. Translated by Paul Patton. New York: Columbia University Press.

Deleuze, Gilles. 1990. *The Logic of Sense*. New York: Columbia University Press.

Deleuze, Gilles. 1988. *Bergsonism*. New York: Zone Books.

Galloway, Alexander R. 2006. *Gaming: Essays on Algorithmic Culture*. Minneapolis: University of Minnesota Press.

Holland, J. John. 1998. *Emergence: From Chaos to Order*. Oxford: Oxford University Press.

Huizinga, Johan. [1938] 1994. *Homo ludens: Vom Ursprung der Kultur im Spiel*. Rowol, Germany: Reinbek.

Juul, Jesper. 2006. *Half-Real: Video Games between Real Rules and Fictional Worlds*. Cambridge, MA: MIT Press.

Lunenfeld, Peter. 2000. *Snap to Grid: A User's Guide to Digital Arts, Media, and Cultures*. Cambridge, MA: MIT Press.

Nash, John F. 1997. *Essays on Game Theory*. London: Edward Elgar.

Neumann, John von, and Oskar Morgenstern. 1953. *Theory of Games and Economic Behavior*. Princeton, NJ: Princeton University Press.

Ostwald, Michael J. 1997. "Structuring Virtual Urban Space." In *Intelligent Environments*, edited by Peter Droege, 451–482. Amsterdam: Elsevier.

Ryan, Marie-Laure. 2006. *Avatars of Story*. Minneapolis: University of Minnesota Press.

Salen, Katie, and Eric Zimmermann. 2004. *Rules of Play: Game Design Fundamentals*. Cambridge, MA: MIT Press.

Smith, Jonas Heide. 2006. "The Games Economists Play: Implications of Economic Game Theory for the Study of Computer Games." *Game Studies* 6 (1). Available at http://gamestudies.org/0601/articles/heide_smith. Accessed 31 August 2009.

Walther, Bo Kampmann. 2007a. "Pervasive Game-Play: Theoretical Reflections and Classifications." In *Concepts and Technologies for Pervasive Games: A Reader for Pervasive Gaming Research*, vol. 1, edited by Carsten Magerkurth and Carsten Röcker, 59–83. Aachen, Germany: Shaker.

Walther, Bo Kampmann. 2007b. "Pervasive Gamespaces: Gameplay out in the Open." In *Space Time Play: Computer Games, Architecture, and Urbanism. The Next Level*, edited by Friedrich V. Borries, Steffen P. Walz, and Matthias Böttger, 290–293. Berlin: Birkhaüser.

Walther, Bo Kampmann. 2003. "Playing and Gaming: Reflections and Classifications." *Game Studies* 3 (3). Available at http://www.gamestudies.org/0301/walther. Accessed 31 August 2009.

Wark, McKenzie. 2007. *Gamer Theory*. Harvard: Harvard University Press.

Žižek, Slavoj. 2008. *Violence*. New York: Profile Books.

14 Trying to Be Calm: Ubiquity, Cognitivism, and Embodiment

Simon Penny

In 1995, Mark Weiser and John Seely Brown proposed a "calm," backgrounded technology as a reaction to the laborious and foregrounded nature of 1990s computer systems and the technofetishism exemplified by mid-1990s virtual reality. This chapter traces discursive and technological transitions between the decade of "virtuality" (1990s) and the decade of ubiquity (2000s). It proposes that the notion of virtuality was in part a product of an incomplete technology. It also outlines the role of the cognitivist paradigm in shaping notions of computation and virtuality through the 1990s and draws attention to the increasing importance of discourses of embodiment in both human–computer interaction (HCI) and media arts since the early 1990s. I observe the key role of media artists in proposing and developing new modalities of embodied interaction and distinguish two quite different classes of technology that are often grouped under the rubric *ubiquitous computing.* I argue that the ongoing paradigm shift toward embodied and performative cognitive perspectives is critical to resolving theoretical and (interaction) design challenges inherent in the development of ubiquitous technology.

After Virtuality

I propose that discourses of technological "virtuality" during the 1990s are attributable in large part to the vestigial condition of interface technologies during that decade, a condition that was theoretically supported by the prevailing cogntivism. Computers, in their new roles as interactive multimedia systems, were inadequately supplied with interfaces to the physical world; the previously "normal" roles for computers did not call for such interfaces. This disjunction between comparative sophistication of computational capabilities and the relative paucity of interface capabilities led to the notion of the (computational) virtual and the confused rhetorics of virtuality. In hindsight, we might say that the 1990s furor around the "virtual" was symptomatic of this technological imbalance, that much of the research work and grassroots development of the 1990s was directed at correcting that imbalance, and that the current era of ubiquitous computing evidences the effectiveness of that correction.

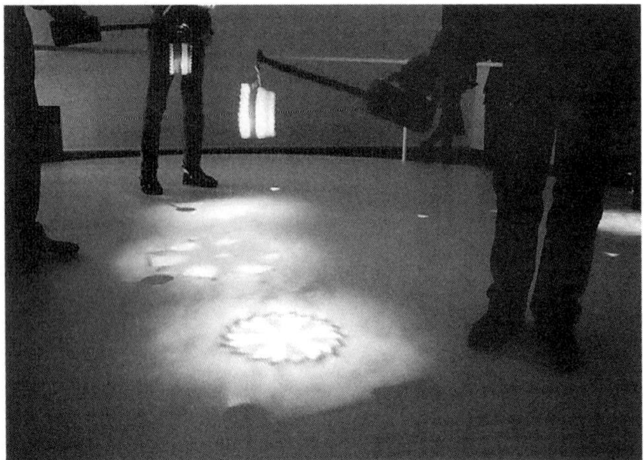

Figure 14.1
Narcis Pares, Roc Pares, and Perry Hoberman, *El bal de Fanalet/Lightpools* (1998). This work combined sonar-based tracking and interactive artificial life–based graphics with artifacts derived from Catalan popular culture. Permission kindly granted by Pares, Pares, and Hoberman.

The 1990s saw an explosion of creative research in interactive and immersive art, catalyzed by the increasing availability of domestic and "prosumer" (professional–consumer) computer-based media technologies and fueled by burgeoning rhetorics of cyberculture (see figure 14.1). The realm of the arts was a highly charged vortex for this work as the traditional commitment to material immediacy and finely crafted sensorial effect abruptly confronted a technology framed as abstract immaterial manipulation of information. Over that decade, media-arts practitioners played a key and vigorous role in diagnosing, imagining, and developing interface technologies and new modalities of engagement. Capabilities of real-time interaction and databasing made central the questions of the aesthetics of (hyper)narrative and the embodied experience of the digital. A desire to reconcile the sensibilities of arts practices and the capabilities and constraints of emerging computational media technologies was as important as an exploration of the potential of the new technologies themselves. It was a radically interdisciplinary moment, bringing together artists, computer scientists, critical and media theorists, and others driven by the traditions of open intellectual inquiry and interdisciplinarity in the arts and by the previous thirty years of "art and technology" practice (see figure 14.2).

The transition from the period of virtuality to the period of ubiquity was a result of the maturation of interface technologies absent from the technological palette of the 1990s. Since then, various technologies linking the data world with the lived physical world—sensing and tracking technologies (such as micro electro-mechanical sys-

Figure 14.2
Simon Penny, *Petit Mal—Autonomous Robotic Artwork* (1993–1995). Shown here in the Smile Machines Exhibition (curator Anne-Marie Duguet), Transmediale 2006, Berlin.

tems (MEMS) accelerometers, machine vision, laser scanners, global positioning system (GPS) devices, radio-frequency identification (RFID) tags) and mobile communications technologies—have been developed and deployed. This development had the effect of nesting the "virtual" back into the lived physical world, revealing the panic to be focused around an explosive and messy technological transition period.[1] This belated integration of data with the world caused "the virtual" to evaporate. The transition from virtual reality to more nuanced augmented- and mixed-reality modes deploying virtual reality's stock-in-trade tracking and simulation techniques indicates that ubiquitous computing is less the kind of antithesis of virtual reality that Weiser envisaged and more of a continuity.

At the same time that HCI moved out beyond the research lab, human interaction with the world and with technology was addressed more intensively—as is evidenced by the rapid expansion of HCI, computer-supported cooperative work (CSCW), and related areas of research. The study of HCI became increasingly interdisciplinary as psychologists, anthropologists, and sociologists became involved. As recognition of the shortcomings of the cognitivist paradigm became more widespread, new modes of cognitive science grappled with the embodied, enactive, situated, and social dimensions of cognition (Varela, Thompson and Rosch, Suchman, Hutchins). Neuroscience research revealed new dimensions of the mind–body relation (Edelman, Ramachanran, Sacks, and so on). Conventional philosophy of mind has been challenged on these bases by Lakoff and Johnson, Clark, Thompson, and others. This movement met media artists coming the other way, as it were—exploring the application of computational technologies to embodied, material, and situated cultural practices. The crafting of embodied, sensorial experience is a fundamental expertise of the arts, an expertise that is as old as human culture itself.[2] Various topics of critical discourse that had been lumped in with discussion of the virtual have persisted, and it has become clear in particular that many of the aesthetic projects of "media artists" are inherently concerned with the central issues of ubiquity.[3]

Ubiquity: Figure and Ground

Mark Weiser, John Seely Brown, and others made clear their motivations for a "calm technology" that recedes from attention, but the term *ubiquitous computing* is applied to two quite different types of technology. One is industrial and embedded, effectively invisible and accessed by experts. The other is a consumer commodity, very visible and demanding of attention, but nonetheless affording sophisticated data-gathering capabilities to paying customers. Although the two categories have much in common technologically, they are very different in their relation to the social.

Intelligent buildings, augmented spaces, and complex machines as well as communications networks themselves involve distributed and networked "embedded" technologies composed of small, low-power units, in practice invisible, with no (immediate) human interface—no screen, no keyboards (perhaps a light-emitting diode (LED)). These systems have been integrated into existing technologies, edging them a little farther along the mechanically causal–homeostatic–adaptive trajectory, quasi-organisms with digital nervous systems. Cars, planes, refineries, hospitals, bridges, utility infrastructures, seismic fault lines, and national borders are now increasingly digitally instrumented. Engines run a little smoother and cleaner; industrial workplaces have fewer workers and fewer accidents due to human error; illegal immigrants are intercepted more efficiently.

In consumer goods, the obsession with the interface does not seem to have abated; the ecstasy of computation—if not the ecstasy of communication—seems to have become a fixture of popular culture. Although miniaturization and wireless networking have indeed moved "out into the physical world," they have not resulted in "repositioning [computing] in the environmental background" (Ulrik Ekman, introduction to this volume). Rather, the miniaturized but intensified interface, attention demanding and insistent, is foregrounded. Although the technological infrastructure (mobile phone reception, etc.) has indeed become ubiquitous, on the level of human experience many technologies reinforce a discontinuity between the data world and the physical world.

Mobile wireless technology has certainly become ubiquitous, but perhaps not in the way Weiser hoped. The words *ubiquitous, pervasive, embedded* have an ominous ring; they carry negative connotations of an oppressive informational monoculture or monopolistic order, perhaps because of their deployment in military jargon. Although the technical modalities of the technology are novel, the purposes to which they are put retain functions of surveillance and control. It is not just a question of to what ends the technology is deployed and for whom or against whom it is working, but of to whom the systems are visible and to whom they are invisible.

Skeuemorphs Rule, OK?

David Mindell reminds us: "Our computers retain traces of earlier technologies, from telephones and mechanical analogs to directorscopes and tracking to radars" (2002, 321). The physical conformation and functionality of the machine we use is determined by the history of technologies from which it arose. Interactive multimedia, we must recall, is the child of Cold War computing research. The Semi Automatic Ground Environment system put soldiers with keyboards and lightpens in front of monitors to accomplish the complex pattern-recognition functions that the system could not achieve autonomously. This constellation of technologies was the model for the keyboard–mouse–monitor paradigm. The fact that this harnessing of flesh to machine was later clad in the rhetoric of liberation in the heyday of interactive multimedia remains deeply ironic.

Why did the computer, which once was a basement-size machine staffed by attendants, morph into a desktop machine? The historical answer is that it was applied to the kinds of tasks that people who sit at desks do when sitting at desks. The desktop computer was functionally an enhanced typewriter and calculator with added filing-cabinet functionality. It follows then that it is particularly useful and relevant for activities that resemble office desk activities, such as record management, accountancy, and letter writing but is decreasingly appropriate for activities whose social and architectural placement diverges from that scenario. Many human activities, including cultural and art-making activities, do not resemble office work in their physical contexts, methodologies, or goals.

For the past generation, we have managed with computer technology that, for all its touted user-friendliness, has continued to demand that we preprocess our thoughts and experiences into a kind of keystroke mush that is easily amenable to these machines' limited *a–d* capability. If we are to pursue the fundamental goals of Weiser's ubiquity, it means developing computational technology past the stage that we and it appear to have got codependently stuck in—tolerating a technology that must be spoon fed with little alphanumeric streams. After thirty years of personal computing, I mercifully no longer have to put myself in work position at my workstation, from which I could not move even a few feet without breaking my connection with the machine by losing contact with screen and keyboard. But why, having finally freed ourselves from the bondage of the desktop, do we tolerate having to poke unidigitally at a miniature QWERTY on our mobile devices? What a profound failure of imagination!

Trying to Be Calm

There is a significant difference between enhancing the control systems of existing machine complexes and the enmeshing of computational processes with human cultural and biological processes. I have distinguished between, on the one hand, clandestine, faceless technologies that involve distributed units in a larger control array that itself is embedded in a larger machine complex and, on the other hand, garrulous, clingy technologies close to the body. Neither of these technologies seems particularly *calm*. Beyond embedded miniaturization (microcontrollers), location (tracking), and transmission (Internet and wireless communication), how far have we come along the trajectory to *calmness*? Is automated processing of logical operations necessarily applicable and an asset in every aspect of life? Are there aspects of our lives where digital intrusion might be utterly undesirable? (Do I need "blueteeth" that notify my dentist directly when they sense decay? Probably not. I certainly don't feel the need for pop-up ads on the periphery of my vision when I'm wearing my sunglasses.) To ask this question is to challenge the marketing rhetoric of the computer industry, to challenge the assumption of the desirability of the intrusion of computation everywhere: that automated processing of logical operations is necessarily applicable and an asset in every aspect of life. Computation is not value-free cognitive bedrock. There is nothing "neutral" about the culture of computation, even if we are naturalized to it.

Although such issues are not necessarily foregrounded in everyday use of consumer devices, we should review the aspirations of ubiquitous computing and its current implementations and consider the desirability of the current trajectory. In what more or less subtle or insidious ways does the bending of human activities to the needs of a not entirely calm technology stain or perturb the richness of those practices? I am thinking here of skilled embodied practices in particular—practices that have developed organically over generations, subtly adapted to the complex richness of human formation, where artifacts have coevolved in ways that adapt and optimize subtleties of human sensorimotoric capabilities, which may never have been nor have had to be made explicit. Consider two examples, one high, one low: the culture of the violin and the culture of the household kitchen. What makes a Stradivarius so much more of a violin than a cigar box with a rubber band stretched over it? The special quality of such an instrument is that it has been formed through an extended period of interplay between artisans and players. A history of coevolution between the material specificities of the artifact and the repertoire, an increasingly refined attunement between the embodied intelligences of the artisan and the musician. A kitchen likewise evolves as a workplace through use—chains of intuitive design tweaks—a subtle interplay between the ingredients, artifacts, and procedures of specific cuisines, spatial layouts, and its users physical capabilities.

In such contexts, the application of digital technologies almost always has the effect of "thinning out" the experience in question, and this effect is due in part to a preoccupation with problem solving on the symbolic plane and the ensuing elision of the situated, embodied action. This syndrome maps onto imperatives of computer engineering—modularity/reductivism, standardization/generality, optimality/efficiency—and instrumentality in general. These criteria are valid in their "home territory"—I want my laptop battery to have maximum life, I want my file to be compatible, I do not want anyone taking aesthetic liberties with the shape of an airplane wing. But the validity of these criteria wanes as they are applied in territories farther from home. Optimization of *King Lear* or Beethoven's Fifth by elimination of redundancy is an inherently ludicrous proposition.

The Profundity of Material Being

The term *human factors* speaks volumes about the engineering mindset—as if the qualities of human embodiment were peripheral "implementation details." This view is veiled cognitivism in the sense that thinking is conceived of as abstract symbol manipulation and is taken to be an end in itself rather than part of the process of ongoing lived being. Combined with a rather Victorian characterization of human perception and action and inflected with dualism, serial processing (input–output) and cognitivism inform much computational thinking. The crisis of the cognitivist model (heralded by the faltering of artificial intelligence) led to renewed attention to embodied, situated, and material aspects of cognition. This new cognitive science is immediately relevant to the still-vexed "human factors" aspect of ubiquitous computing precisely because it addresses aspects of human experience pertinent to the development of richer and more subtle, if not calmer, technologies of interaction.

Escape from the cognitivist cul-de-sac demands a wholesale paradigm shift and a new set of axiomatic assumptions: mind and body are not separate or separable; "self and world" is likewise an invidious distinction; intelligence is making sense of the world; thinking occurs at the fingertips and in the soles of the feet, in the process of interaction with the world. Calm, embedded, context-aware technology implies a phenomenological understanding of being-in-the-world or, rather, of a performative "doing-in-the- world," of situated sensorimotor action. To come to understand the emergence of meaning through a temporal process of bodily interaction with things and people in the world is to engage what Andy Pickering (1995) has called "the mangle of practice." In his book so titled, Pickering captures a key aspect of the paradigm shift I am arguing for in his distinction between what he calls the "representational idiom" and the "performative idiom." In these terms, the cognitivist paradigm is firmly rooted in the representational idiom. I propose that the pursuit of ubiquity demands a postcognitivist approach attending to embodiment, to the performative relation to artifacts and the world, and to the relation of cognition to social and cultural formations. In the next section, I give an introduction to such perspectives via a discussion of the work of Edwin Hutchins.

Cognition Distributed and Embodied

In 1995, Edwin Hutchins published a remarkable work of interdisciplinary scholarship that combined anthropological fieldwork with cognitive science and computational theory. He analyzed the group activity of navigation on a ship's bridge as a case of "distributed cognition," in which a group of people performing specific roles, communicating with each other in specific ways, and using a highly developed set of tools perform computational tasks. In a more recent paper, "Imagining the Cognitive Life of Things," Hutchins makes some remarkable observations on cognition in the wild, which warrant quotation at length:

> In the last chapter of *Cognition in the Wild* . . . I argue that cognitive science made a fundamental category error when it mistook the properties of a person in interaction with a social and material world for the cognitive properties of whatever is inside the person. One enduring problem with this claim is that it demands a description of how cognitive properties arise from the interaction of person with social and material world. *Cognition in the Wild* provides a profoundly incomplete answer to this question. . . . For the most part, the cognitive processes described in *Cognition in the Wild*, and in other treatments of distributed cognition, are presented without reference to the role of the body in thinking. That is, in spite of the fact that distributed cognition claims that the interaction of people with things is a central phenomenon of cognition, the approach has remained oddly disembodied. (2010)

I want to dwell on Hutchins's laudable self-criticism because it is a useful example of the slow process of denaturalizing axiomatic assumptions (in general and in cognitive science) and is exemplary of the paradigm shift occurring in cognitive studies. *Cognition in the Wild* (Hutchins 1995) can be read as an attempt to recuperate a functioning and historically coherent system to computationalism. As Philip Agre puts it, "A computer . . . does not simply have an instrumental use in a given site of practice; the computer is frequently about that site in its very design. In this sense computing has been constituted as a kind of imperialism; it aims to reinvent virtually every other site of practice in its own image" (1997, 131). When Hutchins translates one activity into the terms of another, explaining navigation in terms of computation, the authority of this translation is given by the (presumed) authority of the discourse of computation. The ship crew's ability, their training and process, their tools and artifacts were demonstrably effective long before computational explanation—recall that the expressed purpose of Babbage's difference engine was to calculate tide tables for the British navy—aids to precisely the kind of navigation Hutchins observed.[4]

In what way and for whom did *Cognition in the Wild* "explain" the procedures of coastal navigation, or, to put it another way, what is the power of the computational explanation? An unreconstructed computational explanation would necessarily explain observed phenomena in functionalist terms (Putnam 1967, since recanted). Functionalism asserts that a mental state is constituted by the causal relations that it bears to sensory inputs, behavioral outputs, and other mental states. Cognitivism is just one (computational) version of functionalism. Functionalism has a rather industrial if not von Neumannesque cast in its reliance on the idea of serial processing, inputs, and outputs.[5] The cognitivism of *Cognition in the Wild* is more nuanced. Cognition, for Hutchins, is embedded in artifacts and practices and is shared among actors, but it is still understood as computation. As cognitive science reaches out farther and farther into cultural realms where computation is an increasingly alien concept, distinctions between technical and popular usages become increasingly hazy, and the imperializing project of computer culture insidiously persists.[6]

Hutchins recognizes that "interactions between the body and cultural artifacts constitute an important form of thinking. These interactions are not taken as 'indications' of invisible mental processes, rather they are taken as the thinking processes themselves" (2010). This is reminiscent of remarks made by Hubert Dreyfus many years earlier in his phenomenological critique of artificial intelligence: "My personal plans and my memories are inscribed in the things around me just as are the public goals of men in general" (1992, 266). John Sutton has similarly noted more recently that "thought is not an inner realm behind practical skill, but itself an intrinsic and worldly aspect of real-time engagement with the tricky material and social world" (2008, 50). To permit that bodily motion may constitute the medium of thinking is a radical assertion for a rehabilitated cognitivist but will come as no surprise to the dancer or practitioner of martial arts or to any thoughtful person who does rock climbing or hangs out the laundry. But we must not underestimate the profundity of this sea change in cognitive science; it indicates a hard-won emancipation from naturalization to the tenets of artificial intelligence. Philip Agre lucidly documents his own such emancipation. He credits his reading of Michel Foucault's *The Archeology of Knowledge* specifically and poststructural writing generally as an epiphany: "They were utterly practical instruments by which I first became able to think clearly and to comprehend ideas that had not been hollowed out through the false precision of formalism" (1997, 148–149).

It is precisely this "false precision of formalism" that hollows out embodied knowledge. As Aldous Huxley observed long ago, "In a world where education is predominantly verbal, highly educated people find it all but impossible to pay serious attention to anything but words and notions" (1954, quoted in Pickering 2008). Numerous students of embodied cognition, from Michael Polanyi to Evan Thompson, have stated what practitioners and teachers of embodied cultures have always known: the skills of bodily know-how are notoriously hard to document; such thinking is inherently nontextual and nonintersecting with textual representation and text-based reasoning. Dreyfus, after Polanyi, refers to such knowledge as "muscular gestalts" (1992, 249). John Sutton notes in regard to the potter's skill: "Because this kind of expertise relies on an immense reservoir of practical skill memory, embodied somehow in the fibres and in the sedimented ability to sequence technical gestures appropriately, verbal descriptions of it (by either actors or observers) will be inadequate. . . . [W]hat the expert remembers is in large part consciously inaccessible as well as linguistically inarticulable" (2008, 49). Agre expresses the complementary point when he observes that computational fields "concentrate on the aspects of representation that writing normally captures. As a result, theories will naturally tend to lean on distinctions that writing captures and not on the many distinctions that it doesn't" (2003, 290). It is precisely this discontinuity that creates a deep tension in the modern academy between the pedagogy of the textuosymbolic regime, on the one hand, and the pedagogy of the arts and other embodied practices, on the other—accounting for the failure of interdisciplinarity noted earlier.

Such (embodied) thinking is not computational in the usual sense, so any attempt to recuperate it to the world of computation has to force it through several transmogrifications to fit a linear, atemporal, Boolean mode of representation. The framing of group performance on a ship's navigation bridge as distributed computation in a computational–cognitivist worldview was a tour de force by Hutchins. Yet, as he himself notes, such analysis rendered the bodily dimensions of thinking irrelevant or invisible:

> The processes that underlie the "Aha!" insight remain invisible to a computational perspective in part because that perspective represents everything in a single mono-modal (or even a-modal) system. A careful examination of the way the body engages the tools in the setting, however, helps solve the mystery of how the discovery was made, and why it happened when it did. The insight was achieved in and emerged out of the navigators bodily engagement with the tool. (2010)[7]

Hutchins comes close to Mark Johnson's (1990 work and also to Johnson's work with George Lakoff (Johnson and Lakoff 1999) regarding the origins of abstract concepts in embodied experience when he notes: "Motion in space acquires conceptual meaning and reasoning can be performed by moving the body" (2010). Here is revealed a fundamental cognitive cauterization among all but the most sensitively designed interfaces and interactive systems—a situation that has beleaguered digital-arts practices: they ignore and erase bodily engagement of the sort that complements material artifacts and tools developed over years or generations and, taken together, facilitate bodily reasoning. The navigator's hoey, the engineer's slide rule, the machinist's caliper, the carpenter's square are amenable to computational explanation because (loosely) what is involved is a relatively simple translation of geometry to algebra. The painter's brush, the violinist's bow, the harvester's scythe, and so many other artifacts are complex and sophisticated devices for thinking with because they have evolved in a deep structural coupling with the basic rhythms and modalities of neural circuits and sensorimotor loops. They are prosthetics that integrate with the user at a deep and more organic level precisely because they do not involve a translation into and out of mathematicological computation. On the subject of artifacts, Hutchins notes: "By interacting with particular kinds of cultural things, we can produce complex cognitive accomplishments while employing simple cognitive processes" (2010).[8] Aspects of the environment are deployed as off-board memory, and, consistent with Hutchins's notion of distributed cognition, computation is offloaded, too.

But in framing the situation in this way, are we not reinstating precisely the computationalist bifurcations we sought to avoid? Not simply of storage and processing, but of the world and representation? Lambros Malafouris asserts that it makes little sense to speak of one system representing the other: "Although we may be well able to construct a mental representation of anything in the world, the efficacy of material culture in the cognitive system lies primarily in the fact that it makes it possible for the mind to operate without having to do so, ie, to think through things, in action, without the need of mental representation" (2004, 58). Micronesian canoeists gather knowledge about undersea geography colloquially "through the seat of their pants" (if they're wearing any), but more accurately through a subtle integration of proprioceptive and vestibular cues related to the movement of their craft (canoe, catamaran) as a prosthetic extension of their embodiment. Hutchins goes on rightly to observe: "From the perspective of formal representation of the task, the means by which the tools are manipulated by the body appear as mere implementation details" (2010).[9]

The phrase "implementation details" tells the score before the game begins. It belies a commitment to dualism that will automatically render invisible or irrelevant aspects of embodiment. Explanation of a group human activity in terms of computation will inevitably render invisible the significance of embodied practice because the irrelevance of embodiment is axiomatic to the rationale of the discipline. *Implementation details* is a phrase that stands in for an entire corpus of disciplinary rationalizations to justify the disembodiment of artificial intelligence, as first articulated by Herbert

Simon: "Instead of trying to consider the 'whole man,' fully equipped with glands and viscera, I should like to limit my discussion to Homo Sapiens, 'thinking man'" ([1968] 1969, 65). This arbitrary and convenient "limit" in the "root document" of cognitivism is a veritable Pandora's box that permitted the excision of embodied situated materiality from artificial intelligence and cognitive science for a generation. The devil is not so much in the (implementation) details as in the desire to ignore them. *Implementation details* cannot be swept under the rug. Like *human factors,* this term has allowed technical community to sidestep the overarching importance of human culture—engagement of which would of course demand a challenging interdisciplinarity that always has the awkward potential of destabilizing axiomatic assumptions.[10]

Conclusion

Two decades ago, at the emergence of the "reactive robotics" movement, Rodney Brooks critiqued the reigning representationalism in his pithy assertion that "the world is its own best model" (1991, 15), a sentiment that was sympathetic to emerging paradigms of embodied, situated, and distributed cognition and to Dreyfus's phenomenological critique of artificial intelligence. By virtue of evolutionary selection, there is direct cognitive correlation between the world and the bodily experience of it. This correlation results in a kind of (performative) knowledge and (non)cogitation irreconcilable with the cogntivist "physical symbol system hypothesis."[11] But it is this embodied, situated knowledge that provides the basis for precisely such cogitation as well as for introspection.[12] It is the lived solution to the symbol grounding problem (Harnad 1990). This double—that the world is its own best model and that there is direct (non) cognitive correlation between the world and the bodily experience of it—is the core of the postcognitivist position. It is a true paradigm shift that must be thoroughly internalized if real progress is to be made in the development of "calm" technology.

The period in which (ubiquitous/consumer/computer/digital) technology could be (and needed to be) developed in vacuo, in the lab, is resoundingly over. This technology must now be considered for what it demonstrably is: an integrated component of social and cultural fabric, just like automobiles and telephones. In my opinion, a rigorous engagement of postcognitive perspectives offers the prospect of new approaches to "calmness," context awareness, and other murky "human factors" that have to date stymied the project of ubiquity.

Notes

1. Many theorists have deployed the term *virtuality* in rather abstract ways—for instance, Brian Massumi (2002). In my discussion here, I stay close to practices of interaction with sensor and data-driven technological systems.

2. It is a telling and persistent failure of interdisciplinarity—directly pertinent to the development of ubiquitous computing—that although media artists were at forefront of such research, the two communities had limited connection.

3. As Merlin Donald argues, this "mimetic" intelligence is fundamental to human culture, and much cutting-edge research was done by artists in this period. Certain initiatives stand out as beacons through the 1990s—such as the artist-in-residence program at the Xerox Palo Alto Research Center, the Ars Electronica Futurelab, V2 in Rotterdam, ZKM, the Banff New Media Institute, the Australian Network for Art and Technology, and, more recently, Intel Labs.

4. To claim navigation on the deck of a ship at sea in the name of cognitivism is in this way analogous to Columbus's claiming Hispaniola in the name of the queen of Spain while rather obstinately ignoring the obvious fact that the land was already claimed, named, and occupied.

5. There are, of course, theories of cognition that dispute not simply such seriality, but the very existence of "inputs" and "outputs" as phenomena in the organism (as opposed to representations imposed by the observer)—for instance, the autopoietic theory of Humberto Maturana and Francisco Varela (1980) or the second-order cybernetics of Heinz von Foerster (2002).

6. A phenomenon I have referred to elsewhere as a Trojan Horse effect; see Penny 2008b.

7. Navigators talk of "thinking like a compass." Hutchins notes, "The bodily anticipation of clockwise rotation becomes a somatic anchor for the concept of increasing bearing number value" (2010, 445)—that is, a clockwise bodily twist corresponds to increasing numerical value.

8. This statement is akin to any of a number of approaches in philosophy of mind and cognitive archaeology that talk of offloading memory or computation or both onto a structured environment, such as Andy Clark and David Chambers's (1998) extended-mind hypothesis, Merlin Donald's (1991) exograms, and David Kirsh and Paul Maglio's (1995) epistemic actions.

9. Philip Agre makes a similar argument: "A theory of cognition based on formal reason works best with objects of cognition whose attributes and relationships can be completely characterized in formal terms" (1997, 143). In the study of material culture, little can be "completely characterized in formal terms."

10. This reticence is understandable in terms of the construction of the technical disciplines and academia in general. Interdisciplinarity in such contexts is generally meek and unadventurous precisely because of the fear of moving beyond one's own valorized and specialized expertise (see Penny 2008a). That is not to say that innovative efforts have not been made in some quarters—the humanistic informatics movement arising in Scandinavia in the 1990s and some aspects of what is referred to as "digital humanities" in the United States and elsewhere. The Informatics Department at the University of California, Irvine, is notable within schools of computer science in the United States for its openness to perspectives from anthropology and sociology.

11. "A physical symbol system has the necessary and sufficient means for general intelligent action" (Newell and Simon 1976, 116).

12. This idea is related to the notion of the "cognitive unconscious" as developed by Johnson and Lakoff in *Philosophy in the Flesh* (1999).

References

Agre, Philip. 2003. "Writing and Representation." In *Narrative Intelligence*, edited by Michael Mateas and Phoebe Sengers, 281–303. Amsterdam: J. Benjamins.

Agre, Philip. 1997. "Towards a Critical Technical Practice: Lessons Learned in Trying to Reform AI." In *Social Science, Technical Systems, and Cooperative Work: Beyond the Great Divide*, edited by Geoffrey C. Bowker, 131–157. Mahwah, NJ: Lawrence Erlbaum.

Brooks, Rodney. 1991. "Intelligence without Reason." MIT Artificial Intelligence Laboratory Memo no. 1293, April.

Clark, Andy, and David Chalmers. 1998. "Extended Mind Hypothesis." *Analysis* 58:10–23.

Donald, Merlin. 1991. *Origins of the Modern Mind: Three Stages in the Evolution of Culture and Cognition*. Cambridge, MA: Harvard University Press.

Dreyfus, Hubert L. 1992. *What Computers Still Can't Do: A Critique of Artificial Reason*. Cambridge, MA: MIT Press.

Harnad, Stevan. 1990. "The Symbol Grounding Problem." *Physica D* 42:335–346.

Hutchins, Edwin. 2010. "Enaction, Imagination, and Insight." In *Enaction: Toward a New Paradigm for Cognitive Science*, edited by John Stewart, Olivier Gapenne, and Ezequiel A. Di Paolo. Cambridge, MA: MIT Press, 2010. 425–450.

Hutchins, Edwin. 1995. *Cognition in the Wild*. Cambridge, MA: MIT Press.

Huxley, Aldous. 1954. *The Doors of Perception*. New York: Harper.

Johnson, Mark. 1990. *The Body in the Mind*. Chicago: University of Chicago Press.

Johnson, Mark, and George Lakoff. 1999. *Philosophy in the Flesh*. New York: Basic Books.

Kirsh, David, and Paul Maglio. 1995. "On Distinguishing Epistemic from Pragmatic Actions." *Cognitive Science* 18:513–549.

Malafouris, Lambros. 2004. "The Cognitive Basis of Material Engagement: Where Brain, Body, and Culture Conflate." In *Rethinking Materiality: The Engagement of Mind with the Material World*, edited by Elizabeth DeMarrais, Chris Gosden, and Colin Renfrew, 53–62. Cambridge, UK: McDonald Institute for Archaeological Research.

Massumi, Brian. 2002. *Parables for the Virtual: Movement, Affect, Sensation*. Durham, NC: Duke University Press.

Maturana, Humberto, and Francisco G. Varela. 1980. "Autopoiesis: The Organization of the Living," In *Autopoiesis and Cognition: The Realization of the Living*, 63–123. Dordrecht, Netherlands: Reidel.

Mindell, David A. 2002. *Between Human and Machine: Feedback, Control, and Computing before Cybernetics*. Baltimore: Johns Hopkins University Press.

Newell, Allen, and Herbert A. Simon. 1976. "Computer Science as Empirical Inquiry: Symbols and Search." *Communications of the ACM* 19 (3): 113–126.

Penny, Simon. 2008a. "Bridging Two Cultures—towards a History of the Artist–Inventor." In *Artists as Inventors, Inventors as Artists*, edited by Dieter Daniels and Barbara U. Schmidt, 142–157. Ostfildern, Germany: Hatje Cantz.

Penny, Simon. 2008b. "Experience and Abstraction—the Arts and the Logic of the Machine." *FibreCulture* 11. Available at http://eleven.fibreculturejournal.org/fcj-072-experience-and-abstraction-the-arts-and-the-logic-of-machines. Accessed 24 January 2012.

Pickering, Andrew. 2008. "Against Human Exceptionalism." Unpublished paper, University of Exeter.

Pickering, Andrew. 1995. *The Mangle of Practice: Time, Agency, and Science*. Chicago: University of Chicago Press.

Putnam, Hilary. 1967. "Psychological Predicates." In *Art, Mind, and Religion*, edited by William H. Capitan and Daniel Davy Merrill, 37–48. Pittsburgh: University of Pittsburgh Press.

Simon, Herbert A. [1968] 1969. *The Sciences of the Artificial*. Karl Taylor Compton Lectures. Cambridge, MA: MIT Press.

Sutton, John. 2008. "Material Agency, Skills, and History: Distributed Cognition and the Archaeology of Memory." In *Material Agency: Towards a Non-Anthropocentric Approach*, edited by Carl Knappett and Lambros Malafouris, 37–55. New York: Springer.

Von Foerster, Heinz. 2002. *Understanding Understanding*. New York: Springer.

Weiser, Mark, and John Seely Brown. 1995. "Designing Calm Technology." Available at http://sandbox.xerox.com/hypertext/weiser/calmtech/calmtech.htm. Accessed 14 August 2009.

15 Of Intangible Speed: "Ubiquity" as Transduction in Interactivity

Ulrik Ekman

In-Formational Events: Right before Concretizing Ubiquitous-Computing Interactivity

The cultural movements and events of the epoch emerging with the unfolding and embedding of modes and variants of ubiquitous computing (ubicomp) across a great many regions of the world (notably in Southeast Asia, Europe, and the United States) are still a matter of a history of the present.[1] In that sense, this coemergence of culture and technics does not yet belong to a well-defined period or to a field with clearly drawn contours. Rather, it still remains a somewhat undecidable matter of a dynamic eventuality and a spacing whose structurations and formations are perhaps in the main to come. As such, this coemergence seems to put quite some emphasis on issues of anticipation, inventions of the other, and new individuations—and perhaps this is the reason why a number of researchers today hesitate for a moment in considering whether ubicomp culture exists for real or remains but an inspired vision.[2] Nonetheless, as also attested to by the great many valuable and thought-provoking contributions to this volume, the general remarks respecting this field in the introduction, and the myriad quite remarkable actual developments in technical cultures during the fifteen years after Mark Weiser's early work on ubicomp culture,[3] ubicomp is already a "technical fact" (Leroi-Gourhan 1943b). That is, if universal technical dynamics exist as tendencies, operating independently of the human or ethnic groupings that are nevertheless the only forms through which they are concretized, ubicomp, as such a dynamical tendency, has already begun specific and differentiated concretization in several groups—for example, as total media in Chinese culture, as an overtly personalized and pervasive mobile technoculture in Japan, and as a more infrastructural project in European culture—and is thus to be approached as a technical fact. Insofar as we participate in ubicomp in one or more ways, it is already our artificial envelope, our interposed membrane, or that curtain of objects through which we try to assimilate the exterior milieu (Leroi-Gourhan 1945). In other words, ubicomp is already a movement within the interior milieu (of individuals and their memories, of social cultures and their past, as well as of current technics with its databases and rather capacious storage devices) that is in the process of gaining a foothold in the exterior milieu (animals, vegetation, landscape, locations, spaces, geography, climate). As such, ubicomp is already a mode of survival by other means, more or less inhuman.

This technical tendency is evidently concretized along with and within a certain history of technics and culture, specifically after World War II. In the broad sense, ubicomp culture no longer refers primarily to the first of the three waves of cybernetics capably outlined by Katherine Hayles in *How We Became Posthuman* (1999, 50–130)—that is, the 1945–1960 period drawing upon homeostasis as a central concept—except that its key notion of information is still very much with us considering that Claude Shannon and Warren Weaver's (1949) mathematical theory of communication is hardly less in force today. It would also seem as if the second period (1960–1980), centrally involved with reflexivity as a key concept, is largely a matter of the past. It might even seem as if we are now in several respects beyond or at the outer edges of the third period (from 1980 onward) emphasizing virtuality. However, we may be moving quite a bit too fast here because a number of important efforts from both are still with us and quite decisively so. Perhaps the early notions of reflexivity—such as Heinz von Foerster's (1984) work on observing systems—have indeed been displaced, but we still live with vast bodies of cultural research and technics that draw upon self-organization as a paradigm; witness the continued influence today of second-generation cybernetics, late systems theory, autopoiesis, and versions of more or less radical social constructivism, for instance. Likewise, the hypostatizings of virtual reality, from the mid-1960s through the 1990s, with its transcendental ideal of simulation and its alleged "escape from the meat," perhaps seem ghostly relics today.[4] But virtuality today remains the paradigm for the development of ubicomp culture, albeit now accompanied by certain important modifications and competing approaches. A physical turn after the new millennium slowly but surely seems to have permitted a greater unfolding of embodied virtuality under the aegis of a pursuit of a mixed reality, including augmented reality as well as augmented virtuality, a real environment as well as a virtual environment. Even if virtuality is with us as a paradigm, however, it is not yet entirely clear how to navigate among approaches to it as different as, say, Paul Milgram and Fumio Kishino's (1994) technical notion of the virtuality continuum, Giorgio Agamben's hyper- or postphenomenological notions(Agamben 1998; Agamben and Heller-Roazen 1999, 177–242), Jacques Garelli's (1991) notion regarding a prepersonal reservoir of manifold potentialities for more or less bare life forms, or a Deleuzian transcendental empiricism affirming virtuality as an idea of multiplicitous differentiation/differenciations that is real as potential but not as actual (Deleuze 1993, 208–221).

It might well be that the common denominator here is that the idea of ubicomp solicits, in a quite transdisciplinary manner, a very thorough technocultural augmentation—an expansion, widening, or delimitation that goes so far as to stage new reality effects. Hayles's rehistoricization of cybernetics was and still is quite acute in that respect: virtuality qua "ubiquity" concerns a "computational universe" for and with contemporary network societies, whether this universe be thought along the lines of an all-encompassing continuum, an irreducible (negative) theological reserve of dissemination-granting phenomena, a plane of pure immanence whose singularities open onto dynamic differential syntheses, or something else again. No doubt, both "ubiquity" and "pervasiveness" call for ongoing deconstruction and reconstruction of their ontological and metaphysical remainders (their altogether abstract idealizations, their excessively essential extensions), but certain other traits of a contemporary diagnosis are perhaps just as interesting: we seem to be situated historically and paradigmatically between 1985 and 1995 still, between paradigms of reflexivity and virtuality—no matter that both have undergone quite some revision. If this situation remains a fertile ground today, it is probably because it involves a return of the transcendental/empirical divide, with a difference. In other words, ubicomp culture appears at one and the same time to call for a new mode of cybernetic and human self-organization capable of a wider, more complex, and more smoothly and finely differentiated relationality with the other[5] as well as for a new mode of machinic and sociocultural heterogenesis capable of a wider range of individual emergences and differential syntheses, including technical systems, subjectivity effects, and social formations.[6]

We surely have at this point approached but little of a culture living with open machines so as to have these machines generate and operate as a computational universe. There is today, however, a remarkable tendency to pursue out-of-the-box computing, to live with and within an expansion of information-intensive environments or milieus. These environments do develop along with a culture of living with mixed realities, which begins to demonstrate that we will now continue to operate with the concreticization of embodied as well as more abstract virtualities, providing at least some kind of a counterweight to Hayles's convincing earlier critique of a strong tendency in information science to favor a posthuman ideal of transcendental disembodiment.

The recent work by Paul Dourish (2001b) furnishes one good example of such a counterweight in that it draws upon the thought of the phenomenological lifeworld (from Edmund Husserl through Alfred Schütz) so as to revisit *in* our existing everyday culture the historical traces of the interactions and interaction designs with which we now live in a ubicomp culture—from the electric through the symbolic, textual, and graphic to the explorations during the past fifteen years of embodied interaction with tangible and social computing. Other concrete examples of this counterweight come to mind, such as the developments of tangible or ambient computing and shared workspaces by Hiroshi Ishii (1997) and others; pervasive-gaming projects such as those by Blast Theory (2011; see also Bo Kampmann Walther's contribution to this volume, chapter 13); the motion-control mode of operation for the Wii console along with its gestural-recognition system; recent developments in augmented reality and locative awareness from SixthSense, Layar, and Earthmine (see Timothy Lenoir's contribution to this volume, chapter 34); and a great many interactive and responsive architectural environments (Bullivant 2006). However, more abstract virtualities remain with us as well because virtual reality is still an active research field: the major part of the gaming industry still favors virtuality qua immersive three-dimensional worlds of a certain illusionist realism; phenomena such as *Second Life* still demonstrate a considerable cultural pull; and a concreticization of ubicomp culture may very well be assimilated in large part by developments of abstract platform services such as those we see emerging today, also via the Institute of Electrical and Electronics Engineers, under the rubric of "cloud computing" (Ahson and Ilyas 2011; Buyya, Broberg, and Goscinski 2011).

Insofar as these projects bring forth an everyday culture of living with the mixed realities of information-intensive milieus, they begin to indicate that ad hoc dynamic exchanges among technical and human types of context awareness present both a daunting task (for humans and machines alike) and a source of surprise (welcome or not). Perhaps it is still too early to say whether and how this technical tendency will be concretized as a new set of overtly unfolded modes of living with ubicomp or rather as a more calm technical culture—that is, with a higher degree of embeddedness of context-aware computational units (already vastly outstripping the number of stand-alone computers).[7] However, the varied specialization, the sheer number, and the increasing mobility of computational units have in any case already begun to problematize the notion of the modern computer as a universal machine, and it is an open question what will emerge from this inclination toward a dynamics of multiplicitous singularization.

In this larger staging of a ubicomp culture in the making, one limited but still rather extensive and complex problematic, which is a focal point in this text, concerns the change of notions of interactivity now solicited.[8] The widening of the technocultural field called for in the development of ubicomp is very well illustrated by the demand for and subsequent actualization of new kinds of context awareness, on both human and technical sides; it also quite obviously entails a similar kind of widening of the field for human–computer interaction, whether the latter concerns individual or social human groupings and calm and embedded or more overtly noticeable systems.[9] Moreover, in this widening, one finds today the same kind of transdisciplinary challenge that was explicit in Mark Weiser's early work; witness his ways of drawing upon not just computer science but also, and just as significantly, an entire array of disciplines from the human and social sciences. Here, technical and sociocultural studies can only coevolve, if at all, and the development of interaction designs for "ubiquity" must first and last concern interaction designs for *individuations* of technics and cultures, systems and devices, as well as persons and socialities. It must concern individuations because this coexistence and coevolvement hinge on experiments with environmental and internal systemic technical integration of anthropic difference as well as on experiments with human cultural integration of the differences of technical systems as such and as environmental curtains of objects opening onto technical tendencies. In the case of ubicomp culture and more generally, then, the Simondonian notion of "individuation" hints at the very processing at stake in that coevolutionary becoming of human culture and technics that involves a certain early supersaturation of their being:

> Individuation corresponds to the appearance of stages in the being, which are the stages of the being. It is not a mere isolated consequence arising as a by-product of becoming, but this very process itself as it unfolds; it can be understood only by taking into account this initial supersaturation of the being, at first homogeneous and static, then soon after adopting a certain structure and becoming—and in so doing, bringing about the emergence of both individual and milieu—following a course in which preliminary tensions are resolved but also preserved in the shape of the ensuing structure; in a certain sense, it could be said that the sole principle by which we can be guided is that of the conservation of being through becoming. (Simondon 1992, 301)

Development of these interaction designs for the individuations of ubicomp cultures still seem to hover at the limit between approaches through organization and emergence, respectively. It is far from easy to discern whether these interaction designs are to cater to a computational and cultural universe in which individuations take place mostly as matters of self-organization or, rather, as heterogenesis and whether their paradigms for handling complexity should be incorporated from theories of autopoeisis or emergence, for example. Staying with this insight, however, is already to have missed the important point that these individuations are in any case hardly ever a matter of a theoretical a priori, a knowing intentional plan, a controlled coding of input and output, but rather a matter of an ontogenetic dynamics and its relationality playing themselves out in practice and then primarily in the domains of living sensation and inscriptory registration.[10] In other words, in such a situation of interaction designs for ubiquity, one can at best affirm an event to come, and this event is then the "principle," grasped and known fairly late as an after-effect.

Moreover, for that to happen, interaction designs for ubiquity would need to be "in-formed," and this intervention of information, which will provide actual structuration and formation, is not anticipatable (logically, materially, mathematically). Hence, both actual memories and memory in general might give way: a weak emphasis on opening onto an other invention is not without its justifications, for the dynamic and productive interrelation (de)constitutive of culture and ubicomp may very well be inscribing new differences in more ways than one. If this kind of disparate and tensely uncertain situation is at stake, then experimental interactions take place before their design and in relation to a structurally older and immanently broader interactivity.

The currently ongoing concreticization of the relationality in the interactivity of a ubicomp culture thus cannot but raise new questions concerning human and technical individuation, not least respecting the putting in parenthesis of the sense and sensation of the world, the reach and intensity of the haptics of affective control societies (Bogard 2007; Deleuze 1995), more or less inhuman and asystemic context awareness and technological embeddedness, movements in mixed realities that need not abide by any existential notion coupling life and technics, and organology or inorganic life.[11] These questions are being raised via so many calls for ubiquity, pervasiveness, thoroughness, ubiquity, and ambience, and no matter how any actualization of all this maps out, such a technocultural augmentation cannot but lead, however briefly and fleetingly, to reconsideration of a notion of "information" that is considerably broader than that traditionally inherited from computer science.

In this coming interactivity, the concern is suddenly very little a matter of measuring information entropy—that is, approaching it as a message endowed with technical meaning and a numerical measure (base 2 logarithm of *N*) of the uncertainty of an outcome (Shannon and Weaver 1949). Rather, uncertainty momentarily prevails; the disseminative contextuality of "information" haunts once again; and it is not immediately decidable whether the "information" at stake is perhaps instead a matter of semiotics, sensation, and affect or of an influence leading to behavioral or biological transformation or of data and records on a material substrate or of a trait of *phusis*. At the very edge of any organizational process in a ubicomp culture, one would thus reconsider "information" vis-à-vis the notion of "a difference that makes a difference" (Bateson 1972), but also the careful openness inherent in Shannon and Weaver's earlier formulations—that is, as in the kind of passage where Shannon acknowledged that it "is hardly to be expected that a single concept of information would satisfactorily account for the numerous possible applications of this general field" (Shannon 1993, 180) and where Weaver (1949) was led to a tripartite analysis of information, including not only technical problems concerning quantification and semantic problems relating to meaning and truth, but also certain influential problems respecting the impact and effectiveness of information on human behavior.

The wager here is that when approaching interactivity in a ubicomp culture as partaking of a history of the present, you would necessarily have to reoperationalize your approach to "information" in a finely differentiated fashion. More specifically, this reoperationalization may well involve not just a reinscription of the issues of semantics, contextualization, and the neurophysiology of the brain found in Donald MacKay's (1969, 1980) earlier work on information theory. Nor would it be just a matter of rewriting Raymond Ruyer's (1954, 1958) thought of a necessarily embodied and morphogenetic survey of information in a universe of information. It is also and perhaps most of all a matter of rethinking Gilbert Simondon's critique of earlier cybernetics in his presentation of "in-formation" as a transductive generation between two heterogeneous series of signs and signals.

Hence, if you are led to engage with in-formative interactivity, differing *différance* singularly there for an instant, so as to transduce contemporary culture and ubicomp technics, this engagement always happens on the outside inside via a structural germination, crystallization, or morphogenetic potential, just as it remains a question of the preindividual (a supersaturation of being already in there). To the limit of technology and its individuation, inventions of the other move as matters of involutionary mutation or, more generally, as an infolding of a different structural potential—anthropic, perhaps. Interactivity of the new—whether a question of preindividual components in psychic, social, biological, technical, or environmental individuations—concerns no pure revolution or inventive genius, but a relational refolding that makes another difference qua a transduction. Innovative interactivity with culture and ubicomp technics thus always concerns preindividual remainders, and access cannot but happen through the already-there, showing that Meno's aporia is with us in the twenty-first century, too,[12] not least as a condition of the kind of general, quasi-transcendental phenomenology of technical tendencies and machines in concreticization that Simondon already projected.

An opening onto the uncertainty of the preindividual in ubicomp culture—here as an inventive path of interaction, interaction design, and interactivity—moves across memory and an adoption of a strange future past, already there *in* so many inscriptions and traces, but not as lived and in each case already gone elsewhere transductively and at a structurally older speed (figure 15.1). Perhaps interactive media art in its frequent revisitation of a great many modern and classical distinctions of *ars*, *techné*, and science is not the least promising path toward approaching and exploring relevant bits and parts of such an "already there." In particular, the early projects of Canadian media artist David Rokeby (2011) may stay a privileged kind of remainder from which may still come new individuations for the current epoch, not just because *Body Language* (1984–1986) and its differentiated sequels in *Very Nervous System* (*VNS*, 1986–1990)[13] go back forward through their history of interactive media art, but also because these projects seem to return today as having incorporated what is as if "right before" (ahead of) contemporary interactions, interaction designs, and interactivity in a ubicomp culture (see Rokeby 2000, 2010). Rokeby's *VNS* stands out now, once more, as a thought-provoking precursor.

That is not to say that it is entirely up to date. As an interactive environment whose development started in the early 1980s, *VNS* does not address the kind of development we have seen of the Internet, nor does it begin to work with the kinds of servers providing Internet backhaul to wireless connectivity or all the mobile computing and more or less autonomous ad hoc networking of myriad small, smart devices that we see unfolding more and more today. Nevertheless, Rokeby's project is remarkable

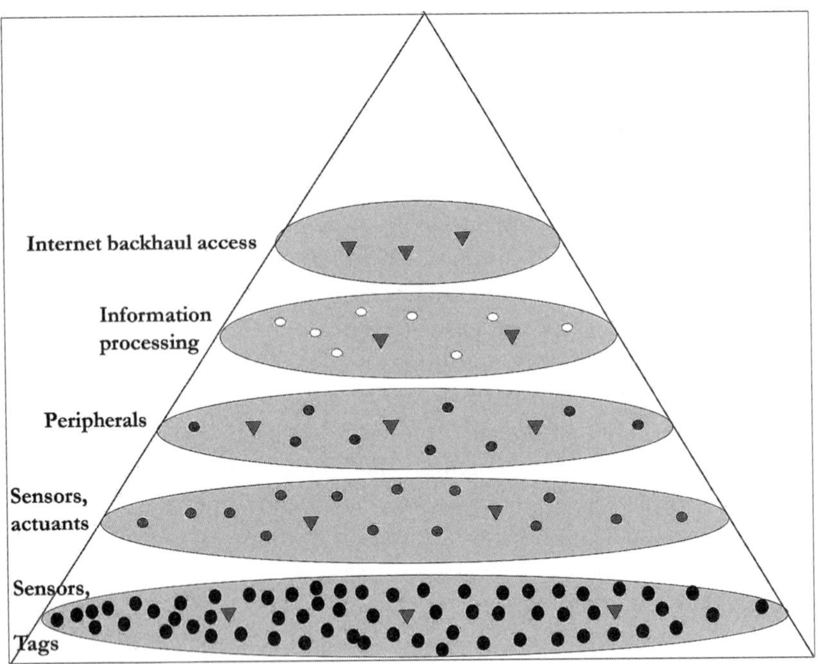

Figure 15.1
Ubicomp layers.

because it may evoke and give you occasion to delve further into what is at stake today in the tagging of our lifeworld now under way everywhere, the sensors in place everywhere, the smart actuants in touch with these sensors, the increasing information access to the world via a great many peripherals, the kind of rather sophisticated information processing going on, for the most part quite invisibly, and not least a sense of what living with a moving and dynamic ubicomp interactivity amounts to.

Interactions—Right before Me

Almost all the time, the interactions between you as an individual and *VNS* as a single interactive environment would tend to leave both unaltered in the main. *VNS*'s assemblage of video cameras, image processors, computers, synthesizers, and sound system would go on as installed and programmed so as to perceive your position, your body contours, and your body movements, not ceasing to pass these elements through its special software to engender the performative presentation of quite complex soundscapes or music or both (figure 15.2). You would hardly notice the sensations of being with *VNS* in this environment but rather would keep perceiving and grasping your

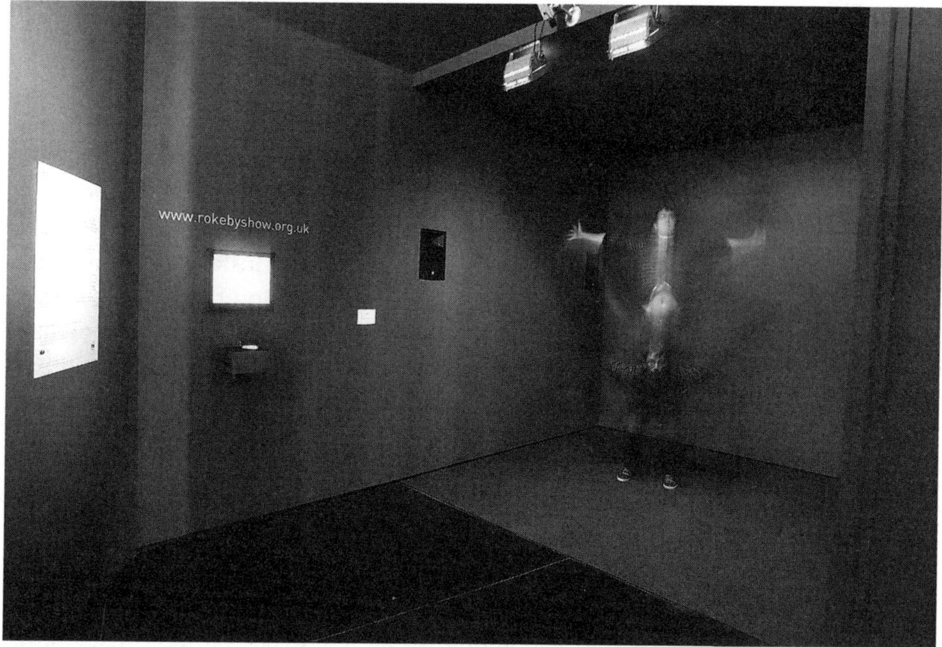

Figure 15.2
Installation, tendentially embedded, and a single human interactant going through vertical kinesthetic experiments. David Rokeby, *Very Nervous System* (1986–1990). Installation view at Foundation for Art Creative Technology (FACT), Liverpool. Photograph by Nathan Cox. Permission kindly granted by FACT.

situation quite clearly, including the dimensions of the room and the identifiable pieces of equipment. Even when your movements turn into a symphony, a jazz song, or the sound of water droplets, these things present themselves as conceptual or semiotic aspects. Even though you may move around horizontally or make slight vertical jumps, doing so remains subject to smooth kinesthesia and works well enough with your body scheme to confirm your current body image.

It is remarkable, however, how far this installation has moved toward a mutually (de)constitutive interactivity for human and computational interactants. *VNS* and you are quite evidently involved in an admirably embodied and inexact control dynamics,[14] or, as Rokeby formulates this relationship,

Body movement is rich, complex, and full of subtlety and ambiguity. Early computer art used random number generators to provide variety and complexity. I replaced the random number generator with the complexity of sentient human response. It is important to understand that *Very Nervous System* is not a control system. It is an interactive system, by which I mean that neither partner in the system (installation and person) is in control. . . . The changing states of the installation are a result of the collaboration of these two elements. The work only exists in this state of mutual influence. (1996)

For the most part, then, you interact, and so does *VNS*, but the relational exchanges and their dynamics tend to leave individual and systemic perception quite undisturbed, and there is seemingly no contact with your preindividual remainders or with other potential inventions lurking *in VNS*'s embedded and overtly present technics.

Nonetheless, it is quite frequently the case that you move *VNS* by becoming provocatively imperceptible to it and that you come to feel the installation as a matter of sensation. It may well be that *VNS* just ignores this sensation by reducing it to its existing mode of operation for its context awareness and its interaction design, perhaps by drawing in part upon its randomization process. Likewise, you might assimilate this sensation to an everyday context awareness that not only would have this sensation be liable to sense but would have it make sense and become an already-known emotion. In any case, it is remarkable how far the interactions between you and *VNS* are already into a "physical turn" that grants another kind of privilege to the real environment and augmented-reality elements. In that sense, interactions are here already a matter of moving in and operating with what Weiser preferred to call "embodied virtuality"—that is, not an immersive and three-dimensional simulative virtual reality bringing you into computing on its terms, but rather a lifeworld in which virtuality is brought out to be incorporated on more or less human terms. Interactions between *VNS* and you are thus already oriented toward tangible computing and living human embodiment to a different degree and in more ways than was the case during the first two waves of computing (mainframes and personal computers), which went quite far toward abstractly universal computing and a pacification and marginalization of living human embodiment. In this case, the artist's own formulations are surprisingly precise and suggestive. In one of his explanations of how he is working with and against contemporary trends in computing, David Rokeby states outright that he objects both to the crushing weight of all the general hype surrounding interactivity and virtual reality and to that hype's implicit transcendental distancing and denigration of the body:

> The computer as a medium is strongly biased and so my impulse while using the computer was to work solidly against these biases. Because the computer is purely logical, the language of interaction should strive to be intuitive. Because the computer removes you from your body, the body should be strongly engaged. Because the computer's activity takes place on the microscopic scale of silicon wafers, the encounter with the computer should take place in human-scaled physical space. And because the computer is objective and disinterested, the experience should be intimate. (Rokeby 1996)

Perhaps some of this media intimacy will make itself felt; perhaps not all sensate complexity will be reduced. Then *VNS* will register as error, certain of its perceptual delimitations. You may well go on feeling different about the installation, not least because its degree of embeddedness (in terms of architecture or darkness, or both) affords only a marginal visuality (as in closed-circuit television or certain kinds of surveillance art). Your sensation then involves considerably more of an indeterminate auditory spacing, recalling that hearing enjoys a special privilege in our kind of embodiment and is at the same time a threat, being a question of an incessantly open attunement to the world (*Stimmung*). This sensation is something to be explored first and last as matters of haptics: your left hand may momentarily seem to manipulate an entire brass section, while the right hand evokes deep bass vibrations, both of which affirm you emotionally, for the outcome is in all likelihood a soundscape or a piece of music that is coherent and so far beyond your usual capability, unless you are an accomplished musician, that you want to listen to it and repeat it. In that case, the surprise of another structural germ is passed by, something structurally older than your current organization of sensation and emotion dwindles away from concreticization, here as a multifaceted fabric or weave of a soundscape that remains to come into contact. In other words, in the internal relation of the individual and its preindividual components, the latter is brushed up against, albeit tangentially and without inventing an individuation with another sense of the world.

Even in such a movement toward felt affirmation of auditory and haptic mastery between you and *VNS*, however, a momentary disturbance has already inserted itself even when this disturbance seems run over by a known emotion, an identifiable sensation, and a habitual operation of the senses of hearing and touch. Thus, the engagement of you with *VNS* and vice versa in a mixed ubicomp reality is less a perceptual and not even a sensing matter, but rather more of a nakedly living tactility and a bare systemic registration of perturbation—that is, a matter of a certain transductive "being in touch." *In* sensation and registration, impersonal affectivity and motricity are at play (figure 15.3). When Rokeby reports having observed a blind boy who simply jumped back as if hitting a physically erected wall when he tried to enter the unmarked environment of *VNS*, this did not happen because the boy's senses of hearing and touch were operative as such, however acutely. It happened rather because the interactions involved contact with enveloping interactivity.[15] This event was then an affective and sensorimotor event that was not just the boy's individually, but one in which hearing was first another protosensory touch and an auditory spacing with a vibrant force of tactility to whose touch he had to be responsive. Perhaps this inventive jolt backward is not entirely unlike what happens when modules in the *VNS* software run into potentially productive internal errors or some of the system wires cross, causing a crash that requires another startup.

Not always, but often enough, in each case unexpectedly, interactions problematize the self-assured sensation or well-functioning registration of being in the world here and now. They are not exactly understood, grasped, or perceived interactions. Nor

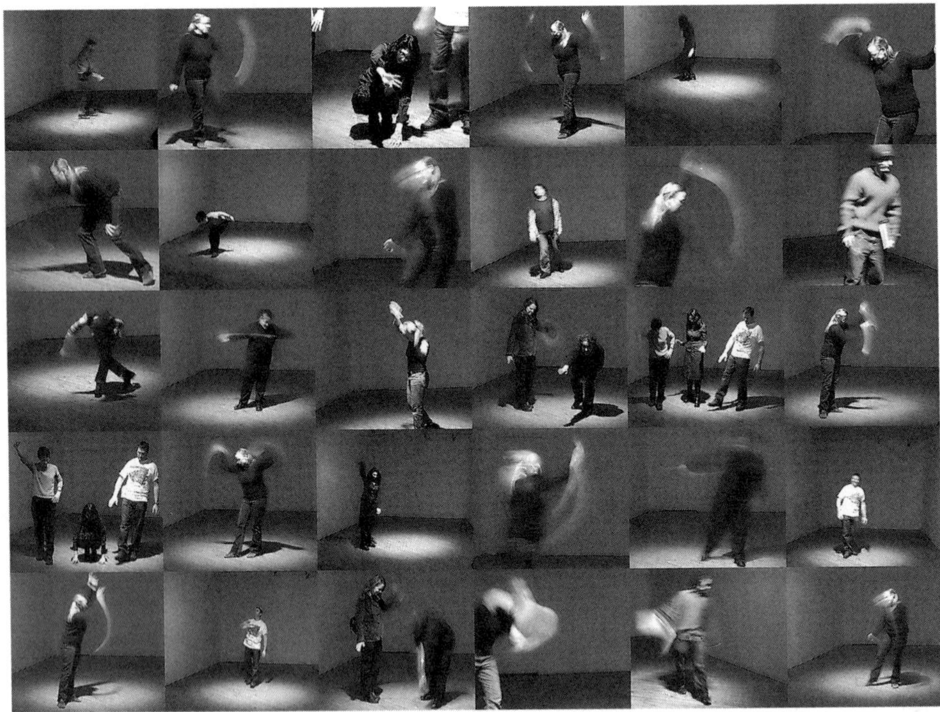

Figure 15.3
An array of kinesthetic experiments with *Very Nervous System* at Foundation for Art Creative Technology (FACT) in Liverpool, 2007. Image array design by Mike Carroll. Photograph courtesy of FACT (Risa Horowitz, William Eakin, and Elizabeth Garlicki).

are they felt and sensed as such: rather, they somehow involve contact with another affectivity or relationality that moves *in* sensation and as if structurally earlier—hence, the affect or registration right "before" you, right "before" those with you and around you, and "before" any programmed input. What moves relationally and affects in such interactions would approximate an invention of the living human and technical other because such interactions problematize individual or socioethnic genetic memories of sensate life, sensations, and their semanticization, along with specific technical memories of impressions and coded inscriptions in individual retentional apparati (e.g., peripherals, random-access memory, hard drives).[16] They are different interactions because they *affect* sensation or registration with delays and relays of an impersonal "you," a "one," or a crystalline "it," engaged as an other already *in* a "me," an "us," or an organized "apparatus." In other words, these interactions care for the invention of another relation—internal to sensation and registration. This relation constitutes transindividual components along with your psychic individuation, the social individuation involving you among others, just as it constitutes other technical tendencies along with the individual technical apparati of *VNS* with which you currently exist.[17] This development by no means precludes that movement is appropriated kinesthetically or by existing units of mobile technology or that affectivity and the force of another relationality are assimilated in well-organized ways in individual sensation and registration—and, in fact, this assimilation is almost always what takes place, for you, those individuals around you, and for *VNS*.

Interaction designs—your individual and social designs and those of more or less "intelligent" systems such as *VNS*—intermittently turn the inside out of any individually stable and sensible moods or registrant attunements to what is to happen and take place. Instead of becoming "liable to sense" (Nancy 1997, 62), providing identifiable sensations or a territorial and temporally well-framed affect[17] or an existing technical fact, some earlier ones or some other traces of things already operative *in* these existing interaction designs introduce a disturbance of vital affectivity and technical relationality. This disturbance is on the move in the blind boy's jump and in your astonishment at the speed and intricacy of the interactivity, in your flight from the installation room, in your momentarily being paralyzed or suspended in awe. It is on the move in the arrival of those internal errors or registered limits that lead *VNS*'s very inexact control and dependence on human interactants to be developed in other ways and toward another kind of mutual context awareness. This disturbance of vital affectivity and technical relationality would also thus have complicated the lines of development that took off in 1982 while Rokeby was designing *Body Language* by combining an Apple II computer, circuitry components to analyze images from an ordinary video camera, a little low-resolution device with sixty-four light sensors, and a rudimentary sound system. Now it would perhaps not stop at Rokeby's use of Mac G4 machines, high-quality video cameras, and the advanced Max software programming of *VNS* as a manifold of dynamically changing "behaviors," so many electronically and algorithmically constructed musical "personalities." It would provoke more than the twenty subroutines looking out of the video cameras at your body so as to take playing cues from your movements to suggest to the sound and instrument database whether a given sort of instrument (say, an electric guitar, a drum, a brass section) should play on offbeats, double its rhythm if you move faster, and so on. Thus, it would perhaps come to involve a wired system and/or a *soft VNS* programming with another kind of affective computing, another kind of concreticization of relations with weight, temperature, body location, posture, movement, gesture, facial expression, emotive signals.

In each case, this disturbance then comes as an earlier difference dynamically deferring and displacing the designed time and place for technical and human individuation. It concerns the invention of a new (because a germlike "older") internal context awareness along with an associated milieu for interactions. As an inventive disturbance, it is the connectivity unfolding between, on the one hand, preindividual components and their embodied human context awareness (psychic and social), the context awareness of embedded ubicomp systems, and, on the other hand, associated milieux.[19] This unfolding is "nervous" to the point of problematizing contextual or epigenetic memory. It does not rest with the conservation or perpetuation of individual memories beyond the individual—via the exteriorization of all those traces (from knapped flint through texts to relational databases and telesurgical inscriptions) through which comes the task to change the conditions for another vital individuation.[20] Rather, the unfolding's "nervousness" further intensifies the lifeworld and information-intensive environments by inscribing a different technical *force*, another technical tendency to become fact, in the time and place of self-affectivity and feedback.

Interactivity among psychic individuations and in the sociality individuating itself transindividually with these individuations only rarely ceases. It remains ongoing almost everywhere, all the time, without actually altogether altering the movement and number of living and technical reality. Any nervously prosthetic exscription of epigenetic interaction designs, including the exscriptions of anthropologically embodied nervous systems along with the sensor networks and actuants of embedded ubicomp (cabled and wireless variants, radio-frequency identification, and components, not least),[21] either fails and crashes or reaffirms the operative organizations of forces and potentials in technical memory. Hence, for the most part, interactivity in life and technics concerns maintenance and reproduction of the sense and sensation of established psychic and social individuations, of the affectivity of nervous or epigenetic memories, and of the more or less forceful inscription of technological memory (epiphylogenesis, or inorganic organized entities qua mediating relations between an individuation and its material environment).

On occasion, however, even epiphylogenetic memory is problematized by transductive potentials in inscriptory technical forces. Life and technics become in-formative; they mutate quite inventively (biotechnology, genetic engineering, nanotechnology, and quantum computing are perhaps to the point), and this mutation appears to take place in a decidedly mixed reality,[22] in another time and at another speed of movement, while potentials are actualized as forces in tension (metastability, disparation).[23] To the extent that transduction *is* ubiquitous, there is a *différance* of *différance* moving—that is, a wider historiality and structural potential in technics than grammaticization. Now, this wider potential not only delimits technological memory inventively but may also well come to affirm with another mixed reality of *phusis* that the essence of technology is nothing technological, not even a vast machinic synthesizer modalizing the continuous variations of becoming.[24] Mixed realities and embodied vitualities with ubicomp, if there are any, can perhaps in-form life with technological memory so as to open it in involutionary ways to outsides inside indi-

Figure 15.4
Being among: *Very Nervous System*, the pedestrians of Potsdam, Germany, and David Rokeby (1993). Photograph courtesy of David Rokeby.

viduation (technical individuation included), but then only to raise again the question whether this other, "older" speed of transductive dynamics and energies will ever have been tangible to any technesis—"mine," "yours," and "ours" least of all. Perhaps this speed is at most vibrating in the air when a óne is moving ever so differently among others and alongside *VNS* as partaking of an environment in a ubicomp culture (figure 15.4).

Interaction Designs—Right before You

Just as the individual interactions between me and Rokeby's *Very Nervous System* almost always leaves embedded and untouched the preindividual remainders whose actualization would permit of an involutionary individuation of either or both of us, so our relations with the environment only rarely, if ever, involve getting into contact with the potentially productive tensions lurking in habitual or programmed modes of context awareness. *VNS* operates mostly undisturbed by the states of its environment, including interactions with me, other human interactants, and other technical systems passing through (e.g., cameras, mobile phones, iPods, notepads, which are also not

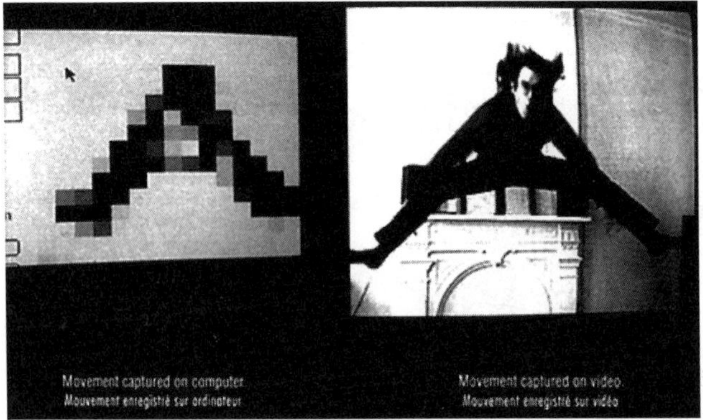

Figure 15.5
David Rokeby, *Very Nervous System*, video camera registering jump. Photograph courtesy of David Rokeby.

directly offered any obvious connectivity to or significant disturbances from *VNS*). It is thus as if even the early version of *VNS* and its very simple environmental relationality sufficed: we might be standing still—again back in 1982, at the point when Rokeby was developing his piece called *Body Language* and at that time combined an Apple II computer, circuitry components to analyze images from an ordinary video camera, a little low-resolution device with sixty-four light sensors, and a rudimentary sound system (figure 15.5).

Likewise, both I and others might well tend to walk through the museum space untouched, most evidently when we either do not enter the black cube usually framing the installation or rapidly leave it again without noticing anything. Here one would at most talk of a static genesis or a rather strict repetition of the same that reinstates the kind of context awareness proper to the interaction designs of the *VNS* system and of our body schemes.

On occasion, however, interactivity almost begins to design. Electrical shutdowns, interference from other technical installations, too much dust, excessive lighting, overheating, and certain human actions triggering software bugs and glitches provide types of environmental relationality that bend and break the edges of context awareness in *VNS*. A set of very strange and downright unrecognizable movements by other interacting inhabitants along with an equally strange and disruptive musical soundscape may momentarily afford intensities of affect that make you lose your bearings and sense of kinesthesis. You become uncertain of the spacing of this space, just as epigenetic memory seems problematized for a split second. This is not just because you are unsure and unable to recall how to behave socially in this context, but also because an imperceptible interruption from the technics of this artifactual milieu meets no recollected response in your lived or living embodiment: you do not know how to move; your sensorimotor apparatus passes through a suspension.[25] Environmental interactivity almost *designs* there and then: both *VNS* and you are almost in-formed; a structural germ materializes from relations with the associated environment to make itself registered or felt. However, even though certain types of preindividual disparation seem to present themselves at and as the edge of your context awareness and that of *VNS*, they go away and stay immanently inert, as is most often the case. This preindividual disparation meets with no actual assemblage or organization but withdraws at the edge of context awareness as nonconcretized and nonintegrated forces and energies in tension. *VNS* restarts or continues with the same kind of context awareness, with its existing interaction design. Perhaps something akin to this maintenance of existing interaction design and already-operative context awareness (social, living, technical, and environmental) was at stake for the woman who stopped my solitary and rather lengthy interactive exploration of *VNS* and myself at the opening of its exhibition at Skive Art Museum in Denmark a while back. She was drawn to the installation environment but stopped at its very limit to ask me whether I was part of the artwork and whether entrance was permitted, but then she rejected the setting and walked away—in spite of my reassuring affirmations and an invitation to join.[26]

However, even rather rapid flight and outright rejection are likely to lead to minimally concretized remainders of preindividual singularities because ontogenesis of environmental relationality is irreversibly ongoing or catastrophically entropic. In a number of cases, in-formations via relations to information-intensive environments thus also go further toward transductive individuation. Even the quite limited subset of environmental relationality at stake between *VNS* and human interactants regularly deconstitute and reconstitute with an altered context awareness, a different interaction design, another type of social and technical memory. This is almost always a matter of a very partial, finite, and low-key introjective movement at the level of technical and social memorization, as if it were quite erroneous or poisonous and in any case a matter of foreign technical and social bodies.

When human interactions introduce *VNS* to environmental relations that exceed the wired or programmed interactive possibilities for its video camera or its software, and when these relations are not simply beyond the reach of the systemic capabilities for registration, this situation does not lead to a full-scale dynamic and ontogenetic integration of difference so that *VNS* individuates differently, changing its context awareness and its interaction design. Rather, it leads to actualization of some rather peripheral and internal inscriptions of difference—rarely as hardware errors, but more often as rather short and cryptic log files or perhaps a more massive feedback pattern such as complete memory dumps.

VNS's contributions to an interactive and information-intensive environment quite frequently lead human individuals and small social groups to encounter a structural germ of another sort of relationality, but then even if this germ does entail a certain in-formation, its actualization is far from overt articulation or perceptible appropriation. Rather, when a small group of people do stay with each other to be surrounded by the environment of *VNS*, they tend to hesitate for a short while and to move only little (and then slowly), dimming interactions with a technical otherness by drawing mainly upon memories of social conventions for shared bodily presence and movement in public or other open spaces. Other kinds of social and technical interactivity most often easily succumb to individual instances of familiarity with the environment or its staging of expressive potential or succumb to instances of prior thorough kinesthetic training and bodily virtuosity (figure 15.6).

In this way the human interactants do not exhaust the interactive possibilities already in *VNS*'s interaction design—even the subset of the musical "personalities" activated become operative only in part and then as rather liminal and vague contextual markers for the human interactants. According to conventional framings, behaviors, and patterns of movement in most modern art museums, no one touches the camera, follows the wires, pushes the speakers, finds the computer, or begins to delve

Figure 15.6
Very Nervous System with female dancer and others, Rennes, France, 1988. Photograph courtesy of David Rokeby.

into the computer's hardware configuration and the coding of the software. A structural germ of social and technical in-formation is thus introjected in the interactants' body schemes, but as a mutedly foreign and disparate multiplicity, as a miniscule set of distributed tensions with little internal relationality or consistency. This germ hovers socially at the edge of an actualization of another mode of social formation, a vague sort of social context awareness just hinting at a different way of being among and with each other. Technically speaking, it insinuates, from rather deep within the affectivity of this small sociality on the move, a different way of comporting oneself as a social body, of surviving with other and more inhuman means. But this awareness remains an extraordinarily peripheral and tacit context awareness shrouded by affects already inscribed in interaction designs qua body schemes: a low-key intersubjective sense of danger, anxiety, and paranoia. It stays something that does not go on to infold with so many living bodies another social "one" or a technical "it" with which to move and thus at most becomes an irritation of the sensorimotor apparati, a minor series of autoimmune problematics or a short-term matter of interoception for each interactant.

Certain transductions in the field of environmental relationality do remain open to different individuations, but rarely, if ever, does this happen as an outright mutation. Interactivity, moving quite tangentially because intangibly embedded and too fast or too slow in its energetic waves and particles for any established human social "us" or for a factual technical system such as *VNS*, may transduce both differently and not always catastrophically or entropically. Outside–inside perceptual contact or recognizable input—in other words, interactivity in an individual–environment relation of a sensate, plural human "you" and a minimally context-aware technical fact such as *VNS*—may deconstitute both involutionarily, inventively problematizing epigenetic memories of social interaction and systemic interaction designs fed by a video camera. A differently impersonal "one" and an "it" may then be incorporated in and as the body schemes of such a "you"; a differently technical tendency may then be concretized in such a system as *VNS*—maybe more anthropomorphic in the dynamics of its interaction design, maybe not.[26]

This transduction happens at a different and new speed (because older), which is in any case less a matter of an agency than a constellation of disturbingly vibrant difference coming to presence, perhaps vitally so. Even if the transduction involves an agency, it arrives from an impersonal field of singularities—perhaps as a machinic assemblage or perhaps, with some delay and displacement, as an organization of lived and living embodiment with certain sociality and subjectivity effects. Each case would call up the actualization of an unknown type of context awareness of mixed realities. With a small jolt in the system architecture, *VNS* and its interaction design would be reprogrammed—in all likelihood by Rokeby and on the basis of earlier crashes, limitations, logs, and observations, but perhaps also by other teams of hardware and software engineers providing components, modules, and applications—thus introducing a set of "personalities" with a different technically registering context awareness. The epigenetic memory and technical existence of some human group would be turned inside out so that everybody relates differently to himself or herself in the interior milieu of culture, relates differently to the exterior milieu via a changed curtain of objects. This turning inside out might be small scale, but it would nonetheless involve concrete compartmental bodily changes beyond easy habituation: the arrival and infolding of another kind of affectively sensate context awareness of mixed realities, a set of changes in human sensorimotor apparati wrought by another technical tendency masked as affectivity. There and then the question remains open whether a new environmental relationality of a human culture and technics emerging with ubicomp also involves a new environment and another climate.

Interactivities: Right before It

Entropy and crashes, war and strife, death and malaise can all too well prohibit inventive problematization of individual memory, as can defensive fear and trembling, maintenance of social codes or conventions, and drops toward sheer inertia (just *no future*). Nevertheless, the interactions of *VNS*, you, and others afford such structural germs or relations with preindividual components as might lead to the invention of individuations qua new psychic and social organizations, along with new technical assemblages. Maybe preindividual potentials for your psychic and social individuation are left neutrally undisturbed in the interactions, not even crystallizing, or they remain in a state of inorganic life. But otherwise you are interacting haptically, via primordial tactility, with transductions that provide another affectivity for your psychic and social modalities of living, thus making you feel differently while "reorganizing" your personal and social life in ways that make a difference—to you, to those around you, and to the modalities of your living on with a more or less open ubiquitous technics. In this living on, moreover, technical tendencies are concretized in another way, and perhaps even new ones begin to become facts.

Transductive interactions, individual and social, are exposed to mnemonic, retentional control—whether this control be a matter of prescribing technically so many organizational psychological envelopes or social constructions of normativity and conventionality, more or less institutional. In each case, this retentional control may involve affective information control (as in processes of neuromarketing preforming secondary retentions) as well as polysemantic coding of sensation (as in multimodal interfacing processes preforming primary retentions). On a preindividual plane of structural germs, however, neither sensation nor affectivity will for that reason necessarily have to cease decoding semiosis or developing another nervous system, even if their impact may have to involve collective and individual trauma, pain, and mnemonic caesura. Within and during the embodied interactions engaging you and others along with *VNS*, internal relations with preindividual elements may have all interactants, human and technical, become other, folding inside out to pass to the limit of any organology (natural, artifactual, or psychosocial). Even so, this development is but a trace of a reserve of preindividual processing that is always already on the move at another speed, at work elsewhere with machinations in metastable domains, in other intense events inscribed with technical tendencies.

Barring environmental disaster or lack of operational relationality, both of which remain possible, the interactivity involving *VNS* and its interactants may well affirm the actualization of another in-formed environment. The climate and other crystalline circumstances permitting, we might be engaged in a veritable mutation of ourselves and the associated environment, both going outside–inside toward a different contextualization of the interaction designs in operation, while epigenetic memory trembles. If the relationality of individuations and environments does not just dwindle or withdraw from this mutation, an impersonal "one" and an environment come into contact with an innovative kind of context awareness. In other words, a lifeworld is meshing with a ubiquitously embedded and unfolded computational technics. As evoked by the coupling of the words *nervous* and *system* in Rokeby's title, this meshing would constitute an originary contact in "life," understood here as *différance* of genetics and technics, as the history of nervously prosthetic inscription and (tertiary) retentional systematization. This inventive contact with an other of operative types of interaction design and context awareness may well be questioning yet again the *anthropos*, at the limit of existing technically, because its inscription transduces both sides of the distinction between the human and the ahuman. Naturally, however, the forces and affects dynamically at play in this arriving technical and genetic context awareness may be reduced to intelligible embodied moods, attunements, and emotions. Moreover, they may come to generate relatively stable and appropriable formations of sensation, passing on through percepts so as to make sense. Nonetheless, somewhere, for a while, these forces and affects maintain a remainder of energetically technical environmental involution, perhaps vital and liable to be disseminated.

There might not be sufficient energy, not enough dynamic forces, or not the right kind of either. Nevertheless, the in-formational processing of the other latent in and as a preindividual interactivity—something involving the technics of *Very Nervous System*, its context awareness and environmental interaction design, our context awareness and body schemes, and a multitude of vital and inorganic movements in our affectivity and motricity, but not exactly ours—may come to relate in a different mixed reality and in an event and a movement of a new type of individuation. If this early project by David Rokeby does not continue on with deadly inert stasis or entropy or with strictly technical becoming or with precoded or probabilistically stabilized information, it stages a theater of production—with us. It may have come-into-presence new individuations as it propagates electric, electronic, sensorimotoric, and affective relations of interactivity of relevance for current mixed realities with ubicomp. Its mixed-reality interactivity does not cease to partake—via the forces and movements in electricity, silicon, and carbon—of the physical time of the degradation of matter, becoming more or less expansive. It does so as technical events and movements—as the inauguration of an other, technical timing—qua the differences and deferrals of so many inscriptions in the nonliving—through which any human would have to be delimited vis-à-vis *phusis*. It also may care for the coming of another being in touch, however: an emergence of another difference from nonlife, an alternate deferral of entropy that is of the living, including human modes of living nervously through and with technical time. In that case, this emergence not only pertains to the processual propagation of an unprecedented transduction but also concerns the trace—as if almost nothing and always already elsewhere in another event—of the other speed of ontogenesis qua the quite intangible and unceasingly mobile processing of transduction on and as the edge of technical memorization.

Notes

1. In the title of my chapter, I am alluding to the relationality of transduction as thought by Gilbert Simondon. Several avid readers of Simondon tend to agree on working with this notion in a shorthand version, defining it as a primary relationality constitutive of the two terms that it relates (Hansen 2006, ix; Hayles 2002, 298; Stiegler 1994, §5). I agree with Muriel Combes, who calls transduction the "mode of unity of being through its diverse phases, its multiple individuations" (1999, 15). I also find helpful Adrian Mackenzie's explanatory comment respecting this notion: "For the process of transduction to occur, there must be some disparity, discontinuity or mismatch within a domain; two different forms or potentials whose disparity can be modulated. Transduction is a process whereby a disparity or a difference is topologically and temporally restructured across some interface. It mediates different organizations of energy" (2002, 25). A more detailed treatment of transduction as individuation in process by Simondon himself also exists (Simondon 1964, 18–22; 1992, 315). *In-formation* is thought here as processually or operationally productive, as an ongoing "in-forming" or as dynamic "involution" in a Simondonian sense. Thus, information is not given, formed, or structured but rather, prior to this, *is* transductively between two heterogeneous series of signs and signals (Simondon 1989, 126–127).

2. *Individuation* refers throughout to this notion as it appears in the thought of Simondon (1964, 1989, 2001).

3. The treatment of ubicomp culture in this text assumes as a familiar heritage the more influential texts by Mark Weiser and his colleagues (Weiser 1991, 1993, 1994, 1997a, 1997b, 1999a, 1999b, 2001l; Weiser and Brown 1995, 1996; Weiser, Gold, and Brown 1999). The past decade and a half has not been at a standstill, so several interesting reconsiderations of Weiser's vision

and the status of contemporary technocultural developments are now available (e.g., Bell and Dourish 2007; Hargraves 2007).

4. The reference here is broadly discursive to the research field but also more specific to part of the early work by I. E. Sutherland (1965), William Gibson (1984), and Jaron Lanier (Lanier and Biocca 1992), respectively.

5. Three indications should begin to give an idea of the reach of this call in this field of research. Hayles's work toward a more seamless integration of humans and machines is one important case in point—that is, her notion of constructing a "posthuman" subjectivity that remains finite and embodied and that lives with technics in a material world of great complexity (1999, 5; 2002; 2005a; 2005b). Mark Hansen's latest work displays a certain convergence with this notion, rethinking Maurice Merleau-Ponty's existential phenomenology of the body along with insights from contemporary cognitive science and interactions with new media art in order to delineate and affirm the expanded scope accorded to a holistically embodied human agency that can exist only in conjunction with technics (2006, 2–3, 20). Bernard Stiegler's quite extensive work on technics and time, from *The Fault of Epimetheus* (1998; see also Stiegler 1996, 2001) onward, can perhaps be read only as part of a continued effort to develop "a general organology" with a view to a human history that consists in a series of potentials, tensions, displacements, and inventions among three large organizational formations: the body with its physiological organization; artificial organs (technics, objects, tools, instruments, works of art); and social organizations.

6. I obviously have in mind the legacy of Gilles Deleuze and not least of Deleuze and Félix Guattari. While we wait for a more sustained and convincing study of Deleuze, Guattari, and the open machines, it will have to suffice to point to the tangential kinds of work done on the topic (De Landa 2002, 2006; Galloway 2004; Galloway and Thacker 2007; Massumi 2002).

7. I am alluding here to Weiser and Brown's call for ubicomp as both calm and embedded (Weiser and Brown 1995, 1996).

8. My emphasis on the different kinds of ontogenetic relationality involved in interactivity should indicate that I point here toward traits at the outer inventive edge of life and technics, which also means outside of most current attempts at definitions. Hence, I affirm but also delimit the hegemony and usefulness of definitions that approach interactivity as feedback loops involving messages, as in mathematical communications theory (Shannon and Weaver 1949) and as a general notion of all modern forms of media-based communication and interaction, responsive as well as participatory, which complete themselves between man and machine as well as between individuals (Daniels 2002)— technological reflections back to us of our actions or decisions, as in models of navigable structures, medial inventions, transforming mirrors, and automata (Rokeby 1995). As far as this one notion goes, I tend in this text to think more along the lines of Alberto Toscano's (2007) approach to interactivity as transduction qua a physical, biological, mental, and social operation whereby an activity propagates itself within a domain and qua the introduction of a structural germ catalyzing the actualization and reciprocal interaction of some virtualities hitherto remaining at the preindividual level. Or I think along the lines of Brian Massumi's (1995) early approach to interactivity as an active space and time involving reciprocal

variations not reaching equilibrium—that is, as something involving forces of interaction among dynamic elements that have the space and time to become other through an involutionary movement.

9. Witness the very interesting and still unresolved general discussion in this field respecting atmospheres, ambience, ambient media, and ambient technology (Cai and Abascal 2006; Dourish, Brewer, and Bell 2005; Hawk, Rieder, and Oviedo 2008). See also the contributions in this volume by Michael Bull, Torben Sangild, Ulrik Schmidt, and Gernot Böhme (chapters 6, 7, 8, and 27).

10. See also Hansen's contribution in this volume (chapter 1) for an account of types of microsensation at stake in this context.

11. Here I do not have in mind the notion of inorganic life still discussed polemically among physicists, astronomers, and others. I am referring instead broadly to Deleuze's deployment of the concept to designate a vitalist materialism, also described by Alan Badiou as an ontology in his treatment of the kinship between Deleuze's thought and the Stoics' (2000, 12).

12. How can you know when you have arrived at the truth when you do not already know what the truth is? You can search neither for what you do know because you already know it nor for what you do not know because you do not know what you are looking for. Is truth, then, never acquired, but only recollected? Is this "recollection" from the past lives of the immortal soul? Compare Plato's *Meno* (1997, 880, 80d–81d).

13. For more information on *Body Language*, see http://homepage.mac.com/davidrokeby/body.html, accessed 15 May 2009; and for more information on *Very Nervous System*, see http://homepage.mac.com/davidrokeby/vns.html, accessed 15 April 2011.

14. I agree with Erkki Huhtamo (2000) that one key reason why this early project by Rokeby demands a second engagement, after the hypostatization of the "interactive" character of new media art in the 1990s, is that it introduces a far more complex notion of interactivity than do most other projects. What is at stake is something "metainteractive" precisely because both *VNS* and interactants remain open: there are no simple one-to-one relationships at stake or any easy feedback loops methodologically approachable via earlier cybernetic theory. For an interesting treatment of the notion of "inexact control," see Roberto Simanowski's interview of David Rokeby (Simanowski 2003).

15. I am evoking touch not just as one sense among others, but as that protosensate tactility or haptic envelope of the skin that Didier Anzieu (1989, 1990) had in mind when articulating his existential notions of the "skin ego" and the psychological envelope.

16. I evoke throughout this text notions of genetic, epigenetic, and epiphylogenetic memory, with reference to Simondon and the way in which these notions appear in Stiegler's work (see Stiegler 1994, §24; 1998, 134–141). It should be relatively apparent that a considerable part of the drive behind my text concerns a certain disagreement with respect to the altogether general reach of the problematic of memory for Stiegler. That is, the tentative emphasis I place here on the energy and dynamics of transduction and inventions other than our individual life form and the technical tendencies with which we currently exist environmentally opens onto

a new and immemorial manifold of contacts that, if it does not meet death and technological entropy, is of another speed of forces and materials to be assembled. This new because much older invention might concern something closer to us and "our" technics than Deleuze's plane of pure immanence and his privileging of molecular Darwinism (macrocosmic processes in microbiology as the path toward a superhuman ethics). However, this closeness or approximation does not imply a withdrawal to an egological existential phenomenology (of the body), a holistic and organic neohumanism, and an assumption of an agency pre-residing over the numerous distributed bodily systems and processes in a given individual. Perhaps mixed realities of the inhuman have yet to be invented and concretized as a dynamics of openly inorganic life and machinics that transduces virtuality differently between molecular becoming and self-organization.

17. Compare Simondon's thought of the transindividual as an epigenetics traversing the inter-individual and the preindividual: "Life is a specification, a principal solution, complete in itself, but leaves behind a residue apart from its system. It is not as a living being that man brings with him what is spiritually individuated, but as a being that contains in it the preindividual and the prevital. This reality can be called the transindividual. It is neither of a social nor an individual origin; it is deposited in the individual, carried by it, but it belongs to it and is not made a part of its system of being as individual. One should not speak of tendencies of the individual that carries [*sic*] it towards the group; because these tendencies are not properly speaking tendencies of the individual as an individual; they are the non-resolution of potentials that have preceded the genesis of the individual. The individual has not individuated the preceding being without remainder; it has not been totally resolved in the individual and the milieu; the individual has conserved the preindividual within itself, and all individual ensembles have thus a sort of non-structured ground from which a new individuation can be produced. The psychosocial is the transindividual: it is this reality that the individuated being transports with itself, this load of being for future individuations" (1989, 192–193).

18. I am distinguishing between an "affect" turning into a sensate emotion interior to an individualized being, thus affording perception and grounds for action, and "affectivity," which remains heterogeneous to individualized reality as a relation between an individualized being and the preindividual milieu. To that extent, I agree with Simondon that affectivity indicates an ideality greater or vaster than the individualized being, not just the function of interior structures (Simondon 1989, 107–108).

19. For further treatments of locative art and context awareness, see Christiane Paul and Malcolm McCullough's chapters in this volume (chapters 23 and 26) and parts of Dourish's work (2001a).

20. The allusion here respecting prosthetics, exteriorization, and hominization is to Andre Leroi-Gourhan (1943a) as read by Jacques Derrida (1976) and to Derrida as read by Stiegler (1998, 137).

21. As regards the question of sensor networks, more or less nervous and ad hoc organizational, consider Falko Dressler's (2008) relatively recent work. For an in-depth treatment of the current problematics of radio-frequency identification in the environment, see Hayles's contribution in this volume (chapter 31).

22. In brief, I have in mind an in-forming assemblage of embodied virtuality that goes beyond the information-theoretical notion of augmented reality found in the (now classic) work of Ronald Azuma (1997). That is, it extends beyond and remains more intensive in its implications for interactants than a system that (1) combines the real and the virtual, (2) is interactive in real time, and (3) is registered in three dimensions.

23. Compare Simondon's illustrative definition at the level of perception: "There is disparation when two twin sets that cannot be entirely superimposed, such as the left retinal image and the right retinal image, are grasped together as a system, allowing for the formation of a single set of a higher degree which integrates their elements thanks to a new dimension" (1964, 228). However, disparation and metastability concern the more general relation of individuation and preindividuality, and here Deleuze's early appreciation may offer a more suggestive approach: "Gilbert Simondon has shown recently that individuation presupposes a prior metastable state—in other words, the existence of a 'disparateness' such as at least two orders of magnitude or two scales of heterogeneous reality between which potentials are distributed. Such a pre-individual state nevertheless does not lack singularities: the distinctive or singular points are defined by the existence and distribution of potentials. An 'objective' problematic field thus appears, determined by the distance between two heterogeneous orders. Individuation emerges like the act of solving such a problem, or—what amounts to the same thing—like the actualisation of a potential and establishing of communication between disparates" (1993, 246). I agree with Toscano with regard to approaching preindividual being as affected by disparation qua the tension between incompatible and still unrelated dimensions of potentials in being (2005, 139). As a process, disparation integrates disparity or difference into a combined, coordinated system.

24. The latter reference regarding the machinic synthesizer is to Deleuze and Guattari (1987, 343). Otherwise, I am here signaling my agreement with Stiegler that technics and time solicit a thought widening out from the early Derrida's *différance*, just as I affirm Stiegler's critical take on Simondon's thought of technical individuation (i.e., the remainder of modern humanism and anthropocentrism that has Simondon refrain from acknowledging that hominization was always technical). See also my treatment of the early work by Stiegler, including its Simondonian reserve (Ekman 2007). However, here, I am also signaling my disagreement with Stiegler's reinscription of the same type of problem with which he reproaches Derrida, now at one remove—that is, on the other side of the life/technics difference. Instead of calling for a resolutely thorough technicization that stretches to the limit of the inorganic (life) without addressing the relation of technical time and the time of becoming (or the [de]gradation of movement and matter), I would assert the need to recall that other time and its older speed, along with Martin Heidegger's insistence—and, later, Derrida's—that the essence of technology is nothing technological.

25. *VNS* as an "interactive environment" shares with mixed reality the important trait of enabling a transformation of the focus of interaction and interaction design. Interaction and interaction design no longer concern primarily a precise location, but the whole environment. Interaction is no longer primarily a face-to-screen exchange but dissolves itself in the surrounding space and objects so that we are decidedly dealing with a post–graphical user interface, postwidget, postmouse phenomenon—that is, smart environments, ambient and tangible computing, and a more peripheral human awareness. Engaging with an information system is no longer

primarily a conscious and intentional act but involves a more vague and haptic sense of the environment as a space of moving interactivity: interactive media art for a ubicomp context tends toward a reinvention of a haptic culture, one in which primordial tactility and touch are granted another kind of privilege than in the strictly hegemonic visual culture to which we allegedly still adhere.

26. It might have made a difference, I thought later, if *VNS* had been less embedded, less of a manifold of musical virtuosity, less intricately randomized. In this situation with the woman at the exhibit, it might have made a difference if more people had been assuredly present or if I had either not affirmed quite as readily that I was part of the artwork or if I had had the chance to articulate at least some of the various things at stake in that statement. At any rate, I am relatively sure that *VNS*, not being a matter of artificial life, strictly speaking, no longer registers me as part of its operations, if it is still working somewhere, but I am quite sure that *VNS* and its milieu are still on their designing way through me, inside out, still changing "my" context awareness and environmental relationality.

27. See the contributions in this volume by Tom Cohen, John Johnston, and Timothy Lenoir (chapters 32, 33, 34) for further and more elaborate questioning of tendential anthropocentrism in existing research and technics.

References

Agamben, Giorgio. 1998. *Homo Sacer: Sovereign Power and Bare Life*. Translated by Daniel Heller-Roazen. Stanford, CA: Stanford University Press.

Agamben, Giorgio. 1999. *Potentialities: Collected Essays in Philosophy*. Edited, translated, and with an introduction by Daniel Heller-Roazen. Stanford, CA: Stanford University Press.

Ahson, Syed, and Mohammad Ilyas. 2011. *Cloud Computing and Software Services: Theory and Techniques*. Boca Raton, FL: CRC Press.

Anzieu, Didier. 1990. *Psychic Envelopes*. Translated by Daphne Briggs. London: Karnac Books.

Anzieu, Didier. 1989. *The Skin Ego*. Translated by Chris Turner. New Haven, CT: Yale University Press.

Azuma, Ronald T. 1997. "A Survey of Augmented Reality." *Presence: Teleoperators and Virtual Environments* 6 (4): 355–385.

Badiou, Alain. 2000. *Deleuze: The Clamor of Being*. Translated by Louise Burchill. Minneapolis: University of Minnesota Press.

Bateson, Gregory. 1972. *Steps to an Ecology of Mind*. San Francisco: Chandler.

Bell, Genevieve, and Paul Dourish. 2007. "Yesterday's Tomorrows: Notes on Ubiquitous Computing's Dominant Vision." *Personal and Ubiquitous Computing* 11 (2): 133–143.

Blast, Theory. 2011. "Blast Theory." Available at http://www.blasttheory.co.uk/bt/index.php. Accessed 5 April 2011.

Bogard, William. 2007. "The Coils of a Serpent, Haptic Space, and Control Societies." *C-Theory 1000 Days of Theory*, td057. Available at http://www.ctheory.net/articles.aspx?id=581. Accessed 1 June 2009.

Bullivant, Lucy. 2006. *Responsive Environments: Architecture, Art, and Design*. New York: V & A.

Buyya, Rajkumar, James Broberg, and Andrzej M. Goscinski, eds. 2011. *Cloud Computing: Principles and Paradigms*. Hoboken, NJ: Wiley.

Cai, Yang, and Julio Abascal. 2006. *Ambient Intelligence in Everyday Life*. Lecture Notes in Computer Science, no. 3864. Berlin: Springer.

Combes, Muriel. 1999. *Simondon individu et collectivité: Pour une philosophie du transindividuel*. Paris: Presses Universitaires de France.

Daniels, Dieter. 2002. "Strategien der Interaktivität." Available at http://www.hgb-leipzig.de/daniels/vom-readymade-zum-cyberspace/strategien_der_interaktivitaet.html. Accessed 1 July 2009.

De Landa, Manuel. 2006. *A New Philosophy of Society: Assemblage Theory and Social Complexity*. London: Continuum.

De Landa, Manuel. 2002. *Intensive Science and Virtual Philosophy*. London: Continuum, 2002.

Deleuze, Gilles. 1995. "Postscript on Control Societies." In *Negotiations, 1972–1990*, translated by Martin Joughin, 177–182. New York: Columbia University Press.

Deleuze, Gilles. 1993. *Difference and Repetition*. Translated by Paul Patton. New York: Columbia University Press.

Deleuze, Gilles, and Félix Guattari. 1987. "1837: Of the Refrain." In *A Thousand Plateaus: Capitalism and Schizophrenia*, translated by Brian Massumi, 310–350. Minneapolis: University of Minnesota Press.

Derrida, Jacques. 1976. *Of Grammatology*. Translated by Gayatri Chakravorti Spivak. Baltimore: Johns Hopkins University Press.

Dourish, Paul. 2001a. "Seeking a Foundation for Context-Aware Computing." *Human–Computer Interaction* 16 (2–4): 229–241.

Dourish, Paul. 2001b. *Where the Action Is: The Foundations of Embodied Interaction*. Cambridge, MA: MIT Press.

Dourish, Paul, Johanna Brewer, and Genevieve Bell. 2005. "Special Section: Ambient Intelligence–Information as a Cultural Category." *Interactions—New York* 12 (4): 31–33.

Dressler, Falko. 2008. *Self-Organization in Sensor and Actor Networks*. Hoboken, NJ: Wiley.

Ekman, Ulrik. 2007. "Of Transductive Speed—Stiegler." *Parallax* 13 (4): 46–63.

Galloway, Alexander R. 2004. *Protocol: How Control Exists after Decentralization*. Cambridge, MA: MIT Press.

Galloway, Alexander R., and Eugene Thacker. 2007. *The Exploit: A Theory of Networks.* Minneapolis: University of Minnesota Press.

Garelli, Jacques. 1991. *Rythmes et mondes : au revers de l'identité et de l'altérité.* Grenoble: Ed. Jérôme Millon.

Gibson, William. 1984. *Neuromancer.* New York: Ace Books.

Hansen, Mark B. N. 2006. *Bodies in Code: Interfaces with Digital Media.* New York: Routledge.

Hargraves, Ian. 2007. "Ubicomp: Fifteen Years On." *Knowledge, Technology & Policy* 20 (1): 3–10.

Hawk, Byron, David M. Rieder, and Ollie Oviedo, eds. 2008. *Small Tech: The Culture of Digital Tools.* Electronic Mediations. Minneapolis: University of Minnesota Press.

Hayles, N. Katherine. 2005a. "Computing the Human." *Theory Culture Society* 22 (1): 131–151.

Hayles, N. Katherine. 2005b. *My Mother Was a Computer: Digital Subjects and Literary Texts.* Chicago: University of Chicago Press

Hayles, N. Katherine. 2002. "Flesh and Metal: Reconfiguring the Mindbody in Virtual Environments." *Configurations* 10:297–320.

Hayles, N. Katherine. 1999. *How We Became Posthuman.* Chicago: University of Chicago Press.

Huhtamo, Erkki. 2000. "Silicon Remembers Ideology." Available at http://homepage.mac.com/davidrokeby/erkki.html. Accessed 15 August 2009.

Ishii, Hiroshi. 1997. "Tangible Bits: Towards Seamless Interfaces between People, Bits, and Atoms." Available at http://tmg-orchard.media.mit.edu:8020/SuperContainer/RawData/Papers/331-Tangible%20Bits%20Towards%20Seamless/Published/PDF. Accessed 15 September 2009.

Lanier, Jaron, and Frank Biocca. 1992. "An Insider's View of the Future of Virtual Reality." *Journal of Communication* 42 (4): 150–172.

Leroi-Gourhan, André. 1945. *Évolution et techniques: Milieu et techniques.* Paris: Albin Michel.

Leroi-Gourhan, André. 1943a. *Évolution et techniques.* Paris: A. Michel.

Leroi-Gourhan, André. 1943b. *Évolution et techniques: L'homme et la matière.* Paris: Albin Michel.

MacKay, Donald M. 1980. *Brains, Machines, and Persons.* Grand Rapids, Mich.: William B. Eerdmans.

MacKay, Donald M. 1969. *Information, Mechanism, and Meaning.* Cambridge, MA: MIT Press.

Mackenzie, Adrian. 2002. *Transductions: Bodies and Machines at Speed.* London: Continuum.

Massumi, Brian. 2002. *Parables for the Virtual: Movement, Affect, Sensation.* Durham, NC: Duke University Press.

Massumi, Brian. 1995. "Interface and Active Space." Available at http://www.anu.edu.au/HRC/first_and_last/works/interface.htm. Accessed 15 May 2009.

Milgram, Paul, and Fumio Kishino. 1994. "Taxonomy of Mixed Reality Visual Displays." *IEICE Transactions on Information and Systems* E77-D.12: 1321–1329.

Nancy, Jean-Luc. 1997. *The Sense of the World.* Translated and with a foreword by Jeffrey S. Librett. Minneapolis: University of Minnesota Press.

Plato. 1997. *Complete Works.* Edited by John M. Cooper and D. S. Hutchinson. Indianapolis, IN: Hackett.

Rokeby, David. 2011. "David Rokeby." Available at http://homepage.mac.com/davidrokeby/home.html. Accessed 1 April 2011.

Rokeby, David. 1996. "Lecture for 'Info Art,' Kwangju Biennale." Available at http://homepage.mac.com/davidrokeby/install.html. Accessed 15 May 2009.

Rokeby, David. 1995. "Transforming Mirrors: Subjectivity and Control in Interactive Media." In *Critical Issues in Electronic Media,* edited by Simon Penny, 133–158. Albany: State University of New York Press.

Ruyer, Raymond. 1958. *La genèse des formes vivantes.* Paris: Flammarion.

Ruyer, Raymond. 1954. *La cybernétique et l'origine de l'information.* Paris: Flammarion.

Shannon, Claude Elwood. 1993. *Claude Elwood Shannon: Collected Papers.* Edited by N. J. A. Sloane and Aaron D. Wyner. New York: IEEE Press.

Shannon, Claude Elwood, and Warren Weaver. 1949. *The Mathematical Theory of Communication.* Urbana: University of Illinois Press.

Simanowski, Roberto. 2003. "Interview with David Rokeby: *Very Nervous System* and the Benefit of Inexact Control." *dichtung digital* 1. Available at http://www.brown.edu/Research/dichtung-digital/2003/issue/1/rokeby/index.htm. Accessed 24 September 2008.

Simondon, Gilbert. 2001. *Du mode d'existence des objets techniques.* Paris: Aubier.

Simondon, Gilbert. 1992. "The Genesis of the Individual." In *Incorporations,* edited by Jonathan Crary and Sanford Kwinter, 296–319. New York: Zone.

Simondon, Gilbert. 1989. *L'individuation psychique et collective.* Paris: Aubier.

Simondon, Gilbert. 1964. *L'individu et sa genèse physico-biologique.* Paris: Presses universitaires de France.

Stiegler, Bernard. 1998. *Technics and Time.* Vol. 1: *The Fault of Epimetheus.* Translated by Richard Beardsworth and George Collins. Stanford, CA: Stanford University Press.

Stiegler, Bernard. *Technics and Time. Disorientation.* Vol 2. Translated by Stephen Barker. Stanford, CA: Stanford University Press, 2009.

Stiegler, Bernard. *Technics and Time: Cinematic Time and the Question of Malaise.* Vol. 3. Translated by Stephen Barker. Stanford, CA: Stanford University Press, 2011.

Stiegler, Bernard. 1994. "Temps et individuation technique, psychique, et collective dans l'oeuvre de Simondon." *Multitudes* 20 (6). Available at http://multitudes.samizdat.net/Temps-et-individuation-technique. Accessed 27 August 2009.

Sutherland, I. E. 1965. "The Ultimate Display." In *Proceedings of Ifip 65*, vol. 2, edited by Wayne Alexander Kalenich, 506–508. Washington, DC: Spartan Books.

Toscano, Alberto. 2007. "Technical Culture and the Limits of Interaction." In *Interact or Die!* edited by Joke Brouwer and Arjen Mulder, 198–205. Rotterdam: NAi.

Toscano, Alberto. 2005. *The Theatre of Production: Philosophy and Individuation between Kant and Deleuze*. New York: Palgrave Macmillan.

Von Foerster, Heinz. 1984. *Observing Systems*. 2nd ed. Systems Inquiry Series. Seaside, CA: Intersystems.

Weaver, Warren. 1949. "The Mathematics of Communication." *Scientific American* 181 (1): 11–15.

Weiser, Mark. 2001. "Whatever Happened to the Next-Generation Internet?" *Communications of the ACM* 44 (9): 61–70.

Weiser, Mark. 1999a. "How Computers Will Be Used Differently in the Next Twenty Years." 1999 IEEE Symposium on Security and Privacy, 9–12 May, 1999, Oakland, California. IEEE Computer Society, online publication, 234–235.

Weiser, Mark. 1999b. "The Spirit of the Engineering Quest." *Technology in Society* 21 (4): 355–361.

Weiser, Mark. 1997a. "It's Everywhere. It's Invisible. It's Ubicomp." *Training & Development* 51 (5): 34–35.

Weiser, Mark. 1997b. "Software Engineering That Matters to People." In *Proceedings of the 1997 International Conference on Software Engineering*, 538. New York City: ACM Press.

Weiser, Mark. 1994. "The World Is Not a Desktop." *interactions* 1 (1): 7–8.

Weiser, Mark. 1993. "Some Computer Science Issues in Computing." *Communications of the ACM* 36 (7): 75–84.

Weiser, Mark. 1991. "The Computer for the 21st Century." *Scientific American* 265 (3): 94–104.

Weiser, Mark, and John Seely Brown. 1996. "The Coming Age of Calm Technology." Available at http://nano.xerox.com/hypertext/weiser/acmfuture2endnote.htm. Accessed 15 August 2009.

Weiser, Mark, and John Seely Brown. 1995. "Designing Calm Technology." Available at http://sandbox.xerox.com/hypertext/weiser/calmtech/calmtech.htm. Accessed 14 August 2009.

Weiser, Mark, Rich Gold, and John Seely Brown. 1999. "The Origins of Ubiquitous Computing Research at PARC in the Late 1980s." *IBM Systems Journal* 38 (4): 693–696.

16 Interaction as a Designed Experience

Lev Manovich

How do designers of information technology understand the interaction between the users and devices today? How do they design user interfaces? In this chapter, I analyze the shift in information-technology design that took place between 1998 and 2007. Contrary to ten years ago, today the designers no longer try to make the interfaces invisible. Instead, the *interaction is treated as an event*—as opposed to a "nonevent" per the previous "invisible interface" paradigm. Put differently, using personal information devices is now conceived as a carefully orchestrated *experience* rather than only a means to an end. I discuss different aspects of this new interface paradigm using the examples of Apple OS X, the LG Chocolate, and the iPhone.

If you recall the very first mobile phone you owned—let's say at the end of the 1990s or maybe even the first years of the 2000s—and compare it to the phone you have (or wish to have) today, the difference in design is striking.

The change in the design of mobile phones is just one example of a larger trend that I call "aestheticization of information tools." The trend began around 1996–1998 (1996: *Wallpaper* magazine [see *Wallpaper.com* n.d.] was launched and Collete [see Collette n.d.], the first store for hip design products, opened in Paris; 1997: the opening of Guggenheim Museum Bilbao; 1998: the introduction of the first iMac). It can certainly be connected with the democratization of design, the rise of branding, the competition in global economy, and other larger socioeconomic shifts. However, there are also particular reasons for it—nonreducible to these other forces.

Until the mid-1990s, only people working in particular jobs spent all their time interacting with information. In addition, these interactions were limited to work spaces and times; they were not spilling into leisure and other nonwork activities. The rise of the information society has greatly increased the proportion of people whose work involves information processing. At the same time, during the 1990s interacting with information via computers and computer-based devices gradually entered people's lives outside of work. The computer and other devices built on top of it, such as the mobile phone, came to be used for all kinds of nonwork activities because of its inherent multifunctionality and expandability: entertainment, culture, social life, communication with others. As a consequence, work and nonwork, professional and personal met within the same information-processing machines—the same physical objects, same hardware and software interfaces, and in some cases even the same software.

As these machines came to be redefined as consumer objects to be used in all areas of people's lives, their aesthetics were altered accordingly. The associations with work and office culture and the emphasis on efficiency and functionality came to be replaced by new references and criteria. The latter include being friendly, playful, pleasurable, expressive, and fashionable; signifying cultural identity; being aesthetically pleasing; and being designed for emotional satisfaction. The modernist design formula "form follows function" accordingly came to be replaced by new formulas such as "form follows emotion"—adopted by major companies, as in the world famous Frog design ("Getting Emotional" n.d.), which happened to introduce the first Macintosh computers.

Aestheticization of Interfaces

Something else has happened in this process. Until the first decade of the twenty-first century, the design of user interfaces was often ruled by the idea that the interface should be invisible. In fact, the really successful interface was supposed to be the one that the user does not notice. This paradigm made sense until the mid-1990s—that is, during the period when people used information devices on a limited basis outside of work. But what happens when the quantity of these interactions greatly increases and information devices become people's intimate companions? The more you use a mobile phone, a computer, a media player, or another personal information device, the more you "interact with an interface" itself.

Regardless whether designers realize this connection consciously or not, the design of user interaction today reflects this new reality. The designers no longer try to hide the interfaces. They treat the interaction *as an event* rather than as an invisible "non-event." As noted earlier, the use of personal information devices is now conceived as a carefully orchestrated *experience* rather than only a means to an end. The interaction explicitly calls attention to itself. The interface engages the user in a kind of game. The user is asked to devote significant emotional, perceptual, and cognitive resources to the very act of operating the device.

OS X

Today a typical information device such as a mobile phone has two kinds of interfaces. One is a physical interface such as buttons and the phone cover. The second is a media interface: graphical icons, menus, and sounds. The new paradigm that treats interaction as an aesthetic and meaningful experience applies equally to both types of interfaces.

The most dramatic example of the historical shift in how interfaces are understood is the difference in user interface design between the successive generations of the operating system (OS) used in Apple computers—OS 9 and OS X. Released in October 1999, OS 9 was the last version of Mac OS still based on the original system that came with the first Macintosh in 1984. The look and feel of the interface for the OS 9—the strict geometry of horizontal and vertical lines, the similarly restrictive palette of grays and white, simple and businesslike icons—speaks of modernist design and "form follows function" ideology. It fits with gray suites, office buildings in international style, and the whole twentieth-century office culture.

The next version of the OS introduced in 2001, OS X, was a radical departure. Its new user interface was called "Aqua." Aqua's icons, buttons, windows, cursor, and other interface elements were colorful and three dimensional. They used shadows and transparency. The programs animated when started. The icons in Dock playfully increased in size as the user moved a cursor over them. And if in OS 9 the default desktop backgrounds were flat, single-color monochrome, the backgrounds that came with Aqua were much more visually complex, more colorful, and more assertive—drawing attention to themselves rather than trying to be invisible.

In OS X, the interaction with the universal information-processing machine of our time—a personal computer—was redefined as an explicitly aesthetic experience. This aesthetic experience became as important as the computer's functionality (in technical terms, "usability"). The word *aesthetics* is commonly associated with beauty, but this meaning is not the only one relevant here. Under OS X, the user interface was aestheticized in the sense that it was now explicitly to stimulate and appeal to the senses rather than to engage the users' cognitive processes only.

The transformation of Apple from a company that was making hardware and software to a world leader in consumer product design—think of all the design awards won by the iMac, the Powerbook, the iPod, and other Apple products—is itself the clearest example of what I have called the "aestheticization of information tools." Here it is relevant to recall another classical meaning of the term *aesthetics*: the coordination of all parts and details of an artwork or a design—lines, forms, colors, textures, materials, movements, sounds. (I talk about classical aesthetics because twentieth-century art often aimed at opposite effects—shock, collision, and establishment of meaning and aesthetic experience through montage rather than through unification of parts). The critical and commercial success of Apple products and the truly fanatical feelings they evoke in many people have to a large extent to do with the degree of this integration, which until now has not been seen in commercial products in this price range. In each new product or version, the details are refined until they all work together to create a rich, smooth, and consistent sensorial whole. This refinement also applies to the way the hardware and software work together. For example, think of the coordination between the circular movement of the user's finger on the track wheel of the original iPod and the corresponding horizontal movement of menus on the screen (which borrows from the OS X column view).

In the beginning of the 2000s, other personal-technology companies had gradually begun to follow Apple in putting more and more emphasis on the design of their products across all price categories. Sony started using the "Sony Style" phrase. In 2004, Nokia introduced its first line of "fashion phones" ("Nokia" n.d.), declaring that personal technology can be "an object of desire" (two years later this correlation became true for the whole mobile phone market). By investing in the industrial designs of their consumer products, Samsung was able to move from being an unknown supplier to becoming a top world brand. Even the companies whose information products were almost exclusively used by professionals and business users started to compete in the design of their products. For instance, the new 2006 version of the BlackBerry smartphone, popular with businesspeople and professionals, was introduced with the slogan "BlackBerry Pearl—Small, Smart, and Stylish."

Interaction as Theater; Interaction as Experience

In retrospect, we can see that the aestheticization (or, perhaps, the theatricalization) of the user interfaces of laptops, mobile phones, cameras, and other mobile technology that took place approximately between 2001 and 2005 was prepared conceptually in previous decades. Based on the work done in the 1980s, computer designer and theorist Brenda Laurel published her groundbreaking book *Computers as Theater* in 1991. She called the interface "an expressive form" and compared it with a theatrical performance. Using Aristotle's *Poetics* as her model, she suggested that interaction should lead to "pleasurable enjoyment" (93–95).

The notion of interaction as theater brings an additional meaning to the idea that a mobile phone engages its user in a kind of game or play, noted at the beginning of the chapter. In suggesting this relationship, I am thinking of how the buttons on the LG Chocolate suddenly appear, glowing in red, when you switch the phone on; or how when you select an option on the same phone, it confirms your selection by replacing the current screen with a whole new graphic screen; or how pressing the cover of a Motorola Pebble opens the phone in an unexpected and unique way. In other words, I am referring to a variety of ways in which the current generation of mobiles responds to user actions in a surprising and often seemingly exaggerated manner. (This mode of response applies to both physical interfaces and media interfaces). The notion of interaction as theater makes us notice another dimension of this playlike behavior. As I describe in more detail later, using the example of switching on the LG Chocolate mobile, the various sensorial responses that a mobile generates in response to our actions are often not single events but rather constitute entire sequences of effects. As in a traditional theatrical play, these sequences unfold in time; various sensorial effects play on each other, and it is their contrast as well as the differences between the senses being addressed—touch, vision, hearing—which together add up to a complex dramatic experience.

In 1991, when Laurel published her book, the use of technology products was still limited to particular professions, but at the end of the decade these products were becoming mainstream items of the consumer economy, as the iMac designers clearly recognized. And this economy as a whole was undergoing a fundamental change. In their 1999 book *Experience Economy: Work Is Theater & Every Business a Stage*, Joseph Pine and James H. Gilmore argue that the consumer economy was entering a new stage where the key to successful business was delivering experiences. According to the authors, this new stage followed previous stages centered on goods themselves and, later, on services. The authors state that to be successful today, a company "must learn to stage a rich, compelling experience" (30). If Laurel evokes theater as a way to think about the particular case of human–computer interaction, the authors of *Experience Economy* suggest that theater can be a metaphor for understanding the interaction between consumers and products in the new economy in general.

The aestheticization (the term I prefer) of the hardware design and the user interfaces of information products that took place throughout the computer industry in the first decade of the new millennium fits very well with the idea of an "experience economy." Like any other interaction, *interaction with information devices became a designed experience.* In fact, we can say that the three stages in the development of the computer's user interfaces—the command-line interface, the classical graphical user interface of the 1970s through the 1990s, and the new sensual and entertaining interface of the post–OS X era—can be correlated with the three stages of the consumer economy as a whole: goods, services, and experiences. Command-line interfaces "deliver the goods" —that is, they focus on pure functionality and utility. The graphical user interface adds "service" to interfaces. And at the next stage, interfaces become "experiences."

Experience Design in the LG Chocolate

The idea of the experience economy works particularly well to explain how the physical interaction with technology objects—as opposed to their physical forms and screen interfaces only—was turned into the stage for delivering rich sensorial and often seductive experiences. For instance, early mobile phones did not have any covers at all. The screen and the keys were always there, and they were always visible. By the middle of the 2000s, the simple acts of opening a mobile phone or pressing its buttons were turned into real microplays: very short narratives complete with visual, tactile, and three-dimensional effects. In the short history of mobile phones, particular models

Figure 16.1
LG Chocolate. Photograph by the author.

whose commercial and critical popularity can be attributed to a significant degree to the innovative sensorial narratives of interaction with them include the Motorola RAZR V3 (2004) and the LG Chocolate (2006; the actual model number is LG VX-8600) (figure 16.1).

More than one million units of the LG Chocolate sold in only eight weeks following its introduction. This phone offered a unique (from a 2006 point of view) interactive narrative that can be called a real *Gesamtkunstwerk*—directly engaging the three senses of sight, sound, and touch and evoking the fourth sense of taste through the phone's name and color. When the phone is closed and off, it appears as a solid monochrome shape, with its display and touchpad completely invisible. It is a mysterious Thing. When you switch the phone on, the whole multimedia drama unfolds. The Thing gradually awakens. Previously invisible buttons suddenly appear in a glowing red color. The screen lights up, and it begins to play an animation. As the short animation unfolds to its finale, the phone suddenly vibrates at exactly the same time when the LG logo comes into the screen.

Given that the process of aestheticization of information tools started only less than a decade ago, I am sure that what we have seen so far constitutes just initial shy steps. More wild effects and experiences that we cannot even imagine today wait for us in the future.

Supermodernism: The Aesthetics of Disappearance

As iMac (1998) and OS X (2001) demonstrate, the aestheticization of the information-technology paradigm was applied equally to designs of information products and to designs of their user interfaces—that is, to both "hardware" and "software." In fact, although the first iMacs (1998–1999) and OS X (2001–) were released at different points in time, their share certain aesthetic features: bright clear colors, use of transparency/translucency, and rounded forms. And although both aim to remove the standard twentieth-century view of information technology as cold, indifferent to human presence, suited only for business, they at the same time cleverly exploit their technological identity. The translucency of the iMac plastic case, the Dock magnification, and the Genie effects in Aqua interface stage technology as magical and supernatural.

In this respect, it is relevant that a number of subsequent designs of Apple products —the Titanium and Aluminum PowerBooks (2001, 2003), the iPod and iPod Shuffle (2001, 2005), the Mac Mini (2005), the accompanying power cables, earphones, and so on—adopted very different minimal aesthetics. In this aesthetic, the technological object seems to want to disappear, fade into the background, and become ambient rather than actively to attract attention to itself and its technological magic, like the original iMacs. Whether consciously or not, these Apple designs communicate or, rather, foretell the new identity of personal information technology that today is still in development—the actual practical disappearance of technological objects so that they become fully integrated into other objects, surfaces, spaces, and clothes. This is the stage of ubiquitous computing in which a technological fetish is dissolved into the overall fabric of material existence. The actual details of this potential future dematerialization will most likely be different from how it is imagined today, but the trend itself is clearly visible. But how to stage this future disappearance using the technology available today? The Apple designs of the first part of the 2000s can be understood as responses to this challenge. Their particular aesthetic historically occupies an intermediate, transitional stage—between the stage of technology as a designed lifestyle object (exemplified by Apple iMacs from 1998 on or by Nokia's Fashion collection of mobiles [2004–]) and its future stage as an invisible infrastructure implanted inside other objects, architectural forms, and the human body.

In 1998, Dutch architecture theorist Hans Ibelings published a slim but soon to become influential book titled *Supermodernism* in which he identified a similar aesthetics of disappearance in the architecture of the 1990s—as exemplified by the Foundation Cartier in Paris (Jean Nouvel, 1994), the SBB Switchtower in Basel (Herzog & De Meuron, 1994–1997) (figure 16.2), and the French National Library in Paris (Dominique Perrault, 1989).

According to Ibelings, supermodern aesthetics "is characterized mainly by the absence of distinguishing marks, by neutrality" (1998, 88). This aesthetics stands in opposition to the previous architectural aesthetics of the 1980s and early 1990s: "Whereas postmodernist and deconstructionist architecture almost always contain a message, today architecture is increasingly conceived as an empty medium" (88). But although architecture as "an empty medium" on purpose avoids communicating

Figure 16.2
Herzog & De Meuron's SBB Switchtower in Basel, 1994–1997. Photograph by the author.

messages and oversignifying, it does something different and new instead. It creates unique sensorial experiences. The large, open, and empty interior volumes, the use of translucency and transparency, the employment of a variety of new materials and finishes that create finely focused sensorial effects—all these tactics have been deployed by supermodern architects to craft unique spatial experiences, where the experience one can have by being inside a particular building cannot be duplicated anywhere else.

In retrospect, we can correlate supermodern aesthetics with the rise of "experience design"/"experience economy" in the second half of the 1990s. We can also see it as already partially employing the new logic of architecture that becomes fully operational in the next decade—that is, the arrival of "signature" buildings by brand-name architects—crucial for branding cities and companies alike. Canonical supermodern buildings used simple geometric volumes that offered subtle sensorial effects inside and tried to disappear when seen from a distance. The canonical brand architecture of the 2000s appears to work differently—its easily identifiable and unique forms function as icons designed for media communication. At the same time, however, much like supermodern buildings, iconic signature buildings also function as spatial destinations—that is, they offer unique sensorial experiences inside. The complex and dynamic forms of Frank Gehry's buildings—such as Guggenheim Bilbao, Los Angeles Disney Hall, and Strata Center at MIT—are perfect examples of this double function: they look dramatic and unique when photographed, and at the same time they promise a unique spatial experience that requires a physical visit.

Ibelings was looking only at architecture, but ten years later we can say that the same supermodern aesthetics was put forward by Ive and his team when designing Apple products in the first half of the 2000s. The newly developed materials and finishes, the flat and largely empty surfaces uninterrupted by multiple buttons or screws (in contrast to a great many typical technological objects), the monochrome appearance that visually emphasizes the shape as a whole, the rounded corners, the glow of the Apple logo, which creates a three-dimensional effect, and the simplicity of the overall three-dimensional form—all these techniques work together to create a powerful impression that the object is about to fade and completely dissolve. And at the same time, the same object—a laptop, monitor, or iPod—creates another spatial experience that, in spite of the dramatic differences in size between these objects and architectural buildings, is a perfect analog of that "new spatial sensibility" that Ibelings found in supermodern buildings. The object confronts you with a "boundless and undefined space," a space, however, that "is not an emptiness but a safe container, a flexible shell" (Ibelings 1998, 62).

Ibelings has speculated about the different reasons for the emergence of a supermodern aesthetics in architecture, but in the case of personal-information technologies, the spatial form that is simultaneously "boundless" and "undefined" and also "a safe container, a flexible shell" seems to me a perfect metaphor for the key meanings of these technologies, as intended by Apple, Nokia, and other progressive (i.e., attuned to current lifestyles and cultural trends) technology/design companies in the 2000s: mobility, flexibility, and a lack of predefined boundaries or limits. The last meaning, however, also happens to define a modern computer in theoretical terms—a universal machine that via software can simulate unlimited number of other machines and tools and, again via software, is infinitely expandable. But how do you find a visual and/or spatial expression for such a metamachine? This is one of the challenges of contemporary aesthetics. The supermodernist aesthetics of recent Apple products as designed by Ive and his team has so far been one of the more successful solutions to this fundamental challenge.

References

Colette. n.d. Web site available at http://www.colette.fr. Accessed 1 April 2010.

"Getting Emotional with . . . Hartmut Esslinger." n.d. *Design & Emotion—Marco van Hout.* Available at http://www.design-emotion.com/2006/08/15/getting-emotional-with-hartmut-esslinger. Accessed 1 April 2010.

Ibelings, Hans. 1998. *Supermodernism: Architecture in the Age of Globalization.* Rotterdam: NAi.

Laurel, Brenda. 1991. *Computers as Theatre.* Reading, Mass.: Addison-Wesley.

"Nokia Fashion Phones Launched." n.d. *www.3g.co.uk.* Available at http://www.3g.co.uk/PR/Sept2004/8307.htm. Accessed 1 April 2010.

Pine, B. Joseph, and James H. Gilmore. 1999. *The Experience Economy: Work Is Theatre & Every Business a Stage.* Boston: Harvard Business School Press.

Wallpaper.com—International Design Interiors Fashion Travel. n.d. Available at http://www.wallpaper.com. Accessed 1 April 2010.

V Being Moved Live

17 Liveness, Presence, and Performance in Contemporary Digital Media

Jay David Bolter, Blair MacIntyre, Michael Nitsche, and Kathryn Farley

Social media, such as Facebook and YouTube, and the mixed-reality and augmented-reality applications now enabled by smartphones are among the most compelling new manifestations of digital media.[1] Contemporary digital-media theory does not adequately account for these new forms. One reason why is that digital-media theory is dominated by the canon of procedurality: the essence of the digital medium lies in the fact that it executes a procedure in code. To understand collective and social-media forms, we supplement the notion of procedurality by exploring the performative character of digital media. Just as all digital-media artifacts are procedural, there is a sense in which they all are performative. And just as concepts from performance studies can deepen our understanding of digital media, performance studies itself can benefit by taking digital media as an object of study. (For an introduction to performance studies, see Schechner 2002.) Since the publication of Philip Auslander's *Liveness* ([1999] 2008), scholars in performance studies have conducted a vigorous debate about whether contemporary mass media have altered or even nullified the cultural category of live performance. Auslander's book regarded television as the "culturally dominant" medium, but that position clearly needs to be revised to account for digital media, especially social media and mixed reality as well as the hybrid forms of film, television, print, and the digital.

Machinima Futurista: Multiple Representational Practices

Just a year or two ago the massive multiple online (MMO) environment Second Life enjoyed enormous cachet as a social application that promised to redefine our digital world. It was fashionable for museums, universities, businesses, and even a few national governments to have an "island" in Second Life. By extrapolating the exponential growth curve, the claim was made that a few years from now everyone who had managed to have a presence in "first life" would have one in Second Life, too. Today, again because of the predictable desire not to be behind the digital curve, it is fashionable to claim that Second Life is a dying world. In fact, although growth in

Second Life may have peaked, there remains a substantial community of participants, tens of thousands at any time, who seem to derive meaning from the opportunity for social interaction and for constructing media objects (clothes, action scripts, buildings, vehicles, and so on) in this virtual world.

Second Life enthusiasts and critics were always wrong, however, in characterizing Second Life as an alternative to our terrestrial social world. Like other manifestations of cyberspace before it, Second Life could not maintain its isolation from the rest of our world. A decade ago theorists such as N. Katherine Hayles (1999) and others called into question the notion that digital technology could offer its users a pure virtuality that allowed them to escape not only their bodies, but also their cultural and social positions. As part of the "second generation" of Internet applications, along with the Web 2.0 sites such as Facebook and YouTube, Second Life makes the notion of pure virtuality even less plausible than it was a decade ago. There are many ways in which Second Life is implicated in our world of social and cultural exchange, not the least of which is the monetary system. Linden dollars are interconvertible with US currency, which links Second Life (very modestly) into the world economy. Many businesses, universities, and other organizations still maintain a presence in Second Life. Numerous blogs and supporting sites weave this virtual world into the web of social media. For all these reasons, Second Life is not so much an alternative to first life as an extension of it. Its relationship to the economic and social world that we inhabit is metonymic rather than metaphoric.

At the Georgia Institute of Technology, we have been exploring ways in which Second Life can be put into a metonymic relationship not only with our world's cultural dimensions, but also with its physical dimensions. Or, more accurately, we have explored how to establish a relationship between Second Life as a medium and the other media that we already see embedded in our world. Faculty and students in the Augmented Environments Lab modified the Second Life client to allow avatars to appear to enter the physical world (figures 17.1 and 17.2).

The avatars are not actually inserted in the world, of course, but rather into the video stream of a camera trained on the world. Humans in the world cannot see the avatars in front of them; they have to look at a video monitor to view the composite.

The effect in the video stream is of a hybrid representational practice of graphic animation and live action, and there is a long tradition of such hybrids in film from Winsor McCay's *Gertie the Dinosaur* (1914) to Bob Zemekis's *Who Framed Roger Rabbit* (1988) and other more recent films. An important difference is that the blending of the avatars with the video stream happens in real time, not in postproduction, as is usual for all filmic examples. The human participant who controls the avatar does so at the same time as the human actors move in the scene. Real-time control allows for performances in which the live actors and avatars can interact and even

Figure 17.1
A Second Life avatar stands in an interior (office) environment. From the Augmented Environment Lab, Georgia Institute of Technology, http://arsecondlife.gvu.gatech.edu.

Figure 17.2
A Second Life avatar stands on the grass. From http://arsecondlife.gvu.gatech.edu.

improvise. This blending of avatars and live actors can also be used to create machinima pieces, which can be "recorded live"—a moment-to-moment recording of a performer manipulating a game engine. This configuration was used in the production of *Machinima Futurista* (2007) by Jenifer Vandagriff.

Machinima Futurista is a remediation of the programmatic Futurist film *Vita Futurista* (1916) by Arnaldo Ginna and others. The original, one of a handful of films made by the Futurists, has not survived, except for verbal accounts and a few film stills. According to the accounts, there were approximately eight separate scenes in the original, most of which depicted conflict between the Futurists and the "passéists," and had endearing titles such as "The Futurist Lunch" (see figure 17.3 for Vandagriff's version), "The Futurist Falls in Love with a Chair," and "How a Futurist Sleeps" (see figure 17.4 for Vandagriff's version; see also Kirby and Kirby 1986, 120–142).

Machinima Futurista is a response to the naive claim of the original *Vita Futurista* to establish a new and appropriately modern mode of living. A standard interpretation of the historical avant-garde (the Futurists and Dadaists) is that they were striving to debunk the aestheticism of the nineteenth century and envision a new kind of art as life praxis (Bürger 1984). In *Machinima Futurista*, the passéists are by and large live-action characters, and the Futurists are Second Life avatars. Making the Futurists into avatars seems somehow appropriate because it captures the playful sense of separation, of otherness, that the Futurists represented. By appropriating the material of the origi-

Figure 17.3
"The Futurist Lunch." Screen still from 1916 film *Vita Futurista*.

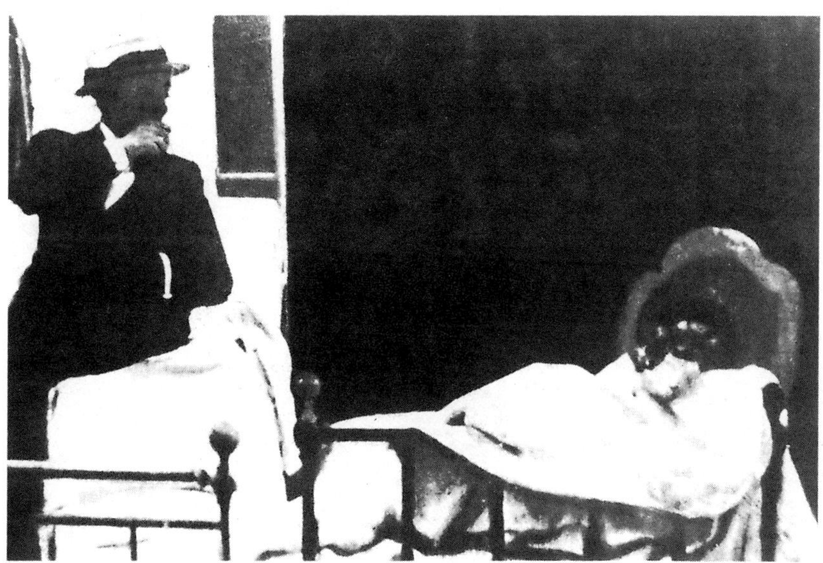

Figure 17.4
"How a Futurist Sleeps." Screen still from 1916 film *Vita Futurista*.

nal film and casting it as a Second Life performance, Vandagriff's piece gently parodies the notion that Second Life (or digital media in general) can provide the field of a new kind of avant-garde life praxis. Reaching back into the history of film and art in the early twentieth century, *Machinima Futurista* questions the cultural status of digital media in our time (figure 17.5).

Vandagriff's piece enacts a world in which the two orders of representation collide. The two regimes of live action and three-dimensional graphics remain formally as well as symbolically at war with each other. Live-action video is the older medium, which is now being invaded by avatars from the new medium. *Machinima Futurista* is not augmented reality or mixed reality per se; it is instead a video recording of a mixed-reality performance. As such, it exists in that curious space that we have known since television or, indeed, since the actualités of the Lumière brothers—the space of performances that are "recorded live." Actions that are recorded without substantial post-production editing seem to enjoy a status different from that of films (such as *Gertie the Dinosaur* or *Who Framed Roger Rabbit*) and of other digital media that are constructed frame by frame or by a process of overlays.

It is interesting to consider how both the categories "live" and "recorded live" are understood in digital-media forms. Liveness has usually been associated with performance or the special construction or framing of an event, which is why liveness became an important term of contestation in performance studies. On television, even

Figure 17.5
Screen still of a scene combining Second Life avatars and live actors.

a natural disaster or war is brought to us "live" by a television news organization. So liveness in the digital realm might be argued to be the combination of immediate presentation and an awareness of performance, and the question of liveness in digital media belongs to the larger question of the performativity of digital media.

Procedurality and Performativity

The dominant analytic category in digital-media theory today is "procedurality." According to most game studies theorists, games are essentially procedural (for example, Bogost 2007). In *The Language of New Media* (2001), Lev Manovich contends that software studies should replace media studies. The interactive–narrative community is pursuing what it calls "procedural narrative." For all these theorists and others, the key quality of the digital as a medium is the fact that each digital artifact runs code, quasi autonomously, according to an algorithm. Interactivity is still perhaps the most popular term in our culture's description of digital media, but proceduralists often criticize the term as vague. What seems important to them is not merely that the user interacts with a digital artifact, but that she interacts according to a procedure embodied in code.

In this view, interactivity becomes a dimension or expression of procedurality. The interface is the face that the artifact presents to the user, player, or viewer. The procedure, the code, is what lies beneath the surface. Interactivity describes the relationship between a human user and a coded artifact. The user of an interactive application is represented by a variable in the main event loop, which triggers one or more of the possible programmed responses. An application is therefore interactive if the user can insert herself into the event loop so that the application's outputs are coupled with the user's moment-to-moment inputs.

If this is what the term interactivity means for most digital-media theorists and practitioners, it means something quite different in communication studies, where it implies communication between or among human subjects. The telephone is an interactive medium; broadcast radio is not (Holmes 2005). Email is an interactive communication; a single-player videogame is not—no matter how intricate the interactions between the code and player, no matter how "believable" the characters in the game might be. Interactivity in the digital realm is interpersonal and sometimes even intersubjective communication.

An approach based on performance studies can encompass both of these definitions. It does not exclude the possibility of procedural interactivity, but it shows that the procedural view is incomplete. Performance studies is intensely interested in issues of the subject and intersubjectivity, whereas the procedural view has very little interest in either. The procedural view is especially uninterested in the intersubjective relationships that are mediated by digital artifacts because the second subject generally only gets in the way of a pure appreciation of the procedure. For most game studies theorists, what matters is that a game is a rule-based activity, and what makes videogames unique is that the player can play directly against the rules, as embodied in digital code. Likewise, for interactive narrativists, the goal is a system in which the computer does the moment-to-moment writing: constructing the characters and situations against which the player can react. In both cases, the computer is the second subject.

The irony is that procedurality is dominant in digital theory at precisely a moment when digital-media forms are expanding in ways for which procedurality cannot account. Ten or even five years ago, single-player videogames were perhaps the dominant digital-media form, almost the only commercially successful form of digital entertainment (other than Internet pornography, which can, in its own ironic way, be regarded as procedural). The popularity of single-player videogames continues, but MMO games now compete with single-player games for cultural interest and market share. And MMO games are interpersonal forms, some of which, such as World of Warcraft, have hundreds of thousands or even millions of players. Furthermore, the story of the past decade is not the single-player videogame or even the MMO game, but the development of general social media, such as Facebook, YouTube, and Wikipedia. Social media are interpersonal and procedural at the same time. The user does not interact solely with the code; instead, the code defines the forms of communication that she can engage in with other users. Social media (and even email and chat) are communication rituals enabled and constrained by code. The user is cast in the role of a performer who is performing for others and often for herself as well.

For these reasons, we propose to supplement the notion of procedural interactivity with concepts of digital performance and performativity. We draw systematically on performance studies in order to enrich digital-media studies.

The Performative Character of Digital Media

The advent of social media, which can be dated back at least to textual chat rooms, and MUDs and MOOs of the 1990s, made it clear that digital forms could be performative. Just as Judith Butler and others were arguing for the performativity of gender throughout our culture, numerous researchers were focusing on gender bending, and other forms of gender construction were going on in multiuser domains and various chat applications, refuting the cyberspace purists who claimed that by entering the world of digital communication we left our bodies behind. The explosive growth of social media in the past decade has made performance perhaps the most common way of engaging the digital. Facebook, MySpace, and many other social Web sites involve tens of millions of participants daily in rituals of identity construction. Facebook is such a ritual or, indeed, an expanding set of such rituals: setting up your Facebook page, adding images, writing on friends' walls, sending a message to friends, and so on. Twitter encourages its users to make a performance out of their daily activities and to report copiously to their followers in 140-character tweets. These social applications are usually reciprocal. Agreement to being a "friend" on Facebook is an agreement on mutual performativity. I agree to be your audience if you agree to be mine.

Facebook began as a simple and relatively well-defined communications ritual, but it has proven remarkably flexible in adding communicative goals to its original purpose (which was flirting and networking among college students at Harvard). Each new Facebook application adds a different—although not radically or disruptively different—ritual activity. The successful new applications are those that provide enough structure to render the ritual intelligible while allowing enough flexibility to be appropriated by the users. This is true of social media in general. In all social media, the user is still inserting herself into the code, still becoming part of a procedure, but the procedure does not completely describe or circumscribe her performance.

The premier video portal of the Internet, YouTube, is also one of its most important performative sites. YouTube is extremely varied as well, and its success certainly rests in part on its adaptability. The original conception, however, remains. The motto of YouTube is "Broadcast yourself," which millions of users have interpreted to mean not only "You do the broadcasting," but also "You broadcast a version of yourself." The classic YouTube video is the "talking head," in which a user directly addresses her Webcam and its implied audience. YouTube is narcissistic performance video as general culture practice.

Social media started on the Web and were accessed on desktops and laptops, but now because of mobile phones they are extending themselves throughout our lived environment. Digital-media forms that combine the physical and virtual enable a different kind of performance, at least in the sense that the audience is (potentially) present and visible. Recent mixed-reality game devices such as the Nintendo Wii or, even better, Guitar Hero attest to the popularity of shared physical performances. Geocaching and location-based games depend on Global Positioning System technology to stage performances sometimes for single players, but more often for groups of players in physical settings from mountaintops to urban streets. And alternate-reality games (ARGs)—a genre that has emerged in the past ten years—combine multiple media forms (Web sites, emails, telephones, even films) with encounters in the physical world. The early ARGs offered players elaborate and esoteric puzzles to unravel, but the genre has since expanded to include games with social themes, such as World without Oil.[2] In this game, which ran for a month in the spring of 2007, players were invited to imagine a world in which oil prices rise tremendously and then to act on what they foresaw would happen. Thousands of players posted blog entries or made videos portraying the consequences of each new price rise on their neighborhood or town. Some even went on to practice energy conservation in acts such as riding their bicycles to work.

Unlike ARGS, flash mobs constitute a form of physical performance in which no mediating digital technology appears necessary. In a flash mob, the participants assemble in a public space, offer a playfully obscure performance, and then disperse. For the mob whose YouTube video is entitled *Frozen Grand Central Station*,[3] two hundred mobbers froze in various poses in the station to the bewilderment of the passersby on the way to and from their trains. Flash mobs are in some ways the contemporary analogs of happenings or even Fluxus events of the 1960s and bear a distant relation to the performances of the Futurists and Dadaists of the historical avant-garde. But they are different in being utterly popular, and their popularity comes from the fact that they rely on digital communication networks for the organization and their publication. Although a Flash mob such as *Grand Central Station* is a live performance, it is called into existence by Short Message Service or emails, which alert the participants to the time and place. A recording of the flash mob is subsequently distributed as one or more produced YouTube videos and can reach a huge audience. The flash mob itself can then promote repetitions and move from unique event to genre: for example, there are now several videos on YouTube showing freezing-in-place mobs in other cities. In this sense, the flash mob suggests how the digital forms can become an ironic fulfillment of the avant-garde desire for a new kind of artistic performance as life praxis.

Flash mobs can be seen as an example of a larger trend, in which the whole world becomes available for the reception and production of mediated performance. As the world itself becomes replete with media, Mark Weiser's (1991) original notion that we will live in an age of ubiquitous computing needs to be amended: our world will be, indeed is now, one of ubiquitous media. If the world is replete with media, every moment is one of potential "live-recorded" performance.

The performative quality of social media and of mixed-reality games and events is clear. But even the single-player videogame can be understood as performative. Videogames are tests of performance in the operational sense of the term: the player is challenged to compete and win, usually by destroying enemies or by overcoming obstacles and collecting points. In *Perform or Else* (2001), Jon McKenzie argues that performance as productivity should also be part of performance studies. But we can also contend that single-player videogames stage a performative situation in the conventional sense of performer and audience. In this case, the player can be both performer and audience through a split subjectivity. The player watches herself play and takes pleasure from the performance, and the videogame, unlike a traditional stage performance, typically facilitates this reflective activity. Many "first-person shooters" offer an over-the-shoulder view of the player as character or even a full third-person view in cut-scenes as well as the opportunity to replay significant events.

Reflectivity is a key to the psychology of mainstream single-player games. These games provide the subject with an opportunity to see herself through an idealized, mediatized reflection. We can find a parallel to an earlier media form that explored the concept of the recorded-live performance: video art of the 1970s. In her essay "Video, the Aesthetics of Narcissism," Rosalind Krauss (1976) argues that the cardinal feature of the video art of such pioneers as Vito Acconci and Richard Serra was the study of split subjectivity that the technology enables, when the artist can monitor her own performance. According to Krauss, the closed-loop of the video camera and monitor became the psychology of the medium. The same can be said of the digital closed-loop of videogames. Videogames are a kind of narcissistic bracketing out of the world as the player falls into self-absorbed performance.

At the same time, the videogame has also led to the overtly performative genre of machinima. The classic machinima videos, such as the Red vs. Blue series by Rooster Teeth Productions, were performances that took place inside a game—in this case, the Halo series. Machinima is a creative misappropriation of the games themselves or of game engines, which were released to the developer community so that it could develop new levels for narcissistic play. Machinima breaks the digital loop, however, because it is made with the assumption of an audience rather than the split subject of the single-player game.

Liveness and Presence

The example with which we began, *Machinima Futurista*, is both a machinima piece and the record of a mixed-reality performance, in this case a record of the interaction of several human actors and an avatar operator. *Machinima Futurista* combines the traditional notion of immediacy with a digital-mediated version of liveness. The avatars are live, too, in the sense that they participate in the action at the same time as the human actors. We also noted at the outset of this chapter that the issue of the ontology of live performance has been debated for years in the performance studies community. For some in performance studies (and presumably for many in the theater itself), the immediacy or presence of live performance is what separates it from the contemporary mass and popular media. Peggy Phelan has articulated this idea: "[The] only life of performance is in the present. Performance cannot be saved, recorded, documented, or otherwise participate in the circulation of representations of representations; once it does so, it becomes something other than performance" (1993, 146).

The title of Phelan's book, *Unmarked: The Politics of Performance*, makes the political claim that theater might free us from the commodification of culture that pervades—for example, the Hollywood film industry and television. However, Philip Auslander questions the idea that performance can escape from the cultural web of media and mediation: "Live performance is becoming progressively less independent of media technology. . . . It is not realistic to propose that live performance can remain ontologically pristine or that it operates in a cultural economy separate from that of the mass media" ([1999] 2008, 45).

Because Auslander regards television as the culturally dominant medium that works its way into our reception of live performance, he sees little hope for the future of such performance. In the economy of repetition, live performance is little more than a vestigial remnant of the previous historical order of representation, a holdover that can claim little in the way of cultural presence or power ([1999] 2008, 46). Auslander does not include digital media in his analysis, originally published in 1999, and even though the second edition (2008) pays somewhat more attention to the digital, it still does not address online games or social media as new fields for popular performance. If we do pay attention to the digital, then live performance no longer seems to be a vestigial remnant but becomes instead an increasingly common social practice. But Auslander's point remains valid, because this new kind of performance practice has no interest in remaining ontologically pure. Digital performance welcomes various forms of mediation, including hybrid combinations of media and the physical world.

This is not to say that those working in digital forms always follow the same performative strategy. *Machinima Futurista* in fact references two opposing strategies. The avatars from Second Life are ordinarily performing in a wholly virtual world; in *Machinima Futurista*, they are suddenly thrust into our world, where they look out of place and comical. Second Life is a 3D graphic online environment, which is sometimes called "desktop VR," and although Second Life does not offer immersive VR, which requires a headset or cave apparatus to simulate the visual surround, it does evoke the ontology of VR. The goal of VR is to create an alternative visual world in which the user can immerse herself. The virtual world is live in the procedural sense that it responds to the moment-by-moment changes of the user's orientation and position. As a result, the user should feel "present" in the virtual world.

The notions of "presence" and "liveness" are closely related. It is well known that Jacques Derrida argues that the metaphysics of presence has been a key and troubled notion throughout the history of Western culture. In the context of the performance studies debate, however, Phelan still seems to be suggesting that performance today can achieve a presence that goes beyond mediation. And Auslander is arguing that our mediated culture always intervenes to close off the possibility of presence. It is ironic in the context of this debate that the VR community has its own version of presence and even its own eponymous journal to study presence. For the VR community, presence is defined as the extent to which the user feels that she is "there" in the environment depicted (Slater and Steed 2000). It has also been defined negatively—as the sense of the absence of mediation (Lombard and Ditton 1997). In both definitions, the goal is unproblematic, although difficult to achieve. Testing the relationship between the technology and the user's experience of presence is the main subject of the journal *Presence: Teleoperators and Virtual Environments*.

In Phelan's terms, of course, VR is the perfect opposite of performative presence. A VR environment is nothing but a representation of representations. If it gives the user the feeling of the absence of mediation, it does so only by achieving a complex coordination of technologies of graphics, sound, and tracking. If anything, VR seems to confirm Auslander's understanding of the new digital context: that there is no escaping mediation even in the pursuit of liveness or presence. VR can in fact be understood as a mediated performance technology. The conceptual relationship between VR and videogames has always been close, and a VR application calls on the user to perform like a player in a videogame. Many popular videogame genres (especially first-person shooters and role-playing games) put the players in a desktop VR: screen-based three-dimensional graphics that hold out the promise of visual immersion. Such videogames want the user to lose herself in the game world, to feel present there. However, most VR applications, like single-player videogames, are closed-loop systems. The user finds herself alone in a procedurally generated world. The experience is narcissistic. VR environments are mirror worlds in which the user can construct an ideal version of herself. The user often has magical powers—for example, she can fly—and she is ultimately present only to herself.

Mixed-reality applications stage a different kind of performance. The user interacts not only with the computer, but also with other aspects of the physical world, which are not fully procedural. Pervasive games, location-based games, and even some ARGs involve the contingency of everyday life. All these digital experiences are far more likely to be interpersonal and intersubjective. Players in ARGs, for example, seldom work on the puzzles alones, and many of the games are organized around social media such as blogs. As mixed-reality applications literally take the (high-tech) blinders off the user and expose her to the world, they open up the procedural loop by enabling performances in which the performer and audience are not necessarily or even generally the same person. The ontology of mixed reality is therefore different from that of VR. Designers of mixed-reality applications are not trying to create seamless virtual worlds in which the technology of mediation is concealed. Instead, the technology for overlaying graphics and establishing communication is openly acknowledged: projected video, mobile phones and personal digital assistants, and even the headset of augmented reality typically do not disappear from the user's conscious view. As a result, the kind of presence or liveness engendered differs from that of VR. The players of an ARG or a pervasive game are present to each other through a series of mediating technologies and sometimes in person. They understand their experience in terms that Auslander defines as the liveness of rock concerts and other mediated productions. Technological mediation does not destroy or invalidate liveness for them; instead, the creative use of the technology contributes to the liveness of the experience.

Notes

We are drawing on the work of a number of colleagues in two interlocking research groups: Digital Performance Initiative (including Kathryn Farley, Melissa Foulger, Blair MacIntyre, Michael Nitsche, Jay David Bolter, Rebecca Rouse, Shashank Raval, and Jenifer Vandagriff) and the Augmented Environments Lab (directed by Blair MacIntyre and including Maribeth Gandy, Evan Barba, Alex Hill, and Kim Spreen). This work has been supported by the GVU Center and the Wesley New Media Center, both in the Georgia Institute of Technology.

1. In this discussion, we do not emphasize the distinction between the terms mixed reality and augmented reality. We use mixed reality as the more general term for any application that involves enhancing the user's experience of her physical environment with digital information, images, or sound. For the classic discussion of the difference between VR, mixed reality, and augmented reality, see Milgram and Kishino 1994.

2. See http://en.wikipedia.org/wiki/World_Without_Oil.

3. See http://youtu.be/jwMj3PJDxuo.

References

Auslander, Philip. [1999] 2008. *Liveness: Performance in a Mediatized Culture.* 2nd ed. London: Routledge.

Bogost, Ian. 2007. *Persuasive Games: The Expressive Power of Videogames*. Cambridge, MA: MIT Press.

Bürger, Peter. 1984. *Theory of the Avant-Garde*. Translated by Michael Shaw. Minneapolis: University of Minnesota Press.

Hayles, N. Katherine. 1999. *How We Became Posthuman*. Chicago: Chicago University Press.

Holmes, David. 2005. *Communication Theory: Media, Technology, Society*. London: Sage.

Kirby, Michael, and Victoria Nes Kirby. 1986. *Futurist Performance*. New York: PAJ.

Krauss, Rosalind. 1976. "Video, the Aesthetics of Narcissism." October 1 (Spring): 50–64.

Lombard, Matthew, and Theresa Ditton. 1997. "At the Heart of It All: The Concept of Presence." *Journal of Computer-Mediated Communication* 3 (2). Available at http://jcmc.indiana.edu/vol3/issue2/lombard.html.

Manovich, Lev. 2001. *The Language of New Media*. Cambridge, MA: MIT Press.

McKenzie, Jon. 2001. *Perform or Else: From Discipline to Performance*. New York: Routledge.

Milgram, Paul, and Fumio Kishino. 1994. "A Taxonomy of Mixed Reality Visual Displays." *IEICE TRANSACTIONS on Information and Systems* E77-D.12: 1321–1329.

Phelan, Peggy. 1993. *Unmarked: The Politics of Performance*. New York: Routledge.

Schechner, Richard. 2002. *Performance Studies: An Introduction*. 2nd ed. New York: Routledge.

Slater, Mel, and Anthony Steed. 2000. "A Virtual Presence Counter." *Presence: Teleoperators and Virtual Environments* 9 (5): 413–434.

Vandagriff, Jenifer, director. 2007. *Machinima Futurista*. Georgia Institute of Technology.

Weiser, Mark. 1991. "The Computer for the 21st Century." *Scientific American* 265 (3): 94–104.

18 Sinews of Ubiquity: A Corporeal Ethics for Ubiquitous Computing

Susan Kozel

This reflection on ubiquitous computing is written from the perspectives of performance and phenomenology—in particular, the dance and choreographic practices that shape the creation of responsive systems from large public art installations to intimate devices worn under clothes and on skin. The kinesthetic awareness of dance combines with the corporeal methodology of phenomenology, and both play a role in crafting an ethics, but this reflection on ubiquitous computing is also knitted with an understanding of how we exist within and move through the world. As such, the infrastructure of ubiquity is also considered: not the circuits, local-area networks, and software, but the corporeal and philosophical sinews of ubiquity that have meaning on ontological, aesthetic, and methodological levels. Calling the ethical approach offered in this chapter "corporeal" means more than simply considering how ubiquitous systems impact bodies; the aim is to re-embody the very understanding of ubiquitous computing in our lives as if it were, in Hélène Cixous words, "the blood flow in the veins between the bodies" connecting a life with another, one community to the other (1998, 3).

To arrive at a consideration of ethics by the end of this chapter, it is necessary to travel a route that sketches specific interpretations of ubiquity and tactility. It is true that a play across the terms *ubiquitous computing* and *ubiquity* in broader philosophical and experiential senses occurs throughout the chapter. This is deliberate. Further, the corporeal ethics proposed here is based on an expanded understanding of tactility as that which is *palpable*. This construction of palpability requires a role for that which is normally just beyond our perception and our awareness: the *invisible* and *oblivion*. Ubiquity implies selection. What to notice? What to overlook? These are the basic questions behind Mark Weiser's suggestion that ubiquitous computing, in its most desirable manifestation, is "calm." A calm technology, according to his now classic formulation, moves easily from the periphery of our attention to the center and back (Weiser and Seely Brown 1996). It effectively goes quiet or becomes less noticeable when it is on the periphery and when one's affective state does the same. On a more profound level, the question "What to notice?" becomes "What to remember?" and

"What to forget?" This construction opens space for considering the seemingly abstract philosophical terms of oblivion (Augé 2004) and the invisible (Merleau-Ponty [1968] 1987), which actually have quite pragmatic applications not just for staying sane with computers all around us, but for seeing the poetry of life. Reflections on Spinozan philosophy (Deleuze 1988) act to balance the poetic and fleshly thought of Maurice Merleau-Ponty with an affirmation of bodies as kinetic and vital.

Some may question the transition from Merleau-Ponty to Gilles Deleuze in the light of a concern for the compatibility between these two philosophical approaches. Merleau-Ponty's late and less-read work (*The Visible and the Invisible* [1968] 1987) offers a phenomenological orientation that is dynamic and fluid, far removed from entrenched notions of phenomenology as reinforcing a narrowly defined ego, subject, or "body proper." The Deleuzian approach to Benedictus de Spinoza, in its celebration of the latter's practical philosophy, is synchronously a pragmatic and, I would argue, deeply experiential account of fluid corporeality affected by ubiquitous systems.

Performance

> In what we call reality, I stumble between strange states and events. Moments follow one another in a long unbroken succession. High and low, long and short, fast ad slow, clamorous and silent. For me, composition is a means of bringing order to chaos and creating meaning from all the tumbling fragments.
>
> —Efva Lilja, *Dance—For Better, For Worse*

Ubiquitous computing is relational and corporeal. It is temporal and intercorporeal. Embedded in our lives, it is touched, seen, lived in, or with. We perform the narratives of daily life, and ubiquitous systems[1] respond while subtly shaping our performance with theirs. Worn over time, these systems bump against us, causing pleasure or annoyance. They are about exchange and perception. Our relationships are increasingly mediated by something designed: our bodies combine and exchange with each other through layers of fabric, machinery, and chemicals; with modulations of velocity and distance; impacting imagination, memory, affluence, and aspirations. Our devices and systems are integrated into the fabric of our existence, worn on our skin, mobile, networked, and almost always "on."

Even when we aren't wearing our ubiquitous devices, we enter into public spaces animated by ubiquitous systems. I can almost feel the presence of a peripheral computer system, like the breath on the back of my neck, as I walk into a room. Is there an electromagnetic field? A tacit intelligence? Is the space crosscut with computer vision or permeated by affordances for networking? Instead of viewing a public place as having a network the way a building has walls and a park has paths, we see a space as offering the potential for networking, for imminent and immanent movement. The tangible gives way to the intangible; the actual is porous with the virtual. It is possible to inquire, in the spirit of Merleau-Pontian phenomenology, What happens when I am aware of something that is aware of me? Like the seeing–seen articulated in Merleau-Ponty's ([1968] 1987) late writings, I am aware of being in someone's or something's awareness. My skin prickles. I feel comforted, surprised, or irritated. I feel the relief of connectivity or the creepy sense of being surveilled.

"Seeing myself seen" is not an inconsequential sensation: it is the basis of an ontological engagement with the world and everything in it. If I am the object of another's gaze or touch as well as seeing or touching my surroundings, I am open to a fluid and responsive relationship with the world, far removed from both a position of mastery and a state of subjugation. This is the first step toward an ethics; and, at the same time, these alive spaces and corporeal exchanges are the stuff of performance. There is a sort of loop in this chapter, like a feedback loop: from bodies in performance with ubiquitous systems or devices, to philosophical concepts regarding the invisible and oblivion that emerge directly from this experience, to an ethics of corporeality based on the palpable to the everyday performance of life with and through ubiquitous computing. The starting point of artistic performance and the end point of daily performance converge, wherein notions of beginning and ending lose distinction. As such, this convergence is a reflection not of ubiquitous computing, but of ubiquitous corporeality, not *ubicomp* but *ubicorp*. The shift to be made here is from the system to the performance within the system: bodies are ubiquitous; they may be digital, distanced, or distracted, but they are present. It is possible to view this assertion as banal and profound in equal measures—we live in the world through our bodies; perception and meaning are constructed through embodied exchanges with the world. Ubicorp is a precondition for ubicomp; ubicorp can keep ubicomp grounded.

Considering ubiquity from the perspectives of embodiment and performance means that I have a particular investment in the configurability and affordances of a system, and I see the outputs of media and gesture as a choreography across bodies and hardware/software. I also see all ubiquitous systems as providing scope for social and personal improvisation. As I look for flexibility, agency, and configurability, important for performance and for life, a fundamentally ontological question emerges: Can my state of being and the state of being of these systems extend to include improvisation not just in the narrow rhythmic exchanges of rapid action, but in sleep and stillness, in contemplation and communion? This extension amounts to extracting ubiquitous computing from the domain of accelerating economic productivity so that it can be more useful in the performance of life.

Ubiquitous systems mimic the holistic web that connects all components of the world; we cannot help but respond to one another, for we all are networked on subtle and not so subtle levels. My actions impact you, even if I may choose to ignore this impact most of the time. The same is true of the systems of the body: one's skeletal system registers the presence and the state of well-being of the nervous system, digestive system, respiration, and psyche. A ubiquitous system registers—sometimes indiscriminately—the presence of beings who enter it. A revealing moment when working with a new sensing system for an installation or performance, both practically and philosophically, is when background noise needs to be extracted from it. A camera-based sensing system must be calibrated by its software designers to judge what is simply noise in order to identify meaningful changes in the environment. An acoustic example relevant to artistic as well as security systems is the need to filter out the background hum of ambient noises in the room, such as ventilation or air conditioning, so that the sound of footsteps can be detected. Once again, ubiquity implies selection. *What can we, should we, do we notice? What can we, should we, do we overlook?* The act of filtering out is an act that defines performance. Performance can be seen to depend on the preposition *as*: if I choose to see my movement as performance, then it is (Kozel 2007, 68; Schechner 2003, 30). Here the *as* is broadened to include whether we design and calibrate a system to notice a certain kinetic presence or expressive mode: what we deem to be worthy of noticing is the performative, and a ubiquitous system can be a palpable, performing being. The performative is defined in relation to that which we choose to forget, or simply not to see, but which maintains its own mode of presence as oblivion or invisibility.

This definition of performance may seem mechanical or technologically determined, but at the root of it is a reflexivity, an awareness that a decision needs to be made on whether to notice or not to notice the performance of an action. The boundaries of any definition need to be distinguished; hence, when we are reflecting on ubiquity and performance, the question of what is *not* a performance becomes significant. Are unaware or unnoticed acts not performed? Is there a level of action that is not performed, but just is? I suggest there is always an ontologically raw domain of presence, expression, and action that is pre-performative, but maybe I believe so because I yearn for a domain that is free from the necessity or compulsion to act and to reflect. I yearn for the off switch. Perhaps this yearning can be satisfied not by delving explicitly into the nonreflective or nonperformative, but by exploring the forgotten or unnoticed—that is to say, oblivion and the invisible. Performance needs to occur in relation to its other, but perhaps its other is not nonperformance.

Oblivion

> [T]he value of life in its quotidian unfolding and the meaning we find in such life are animated by a constant, fragile calculus of remembering and forgetting, a constant tug and pull between memory and oblivion, each an inverted trace of the other.
>
> —James Young, foreword to Marc Augé's *Oblivion*

There is a subtle relationship between what we perceive and what we forget. If we do not notice something, then is it necessarily forgotten? And what is forgetting? It is not simply erasure, according to Marc Augé's wonderful rumination on memories. "Oblivion," he writes, "is the life force of memory and remembrance is its product" (2004, 21). Oblivion, along with the invisible, is the animating force of ubiquity, and both contribute to an ethics based on the palpable. Ubiquity cannot be defined separately from those who exist within its domain, and, as such, it cannot be everywhere, always, pervasively "on" because we are not always "on," and sometimes we elude detection, even within ourselves. Refiguring ubiquitous computing in terms of the ebbs and flows of forgetting helps us find a creative, corporeal, and ethical way to live while being sensed, tracked, and anticipated by others. The absences or gaps that constitute forgetting provide the space to navigate the meaning of what one has remembered, just as the negative spaces or blind spots constitute a system almost as much as its concrete data or specific functions do. And if memories, generally thought of as visual images, are linked to muscular and thermal sensations (Young 2004, vii), then oblivion is corporeal, too.

Augé considers three components of memory that bind it with oblivion. These components help to make a difficult notion a little more intuitive, and they open space for his thought to be applied to ubiquitous systems: first, memory is plural; second, we should not consider the trace of memory, but instead what is traced; third, the connections between memories are more important than the memories themselves (2004, 23).

Ubiquity, like memory, is not a unified cloud; it is a multiplicity, or, as Augé says, "memory is plural" (2004, 23). Each of us exists at a convergence of multiple ubiquitous systems—even competing systems: what may be helpful coming from one system may become an annoyance or a hazard coming from many. Mark Weiser and John Seely Brown characterize ubiquity as not just computation embedded in the world, but "many computers sharing each of us." This unlikely turn of phrase is constructed in parallel to the older phenomenon of the mainframe computer, where "many people share a computer" (Weiser and Seely Brown 1996). The notion of computers sharing us or pulling us in many directions need not be a cause for concern in itself if we realize that this is how our memories function and that, following Spinoza, our bodies themselves are plural. Bodies and minds are not forms, substances, or subjects, but rather modes, which is to say complex relations of speeds and slowness combined with the ability to affect and to be affected (Deleuze 1988, 124). The problem with ubiquitous systems is not their proliferation per se, but that they are not sufficiently flexible to adopt the range of speeds and affects that reflect the bodies within them. When Augé indicates that memory is not about the trace, but about "what is traced," and that these traces are always connected, we gain a greater sense of the plurality of memory and ubiquity. Ubiquitous systems navigate intercorporeal trajectories of not just *any* body, but *many* bodies, and the focus is less on concrete traces than on the ebb and flow of what or who are traced. The tendrils of oblivion, as they blur the edges of memory, take shape in the attempt to recapture childhood memories, according to Augé. These remembrances, if we try to capture them explicitly, are ghostly, fleeting, vanishing, offering incongruous details rather than the clarity and certitude we desire. More significant, when we attempt to recapture distant memories, we discover that they have been reshaped by the tales of others who integrate them into their own narratives. My traces mingle and are repatterned by others' traces. My forgetting merges with your forgetting, and the result is remembrance.

Invisibility

In a way her work was invisible. It consisted of extracting a story from the unconnected shots the directors brought her. She usually made them coherent by excising the greater part of them.
—Jens Christian Grøndahl, *Silence in October*

This section on the invisible really should be blank. You can fill it in with your own sense of what it is that you cannot see, but what is intimate to everything you perceive, think, and do. Merleau-Ponty writes that the invisible is the lining of the visible; it is what gives texture, flesh, meaning, and richness to life. The invisible is not an "absolute invisible"; rather, "it is the invisible *of* this world, that which inhabits this world, sustains it, and renders it visible, its own interior possibility, the Being of this being" ([1968] 1987, 151). The invisible and oblivion are the latitude and longitude of ubiquity. They are its metaphysics. Oblivion means that these systems exist over time and that forgetting is inherent; the invisible means that they exist through space and that not all can be seen or perceived. There is some comfort in this notion because human beings are more at ease (in our profoundly neurotic ways) with not remembering or not seeing everything, whereas systems will try always to achieve both but will fail.

As a dancer, I approach the notion of ubiquity with considerable suspicion. I need to see in ubiquitous computing the possibility for the unexpected, for it to deliver more than simply a sleeker, more automated version of our current body–world relations, and I do not want only calmness from it. This need can be articulated both philosophically and pragmatically: philosophically, the need for the unexpected is a desire for innovation, difference, or quite simply crevasses in the visible where the invisible makes itself known; pragmatically, a dancer's need to provide scope for innovative physical and affective expression means that preprogrammed systems are too often dampening or constraining of creative ingenuity, particular corporeal, or gestural expression. I look for textures of corporeality in computation: gesture, affect, perception, motility, kinesthesia, synesthesia, intersubjectivity, otherness—which includes the strangeness of innovative expression as well as a wide range of corporeal materialities that are offered by many responsive computational systems.

We cannot know, perceive, or think everything. If we could, we would lose most of the magic of life, what makes us human or causes us to glance out the same window each morning to see what the day looks like. Difference is like an unfolding of moments of the invisible into the visible. That which is different calibrates us, that which we do not yet know animates and gives life to what we do know. Ubiquitous computing can be seen as orchestrating a convergence of differences. In its best manifestations, a ubiquitous system lets differences between bodies flourish; more often than not it flattens them. The invisible is ubiquitous, and the opposite is worth articulating: ubiquity is permeated by that which we cannot see. This permeation is both ubiquity's great strength and the source of our deeply rooted fears.

Ethics

Ethics, which is to say, a typology of immanent modes of existence, replaces Morality, which always refers existence to transcendent values.

—Gilles Deleuze, *Spinoza: Practical Philosophy*

The ethics offered here is an ontological understanding of bodies in the world. Instead of offering rules for designing or implementing ubiquity, this ethics distills a sense of corporeal engagement that is expansive enough to include systems and bodies, and generous enough to recognize unexpected implications of a system designed to inhabit the lifeworld with beings. I draw this corporeal ethics from specific components of Merleau-Ponty and Deleuze's thought and filter it through the practical and experiential lens I have gained through being a dancer in responsive systems. I turn to Deleuze to provide an alternate construction of bodies that is deeply kinetic and respectful of movement, permitting the inclusion of systems and machines under the definition; I turn to Merleau-Ponty to provide poetry and palpability, desire and absence. In short, Merleau-Ponty puts flesh on Deleuze's somewhat abstracted kinetics, and together they paint a picture—not without tensions, of course—of what is really at stake when we inhabit ubiquitous systems.

The palpable is more than the tactile or the visual; it evokes Merleau-Ponty's deeper sense of flesh and the entwinement between oneself and the world. I do more than touch the world and others; they are part of me, and I am part of them: through palpation, I become closer to the world, but I do not consume or overlap with it. Palpation implies touch; for Merleau-Ponty, it is the synesthetic touch of vision, but, more significant, it is a wider mode of sensing in which what is immanent opens outward to be receptive of the world. I am inside out, Merleau-Ponty writes; I live a sort of "pact" between myself and things "according to which I lend them my body in order that they inscribe upon it and give me their resemblance" ([1968] 1987, 146). The things that inscribe us include ubiquitous systems. When something is palpable, it is present to us in many dimensions: the peripheral and invisible as well as that which is central and visible, something we sense in our bones and flesh as well as through more clearly defined channels. The somatic is in the domain of the palpable, as is the kinesthetic. In order to palpate the world, I have to do so with "a certain hollow, a certain interior, a certain absence, a negativity that is not nothing" ([1968] 1987, 151) because my perception and, indeed, my being are structured in such a way that I am always formed and shaped by what is external to me; in fact, I need that outside to my inside. If we integrate this notion of the palpable with the argument from the previous part of this chapter, we see that oblivion and the invisible are woven into the palpable; they are part of the certain absence. I am open to the ubiquitous systems that I deploy or inhabit: they become part of my body.

An illustration of how dancers communicate while in performance brings this integration to life. Dancers rarely look at each other directly when performing for an audience, but their connection and contact with each other is constant whether they actually touch or not. They know where other dancers and audience members are in space and sense the rhythms of all. Affect is shared, as are vitality and intention. Dancers exert a kinesthetic pull that is deeply elastic and, although ostensibly invisible, is entirely real. The music and the space are also palpable presences that do more than structurally or rhythmically shape movement; a building can inform movement, palpably imbuing movement with qualities or memories.[2] Returning to Cixous's words, we can say that it is as if blood flows in veins or tendrils between dancers; the space becomes alive with palpation. The sensing that occurs is multimodal and pervasive; this level of subtle awareness and responsivity is a corporeal analogy relevant to even the most sophisticated ubiquitous sensing system.

Elaborating Deleuze's account of Spinoza provides an understanding of kinetics, affect, and vitality that lends breadth to an ethics of the palpable. A body is defined according to two propositions: one is kinetic and the other is dynamic. The kinetic aspect of a body is that it is composed of an infinite number of particles in relations of motion and rest, speed and slowness; the dynamic aspect is that a body affects other bodies and is affected by other bodies. It has the capacity for affecting and being affected, not unlike the dynamic of the seeing–seen. The extent to which Spinozan bodies, originally formulated in the seventeenth century, can include responsive computational systems is uncanny: sensing systems operate according to feedback loops whereby they can be affected by the presence of something, usually us, and in turn affect our behavior for better, as in enhancing creativity or facilitating expression, or for worse, as in external surveillance of our movement to help others decide whether we are suspect persons. Ubiquitous systems are dynamic in that they are ways of facilitating or manipulating human affective states; they are kinetic in that they operate by constantly updating themselves, identifying motion and rest, constantly scrolling code or detecting presence.

Deleuze elaborates Spinoza's *Ethics* (2000) not in familiar religious or legal terms of good and bad as fixed notions producing rules or laws, but in terms of what increases or diminishes a body's vitality: "When a body 'encounters' another body, or an idea another idea, it happens that the two relations sometimes combine to form a more powerful whole, and sometimes one decomposes the other, destroying the cohesion of its parts" (1988, 19). We can see a ubiquitous system as another body—and its effects on us are actually affects; "we experience joy when a body encounters ours and enters into composition with it, and sadness when, on the contrary, a body or an idea threatens our own coherence" (19). If we regard our systems as bodies encountering our bodies, then the stakes are much higher: badly designed, invasive, or annoying systems act to cause a "decomposition of our self" with the associated affects of sadness and a reduction of vitality.

An implicit materiality resides in the ideas of composition and decomposition, opening an important dimension to our engagement with ubiquitous systems, which is what they may do to our bodies on a physical level. Ongoing debates relevant to this question include whether mobile phones damage our brains, the physiological and emotional impact of "sick buildings" ("intelligent" because they save energy by circulating less air) have a the physiological and emotional impact, the effect that a systemic hum or thrum has on our well-being, and how fluorescent lighting might diminish our vision, energy, and cognition. "All the phenomena that we group under the heading of Evil, illness, and death, are of this type: bad encounters, poisoning, intoxication, relational decomposition" (Deleuze 1988, 22). According to many ethical, political, and ideological approaches to contemporary life, this rather basic level of well-being is frequently elided in the interests of complex debates on rights, privileges, laws, and freedoms. When we think of whether our body achieves a state of composition or decomposition in encountering another body (or system), we have a way of accounting for well-being on both corporeal and civic levels.

Is it possible not only to attain a state of calm within ubiquitous systems, but perhaps also to achieve a state of vitality—by which we understand an enhancement of our mental, physical, emotional, and spiritual well-being? Relational decomposition, an adverse effect on any body that is counter to our vitality, is an excellent way of understanding our reaction to a poorly designed system: our focus is split, our imagination is curtailed, our creative potential is reduced to damage limitation, our engagement with others is stilted. From a dance perspective, this distinction between vitality and decomposition is the difference between a choreography that flows and leads us—the audience as well as the dancers—to new states of physical and creative expression and a choreography that is pleasing but somehow without lasting impact. The installation *trajets* (2000, 2007), which had the goal of sensing the paths of a group of people while activating video imagery and screen movement in response to their trajectories, was expanded from its original technological configuration seven years after it was first devised. Although the first version was not adverse, the second system for sensing and response (involving hardware, software, and video control) exemplified a stronger Spinozan sense of bodies entering into composition with one another. The installation was, without too much of a stretch to the imagination, a body.[3] The people inside it were bodies. The newer system affected people far more vividly: different qualifiers came from different people—*beautiful, meditative, poetic, transformative*. People stayed in it for longer, social groupings formed, and a wider range states of engagement were evident. People who were not dancers found themselves drawn into spontaneous and sometimes sustained improvisations with screens, drawn further into interactions based on a sense of joy.

If Spinoza's *Ethics* can be seen to be an "ethics of joy" where "only joy is worthwhile, joy remains, bringing us near to action, and to the bliss of action" (Deleuze 1988, 28), it is also important to chart the opposite: what happens when we enter into relational decomposition. When the latter happens, we are most separated from our powers of acting; we become alienated as if under the control of a "tyrant." Is this overstating things? Who has not felt, even in a small way, tyrannized by an interface or a system? Whether this system is the automated bank teller that swallows one's bank card or a QWERTY keyboard that causes wrist and neck pain or a neighbor's car alarm short-circuiting in the middle of the night, it is an external body that does not agree with our own bodies. "It is as if the power of that body opposed our power, bringing about a subtraction or a fixation; when this occurs, it may be said that our power of acting is diminished or blocked" (Deleuze 1988, 27). The result is sadness. I like to emphasize the composition of powers produced by *trajets*—that wonderful combination of vitality, dynamism, and joy—but, of course, affective range is never homogeneous in art or in ethics, and there were instances of a relational decomposition in the installation or a decrease in vitality on the part of at least one person, an elderly lady. The 2007 exhibition was in Barcelona, and something about the verticality of the moving screens and the dark environment made her think of being in prison under the fascist regime. This reaction was equally powerful and equally Spinozan.

Integrating Merleau-Ponty's insight with Deleuze's, I argue that ubiquitous computation all around us is not just a series of systems and devices; these systems and devices are bodies entering into contact with our bodies, with the result of increasing or decreasing vitality. Further, our bodies are composed in such a way that these systems become part of our very flesh. We are incomplete at all times, living an interiority that is defined by the invisible and oblivion. This means that the stakes are much higher when we build and deploy ubiquitous systems: we are not just making extensions of bodies; we are also permeating our bodies with computational bodies due to our porosity. Our very fabric and all of our relations with others and with

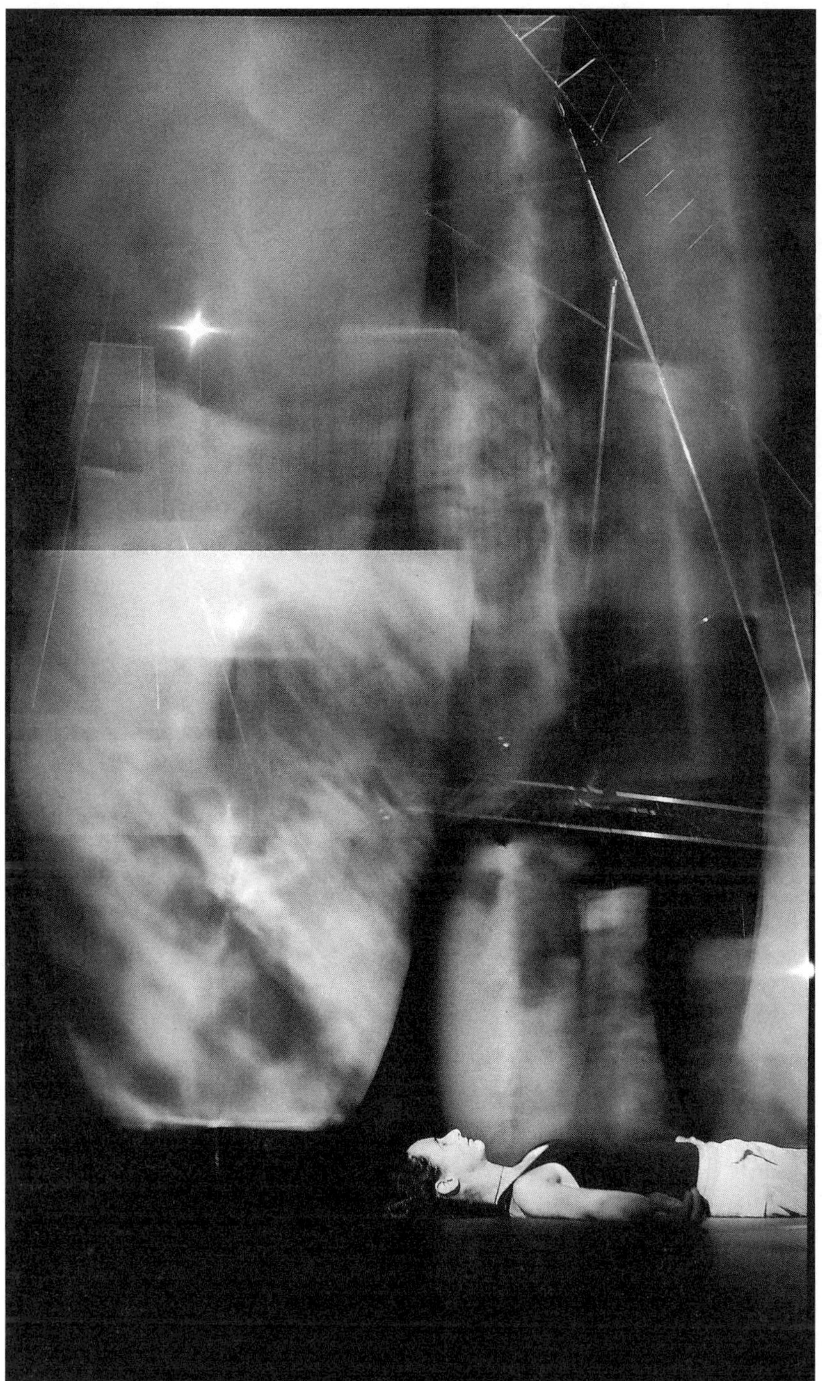

Figure 18.1
Franck Le Blanc, *Trajets Diptyque* (2007). Permission kindly granted by the artist.

Figure 18.2
Laurent Sales, *Trajets* (2005). Video still image. Permission kindly granted by the artist.

the world are shaped by what we build. We palpate others and the world, even caress them, with what we build.

The corporeal ethics sketched here reveals to what extent it is too simple to construe bodies as matter and ubiquity as somehow unseen, embedded, computational intelligence. This oversimplification is unhelpful in the way that most dualisms are unhelpful because they reduce and polarize. Instead of assuming a tension between corporeality and ubiquity, we would find it more compelling to probe ubiquity from a position of embedded corporeality. This is the point of asking a dancer to discuss ubiquity.

The real agenda behind this chapter's philosophical and performative rumination is the enhancement of human creativity, the expansion of human motion and expressivity. This expansion leads to a convergence between intuition and creativity, expression and embodiment, joy and life. I want my technologies to foster and facilitate this convergence. Of course, ubiquitous systems do not actually produce creativity, but they might contribute to shared affective, perceptual, expressive, intuitive, and embodied states that open onto creativity rather than the opposite. In this sense, Weiser gets us part of the way there, but there is more to ubiquitous computing than calmness.

Notes

1. The systems referred to include any networked system for tracking, connecting, or sensing human activities such as mobile phones, components of smart buildings (heating, lighting, air circulation, and other presence-detection functions), public-security systems, Global Positioning System devices, and Wi-Fi-enabled devices, but also more innocuous devices such as domestic sprinkler systems, car alarms, and children's toys.

2. The idea that a building can inform movement was the motivation for the *Yellow Memory* performance where the memories of the Gothic building that houses the Ukrainian Institute in New York City informed the movement vocabulary. Svitlana Matviyenko, dramaturgy; Inka Juslin, choreography; Susan Kozel, dance (2009).

3. *Trajets* was codirected by Gretchen Schiller and myself in collaboration with Robb Lovell, Pablo Mochcovsky, Scott Wilson, and Shaun Roth.

References

Augé, Marc. 2004. *Oblivion*. Translated by Marjolijn de Jager. Minneapolis: University of Minnesota Press.

Cixous, Hélène. 1998. *First Days of the Year*. Translated by Catherine A. F. MacGillivray. Emergent Literatures. Minneapolis: University of Minnesota Press.

Deleuze, Gilles. 1988. *Spinoza: Practical Philosophy*. Translated by Robert Hurley. San Francisco: City Lights.

Grøndahl, Jens Christian. 2000. *Silence in October*. Translated by Anne Born. Edinburgh: Canongate.

Kozel, Susan. 2007. *Closer: Performance, Technologies, Phenomenology*. Cambridge, MA: MIT Press.

Merleau-Ponty, Maurice. [1968] 1987. *The Visible and the Invisible*. Translated by Alphonso Lingis. Evanston, IL: Northwestern University Press.

Lilja, Efva. 2004. *Dance—For Better, For Worse*. Stockholm: ELD.

Schechner, Richard. 2003. *Performance Theory*. New York: Routledge.

Spinoza, Benedictus de. 2000. *Ethics*. Edited by G. H. R. Parkinson. Oxford: Oxford University Press.

Weiser, Mark, and John Seely Brown. 1996. "The Coming Age of Calm Technology." Available at http://nano.xerox.com/hypertext/weiser/acmfuture2endnote.htm. Accessed 15 August 2009.

Young, James E. 2004. "Foreword." In *Oblivion*, by Marc Augé, vii–xii. Minneapolis: University of Minnesota Press.

19 Affective Politics in Urban Computing and Locative Media

Anne Galloway

In the late 1980s, researchers began working on a "postdesktop" paradigm for human–computer interaction known as "ubiquitous" or "pervasive computing." Combining any number of mobile, networked, and context-aware technologies, this vision hinges on the possibility of embedding computational capacities in the objects and environments that surround us. Following Mark Weiser's (1991) vision of twenty-first-century computing and Weiser and John Seely Brown's (1997) model of "calm technology," researchers have worked to integrate computation into our everyday lives in ways that make it difficult to identify when and where we interact with these systems. For example, many of us are aware of or have used Global Positioning System (GPS) technologies in our vehicles or radio-frequency identification technologies in public-transportation passes such as London's Oyster card and Hong Kong's Octopus card. When sensor technologies are added to the mix, these systems can measure and monitor everything from environmental conditions such as air pollution or noise levels to bodily functions such as heart rate or temperature and connect such data to any number of applications or services. But people are also surrounded by thousands of computational devices that they cannot see or do not recognize. Although these technologies are certainly not infallible, interaction with such systems is generally so seamless that it is easy to overlook the significant infrastructure that underpins their management and use.

By the early 1990s, sufficient engineering and computer science advances had been made to bolster the claim that although the era of pervasive computing might not have yet arrived, it almost certainly would in the future. When research in these areas began to spread from university and corporate research labs to the popular imagination, there was an almost immediate reaction against such a totalizing vision of technological penetration of everyday life. In North America and Europe in particular, privacy concerns emerged front and center as commentators envisioned a world of absolute surveillance. Even within the human–computer interaction research community, responses were mixed. In the mid-1990s, strong criticism emerged, and researchers debated the pros and cons of developing such "dangerous" technologies (see, for example, Doheny-Farina 1994 and Porush 1995). However, technological limitations at the time still allowed researchers to claim that these social concerns were theoretical rather than actual, and the matter faded from public consciousness again until the early 2000s.

By the turn of the twenty-first century, mobile phone penetration was globally on the rise, and a vision of ubiquitous information and communication technologies no longer seemed a fantasy. Technologies that had not existed even five years earlier were becoming commonplace, and, firmly embedded within broader consumer desires for convenience and comfort, the pervasive computing vision began to roll out with unprecedented vigor. Industries and governments began heralding the coming "Internet of Things," where the global supply chain would be managed in ways that would create "smart objects" or a Web presence for consumer goods and personal objects. Popular media again tended to focus on the surveillance possibilities, and ubiquitous- or pervasive-computing discourse began to take on a distinctly dystopian tone. However, at the same time, new agendas in urban computing and locative media research and practice emerged to present a utopian countervision (see, for example, Proboscis 2009; Urban Atmospheres n.d.).

These research agendas importantly challenged the discursive construction of pervasive computing as "everywhere" by actually locating these technologies "somewhere." In doing so, urban-computing and locative-media discourse also stressed active engagement with new technologies to create more meaningful relations with the people, places, and objects that surround us. This call for collaborative, participatory, and creative action can be understood as a driving force behind an affective politics of urban computing and locative media, and after providing a brief introduction to exemplary discourses and practices, this chapter takes a closer look at how people's capacity to move and be moved both shapes and is shaped by new technologies. I am interested more specifically in how these affective politics embody a broader move from a disciplinary society's "power over" to a control society's "power to" as well as in how urban computing and locative media are enacted as both promise and threat.

A Brief History of Urban Computing and Locative Media

Urban computing is effectively a subset of ubiquitous or pervasive computing—a professional research agenda in engineering, computer science, human–computer interaction research, and design practice. In addition to researchers and "users" of urban computing, the actors at hand include publics and public spaces, corporate research laboratories, universities, conferences, workshops, academic journals, articles, Web logs, and so on. In 1999, before the launch of the Institute of Electrical and Electronics Engineers' *Pervasive Computing* journal, the First International Symposium on Handheld and Ubiquitous Computing took place in Karlsruhe, Germany. The second symposium was held in Bristol, United Kingdom. In 2001, the First International Conference on Ubiquitous Computing (known as "UbiComp 2001") replaced this series with the mandate to "bring together research practitioners in all disciplines developing the new paradigm of computing off-the-desktop that moves towards the notion of a disappearing or invisible computer" ("First International" 2001). At UbiComp 2003 in Seattle, architecture professor William J. Mitchell gave the keynote presentation on his book *Me++: The Cyborg Self and the Networked City* (2003), and both the multidisciplinary and urban dimensions of ubiquitous computing emerged front and center. In other words, "off the desktop" effectively became "in the city."

In July 2004, the Urban Atmospheres Research Project at Intel Research Berkeley held a one-day event called "Street Talk: An Urban Computing Happening." It announced a "gathering for an event to expose, deconstruct, and understand the challenges of this newly emerging moment in urban history and its dramatic influence on technology usage and adoption" (Urban Atmospheres 2004). The wide-ranging interests and alliances of urban computing were reinforced by international (North American, European) participants from industry (Intel, Microsoft), academics (anthropology, architecture, art and design, computer science, performance studies, sociology, urban studies), as well as independent artists and activists (including the Billboard Liberation Front) working in and around public spaces. Also present in the audience were representatives from the likes of NASA, France Telecom, Ricoh, IDEO, Nortel, and the Institute for the Future (an American nonprofit technology-foresight group). At a one-day workshop called "Ubicomp in the Urban Frontier" at UbiComp 2004 (in Nottingham, United Kingdom) the range of participants continued along the same lines, furthering the promise and expectation of broader stakeholder involvement.

In 2005 and 2006, the Intel researchers again collaborated with academics working in architecture and computer science to lead two more UbiComp workshops: "Metapolis and Urban Life" (in Tokyo) and "Exurban Noir" (in Orange County, California). The former sought to explore "urban projects for which the urban is not merely a palimpsest of our desires but an active participant in their formation" and to transform new technologies "into experiences that matter" (Paulos, Anderson, Chang, et al. 2005). The latter attempted to rise collectively to the "challenge of understanding the relationship between future technology comforts and social discontent" (Anderson, Burke, Paulos, et al. 2006). Building on the former, the University of California at Berkeley ran a "Metapolis" undergraduate class in architecture and new media in 2006, cotaught by academic (architecture) and industry (Intel, IDEO) partners. Also in 2006, the Center for Virtual Architecture, the Institute for Distributed Creativity, and the Architectural League of New York organized a public symposium called "Situated Technologies" that addressed how ubiquitous computing stood to reshape architecture and urbanism. In 2007 and 2008, *Everyware* author Adam Greenfield (2006) and designer Kevin Slavin taught a course called "Urban Computing" as part of New York University's Tisch School for the Arts' Interactive Telecommunications Program. Between 2007 and 2010, the organizers of the "Situated Technologies" event published a series of critical pamphlets, beginning with *Urban Computing and Its Discontents* (2007) by Adam Greenfield and architecture and media studies professor Mark Shepard. During the same period, in what I have elsewhere described as the "rise of the sensor citizen" (Galloway 2008), urban computing took a distinctly political turn with an increased interest in how these technologies might be mobilized to support a "citizen science."

Meanwhile and running parallel to the development of urban computing, locative media emerged from more artistic and explicitly political efforts. Christiane Paul (chapter 23 in this volume) provides an exemplary overview of a range of locative media, and Susan Kozel (chapter 19) outlines a corporeal ethics for ubiquitous computing, but I wish to draw attention to the politics mobilized by locative-media practitioners and projects. Whereas urban computing most often finds expression in high-profile academic conferences and classrooms, locative media manifest themselves in online forums, public workshops, and art festivals. Ben Russell's seminal *Headmap Manifesto*, subtitled *Know Your Place*, was first published in 1999 (reissued as *Headmap 3 Redux* in 2007). The original document comprised thirty-four pages of fragmented text and poetic ideas about location-aware devices, including the claim that "what was once the sole preserve of builders, architects and engineers falls into the hands of everyone: the ability to shape and organise the real world and the real space." Although the term *locative media* was initially coined by Karlis Kalnins as a "test category" for processes and products coming from the Locative Media Lab, an international network of artists and activists working with GPS and mobile technologies, locative-media practitioners were quick to distinguish their work as being enabled by technology rather than enabling technology, which was seen to be an academic, industry, and military activity. Russell later worked the manifesto's ephemeral and fragmented ideas into the introduction to the Locative Media Lab's *Transcultural Media Online Reader* to explain that

> locative media is a term that ties together a set of questions, critical perspectives and practices. Its catalytic premise was civilian awareness and engagement with a particular "operational construct" with military origins. . . . [The term] [l]ocative media is many things: A new site for old discussions about the relationship of consciousness to place and other people. A framework within which to actively engage with, critique, and shape a rapid set of technological developments. A context within which to explore new and old models of communication, community and exchange. A name for the ambiguous shape of a rapidly deploying surveillance and control infrastructure. (2004, para. 3)

The 2003 "RIXC Locative Media Workshop" took place in "a semi-abandoned former Soviet military base on the Baltic coast of Latvia," where a "diverse group of artists [came together] to contemplate, amongst other things, how to appropriate the

American military technology of GPS in the ruins of this former military city" (Tuters n.d., para. 1). Subsequent online discussions described locative-media practitioners as "keeping the technologies close to the ground, available for hacking, re-wiring and re-deploying in non-authoritarian ways" (Albert 2004, sec. 5, para. 1), and in 2004 Drew Hemment drew out the kind of politics he saw as locative media's primary contribution:

> Where the focus is placed upon the social before the spatial, either in the creation of open tools or in user-end applications, it becomes something fundamentally different. Like surveillance, locative media is [*sic*] a social project, but the grass-roots, social networks it advocates offer a critical distance to the system of domination of the control society. Locative media exults in the pleasure of locating and being located, and finds in this the basis for an emergent sociality—driven not by marketing but by networks of reciprocity and trust—as well as new ways of representing, relating to and moving in the world. . . . Locative media indicates how [location-based technologies] may be used not for pinning down but for opening up. (para. 5)

As we can see, locative-media discourse tends to be explicitly political, but the more academic discourse of urban computing can be seen to be equally if perhaps differently critical, and it is worth reminding ourselves of the significantly common ground between the two. Just as urban computing does not represent "pure" academic or industry research, locative media do not represent "pure" art or activism—especially if we believe that such activities are mutually exclusive or necessarily politically opposed. Despite their differences, what brings urban computing and locative media together is a shared interest in and commitment to a strongly collaborative, participatory, and creative use of new technologies. However, in the rest of this chapter I unpack the politics that accompany these interests—especially insofar as they promise "critical" positions—and ask how or if they can succeed in "subverting the dominant hegemony" and "contributing to the construction of new subjectivities" (Mouffe 2007, 5). With this in mind, I begin with a brief discussion on how technosocial hopes, expectations, and promises relate to affective politics.

New Technologies, Expectations, and Affective Politics

Just as a sociology of translation and actor–network theory (Callon 1986; Latour 2005; Law and Hassard 1999) during the past decade or so have grown in influence both within and beyond science and technology studies, the constitutive, performative, and generative qualities of social expectations have increasingly been recognized as playing important and intriguing roles in technological innovation (Brown, Rappert, and Webster 2000; Hedgecoe and Martin 2003; Brown and Michael 2002; Borup, Brown, Konrad, et al. 2006). Technosocial expectations are considered to be highly situated in the sense that they occupy particular spatial geographies and demonstrate particular temporal patternings. And yet, as Mads Borup and his colleagues explain,

"Expectations play a central role in science and technology not least because they mediate across boundaries between different scales, levels, times and communities" (2006, 293).

A sociology of expectations looks to the affective roles of imagination and desire in shaping technological change. Like most complex relations, expectations are generative in the sense that they

> guide activities, provide structure and legitimation, attract interest and foster investment. They give definition to roles, clarify duties, offer some shared shape of what to expect and how to prepare for opportunities and risks. Visions drive technical and scientific activity, warranting the production of measurements, calculations, material tests, pilot projects and models. . . . They play a central role in mobilizing resources both at the macro level, for example in national policy through regulation and research patronage, and at the meso-level of sectors and innovation networks, and at the micro-level within engineering and research groups and in the work of the single scientist or engineer. (Borup, Brown, Konrad, et al. 2006, 286)

Expectations are also performative in the sense that they attract interest from potential allies, define roles, and "build mutually binding obligations and agendas" (Borup, Brown, Konrad, et al. 2006, 286). As a sociology of translation would have it, expectations are "central in brokering relationships between different actors and groups" (289), and this scenario raises interesting questions about relations between imagination, materiality, and embodiment in technological innovation. It also explicitly ties expectations to affect because affective contagion (or lack thereof) increasingly plays a central role in the eventual acceptance or success of particular technologies.

Although ubiquitous computing, like all computing, can be seen to be historically embedded within complex global assemblages of military, industry, government, and public interests—including a fundamental belief in technological progress—it also currently occupies spaces that hinge on a specific future yet to happen or generic futures that *may not ever* happen. Borup and his colleagues further claim that "novel technologies and fundamental changes in scientific principle do not substantively pre-exist themselves, except and only in terms of the imaginings, expectations and visions that have shaped their potential" (2006, 285). Or as Bruno Latour rather elegantly explains:

> To say something is constructed means that it's not a mystery that has popped out of nowhere, or that it has a more humble but also more visible and more interesting origin. Usually, the great advantage of visiting construction sites is that they offer an ideal vantage point to witness the connections between humans and non-humans. Once visitors have their feet deep in the mud, they are easily struck by the spectacle of all the participants working hard at the time of their most radical metamorphosis. . . . Even more important, when you are guided to any construction site you are experiencing the troubling and exhilarating feeling that things *could be different*, or at least *they could still fail*—a feeling never so deep when faced with the final product, no matter how beautiful or impressive it may be. (2005, 88–89)

All of this reinforces the idea that pervasive computing involves persistent tensions between pasts, presents, and futures that make certain identities and objectives possible or probable and others impossible or improbable. Expectations can be positive or negative and are often, especially in the case of technoscience, put in terms of utopian or dystopian futures. Expectations in such cases are also associated with the belief that technoscientific progress is both a requirement and a promise, where practitioners, advocates, and adversaries of pervasive computing assume a certain technological inevitability and feel obligated to deliver the best possible product, service, or alternative solution in response to that inevitability.

To question ubiquitous computing today is to visit a few ruins and a host of construction sites as well as to follow "future abstractions [and] expectant projections that alter the now" in ways that involve "the future working back on the present" (Borup, Brown, Konrad, et al. 2006, 289). As these "wishful enactments of a desired future" are made real—or actualized—through a range of embodied interactions and material objects, "promissory commitments become part of a shared agenda and thus require action" (289). In these ways, future-oriented visions of ubiquitous computing can be seen to work primarily in the present to shape current relationships and to provide particular orientations toward the past, present, and future.

Put another way, technoscientific uncertainty is often countered by certain values and desires. Of particular interest here are the expectation that ubiquitous computing will be everywhere and beyond our control as well as the promise of urban computing and locative media to situate these technologies somewhere and within our control. Technoscientific and technosocial expectations actually involve tensions between what Michel Foucault calls "regimes of truth" and what Tiago Moreira and Paolo Palladino call "regimes of hope." As Foucault remarks, "'Truth' is to be understood as a system of ordered procedures for the production, regulation, distribution, circulation and operation of statements. 'Truth' is linked in a circular relation with systems of power which produce and sustain it, and to effects of power which it induces and which extend it. A 'regime' of truth" (1980, 133). A "regime of hope," in contrast, involves similar processes that evoke and invoke hope. This metaphor is most often associated with and indeed very well suited to emerging biotechnologies that stand to redefine life and death. As Moreira and Palladino summarize, "The 'regime of hope' is characterized by the view that new and better treatments are always about to come, being tested, 'in the pipeline.' . . . The 'regime of truth,' on the other hand, entails an investment in what is positively known, rather than what can be" (2005, 67).

Nik Brown more explicitly draws out the political and ethical dimensions of this parasitic relationship (cf. Serres 1982) between regimes of truth and hope. He claims that biotechnologies are not currently debated in terms of evidence or truth but instead involve discussions about "abstract future-oriented values representing a shift towards more aesthetic and symbolic references" (2007, 244) as well as a shift "from authority to authenticity" (Brown and Michael 2002, 259). This suggests that new biotechnologies are increasingly positioned not as evidential problems but as affective ones, where many different actors are assembled to negotiate affective roles. Although urban computing and locative media are obviously different kinds of technoscience, the metaphor of hope plays an important role in managing expectations in those domains as well. As Nik Brown and Alison Kraft explain,

> Futures and expectations are, by and large, shared attributes that in some circumstances can become embedded in what we might call "communities of promise." . . . Communities of promise are highly complex and multi-authored enterprises. It is rarely ever possible to ascribe responsibility for expectations to one actor rather than another. . . . [D]ifferent participants in a community of promise "conspire" or "collaborate" in the authorship of a future. . . . Agency is also complex across time as well as across present communities of promise. There are no "first causes" but rather a long and complex prefiguring of expectations through events, practices, statements and promises stretching through time. (2006, 323–324)

And, as suggested earlier, these prefigurings refer to particular interests invested in the present or in present potentials: "To enable hope requires the coordination and management of the conduct of individuals and groups so that a particular future may come into being" (Novas 2006, 291). If a particular translation has been successful, certain identities and associations become irreversible or path dependent. If truth can be loosely tied to materiality and hope to imagination, then expectations can be seen as relational objects that act as "bids" or tenders on the future (Berkhout 2006). These bids and expectations are understood to be conditional and flexible and are integral to the complex material and symbolic transformations that occur in processes of translation and that bring about particular associations.

The situatedness of associations should also compel our attention to the situatedness of expectations. As N. Katherine Hayles points out in regard to artificial-intelligence research paradigms,

> Whether or not the predicted future occurs as it has been envisioned, the effect is to shape how "human being" is understood *in the present*. . . . [T]he relation between humans and intelligent machines thus acts as a strange attractor, defining the phase space within which narrative pathways may be traced. What becomes difficult to imagine is a description of the human that does not take the intelligent machine as a reference point. . . . The future echoes through our present so persistently that it is not merely a metaphor to say the future has arrived before it has begun. When we compute the human, the conclusion that the human being cannot be adequately understood without ranging it alongside the intelligent machine has already been built into the very language we use. (2005, 132, 148)

With regard to the case of pervasive or ubiquitous computing, such a perspective suggests that expectations or promises concerning urban computing and locative media have more to do with present technosocial concerns—including social networking, participatory culture and politics, health monitoring and environmental sensing—

than they with future predictions. Expectations about urban computing and locative media likewise shape how we approach research in these areas today, along with our very definitions of and how we understand relations between humans, computers, and everyday urban life. Ben Anderson (2006) also explains that hope emerges from particular encounters, and in the case of urban computing and locative media I have alluded to the particular kinds of hope that emerge from the capacity to reconfigure a potential dystopian future with the possibility of a utopian one. For example, in a post-9/11 world, ubiquitous computing often evokes a future in which three models of power—panopticism (Foucault 1977), control (Deleuze 1997) and bare life (Agamben 1998)—come together under the mandate of machinic protocols to manage everyday life more effectively. Given such restrictive scenarios, urban-computing and locative-media projects instead try to offer people the ability to create richer and more meaningful connections to the people, places, and things around them. Furthermore, in an era marked by environmental degradation, we can see ubiquitous sensor technologies being employed in projects that attempt to move citizens to new kinds of political action involving the monitoring and tracking of environmental conditions.

The Promise and Threat of Urban Computing and Locative Media

Inke Arns also connects ubiquitous computing to the control society (chapter 22 in this volume), and I would like to draw out some of the ways in which urban computing and locative media's affective politics comprise both promise and threat (cf. Seigworth and Gregg 2010). I described earlier how expectations and promises affect technological change, and I discussed the rise of urban computing and locative media as distinct but related promises put forward to challenge expectations of a more dystopian future of ubiquitous computing. More specifically, where visions of pervasive computing have tended to conjure images of absolute technological penetration everywhere, locative media and urban computing have promised to situate new technologies in particular places by connecting stories to them or extracting data from them. Furthermore, the affective politics that have accompanied and indeed driven both approaches are characterized by expectations of individual agency and public good that are seen to challenge fears of surveillance and top-down control.

However, although urban computing and locative media can indeed function as "regimes of hope," their prefiguring of futurity also clears a space–time for movement in much the same way a society of control is characterized by "power to" (Deleuze 1997) rather than "power over" (Foucault 1980). For example, Brian Massumi suggests that "our degree of freedom at any one time corresponds to how much of our experiential depth we can access toward a next step—how intensely we are living and moving" (2002, 214), and urban computing and locative media are also characterized by their desire and ability to extend and transmit urban experience, either by providing greater depth of knowledge and awareness of a space or by overlaying information on existing places and objects. So just as the microscope is expected to compensate for the limitations of the naked eye, ubiquitous computing is expected, at least in part, to overcome the constraints of the physical world or space–time. Rather than being detached from the world around us, we are expected to become more deeply embedded in it. Knowledge similarly becomes a matter of knowing interiority or what is going on *inside of* or *under* the surface of things. In this vision of the city or local environment as an interaction design space, urban computing and locative media also extend *over* the entire built and natural environment, enacting another layer of exteriority to be experienced. The extensibility and transmissibility of the city (or of part of it) and an increased ability to be embedded within it are foundational elements of the affective politics at hand.

Following Ash Amin and Nigel Thrift (2002) as well as John Urry (2003), Mike Michael describes this complex enactment of spatiality as a matter of disclosure, where new technologies work to open up rather than enclose places (2006, 113–115), thereby performing what Mike Crang (2000) calls a "transmissible" space. The rich potential of these experiences also recalls a "deepening" of meaning (Latour 2005) in terms of increased connections or an augmenting of what Michael also calls the "density of spaces" (2006, 117). Nonetheless, many urban-computing and locative-media projects also—whether on purpose or by accident—position everyday places and social interaction as somewhat lacking or in need of improvement. It also seems that some practitioners believe that everyday life has already been irrevocably and perhaps rather unfortunately colonized by information and communication technologies. They promise, then, to improve the quality of our future interactions by enabling us to make contact (only) with other people and places of our own choosing.

Indeed, when the city becomes a technological platform, certain social possibilities and potentialities are able to multiply. In these "critical" scenarios, the real (i.e., lived, vital) world is inseparable from the digital world. People with the proper technological capacities are able to live in each time and space of the places to which they have access; past and future events are made present; they can move and be moved in many directions. However, this story and the "critical" future it expects also bracket out the possibility of what happens, for example, if these technologies are unequally distributed. The very development of urban-computing and locative-media applications has depended on stable and affordable access to technological infrastructure, and people without the proper preexisting technosocial capacities get stuck in an incomplete present, without the sense of potential afforded by memories and dreams, never quite able to experience or live a fully augmented life. These expectations and promises also preclude technological failure (Will we all be doomed to a less than full life? Will our very lives break down?) as well as any unintended consequences (What if we drown in these depths of field? What if we want to forget? Or what if someone else chooses for us?). Where Chantal Mouffe (2007) seeks counterhegemony and new subjectivity from critical aesthetic expression, urban computing and locative media speak almost the same language of the capitalist–military–industrial enterprise from which they also seek to distance themselves.

This brings me to one of the most intriguing aspects of urban-computing and locative-media projects: how they suggest that the "political" is actually quite complex and conflicted as well as how critical distance (positionality) always already chafes against timing, tempos, and rhythms (mobility). This sense of affective politics is akin to notions of "controlled falling" (Massumi 2002) or to highways that permit freedom of movement within clearly prescribed boundaries (Deleuze 1998). As Massumi argues, "Capitalism starts intensifying or diversifying affect, but only in order to extract surplus-value. It hijacks affect in order to intensify profit potential. It literally valorises affect" (2002, 224). I see the same happening in much urban-computing and locative-media discourse and practice, and, like Massumi, I am troubled and confused by an apparent "convergence between the dynamic of capitalist power and the dynamic of resistance" (Massumi 2002, 224). Given this ambiguity, the crucial point I wish to make about the affective politics at hand is, as Gregory Seigworth and Melissa Gregg point out, "that there are no ultimate or final guarantees—political, ethical, aesthetic, pedagogic, and otherwise—that capacities to affect and to be affected will yield an actualized next or new that is somehow better than 'now'" (2010, 9–10).

Because an affective politics is necessarily processual, we are faced not with the predicament of choosing between the (absolute/final) absence or presence of something "good" or "bad," but rather with being modulated through greater or lesser intensities of each. It is in this way that urban computing and locative media emerge as both promise and threat. These concatenations of humans and nonhumans make it difficult to distinguish productively between subject and object, interior and exterior, proximity and distance—and perhaps that is where an affective politics most starkly contrasts with more traditional neoliberal understandings of the "political." If pervasive or ubiquitous computing can be seen as having power "over" us—extending everywhere and all the time, enclosing bodies or encouraging bodies to enclose themselves—then urban computing and locative media (re)present control and the power "to" escape, change, and so on. In this scenario, things may get better, but they may get worse. There is indeed (political) hope to be found here, but the collaboration, connection, participation, and enrichment that are so often promised in critiques of or resistance to pervasive computing should not be assumed and cannot be assured. The most "critical" projects are always already embedded within the systems they seek to resist, and I suggest that as long as we allow our efforts to fall into either the dystopian camp or the utopian camp, then we are stuck with ideologies that perpetuate disciplinary power over us. I believe that approaching new technologies from the perspective of control does not dilute the critical project as much as it forces us to acknowledge the limits of our critiques. Hope, however fragile, affects people in unexpected and unpredictable ways; urban-computing and locative-media projects have suggested alternate paths for ubiquitous computing, not good or bad, but gloriously better, horribly worse, and everywhere in between.

References

Agamben, Giorgio. 1998. *Homo Sacer: Sovereign Power and Bare Life*. Translated by Daniel Heller-Roazen. Stanford, CA: Stanford University Press.

Albert, Saul. 2004. "Locative Literacy." *Mute*, 12 July. Available at http://www.metamute.org/en/Locative-Literacy. Accessed 17 November 2010.

Amin, Ash, and Nigel Thrift. 2002. *Cities: Reimagining the Urban*. Cambridge, UK: Polity.

Anderson, Ben. 2006. "Hope for Nanotechnology: Anticipatory Knowledge and the Governance of Affect." *Area* 39 (2): 156–165.

Anderson, Ken, Anthony Burke, Eric Paulos, and Amanda Williams. 2006. "Exurban Noir." Available at http://drzaius.ics.uci.edu/meta/exurban-noir. Accessed 17 November 2010.

Berkhout, Frans. 2006. "Normative Expectations in Systems Innovation," *Technology Analysis & Strategic Management* 18 (3–4), 299–311.

Borup, Mads, Nik Brown, Kornelia Konrad, and Harro Van Lente. 2006. "The Sociology of Expectations in Science and Technology." *Technology Analysis & Strategic Management* 18 (3–4): 285–298.

Brown, Barry, Richard Harper, and Nicola Green, eds. 2001. *Wireless World: Social and Interactional Aspects of the Mobile Age*. London: Springer.

Brown, Nik. 2007. "The Aestheticisation of Futurity: From Facts to Values—Authority to Authenticity." In *Tensions and Convergences: Technological and Aesthetic Transformations of Society*, edited by Reinhard Heil, Andreas Kaminski, Marcus Stippak, Alexander Unger, and Marc Ziegler, 237–252. Bielefeld, Germany: Transcript/Transaction.

Brown, Nik, and Alison Kraft. 2006. "Blood Ties: Banking the Stem Cell Promise," *Technology, Analysis & Strategic Management* 18 (3/4): 313–327.

Brown, Nik, and Mike Michael. 2002. "From Authority to Authenticity: The Changing Governance of Biotechnology." *Health, Risk, & Society* 4 (2): 259–272.

Brown, Nik, Brian Rappert, and Andrew Webster, eds. 2000. *Contested Futures: A Sociology of Prospective Techno-Science*. Aldershot, UK: Ashgate.

Callon, Michel. 1986. "Some Elements of a Sociology of Translation: Domestication of the Scallops and the Fishermen of St Brieuc Bay." In *Power, Action, & Belief: A New Sociology of Knowledge?* edited by John Law, 196–229. London: Routledge & Kegan Paul.

Crang, Mike. 2000. "Urban Morphology and the Shaping of the Transmissable City." *City* 4 (3): 303–315.

Deleuze, Gilles. 1998. "Having an Idea in Cinema (On the Cinema of Straub-Huillet)." Translated by Eleanor Kaufman. In *Deleuze and Guattari: New Mappings in Politics, Philosophy, and Culture*, edited by Eleanor Kaufman and Kevin Jon Heller, 14–19. Minneapolis: University of Minnesota Press.

Deleuze, Gilles. 1997. *Negotiations: 1972–1990*. Translated by Martin Joughin. New York: Columbia University Press.

Doheny-Farina, Stephen. 1994. "Default = Offline, or Why Ubicomp Scares Me." *Computer-Mediated Communication Magazine* 1 (6): 18.

Foucault, Michel. 1980. *Power/Knowledge: Selected Interviews and Other Writings, 1972–1977*. Edited by Colin Gordon. New York: Pantheon.

Foucault, Michel. 1977. *Discipline and Punish: The Birth of the Prison*. Translated by Alan Sheridan. New York: Pantheon Books.

Galloway, Anne. 2008. "The Rise of the Sensor Citizen: Community Mapping Projects and Locative Media." *Receiver* 21. Available at http://www.receiver.vodafone.com/the-rise-of-the-sensor-citizen. Accessed 17 November 2010.

Greenfield, Adam. 2006. *Everyware: The Dawning Age of Ubiquitous Computing*. Berkeley, CA: New Riders.

Greenfield, Adam, and Mark Shepard. 2007. *Urban Computing and Its Discontents*. Situated Technologies Pamphlets 1. New York: Architectural League of New York.

Hayles, N. Katherine. 2005. "Computing the Human." *Theory, Culture, & Society* 22 (1): 131–151.

Hedgecoe, Adam, and Paul Martin. 2003. "The Drugs Don't Work: Expectations and the Shaping of Pharmacogenetics." *Social Studies of Science* 33 (3) (2003): 327–384.

Hemment, Drew. 2004. "The Locative Dystopia." *Nettime*, 9 January. Available at http://www.nettime.org/Lists-Archives/nettime-l-0401/msg00021.html. Accessed 17 November 2010.

Latour, Bruno. 2005. *Reassembling the Social: An Introduction to Actor–Network Theory*. Oxford: Oxford University Press.

Law, John, and John Hassard, eds. 1999. *Actor Network Theory and After*. Oxford: Blackwell.

Massumi, Brian. 2002. "Navigating Movements." In *Hope: New Philosophies for Change*, edited by Mary Zournazi, 210–243. London: Routledge.

Michael, Mike. 2006. *Technoscience and Everyday Life*. Oxford: Oxford University Press.

Mitchell, William. 2003. J. *Me++: The Cyborg Self and the Networked City*. Cambridge, MA: MIT Press.

Moreira, Tiago, and Paolo Palladino. 2005. "Between Truth and Hope: On Parkinson's Disease, Neurotransplantation, and the Production of the 'Self.'" *History of the Human Sciences* 18:55–82.

Mouffe, Chantal. 2007. "Artistic Activism and Agonistic Spaces." *Art & Research: A Journal of Ideas, Contexts, and Methods* 1 (2): 1–5.

Novas, Carlos. 2006. "The Political Economy of Hope: Patients' Organizations, Science, and Biovalue." *BioSocieties* 1:289–305.

Paulos, Eric, Ken Anderson, Michele Chang, Anthony Burke, and Tom Jenkins. 2005. "Metapolis and Urban Life." Available at http://www.urban-atmospheres.net/Ubicomp2005. Accessed 17 November 2010.

Porush, David. 1995. "Ubiquitous Computing vs. Radical Privacy: A Reconsideration of the Future." *Computer-Mediated Communication Magazine* 2 (3): 46.

Proboscis. 2009. "Urban Tapestries." March 11. Available at http://urbantapestries.net. Accessed November 17, 2010.

Russell, Ben. 2007. *Headmap 3 Redux*. Available at http://www.banffcentre.ca/bnmi/programs/archives/2003/wireless_laboratory/presentations/wireless_head_map_banff.pdf. Accessed 17 November 2010.

Russell, Ben. 2004. Introduction to *Transcultural Media Online Reader*, by Locative Media Lab. Available at http://web.archive.org/web/20060720212044/locative.net/tcmreader/index.php?intro;russell. Accessed 17 November 2010.

Russell, Ben. 1999. *Headmap Manifesto: Know Your Place*. Available at http://tecfa.unige.ch/~nova/headmap-manifesto.PDF. Accessed 17 November 2010.

Seigworth, Gregory J., and Melissa Gregg. 2010. "An Inventory of Shimmers." In *The Affect Theory Reader*, edited by Melissa Gregg and Gregory J. Seigworth, 1–25. Durham, NC: Duke University Press.

Serres, Michel. 1982. *The Parasite*. Baltimore: Johns Hopkins University Press.

Tuters, Mark. n.d. "[TCM 1] The Trans-Culture Mapping Network & the Icelandic Workshop." Available at http://www.rixc.lv/reader/txt/txt.php?id=173&l=en&raw=1. Accessed 17 November 2010.

"First International Conference on Ubiquitous Computing [30 September–2 October 2001]." 2001. Available at http://www.ubicomp.org/ubicomp. Accessed 17 Nov. 2010.

Urban Atmospheres. 2004. "Street Talk: An Urban Computing Happening." 16 July. Available at http://www.urban-atmospheres.net/StreetTalk. Accessed 17 November 2010.

Urban Atmospheres. n.d. "Citizen Science." Available at http://www.urban-atmospheres.net/CitizenScience. Accessed 17 November 2010.

Urry, John. 2003. *Global Complexity*. Cambridge, UK: Polity.

Weiser, Mark. 1991. "The Computer for the 21st Century." *Scientific American* 265 (3): 94–104.

Weiser, Mark, and John Seely Brown. 1997. "The Coming Age of Calm Technology." In *Beyond Calculation: The Next Fifty Years of Computing*, edited by P. J. Denning, 75–85. New York: Copernicus.

20 Machinic Sutures: From Eighteenth-Century Physiognomy to Twenty-First-Century Makeover

Bernadette Wegenstein

In this chapter, I develop the notion of "machinic suture" in the context of a historical analysis of what I call "the cosmetic gaze." If the term *cosmetic gaze* refers to how humans have come to experience their bodies and those of others as incomplete projects, awaiting the intervention of whatever technologies of enhancement are available in order to better approximate their true self or natural potential, *machinic suture* names the operation through which the supposedly prior or pure aspects of selfhood—my true self, how I desire to be, my body—have become so via the performative influence of augmented realities. These concepts thus complement the growing theoretical discussion around ubiquitous computing—not, however, because they presuppose physically ubiquitous computational machines, but rather because digital technologies have adapted themselves so easily to the operations of machinic sutures, operations that have been in effect in a variety of technological regimes for a very long time.

To this extent, the concept of machinic suture supports the implicit and explicit position taken by many of the scholars included in this volume that the concept of virtuality on its own fails to account for the phenomena and experiences associated with the rise of ubiquitous or pervasive computing. Far from an endorsement of constructivism, in other words, the concept of machinic suture undergirds the realization that bodily experiences take place in and by means of mediated environments and that mediated environments are thoroughly embodied affairs. To state this is not to undermine the importance of virtual environments, however. Although I may agree with Jay David Bolter and his colleagues in their assertion that "the ontology of mixed reality is therefore different from that of [virtual reality]" (chapter 18 in this volume), I must nonetheless clarify that the existence and pervasiveness of both contribute to the current nature of the machinic suture. Likewise, if a philosophical sequitur of the analysis of ubiquitous computing is, as Mark Hansen (2006) indicates, that *all reality is mixed reality*, the conceptual distinction between mixed reality and machinic suture is that whereas the former refers primarily to a technical state of affairs, the latter describes the internal influence of such states of affairs on subjective formation.

Susan Kozel's contribution to this volume (chapter 19) reinforces the growing emphasis on the embodied nature of even potentially virtual experiences with her coinage of the term *ubicorp* (ubiquitous corporeality) as a counterbalance to *ubicomp*. Cognizance of the fact that "ubicorp is a precondition for ubicomp" leads us to the question of what she calls "corporeal ethics" because "ubiquitous computing all around is not just a series of systems and devices, [but] bodies entering into contact with our bodies, with the result of increasing or decreasing vitality." Although the standard of vitality certainly poses the ethical question in stark terms by proposing a measure for ethical judgments about the effects of machinic sutures on subjective formation, it does not necessarily make such assessments any easier. Whether the decision to undergo surgical interventions under the sway of the cosmetic gaze increases or decreases vitality is a thorny question, made thornier by the ambiguity of the concept of "vitality" itself. But there can be no doubt that the formulation of an ethical question at the heart of ubiquitous computing is of great importance.

A final connection to note comes from Anne Galloway's contribution, immediately preceding this one, on the artistic practice known as "locative media." If we grant that sense of place in space is a core aspect of any phenomenological understanding of selfhood, to what extent and in what ways might the increasing ubiquity of locative technologies such as Global Positing System devices and handheld computers constitute a new machinic suture? If my imagining of where I currently am in relation to a destination or provenance takes the form of a page from Google Maps or the navigational screen of a TomTom, then my basic sense of place is already the effect of a complex interaction between memory, sense perception, satellite communications, and a digital interface.

In the historical vignettes and case studies discussed here, I trace a few instances of how machinic sutures have structured the cosmetic gaze. The point of this exploration is to show that if examples of ubiquitous computing such as facial-recognition software have extraordinary potential for structuring the cosmetic gaze today, it is only because they are instances of a machinic suture that has long been at work informing how bodies perceive themselves as well as their most intimate potentials.

The Science of Nineteenth-Century Physiognomy

When it comes to people, we almost can't help violating the proverbial prohibition against judging a book by its cover. Cultures are continually motivated—religiously, scientifically, or empirically—to find a "pure language" (Zelle 1993, 52) with universal rules for reading and interpreting authoritatively the connection between the inside of a person, his or her "character" or "soul," and his or her outer appearance as well as to locate the technology that would be most truthful and helpful in this attempt. If we understand "inside" and "outside" in the sense of a Deleuzian *assemblage* that has neither base nor superstructure (Deleuze and Guattari 1987, 90), the idea behind this universal language would be to "read" a person through and through—the outcome of which would be a human "plane of consistency," where character and appearance merge into the *person*. It should be evident that the series Ulrik Ekman articulates in his introduction to this volume—wherein Gilbert Simondon's notions of disparation and transduction inform Gilles Deleuze and Félix Guattari's machinic assemblage, which in turn influences Mark Hansen's own rethinking of mixed realities—is fully operative here. The machinic suture deployed at the core of the cosmetic gaze fuses the physical perception of bodies with an implicit moral matrix; informing the mixed reality as relation of a preindividual field and an informative event, in other words, the machinic suture precedes and makes possible the very individual in the act of perceiving his or her own or another person's body.

US phrenologist Samuel R. Wells, a traveling professor who offered popular lectures on phrenology and analyzed heads across the United States in the late nineteenth century, expressed judgment of character when he proposed that the white man's "prominent" and "high" forehead is a sign of wisdom and intellectuality ([1895] 1971, 5). This forehead is contrasted to the forehead of the "lowlander" (not named), shown from a straight profile (figure 20.1), which—just from its representation in the portrait—looks shorter and emphasizes the more "observant and practical" character trait, supposedly resulting from the predominating lower part of the forehead.

Figure 20.1
The forehead of the "lowlander." From Wells [1895] 1971, 5.

Hepworth Dixon is here the example of a "thoughtful"-looking man, whereas the unnamed lowlander is merely observant and hence lacking a certain reflective capacity. This desire to see through the "mask of the face" was in part driven by a "science of the mind" emerging in the later nineteenth and early twentieth centuries (Hartley 2001, 3); in the science of physiognomy, apart from the measuring of heads and bodies, photographs were used as "objective examples" of various categories of minds, like the Italian criminal-anthropologist Cesare Lombroso's (1835–1909) collection of "criminals" (figure 20.2).

This album stems from the fifth and last edition of Lombroso's tome on criminal anthropology, *Criminal Man* (Lombroso and Ferrero [1896–1897] 2006, 202), featuring illustrations and photographs not only of criminal types, but also ethnic types such as Germans and others. Lombroso did not take these photographs himself; rather, as he reports, colleagues from around the world would send him their collections in order to increase the criminal anthropologist's master database. Lombroso used his database for his theory of *atavism*, "primitive man," in which the physiognomical proximity to the animal becomes the indicator for the character.

A contemporary of Lombroso, Sir Francis Galton (1822–1911)—a cousin of Charles Darwin known mostly for his advances in statistics, twin studies, and the method of finger printing—was very impressed by Darwin's insights, and so in his 1869 treatise *Hereditary Genius* he set out to prove that human faculties are not divine givens but transmitted from generation to generation. Galton developed a particular technology to prove his point: the method of *composite portraiture* (figure 20.3). With this method, he produced typologies of races, allowing a comparison between the average faces of parental generations with that of their offspring, supposedly revealing the real character of single individuals as criminal, ill, or healthy people (1883, 9).

Composite portraiture, hence, becomes a true *physiognomical* technology by ostensibly presenting the essence of a person's inborn character. Or, to put it into a Deleuzian language, the *tool* of the composite portraiture defined the machinic assemblage of the nineteenth century, when the judgment residing at the fault line between outer appearance and inner essence took the form of a purported science trying to read the mind from the outside. We might say that this trend continued throughout the twentieth century medically, cognitively, psychoanalytically, and visually, with more and more accurate *tools* to render the internal sphere of the mind—for instance, via brain-imaging technology.[1] But Wells, Galton, and Lombroso were not the first ones to believe in the signs of the *kalókagathia*, the intrinsic relationship between moral goodness and a beautiful or trustworthy appearance. Such a belief, which had been deeply implemented into the Western consciousness from antiquity onward, was highly dependent on a religious determinism in which the relation between the good and the beautiful were believed to have been fixed by God.

28 Album of Criminal Photographs
Editors' note: Photography became a modern tool of criminal investigation in the late nineteenth century, allowing police to identify repeat offenders. Lombroso believed that he could identify born criminals solely from photographs sent to him from colleagues around the world.
Source: Lombroso, *L'uomo delinquente*, edition 4.

Figure 20.2
Atlas of illustrations and photographs of criminal types. From Lombroso, Criminal Man, 1876.

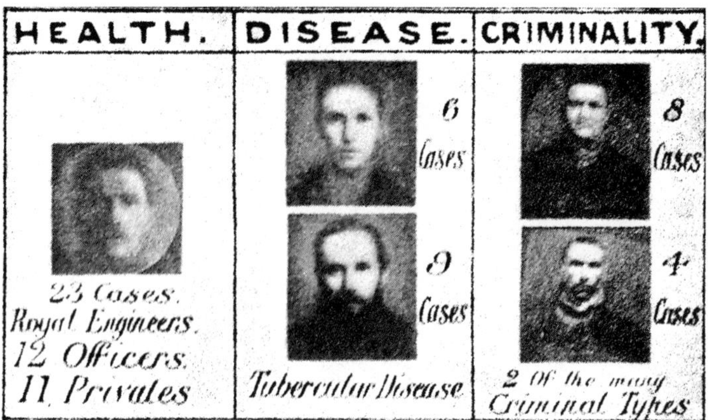

Figure 20.3
Specimens of composite portraiture: health, disease, criminality. From Galton 1883, 9.

The Concept of *Kalókagathia*: "The Good and the Beautiful"

Although in Plato's times the term *kalókagathia* or *kaloi kagathoi* (its more common use) referred to "gentlemanly nobility"—that is, to someone who was raised right or possessed the proper culture,[2] the term itself is not that easy to track down,[3] having gone through a series of vicissitudes from antiquity to the age of Enlightenment ethics in the first half of the eighteenth century, when it was finally fused into the concept of the "beautiful soul" (Norton 1995). This is also the time that the Swiss theologian and physiognomist Johann Caspar Lavater (1741–1801) produced his *Physiognomische Fragmente zur Beförderung der Menschenkenntnis und Menschenliebe* (*Physiognomical Fragments for the Promotion of the Knowledge and Love of Man*) (the original published in 1775–1778, the translation in 1789), a best seller in its time, deeply indebted to the theological notion of *kalókagathia.*

Lavater, unlike Galton—who had proposed to replace religion with eugenics—founded his physiognomy on the belief in divine determination of character, that there is a direct connection between morality and outer appearance: "Beauty and ugliness have a strict connection with the moral constitution of Man. In proportion as he is morally good, he is handsome; and ugly, in proportion as he is morally bad" (1788, 135).[4] Lavater comes to this conclusion by careful logical deduction: morally beautiful states of being express themselves beautifully on the body, particularly on the face. Morally ugly or bad states of the soul accordingly express themselves through a negative countenance. In other words, the face is a general expression of a current state of mind, just as in the classic art of rhetoric, in which the face is supposed to underline and express a speaker's feelings.[5] This means that, for Lavater, whether we are good or bad people is not merely a question of inborn beauty or ugliness; rather, the movement has to be inverted: what is in someone's soul will most likely be visible on his countenance. But Lavater also limits his position immediately by pointing out that virtue beautifies and vice uglifies, hence intensifies what is already there to begin with. That said, even Lavater admits that socioeconomic circumstances such as climate, profession, illness, and profession are influential on the appearance. Moreover and most important, improvement for Lavater is always possible and desirable. Despite the fact that certain predispositions of the mind and body are inherited, you *can* better yourself: "That the whole bony system with the fleshy parts, the whole frame taken together—figure, colour, voice, gait, smell—everything, in a word, has a relation to the face, and is liable to degradation or improvement[6] together with it" (1789, 147–148).

I want to emphasize the linkage of appearance and attitude based on *aesthetic and moral judgment* in all of these historical examples. This judgment has sunken into the various historical moments discussed here as a way of looking for what has been marked as "better" by an authoritative gaze coming from the eyes not only of such physiognomists as Johann Caspar Lavater, such phrenologists as Samuel Wells, such anthropologists as Cesare Lombroso, and such scientists as Sir Francis Galton, but even such men as the official racial theorist of the National Socialists, Hans F. K. Günther (1891–1968), who established a theory of the superiority of the Nordic race based on anthropometrical data.[7]

These historical examples showcase that the search for the perfect or bettered self or both is framed in moral terms as a desire to make outward appearances conform to a truer, inner self that somehow represents more accurately a person's character. Although the purity of that inner character was assumed in these historical cases, the technologies through which self-imagining and ultimately self-enhancement are made possible have changed. Whereas the historical examples showcase an assemblage of images, of which all strata can still be experienced (by superimposition, by contrasting "before" and "after"), the more integrated technologies of the twenty-first century have blurred the lines of the assemblage to attempt the completion of a "Nature–Society machinic assemblage" (Deleuze and Guattari 1987, 90).

As I mentioned earlier, the cosmetic gaze refers to how the act of looking at our bodies and those of others is already informed by the techniques, expectations, and strategies of bodily modification. As shown in the historical examples, the cosmetic gaze is also and perhaps most important a moralizing gaze, a way of looking at bodies as awaiting an improvement, physical and spiritual, that is already present in the body's structure as an absence or a need. To the extent that the cosmetic gaze represents an urge to self-realization or self-perfection, that urge or drive is always structured by the organization or mediation through which embodiment is historically enabled. In other words, the very true self on which any sort of self-enhancement is justified is itself nothing other than the reification of a historically and culturally specific technological mode of mediation, through which a given body comes to know itself and to perceive itself as lacking and needing just this "fix" to achieve itself. This realization thus permits us to ask how the cosmetic gaze is manifested in today's culture of the quick fix, how it is commodified, and how it informs those who operate with it, quite literally, as the "aesthetic surgeons" or software-program engineers of "beautification engines."[8]

In a media culture like ours, characterized at least in part by the environment of ubiquitous computing, we find the cosmetic gaze assembled into in its operative toolkit, as we can see with such games as *Sims 1, 2,* and *3,* where children can create a rounder jaw, a more even forehead than that of the lowlander, and a smoother and lighter skin color than that of Lombroso's criminals or where they can play God by modifying nose sizes as well as character traits—all examples of the possibility of improvement that Lavater raised in his physiognomy: slight or drastic changes that suit our bodies or our character better than the "original."

But as Mark Hansen points out, any reality is a mixed reality (2006, 8), for which the dream of total immersion that has preoccupied the moving image at least since André Bazin's "reality thirst" had to be abandoned. The question is not the mixture of realities per se, but how we proceed seamlessly from one to the other reality. In the next two sections, I look more closely at two areas of proliferation of today's cosmetic gaze: cosmetic surgery patients, who presumably know their faces and have decided to reinvent them with the help of surgeons, hence creating a new reality for themselves; and the virtual creation of existing faces by the faceprint software program used by the UK police to create "identikit" pictures, hence rewriting a reality as experienced by an eyewitness.

Cosmetic Surgery

Susan and Pat, two housewives from New Port Beach, one of the top global environments of the cosmetic surgery industry, told me in an interview (in the documentary film *Made Over in America* [Wegenstein and Rhodes 2007]) that for them the motivation to undergo cosmetic surgery was not to look like an entirely different person, but to look and feel "subtly refreshed" (figure 20.4).

Susan emphasized that the overall goal for her was to make life "easier: "it's just sort of easier in a way, and it's feminine and just fun when your clothes fit you well and you look good. You know, you put on a dress, and it's nicer to have a strap-dress and then have a curvy figure, and just do it easy." In fact, Susan mentioned that on the "job market" for becoming a spouse there is no doubt that this refreshed look helps, too, when "lots of men in this area are health conscious and are looking for women with the same thoughtfulness and self-respect." What is striking about these

Figure 20.4
Susan: "We don't want to look like an entirely different person." Film still from *Made Over in America* (Wegenstein and Alan 2007). Courtesy of Icarus Films.

statements is how cosmetic surgery, an invasive surgical procedure under the influence of anesthesia, gets listed as "healthy." Within makeover discourse, "healthy" has come to mean "beautiful" in the neo-Darwinian sense of a genetically predetermined desire to procreate and guarantee one's offspring with the healthiest—that is, most beautiful—partner (see Thornhill 1998 on Darwinian aesthetics).

Susan's friend Pat is between twenty and thirty years older. It is hard to tell, though. Her surgery is still an example of a drastic intervention and reinvention of her face and is reminiscent of the "face-lift" popular after the World War II, when women became particularly concerned with aging (figure 20.5). The common "face-lift" helped them feel better about themselves and their world rather than changing their faces (Tyler May 1988). Pat's look adheres to the logic of the "Old New Face," as the popular dermatologist and beauty-product-line developer Patricia Wexler, MD, puts it, pointing to the example of Ivana Trump: "When she got a totally new face in the early nineties—a new jawline, a new eyebrow arch—that was a *new* face. She is now aging as a whole different person. The new version of the New Face is that it shouldn't look new. It should look like you. It should look like the *old* you" (quoted in Van Meter 2008). The new face, that "subtly refreshed" version of yourself that Susan wanted, is supposed to look like you "four films ago," in Hollywood jargon. In other words, the new face is an evolutionary likely resemblance of you or a "fantastic approximation," as Jonathan Van Meter (2008) has it.

Figure 20.5
Pat: "I have had cosmetic surgery done and am making no secret of it." Film still from *Made Over in America* (Wegenstein and Alan 2007). Courtesy of Icarus Films.

E-FIT

After World War II, *physiognomy* became a taboo word, especially in German-speaking countries.[9] Recent decades, however, have witnessed a renewed upsurge of (scientific) interest in bodily beauty and the universality of our experience of perceiving beauty. Interestingly and not surprisingly, much of this research on *average* faces is based on the use of computer-generated "composite faces." Judith Langlois and Lori Roggman (1990), for instance, used a digital morphing program to create averaged composite faces in the early 1990s. Several faces were photographed, and then each was represented by 512 × 512 numeric gray values. These matrices were arithmetically averaged, and on the basis of them a series of achromatic composite facial images was created. The result of Langlois and Roggman's research suggested that beautiful faces are actually average faces (figure 20.6).

Victor Johnston, however, challenges Langlois and Roggman's findings with the argument that "the overlay averaging procedure used in these studies could blur facial details, increase symmetry, and change proportions . . . and that as a result all factors could enhance attractiveness" (2008). In other words, Johnston challenges the operativity of Langlois and Roggman's composites, pointing to their own restrictions as applying a way of looking that is already informed by the technologies of bodily makeover—in this case the averaging composites' production of "more beautiful" faces. Johnston, however, is an evolutionary psychologist and not a cultural theorist, so for him this chal-

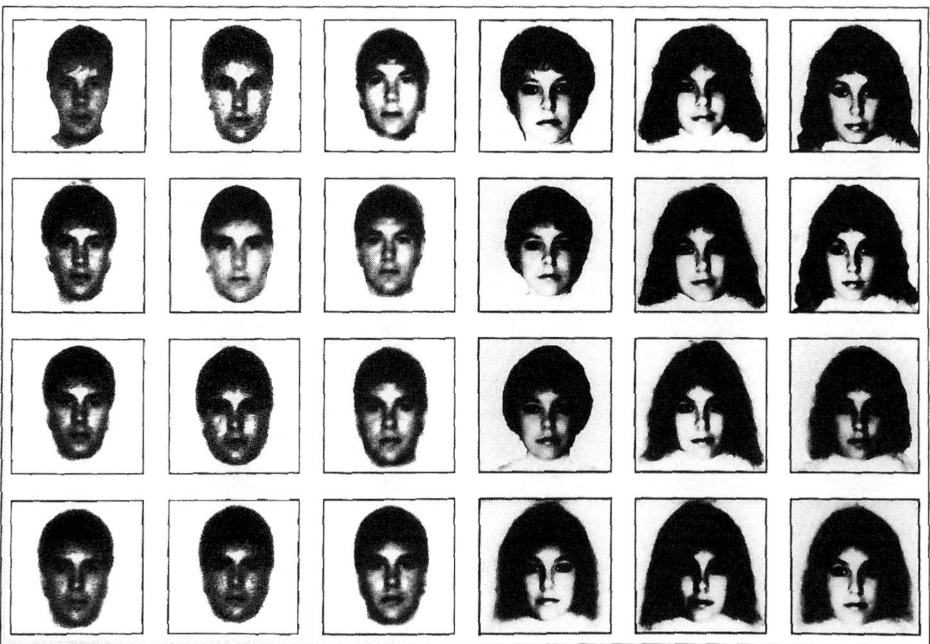

Figure 20.6
Composite Faces. From Langlois and Roggman 1990, 115–121.

lenge can be overcome. In collaboration with Melissa Franklin, he developed a computer program that allows individuals to "evolve" their most attractive facial composite—just like Susan and Pat "evolved" their most attractive inner self by subtly refreshing their look and turning their outer clock a few years back (figure 20.7). What Johnston finds is that from an evolutionary perspective, which correlates beauty and mate choice with sexual fitness, attractive female faces are not average, but "display features indicative of higher levels of pubertal estrogens (full lips) and lower levels of androgen exposure (short narrow lower jaw and large eyes) than average females" (Johnston 2008).

In figure 20.7, the "average female face" (left) and its "attractive and younger looking female corrective" (right) differ in the elevation of the lower jaw and lips, according to Johnston and Franklin (Johnston 2008). As a result, the eyes seem larger, the lips fuller, and the cheekbones higher in the modified face, as if the face had been pumped with pubertal estrogens.

The software program E-FIT is based on Johnston and Franklin's evolutionary faces. E-FIT was developed in Edinborough, Scotland, by the company Visionmetric, which

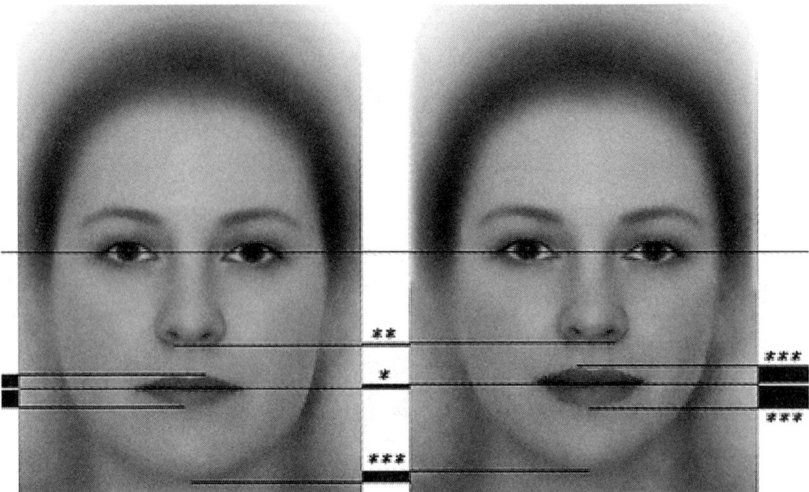

Figure 20.7
"Difference between average and attractive female faces." From Johnston 2008.

specializes in facial-identification software. Rather than looking for the average, as in Langlois and Roggman's research based on the facial composite, E-FIT enables the creation of an individual and unique face that has never existed except in the memory of an eyewitness. Chris Solomon, a software engineer who programmed E-FIT, explains:

> The system is trained on about 2,500 images of men and women of various ethnicities.[10] The processing we do enables us to understand the dominant or key ways in which faces differ from the average face, i.e., an average of all those that are used in the database. We are then able to produce new faces, which are a random combination of all these key components. As such, the system no longer needs the original pictures. It has learned how to create faces belonging to a given group and can in fact produce a near infinite number of "new" faces. All the faces you create are "virtual" in the sense that they are not made from individual elements of real faces but nonetheless look real.[11]

The first choice to make within E-FIT's logic is that of gender and ethnicity. When it comes to ethnicity, however, the pool of images is limited to such stereotypical categories as "Oriental," "eastern European," "black," "white," and so on. The system can learn to deal with an ethnicity only when it has been trained on it, as Solomon says. So, for instance, the system does not have "eastern European women" as a category because Visionmetrics does not have sufficient sources for such images: eastern European women do not constitute a risk category for crime in the United Kingdom.

The next step is to "write" the face in question into E-FIT's evolutionary mode (figure 20.8). The witness is now asked to view groups of computer-generated faces. She rejects the worst matches and selects the best groups. As the program itself says,

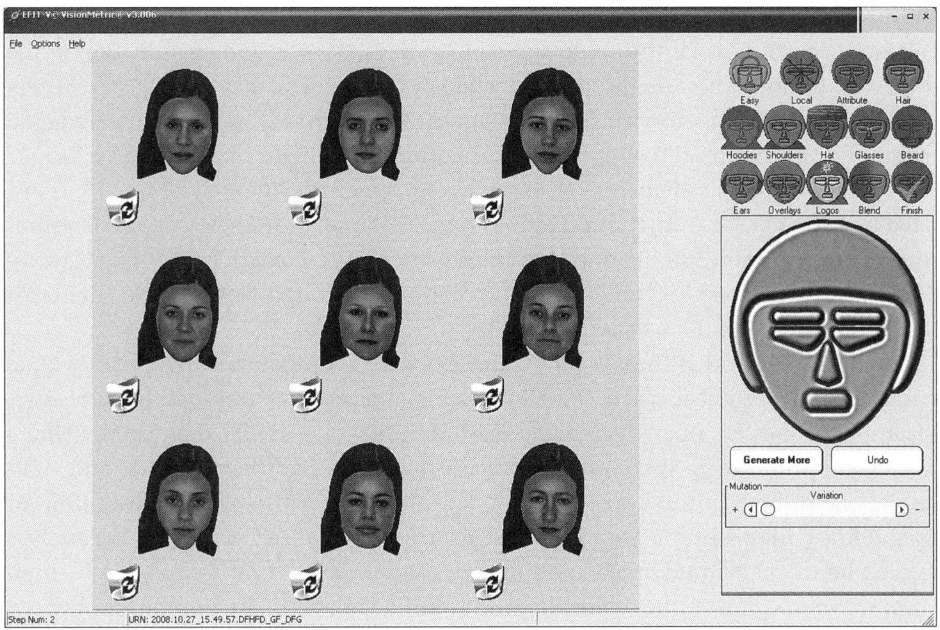

Figure 20.8
E-FIT screen shot. Courtesy of Visionmetrics.

it "takes account of these decisions and gradually evolves the face closer to the target." A mutation glider controls the amount of variation between the groups of faces displayed. Once the witness thinks she recognizes a facial template, she freezes it.

The next steps involve the application of "local tools," which narrows the facial accessories and other accessories, such as the choice of hats. The categories are interestingly limited, not to say a pastiche of material and functional ethnic descriptions as they appear in the cultural imaginary: the choices are "African," "bandana," "Indian," "helmet," "woolen," and so on. Finally, the dynamic overlay tool enables one to insert such realistic effects as aging lines, wrinkles, eye bags, prominent cheekbones, double chin, and so on. In the overlay tool, one can also adjust the age and create an "aging video."

E-FIT presupposes that there is a "real image pool" out there. As Solomon explains, the software is designed to "learn" on the basis of these character, gender, and ethnic types but creates completely new "virtual" faces. But similar to Susan and Pat, the real pool from which the data are drawn is already a result or retroactive projection of the technological interventions themselves. These interventions can be called "machinic sutures" insofar as they act to sew together a real body's process of becoming with an ideal whole whose existence is presupposed by the technology's deployment in the first place. In this sense, the series cited earlier—from disparation to transduction to mixed reality and now to machinic suture—achieves full theoretical operativity. Gilbert Simondon explains the conceptual pair of disparation and transduction in the following terms: "There is disparation when two twin sets that cannot be entirely superimposed, such as the left retinal image and the right retinal image, are grasped together as a system, allowing for the formation of a single set of a higher degree which integrates their elements thanks to a new dimension" (1995, 203 n. 15, translated by Ulrik Ekman in the introduction to this volume). Adrian Mackenzie develops this line of reasoning, stipulating that transduction "is a process whereby a disparity or a difference is topologically and temporally restructured across some interface" (2002, 25, quoted by Ekman in chapter 16).

The essential point is that disparate images exist as components in a preindividual stage; individual subjects then come into being as a result of transductive processes. Machinic sutures are operative when, as is often the case, rather than there being a transduction involving two purely biological instances like that of a left and right retina, one or both of the disparate poles depends on a technological intervention or nonarbitrary intervention. Susan and Pat refer to an idealized version of themselves created by the globalized application of the cosmetic gaze, itself formulated by multiple, sedimented machinic sutures between real bodies and technologically enhanced images. In the case of E-FIT's facial composites, the disparation–transduction process is operative at multiple levels: facial samples are chosen on the basis of stereotypical categorizations of real population pools and in turn digitized and morphed into virtual models that in turn inform the expectations and judgments of real perceptions. Even the reality that Solomon claims to have trained the system on is inextricably mixed, already informed by our moral judgment and by a cosmetic gaze that knows, for instance, how to distinguish eastern Europeans from other Europeans. In this regard, it is not surprising that Visionmetrics is waiting for input from around the world, just as Lombroso was collecting the photographs or criminals that people sent him from around the world. Says Solomon, "If you know of any potential sources for such pictures of Eastern European women, let me know."[12]

If the cosmetic gaze is the mechanism through which the body appears as always subject to enhancement or transformation in order to become what it really is, then the deployment of both old and new technologies must be seen as the machinic sutures that bond the virtual, ideal, and also ideologically motivated images with the very possibility of their realization. Although the ideological categories so prevalent in the nineteenth-century examples no longer stick out with the same clarity as they did in, for instance, Galton's composites or Lombroso's albums of criminals, these categories persist today and have not ceased to inform our very perception of the bodies we both see and wish to be. If anything, today's makeover culture has come ever so close to the Lavateran notion of *kalókagathia*, not only in the sense of a judgment of character, but, more important, in the sense of an improvement of soul and appearance that the theologian believed in when he wrote, "If man may be liable to fall, he is able to rise again, and capable of attaining an elevation of virtue superior even to that from which he fell" (Lavater 1789, 148).

Notes

This chapter is a short version of "Machinic Suture: Twenty-First-Century Technologies of Makeover Beauty," chapter 3 in my book *The Cosmetic Gaze: Body Modification and the Construction of Beauty* (Cambridge, MA: MIT Press, 2012).

1. C. U. M. Smith (2008) argues that visual thought is and has always been at the core of neurobiological science.

2. Henry Liddle and Robert Scott reference *kalókagathia* as "nobleness and goodness," the original denotation of *kalós kagathós* as the "perfect gentleman," and a second denotation as the "perfect character in a moral sense" (1961). See also Jüthner 1930.

3. The compound noun was actually used only in the apocryphal *Definitions*. Plato referred only to *kaloi kagathoi* or alluded to the concept as such.

4. This quote is from fragment sixteen, "Of the Harmony between Moral Beauty and Physical Beauty," which is a translation from the German fragment number nine.

5. To back himself with classical rhetoric, Lavater in fact quotes book XI.3.72 of Quintilian's *Institutio Oratoria*: "The face is the most dominant part of the head. It is by means of it that we are submissive, threatening, charming, sad, funny, proud, and humble. . . . Even before we speak, by it we express love and hatred, from it we understand many things. Often enough, the face is equivalent to all the words we could possibly use" (quoted in Lavater 1775–1778, 59, fragment 9, "Von der Harmonie der moralischen und körperlichen Schönheit," translation by Christopher Celenza).

6. The German original uses the verbs *verekeln* (to make something disgusting), *verschlimmern* (to worsen), and *verschönern* (to beautify).

7. For reasons of space, I cannot develop this point any further. For more, see "Tracing the Cosmetic Gaze: From Eighteenth-Century Physiognomies to Racial Theories of the Third Reich," chapter 1 of Wegenstein 2012.

8. See the *New York Times* article on the beautification software program developed by Tommer Leyvand at Tel Aviv University, "The Sum of Your Facial Parts" (Kershaw 2008).

9. I thank Nora Ruck, my coauthor in the publication "Physiognomy, Reality TV, and the Cosmetic Gaze" (Wegenstein and Ruck 2011), for her input on this section.

10. Not criminals, but "regular" people.

11. Email exchange with the author, 24 February 2009.

12. Email exchange with the author, 24 February 2009.

References

Deleuze, Gilles, and Félix Guattari. 1987. *A Thousand Plateaus: Capitalism & Schizophrenia.* Translated by Brian Massumi. Minneapolis: University of Minnesota Press.

Galton, Francis. 1883. *Inquiries into Human Faculty and Its Development.* London: Macmillan.

Hansen, Mark. 2006. *Bodies in Code: Interfaces with Digital Media.* New York: Routledge.

Hartley, Lucy. 2001. *Physiognomy and the Meaning of Expression in Nineteenth-Century Culture.* Cambridge, UK: Cambridge University Press.

Johnston, Victor S. 2008. "Facial Beauty and Mate Choice Decisions." Unpublished article on file with the author.

Johnston, Victor S., and Melissa Franklin. 1993. "Is Beauty in the Eye of the Beholder?" In *Ethology and Sociobiology,* Vol. 14 (3): 183–199.

Jüthner, Julius. 1930. "Kalogathia." In *Charisteria: Alois Rzach zum achtzigsten Geburtstag dargebracht,* 114–115. Reichenberg, Germany: Gebrüder Stiepel.

Kershaw, Sarah. 2008. "The Sum of Your Facial Parts." *New York Times,* 9 October.

Langlois, Judith H., and Lori A. Roggman. 1990. "Attractive Faces Are Only Average." *Psychological Science* 1:115–121.

Lavater, John Caspar. 1789. *Essays in Physiognomy Designed to Promote the Knowledge and Love of Mankind.* Vol. 1. Edited by Thomas Holloway. Translated by Henry Hunter. London: Murray and Highley.

Lavater, Johann Kaspar. 1775–1778. *Physiognomische Fragmente zur Beförderung der Menschenkenntnis und Menschenliebe* (Physiognomical Fragments for the Promotion of the Knowledge and Love of Man). Leipzig: Weidmanns Erben und Reich.

Liddle, Henry George, and Robert Scott. 1961. *Greek–English Lexicon.* Oxford: Oxford University Press.

Lombroso, Cesare. *Album of Criminal Photographs.* In *Criminal Man* (*L'uomo delinquente*). 1876. Translated by Mary Gibson and Nicole Hahn Rafter. Durham: Duke University Press, 2003.

Lombroso, Cesare, and Guglielmo Ferrero. [1896–1897] 2006. *Criminal Man.* Translated and with an introduction by Mary Gibson and Nicole Hahn Rafter. Durham, NC: Duke University Press.

Mackenzie, Adrian. 2002. *Transductions: Bodies and Machines at Speed.* London: Continuum.

Norton, Robert E. 1995. "The Eighteenth Century and the Hellenic Ideal of *Kalokagathia.*" In *The Beautiful Soul: Aesthetic Morality in the Eighteenth Century,* 100–136. Ithaca, NY: Cornell University Press.

Simondon, Gilbert. 1995. *L'individu et sa genèse physico-biologique.* Grenoble, France: Éditions Jérôme Millon.

Smith, C. U. M. 2008. "Visual Thinking and Neuroscience." *Journal of the History of the Neurosciences* 17 (3): 260–273.

Thornhill, Randy. 1998. "Darwinian Aesthetics." In *Handbook of Evolutionary Psychology*, edited by Charles B. Crawford and Dennis L. Krebs, 543–572. Mahwah, NJ: Lawrence Erlbaum.

Tyler May, Elaine. 1988. *Homeward Bound: American Families in the Cold War Era*. New York: Basic Books.

Van Meter, Jonathan. 2008. "About Face." *New York Magazine*, 11 August. Available at http://nymag.com/news/features/48948. Accessed 23 April 2010.

Wegenstein, Bernadette. 2012. *The Cosmetic Gaze: Body Modification and the Construction of Beauty*. Cambridge, MA: MIT Press.

Wegenstein, Bernadette, and Geoffrey Alan Rhodes, directors and producers. 2007. *Made Over in America* (documentary film). Brooklyn, NY: Icarus Films.

Wegenstein, Bernadette, and Nora Ruck. 2011. "Physiognomy, Reality TV, and the Cosmetic Gaze." *Body & Society*, Vol. 17 (4): 27–55.

Wells, Samuel R. [1895] 1971. *How to Read Character: A New Illustrated Handbook of Phrenology and Physiognomy for Students and Examiners with a Descriptive Chart*. Rutlant, VT: Charles E. Tuttle.

Zelle, Carsten. 1993. "Soul Semiology: On Lavater's Physiognomic Principles." In *The Faces of Physiognomy: Interdisciplinary Approaches to Johann Caspar Lavater*, edited by Ellis Shookman, 40–64. Columbia, SC: Camden House.

VI Context Awareness

21 Feeding the Serpent Its Own Tail: Counterforces to Tactile Enclosure in the Age of Transparency

Inke Arns

Giedion, Mendelsohn, Corbusier turned the abiding places of man into a transit area for every conceivable kind of energy and for electric currents and radio waves. The time that is coming will be dominated by transparency.

—Walter Benjamin, "The Return of the *Flâneur*"

The coils of a serpent are even more complex than the burrows of a molehill.

—Gilles Deleuze, "Postscript on the Society of Control"

With a fictitious newspaper report allegedly appearing in the year 2067—bearing the headline "Anna Kournikova Deleted by Memeright Trusted System"—David Rice (2001) pursued to a logical end the situation of transparency coupled with the ever stricter persecution of copyright infringements we are witnessing today. The perfidiously phrased newspaper report details the death of former professional tennis player and model Anna Kournikova. Kournikova, having had her looks protected against illegal look-alikes, had been identified as an imitation of herself (an "illicit copy") while on an unofficial trip to the Pacific Rim and thereupon eliminated by a potent microwave beam from a satellite operated by the Memeright Trusted System.

David Rice's story perfectly illustrates the change from the enclosing milieu of the disciplinary society to the flexible modulations of the society of control. Whereas the disciplinary societies described by Michel Foucault (1977) are characterized by built enclosures (the prison, the school, the factory, the hospital), the control societies of today are permeated by continuous modulations. These, soft modulations resemble a "self-transmuting molding continually changing from one moment to the next, or like a sieve whose mesh varies from one point to another" (Deleuze 1995, 179). Both coils and burrows are "apparatuses of capture; in burrows or coils, either way, you are caught" (Bogard 2007). Burrows, however, are "rigid, arborescent structures, assembled as series of confined spaces or interiors. . . . Serpents' coils, on the other hand, are meshes rather than series. A more flexible form of enclosure than burrows, they adjust to the body as it moves and wherever it moves" (Bogard 2007). As suggested by Gilles

Deleuze's analysis, today "rigid mechanisms of enclosure are giving way to supple ones that have lost none of their power to constrict the body. The new mechanisms can position and fix the body independently of its location" (Bogard 2007). With coils as a kind of mobile confinement, "control is more intensive, enclosure more supple, and confinement to fixed interiors redundant" (Bogard 2007).

Control society's supple mold has three distinctive attributes: (1) transparency (diaphanousness or invisibility that eludes direct sensory perception); (2) immateriality (as the connection between individual materialities), and (3) performativity ("Code is Law,"[1] computer code becomes the law). These three in turn create a so-called fourth attribute, "smooth space" (Deleuze and Guattari 1987, 493) or "haptic space" characterized not by (pan)optic visuality and distance perception, but by haptic visuality within a close-range space.

Transparency

Today, the age of transparency that Walter Benjamin in 1929 optimistically considered to be emerging in the glass buildings designed by his architect contemporaries seems to be ambiguous. For one thing, not only light waves pass through the transparent buildings, but any number of electromagnetic waves deriving from a very diverse range of technical sources.[2] For another, the notion of "transparency"—with its double meaning of visibility and invisibility or with the ambivalence of the panoptical and the postoptical (see Arns 2005)—turns out to be very suitable for the characterization of contemporary performative (information) architecture and spaces. Michel Foucault's (1977) notion of panopticism is derived from Jeremy Bentham's "panopticon," the blueprint for a perfect prison that makes the inmates of a circular prison permanently visible to a warden placed in the middle. However, I use the term *postoptical* to denote all the digital data streams and (programmed) communication structures or architectures that are monitored at least as easily as such prisoners yet consist of visual information in only a very small part ("dataveillance").

Although in everyday usage the term *transparency* stands for simplicity, clarity, and controllability through viewability (as suggested, for example, by the names "Transparency International"[3] and "Prozrachnyi Mir" [Transparent World]),[4] in computer science it means the very opposite—namely, invisibility and information concealment. A "transparent" interface is one that the user can neither detect nor notice. Although this concealment of (superfluous, excessive) information is often expedient in terms of reducing complexity, it can also lull the user into a false sense of security: the invisibility of the interface suggests a direct view of something, an unimpaired transparency in which it would be foolish, of course, to believe. For that reason, Lev Manovich writes: "Far from being a transparent window into the data inside a computer, the interface brings with it strong messages of its own" (2001, 65). Making this "message" visible is a matter of directing attention to the transparent "windowpane" itself. Just as at the press of a button the glass facades of buildings can be transformed from transparent to translucid—that is, semitransparent or semiopaque surfaces—and thus become visible, "making the message visible" is a question of wrenching the transparency out of postoptical information–technical structures. Applied analogously to communication networks, it would be a matter of making opaque and therefore perceptible the transparent distribution structures of economic, political, and social power. It is ultimately a matter of restoring to the information-technology-based notion of transparency the original meaning of clearness and controllability through visibility.

Immateriality

The more regulated by software everyday things become, the less accessible they are to sensory perception in our everyday dealings with them. However, the fact that they are vanishing from sight does not mean that they are not there. On the contrary, the increasingly programmed world surrounding us means that rules, conventions, and relationships that are basically changeable and negotiable are being translated into and fixed in software. Recorded in software, immaterial structures are at least—and herein lies the paradox—as permanent and perhaps even more powerful than material structures and architecture. The secret (and uncanny) making invisible of the world through software deployment not only leads to a withdrawal from visibility and perceptibility but also means that structures become immaterial. In this case, however, the term *immaterial* does not imply that these structures are any less effective than their solid counterparts. To take *immaterial* to mean the opposite of *material* would be to wholly misread the term (see Terranova 2006, 31). Rather, one must learn to grasp the immaterial as something that turns "qualitative, intensive differences into quantitative relations of exchange and equivalence" (Terranova 2006, 31). The immaterial establishes relations between isolated materialities—things and people, wares and individuals, objects and subjects—and in this way is able to compute profiles, for instance, of consumers or movements at very high speed.[5] At every given second, the immaterial is *somewhere* (as opposed to nowhere), between the things. It encloses the materialities, elastically changes shape, agilely follows objects and bodies, and constantly establishes connections. The immaterial is admittedly not that "what holds the world together in its innermost self," as described in Goethe's *Faust*, but it forges together the things in the world by interrelating them and does so more efficiently than rigid structures were ever able to. Thus, software turns out to be a very hard substance, and immateriality to be quasi-factitious materiality that most of the time eludes our (visual, tactile) sensory perception.

Performativity

Programmed structures consist of two kinds of texts: a visible, "front end" (the graphical user interface) and an invisible, transparent, "back end" (the software or program code). These texts are to each other as phenotext is to genotext in the sphere of biology. The surface effects of the phenotexts (graphical user interfaces) are called up and controlled by the texts (program codes or source texts) effective below the surface. The characteristic attribute of program code is that it unites saying and doing (action); in other words, code as a performative speech act is not a description or representation of something but instead affects directly, sets in motion, times effects. Code does what it says.

However, code affects not only the phenotexts—that is to say, the graphic user interfaces. Coded performativity has equally direct and even political effects on the (virtual) realms through which we move. "Program code increasingly tends to become law," according to Lawrence Lessig (2000). Today, control functions are integrated directly in the architecture of the network—namely, in its code. In *Code and Other Laws of Cyberspace* (1999), Lessig uses the Internet provider America Online (AOL) as a compelling illustration of the way in which program architecture can hinder, with the aid of the code that defines it, any form of virtual "rebellion," for instance, and largely control the users. Graham Harwood describes this transparent world as an "invisible shadow world of process" (2001, 47). It is a world with direct and also political consequences for the virtual and real spaces in which we move today: by stipulating what is possible in these spaces and what is not, it mobilizes or, as applicable, immobilizes its users. The question of permeability—Access? When and for whom?—is central for contemporary spaces and closely linked to the notion of performativity (see Arns 2005). "The conception of a control mechanism giving the position of any element within an open environment at any given instant (whether animal in a reserve or human in a corporation, as with an electronic collar), is not necessarily one of science fiction," writes Gilles Deleuze. "Félix Guattari has imagined a city where one would be able to leave one's apartment, one's street, one's neighborhood, thanks to one's (dividual) electronic card that raises a given barrier; but the card could just as easily be rejected on a given day or between certain hours; what counts is not the barrier but the computer that tracks each person's position—licit or illicit—and effects a universal modulation" (1995, 181–182).

So-called radio-frequency identification (RFID) technology, for example, makes possible a tracking of the very kind described in the previous paragraph (see Hayles, chapter 31 in this volume; "Radio Frequency" n.d.). RFID tags are tiny radio labels, passive wireless transmitters, able to send and save information, which are expected to become replacements for barcode labels. They are already in use in goods logistics, human surveillance, and antitheft protection. In response to a weak wireless energy pulse, RFID tags return to a reading device the information stored on them. The connection is already possible over a distance of up to several hundred meters—without the bearer of the tag even noticing. In addition, the technology enables objects to be unambiguously identified worldwide; in addition to the unnoticed reading out of information, this capability is a further significant attribute distinguishing RFID from a conventional barcode. RFID allows goods flows to be retraced without gaps and thus opens up whole new dimensions of data mining (for instance, through the compilation of consumer profiles). If one considers the potential deployment of RFID technology on and inside people—say, via passports or health insurance cards provided with RFID chips on which biometrical data are stored or via RFID tags with biometrical data implanted below the skin (see "Wo gibt es RFID?" n.d.)—then new forms of ubiquitous control are conceivable.

Haptic Space

David Rice's Anna Kournikova was detected and eliminated thanks to her moving about in "haptic space." Drawing on Deleuze and Guattari's concept of "smooth space" (1987, 493), Laura U. Marks (2004) has suggested that whereas panoptical regimes (Foucault's disciplinary societies) relied on optical visuality based on distance perception, postoptical regimes (Deleuze's society of control) rely on "haptic visuality," involving close-range space. This haptic space is characterized by a lack of distance and immediate connectedness of the body to its surroundings. The body is continuously enveloped by a "self-transmuting molding" (Deleuze 1995, 179), which is changing shape at any time, filling up cavities as they form. Envelopment of such perfection hinders (and this is where performativity comes in) forward movement at least as efficiently as built enclosures do and perhaps even more so.

The age of transparency is marked by a dual structure of the panoptical and the postoptical,[6] with a growing tendency toward the latter. On one side, panoptical visibility is being continuously enhanced in state and private-sector structures of surveillance satellites (see Parks 2005). On the other side, in parallel with this panoptical visibility, the technical structures that observe and act performatively have increasingly withdrawn into invisibility (embeddedness, ubiquitous computing). In many cases, performative structures are recognizable only by their effects but are no longer necessarily visible. Software, for example, eludes human perception because it involves "inconspicuous" performative (geno)texts lying below the visible surfaces (phenotexts) that generate them. We are confronted, as Marks (2004) has formulated, with a dialectics of optic and haptic visuality, of distance perception and close-range space. However, control society is increasingly based especially on the latter, haptic space: "And you understand why McLuhan saw in the era of the great electronic media an era of tactile communication. We are closer here in effect to the tactile than to the visual universe, where the distancing is greater and reflection is always possible" (Baudrillard 1983, 123–124). In the case of Rice's fictional Kournikova, reflection occurs only after the fact.

How can political or artistic action or both be articulated in such haptic, close-range spaces that have become imperceptible, withdrawn from direct view? In view of this software-assisted disappearance of the world, where and how can potential spaces of the political (re)emerge? Various media, net, and software art projects have in recent years developed approaches that make opaque (that is, perceivable) the transparent structures of economic, political, and social power distribution in communication networks (see Arns 2002a, 2005, 2008). The concern of such projects is to transpose information-technical structures from a state of transparency to one perceptibility. In an age of software-assisted implosion of the political, this first step alone is eminently political. One way of making sense of a transparent and complex world that increasingly withdraws from human perception is—if we remember David Rice's story about Anna Kournikova—*storytelling.*

Within media and net activism, it is not only the technical hacks and the hardcore programming code—the *fact*, if you will—that are performative in the sense of Austin's speech-act theory, but also the narratives—the *fiction*. Narrative and counternarrative not only assign meaning to the disparate, unconnected elements of the world we perceive, but also, as performative text, also have the potential to mobilize people. Fiction has an effect on those it is being told to as well as on those who are engaged in further distributing it. By infusing and releasing these stories (hoaxes) into the mass media (i.e., by hacking the mass media), it becomes possible to launch a certain topic and to reach a global media audience. The Swiss–Austrian artist duo UBERMORGEN.COM are masters of storytelling in, with, and through the media.[7]

UBERMORGEN.COM: The *EKMRZ Trilogy*

Hans Bernhard, after leaving the corporate art group etoy (see Arns 2002b; Wishart and Bochsler 2002), "the first street gang on the information super highway",[8] which he had cofounded in the early 1990s, started the company UBERMORGEN.COM with Maria Haas, registered in Germany, Austria, Switzerland, and Bulgaria. Bernhard and Haas describe UBERMORGEN'S activities as "media hacking" wherein it distributes its contents via guerilla marketing tactics and so-called shock marketing. However, it is storytelling that is at the very core of these media-hacking activities.

"*202.345.117 years until GWEI fully owns Google.*"[9] This surprising yet poetic statement opens the first part of UBERMORGEN.COM's *EKMRZ Trilogy*, entitled *GWEI—Google Will Eat Itself* (2005–2008) (figure 21.1). Together with colleagues Paolo Cirio and Alessandro Ludovico,[10] UBERMORGEN tackles the trinity of EKMRZ ("e-commerce") giants that survived the crash of the dotcom boom and are now almost generic names for unique business models—and monopolies—on the Internet: Google, Amazon, and eBay. *The EKMRZ Trilogy* looks at the monopolists' distinctive business models and proposes creative ways to "short-circuit" the immaterial wiring of these models. By obediently turning themselves into the ultimate torchbearers of the Google advertising system, UBERMORGEN.COM made Google "eat itself" and thus made themselves

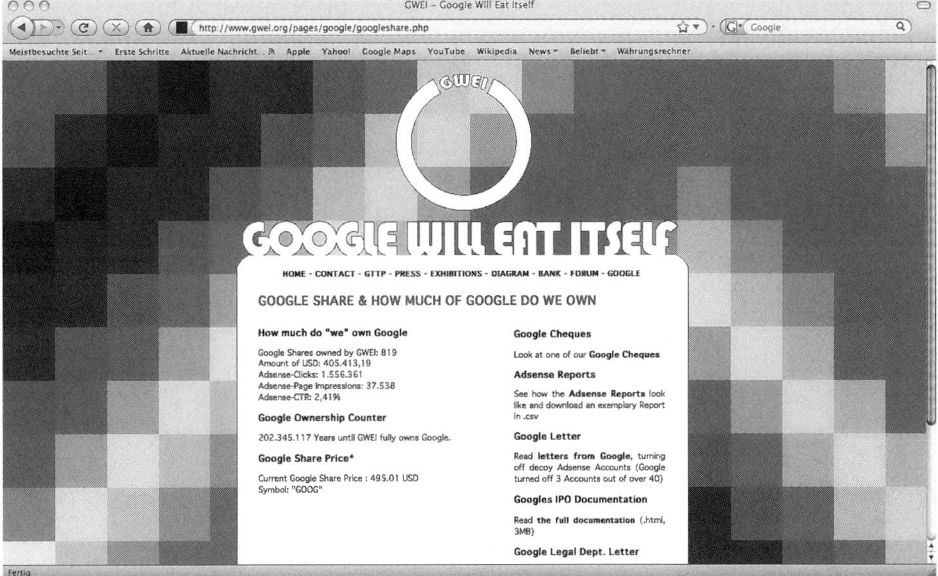

Figure 21.1
GWEI—Google Will Eat Itself, part I of the *EKMRZ Trilogy* (2005–2009). Screenshot. Permission kindly granted by UBERMORGEN.COM.

Google owners in a remote future. They also performed another kind of hack on the Amazon system by shamelessly downloading the digital content of thousands of books. Within *The EKMRZ Trilogy*, eBay, in turn, is made to play the tune of e-commerce, created by transforming eBay user data into the dull yet hypnotic soundtrack of ubiquitous online micropayments.

GWEI—Google Will Eat Itself generates money by serving Google text advertisements on a network of hidden Web sites. With this money, the artists automatically buy Google shares: "We buy Google via their own advertising! Google eats itself—but in the end we own it! By establishing this autocannibalistic model we deconstruct the new global advertisement mechanisms by rendering them into a surreal click-based economic model."[11] The artists have calculated that it will take exactly 202.345.117 years until GWEI fully owns Google. By rerouting some of the immaterial wires of the digital-information economy, it is thus potentially possible to hack the system—no matter that the result will only be visible more than two hundred million years later.

"We have stolen the invisible."[12] This confession opens the story of the second EKMRZ hack, *Amazon Noir—The Big Book Crime* (2006–2007) (figures 21.2 and 21.3), which involves assaults on stage coaches filled with digital gold and the somber highwaymen of the information superhighway. The project exploited Amazon's "Search inside the Book" feature—a service that allows customers to search for keywords in the full texts of the 250,000 books in its catalog. Between July and October 2006, EKMRZ "stole" three thousand digital books were from the Amazon Web site by targeting weaknesses in the "Search inside the Book" feature. A specially programmed software "bombarded the Search Inside™ interface with multiple requests, assembling full versions of texts and distributing them across peer-to-peer networks (P2P)" (Dieter 2007). Michael Dieter points to the fact that far from being a purely malicious and anonymous hack, the, "heist" was publicized as a tactical-media performance—based, one should add, on a script that recalls a spaghetti Western:

> The Bad Guys (The Amazon Noir Crew: Cirio, Lizvlx, Ludovico and Bernhard) stole copyrighted books from Amazon using sophisticated robot-perversion technology coded by supervillain Paolo Cirio. A subliminal media fight and a covert legal dispute escalated into an online showdown with the heist of over 3,000 books at the centre of the story. Lizvlx from UBERMORGEN.COM had daily shoot-outs with the global mass media, Cirio continuously pushed the boundaries of copyright (books are just pixels on a screen or just ink on paper), Ludovico and Bernhard resisted

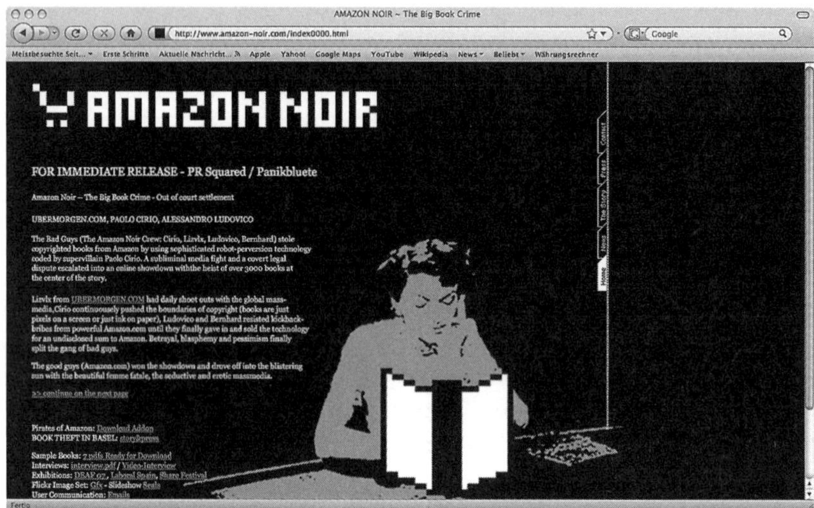

Figure 21.2
Amazon Noir—The Big Book Crime, part II of the *EKMRZ Trilogy* (2006). Screenshot. Permission kindly granted by UBERMORGEN.COM.

Figure 21.3
Amazon Noir—The Big Book Crime, part II of the *EKMRZ Trilogy* (2006). Diagram. Permission kindly granted by UBERMORGEN.COM.

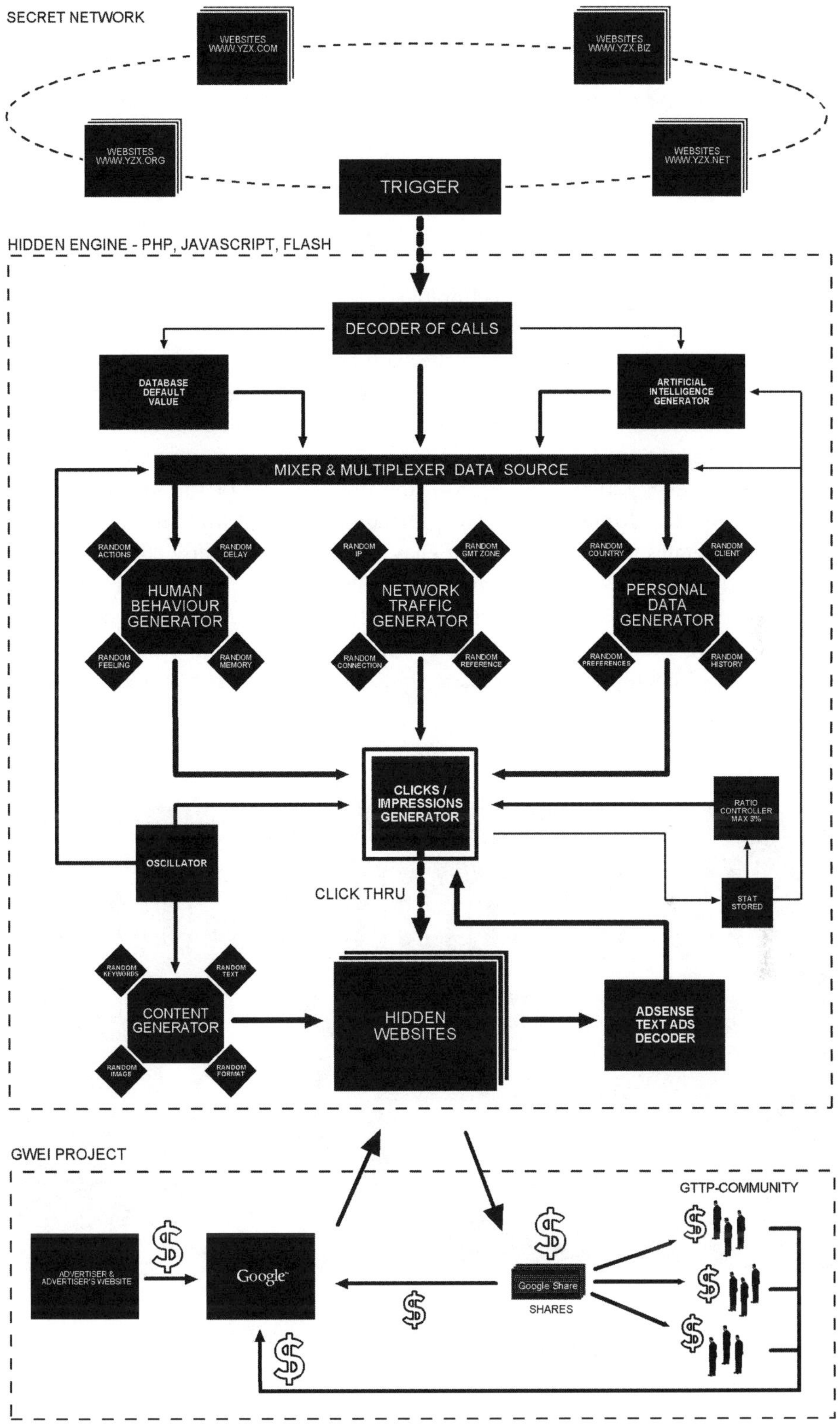

SECRET NETWORK

WEBSITES WWW.YZX.COM

WEBSITES WWW.YZX.BIZ

WEBSITES WWW.YZX.ORG

WEBSITES WWW.YZX.NET

TRIGGER

HIDDEN ENGINE - PHP, JAVASCRIPT, FLASH

DECODER OF CALLS

DATABASE DEFAULT VALUE

ARTIFICIAL INTELLIGENCE GENERATOR

MIXER & MULTIPLEXER DATA SOURCE

RANDOM ACTIONS

RANDOM DELAY

HUMAN BEHAVIOUR GENERATOR

RANDOM FEELING

RANDOM MEMORY

RANDOM IP

RANDOM GMT ZONE

NETWORK TRAFFIC GENERATOR

RANDOM CONNECTION

RANDOM REFERENCE

RANDOM COUNTRY

RANDOM CLIENT

PERSONAL DATA GENERATOR

RANDOM PREFERENCES

RANDOM HISTORY

CLICKS / IMPRESSIONS GENERATOR

RATIO CONTROLLER MAX 3%

OSCILLATOR

STAT STORED

CLICK THRU

RANDOM KEYWORDS

RANDOM TEXT

CONTENT GENERATOR

RANDOM IMAGE

RANDOM FORMAT

HIDDEN WEBSITES

ADSENSE TEXT ADS DECODER

GWEI PROJECT

GTTP-COMMUNITY

ADVERTISER & ADVERTISER'S WEBSITE

$

Google™

$

$

Google Share

SHARES

$

$

$

$

kickback-bribes from the powerful Amazon.com until they finally gave in and sold the technology for an undisclosed sum to Amazon. Betrayal, blasphemy and pessimism finally split the gang of bad guys. The good guys (Amazon.com) won the showdown and drove off into the blistering sun with the beautiful femme fatale, the seductive and erotic massmedia.[13]

Dieter suggests that the extensive use of imagery and iconography from the noir genre should be seen as an explicit reference to the increasing criminalization of copyright violation through digital technologies. At the same time, the term *noir* also refers to the fact that it is increasingly difficult (in *Amazon Noir,* as in real life) to distinguish between the "bad guys" and the "good guys." The politics of file sharing, Dieter continues, essentially depend on the "command of imaginaries": *Amazon Noir* specifically "dramatizes these ambiguities by framing technological action through the fictional sensibilities of narrative genre" (2007).

The Sound of eBay (2009) (figure 21.4), the final chapter of the *EKMRZ Trilogy,* provides us with the ultimate soundtrack of e-commerce that underlies most online activities. It generates unique songs from eBay user data. When any eBay user name and email address are entered and "generate" is clicked, a "score-file" is created from the data harvested by the software, and this file is then transformed "into your unique but uniform song and presented in teletext porn style!"[14] UBERMORGEN.COM continue in their inimitably overenthusiastic style: "We love it! *The Sound of eBay* is

Figure 21.4

The Sound of eBay, part III of the *EKMRZ Trilogy* (2008–2009). Screenshot. Permission kindly granted by UBERMORGEN.COM.

our affirmative low-tech contribution to the ATOMIC soundtrack of the peer-to-peer hyper-catastrophic shock-capitalism. reference: Peter Weibel's song *Sex in der Stadt* (Sex in the City) from 1982—Hotel Morphila Orchester, where PW, 'raps' (sings) sex-ads from a newspaper."[15] Indeed, Peter Weibel's singing of sex ads[16] provides an interesting frame of reference for this project: it is about reading the underlying texts of our surroundings and reproducing them in real time, like a parallel reading (input) and automatic writing (output) that recalls the surrealist writing experiments of *écriture automatique* or glossolalia (speaking in tongues). We are also reminded of other artistic performances: for example, Gebhard Sengmüllers's *TV Poetry* (1993–1994),[17] Igor Stromajer's *Oppera Internettikka* (since 1998),[18] and Christophe Bruno's *Human Browser* (2004).[19] These projects limit the factor of intentionality—that is, the active role of the artist—in favor of casting themselves in the role of a medium through which *language speaks*. The artist appears as an entity loaded with preexisting language that cannot utter anything but the discourse of the Other. Jacques Lacan (1966) defines this repetition as the "insistence of the letter" (*l'instance de la lettre*)—that is, the compulsive repetition of certain signifiers or letters despite the subject's conscious attempts to repress them. "Repetition," he writes, "is fundamentally the insistence of speech" (1993, 242). However, in *The Sound of eBay* it is not the voice of the radically decentered subject that produces language utterances, but a software program that generates a catchy eight-bit musical soundtrack from eBay user data. It reminds us that underneath the shiny surfaces and glossy interfaces there is a layer of performative code and precious personal data that performs the constant modulations crucial for the functioning of today's society of control.

Feeding the Serpent Its Own Tail

In their *EKMRZ Trilogy*, UBERMORGEN.COM formulates dark visions of the "information society" and then turn these visions into highly entertaining, blithe narratives about the age of transparency, using the format of film scripts, adventure novels, and tabloids. By forcing Google to eat itself, by stealing the invisible, and by making eBay's code play stupid tunes it was not supposed to play, UBERMORGEN is short-circuiting (for real because these hacks are not merely stories) the three online services' internal wirings, which in fact constitute a part of the "self-deforming cast" of the society of control. Supple, constantly self-adapting modulations envelop the bodies and objects moving about in "haptic space." This postoptical haptic space, however, is transparent, invisible. Therefore, it cannot be observed by visual means. It can be resisted only by "*participating in the very activity that is being denounced precisely in order to denounce it*" (Owens 1980, 79, emphasis in original)—that is, by reverse coding, hacking, and engineering tools for resisting network domination. Counterforces to tactile enclosures have started to emerge on the horizon (net activism, software art). Let us see what happens if we feed the serpent more of its own tail.

Notes

1. "Code is Law" is Lawrence Lessig's motto, coined in *Code and Other Laws of Cyberspace* (1999).

2. See the exhibition catalog *Waves—the Art of the Electromagnetic Society* (Medosch, Smite, Smits, et al. 2008; also *Waves*[2006] at http://rixc.lv/06).

3. Transparency International is an organization combating corruption worldwide; see http://www.transparency.org.

4. This Russian company supplies high-resolution satellite images of earth for private business purposes; see http://www.transparentworld.ru.

5. "The digital language of control is made up of codes indicating whether access to some information should be allowed or denied. We're no longer dealing with a duality of mass and individual. Individuals become '*dividuals*,' and masses become samples, data, markets, or '*banks*.'" (Deleuze 1995, 180).

6. I refer to the present as a postoptical age in which program code—which might also, with reference to Walter Benjamin, be described as a "postoptical unconscious"—is becoming "law" qua performative text. See Benjamin 1985, 243.

7. For more on UBERMORGEN's most famous project to date, *Vote-Auction—Bringing Democracy and Capitalism Closer Together* (2000), see http://www.vote-auction.net.

8. From http://www.hijack.org.

9. From http://gwei.org/index.php.

10. Italian programmer Paolo Cirio and *Neural.it* editor Alessandro Ludovico worked with UBERMORGEN.COM on *Google Will Eat Itself* (2005) and *Amazon Noir* (2006), but not on the *Sound of eBay* (2008–2009).

11. From http://www.ubermorgen.com/EKMRZ_Trilogy.

12. From http://www.amazon-noir.com/TEXT/Thieves_of_the_invisible.pdf.

13. From http://www.ubermorgen.com/EKMRZ_Trilogy.

14. From http://www.sound-of-ebay.com/pdfs/SoE_Press_Release_no_1.pdf.

15. From http://www.ubermorgen.com/EKMRZ_Trilogy.

16. See http://www.youtube.com/watch?v=rvIMbUGo9Fk.

17. See http://www.gebseng.com.

18. See http://www.intima.org/index_1995-2007.html.

19. See http://www.christophebruno.com/?p=83.

References

Arns, Inke. 2008. "Transparent World. Minoritarian Tactics in the Age of Transparency." In *Un_imaginable*, edited by Dennis Del Favero, Ursula Frohne, and Peter Weibel, 20–35. Karlsruhe, Sydney, and Pittsburgh: ZKM Center for Art and Media, iCinema Center/University of New South Wales, and University of Pittsburgh.

Arns, Inke. 2005. "Read_me, run_me, execute_me. Code as Executable Text: Software Art and Its Focus on Program Code as Performative Text." In *Media Art Net 2: Key Topics*, edited by Rudolf Frieling and Dieter Daniels, 197–207. New York: Springer. Also available at http://www.mediaartnet.org/themes/generative-tools/read_me. Accessed 20 January 2012.

Arns, Inke. 2002a. *Netzkulturen*. Hamburg: Europäische Verlagsanstalt.

Arns, Inke. 2002b. "This Is Not a Toy War: Politischer Aktivismus in Zeiten des Internet." In *Praxis Internet: Kulturtechniken der vernetzten Welt*, edited by Stefan Münker and Alexander Roesler, 37–60. Frankfurt am Main: Suhrkamp.

Baudrillard, Jean. 1983. *Simulations*. New York: Semiotext(e).

Benjamin, Walter. 2005. "The Return of the *Flâneur*." In *Walter Benjamin: Selected Writings*, vol. 2, translated by Rodney Livingstone and others, edited by Michael W. Jennings, Howard Eiland, and Gary Smith, 262–267. Cambridge, MA: Harvard University Press.

Benjamin, Walter. 1985. "A Small History of Photography." In *Walter Benjamin: One Way Street and Other Writings*, translated by Edmund Jephcott and Kingsley Shorter, 240–257. London: Verso.

Bogard, William. 2007. "The Coils of a Serpent, Haptic Space, and Control Societies." *C-Theory*. Available at http://www.ctheory.net/articles.aspx?id=581. Accessed 20 January 2012.

Deleuze, Gilles. 1995. "Postscript on the Society of Control." In *Negotiations, 1972–1990*, translated by Martin Joughin, 177–182. New York: Columbia University Press.

Deleuze, Gilles, and Félix Guattari. 1987. *A Thousand Plateaus: Capitalism and Schizophrenia*. Translated by Brian Massumi. Minneapolis: University of Minnesota Press.

Dieter, Michael. 2007. "Amazon Noir: Piracy, Distribution, Control." *M/C Journal—A Journal of Media and Culture* 10 (5) (October). Available at http://journal.media-culture.org.au/0710/07-dieter.php. Accessed 20 January 2012.

Foucault, Michel. 1977. *Discipline and Punish: The Birth of the Prison*. Translated by Michael Sheridan. New York: Vintage.

Harwood, Graham. 2001. "Speculative Software." In *DIY Media—Art and Digital Media, Software—Participation—Distribution*, edited by Andreas Broeckmann and Susanne Jaschko, 47–49. Berlin: Transmediale.01.

Lacan, Jacques. 1993. *The Seminar*. Book III: *The Psychoses*. Translated by Russel Grigg. London: Routledge.

Lacan, Jacques. 1966. "The Insistence of the Letter in the Unconscious." *Yale French Studies* 36–37:112–147.

Lessig, Lawrence. 2000. "Stalin & Disney: Copyright Is Killing the Internet." *Rohrpost*, 30 May.

Lessig, Lawrence. 1999. *Code and Other Laws of Cyberspace*. New York: Basic Books.

Manovich, Lev. 2001. *The Language of New Media*. Cambridge, MA: MIT Press.

Marks, Laura U. 2004. "Haptic Visuality: Touching with the Eyes." *Framework, the Finnish Art Review*, No. 2, 79–82.

Medosch, Armin, Rasa Smite, Raits Smits, and Inke Arns, eds. *Waves—the Art of the Electromagnetic Society*. Bönen, Germany: Kettler, 2008.

Owens, Craig: 1980. "The Allegorical Impulse: Toward a Theory of Postmodernism." *October* 13:59–80.

Parks, Lisa. 2005. *Cultures in Orbit: Satellites and the Televisual*. Durham, NC: Duke University Press.

"Radio Frequency Identification Technology (RFID)." n.d. *Wikipedia*. Available at http://en.wikipedia.org/wiki/RFID. Accessed 20 January 2012.

Rice, David. 2001. "Anna Kournikova Deleted by Memeright Trusted System." *FutureFeedForward*. Available at http://www.futurefeedforward.com/front.php?fid=33. Accessed 20 January 2012.

Terranova, Tiziana. 2006. "Of Sense and Sensibility: Immaterial Labour in Open Systems." In *Curating Immateriality*, edited by Joasia Krysa, 27–36. New York: Autonomedia.

Wishart, Adam, and Regula Bochsler. 2002. *Leaving Reality Behind: Inside the Battles for the Soul of the Internet*. London: Fourth Estate.

"Wo gibt es RFID?" n.d. Available at http://www.foebud.org/rfid/wo-gibt-es-rfid. Accessed 20 January 2012.

Plate 1 (figure I.1)
A young woman and an *Under Scan* video portrait exchanging greetings in the streets of Leicester, UK (2006). *Source:* Photograph courtesy of Rafael Lozano-Hemmer.

Plate 2 (figure I.2)
A laying bare of the surveillance and tracking grids in *Under Scan* (2008), Trafalgar Square, London. *Source:* Photograph courtesy of Rafael Lozano-Hemmer.

Plate 3 (figure I.3)
Pervasive augmented-reality gaming with Third Echelon. *Source:* Photograph courtesy of Earthmine/Layar.

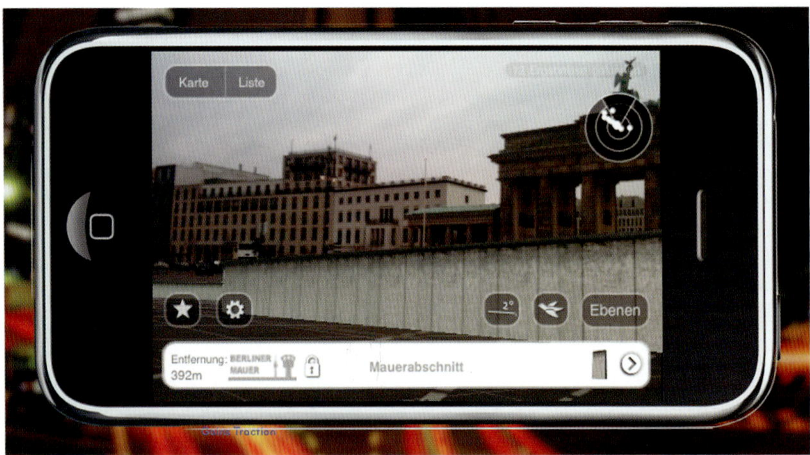

Plate 4 (figure I.4)
Historical augmented-reality context awareness in Berlin. *Source:* Photograph courtesy of Earthmine/Layar.

Plate 5 (figure I.5)
Locative and context-aware augmented-reality advertising for the *Prince of Persia* game. *Source:* Photograph courtesy of Earthmine/Layar.

Plate 6 (figure I.6)
Becoming aware of embeddedness and systemic context awareness in Rafael Lozano-Hemmer's *Under Scan*, Leicester, UK (2006). *Source:* Photograph courtesy of Rafael Lozano-Hemmer.

Plate 7 (figure 4.1)
David Rokeby, *Sorting Daemon* (2003). *Source:* Permission kindly granted by the artist.

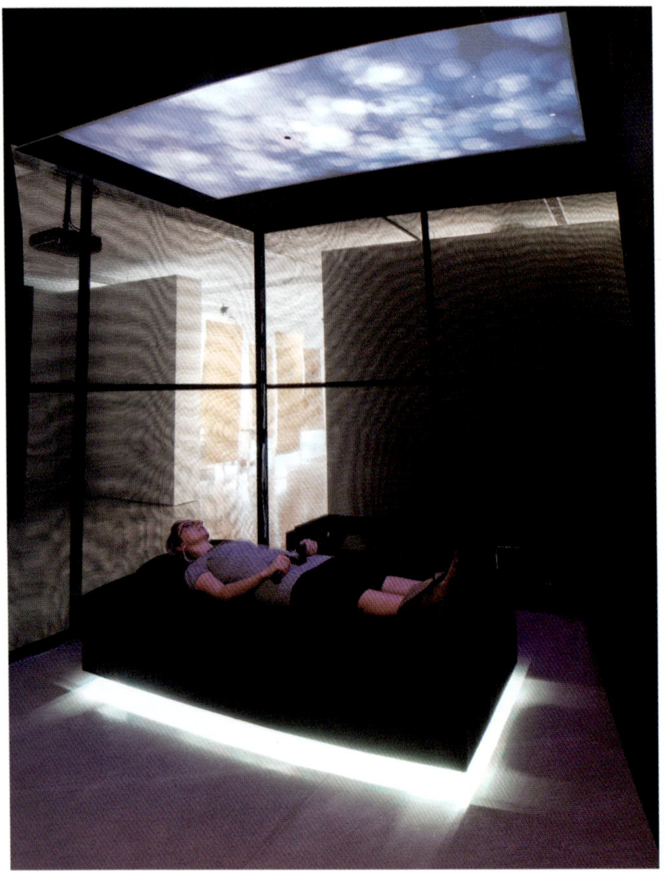

Plate 8 (figure 4.2)
George Poonkhin Khut, with David Morris-Oliveros, *The Heart Library Project* (2009). *Source:* Permission kindly granted by the artist.

Plate 9 (figure 10.1)
Tokyo, the ubiquity of mobile phones. *Source:* Larissa Hjorth 2004.

Plate 10 (figure 10.2)
Three generations and remediations of personalized media (*keitai* version). *Source:* Larissa Hjorth 2004.

Plate 11 (figure 10.3)
Technocute personalization. *Source:* Larissa Hjorth 2004.

Plate 12 (figure 14.2)
Simon Penny, *Petit Mal—Autonomous Robotic Artwork* (1993–1995). *Source:* Shown here in the Smile Machines Exhibition (curator Anne-Marie Duguet), Transmediale 2006, Berlin.

Plate 13 (figure 15.2)
Installation, tendentially embedded, and a single human interactant going through vertical kinesthetic experiments. David Rokeby, *Very Nervous System* (1986–1990). *Source:* Installation view at Foundation for Art Creative Technology (FACT), Liverpool. Photograph by Nathan Cox. Permission kindly granted by FACT.

Plate 14 (figure 15.3)

An array of kinesthetic experiments with *Very Nervous System* at Foundation for Art Creative Technology (FACT) in Liverpool, 2007. *Source:* Image array design by Mike Carroll. Photograph courtesy of FACT (Risa Horowitz, William Eakin, and Elizabeth Garlicki).

Plate 15 (figure 17.1)

A *Second Life* avatar stands in an interior (office) environment. *Source:* From the Augmented Environment Lab, Georgia Institute of Technology, http://arsecondlife.gvu.gatech.edu.

Plate 16 (figure 18.1)
Franck Le Blanc, *Trajets Diptyque* (2007). *Source:* Permission kindly granted by the artist.

Plate 17 (figure 18.2)
Laurent Sales, *Trajets* (2005). *Source:* Video still image. Permission kindly granted by the artist.

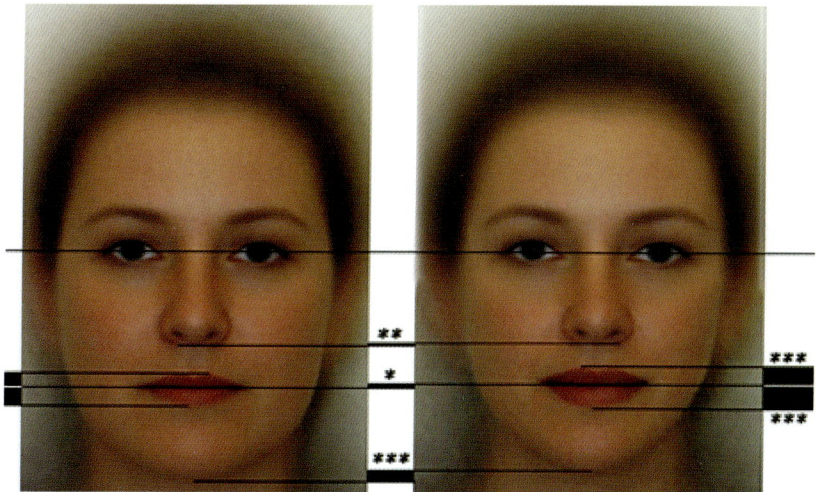

Plate 18 (figure 20.7)

"Difference between average and attractive female faces." *Source:* From Johnston 2008.

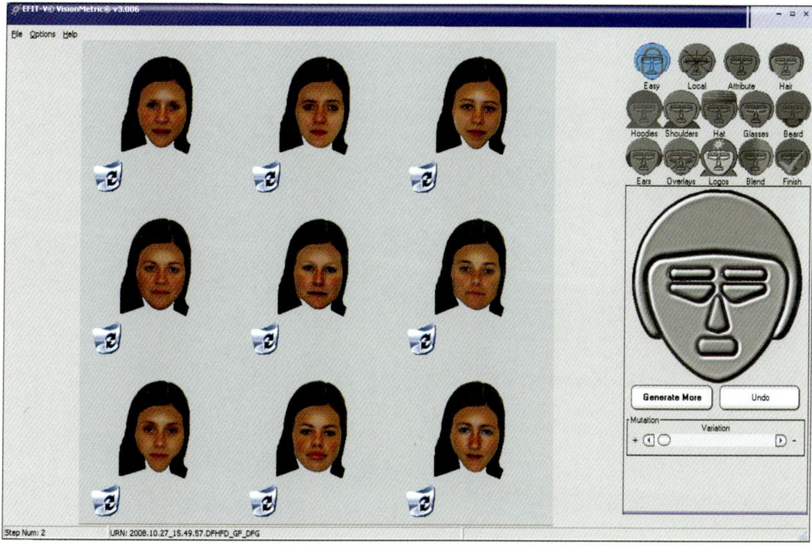

Plate 19 (figure 20.8)

E-FIT screen shot. *Source:* Courtesy of Visionmetrics.

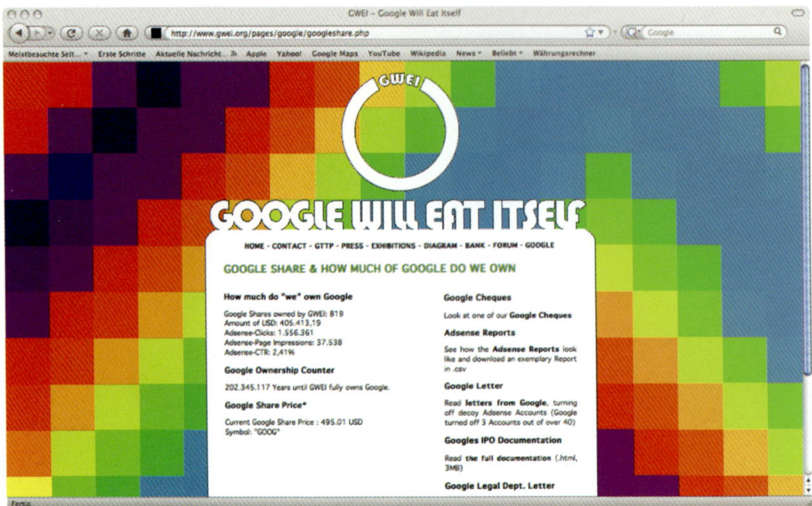

Plate 20 (figure 21.1)

GWEI—Google Will Eat Itself, part I of the *EKMRZ Trilogy* (2005–2009). *Source:* Screenshot. Permission kindly granted by UBERMORGEN.COM.

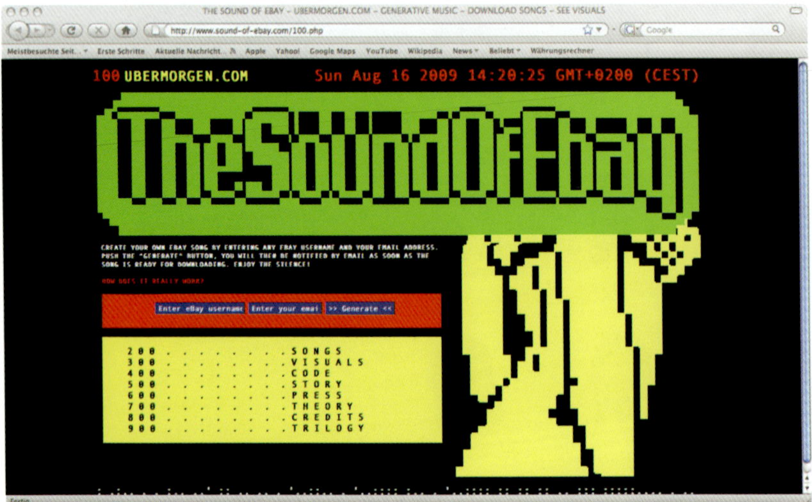

Plate 21 (figure 21.4)

The Sound of eBay, part III of the *EKMRZ Trilogy* (2008–2009). *Source:* Screenshot. Permission kindly granted by UBERMORGEN.COM.

Plate 22 (figure 22.2)

C5 and Jack Toolin, *The Perfect View*, C5 Media Player, screenshot; *N 37 49.130 W 083 34.847, Kentucky*, 30 × 68 × 2.5″ triptych (photography, satellite aerial imagery, three-dimensional computer graphic imagery). *Source:* Courtesy of Jack Toolin.

Plate 23 (figure 22.3)

Preemptive Media (Beatriz da Costa, Jamie Schulte, Brooke Singer), *Area's Immediate Reading* (*AIR*), 2006. Prototypes of portable air-quality measurement kits to monitor various air pollutants, accompanied by data visualizations of the findings. *AIR* is a process-oriented, socially based artwork that integrates the community into the creation and presentation of the work. *Source:* Photograph courtesy of Preemptive Media.

Plate 24 (figure 24.2)

Timm-Oliver Wilks, Thorsten Kiesl, and Harald Moser, *garden of eden* (2007). *Source:* Permission kindly granted by the artists.

Plate 25 (figure 27.1)
Eduardo Kac, *Genesis* (1999), transgenic work with artist-created bacteria, ultraviolet light, and Internet. Video (detail), edition of 2, dimensions variable. *Source:* Courtesy of the Collection Instituto Valenciano de Arte Moderno, Valencia, Spain.

Plate 26 (figure 27.2)
The *whisper[s]* project and Gretchen Elsner, pieces of interactive clothes (2003–2005), Simon Fraser University, Vancouver. *Source:* Photograph by Elisa Gonzales.

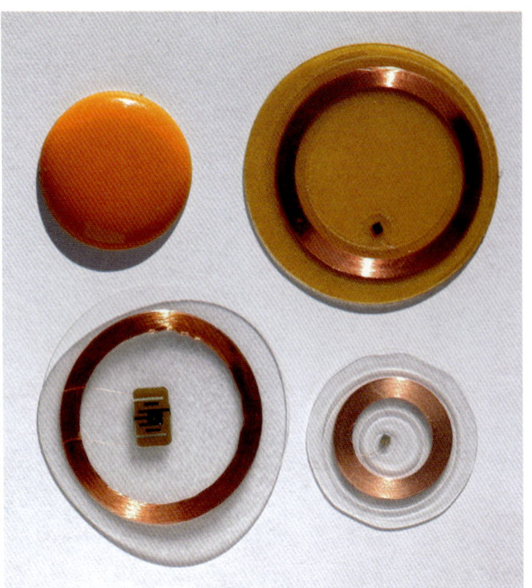

Plate 27 (figure 30.1)

Variety of passive tags. *Source:* Courtesy of Nicholas Gessler and his collection of "Things-That-Think."

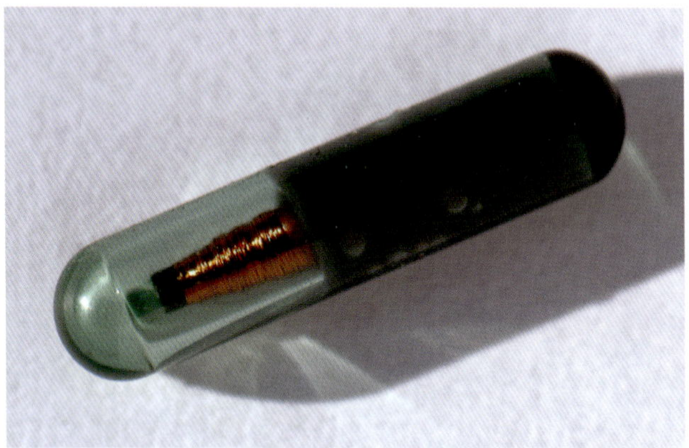

Plate 28 (figure 30.4)

RFID tag in glass capsule intended for implantation in domestic animals (or, as Scott Silverman of VeriChip Corporation suggests, in humans). *Source:* Courtesy of Nicholas Gessler and his collection of "Things-That-Think."

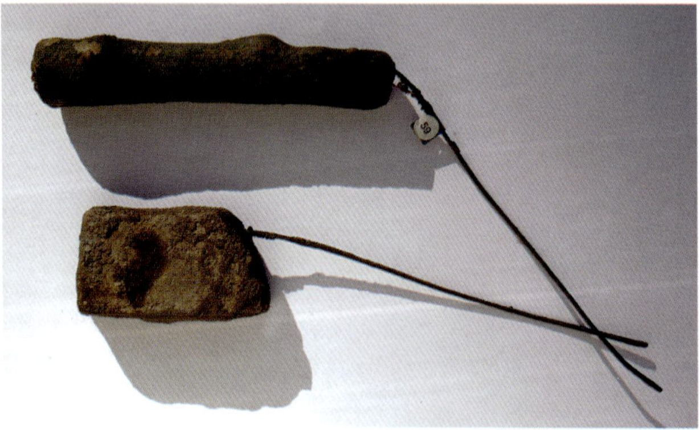

Plate 29 (figure 30.5)

RFID devices such as the ones shown here were coupled with vibration sensors and used by the US military to detect traffic in the Vietnam War. *Source:* Courtesy of Nicholas Gessler and his collection of "Things-That-Think."

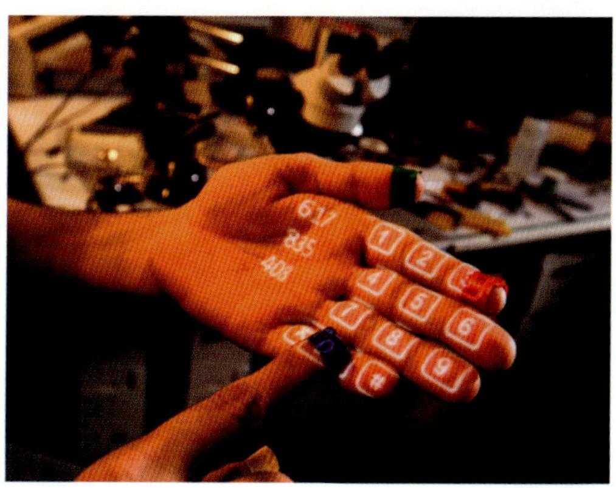

Plate 30 (figure 33.1)

Active phone keyboard overlayed on user's hand, part of Pranav Mistry and Pattie Maes's SixthSense prototype. *Source:* Photograph courtesy of Pranav Mistry.

Plate 31 (figure 33.2)

Camera recognizes flight coupon and projects departure update on the ticket. *Source:* Photograph courtesy of Pranav Mistry.

Plate 32 (figure 33.3)

Camera recognizes news story from the Web and streams video to the page. *Source:* Photograph courtesy of Pranav Mistry.

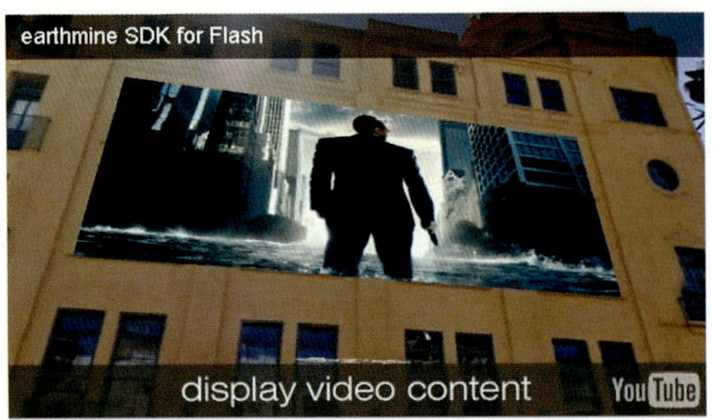

Plate 33 (figure 33.4)
Earthmine attaches location-aware applications (in this case streaming video) to specific real-world locations. Three-dimensional mapping, location-aware applications, and augmented-reality browsers. *Source:* Photograph courtesy of Earthmine/Layar.

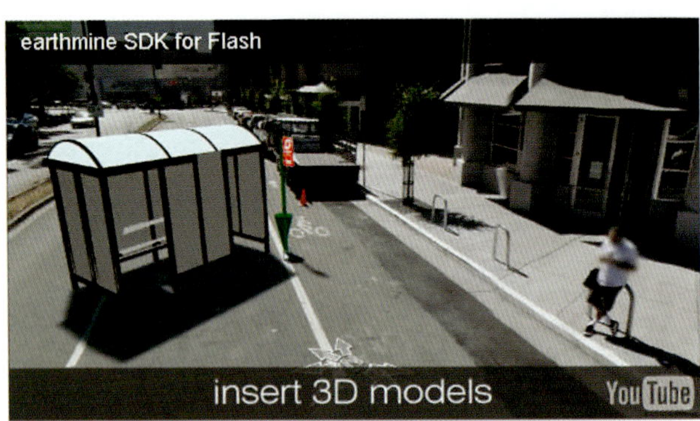

Plate 34 (figure 33.5)
Earthmine enables three-dimensional objects to be overlaid on specific locations. *Source:* Photograph courtesy of Earthmine/Layar.

Plate 35 (figure 33.6)
Layar augmented-reality browser overlays information, graphics, and animation on specific locations. *Source:* Photograph courtesy of Earthmine/Layar.

22 Contexts as Moving Targets: Locative Media Art and the Shifting Ground of Context Awareness

Christiane Paul

In recent years, the concepts of ubiquitous and pervasive computing have gradually counterbalanced, if not superseded, the notion of a predominantly virtual cyberspace as the quintessential model of the "digital environment." Physical computing has always been an important aspect of the history of computation. Yet popular notions of the digital environment from the 1980s on were profoundly shaped by the concepts of virtuality or "cyberspace" developed in novels such as William Gibson's *Neuromancer* (1984) and Neal Stephenson *Snow Crash* (1992). These concepts found their manifestation in the "embodied virtuality" of immersive environments accessed through head-mounted displays and data gloves and were critically analyzed from various theoretical perspectives in books such as Michael Benedikt's collected volume *Cyberspace: First Steps* (1991) and Sherry Turkle's *Life on the Screen* (1995). Although the concepts of virtuality and physical forms of computing are closely connected, ubiquitous computing places emphasis on the embeddedness of microprocessors in every aspect of daily life and on the connectivity and access to social networks enabled by mobile devices. As cyberspace, ubiquitous computing is surrounded by a certain amount of hype and invites a set of critical questions. As Ulrik Ekman points out in his introduction to this volume, ubiquitous computing and pervasive computing are not a clearly demarcated field, and a critique of their idealities has to be undertaken. What exactly does ubiquity mean if large portions of the world remain disconnected from digital networks or are restricted by their governments in their use of these networks? How can we classify the impact of pervasive computing, which ranges from enhanced agency and participation to invasive tracking?

This chapter focuses on ubiquitous computing and pervasive computing—considered an extension of computational processing power into a multitude of everyday scenarios—as they manifest in projects that make use of mobile computational devices. Ubiquitous computing has expanded both the physical manifestations and the concepts of interfaces and enabled new forms of human–software–hardware interaction. A substantial amount of research in the area of "interface" focuses on interface aesthetics as an aesthetics of systems rather than on the aesthetics of interfacing as the (social) practices of interaction. One can argue that there are two major approaches to context awareness: one focusing on the human, embodied, subjective, phenomenological experience; the other being driven by embedded technological systems and their "awareness" or reading of their physical environments and their human inhabitants. These two approaches frequently interconnect because the interpretation of a context by a technological device or system can in turn affect the individual or intersubjective awareness of the person using it.

Mobile computing potentially enables various forms of social interaction and has to be considered in relation to concepts of embodiment, the creation of meaning, as well as individual autonomy and agency. The latter aspects of mobile computing and locative media considerably affect our perception and awareness of environments. One might argue that digital technologies have expanded the agency enabled by our embodied condition: our bodies can function as interfaces in navigating virtual environments; avatars can be understood as a virtual embodiment; wearable computing can establish a technologized connectivity between bodies; and mobile devices can function as technological extension of embodiment, connecting us to location-based information and enhancing awareness of our environment or "social body."

Locative new-media art, which uses locations in public space as a "canvas" for implementing art projects, has become one of the most active and fast-growing areas within the larger field of digital arts. Wireless networks and "nomadic devices" such as mobile phones and personal digital assistants (PDAs) have blurred the boundaries between the translocal (connections between different sites) and the locative or site specific. Camera and video phones, Blackberries, iPhones, and mobile devices with embedded Global Positioning System technology have become new platforms for cultural production, providing an interface through which users can participate in networked public projects and enabling the formation of ad hoc communities. The networked, multilayered informational systems that are supported by digital media are in constant flux and reorganization and seem to embody perfectly the notion of shifting (or even unstable) contexts; depending on the "links" and relations one establishes, any text both is embedded in multiple contexts and provides context for information outside itself.

This essay discusses different approaches to understanding context awareness and tries to identify different categories of locative site-specific media art and their effect on human awareness of the environment. Most of the projects discussed in this text are site-specific (rather than translocal) locative-media projects that allow participants to "leave a mark" on their surroundings, to submit or retrieve site-specific information, or to reconfigure a map. In these cases, the focus of the discussion is context awareness as it is shaped by embodied phenomenological experience. Another group of projects explored here involves system "awareness" of the environment, ranging from "reactive" architectures to embedded surveillance systems or sensors for monitoring environmental factors such as air quality. Responsive locations and architectures seemingly reflect their inhabitants' presence, movements, actions and reactions, profile, tasks and goals, emotions and behavior. These types of projects tend to shift emphasis from increasing human awareness of a site's architecture to a systemic awareness of people's moods or behaviors. Locative-media projects addressing surveillance or environmental issues place emphasis on increasing people's awareness of the larger sociopolitical context of the site, often encouraging or enabling their users to become proactive and engage in local politics.

Context Awareness: Grounding Place and Life

Events in physical space, physical locations, or objects are situated within a field of relations, many of which are usually kept out of sight, separated by space. The immediate transition between different kinds of location-specific information that is made possible by hyperlinked media platforms, in contrast, erases the perception that we have moved between blocks of information that—in the physical world—would be pages and shelves or even cities and countries apart. The spatial distance dividing the center from the margin or the text from its context (e.g., in a book) is subjugated to the temporality of the link; every context is yet another central text or vice versa. Digital media make relations and connections accessible and allow movement between contexts. They undermine the very notion of context, enriching it while rendering the concept of context itself superfluous.

Context is a complex construct: it can be physical (bound to a location), social (connected to human interactions), organizational and economic (attached to structures of governance and systems of value). From a global perspective, context is about location, enriching the specifics of a particular place. From a local perspective, context is about activity and agency, the ability to engage with the location. The slogan "think global, act local," which has become a catchphrase of the information society, points to this relationship. It is interesting to note that the phrase originally appeared in the book *Cities in Evolution* (1915) by Patrick Geddes, connecting ideas of urban planning, social conditions, and education. The increasing interest in the locative and site specific within digital media counterbalances the promise of the "any time, any place" slogan associated with instant, "global" access and connectivity provided by digital networks. At the heart of locative media lies the recognition of the human condition as embodied—the fact that, translocal connectivity and virtual worlds aside, we are always bound to the perception of the world through our bodies.

In his book *Digital Ground: Architecture, Pervasive Computing, and Environmental Knowing* (2004), Malcolm McCullough makes a distinction between "setting" as objective, a priori space and "context" as both the engagement with the setting and the bias that this space creates for the interactions occurring within it (48). Contextual factors play an essential role in any form of interactivity and its quality as well as influence the respective action's intention. "Activity theory"—initiated by Russian psychologists Lev Vygotsky (1896–1934) and his colleagues A. N. Leont'ev and A. R. Luria in the 1920s and 1930s and proposing a model of artifact-mediated and object-oriented action—has become a useful approach to understanding the connections between context, activity, and intentionality.

McCullough points out that networks cannot be separated from location and architecture and that it is equally important to understand informational, physical, and cultural contexts. Context awareness and the ability to improvise in contexts are a necessity for functioning in an information society that finds its extension in mobile media and pervasive computing. According to McCullough, ethnographic fieldwork had become intrinsic to digital-systems development by the late 1990s (2004, 157–159).

Digital Ground illustrates that "grounding place" is an expression of culture and that it is a necessity to ground life in effective contexts in order to have agency (McCullough 2004, 171). Places are always repositories of value (from economic to personal and social) established through interactions. In *Place and Placelessness* (1976), Edward Relph writes, "Places are defined less by unique locations, landscape, and communities than by the focusing of experiences and intention onto particular settings" (141). Relph juxtaposes the *identity of* a place with the personal *identification with* a site. He argues that the identification with a place is as much about subjective "insideness" as about the "outsideness" created by objective boundaries, and he proposes different scales of insideness, among them a "vicarious insideness" created through the arts (50–55). Art can certainly have a major effect on both the identity of and identification with a space, although the degree of its impact will vary substantially depending on the nature of an art project.

The subjective perception of place and the emotional effects of the geographical environment also were the focus of the Situationists' concept of psychogeography, which experienced a revival in the art of the 1980s and 1990s and is particularly relevant to many site-specific mobile media. The Situationist International, a political and artistic movement, emerged in the late 1950s through the fusion of several smaller groups, among them the Lettrist International and the London Psychogeographical Association. In his "Introduction to a Critique of Urban Geography" (1955), Guy Debord writes:

> Psychogeography sets for itself the study of the precise laws and specific effects of the geographical environment, whether consciously organized or not, on the emotions and behavior of individuals. The charmingly vague adjective psychogeographical can be applied to the findings arrived at by this type of investigation, to their influence on human feelings, and more generally to any situation or conduct that seems to reflect the same spirit of discovery.

The subjective and temporal view and experience of the geographical environment or city is captured in Debord's famous "Naked City" map of Paris, which deconstructs the grid of the city and structure of its society by ripping it apart, bringing its marginalized spaces to the center and connecting them by arrows. The arrows give visual form to the Situationists' strategy of *détournement*, a deflection or diversion and distortion that reconfigure an object or situation, resulting in a rerouting of the city's flow.

One can argue that major factors in the subjective view of or identification with a place are immersion into the site and potential engagement with it—factors that can be further discussed by means of the concept of "flow." Not coincidentally, flow is frequently mentioned in McCullough's *Digital Ground* when it comes to satisfactory experiences enabled by pervasive computing. Psychologist Mihály Csíkszentmihályi describes the concept of "flow" as a mental state in which the person is fully immersed in his or her activity by a feeling of energized focus and full involvement and by an experience of success in the process of the activity (Csíkszentmihályi 1990, 1996, 1997, 2003; Csíkszentmihályi and Rathunde 1993, 60) (see figure 22.1). In a state of flow, consciousness is full of experiences in harmony with each other, and action is effortless. Flow in activities allow a person to focus on goals that are clear and compatible and provide immediate feedback (Csíkszentmihályi 1997, 29–30). Csíkszentmihályi's

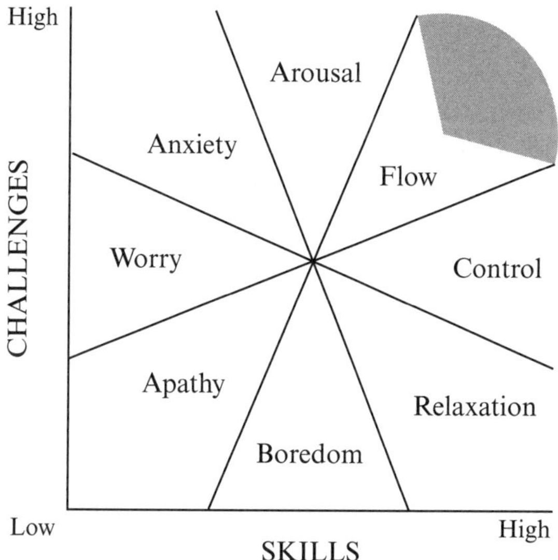

Figure 22.1
Mihály Csíkszentmihályi, flow diagram. Adapted from Massimini and Carli 1988 and Csíkszentmihályi 1990. Permission kindly granted by the authors.

concept has been referenced in a range of fields and has been applied within the field of new media to user experiences in gaming in particular. He identifies several factors that accompany an experience of flow (all of which are not needed to achieve the experience, though), among them a loss of the feeling of self-consciousness, the merging of action and awareness, a balance between ability level and challenge (the activity is neither too easy nor too difficult), and absorption in the activity so that the focus of awareness is narrowed down to the activity itself.

According to Csíkszentmihályi, flow tends to occur when a person's skills are fully involved in overcoming a challenge that is just about manageable, and optimal experiences involve a fine balance between the person's ability to act and the available opportunities for action (1997, 30).

Csíkszentmihályi's theories provide an interesting backdrop for exploring context awareness in relation to locative media because they raise several questions: What role does the awareness of a place's context and of one's self play in the merging of awareness and activity that produces a feeling of flow? Does the identification with a site brought about by context awareness enhance the experience of flow because it induces a merging of context awareness, self-awareness, and activity? Do context awareness and self-awareness enhance or compete with each other? How do mobile devices, which require active engagement and set up or determine the activity in which the user is engaged, affect flow (considering that the experience of flow will depend on whether the user's ability level in interacting with a device matches the challenges of the hardware and software)?

In the rest of the essay, I explore these questions and factors in more detail with regard to different categories of locative-media art. My goal is to investigate whether different forms of locative media might produce different kinds of context awareness. The discussion of projects in the next section focuses on works that are experienced on site rather than on those works that transcend locality and establish global connections. It approaches the projects mostly from the perspective of embodied experience, which frequently intersects with the "awareness" of mobile or embedded technological systems such as Global Positioning System (GPS), radio-frequency identification (RFID), and surveillance devices.

Taxonomies of Shifting Grounds: Context Awareness in Locative Media-Art Practices

Networked mobile devices have opened up new sites for artistic intervention in public space, thereby broadening our concept of so-called public art,, which has traditionally been considered art displayed in public spaces outside of a designated art context or for public performative events. Public art has a long history, is usually authorized and sometimes financed by the government or authority administering the respective space, and has frequently been used by totalitarian regimes for propaganda. However, there also is a history of "guerilla" public art (Bou 2006; Mathieson and Tàpies 2009) —street art that often has an activist, subversive quality and most commonly takes the form of graffiti or tagging.

An important element in all public art is the varying degree of audience participation and agency. Agency manifests itself in the possibilities for influencing, changing, or creating institutions and events or for acting as a proxy. Degrees of agency are measured by the ability to have a meaningful effect in the world and in a social context, which naturally entails responsibilities.

Networked locative media art can be understood as a new form of public art, which can be both translocal (connecting people across geographical locations) and site specific, enhancing or augmenting physical space with contextual information that can be deposited or retrieved or both. Mobile locative media have found a broad spectrum of use in artistic practice that includes the annotation and augmentation of urban spaces or landscapes with information; location-specific narratives; critical engagement with the cultural impact of mobile technologies; and enhancement of the public's agency through data gathering. Many artists and media practitioners have also critically explored the issues surrounding privacy and identity that emerge from mobile-media devices' tracking and surveillance capabilities.

In the rest of this section, different categories of locative media art are examined with regard to their effects on context awareness and their aesthetics. Although this taxonomy of locative media art focuses mostly on projects created for mobile devices, it also includes some projects in which the location is seemingly aware of its inhabitants or passersby. The categories outlined are meant as a flexible diagram rather than as a rigid classification, and so they frequently overlap.

Media Annotations of Cartographic Space—Mapping Experience

Developments in mobile-media technologies have brought about a variety of projects that focus on "augmenting" existing physical spaces and architectures by allowing participants to retrieve or contribute contextual information, be it personal or historical. From a technological point of view, these projects may involve actual augmented-reality systems, in which physical space is augmented by overlayed virtual information or mixed reality, which involves fluid transitions between the physical and virtual realms.

A number of locative-media projects have focused on mapping existing physical spaces and architectures, a phenomenon that Malcolm McCullough explores from a different perspective, as ambient inscription and urban markup, in his chapter in this volume (chapter 26). *PDPal* (2002–) by Scott Paterson, Marina Zurkow, and Julian Bleecker,[1] for example, was a mapping tool accessible on the Internet and downloadable to one's PDA that allowed users to record personal experiences of the Times Square area in New York City and the Twin Cities, Minnesota. Users would create personal maps by marking locations on a geographical map with graphic symbols and giving them attributes and ratings. A similar approach was taken by the British collective Proboscis for *Urban Tapestries* (2002–2004), a research project and experimental software platform for "public authoring in the wireless city" that combined mobile and Internet technologies with geographic information systems technology and enabled people to "author" the environment around them.[2]

These projects facilitate the creation of personal, cultural, or historical context for geographical spaces, thereby developing context awareness with regard to specific locations. At the same time, these works presumably raise the participants' awareness both of the geographical environment's impact on their own emotions and behavior and (through the collaborative maps) of the (ad hoc) community inhabiting and visiting that very place. Context awareness of place is closely intertwined with an awareness of self and community. One can speculate that this merging of context awareness, self-awareness, and activity might generally create an enhanced experience of flow.

Although these media annotations and experiential mappings of personal experience reflect the concept of psychogeography, they do not necessarily go beyond the inherent limitations or assumptions of the traditional map. In her article "Redefining the Basemap" (2006), Alison Sant raises questions regarding the constraints of the base map and the possibilities of "moving beyond the grid," asking whether it is possible to map the city through its use patterns and the rhythms of urban life.

Sant's remarks point to an important factor in the establishment of context awareness: the grounding of context itself. As a network of circumstances or facts surrounding a particular place, event, or situation, context needs to be bound, attached, and tied to its "central text." Traditional cartography and its conventions have the advantage that they provide an easy foundation for grounding context in a setting; however, this cartography limits the potential of locative media to open up new contexts.

Repositioning Cartography—Mapping Experience and Flow

Within the larger field of locative media art, a group of works has focused on the flow of (human) movement through space as a driving factor in the creation of experiential maps. Because the projects in this category place an emphasis on the tracking of flow and trajectories rather than on the annotation of existing architectures and cartography, it does not come as a surprise that most of them rely on GPS-enabled mobile devices.

Amsterdam Real Time (2002)—a project by artists Esther Polak and Jeroen Kee realized in collaboration with the Waag Society—presented "a diary in traces" by tracking sixty volunteers' daily itineraries through the city of Amsterdam over several months.[3] The collective map of these itineraries illustrates overlaps in the frequency of the use of certain routes and reveals which ones are most commonly traveled. *Amsterdam*

Real Time creates a visual context for understanding the "use" of a city as it manifests in the daily routes taken by its inhabitants. This context presumably creates an awareness of patterns of movement, which—if investigated on a larger scale—may potentially give information about the economic and social conditions within the city. *Amsterdam Real Time* does not use the city map as a basis, yet the city map remains a recognizable backdrop to the tracking done in the project. Other projects, such as Teri Rueb's *The Choreography of Everyday Movement* (2001),[4] further remove or even abandon the map, which leads to a change of context. With the topographical anchor removed, the awareness of context shifts from place and larger sociopolitical conditions to the poetics of the line and the movements that created it.

A combination of GPS-supported spatiotemporal mapping and user annotation unfolds in Esther Polak's *MILK* (2003), which originally investigated spatial and temporal representations of the routes of several small-scale Latvian milk farms and of milk transportation throughout Europe.[5] From February to April 2009, Polak traveled to Nigeria and used satellite technology to track the distribution of "Peak" brand milk from Lagos to the capital of Abuja and a nomadic Fulani family of cow herders in Abuja's vicinity. Polak was accompanied by a custom-built robot that was fed the GPS data and drew the people's recorded routes with sand, allowing groups of people to watch the drawing and reflect communally, and their responses were videotaped.[6] Compared to the projects previously discussed, *MILK* is more explicitly focused on the economic conditions of the production and distribution of one particular product and about changes produced by context awareness.

In all of the GPS-based experiential mapping projects mentioned here, the awareness of context emerges less "in the moment" of moving through space itself (although there presumably is an awareness of one's movements being recorded) and more retrospectively in the process of viewing the recorded patterns. Although the media annotations of public space discussed previously enhance spatial context awareness at the site itself, the experiential mapping of movements via GPS emphasizes the spatiotemporal dimension rather than reinscribing cartography. The understanding and role of traditional cartography are not revised but at least repositioned in adding the temporal dimension of the flow of people who are "writing" their own map.

A different take on repositioning of the map, with a more comparative focus, is proposed in the project *Landscape Initiative* (2002–2005) by the San Jose–based art group C5 (1997–2007). The project consists of three parts—*The Analogous Landscape, The Perfect View,* and *The Other Path*—for which the group undertook massive performative expeditions all over the world using GPS tracking (figure 22.2). At the project Web site,[7] visitors can use the C5 GPS Media Player to access the GPS track logs of each C5 member's route in the different manifestations of the project, view associated media documentation (photographs/video), and investigate multiple track logs to compare the landscapes. GPS in itself has created new forms of relationships with the

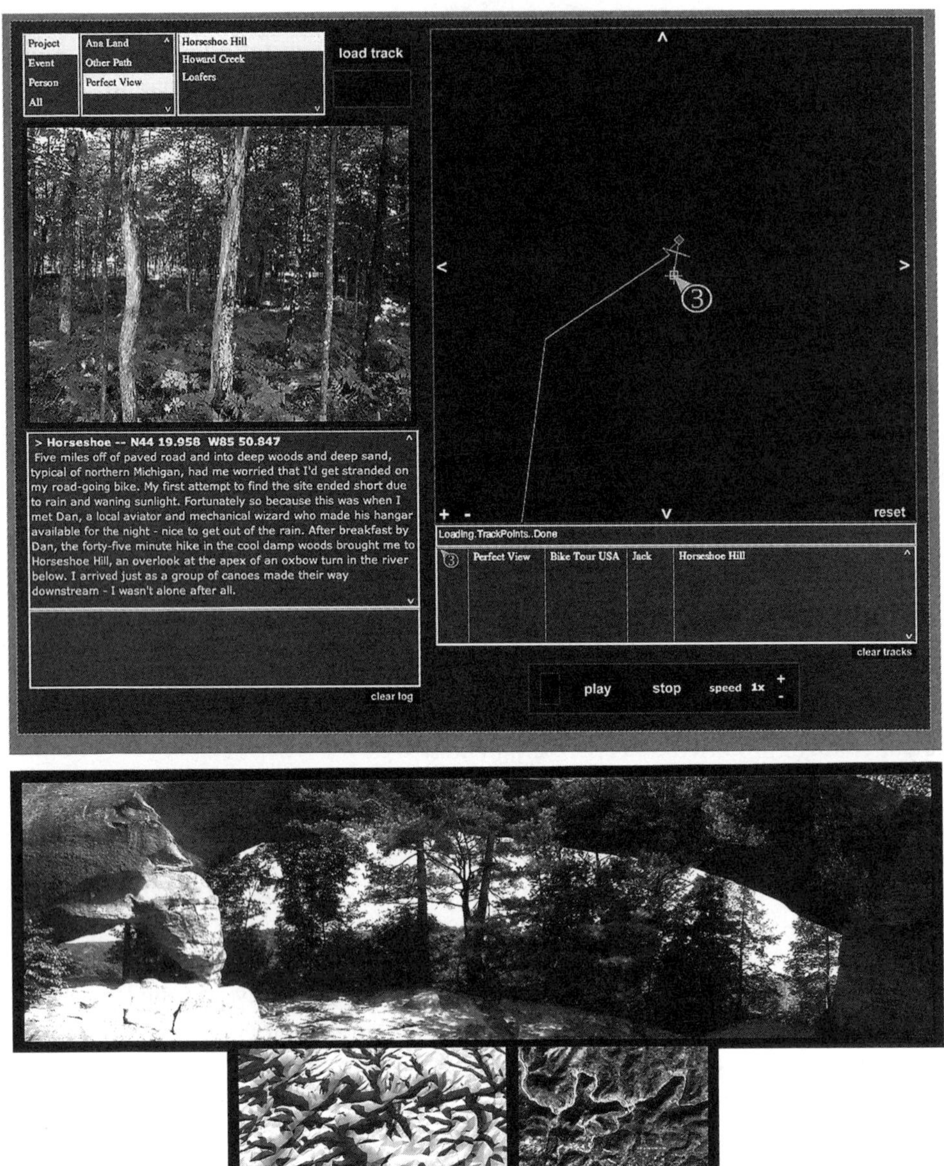

Figure 22.2

C5/Jack Toolin, *The Perfect View*, C5 Media Player, screenshot; *N 37 49.130 W 083 34.847, Kentucky*, 30 × 68 × 2.5″ triptych (photography, satellite aerial imagery, three-dimensional computer graphic imagery). Courtesy of Jack Toolin.

landscape, firmly positioning an individual or object in relation to a specific location while remaining a virtual data set; the Media Player's virtual track logs and overlapping paths form their own kind of landscape, which is rooted in a personal interaction with the actual landscape but translates into a virtual set of data that becomes a potential index of connections. The online project suggests a trajectory from personal experience to a data representation of this very experience and the possible contexts for understanding it.

In terms of Csíkszentmihályi's concept of flow, the mapping of experience and movement over time seems to have very different effects than media annotations of space. In the GPS-supported cartography of movement, meaning presumably emerges mostly in the process of contemplating the map after its creation. There is more of a retrospective self-conscious awareness of contexts of movement (while looking at the map) and less of a merging of action and awareness in the moment of creating the map while moving through space.

Behavioral Awareness—Responding to the Environment

The cartographies of movement created in many GPS-based works find their counterpoint in the projects that use locative media to create an awareness of how one behaves in a given environment. These projects do not necessarily result in maps but initiate engagements with space that invite users to reflect on their patterns of behavior and movements.

Jennifer Crowe and Scott Paterson's performative mobile-media project *Follow Through* (2005), for example, was created specifically for the Whitney Museum of American Art's Fifth Floor Permanent Collection galleries to reflect on behavioral conventions in a museum environment.[8] To experience the work, visitors used portable media players to access the existing audio tour for the fifth-floor galleries and received, in addition to the audio for a specific work, visual instructions to engage in a set of small exercises designed to bring well-established behavioral codes of museum attendance into relief. The exercises consisted of small actions that gallery visitors would casually "perform" on any given visit (such as assuming a certain pose in front of a work or making a specific gesture) and drew attention to common body language in the museum setting.

By contrast, Layla Gaye's *Sonic City* (2002–2004) responded to participants' interaction with urban space through music. The wearable system functioned as a form of interactive music instrument that allowed participants to create a soundscape of electronic music by walking through an urban environment. Creating music on the basis of everyday activities, the project found aesthetic expression for everyday practices.

Although *Follow Through* and *Sonic City* were radically different in their approaches and spatial context, both established a framework for enhancing awareness of context-specific behaviors. One can assume that both projects to some extent disrupted flow by separating action from awareness, making people "step back" and ponder their actions and movements and creating a space for reflection on (subconscious) activities. *Sonic City* enabled its participants to consciously use their awareness of movements to "play" the city, adding a level of intentionality.

Location-Based Storytelling

Context awareness plays out in yet another way in the projects that use mobile devices for a process of location-based storytelling in which participants retrieve elements of a visual or audio narrative at specific locations. In these cases, place becomes the canvas for a documentary, fictional, or semifictional narrative experienced on site (the narrative obviously can range from a more traditional story to a more abstract experiment). This scenario also often unfolds in mobile gaming projects, which are not the focus of the discussion here. In location-based storytelling, the actual historical context of a site can potentially be completely reconfigured, creating a changed awareness of site.

Teri Rueb's project *Core Sample* (2007) used GPS technology to create a factual and fictional interactive audio narrative that mixes natural and processed sounds as well as the voices of former residents to tell a unique story of Spectacle Island in Boston Harbor and to draw attention to its natural soundscape.

By contrast, Julian Bleecker's *WiFi ArtCache* (2003) created a far more abstract "narrative" by transforming a specific location into a form of wireless art repository. The project established an access point for digital animations by creating a free-floating Wi-Fi node that had been deliberately disconnected from the Internet. It investigated the possibilities of wireless, location-based narrative and the production of space itself in that participants needed to be within physical range of the node to retrieve information. In terms of context awareness, the project presumably draws more attention to the demarcation of an invisible yet physical "space for art" and to specifics of the art objects rather than to specifics of the site.

A more documentary approach was taken in a location-aware mobile narrative for the Dublin Liberties neighborhood, *Media Portrait of the Liberties* (2004), by Valentina Nisi, Ian Oakley, and Mads Haahr.[9] The stories were delivered to the audience on location-aware PDAs, and each story could be viewed only when an audience member was situated in the physical place where the story is set. As opposed to many of the other works discussed here, the *Media Portrait* project was accompanied by an extensive user study, which captured the reaction of three broad audience samples: media experts, community members, and nonresidents. Despite being anchored in physical locations, location-based storytelling that uses very rich media content and traditional narration (more than any of the previous categories) might run the risk of competing with the audience's awareness of and focus on the site itself.

Site Awareness—Architectures Reflecting Their Inhabitants

Although the projects in which locations and architectures seemingly reflect their inhabitants' presence, movements, actions and reactions, profile, tasks and goals, emotions and behaviors do not fall in the category of mobile, locative media art, they also need to be considered in relation to context awareness.

In Camille Utterback's *Abundance* (2006), for example—a temporary public installation in San Jose, California, commissioned by ZERO1, the Art and Technology Network —people's movements through City Hall Plaza were captured by a video camera, and at night these captured movements generated a dynamic, visual composition projected on the three-story cylindrical rotunda of City Hall.[10] *Abundance* allowed people to inscribe their presence temporarily into the site's architecture and visualized the "social space" created by people's movements in the plaza. Context awareness presumably was focused on people's behaviors on the site rather than on the context of the building itself. As opposed to some GPS-enabled tracking of the flow of people, where meaning emerges mostly from looking at a completed graphic, *Abundance* created an immediate awareness by functioning as a type of "mirror."

A different type of context was visualized in Q. S. Serafijn's *D-tower* (1998–2004), an art piece commissioned by the Dutch city of Doetinchem and codeveloped by V2_lab.[11] *D-tower* strove to map the emotions of the city's inhabitants by illuminating a physical tower in different colors corresponding to citizens' feelings of happiness, love, fear, and hate as well as to create awareness of the urban landscape as a space inscribed by human perception and emotion.

The previously discussed projects are only a starting point for exploring the much larger field of architectures that reflect inhabitants or even respond to them. There presumably will be an increasing amount of locative-media projects that explore responsive architectures.

Any discussion of architectures—from private homes to institutions, public spaces, border regions, and infrastructures—that are seemingly "aware" of their inhabitants cannot ignore the impact of the pervasive surveillance and tracking technologies that are often linked to the very mobile devices that enable communication and agency. Numerous projects and art exhibitions have critically engaged with these issues in recent years.[12]

Surveillance and Sousveillance—Tracking the Trackers

A growing category of activist locative-media projects has started to address tracking in surveillance and consumer technologies. Issues of surveillance not only raise issues about control, privacy, and rights of the individual but also have to be seen in a larger cultural context of fascination with visibility. The age of Web 2.0 and social-networking technologies in particular has created platforms that allow people to "broadcast" themselves on a continuous basis. One might ask whether the various forms of enhanced awareness of physical, social, and cultural contexts supported by digital technologies enforce people's need to make the world aware of them and be observed by it. In "The Locative Dystopia" (2004), Drew Hemment states that we live in an age of "scopophilia," a mix of voyeurism, exhibitionism, and an ontological need to be observed.

Today's digital mobile devices and locative media have opened up a whole set of new possibilities for activist art and have enhanced the mobility that has always been an important factor in the field of tactical media. One strategy commonly employed by activist projects is to turn technologies against themselves—for example, by making mobile technologies' capacities for monitoring available to the public in a process of "sousveillance," or inverse surveillance, by the public itself.

Annina Rüst's *TRACK-THE-TRACKERS* (2003), for example, created awareness of the proliferation of video surveillance in the urban public sphere.[13] Participants took a mobile unit—a bag containing a laptop, GPS receiver, earphones, and a generic mouse —on a walk through the city and experienced a change of sound whenever they entered the vicinity of a surveillance camera. The sound effect was triggered by a surveillance camera whose locations were being added by participants to a continuously growing database. Similar to previously discussed projects, *TRACK-THE-TRACKERS* allowed the annotation and retrieval of information about public space, yet its intent was distinctly different from that of locative art, which enhances the identification with or historical identity of a site.

Tracking technologies not only are used for surveillance purposes but have also become increasingly commonplace in consumers' day-to-day lives. RFID tags, in particular—which N. Katherine Hayles discusses further in chapter 31 with regard to human agency and meaning—are playing an important role in tracing products. The use of shopping cards—store cards or "membership" cards—to assess and monitor consumer habits are just one example of how personal data are now accessed in order to maximize the effectiveness of information economies. Projects such as *Zapped!* (2004–) by Preemptive Media (Beatriz da Costa, Heidi Kumao, Jamie Schulte, and Brooke Singer)[14] critically address the mass deployment of RFID through workshops, devices, and activities. Among the devices developed by the group is the *Zapped!* Keychain RFID Detector, a keychain that rings when a RFID reader is within range and scanning the airwaves for people's data. The objective of *Zapped!* is to inform people about such tags and to encourage critical response and engagement rather than paranoia.

When it comes to context awareness, the projects discussed here have an ambiguous effect. On the one hand, although they enhance a user's understanding of a site and a larger social and cultural framework, they presumably disrupt or disturb flow and the immersion into and identification with a site: the environment (place and objects) and the surveillance technologies embedded in it might be perceived as "the enemy," which Inke Arns further explores in her chapter on the counterforces to tactile enclosures (chapter 22). On the other hand, the mobile technologies people use to engage in "sousveillance," or inverse surveillance, might have an empowering effect and create an experience of flow with regard to the activity of sousveillance itself. The increasing number of artists using sousveillance tactics—from Steve Mann[15] to Hasan Elahi[16] —the growing number of conferences devoted to or covering the subject,[17] and the creation of World Sousveillance Day in Toronto in 1998 testify to the momentum that concerns about embedded surveillance have gained.

Citizen Science and Environmental Context Awareness

Empowerment also is a key factor in the activist locative projects that employ mobile devices to gather environmental information, such as levels of carbon dioxide and contaminants. These works concentrate on a specific area of the "environmental knowing" that McCullough discusses in *Digital Ground,* where environments are understood as the sum of all present contexts shaped by our expectations that we have for technologies as they arise from location, embodiment, and architectural settings (2004, xv). Examples include the *Participatory Urbanism* (2002–) project developed by Eric Paulos and team from the Urban Atmospheres group at the Intel Research Lab[18] and Paulos's work with the Living Environments Lab, a part of the Human–Computer Interaction Institute at Carnegie Mellon University.[19] Both Intel Research and the Living Environments Lab are working on research in citizen science, which transforms mobile devices from mere communication tools into "networked mobile personal measurement instruments."[20] By authoring, sharing, and remixing new or existing technologies, the project series strives to give citizens more agency in contributing to decision making about their environment. Providing average, nonexpert inhabitants with hardware toolkits and physical sensors that can be easily attached to consumer mobile devices enables them to collect and share data about their surroundings and environment.

Another example of this type of work is Preemptive Media's *Area's Immediate Reading* (*AIR*) (2006), which consists of making portable air-quality measurement kits available to participants to monitor various air pollutants and tracking online the data visualizations that capture the findings (figures 22.3 and 22.4).[21]

Natalie Jeremijenko's *Feral Robotic Dogs* (2004–) project also collects data regarding emissions via hacked and reengineered toy robotic dogs such as Sony's Aibo.[22] In workshops and classes taught at universities and community centers, the dogs are equipped with sensors and then sent out to "sniff out" contaminants. The site conditions are then reported back to the "base" and interested community members.

The projects existing within the larger framework of citizen science strive largely to establish platforms for discussing environmental and energy politics and their

Figure 22.3
Preemptive Media (Beatriz da Costa, Jamie Schulte, Brooke Singer), *Area's Immediate Reading* (*AIR*), 2006. Prototypes of portable air-quality measurement kits to monitor various air pollutants, accompanied by data visualizations of the findings. *AIR* is a process-oriented, socially based artwork that integrates the community into the creation and presentation of the work. Photograph courtesy of Preemptive Media.

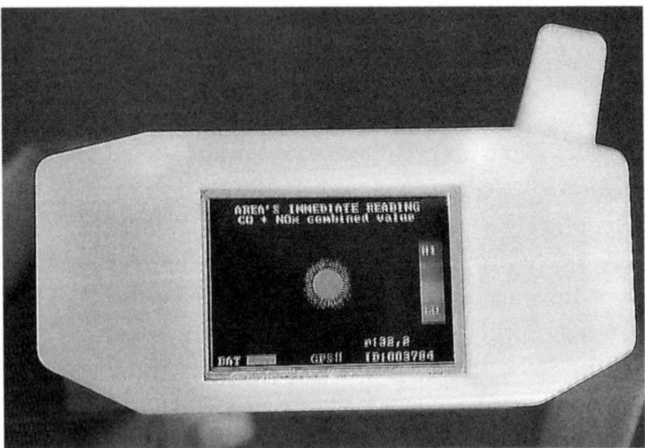

Figure 22.4
AIR device. Photograph courtesy of Preemptive Media.

impact on (natural) sites, health, and social groups in specific regions. At the core of these works lies the necessity to ground life in effective contexts in order to have agency.

Conclusions: Start/Stop Making Sense, or Where Is the (Con)Text?

The locative-media projects discussed here illustrate that context awareness is a highly complex construct influenced by multiple variables. The emphasis on awareness of a specific context—be it geographic, personal, social, cultural—can vary considerably from one category of locative-media works or even one project to another. Whether context awareness and self-awareness enhance or compete with each other and merge with the activity performed by the participant at any given point is dependent largely on the specifics of a project. Expertise, the way in which the content of a locative media project is presented, and the user's relationship to a site influence the degree to which context awareness and the performed activity lead to an experience of flow. Despite the fact that there is no definitive categorization of context awareness in locative media art, one can identify certain tendencies in different project categories and the kind of context awareness they emphasize.

There is no doubt that pervasive computing and locative media have increased the potential for various forms of context awareness. Although this awareness ideally leads to a deeper understanding of our environments and actions and enhances our agency in shaping them, it also involves the risk of losing the respective text/focus in an overload of site-specific, social, spatiotemporal context. Both Anne Galloway's discussion of affective politics in locative media (chapter 20) and Susan Kozel's exploration of a corporeal ethics for ubiquitous computing (chapter 19) in this volume further elaborate on the issues involved.

Do we want an environment in which our buildings broadcast their history and their inhabitants' activities, reflecting energy levels and the general mood of the city, while the city responds to our daily paths, reminds us what we might need, and informs us what we can purchase at any given location, and while our social network keeps us posted on its every move with text messages, tweets, and calls? The art projects discussed in this essay strive to provide focused experiences that create contexts for anchoring "texts" (be they a geography or our behaviors in specific settings). At the same time, there is a danger that multiple forms of mobile connectivity and Web 2.0 social-networking services cumulatively produce a contextual noise of sound bytes that stops making sense and obscures "the text." How many contexts can our sensori-emotional system handle before collapsing into attention deficit? One of the challenges for locative media and ubiquitous computing will be to balance the promise of enhanced context awareness and the danger of sensory and informational overload—to remain on target while the target moves.

Notes

1. See http://www.o-matic.com/play/pdpal.

2. See http://urbantapestries.net.

3. See http://www.waag.org/project/realtime.

4. See http://www.terirueb.net/choregraph/index.html.

5. See http://locative.x-i.net/piens/index.html.

6. See http://www.nomadicmilk.net/full.

7. See http://www.c5corp.com/projects/landscape/index.shtml.

8. See http://artport.whitney.org/commissions/followthrough.

9. See http://www.intelligentagent.com/archive/Vol6_No2_community_domain_nisi_etal.htm.

10. See http://camilleutterback.com/projects/abundance.

11. See http://www.v2.nl/lab/projects/d-tower.

12. Exhibitions include: ctrl[space] (ZKM, Karlsruhe, Germany, 2001); *Anxious Omniscience: Surveillance and Contemporary Cultural Practice* (Princeton University Art Museum, Princeton, NJ, 2002); Open_Source_Art_Hack (New Museum of Contemporary Art, New York, 2002); *Profiling* (Whitney Museum of American Art, 2008).

13. See http://www.t-t-trackers.net.

14. See http://www.preemptivemedia.net/zapped.

15. See http://wearcam.org/index.html.

16. See http://www.trackingtransience.net.

17. See http://www.digitalurbanliving.dk/sousveillance.

18. See http://www.urban-atmospheres.net.

19. See http://www.living-environments.net.

20. See http://www.paulos.net/papers/2008/Ubiquitous%20Sustainability%20(UbiComp%202008).pdf.

21. See http://www.pm-air.net/index.php.

22. See http://www.nyu.edu/projects/xdesign/feralrobots.

References

Benedikt, Michael, ed. 1991. *Cyberspace: First Steps*. Cambridge, MA: MIT Press.

Bou, Louis. 2006. *NYC BCN: Street Art Revolution*. New York: HarperCollins.

Csíkszentmihályi, Mihály. 2003. *Good Business: Flow, Leadership, and the Making of Meaning.* New York: Viking.

Csíkszentmihályi, Mihály. 1997. *Finding Flow: The Psychology of Engagement with Everyday Life.* New York: Basic Books.

Csíkszentmihályi, Mihály. 1996. *Creativity: Flow and the Psychology of Discovery and Invention.* New York: Harper Collins.

Csíkszentmihályi, Mihály. 1990. *Flow: The Psychology of Optimal Experience.* New York: Harper & Row.

Csíkszentmihályi, Mihály, and Kevin Rathunde. 1993. "The Measurement of Flow in Everyday Life: Towards a Theory of Emergent Motivation." In *Nebraska Symposium on Motivation*, vol. 40, edited by Janis E. Jacobs, 57–97. Lincoln: University of Nebraska Press.

Debord, Guy. 1955. "Introduction to a Critique of Urban Geography." In Ken Knapp, *Situationist International Anthology.* Berkeley, CA: Bureau of Public Secrets. Originally published in *Les Lèvres Nues* No. 6, September 1955. Available at http://www.bopsecrets.org/SI/urbgeog.htm. Accessed 21 January 2012.

Geddes, Sir Patrick. 1915. *Cities in Evolution.* London: Williams.

Gibson, William. 1984. *Neuromancer.* New York: Ace Books.

Hemment, Drew. 2004. "The Locative Dystopia." Available at http://amsterdam.nettime.org/Lists-Archives/nettime-l-0401/msg00021.html. Accessed 21 January 2012.

Massimini, Fausto and Massimo Carli. 1988. "The Systematic Assessment of Flow in Daily Experience." In Mihály Csikszentmihalyi and Isabella Selega Csikszentmihalyi, eds. *Optimal Experience: Psychological Studies of Flow in Consciousness.* Cambridge: Cambridge University Press. 266–287.

Mathieson, Eleanor, and Xavier A. Tàpies. 2009. *Street Artists: The Complete Guide.* London: Graffito Books.

McCullough, Malcolm. 2004. *Digital Ground: Architecture, Pervasive Computing, and Environmental Knowing.* Cambridge, MA: MIT Press.

Relph, Edward. 1976. *Place and Placelessness.* London: Pion.

Sant, Alison. 2006. "Redefining the Basemap." *Intelligent Agent* 6 (2). Available at http://www.intelligentagent.com/archive/Vol6_No2_interactive_city_sant.htm. 21 January 2012.

Stephenson, Neal. 1992. *Snow Crash.* New York: Bantam Books.

Turkle, Sherry. 1995. *Life on the Screen: Identity in the Age of the Internet.* New York: Simon & Schuster.

23 Intimacy and Self-Organization in Hybrid Public Spheres

Söke Dinkla

It has become virtually impossible to talk about the public space without recognizing the impact of locative technologies, such as mobile phones, Global Positioning System devices, tracking systems, mobile computers and digital networks. The notion of what is "public" is undergoing a deep transformation in a culture interwoven strongly by ubiquitous computing. In the first years of the twenty-first century, artists began to work with mobile digital technologies that shape the way we are talking about the impact of ubiquitous computing. The term *locative media* was coined as the title for a workshop hosted by the Riga Center for New Media Culture, the Latvian electronic art and media center.[1] "Locative media emerged over the last half decade as a response to the decorporealized, screen-based experience of net art, claiming the world beyond either gallery or computer screen as its territory" (Tuters and Varnelis 2006, 357; see also Russel 1999).

Locative art projects are researching the aesthetic impact of mobile technologies and commenting on their social and political implications. Locative art was a liberation from the permanent pressure to define digital art with respect to its modes and places of presentation, such as museums, festivals, and the Internet. By moving into the public space of the streets, locative art places itself within the tradition of "happenings" and performance art of the 1960s and its emancipatory potentials. At the same time, locative art designs models for living and acting in public spaces increasingly marked by ubiquitous computing.

It is as difficult to define locative art as it still is to define the many different formats of digital art or media art. Should we even talk about "ubiquitous art"? The term *ubiquitous* helps us to describe the new quality of space that we begin to experience in the twenty-first century. The great achievement of the concepts of "ubiquitous" and "pervasive" is that they make clear that there is no virtual world that exists next to the real world. In the "decade of ubiquity" (Simon Penny, chapter 15 in this volume), we are not escaping the real world to become immersed in digital worlds; rather, we learn to move and act within new environments that are thoroughly structured by microprocessors and connectivity. "Ubiquity" means that in every single moment we live, we are able to get connected to other parts of the world, to other spheres of communication, to someone else's emotions, thoughts, and mental microcosms. As Christiane Paul quite correctly points out in chapter 23 in this book, "Ubiquitous computing is surrounded by a certain amount of hype," as in how every new concept tries to grasp the sociotechnical changes that current forms of digital technologies bring about.

Locative art is turning this hype around. It is working with the invisible power of embedded ubiquitous technologies and its dominant tendencies. Instead of simply exploring the technological possibilities, locative art is using and detecting the technology's poetic energy. It opens up the network to the general public, linking it to audiences in a specific time and space (Cubitt 2007). Unlike the ideal unification that the apparent omnipresence of locative digital technology might invoke, we are observing today a growing division into different fragments of public space. At the same time, public and private spaces are being telescoped into each other. These changes prompt us to investigate a different perception of public space. Here, I look at public spaces today as spheres characterized by locative ubiquitous technologies. Although personal mobile technologies such as mobile phones and personal computers have the tendency to intensify the intimacy with the user, separating her perceptions from the specific time and place in which she is moving, locative art works toward an entanglement of both spheres—the communication network and the geographical space. Locative art makes multifaceted comments on the condition of public space. It is challenged to find new strategies for art to move in this constantly reconquered space. What strategies can art develop to be able to work in a critical mode—as a way of commenting on the risks and consequences of the changes happening today in public space?

Public space is a utopian space. In this respect, public space has much in common with digital space. Both are spaces of our desires and imaginations. The art of the twentieth century idealized these spheres to a great extent. With emancipatory power, the Futurists captured the streets of the cities and thus hoped to elude the constraints of the art institutions and at the same time those of an audience they didn't consider capable of provoking social change.

The art after World War II gained energy and inspiration out of those short episodes of rebellion against academicism and traditionalism. With happenings, performances, and Situationist city explorations, artists tested how to treat city streets as artistic material. It was their aim to create situations in which the people could act autonomously and equally, exchanging opinions, exercising their creativity, and not having to follow strict rules.[2]

An important part of these ideas put forth by one of the last major avant-garde movements still clings to the public space today. The public space, particularly in the crisis it is facing today, is being reclaimed as a place where social and political relationships are not narrowly defined but are instead open for negotiation. In democratically legitimated societies, the urban public space is regarded as an egalitarian space, a locus of conversation between equals, freely accessible to all citizens. The fact that reality has long since departed from this idealized image—or perhaps never conformed to it in the first place, as Monika Wagner (2008) asserts—is evident above all from the development of the inner cities, which especially in recent years have been increasingly transformed into regimented and monitored zones dedicated to consumption. Whole city quarters are making way for shopping malls: public space is becoming private space, entangling us in a system of observation and surveillance in a barely concealed manner. These ubiquitous public spaces are cybernetic systems subject to indiscernible rules.

The questions of whether it is possible for art to expose these programmed sets of regulations, to perforate them and create alternative spaces, and how it is to go about this task concern not only the effectiveness and relative importance of art in our society, but also and much more the state and the effectiveness of democracy in postindustrial societies.

Interestingly enough, just at the time when art was feeling the diminishing power of the public space to define anything and either withdrew from that space or seemed to relinquish the utopia of social efficacy by adopting barely visible, minimally invasive strategies, the digital sphere became charged with the utopias no one dared believe in anymore in real space. One of the best-known European platforms was the "Digital City" founded in 1994 by the Dutch group Hacktic Netwerk and the sociocultural center De Balie in Amsterdam. Via a text-based mailbox system, people could discuss issues with one another and with their political representatives. One of the primary aims was to provide Internet access free of charge to the broad public, a goal that was realized in the Netherlands with the help of the federal and municipal governments.

Along with this initiative, a series of projects with structures based on the model of the city came into being on the World Wide Web in the 1990s. The dominant metaphors for the Web at that time were "information highway" and "digital city." Whereas the American highway metaphor emphasizes the Internet's economic potential, such as for use in high-speed business communications, the city metaphor was first brought up in Europe and stresses the Web's sociocultural dimensions. New forms of social and political participation were tested and established in the digital space. And for a short while, the thesis of the vanishing physical city (Mitchell 1995) seemed to come true.

At the same time, digital technology itself promised an emancipatory way to engage users in complex, invisible processes and to make those processes comprehensible and transparent. Already in the 1980s, the first interactive possibilities advocated and facilitated the breakout of digital technology from the universities and research laboratories.

In 1966, artists picked up the thread of earlier works by John Cage, Robert Rauschenberg, Merce Cunningham, David Tudor, and others at *9 Evenings: Theatre and Engineering* at New York's Armory Hall. Using simple forms of digital control, these artists were able to reinforce the indeterminacy of their pieces. They saw the essence of technology as consisting in its invisible, self-organizing function, which allows the artist to withdraw from his status as author of a piece and to delegate some of his tasks to the system instead. In the program for *9 Evenings*, Tudor wrote: "*Bandoneon* does not use any compositional means; it activates, composing itself out of the composite qualities of its instruments."[3]

Metagames

In contrast with technological developments and the concept of "virtual reality," which attempts to make a world inside the computer, where users wear gloves and data suits, art has relied from the outset on "embodied virtuality" (Weiser 1991, 98). Art has formulated and exemplified some of the fundamental qualities of the new digital medium. The first interactive environments were created in the mid-1970s as a combination of closed-circuit-video art installations and computer. In such environments, filmed by a video camera, the exhibition visitor sees her silhouette projected on a large screen, which allows her to operate with various graphic forms. In short game sequences, the user determines the invisible rules and accepts the system as communication partner. A new model of the game emerges, a "metagame" in which we acknowledge the screen as another "reality." Triggered by the player's physical activities, real and computer-generated spaces are intertwined (Dinkla 1997). Terms such as *artificial reality*, *virtual reality*, and *cyberspace* try to capture the special nature of this "space." They stand for the radicalization of the tendencies toward dissolving physical space witnessed in modernism.

The dematerialization of the (art) object is one of the fundamental paradigms presaged by the art of the twentieth century and for which it laid the groundwork. It is now exemplified by digital media. Taking the place of the object is the process—art as both the artist's and the viewer's activities. To a certain extent as a countermovement to the loss of the physical object, various concepts came about for involving the viewer in the realization of the "work"—that is, in the creation of the increasingly abstract processes involved. Closely associated with this trend is the relativization of the role of the artist as sole author of the work. These achievements of the avant-garde must be understood as a massive countermovement against late-capitalist art production. They work against the fetishization of the art object and are of fundamental significance because they open up alternative possibilities, perspectives, and frames of action for art that explore the new conditions of digital systems as society-building forces and that develop from them new forms of intimacy.

The fact that the very same universal machines that shape our globalized societal systems today are the ones that are also generating the antifetishistic tendencies in art is all part of the multifaceted nature of the computer and has become the emblem of digital culture.[4]

The Aesthetics of the Hyperreal

The nonmaterial and functional foundation for digital art is the Turing machine, which is based on releasing mathematical axioms from their representational function. According to this approach, truth and existence can no longer be distinguished by making reference to an outside world but can be based only on the freedom of their axioms from any contradictions. The worlds of imagery and sound generated by the computer are therefore neither representational nor abstract: Jean Baudrillard calls the culture they give birth to "hyperreal"—simulation that "is no longer that of a territory, a referential being or a substance." These worlds instead enlist "models of a real without origin or reality: a hyperreal" (1978, 7).

There thus arises in digital art an aesthetic of the hyperreal. In order to get hold of the hyperreal, to appropriate it, digital art develops strategies for producing proximity and intimacy. It is able to free itself today from its immobility and fixedness in one place and to charge the urban sphere with new communicative contextures. It ties the boundless and amorphous data realm back to the body and the real physical space of the city.

Whereas in the 1990s the model of the city served primarily to facilitate orientation in data space by providing a familiar image to work with, today it is the city space itself that is changing. The city space forms the conceptual framework for (urban) performances such as Jochen Roller and Martin Nachbar's *mnemonic nonstop* (2006). This piece, which consists of a dance performance on stage and a tour through the city, is based on the experiences of the two dancers and choreographers, Roller and Nachbar, in various cities—Berlin, Brussels, Tel Aviv, Zagreb, and Graz. They wandered through these cities off the beaten track, following maps of other cities in order to experience space in a way that would otherwise have been closed to them. Out of these forays emerged a dance performance in which the stage space is overlaid with projected cartographic patterns. Schematic blood-circulation pathways painted in real time on overhead slides do not freeze on the screen but rather ripple over the dancers' bodies like the movable boundary lines of unexplored territories (Cramer 2006). The fiction of the images and dances is repeatedly undermined by documentary reports of the dancers' experiences on their city rambles.

Inspired by the Situationist practice of the *dérive*, Nachbar and Roller invite the audience to take part in a city exploration after their stage performance in which, equipped with a city map of Gazianthep, they stroll through downtown Duisburg, encountering obstacles in the real space. French philosopher Guy Debord developed with the *dérive* a method of aimlessly drifting around a city in order to guide one's attention to things that have previously gone unnoticed. Nachbar and Roller purloin this method of urban exploration, also called "psychogeography," in order, first, to question the fictive space of the stage, the real space of the city, and the value of abstract geographic-orientation systems and then to relate them to one another. That which has occurred in the stage space physically and highly subjectively on the dancers' own bodies is now translated to the outside space as image and intimate experience. When this activity is simultaneously delegated to the audience, the transfer becomes a consistent interrogation of the concept of subjectivity.

How do personal experiences come about in a largely depersonalized structural fabric? The Situationist concept of the *dérive* shapes our behavior on the Internet and is increasingly infiltrating our perceptual habits and behavior in the urban space as well. It forms the conceptual framework in the urban locative gaming situations created by the group Blast Theory. *Can You See Me Now?* (2003) is a game in which players move through a model of the city online while the Blast Theory performers act as runners in the real city. Fitted with sensors and mobile computers, they roam through the urban space. On their mobile computers, they can see the positions of the online players chasing them. Their perceptions as they traverse the city, which are graphically presented on the Web, mix in with the remote participants' interactions. The online world is kind of empty because there is no vehicle traffic. However, with the question "Is there someone you haven't seen for a long time that you still think of?" the virtual space is animated by the imagined person. As the performers in the city chase the online gamers, the answer to the question of who is in control is ambivalent. The game is a complex model of how ubiquitous computing is influencing our perception of mowing through the geographical space and at the same time acting in online environments with distant gamers. Performers and gamers continually change in their relationship to one another. They embody what we perceive today as "floating identities." Their inner logic is to assume as a given the nonexistence of boundaries between various levels of reality.

These different levels of reality are mixed up in a radical way in Blast Theory's *Day of the Figurines* (2006, see figure 2), a "board game" for up to one thousand players using mobile phones.[5] The point of departure is a physical model of an English city with its buildings and protagonists, the figurines, which is set up in a public place. Visitors become players by selecting a figure and giving it a name and specific attributes. The small, brightly painted plastic figures, which seem to hail from another world and another time, are positioned on the game board by the players. They thus become surrogates for the participants, alter egos that are now part of an obscure city set against an architectural backdrop that resembles stage scenery. The seemingly deserted town is a fictional place: a restaurant, an empty shop, a fallout shelter, and a rat research institute are apparently arranged here at random. Just as random is the positioning of the figurines in the alien city.

Over the next twenty-four hours, an intimate communication unfolds. The players constantly receive text messages on their mobile phones asking them to make decisions for their figurines and to determine their actions. They can exchange messages with other players and find objects such as billiard cues, sausages, gas canisters, or corpses with defibrillators. They continually receive enigmatic assignments and are posed with dilemmas. Matt Adams of the Blast Theory group and Gabriella Giannachi describe the events as follows: "Over time, with every day represented by one hour of playing time, the city changes—bars open, the warehouse runs out of fleeces, the parking lot empties—and the health of the players deteriorates—their temples suffer abrasions, hands become sticky, armpits begin to smell. Special incidents occur—a party, a solar eclipse, an explosion, a concert, the imperious exercises of an army—which influence the health and mood of all city residents" (2008, 87).

In the course of the game, the occasionally fanciful and violent happenings in the increasingly eerie city get mixed up in a confusing way with the players' everyday lives. During the time we are playing the game, the route they move through in real quotidian life and their experiences along the way become charged with narrative snippets and episodes from the game. In passing but at the same time with the highest degree of concentration, they are engaged in producing a narration. The game augments and exaggerates the players' feeling of dislocation: events in one place (the physical setting of the board game) are shaped by incidents in several remote locations and vice versa. *Day of the Figurines* works with various embedding mechanisms. It detaches social relationships from their ties in space and time and shows how the complexity of shifting temporal and spatial references leads to a changed communication situation. The game reveals our striving to create social relations and significance even under the most adverse conditions. The prerequisite for such efforts is proximity despite distance. In *Day of the Figurines*, an intimate situation is created by means of a game inserting itself in our daily routine. The game becomes part of our social interactions and interlaces itself with private episodes. Detachment from space–time is followed by a reintegration into a new, intimate coexistence.

Where do we spend time together? We encounter this question again and again in the works of the artist duo M+M (Marc Weis and Martin De Mattia). Their *Song fuer C* (2006) was one of the first films developed expressly for the mobile phone, sounding out the possibilities for the phone to act as broadcast and communication medium. M+M categorize the film, which follows a screenplay by Helmut Krausser, as a "mystery thriller." As we watch the film, equipped with a prototype mobile phone, we move through a shopping mall.[6] By answering questions that appear on the display, we decide which paths the story will take. We become more and more deeply involved in a father's search for his missing 18-year-old daughter. The father hires a female uncover detective who works in disguise in an effort to make contact with the daughter. Various news items, texts and film episodes develop a non-linear narrative fabric, which we can interrupt at any time in order to call up additional information. In the course of the story, one of the protagonists detaches himself from the fictional narrative and encounters us in the real space of the shopping center.

Song fuer C creates a narrative with branchings and links, which we drift through similarly to the *dérive*. The geographic space becomes a mobile storytelling space—a space we discover through our senses of touch, sight, and hearing. Unlike *Day of the Figurines*, the film works with traditional storytelling strategies, fragmenting them in order to develop a new cinematic narrative technique in which fiction, documentary, and reality overlap and crisscross. What is special here is that no breaks occur when transitioning between the various levels. Instead, an imaginative realm emerges with a temporal structure in which the time of the narrative coincides with the time in which the user is living. We make our way through the mobile story, spellbound by new strategies of narration. (For a discussion of new strategies of narration see Dinkla n.d., 2006).

In our finely differentiated postindustrial societies, forms of interpersonal communication are dwindling. At the same time, the space of the public is expanded to a great extent into complex communication networks. This process is not only an expansion of public space; it is not only an augmentation or a mixing of two concepts of space—a "mixed reality" consisting of the real and the virtual environment (Milgram and Kishino 1994). Rather, it is the generation of ubiquitous spheres of communication where new strategies of narration intermingle with traditional ways of representation, psychogeographical explorations, and intimate dialogs between distant users. The defining power of physical places is not only being eroded through the ever wider reach of mobile digital technologies. It is also upheld by these very technologies because it has succeeded in appropriating the strategies and metaphors of the vast digital sphere and making them its own. When we move through the space of the city today, we are also moving through a complex set of sociotechnical interfaces, platforms, networks, and media. The lack of traditional hierarchical structures gives space for artists' ongoing contest or "agon" for democracy (Dietz n.d.; Mouffe 2000).

Public art using mobile digital technologies are at once an aesthetic research project and a political statement. Artists such as M+M and Blast Theory are developing in association with businesses the technology that will in the future dictate the forms of communication available to us. Blast Theory has been working with Sony and the University of Nottingham since early 2000 to develop the new mobile technologies as a cultural space. The artist duo M+M created its project *Song fuer C* in conjunction with Vodafone's research-and-development department and Zurich University of the Arts—an unprecedented cooperation between network operators and scientists.

We can foresee today that the erosion of public spaces, which in recent years have lost part of their communicative function as a locus of democratic public exchange, will now be succeeded by a renewed activation of very specific local spaces. Art is using mobile technologies to activate the sphere of ubiquitous computing, producing new "spaces" that frequently defy description. The "artwork" comes about as a result of the temporary activation of nodes and points as we move past them. We ourselves—embedded in a cybernetic system of broadcast networks, GPS systems, and wireless local-area networks—arrange the urban web into semantic points that generate meaning individually and for a limited time span. But we are no longer the hub at the center of things—we are merely part of the system. We are listeners and storytellers, viewers and actors in a fabric of lines and streams that we navigate in accordance with our personal interests to create specific "event zones." We cooperate, as Michel De Certeau remarks, in temporarily rededicating the rules of the system as rules dictated by our own interests:

> These "ways of operating" constitute the innumerable practices by means of which users reappropriate the space organized by techniques of sociocultural production. . . . [T]he goal is not to make clearer how the violence of order is transmuted into a disciplinary technology, but rather to bring to light the clandestine forms taken by the dispersed, tactical, and make-shift creativity of groups or individuals already caught in the nets of "discipline." (1984, xiv–xv)

In the future, art not only will be concerned with discovering spaces and activating them but will also *generate* them and find forms in which individuals and groups organize themselves into networklike subforms of the public. Art gives the transformation of geographical urban space into ubiquitous spheres a poetic dimension. It creates aesthetic strategies for this transformation. By pointing beyond the space itself, it demonstrates the magic of that space, its power and its potential endlessness. In this way, it personalizes and subjectifies such public ubiquitous-computing spheres. Physically, imaginatively, and medially mediated interactions crisscross, letting us feel tangibly that we are moving through a new kind of space affected by the impact of ubiquitous computing. Reconnecting with the individual and strengthening the self-organizing forces of society are among art's foremost responsibilities.

Notes

1. For more on the Riga Center for New Media Culture, see http://locative.x-i.net/.

2. The Situationists were one of the last classic avant-garde groups of the twentieth century. Founded in 1957, this alliance of European artists and intellectuals was active during the 1960s,

developing guerilla communication methods that influenced the international art scene and pop culture. They worked against the division of life into discrete spheres.

3. From the play program for *9 Evenings: Theatre and Engineering* (1966).

4. This apparent contradiction is still causing fundamental deficits in the analysis and interpretation of as well as the critical discourse on digital art today. This volume can be credited with reducing this deficit by bringing together disparate perspectives, backgrounds, and research approaches because our constant wrestling with the task of finding adequate terminology demands an existential exchange between the disciplines.

5. My description refers to the premiere of *Day of the Figurines* at the First Play Festival at the Hebbel am Ufer theater, HAU2, in Berlin, October 2006.

6. My description refers to the performance of *Song fuer C* at Ars Electronica 2006.

References

Adams, Matt, and Gabriella Giannachi. 2008. "Day of the Figurines von Blast Theory." In *Paradoxien des Öffentlichen*, edited by Söke Dinkla and Karl Janssen, 86–89. Nuremberg: Verlag für Moderne Kunst.

Baudrillard, Jean. 1978. *Agonie des Realen*. Berlin: Merve-Verlag.

Cramer, Franz Anton. 2006. "*Mnemonic Nonstop*: Martin Nachbar and Jochen Roller." In *PubliCity: Constructing the Truth*, edited by Söke Dinkla, 94–99. Nuremberg: Verlag für Moderne Kunst.

Cubitt, Sean. 2007. "Media Art Futures." *Futures* 39:1149–1158.

De Certeau, Michel. 1984. *The Practice of Everyday Life*. Berkeley and Los Angeles: University of California Press.

Dietz, Steve. n.d. "*Public Sphere_S*." Available at http://www.medienkunstnetz.de/themes/public_sphere_s/public_sphere_s. Accessed 23 January 2012.

Dinkla, Söke. 1997. *Pioniere Interaktiver Kunst von 1970 bis heute*. Ostfildern, Germany: Cantz.

Dinkla, Söke. n.d. "Virtual Narrations." Available at http://www.medienkunstnetz.de/themes/overview_of_media_art/narration. Accessed 23 January 2012.

Milgram, Paul, and Fumio Kishino. 1994. "Taxonomy of Mixed Reality Visual Displays." *IEICE Transactions on Information and Systems* E77-D.12: 1321–1329.

Mitchell, William J. 1995. *City of Bits: Space, Place, and the Infobahn*. Cambridge, MA: MIT Press.

Mouffe, Chantal. 2000. *The Democratic Paradox*. New York: Verso.

Russel, Ben. 1999. "Headmap Manifesto." Available at http://tecfa.unige.ch/~nova/headmap-manifesto.PDF. Accessed 23 January 2012.

Tuters, Marc, and Kazys Varnelis. 2006. "Beyond Locative Media: Giving Shape to the Internet of Things." *Leonardo* 39 (4): 357–363.

Wagner, Monika. 2008. "Die Parzellierung des öffentlichen Raums—oder Kunst als sozialer Kitt." In *Paradoxien des Öffentlichen*, edited by Söke Dinkla and Karl Janssen, 24–33. Nuremberg: Verlag für Moderne Kunst.

Weiser, Mark. 1991. "The Computer for the 21st Century." *Scientific American* 265 (3): 94–104.

24 Kuleshov's Display—on Contextual Invisibility

Dietmar Offenhuber

This chapter presents contextual strategies for staging ambient interfaces in public space. Although in existing literature ambient displays are often considered and evaluated as solitary objects, I argue that the experience of an ambient display is not determined in the first place by its intrinsic qualities, but by the way the display is contextually situated. To that end, I investigate six strategies to show how context can be incorporated into the design of ambient displays. Some of these strategies may seem counterintuitive, for they take advantage of some of the effects that designers usually try to avoid. They are meant to incite further experiments and cross-pollination among the fields of architecture, public art, and interaction design.

Invisibility and context are arguably the two central concepts of ubiquitous computing. According to the famous comment by Mark Weiser (1991), the most profound technologies are those that disappear—computers and interfaces become invisible by blending seamlessly into the everyday environment. Although this notion of invisibility, also described as "calm technology," is inherently contextual, the vision of ubiquitous computing reaches out farther: technology should not only be embedded into its context, but also become context aware and consequently burden the user only with information and functionalities relevant for a specific situation. Weiser's vision originally encompassed both the private and public aspects of life; however, most work in ubiquitous computing remains concerned with the personal domain. In the public sphere of urban infrastructure and displays, the ideas of invisibility and context awareness come with a number of conceptual challenges. It can be observed that within the increasingly mediated urban environments, large-scale displays neither blend into their surroundings nor share the contextual qualities found in technology for the personal domain.

This chapter investigates what a contextual public display might look like and, based on existing work, which design strategies can be employed to achieve contextual invisibility. The impact of outdoor displays on public space gains prominence in discussions within the architectural community, but the current debates are based mainly on traditional concepts of the screen as an animated iconographic surface designed to capture attention. As a result, much of the contemporary discourse resembles the discussions around the "architecture of the billboard" from the 1960s and 1970s (Venturi, Brown, and Izenour 1972). To move beyond the already outdated visions of mediated architecture associated with images of Times Square, Las Vegas, and Shibuya, the traditional notion of the display needs to be reconsidered.

Ambient Displays

Inspired by Mark Weiser and John Seely Brown's (1996) notion of calm technology, the concept of the ambient display offers one alternative conceptual framework for the contextual integration of information displays into the built environment. Ambient displays are architectural interfaces that are based on the observation that humans can process a large amount of information in the periphery of their attention (Ishii and Wisneski 1998). Their design is unobtrusive, and the expressive range of their possible states deliberately limited—for example, down to a subtle change in color or visual pattern or a slight movement that can be recognized without the effort of explicit attention. Information is implicitly encoded into the physical properties of the display: the colors of the facade, the arrangement of lines in a digital painting, or reflections from a perturbed water surface (Moere 2008). To capture the viewer's attention, ambient displays rely on a mechanism often referred to as the "Cocktail Party Effect" (Cherry 1966): a mechanism that allows us to carry on conversation in the noisy ambience of a cocktail party but at the same time to become alert when amid the chatter our name is mentioned.

Ambient media systematically investigate design languages that utilize this effect and consider the transition between the viewer's attentive states—an ability that is especially relevant for environments with multiple simultaneous stimuli such as urban public spaces. Although a considerable body of research has been dedicated to the design of ambient displays, critical evaluation shows that these displays do not always perform well as an effective means to deliver information (Shen, Moere, and Eades 2005).

One problem is the metaphorical nature of ambient displays. Most of them require learning the visual language of the display because the way the displayed data are mapped to the display's visual parameters is not obvious (Wisneski, Ishii, Dahley, et al. 1998). This learning effort might be reasonable in the personal realm but is hardly an option for a display in public space. A common response to this problem is reducing the complexity of the displayed information—often down to a binary value that helps with a specific decision, such as a light-emitting diode (LED) integrated into the handle of an umbrella that lights up when rain is expected (as in AmbientDevices' *Ambient Umbrella* [2010]). This might work well for alerting purposes but does not solve the underlying problem of interpretation. Consider, for example, the display of

NOX architect's *D-Tower* (1998–2004), an illuminated, translucent architectural sculpture signaling the emotional state of a city through red and blue illumination (discussed in Bullivant 2005); its message remains ambiguous despite its binary nature. One might wonder, for example, about what the color red represents—Is it happiness or rage? If the metaphorical reference is not obvious and a common convention is missing, the display remains incomprehensible.

A second problem is that most existing work takes only the relationship between observer and display into account while ignoring the situation in which the display is placed. Focusing on the "calmness" of the display medium is not enough to enable peripheral awareness of the display's information because the reception of a visual message depends substantially on the situation in which it is presented: the physical environment, the presence of other information in proximity, and finally the observers' goals and expectations. In this respect, existing heuristics for the evaluation of ambient displays lack an important element because criteria such as the "peripherality of the display" (Mankoff, Dey, Hsieh, et al. 2003) depend largely on context.

The Role of Context

The filmmaker Lev Kuleshov demonstrated in a cinematic experiment that the perceived meaning of what we see is often defined by the context rather than by the content of an image (Mitry and King 2000). He presented a short film showing the blank face of an actor interspersed by footage showing either a bowl of soup, the coffin of a child, or a beautiful woman. Depending on the juxtaposed footage, the audience interpreted the actor's empty facial expression as showing hunger, sorrow, or desire, when in fact they were seeing the same sequence of the actor's face. The effect makes it clear that context is more than a static description of a situation: it is a quality constructed from the interaction with the observer, "an emergent feature of the interaction, determined in the moment and in the doing" (Dourish 2004, 23).

In the next section, I discuss design strategies that are based on the "Kuleshov effect" and that play with the notion of contextual invisibility in order to make media in built environments more articulated and informative and at the same time less obtrusive. These strategies address ways in which displays can be staged effectively by considering properties of the environment and the observers' expectations. Some of the strategies are familiar and well established, whereas others might seem counterintuitive and create situations that designers usually try to avoid. They share some similarities with ambient displays: both emphasize the transition between the foreground and background of attention. Unlike ambient displays, however, the presented examples achieve this blending not through the choice of a "calm" display medium, but through a tight relationship with their local context and so establish "invisibility" by taking advantage of habitual blindness.

Invisibility through Mimicry

The urban environment conveys an abundance of information. At the same time, we also have learned to ignore most of such information through habituation; we have become blind to the messages we encounter in the course of our daily routine. This section focuses on examples that take advantage of this habitual blindness.

According to the artist Heath Bunting, "A good piece of art should in fact be invisible, but immediately incorporated and quickly taken for granted" (quoted in Frieling and Daniels 2005, 264). Among his many explorations in public art, he installed fake pedestrian street signs into subway stations and public spaces. Bunting claimed that even though upside down, these signs lasted for months—a result of their official appearance.

Other artists employed similar strategies—for example, by adding personal objects, such as family photos, into the showrooms of furniture stores (Ruppe Koselleck's *Ich und IKEA: Parasitäre Publikationen* [2007]) or by disclosing controversial information such as an educational institution's suicide statistics disguised as a bus schedule (Leonardo Bonanni's *Untimely Death Bus Schedule—Information Aesthetics* [2010]). Despite their controversial or funny content, these objects perfectly blend into their environment and often go unnoticed (see figure 24.1).

This strategy of mimicry creates what Bill Gaver, Jake Beaver, and Steve Benford (2003) call "ambiguity of context": a situation in which an object offers different meanings depending on the context in which it is observed. As in the example of Marcel Duchamp's *fountain* (1917), an additional layer of meaning is added to an ordinary object. The design of contextual displays should take these different possible readings into account. An information display might have a different function depending on its state or become invisible to those for whom the message is not relevant.

Embracing Unstable Display Media

A traditional display requires a generic, homogenous, and maximally controllable display medium. All influence from the local environment has to be minimized; the appearance of the display should be the same in every light condition. Developers of outdoor LED displays invest considerable effort to compensate for the influence of ambient light. Nevertheless, the outdoor environment remains a difficult setting for dynamic displays, and independence from the environment is not always possible to achieve.

However, unstable and sensitive display media offer an interesting possibility. Architects have learned to work with the aesthetic qualities of materials that age and change their appearance under different environmental conditions, instead of aiming

Figure 24.1
Fly poster in the old market of Bristol.

for pristine and inert surfaces immune to external influences. The same approach can also make sense for urban interfaces—to embrace the spectrum of expression offered by the material under different environmental conditions. One example from contemporary art history is Hans Haacke's *condensation cube* (1963; see Fitzsimmons 1969), a minimalist sculpture in the shape of a sealed-off glass cube containing a small quantity of water, which causes a layer of condensation to cover the cube's walls. Through the continuous cycle of condensation and evaporation, the artwork's appearance changes constantly influenced by environmental variables such as temperature and light. Inspired by this artwork, Amanda Parkes and I developed the ambient display *dewy* (2007; see Parkes and Offenhuber 2008), showing a pixilated pattern of condensation. Although the display allows high-level control over the emerging patterns, the actual appearance of the condensation patterns depends a great deal on external humidity, temperature, and light direction.

Numerous other examples and possibilities show the significance of sensitive display media. Plants are a particularly interesting choice for a display medium: they interact with their environment in many ways, while showing many expressive features, such as phototrophic behavior (Holstius, Kemble, Hurst, et al. 2004) or color change depending on available sunlight. No doubt, ephemeral materials as display media are harder to control and therefore offer less variety for displaying information. In addition, the content of the display will never show the data in their pure form but instead in a form blended with environmental influences. However, if the properties of the display medium are aligned with the subject of the representation, the medium can contribute an additional dimension of expressivity to the display.

Designing with Physical Wear

Despite being a mechanical problem, physical wear has many interesting features. It is a reliable record of an object's interaction history: the location of hollows in an old marble staircase tells us about how people have stepped on it; the shiny parts on the patinated surface of a copper door handle reveal how people prefer to operate it. In that sense, physical wear and patina are an ambient information display, the message of which is explicitly or implicitly taken into account when, for example, judging an object's value and age.

The phenomenon of physical wear also inspired the metaphorical notion of "computational wear" as a representation of a digital object's interaction history, initially demonstrated with the example of digital documents (Hill, Hollan, Wroblewski, et al. 1992). The authors differentiated between active and passive wear—the latter resulting from passive consumption and aging, but the former indicating an active editing or annotating process. As a physical implementation of computational wear, the "history tablecloth" (Gaver, Bowers, Boucher, et al. 2006) preserves luminous imprints of objects placed onto its surface. Beyond the metaphorical reference, there are also projects that incorporate wear in the literal, physical sense. In Ethan Ham's *Email Erosion* project (2006), for example, a physical sculpture is irreversibly consumed based on email activity.[1]

Making physical wear part of the concept is particularly interesting for urban interfaces. In the unprotected outdoor environment, physical wear is a permanent issue, and maintenance is a necessity. Including physical wear in design through choice of appropriate materials can be a way to provide a subtle display of an object's interaction history.

Animism

Animism is the idea that a living spirit inhabits all objects even if they appear lifeless. Originally an archaic religious concept, the notion is still alive, for example, in the visual language of animated cartoons, where inanimate objects might suddenly come to life and act on their own behalf.

This animistic "awakening" of an apparently static object can be a powerful interface metaphor, and it is often used in a very literal way: for example, a seemingly ordinary emergency exit sign in a hallway suddenly comes to life. A number of existing ambient displays use animistic concepts, such as the "*nabaztag*" (Peters 2006), a networked rabbit toy announcing events such as incoming emails, or Kazuhiko Hachiya's ThanksTail (n.d.),[2] a robotic dog tail for cars enabling drivers to exchange friendly gestures. A more subtle way of showing the hidden life of inanimate objects is by manipulating their shadows—for example, in Motoshi Chikamori and Kyoko Kunoh's media-art installation *Kage* (1998), featuring objects with interactive shadows set in a projected spotlight beam, or Andreas Gysin and Sidi Vanetti's *Ombra* (2007), a project animating the shadow of a sculpture on a public plaza. Displays and interfaces more often refer, however, to animistic concepts in a less figurative way. Andreas Zingerle's kinetic display *Atemraum* (2006) presents a wall with a smooth surface that is subtly bulging and retracting and thus appears to be breathing in sync with the observer's respiration.

In many cases, however, animistic metaphors miss an important point by focusing entirely on the anthropomorphic appearance. More important than a cartoonish look is the choreography of the display: only if the display appears lifeless long enough to be regarded as a static object does the animistic awakening have a powerful effect. A constantly babbling cartoon character lacks that "beat."

In the case of animism, contextual invisibility means the existence of a latent reality that becomes apparent only in certain situations. The display has two separate roles—one as a carrier of information and another as a physical object. The commonsense notion of information design demands that these two roles be tightly coupled—the physical object should clearly indicate its function as a dynamic display through its physical and digital affordances (Norman 2002). With the use of animistic metaphors, these affordances are deliberately concealed, and the display assumes a role as a physical object independent from its informational purpose. In terms of ambient media, the moment of transition between these two states is of special interest because the blending between the background and foreground of attention is a crucial function of calm technology (Weiser and Brown 1996). Animistic metaphors can emphasize this shift through a visual language that is almost universally understood.

Indexical Displays

When information is displayed at the scale of the urban environment, the map sometimes becomes the territory. The boundary between object and representation can become blurry when both occupy the same space, and the representation incorporates elements of the visualized phenomenon. On the most basic level, the sky is a perfect example of an ambient display (Wisneski, Ishii, Dahley, et al. 1998). Its sensory appearance conveys an abundance of information that we have learned to decipher by observation. Seen as an ambient display, it is at the same time representation and represented phenomenon, linked by an indexical relationship.

Timm-Oliver Wilks, Thorsten Kiesl, and Harald Moser's public installation *garden of eden* (2007) (see figure 24.2) assembles an array of plants in glass boxes that are

Figure 24.2
Timm-Oliver Wilks, Thorsten Kiesl, and Harald Moser, *garden of eden* (2007). Permission kindly granted by the artists.

filled with toxic air generated according to environmental data from different cities around the world. The air quality is not visualized through a symbol or a graph, but only through its effect on the plant. The condition of the plant suggests something about the quality of the air surrounding it—in terms of Charles Peirce's semiotics, it is an *index* and as such implies a causal relationship.

An even tighter feedback loop between representation and object can be found in Helen Evans and Heiko Hansen's urban-scale visualization project *Nuage vert* (2008). The piece projects a visualization of power consumption in a neighborhood onto the cloud of smoke rising from a power plant that generates the power for this same neighborhood.

This ambiguity is rare in traditional forms of information design, where data and representation are kept strictly separate. Iconic and symbolic types of representation usually prevail: a message is expressed either through visual resemblance or through an abstract symbolic language. In contrast, the two projects described in this section, *garden of eden* and *Nuage vert*, belong to a different class of visualizations that have an indexical character. Whereas traditional information design seeks to minimize ambiguity, in these examples ambiguity actually increases the readability of an information display. Furthermore, the strategy can help to highlight causal relationships if their effects can be directly observed.

Removing the Context

Designing information displays for a public audience usually means lowering the cognitive threshold in order to maximize accessibility. The deliberate exclusion of users by making the presented information deliberately hard to understand may sound nonsensical and paradoxical. However, curiosity is a powerful motivator, and with the right cues this strategy can be a way to encourage the user to learn the conventions of an information interface. Many communication processes in public space play with the simultaneous inclusion and exclusion of different groups of users. The visual codes of graffiti or fashion contain elements that are broadly understood as well as elements that are meaningful only for a certain group.

Alternate-reality games, taking place in physical and virtual public spaces, are driven by obfuscated information. Players collect cues and hints embedded in the urban environment's complex reality. The central principle is that elements of the game should not be recognizable as such but should perfectly blend with the environment (McGonigal 2003). Equally intertwined with everyday activities and "invisible" in the literal sense is Julius von Bismarck's *Image Fulgurator* (2008), a project involving a device for manipulating other people's photographs at the moment they are taken—by projecting an image into the environment at the right moment for a fraction of a second. Although in these examples outsider knowledge is necessary to understand what is displayed, it might make sense to offer hints for the viewer without such knowledge. All it takes sometimes is choosing the right viewpoint—as in Felice Varini's spatial paintings (see Varini, Müller, and López-Durán 2004). Based on the renaissance technique of anamorphosis, the visual elements of Varini's paintings are distributed in space, and they form a coherent picture from only one single viewpoint.

The application of this strategy requires a balancing of accessibility and concealment. In the first place, presence of meaningful information has to be clearly communicated (Skog, Ljungblad, and Holmquist 2003). The power of the strategy is that the task of communication happens on different levels that can be aimed at different groups. For outsiders, the interface might still offer decodable cues and fulfill purposes of alerting or guiding. For the knowing user, without the constraint of general accessibility, the system might offer a higher information density.

Conclusion

The strategies described in the previous sections illustrate different ways to establish an interactive relationship between a display and its context. The presented principles place special emphasis on the moment of transition between background and foreground of attention—the moment when a display is noticed by an observer or fades from her awareness. Depending on the direction of this transition, these strategies fall into two groups. The first group presents strategies for decreasing the contrast between a display and its background: it includes mimicry, the strategic use of unstable display media and physical wear. The display accomplishes mimicry by anticipating the observer's expectations and attentive state. By using an unstable display medium and allowing for physical wear, the display blends with its physical environment. The second group combines strategies that can help to increase the contrast between a display and its background. It includes design strategies that utilize animism, indexical representations, and, to some extent, the deliberate exclusion of the user by removing the context. Animistic qualities can emphasize display agency by creating a surprising transition between its static and animate states. Indexical representations can help to draw attention to the phenomenon and highlight its causal relationships. The removal of context by withholding essential information makes the display stand out by creating a moment of irritation. Some of the presented strategies can go in both directions, either catching attention or blending with the environment—for example, animistic displays or the removal of context. The presented strategies are an invitation to designers to reach beyond the current practices of information and interaction design so as to explore strategies that might seem counterintuitive. They can add a subversive, irritating aspect to public media and can help us see our daily environment with different eyes.

Notes

This chapter is based on a workshop paper presented under the title "The Invisible Display—Design Strategies for Ambient Media in the Urban Context" at UbiComp 2008, Seoul, Korea, 21 September 2008.

1. For information on *Email Erosion*, see http://hizome.org.

2. For ThanksTail, see http://www.petworks.co.jp/~hachiya/works/ThanksTail.html.

References

Bullivant, L. 2005. "D-Tower, NOX, Doetinchem, the Netherlands, 1998–2004, and Son-O-House, Son en Breugel, NOX, the Netherlands, 2000–2004." *Architectural Design* 75 (1): 68–71.

Cherry, Colin E. 1966. On Human Communication: A Review, a Survey, and a Criticism, 2nd ed. Cambridge, MA: MIT Press.

Dourish, Paul. 2004. "What We Talk about When We Talk about Context." *Personal and Ubiquitous Computing* 8 (1): 19–30.

Fitzsimmons, James. 1969. "Hans Haacke." *Art International* 13(7): n.p.

Frieling, Rudolf, and Dieter Daniels. 2005. *Medien Kunst Netz 2: Thematische Schwerpunkte.* Vienna; New York: Birkhäuser.

Gaver, William, Jake Beaver, and Steve Benford. 2003. "Ambiguity as a Resource for Design." In *Proceedings of the Conference on Human Factors in Computing Systems*, 233–240. New York: Association for Computing Machinery.

Gaver, William, John Bowers, Andy Boucher, Andy Law, Sarah Pennington, and Nicholas Villar. 2006. "The History Tablecloth: Illuminating Domestic Activity." In *Proceedings of the 6th ACM Conference on Designing Interactive Systems*, 199–208. New York: Association for Computing Machinery.

Hill, William C., James D. Hollan, Dave Wroblewski, and Tim Mccandless. 1992. "Edit Wear and Read Wear." In *Proceedings of the SIGCHI Conference on Human Factors in Computing Systems*, 3–9. New York: Association for Computing Machinery.

Holstius, David, John Kemble, Amy Hurst, Peng-Hui Wan, and Jodie Forlizzi. 2004. "Infotropism: Living and Robotic Plants as Interactive Displays." In *Proceedings of the 5th Conference on Designing Interactive Systems: Processes, Practices, Methods, and Techniques*, 215–221. New York: Association for Computing Machinery.

Ishii, Hiroshi, and Craig Wisneski. 1998. "AmbientROOM: Integrating Ambient Media with Architectural Space." In *Conference Proceedings of CHI '98*, n.p. New York: Association for Computing Machinery.

Mankoff, Jennifer, Anind K. Dey, Gary Hsieh, Julie Kientz, Scott Lederer, and Morgan Ames. 2003. "Heuristic Evaluation of Ambient Displays." In *Proceedings of the SIGCHI Conference on Human Factors in Computing Systems*, 169–176. New York: Association for Computing Machinery.

McGonigal, Jane. 2003. "This Is Not a Game: Immersive Aesthetics and Collective Play." In *Melbourne DAC 2003 Streamingworlds Conference Proceedings*, 116–125. Melbourne: RMIT University.

Mitry, Jean, and Christopher King. 2000. *The Aesthetics and Psychology of the Cinema*. Bloomington: Indiana University Press.

Moere, Andrew Vande. 2008. "Beyond the Tyranny of the Pixel: Exploring the Physicality of Information Visualization." In *IEEE International Conference on Information Visualisation (IV '08)*, 469–474. Piscataway, NJ: IEEE.

Norman, Donald A. 2002. *The Design of Everyday Things*. New York: Basic Books.

Parkes, Amanda, and Dietmar Offenhuber. 2008. "Dewy: A Condensation Display." In *ACM SIGGRAPH 2007 posters*, n.p. New York: Association for Computing Machinery.

Peters, Luke. 2006. "*Nabaztag* Wireless Communicator." *Personal Computer World* 2 (2006): n.p.

Shen, Xiaobin, Andrew Vande Moere, and Peter Eades. 2005. "An Intrusive Evaluation of Peripheral Display." In *ACM New York*, 289–292. New York: Association for Computing Machinery.

Skog, T., S. Ljungblad, and L. E. Holmquist. 2003. "Between Aesthetics and Utility: Designing Ambient Information Visualizations." In *Proceedings of InfoVis 2003*, 233–240. Piscataway, NJ: IEEE.

Varini, Felice, Lars Müller, and Fabiola López-Durán. 2004. *Points of View*. New York: Springer.

Venturi, Robert, Denise Scott Brown, and Steven Izenour. 1972. *Learning from Las Vegas*. Cambridge, MA: MIT Press.

Weiser, Mark. 1991. "The Computer for the 21st Century." *Scientific American* 265 (3): 94–104.

Weiser, Mark, and John Seely Brown. 1996. "Designing Calm Technology." *PowerGrid Journal* 1 (1): 75–85.

Wisneski, Craig, Hiroshi Ishii, Andrew Dahley, Matt Gorbet, Scott Brave, Brygg Ullmer, and Paul Yarin. 1998. "Ambient Displays: Turning Architectural Space into an Interface between People and Digital Information." In *Proceedings of the First International Workshop on Cooperative Buildings, Integrating Information, Organization, and Architecture*, 22–32. London: Springer.

25 Inscribing the Ambient Commons

Malcolm McCullough

The act of tagging, made popular by Web-based media, has also long existed in a different, more vigorous form in street culture as graffiti. As information media become ambient, what might interaction designers learn from this contrast? This essay examines the relationship between the tagger and the ambient through the notion of a commons. In urban computing, it finds a new middle ground of inscriptions. It finds merit in lower-tech genres of adhesive art and echoes widespread cautions about data-surveillance aspects of higher-tech tagging. It mainly asks for a curatorial role on urban markup and points out a need for an environmental history of information.

Tagging

At this writing, the most eminent visual artist in the United States is a tagger. There may be an *Obey Giant* sticker near you, and by some estimates there are half a million worldwide (figure 25.1). But although already ubiquitous, the work of Shepard Fairey was made much more famous by his Barack Obama campaign poster. Thus, for example, the *Giant* recently appeared at the Institute for Contemporary Art in Boston on one of those big banners that museums hang over their portals.

On the street, a tagger is someone who signs in aerosol. To tag is to spray-paint your name. An information professional, to whom tagging would mean much else, might call this practice a reputation system. Anyone who can sign all over town without getting caught in the act must be a badass. At some animal level, tagging just marks territory and has no civic aspirations. But then it becomes social—defiantly in its choices of site, competitively in which tags are respected and not soon written over by rivals, and culturally in how some signs become noticed by the general populace and even appreciated by critics. Why else would so many art museum gift shops offer coffee-table books of photographs of graffiti?

Citywide, rampant graffiti indicate distress. The sense of neglect that graffiti create tends to invite other troubles. Although such atmosphere has become more widespread in many cities, around Paris in particular, anyone who remembers New York

Figure 25.1
Shepard Fairey, *Obey Giant* (Boston Institute of Contemporary Art, 2009). Photograph courtesy of Joe C., available at http://www.random-pattern.com.

in the 1970s might know it best. There the graffiti reached unprecedented scale, most memorably covering almost all subway cars. In response, railyards got fenced in concertina wire, wide-nibbed markers were taken off the market, and penalties for aerosol signing began to escalate.

As New York made clear in its later recovery from its physical and fiscal nadir of the 1970s, one of the most useful public policies is to fight any appearance of anomie. It is important to assert the existence of a commons. This position was made memorable by the "broken-window theory," introduced in the early 1980s: "Social psychologists and police officers tend to agree that if a window in a building is broken and is left unrepaired, all the rest of the windows will soon be broken. . . . Vandalism can occur anywhere once communal barriers—the sense of mutual regard and the obligations of civility—are lowered by actions that seem to signal that 'no one cares.'. . . Such an area is vulnerable to criminal invasion" (Wilson and Keiling 1982).

Among the side effects of New York's cleanup, more interesting variants of tagging appeared. Adhesive art or "slap tagging," Shepard Fairey's medium, for instance, took off with the use of the "Hello My Name Is" stickers that are commonly used for casual business receptions. Stickers had a past in posters, of course: long before electronic media, posting lithographic bills was the main form of advertising. Thus, most cities have rules about flyposting. But compared to spraying, stickering makes it easier to hit more locations and easier to stay of jail. Still less risky is "reverse graffiti," a new genre of erasure, which simply helps owners remove grime from their walls. Such noncriminality has helped move street art beyond teen angst and into the cultural mainstream, such as museums (Walde 2007). Stylistically, there is something in the air that favors urban markup.

The rise of electronic tagging may not hurt this trend. Many people and organizations of respectable means now have their own use for the word *tagging*. At the moment, the most fashionable form of tagging appears to be Twitter's "hashtags." Tags more generally imply all manner of metadata: smaller identifiers for larger pieces of information. For example, this book may be tagged with an ISBN number, a library catalog number, publisher's information, and so on. Graphics files, particularly in mapping, come with tags about format, version, and origin. The Web, above all, has spread a new sensibility of tagging through its markup languages. Begun as a metaphor on earlier publishers' systems of annotation (metadata) for layout and printing, hypertext markup language (HTML) and extensible markup language (XML) have by now enabled widespread open-keyword file sharing by means of everyday systems such as Flickr and YouTube. The openness is one reason why these sites have exploded in popularity. Anyone can make up a keyword, and there is no such thing as a wrong tag.

In information design and with possible lessons for new forms of urban inscriptions, there follows a debate about bottom up versus top down. Classification schemes traditionally were top down and sought to be comprehensive on their designated topics. A taxonomy (such as the one a library would use to shelve this book in a certain place) is a top-down, tree-structured hierarchy. Or for nonhierarchical classification, an information designer might develop an *ontology*, which is an existence term appropriated from metaphysics to deal with markup languages' capacity for bottom-up schemas. Unlike the aggregate of aerosol tags in Le Bourget or the Bronx, bottom-up tagging online has great capacity for emergence. The complex patterns that arise from very large numbers of very simple elements may stabilize into enduring relationships, and some of those relationships may appear as classification schemes. The coined term *folksonomy* has developed from the concern for the accuracy of emergent taxonomy.

Issues arise in interaction aesthetics. In tagging, unlike so much other invisibly embedded ubicomp, there is no doubt about whether one is a "user." There also is no holdover from workplace usability metrics, where for a livelihood people were willing to put up with crummy technology. Instead, tagging is just plain fun. So in urban computing there may well exist new stylistic motives, other than shopping or drifting anonymously, for going out on the town with no particular destination in mind.

Ambient Commons

The continuum of annotations becomes a cultural domain in itself. Inscriptions, unlike screens that act as portals, make information everywhere slightly different, unobtrusive, persistent, and significant without links to other places—in a word, ambient. This concept differs from usual notions of ubiquity, which tend to imply connections to one same Internet of things, competition for attention, and endless networking.

These shared public qualities give ambient information qualities different from other forms of ubiquity and especially from aspects of "commons." Environmental policy and intellectual property law, to name just two domains, also have uses for the word *commons*. Wherever economic measures favor utility over existence, many pooled resources suffer depletion. This happens despite how systems of value now again acknowledge the greater good.

Tagging the commons thus belongs to a much larger set of cultural discourses. Today, prominent scholars such as the economist Elinor Ostrom and the anthropologist Lewis Hyde (2010) ask whether cultural knowledge itself is such a pooled resource and should be understood as a commons. Under these larger ideological turns, the act of tagging becomes one of ambient cultural awareness. For instance, when Eve Mosher's *HighWaterLine* project (2007)[1] marked anticipated sea levels on the streets of New York (figure 25.2), was that an artistic act, a crime, or merely a public service, like the many other traffic signs that have been officially installed everywhere? Or for an inverse example: if a university official goes around removing flyposted event tags from lampposts, is that an act of social good or a category error mistaking a social commons for signs of neglect? So these are the questions for this essay and this volume. Under what conditions does the act of marking some shared resource add to it or detract from it? Can the act of tagging the city electronically (and not in spray paint) promote some new kinds of cultural stewardship? How do the practices of reading and writing tagged urban places foster any larger ambient awareness?

Furthermore, interaction design becomes essential to the experience of ambient information. Not all information can be available everywhere. Not all information can have the same meaning in multiple contexts. Not all information can be kept at the foreground of attention. Some information acquires significance or legitimacy on the basis of where, how, and from whom it is obtained. Physical and organizational factors shape how convenient, unobtrusive, or satisfying the use of particular information may be.

Here is a third word to consider: the "ambient" is that which surrounds. With respect to information media, it is the inescapable spread of communications, sensors, displays, and memory. It is closely related to this volume's title, *Throughout* (see especially Ulrik Schmidt's essay on ambience and ubiquity, chapter 8). In general, as

Figure 25.2
Eve Mosher, *HighWaterLine* (New York, 2007). Photograph courtesy of Hose Cedeno.

understood by interaction designers, the ambient is a continuum of possibilities for shifts of perception or attention. It belongs to the world of cognition. Once surrounded, many people find cultural value in those possibilities for perceptual shifts even without corresponding shifts of intention or action. Why else would they put screens in so many places and so many things on each screen? Moreover, it is not only images. More and more sidewalks get showered by audio speakers. You can even buy underwater speakers for your swimming pool.

The ambient unfortunately often creates a perception of glut. Because the ambient surrounds, unlike a screen, it is a perception from which you cannot just walk away. As an inescapable nuisance, glut raises notions of pollution, albeit not of a finite resource and only in the eyes and ears of the beholder. Not nearly so dire as atmospheric pollution, information glut may nevertheless be overlooked as one of the most distinguishing aspects of these times. Yet to most, more is better: information is assumed to be an asset. Especially when emergent and socially produced ambient information has become an essential component of what ubiquitous-computing (ubicomp) pioneer Rich Gold (2007) called a "plenitude." The ambient abounds. It is not only widespread access to the net, which is what the term *ubiquity* most often means, but also localized and embedded media: information appliances, art installations, site-specific displays, and the relation of these media to other, nondigital media in those same sites.

Although other essays in this book may well have exposed the ambient for its aspects of old-school behavioral engineering or new fascinations with "persuasive" media, and although this essay needs a complementary one on graffiti and Twitter as pollution, for the moment just imagine an ambient that just *is*. If that sounds like art, where you cannot ask what something is *for*, then is the Ambient a collective artistic production? Or is the better approach through environmentalism: like a forest, the ambient has intrinsic and not just instrumental value. But who are its rangers and stewards?

Urban Markup: A New Middle Ground

In the literature of the ambient commons, there exists a well-known trope on tagging. Written by the urban sociologist Richard Sennett, it is called "the I and the It." This trope fits in a simple question: Does a young man spray painting a subway car in the Bronx *see* that subway car? But it then unpacks to a thesis of urbanism. Sennett, too, remembers New York in the 1970s: "The scale of this graffiti was what made the first impression: there was so much of it. . . . The kids were indifferent, however, to the general public, playing to themselves, ignoring the presence of other people using or enclosed in their space. . . . Transgression and indifference to others appeared joined in these simple smears of self, and with a simple result. The graffiti were treated from the first as a crime" (1990, 205).

Whereas a tagger just shouts "I," the "it" expresses the presence of others past, present, and future through the material forms and constraints of the city. There are limits to personalization. This is the urbanism: working with external circumstances that result from the presence of others pushes one to a higher level. The aggregate of these material expressions constrains each individual contribution. To Sennett, whose more recent work on craft affirms this outlook, an artist working in a civic capacity does see this material commons and does let it shape intentions and expressions, through which the city becomes a medium.

Consider another form of urban inscription. At a culturally opposite extreme from graffiti, New York also features more carved stone inscriptions than many other cities, at least in North America. Whereas newer construction in steel and glass favors other forms of text application—in particular backlit, branded signage—the era of Beaux-Arts sensibilities during which so many of New York's landmarks were built intrinsically favored neoclassical carving. This idiom proved especially apt for the many public cultural institutions that the city was building at the time in response to the unprecedented fiscal wealth and unprecedented social costs of industrialization. Museums, libraries, and schools were built to last and dedicated in stone for the advancement of the people. Yet in almost all aspects and especially as a form of tagging, all this building was quite top down, as if someone wished, at least stylistically, for these edifices to have been decreed by Caesar.

But that was then. Twentieth-century broadcast media soon put this urbanism into uncomfortable tensions, often as mere backdrops for television stand-ups, for a more dispersed, passive, and voyeuristic populace. Most media theory of recent decades has decried this tension. Although this is not the moment to recite any of this debate, it is safe to say that critiques the likes of Paul Virilio or Guy Debord have played much more prominent roles in theories of architecture and urbanism than have aspirations for the commons, such as of the Beaux-Arts.

But that, too, was then. In the fall of 2008 and in alliance with Shepard Fairey posters on the street, the Internet defeated television for control of Washington. Under postbroadcast, Web 2.0, embodied computational culture, all that midcentury televisuality somehow recedes into the past. Now there are thousands of spectacles on demand, not just the one. Is anyone even watching, and are these spectacles the same thing when viewed on a tiny iPhone screen? There the unit of 140 text characters assumes equal power.

So arises a new middle ground of urban cultural participation. No longer content to drift alone in the crowd as a flaneur, the networked urban subject wants to leave a mark and to share it. This collection of essays explores a shift from object signs to subject connectivity or from the "it" to the "we." Urban markup has put that shift in play. Beyond passive consumerism and leading toward either unprecedented personalization (new forms of the "I") or newly networked ambient environmental awareness (new forms of the "It"), urban markup deserves at least as much interpretation as art museums or broadcast media.

Between the former extremes of top-down civic institutional inscription and bottom-up antisocial defiant graffiti, there now has emerged a substantial, unofficial, noncriminal spectrum of practices in tagging. This spectrum is slowly acquiring an aesthetic. Although technocratic telecoms push much of this development, artists' tactical critiques push back. Few persistent editorial entities yet exist, but the turn toward hyperlocal news feeds in the place of defunct print newspaper suggests something. Above all, a curatorial charge arises. If anyone may mark up the city digitally, then who catalogs and conserves the most heartfelt narratives so that the city may become still more of an "it," a new dimension of "we," and serve now more than ever as repository of culture?

Cases in Adhesive Electronics

Locative media, a larger genre, have in a decade grown from a curiosity to a big business. Geodata industries support concerns in environment, infrastructure, logistics, social services, security, and more. The geospatial web increasingly collects and delivers this managed data on demand, often to the very places it documents. Embodied computation gathers and distributes these feeds in uncanny ways. Design business conferences such as Lift and Where 2.0 feature the latest blogjects, mashups, and distributed narrative installations. Research societies offer a technology-specific focus on positioning, sensing, embedding, displaying, and ad hoc networking, to name a few. Some even defend the electronic commons.

Many of these rapidly sharing domains share assumptions about ubiquity and mobility that demand deeper cultural examination. Issues of privacy and surveillance tend to dominate these concerns, but others also exist. For instance, how does so much personalization recast civility? What kinds of information best belong in one place and not everywhere? How might locative media help document and conserve material and energy flows? Does ambient connectivity enhance or distract from environmental awareness or civic participation? The field of urban computing has arisen to explore these concerns.

Because the adoption rate of mobile handheld communication surpasses that of cars or television, handheld communication is rightly considered the most transformative urban infrastructure of the day. Mobile applications of the geospatial Web thus tend to dominate artistic and academic investigations. Not all of those applications are for positional wayfinding, however, as geodata industries too quickly assume. Agendas in social navigation and environmental management also emerge. Even surveillance sometimes turns bottom up.

When a large new field grows around a given focus, some of its smaller, less dominant facets may help reflect its new outlooks. For example, to question ubiquity, it helps to study the situated (Kahn, Scholz, and Shepard 2006). To question mobility, it helps to uphold fixity, such as the expressive urban material constraints that the rude young aerosol tagger ignores. And here, to question the spellbinding high-tech complexity of handheld social networking, consider low-tech and sometimes antisocial tagging.

This essay does so by arbitrarily choosing adhesive art, which is without Global Positioning System technology or Bluetooth, for instance, and by using this choice to ask about shifts in ambient environmental awareness. Can the purpose of handheld electronic media shift beyond communicating for the sake of communicating or personalizing or else tuning out so much of the world, toward helping someone be here now, in the sense of knowing an urban commons?

For years, one signal project for such inquiry has been *Yellow Arrow*. Much like *Obey Giant*, *Yellow Arrow* has been acknowledged by the insider museum culture: in 2008, it was shown in New York's Museum of Modern Art. As interpreted by the *New York Times* in 2006, *Yellow Arrow* was a clearly understandable instance of the geospatial Web, "the Internet overlaid" on the physical world "to make the city more browsable" (Todras-Whitehill 2006). The arrow itself was a palm-size sticker, each of which had a unique alphanumeric code to use in text messaging to and from *Yellow Arrow*'s servers. You could buy a sticker for fifty cents, apply it anywhere you dared (or had permission, said the organization, to keep it legal), and upload a short text comment about that place. Anyone who came across the sticker could then text the indicated code and read your comment or upload another of his or her own. Over the four-year run of the project, a few thousand stickers were applied, mostly in a few pilot cities. Although most arrows were one-offs, which is natural in such a bottom-up authorship format, some civic themes did emerge. In Copenhagen, the main use that emerged was for political campaigning. In Boston, many arrows served bicyclist rights advocacy.

In hindsight (*Yellow Arrow* closed due to reasons of scale and funding), much of the project's appeal came from the interaction aesthetic of physical tagging. Whereas the social-networking aspect may have prevailed at the time—for, indeed, *Yellow Arrow* was seen as a community by some participants and as a way of life by a crazy few—more recent technologies and especially Twitter have taken that experience to new and different levels. Instead, the aspects of physical placement stand out. Here was social networking that was not ubiquitous, that involved the delight of discovery, that tested the cultural and material constraints of the city, and that tapped into the unofficial, noncriminal cool of stickering. "It's been called a game, a form of graffiti, and the largest performance art piece ever attempted," wrote the *Harvard Crimson* (Johnson 2004). *Yellow Arrow* was something you could do on a dare.

Even simpler Web-served tagging systems have occurred. Grafedia first took open-keyword media sharing to the walls. Its assumed medium was handheld picture messaging, although it also allowed small texts and sounds. Having invented a keyword and posted some annotations with it, one would tag in blue chalk to resemble hyperlinked words on the Web and so engage literally and physically in hypertext markup language. This has not become widespread. Far more frequent is to tag a Universal Resource Locator (URL, Web address) with a Quick Response (QR) sticker, which is in effect the two-dimensional barcode. Indeed, in Japan, where QR shows up everywhere from food packages to gravestones, it is well on its way to supplanting the Universal Product Code (UPC, or barcode). The best-known instance worldwide in the geospatial Web has been Semapedia, which links to *Wikipedia* entries. Semapedia generates a smartcode file for any *Wikipedia* article and sends that file for printout for use in tagging. Launched in 2005, Semapedia now has close to ten thousand tags. This is an obvious early instance in curating unofficial markup. Encyclopedias do lack street appeal, however, and although somebody might appropriate Semapedia by generating a smartcode for some other site, at the moment Google yields a null result on a search for "Semapedia abuse."

Contestation in applied electronic tagging instead tends to focus on radio-frequency identification: RFID. This technology has lucrative advantages in supply-chain management, whether in defense contracting or big-box retail, so its rollout has become a fact of life. Today, a search on "RFID sticker" raises a news note that "DAILY RFID has unveiled mini RFID Sticker Tag-08 (measured in dia. 9 mm) for use in most RFID applications, including directly on metallic surfaces. This adhesive RFID Sticker tag can easily be affixed to on flat and clean surfaces with its 3M Glue" (Daily RFID 2008). This note reflects the huge growth of merchandise logistics in China. For instance, in the spring of 2008 Wal-Mart began charging its suppliers a small fine for each palette of goods not tagged with RFID. At a smaller scale, Avery Dennison, the maker of the "Hello My Name Is" sticker, now also operates in "RFID Labeling Solutions."

The electronic-arts fields saw a wave of RFID projects around 2003–2006, when the possibilities of the technology were still becoming understood. For example, Preemptive Media showed a keychain that alerts to RFID sensing and stickers to tag RFID zone warnings for others (Kumao and Preemptive Media 2005). Yet today less new RFID art occurs. *We Make Money Not Art*, a much-read blog on ubicomp art, admits how "RIFD has moved away from my radar in the last couple of years" (Debatty 2008).

Still the challenge remains. Social thinkers rightly shun RFID for how it reifies everyday data surveillance, especially passive personal-identification checks. With RFID on your passport or transit pass, no longer does someone have to ask you for some ID. When coupled with data mining, this data surveillance leads to socially corrosive behavioral tactics, whether on the part of marketers, police, or interpersonal networks. Moreover, as N. Katherine Hayles has probed in this collection (chapter 31), some fundamental changes in cultural perception may accompany any shifts toward normalcy of passive tagging. MediaMatic in Amsterdam thus runs an annual "social RFID hacker camp." Esteemed futurist Bruce Sterling keeps an "arphid watch" on his column, which lately has tracked the scary realities of tracking living things, possible errant humans, such as by implanted Verichip.

For a taste of social fiction, in which RFID plays a more innocent role at tagging, it might help to take a moment to question that most widely assumed social act: Web posting. Imagine nothing server-side. For a case, a system of RFID tags, local flash memory, and off-the shelf reader bracelets might house a threaded urban narrative on a specific theme—say, ethnic history, urban botany, or architectural preservation. To read a different topic, you would buy a different reader off the rack at a local store. With nothing posted centrally, data surveillance might be less likely, paranoia levels might reduce, and participation might become more candid. That does seem difficult to imagine. The temptation would naturally exist to gather all this online in a box on a server farm outside town. Where does that temptation come from? Would there ever be counterexamples? Under what circumstances of noncriminal, nonofficial tagging would posting become taboo?

Toward an Environmental History of Information

In summary, on the topic of urban markup this essay has considered some ideological shifts. The first claim is that a new middle ground has emerged between official and criminal genres of signing. New forms of digital tagging create new roles in who has the right to mark up the city. Some of these roles must turn curatorial. Rote (and likely short-lived) storage of terabytes of all information isn't the answer. Archivists agonize over curating the digital. Markings have run the gamut from the regal to the and from the sacred to the profane. Ways of embellishing everyday space provide remarkable range for cultural critique.

Second, sufficient overlays of contextual marking can allow information media to provide orientation rather than escape from urban environmental awareness. Do these conditions aim toward a new kind of information environmentalism? Do they have a past in urban environmental history? These inquiries now exist. Is there an ambient commons?

Third, the idea of a commons raises useful questions regarding the contexts of ambient information. Ample evidence exists for a rise of site-sensitive social production of information. Conversely, there is clearly evidence of information overload, anxiety, and pollution. Do these trends detract from or contribute to any awareness of something larger and commonly pooled? When the pace and quantity of something so accelerate, changes occur: more is different. For instance, Sennett's trope of "the I and the It" may take new relations. As context distinguishes ambient information from earlier stages of electronic information and puts it in better relations with the longer history of architectural inscriptions, it demands awareness of the city as a constraining medium. This awareness demands better recognition of common-pool cultural resources, which demands an environmental history of information.

But, alas, tags have seldom endured. For example, the handbills, gazettes, and fly-postings of early print cultures such as Georgian London generally and quickly vanished. They received almost no mention from commentators on the everyday of the time, such as Samuel Pepys or Laurence Sterne. Alas, among literate cultures only the stories of the powerful were made permanent. Fewer documents of everyday life survived. And in traditional cultures, ephemeral tagging might be more usual still. The cyclical notions of time support festive practices of adornment, which are to be cleared away and perhaps repeated the next month or even the very next day.

Note

1. For more on *HighWaterLine*, see http://www.highwaterline.org.

References

Daily RFID, press release, December 2008. Available at http://www.rfid-in-china.com/products_667_1.html.

Debatty, Regine. 2008. "RFID Workshop at iMal." Comment on *We Make Money Not Art* (blog). Available at http://www.we-make-money-not-art.com/archives/2008/03/rfid-workshop-at-imal-in.php. Accessed 10 June 2010.

Gold, Rich. 2007. *The Plenitude—Creativity, Innovation, and Making Stuff.* Cambridge, MA: MIT Press.

Hyde, Lewis. 2010. *Common As Air—Revolution, Art, and Ownership.* New York, Farrar, Straus & Giroux.

Johnson, Camille. 2004. "Yellow Arrow Aimed at Building Art Community." *The Harvard Crimson,* 19 November.

Kahn, Omar, Trebor Scholz, and Mark Shepard, eds. 2006. *Situated Technologies.* Pamphlet series. New York: Architecture League of New York.

Kumao, Heidi, and Preemptive Media. 2005. "Zapped." Available at http://www.preemptivemedia.net. Accessed 10 June 2010.

Sennett, Richard. 1990. *The Conscience of the Eye: The Design and Social Life of Cities.* New York: Norton.

Todras-Whitehill, Ethan. 2006. "Making Connections Here and Now." *New York Times,* 25 January.

Walde, Claudia. 2007. *Sticker City.* New York: Thames and Hudson.

Wilson, James, and George Keiling. 1982. "Broken Windows." *The Atlantic Monthly* (March). Available at http://www.theatlantic.com/magazine/archive/1982/03/broken-windows/4465.

VII Mixed Reality

26 The Space of Bodily Presence and Space as a Medium of Representation

Gernot Böhme

Many Concepts of Space?

One of the most attractive aspects of thinking about space seems to lie in contrasting different concepts of space—the space of the physicist, the space of living reality, the space of the stage-set designer; space in psychoanalysis, the space of the landscape planner, the space of the lyric poet. But when different concepts of space are juxtaposed in this way, the question necessarily arises whether there is a unified space in the background—a space that is merely conceived in different ways—or whether there is some common element in the concepts themselves that justifies our grouping them together as concepts of space. Once we have begun to doubt the possibility of a multiplicity of different spaces, we are soon confronted by the question, *What actually* is *space?* or simply *What is space?*—space from which more or less everything is derived and to which more or less everything is related.

There is *one* difference between concepts of space that seems to me undeniable, and it is a difference so great that it seems almost impossible to bridge. It is the difference between the space of bodily presence and space as a medium of representation. The space of bodily presence is essential to my bodily existence because to be bodily present means to find oneself within an environment. Space as a medium of representation, by contrast, has nothing to do with me as a human being but is an abstract schema according to which a multiplicity of different things is represented. What is remarkable is that these two concepts are generally treated as if they were the same, so it is precisely the everyday commingling of them that enables us to speak of *space* in both cases: my bodily presence is conceived as a state of being placed among things, and the order existing between things is understood as the order of their simultaneity—that is, of their reciprocal presence.

It is interesting that in the work of Immanuel Kant, which employs a unified concept of space, this concept of space falls apart, as if by accident, in the course of its exposition.

Kant

In his *Critique of Pure Reason*, Kant defines space as a form of intuition. Because intuition is a representation, its space can be allocated to the concept of *space as a medium of representation*. Space makes it possible to represent a manifold of entities—that is, a multiplicity of entities in juxtaposition. What is striking, however, is that in the passages in which Kant introduces this concept of space in the chapter "The Transcendental Aesthetic," the other concept—the space in which I find myself—also becomes involved: "By means of outer sense, a property of our mind, we represent to ourselves objects as outside us, and all without exception in space" (1929, sec. 2, A 22/B 37). What have these two propositions to do with each other: first, that we represent things as outside us and, second, that we represent them all without exception in space? By saying "outside us," Kant is clearly bringing into play a spatial relationship that characterizes us in our bodily presence. If we apprehend objects as objects outside us, that implies that we perceive them from the perspective of our bodily presence. Although they form part of our environment, their mode of being present is clearly separate from our corporeally experienced inner sphere. This way of experiencing our bodily presence as surrounded by things clearly implies the notions of *centeredness* and *boundary* and, above all, the *difference between inner and outer* and thus also the notion of directions. None of this explains, however, how things are to be understood in relation to each other or whether, as Kant claims, they belong to an order of juxtaposition.

Now, one might object, of course, that Kant is not actually talking here about the body itself and that the difference between inner and outer is really the difference between inner and outer perception. Inner perception is the perception of myself. It takes place through self-affection within the mind. Outer perception is the perception of objects and takes place on the basis of affection by things in themselves. Assuming this difference between inner and outer, then the statement "we represent objects to ourselves as outside us" would mean no more than that these objects are represented as something that we ourselves are not and that must therefore be presented to us by outer affection. The manner in which we represent a manifold of objects to ourselves—Kant would then assert—is such that we juxtapose them in accordance with the form of intuition that he calls "space."

However, Kant cannot be rid of the body quite so easily. And perhaps he does not want to be rid of it because he needs it to make intelligible what he means by "space." On the very next page, under point 1 of the "Metaphysical Exposition" of the concept of space, we read: "For in order that certain sensations be referred to something outside me (that is, to something in another region of space from that in which I find myself), and similarly in order that I may be able to represent them as outside and alongside one another, and accordingly as not only different but as in different places, the representation of space must be presupposed" (1929, A 23/B 38). By now, it is quite unmistakable: Kant is treating space as something in which I find myself—the space of bodily presence. The objects confronting the outer sense are clearly referred to here as objects outside my body. But Kant then says that I represent these objects according to the schema of *things outside and alongside one another*—that is, as objects existing in space as a medium of representation. From the second half of this sentence on, Kant forgets the body for the remainder of the *Critique of Pure Reason*. Things confronting the outer sense are now represented only abstractly, according to the schema of what is mutually external and juxtaposed; the fact that I find myself among these things as a corporeal being no longer plays any part. That is surprising enough because, as objects of cognition, they must be given—that is, given in terms of sense perception. And how can sense perception take place if one were not present? But the compulsion of objectivity causes Kant to forget everything that this bodily presence in the perception of things might perhaps imply; instead, he concentrates exclusively on the relationships between objects. Why then, one might ask, does he in the first place speak of space as the space of bodily presence? He does so, it seems to me, because he draws from that idea an understanding of what it means to be in a place. To be in a place, as we know from bodily experience, means to find ourselves within an environment of things that are experienced as external. And by analogy—whether rightly or wrongly—Kant himself conceives of the mutual externality and juxtaposition of things as a presence in *different places*—namely, in places the difference between which is determined solely by the fact that they are mutually external. But for the concept of space as a form of intuition, is that idea actually necessary? That concept is not supposed to yield anything more than the notion of a manifold in juxtaposition. At any rate, space, for Kant, is to have the function of a medium of representation.

Space as a Medium of Representation

Mathematics treats space as a set with a certain structure. One can be confronted by different spaces depending on their structure. There are, for example, topological space, affine space, and metrical space. A manifold of points can be represented as a manifold of numbers. If in this case each point has one corresponding number, space is referred to as "one dimensional"; if it has two corresponding numbers, it is referred to as "two dimensional"; if it has *n* corresponding numbers, it is referred to as "*n* dimensional." Space qua space has specific structures. Dimensionality is one such structure. If the points in space are determined only by relationships of juxtaposition, then that space is topological; if, in addition, the points are separated by distances, we have a metrical space. The Kantian space of intuition is determined by the form of intuition—that is, by "being alongside," as in, first of all, only a topological space.

In the further course of the *Critique of Pure Reason,* Kant shows how through the effect of the categories of causality and quantity the space of intuition is formed into metrical space. The crucial point here is that through the notion of objects as confronting the outer sense, their relationships are represented as spatial relationships. That is what Kant means when he says that we can know nature only as appearance: objects are appearance insofar as their relationships to each other are represented as spatial relationships in the medium of space. This idea can be extended, in accordance with the theories of Albert Einstein or Hermann Weil, to include the manifold of events. The relationships between events are represented as spatial relationships in a four-dimensional space, time being added as the fourth dimension to classical three-dimensional space. This extension is important because causal relationships between events can thereby also be represented as spatial relationships.

Mathematical spaces, as the subject matter of a science, naturally have value in their own right, but their essential function lies in serving as media for representing relationships within manifolds of objects. It is known, for example, that extensions of concepts—that is, logical classes—can be represented by relationships of including or being included and as areas of intersection, and so on. But all networklike connections between objects—as treated by graph theory, for example—are also of this kind. Although one may not realize it in individual cases, these relationships, too, are represented as relationships in space. If these relationships are themselves particularly abstract or even nonsensory, as in the case of hierarchies or affinities, this manner of representing them in space is referred to as *visualization.* That expression, however, does not really do justice to the matter and has an almost pejorative ring. The fact is that relationships within manifolds of objects are often perceived only through being represented in space. One then speaks of spatial or even graphic models. This awareness—that in relation to some categories of objects one is thrown back on spatial or graphic models—does in a sense reproduce Kant's insight that all knowledge involves concept and intuition. The element of intuition is provided by representation in space.

The Space of Bodily Presence

Just as mathematics is concerned with space as a medium of representation, phenomenology deals with space as the space of bodily presence (see Schmitz 1967–1978; Ströker 1977). In noting this fact, one is made aware of the fundamental difference between the two concepts of space. Mathematics deals with objective, perhaps even eternal entities, phenomenology with subjective data. The space of bodily presence is something deeply subjective, although common to all subjects. The space of bodily presence is the space *within which* each of us experiences our bodily existence: it is "being-here," a place articulated absolutely within the indeterminate expanse of space—*absolutely* in the sense that it is without relation to anything else, especially to things; the "here" is implicit in the intuition of oneself. To the extent that the body is itself given as limited through the encounter with other bodily entities, the difference between the absolute "here" and the expanse of space is the difference between inner and outer. Up to this point, bodily space can still be represented mathematically: it is a centered space with directions, within which environments compose themselves in layers around the center. It can therefore be referred to it as an anisotropic, topological space.

However, this structure of the space of bodily presence as delineated by mathematics misleads us with regard to the true nature of that space. What is crucial is my involvement in this space, its existential character. Bodily space is the manner in which I myself am here and am aware of what is other than I—that is, it is the space of actions, moods, and perceptions.

As a *space of actions*, the space of my bodily presence comprises my scope for actions and movements. It might be called my "*sphaera activitatis.*" As such, it is certainly also centered and is articulated by characteristic physical directions such as *above/below* and *right/left*, but it is larger or smaller depending on the situation—for example, the presence of light or darkness. Bodily space as the space of actions is experienced essentially as possibility, as scope (*Spielraum*).

The *space of moods* is physical expanse insofar as it involves me affectively. The space of moods is atmospheric space—that is, a certain mental or emotive tone permeating a particular environment—and it is also the atmosphere spreading spatially around me, in which I participate through my mood.

The *space of perceptions* is my being among things—that is, the way in which, through perceiving, I am outside myself; or it is expanse insofar as my own presence is articulated through the presence of things.

It might be said that the space of bodily presence is an existential concept in the Kierkegaardian sense: it refers not to the determination of something, but to the "How?" of my existence. Although bodily space is always the space in which I am bodily present, it is at the same time the extension or, better, the expanse of my presence itself. The space of moods is the space that in a sense attunes my mood, but at the same time it is the extendedness of my mood itself. The space of actions is the space in which I can act, but also the scope of my possibilities. The space of perceptions is the space in which I perceive something, but also the expansion of my involvement in things.

Intuitive Space and Virtual Spaces

Having now become aware of the profound differences between space as a medium of representation and the space of bodily presence, one wonders what, if anything, these two concepts have to do with each other and whether it is right to refer to both of them as concepts of space. One strategy for dealing with this situation, which follows the example of Edmund Husserl, is to demonstrate a fundamental connection between them. Elisabeth Ströker (1977), for example, argues that mathematical space is founded in bodily space or, to use her terminology, in "lived space." However, this approach seems to me to underestimate the gulf between the two and to do violence to the freedom of mathematical possibilities of thought and construction. My thesis, by contrast, is that both types of space overlap from case to case and are, as it were, interwoven. Here, I briefly discuss two forms of this overlapping: intuitive space and virtual space.

By *intuitive space* (*Anschauungsraum*)—I take this term from Ströker (1977)—I mean that space in which we intuit our everyday praxis. Intuitive space is not the same as the space of perceptions. It is not just our extended being among things, nor is it space as a form of intuition in the Kantian sense because it is not a medium for the representation of things. In everyday life, we do not represent the things in our environment; we perceive them. However, to some degree we overlay our perception of the environment with patterns of representation. These patterns are ordering schemata, which certainly include Kantian juxtaposition, but also more than that: perspective, object permanence, and other patterns such as those demonstrated by gestalt psychology. These patterns are assimilated culturally, as is proved by reversible figures.

Intuitive space, therefore, is undoubtedly a hybrid entity and is by no means merely a medium in which we convert perceptions into representations. As we conceive or view things, we are certainly out there among them, but we organize our presence according to the patterns of possible representation; that is, we perceive things, but we intuit them as this or that.

Virtual spaces, however, are those types of spaces that are now forcing us to reflect on the difference between space as a medium of representation and the space of bodily presence. In a sense, so-called virtual spaces are not virtual at all but are simply images—that is, two-dimensional or multidimensional media in which a manifold attains representation. In this respect, it is quite immaterial whether what is represented is merely a product of thought or is derived from reality. In particular, it is incorrect to call virtual spaces "virtual" because they simulate reality, for that simulation is nothing but representation; that is, such so-called virtual spaces are images and nothing else. Representational spaces, however, do take on the character of virtual spaces at the moment when they become entwined with the space of bodily presence. In principle, there are two possible ways in which this can happen. One way is enter a space of representation through a representative—that is, to become virtually present in the space of representation through an avatar. This possibility should not, of course, be overestimated because virtual space does not by any means thereby fully become the space of bodily presence. As a rule, virtual space becomes only a space for actions, but it can also be experienced by the player through identification with the avatar—in this example, we are dealing, of course, with electronic games—as a space of moods.

The other possible way in which the space of bodily presence can to some extent be made to coincide with representational spaces is to surround oneself with a representational space by means of a data glove, data spectacles, or an electronic "cave." In this way, too, a representational space becomes a virtual space in that one is in a sense bodily present in it. Here, in contrast to the first case, I do not become bodily present in the space of representation through a representative, but, inversely, the bodily "I" becomes present in a representational space by coupling a representational space to its sensory perceptors. That the virtual space in both cases represents a sort of real life for the person experiencing it is shown in the first case by the affective and biographical importance of the events in the game for the player and in the second by possible bodily reactions, such as nausea, experienced by visitors to caves and simulators.

Virtual spaces, too, therefore involve an intertwinement of representational spaces with the space of bodily presence. Virtual spaces are rightly called such because, although merely representational spaces, they can be experienced as spaces of bodily presence. Virtual spaces should not therefore be referred to as "virtual" simply on account of their character as representational spaces, but only and insofar as a subject becomes in some way involved in them. This possibility, I would like to say in conclusion, is likely to be connected to the fact that an overlaying of the space of bodily presence by patterns of representation is already rehearsed in everyday life—that is, in intuitive space. That is certainly not to say that virtual spaces are limited to these patterns and should in some way approximate reality; rather, it should be possible to simulate a virtual presence in representational spaces of any desired structure.

References

Kant, Immanuel. 1929. *Critique of Pure Reason.* Translated by Norman Kemp Smith. London: Macmillan.

Schmitz, Hermann. 1967–1978. *System der Philosophie III, der Raum.* 5 vols. Bonn: Bouvier.

Ströker, Elisabeth. 1977. *Philosophische Untersuchungen zum Raum.* 2nd ed. Frankfurt am Main: Klostermann.

27 Toward a (Re)Constructed Endosemiotics? Art, Magic, and Augmented Reality

Jacob Wamberg

The term *augmented reality* sometimes refers more narrowly to supplementing the physical world with an extra virtual interface, but in this chapter I use it more broadly in the sense of Lev Manovich's "augmented space" or what in this section of the volume is called "mixed reality": "*overlaying the physical space with the dynamic data*" (Manovich 2006, 223). According to the utopian ring of this conception, through information technology, reality is itself upgraded. Is this just another example of hubris and hype connected to the introduction or expectancy of a new technology that will eventually shrink to the business-as-usual pragmatic use of artifacts? Or are we witnessing a threshold to a genuinely new condition in which the saturation of the environment with information technology does imply a certain not only quantitative, but also qualitative shift in our lifeworld?

This anthology is a sign, of course, that many of us do suspect a certain paradigm shift, and in this essay I suggest a sense in which augmented reality can be located in a utopian genealogy, regardless of whether it will actually improve our lifeworld. My lens is semiotic, suggesting that augmented reality reawakens the index as a primal sign of communication and hereby reactualizes certain layers of communication in nature. Pure indexicality—passive imprints from or pointing toward things—is shared with the exosemiotics of organisms' outer lifeworlds. In augmented reality, however, the index is empowered away from passivity to proactivity, fusing sign with physical influence, and in nature this feature seems to be shared only with the endosemiotics of intracorporeal realms. In the cultural domain, this fusion also recalls the magic of premodern cultures, and the questions therefore arise whether augmented reality fulfills certain repressed utopian desires of art—a category that can be construed as an offspring of magic practices—and, if so, what role art and aesthetics may possibly play in relation to augmented reality. Are they subsumed by it and made superfluous as autonomous domains, or do they take on an active—for instance, critical—position within it? I hope this essay, although not giving a definite answer to these questions, will nevertheless provide some useful material for approaching them.

From Media to Augmented Reality

To introduce the semiotic angle, my thesis, as indicated, is that augmented reality implies a rise of the Peircian index in the form of the physical imprint (Peirce 1960), not least a new kind of index that I designate "proactive." My claim is that the semiotic sphere of human cultures prior to the 1900s was dominated by signs with a marked distance to physical referents: on the one hand, the icon, the structural simulation of objects; on the other hand, the symbol, the codified representation of objects. To put it another way, in handmade and graphic images and in spoken, written, and printed statements of all kinds, even in music, the reference, if any, to concrete physical objects was to an increasing degree indirect because all these signs were produced by the hand, voice, body, and diverse instruments with no physical connection to objects. Moreover, the interpretants, or signifieds, of these signs were often higher- or lower-degree abstractions from the physical environment, such as mythical personages or concepts. It was only after the mind, fed by sensory inputs, had assembled an inner virtual image of some kind—pictorial, literary, mathematical, musical, and so forth—that this image could be transferred to material representation. Likewise, if the sign was going to influence the world, the mind had to react again to this representation and transfer its message to the body and its outer prostheses in instruments and machines—what I here designate "technology" in contrast to "media." In this understanding, signs and their material grounds, the media, were prostheses mainly for the distant senses, sight and hearing (i.e., books, pictures, notes, and even musical instruments and theater stages), and thus they appealed exclusively to the mind that they reflected. What actually moved the world and had material exchanges with it, however, was composed of the body and its prostheses in technology, such as weapons, hammers, wagons, mills, steam engines, and so forth. The mind was thus a necessary relay things had to pass through in order to be both read as and distilled into signs and to move the world (Koefoed Hansen and Wamberg 2005). Therefore, at least in my disenchanted retrospective analysis, just as no cultural image or word was moved or shaped by the world it represented, so it could not in itself move or shape that world after entering its physical form. This is not to say, of course, that signs did not have an indexical quality in premodern times, only that the index was always an imprint of the bodily limb or instrument that made the sign rather than of any extracorporeal or extrainstrumental object.

This particular state of affairs, which prevailed throughout most of cultural history—from prehistorical times to postmedieval modernity—became increasingly challenged, however, with the emergence of the photographic and audio-recording media after 1830. In contrast to the earlier physically indirect and mind-controlled media, these new automatic fora are physically marked and shaped by the visual or auditory phenomena they represent, having indexical imprints from them. Moreover, this indexicality goes through a remarkable evolution, moving from a passive freezing of the past to real-time animated representation of the present and on to a proactive influence on the future. If we focus on the photographic media, the photograph is thus marked by momentary light imprints of particular surroundings; the film captures these surroundings in animation, and television breaks through to the surroundings in real time. In this breakthrough, television in its direct and nonrecorded form acquires the status of an optical prosthesis—a telescope that can turn around corners—more than an old-fashioned medium re-creating something not really "there." In particular, the past and therefore the still cut-off worlds of photo and film are transformed into actual surroundings that are in principle no less observable than the immediate surroundings reached by the naked eye. With direct television, then, the visual (and acoustic) physical environment is markedly extended, turning into a montage of differently located but still, in a physical sense, present realities.

Skeptics of a social constructivist bent—that is, probably most humanist scholars —may object at this point that the intermediation of analog and especially digital technologies found in photographic and audio-recording devices does not allow for any enhanced presence, but quite the opposite: as aspects of the real object are broken down and translated into many layers of signals, the object's presence is displaced and made accessible only through signals that are increasingly symbolic rather than indexical (Derrida and Stiegler 2002, 6, 32). In response to this argument, one might counter that this condition is no less true for the way the "naked" presence of an object is made accessible for consciousness via the human body, translated as it is into light waves and nerve signals that are again collected into brain images with no immediate connection to the object. As both natural and technological "presences" are thus grounded in complicated signal translations, either one can give up the idea of presence altogether (which social constructivists would often prefer), or one can, as I suggest, operate with degrees of presence. The degree of presence is established, however, not in the character of translation (analog or digital, artificial or natural), but in how specifically *icons embedded in time* are reconstructed in a mediated form—with a shared real time as the ultimate point of presence production (a state that is, of course, approached only because of the speed of light but never fully attained either in artificially or naturally mediated presences). Old-fashioned media do not produce this kind of presence simply because they are grounded in the brain's reconstruction of sense impressions via the work of the hand and its instrumental prostheses—a collecting together, a *re-membering*, of many different discontinuous moments that may reconstruct the iconic aspects of an object or event, but not its temporal embeddedness.

In any case, what is obviously missing in the presence production of television is interactivity, the possibility of physically influencing the part of the world we see and hear. This possibility, however, comes in reach with the computer, whose multimedial sign-processing systems can be physically switched together with near or remote physical worlds (Dourish 2001, 140). To be sure, until now we have become accustomed to conceiving of the computer as primarily a virtual technology, so in many ways it is an old-fashioned medium in the sense I described earlier—an aspect stressed by the still very medialike interface comprised by the computer screen with its alternating associations to book page and picture. In this admittedly hypercritical light, the difference between computer and medium consists mainly in the fact that the signs of the computer appear as more radically malleable and furthermore, as we see from the Internet, more rapidly accessible and exchangeable than the signs of earlier media. However, in the framework of augmented reality, the genuinely new quality of the computer is that its more malleable, accessible, and exchangeable sign complexes may be connected directly to the physical world, thereby breaking through or at least making much more porous the relays of consciousness that have hitherto, medialike, acted as security guards between the outer physical environment and the inner virtual world of computers.

At one pole of augmented reality, we find telepresence, which can be understood as the previously desired interactive television, a television in which the prosthetic radius of action extended from remote artificial visual and auditory sense organs to remote artificial body parts that may actually do something with the remote reality. In a particularly subtle artistic interpretation of this possibility, Eduardo Kac's *Genesis* (1999) (see figure 27.1), remote agents could turn on ultraviolet light over Petri dishes via the Internet in order to see what was happening among their coli bacteria. Some of these coli bacteria had had a specially encoded passage from the biblical Book of Genesis, the one referring to the transferral of power over the beasts from God to man, inserted into their DNA material. When the light was turned on, the bacteria not only became remotely visible—emitting cyan in contrast to the yellow of the unmarked bacteria—but also subject to mutations deforming their original message because the same light was also an agent that changed their genetic behavior (see Kac 2005). In this way, the ultraviolet spark indicated both creation and its opposite, a letting-go of divine power together with the Genesis passage indicating that power, gradually corrupting the message to, for example, "LET AAN HAVE DOMINION OVER THE FISH OF THE SEA AND OVER THE FOWL OF THE AIR AND OVER EERY LIVING THING THAT IOVES UA EON THE EARTH."

Apart from a subtle comment on the ambivalent status of human creation—Who is creating whom?—we encounter a new kind of index exchange in this installation. First, by being exposed to the ultraviolet light, the coli bacteria made their visual impression remotely accessible as an icon created by a real-time but still passive index, just as happens in normal photographic media. However, second, the very turning on of ultraviolet light could in itself be considered a proactive index that the remote agent sent off through space, thereby converting her or his computer's media coating of

Figure 27.1
Eduardo Kac, *Genesis* (1999), transgenic work with artist-created bacteria, ultraviolet light, and Internet. Video (detail), edition of 2, dimensions variable. Courtesy of the Collection Instituto Valenciano de Arte Moderno, Valencia, Spain.

icons and symbols into a physical agent that actively interacted with and transformed the world. This is, as it were, an index with a vengeance, an inverted index, not only shaped as passive physical impression of an object, but going back to the object and transforming it instead.

At the other pole of augmented reality—one often referred to specifically by that name or by synonyms such as *pervasive computing* or *ubiquitous computing*—instead of remote locations made accessible through simulation, rather the physically near environment is coated with information technology (Manovich 2006). In this form of augmented reality, the proactive index becomes perhaps even more powerful because mere gestures turn into actions, such as when, for instance, a lowered hand can dim the lights. Through this influential gesturing, we encounter a hyperempowerment of what was originally the weakest form of the Peircian index: the mere pointing in which the only physical connection between body and object is that of space. At the same time, though, the surroundings will be pervaded by networks of computers influenced by near and remote agents of which we have no knowledge or control. As Adam Greenfield puts it with his neologism *everyware*, "Everyware produces a wide belt of circumstances where human agency, judgment, and will are progressively supplanted by compliance with external, frequently algorithmically-applied standards and norms" (2006, 148). The ants video transmitted to Copenhagen from a desert in

New Mexico and dictating, with regular shifts, the rules according to which live actors behaved in Lars von Trier and Niels Vørsel's installation *The World Clock* (1996) can be seen as a metaphorical prediction of such dependence on external standards and norms (Schepelern 2000, 158–164).

In augmented reality, the surroundings may likewise react to your own bodily behavior long before you are conscious of it—as is artistically explored in the Canadian *whisper[s]* project (2003–2005) (see figure 27.2), in which everyware infiltrated diverse pieces of underwear, making, for instance, a vibrator move in one agent's shirt in response to another agent's breathing.[1] In these instances, the indexicality is no longer the result of conscious acts but rather belongs to bodily unconscious or automatic processes. Nevertheless, the indexes are still proactive in the sense that originally weak and remote physical influences not only leave imprints but lead to actual movements and events.

Figure 27.2
The *whisper[s]* project and Gretchen Elsner, pieces of interactive clothes (2003–2005), Simon Fraser University, Vancouver. Photograph by Elisa Gonzales.

The Index before and within Culture

With all due respect to the obvious differences, this reawakened and even empowered indexicality of augmented reality has certain similarities with natural habitats and can indeed be understood, I would claim, as a relinking to natural layers of experience (for an illustration of this idea and the following description, see figure 27.3). In striking contrast to the aforementioned earlier cultural regimes whose signs were nonindexical mediations and whose referents, furthermore, tended to belong to nonpresent realities, sign exchange in nature—among animals and plants and inside organisms—seems always to regard the actual surroundings (Hoffmeyer 2005, 313–315). If we first look at the semiosis in the outer lifeworld of organisms (exosemiotics), the rattling of a rattlesnake is a sign communicated in the physical neighborhood signaling the danger posed by the self-same snake. Bird song is about immediate matters among

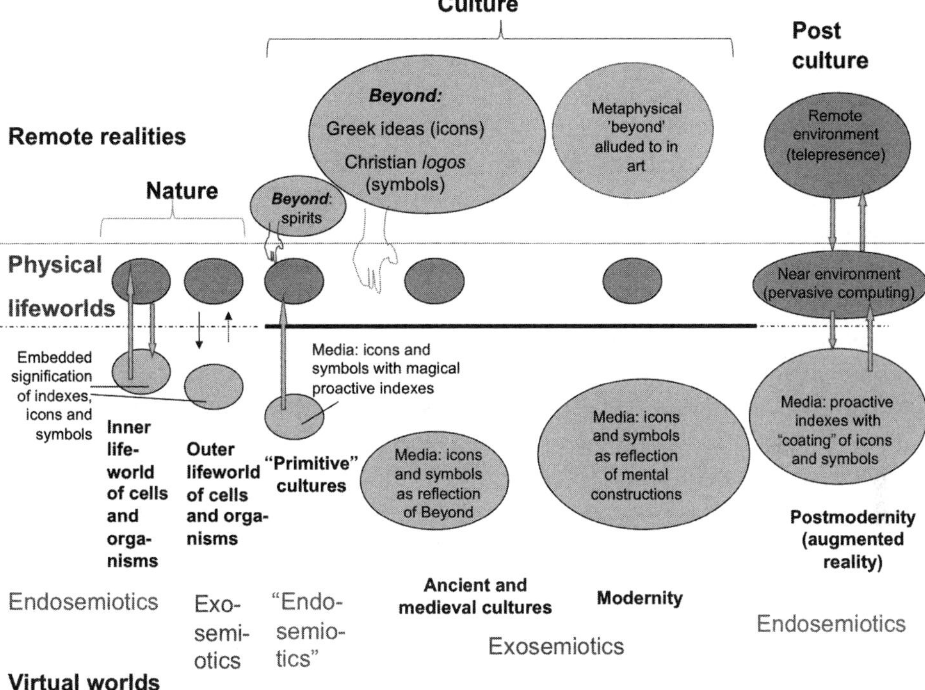

Figure 27.3
Evolution of the relation between virtual worlds and lifeworlds in nature and culture. Illustration by the author.

birds, such as flirtation. The colors and forms of flowers and fruits are aesthetic signals to insects and larger animals, enticing them to spread the plants' genetic material. All these natural signs, then, can be taken as stronger or weaker indexes, either being shaped directly by the object to which they refer (such as the rattling of the rattlesnake) or pointing to objects or organisms in the immediate surroundings (such as bird song). Even if some sort of iconic or symbolic quality is admitted (such as the exquisite shapes of flowers, camouflage that makes an animal disappear in its surroundings, or the "abstract" signs of bird song), it doesn't undermine the observation that the signs still refer to conditions in the tangible environment and therefore also have an aspect of index in the sense of pointing.

In spite of the seeming remoteness of several of the realities included in augmented reality, the aforementioned indexical way in which these realities are made accessible in the immediate surroundings makes it meaningful to say that certain aspects of the remote realities are just as physically present as those met by the naked sense apparatus and therefore that this web of presences forms a kind of neonatural habitat. Furthermore, the reawakened indexicality, in both its space-pointing and physically influential dimensions, reminds us of the environment-directed sign exchange among animals and plants.

But apart from the obvious fact that the reawakened indexes are typically coated and interact with thick layers of icons and symbols—that virtual world that is the specific outcome of human cultures—another crucial aspect of augmented reality is missing in the outer lifeworld of cells and higher organisms: proactivity, the ability to move physically by means of the very sign activity. However, if we are to believe the still controversial founding idea of biosemiotics, this quality is seemingly encountered if we move from the semiotics of the outer lifeworlds (exosemiotics) to the semiotics taking place inside organisms (endosemiotics). The claim of biosemiotics is that intra- and intercellular processes such as DNA–RNA–protein communication, hormones stimulating growth, or alarmones signaling stress are not to be understood solely as complicated automatic reactions—chemical or biophysical—but as also possessing a truly semiotic dimension. In other words, these processes involve molecules behaving as signs to be interpreted by some agent choosing between presented possibilities. However, this agent cannot be the usual relay of consciousness and certainly not one located in a brain; it must rather be some kind of distributed subjectivity (Hoffmeyer 2005, 101–110, 252–259). This, then, is another way of saying that these intraorganismic reactions actually concern proactive index processing, processing in which symbolical signs are directly involved through some sort of combined physicosemiotic interaction in the material action or genesis they trigger.

As far as I can judge, if the proactive indexes of augmented reality are construed as a technological restaging of such natural sign processing, then they have cultural forerunners in the magic signs of "primitive" cultures. These signs concern a desire for reconnecting with the primordial origins of nature, a regressive movement that I would explain by the immaturity of the human child compared to young animals. Because the child is a kind of still-not-finished embryo that has left the womb too early, it will seek to reestablish the womb environment, including its endosemiotic communication, with cultural means. If the structural correspondences between cultural onto- and phylogenesis—that the child reenacts the development that culture as a whole has played through and vice versa (Habermas [1976] 1991, 149)—are taken into account, the first tribal cultures of grown-ups will act in a conceptual space similar to that of the young child. Thus, although I stated earlier that the mediated signs of premodern cultures were rarely indexical in relation to the objects they referred to, this is true only in disenchanted retrospect and definitively untrue if we consider the self-understanding of the makers of religious and magical signs.

More precisely, religion and its images—signs that can be understood immediately as forerunners of the modern domain of "art"—can be seen as a response to a frustration with nature and that part of culture that is comprised by technology. Because nature and its technological prostheses do not seem to be sufficiently powerful in their naked states—that is, the states in which the human being is situated outside the womb—a supranatural world, a Beyond, is contrived that transcends the limitations felt in what is now seen as the "worldly" world. This more powerful Beyond, reestablishing a womblike state, including its endosemiotic connections, may now be activated and made accessible through certain performative contexts. In magic, rituals and signs thus take over those tasks for which nature and technology are in themselves impotent by letting unfulfilled wishes canalize directly through the signs and into the environment—such as happens in, for instance, healing, curbing, prophesying, telekinesis, creating rain, and transcending death. Not only are religious artifacts such as totem figures, fetishes, amulets, and icons intimately or indexically shaped by or connected to the otherworldly regime they represent (for instance, *acheiropoieta*, images created without human hands, such as the holy veil of Veronica [Koerner 1993, 80–126]). Such representations are often claimed to be endowed with a miraculous power to influence from a distance—for instance, heal, injure, confer fertility, occupy with spirits, or make happen other kinds of wish fulfillment—as is continually witnessed in religion's off-shoots in folklore and fairy tales (Frazer [1922] 1963, 12–14; Freedberg 1989, 270–277; Mauss [1950] 1972, 63). Just as they are indexically connected to the Beyond, so they are themselves, as proactive indexes, able to move and activate. All these supernatural remedies, adding up to archaic religion, can thus be construed as a bridge overcoming a gap between human being and world and re-creating that endosemiotic womb from which the child was expelled too early and for which the grown-up is continually longing—a virtual bridge building that may be implied by the very word *religion*, probably etymologically derived from the Latin word *religare*, "to bind" (Lactantius 2003, 4:xxviii, 275–276).

Indeed, I will expand my semiotic perspective at this point because the sign world of icons and symbols per definition fills up a gap between human being and world, evoking an ersatz presence for something not really there. My claim would thus be that the representations of religion are simply a more specialized aspect of this broad-ranging semiotic virtual Other, for if the two domains, semiosis and religion, build bridges to realities not immediately present, the religious representations thus have an accent on zones so remote that they can be termed supernatural—a movement away from the physical surroundings that a modern, more disenchanted analysis would understand historically as an increasing abstraction (Wamberg [2005] 2009, 1:161–186). Thus, considering the most autonomous notions of the religious Beyond, those encountered in Greek–Roman and Judeo-Christian cultures, we see that they are modeled on the very semiotic bridges through which they are revealed—that is, as regimes of completely abstracted, spiritual signs, be it the Platonic Beyond of ideas (supericons) or the Judeo-Christian Beyond of Logos (the superword). Here the real and the virtual occupy roles exactly opposite to that of modern culture, so that what is most real is composed of the Beyond: those ethereal entities—signs and symbols—that precisely were contrived to compensate for a loss of presence felt toward parts of the world not in the immediate physical neighborhood. The sign is not an impression of the thing, but the thing of the sign.

What in archaic cultures still establishes a bridge to the Beyond is, however, an extraordinary, nonabstract quality originally connected to the iconic and symbolic signs—images, signs, and words through which religion is expressed—namely, a left-over endosemiotic power that reestablishes a link to Mother Nature's womb and that may be termed "magical." It is this proactive indexicality, the performing of magical feats, that constitutes the overcoming of the abovementioned frustration with nature and its artificial prostheses in technology. However, because religious evolution can be described as an increasing abstraction, proactive indexical qualities of religious signs are looked upon with growing skepticism, and therefore spiritual communication through icons and symbols—that is, communication that moves dominantly through the relay of consciousness—is promoted at the expense of magic, which is thus marginalized to extraordinary events: miracles. This development was made explicit in the iconoclastic movements of the Middle Ages and the Reformation, which rejected religious images precisely because these images, rather than their now exclusively spiritual—that is, completely abstracted—prototypes were venerated as powerful (Barash 1992).

Whereto Art? The Proactive Index in the Aftermath of Culture

The question I raise in conclusion is whether augmented reality can in certain ways be seen as a fulfillment of the utopian desire connected with these magical aspects of religious images—in other words, their alleged indexical proactivity. This fulfillment would be in line with science-fiction writer Arthur C. Clarke's Third Law of prediction that "[a]ny sufficiently advanced technology is indistinguishable from magic" (1973, 21). Adam Greenfield is in no doubt:

> Folklore is replete with caves that open at spoken command, swords that can be claimed only by a single individual, mirrors that answer with killing honesty when asked to name the fairest maiden in the land, and so on. Why, then, should anyone be surprised when we try to restage these tales, this time with our technology in the central role? Everyware is simply speaking to something that has lain dormant within us for much of modernity and played an overt, daily role in our lives for a very long time before that. (2006, 119)

For Greenfield, then, there is no question that augmented reality places itself in a genealogy of magic and the extraordinary, a genealogy that bypasses the rationality of modernity and thereby simply the genealogy of technology. As indicated earlier, although Greenfield's focus is the less canonically religious folklore and fairy tales, this genealogy can easily be extended to indexical communication with the religious Beyond. Augmented reality thus makes a bridge between the two remotenesses, of which this Beyond is probably a reflection: (1) physically distant locations and (2) the inner virtual world of icons and symbols whose abstractions have broken with the physical environment. Augmented reality can overall be seen as a turn in which the specific outcome of human culture—the virtual world of icons and symbols—has expanded to such a degree that it crushes against the cave wall of the material world and begins to reconnect with that materiality that was desired—but not actually touched, we presume—in magical signs.

But if this genealogy does indeed make sense, then another question inevitably follows: Where is contemporary art to be placed in this genealogy? For, again, art is often and for good reason seen as a secularized follower of religious images, a follower in which the magical and indexical link with the Beyond has not only been exorcised, as in the iconoclastic movements, but exiled from some heaven to humans' metaphysical inner depths (Shiner 2001, 194–196). However, as famously described by Peter Bürger (1974), the project of the historical avant-gardes was to explode this inner exile and catapult art back into the lifeworld or, as in this essay's vocabulary, to augment reality according to the experiences of the former autonomous art. The question therefore arises whether the augmented reality that the postindustrial world is now perhaps entering can be compatible at any analytic level with that augmented reality desired by the avant-gardes, and, if so, what role, if any, is then left for art as a specific domain? In favor of a view of the avant-garde fusion of art and life as compatible with augmented reality, one might mention that both avant-garde art and augmented reality concern a performative turn, a reality in which signs are able to do and vice versa (Fischer-Lichte 2004, 31–42). Duchamp's ready-mades, for example, comprise things fused with a space of significance that becomes visible through their displacement from a "neutral" sphere of bodily use—that is, technology—to a sphere of images. This performative way of being a thing is comparable to the way recorded things are made present in distant spaces through the displacements of teletechnology. Emphasizing the link between archaic magic and augmented reality's proactive index, this performative agglomeration of sign and thing can also be termed "neoprimitive" because it violates modernity's foundational ideology of nominalism, the rationalist dogma of a strict separation of world and concept, *Ding an sich* and *Ding für uns*. The many primitivist movements of modern art may thus designate thematic condensations of a pervasive condition of postmodernity, that of signs being in close indexical contact with the realities they refer to and possibly being able to influence those realities proactively—as was the case with their animistic predecessors in archaic, "primitive" cultures. That magic in large part comprises signs—such as rituals, spells, and voodoo figures—that are allegedly able to act is a feat etymologically reflected in how the word *magic* shares roots with the word *doing* in several languages—for instance, *Zauber* in German (Mauss [1950] 1972, 19).

And yet, if avant-garde utopia and augmented reality are compared, a leftover reaction is that augmented reality still designates just a "technological" sphere facilitating embodied interaction, whereas art concerns focused works or at least denser areas of the lifeworld retaining a surplus quality that should perhaps still be termed "metaphysical." Should the interactive networks of augmented reality actually become so dense in themselves that we can do without such prespecified nodes, such aesthetic events with special life-enhancing qualities?

At least one pathway for art—but perhaps also out of art—seems to be the function of more or less critical affordance for events in augmented reality. As presented by the psychologist of vision James J. Gibson (1979) and elaborated upon by computer theoretician Donald A. Norman ([1988] 1990, 87–104), affordances are characteristics in objects that reveal how those objects may be used, thereby facilitating actions. If, however, affordances are conceived of only as subconscious gateways to actions, it becomes eerily obvious that augmented reality has in fact turned into one giant intracorporeal organism, but one whose movement and distribution of power through automatic mechanisms and choiceless subjects might be the instruments of suspicious interests. Therefore, this vision is not truly endosemiotic, given that it just describes the intracorporeal happenings in terms of a large automaton programmed by cynical subjects instead of in terms of a swarmlike cluster operating according to a distributed subjectivity. Reacting to this nightmare, scholars such as Anthony Dunne suggest that this calm or invisible computing ought to have reinserted a friction with the relays of consciousness, a Brechtian *Entfremdung*, or user-unfriendliness, allowing humans to retain their status as conscious agents ([1999] 2005, 35–36). Following this vision, artistic affordances in the form of aesthetic framings may appear, channeling, avant-garde fashion, a critical and reflective reservoir into our exchange with augmented reality. This is perhaps what a work such as Kac's *Genesis* proposes to do, although still operating in an autonomous artistic space outside the actual creation of life and thereby not being an affordance proper. At least a temporarily useful concept for art and aesthetics may thus be something like Paul Dourish's notion of *coupling* (Dourish 2001, 138–139), a steady switching between what Martin Heidegger termed *Vorhanden* and *Zuhanden* ([1927] 1967, 102–104), between critical deconstruction and indexical alignment.

And yet I do believe that augmented reality signals a new paradigm in which consciousness and its outer representations in icons and symbols cannot in the same way as in modernity keep their autonomy and distance to the physical surroundings they are interacting with. If, as I have suggested, augmented reality does signify a space comparable to a reconstructed endosemiotic realm, we therefore have to invent a new, less dualistic thinking. In this thinking, the dualism between free, autonomous subjectivity and involuntary, automatic subjugation should be mitigated and instead include an agency akin to that found inside the organism—an agency that, for want of better terms, can be called "distributed subjectivity."

Note

1. For more on the *whisper[s]* project, see http://whisper.iat.sfu.ca.

References

Barash, Moshe. 1992. *Icon: Studies in the History of an Idea.* New York: New York University Press.

Bürger, Peter. 1974. *Theorie der Avantgarde.* Frankfurt am Main: Suhrkamp.

Clarke, Arthur C. 1973. "Hazards of Prophesy: The Failure of Imagination." In *Profiles of the Future: An Inquiry into the Limits of the Possible,* 12–21. New York: Harper and Row.

Derrida, Jacques, and Bernard Stiegler. 2002. *Echographies of Television: Filmed Interviews.* Cambridge, UK: Polity Press.

Dourish, Paul. 2001. *Where the Action Is: The Foundations of Embodied Interaction.* Cambridge, MA: MIT Press.

Dunne, Anthony. [1999] 2005. *Hertzian Tales: Electronic Products, Aesthetic Experience, and Critical Design.* London: RCA CRD Research Publications.

Fischer-Lichte, Erika. 2004. *Ästhetik des Performativen.* Frankfurt am Main: Suhrkamp.

Frazer, James George. [1922] 1963. *The Golden Bough: A Study in Magic and Religion.* New York: Macmillan.

Freedberg, David. 1989. *The Power of Images: Studies in the History and Theory of Response.* Chicago: University of Chicago Press.

Gibson, James J. 1979. *The Ecological Approach to Visual Perception.* Boston: Houghton Mifflin.

Greenfield, Adam. 2006. *Everyware: The Dawning Age of Ubiquitous Computing.* Berkeley, CA: New Riders.

Habermas, Jürgen. [1976] 1991. *Communication and the Evolution of Society.* Translated and introduced by Thomas McCarthy. Cambridge, UK: Polity Press.

Heidegger, Martin. [1927] 1967. *Sein und Zeit.* Tübingen, Germany: Max Niemeyer.

Hoffmeyer, Jesper. 2005. *Biosemiotik: En afhandling om livets tegn og tegnenes liv.* Charlottenlund, Denmark: 2005.

Kac, Eduardo. 2005. *"Genesis."* In *Telepresence and Bio Art: Networking Humans, Rabbits, & Robots,* 249–263. Ann Arbor: University of Michigan Press.

Koefoed Hansen, Lone, and Jacob Wamberg. 2005. "Interface or Interlace? Or How Art Is Mediated in Augmented Reality." In Lisbeth Klastrup, Susana Tosca, Raine Koskimaa, and Hanne Sørensen, eds., *Proceedings of the 6th Digital Arts & Culture Conference. Digital Experience: Design, Aesthetics, Practice,* 169–177. IT University of Copenhagen, 1–3 December. Copenhagen: IT University.

Koerner, Joseph Leo. 1993. *The Moment of Self-Portraiture in German Renaissance Art.* Chicago: University of Chicago Press.

Lactantius. 2003. *Divine Institutes.* 7 vols. Translated and introduced by Anthony Bowen and Peter Garnsey. Liverpool, UK: Liverpool University Press.

Manovich, Lev. 2006. "The Poetics of Augmented Space." *Visual Communication* 5:219–240.

Mauss, Marcel. [1950] 1972. *A General Theory of Magic.* Translated by Robert Brain. London: Routledge & Kegan Paul.

Norman, Donald A. [1988] 1990. *The Design of Everyday Things.* New York: Doubleday/Currency.

Peirce, Charles S. 1960. "The Icon, Index, and Symbol." In *Collected Papers,* edited by Charles Hartshorne and Paul Weiss, 2:156–173. Cambridge, MA: Belknap Press of Harvard University Press.

Schepelern, Peter. 2000. *Lars von Triers Film: Tvang og befrielse.* Copenhagen: Rosinante.

Shiner, Larry. 2001. *The Invention of Art: A Cultural History.* Chicago: University of Chicago Press.

Wamberg, Jacob. [2005] 2009. *Landscape as World Picture: Tracing Cultural Evolution in Images.* 2 vols. Aarhus, Denmark: Aarhus University Press.

28 Teleologics of the Snail, or the Errancies of the Equipped Self in a WiMax Network

Bernard Stiegler

We are fretful and concerned: the inhabitants of the earth, our societies everywhere, are ill, suffering, in need of care. And this situation seems for the most part to be due to, besides the effect of a profound transformation of capitalism, to technological disorders that indeed make this transformation possible, from the generalization of media influence to technology transfers in so-called emerging countries, not to mention the generalized connectivity that concretizes globalization as real time and the delegation of decision-making processes to automatic systems of remote control that constitute the infrastructure of what Gilles Deleuze calls "control societies."

And yet a society of humans always bases itself on a technicity in which psychic functions are delegated so as to make social apparatuses. The latter are supported by those *organa* that Plato called *pharmaka*—which he defines as teletechnologies and, as such, as poisons. However, these *pharmaka* are just as much *remedies* as poisons. A system of care is needed to implement such remedies and to avoid their becoming poisons. This system presupposes on the one hand a pharmacopoeia and on the other a medical science for which the knowledge of pharmacists is not sufficient. This medical science is, for Plato, philosophy as the therapy of the soul—that is, as we will see, as dialectics, as the maieutics of dialogue, with the other as well as with oneself as an other—which is called *dianoia.*

Such a philosophy does not distinguish what belongs to the order of the psyche and what belongs to that of the polis as the order of justice, *dike,* and the order of ethics, *aidôs.* This is why it is indistinguishably a *psychotherapy* and a *sociotherapy*—not to mention the fact that it also calls for therapy, in the usual sense of the term, as care for the body, beginning with *gymnastics.* Now, that which this psycho-sociotherapy takes care of before all else is the telos: the *structurally and irreducibly distant as the horizon of all ends forms itself therein*—in the strict extent to which *this end is that of a desire.* This telos, which is also an origin, Plato calls an idea. This plane of ideas, which is the plane of being, is radically separated by Plato, as *chorismos,* from the corruptible world of generation, which is also the plane of becoming and the world of technics. The idea is what Husserl calls *eidos* insofar as it constitutes the intentional core of all phenomena. But such an *eidos* is no longer separate: it no longer calls out for an other world, although it remains essentially far away and inaccessible. Without being separated, it is, however, on another plane than that of experience and thus of existence. This is what I call the plane of consistence—which is on another plane than that of existence; it raises existence beyond subsistence.

However, what I call the plane of consistence is not transcendent or even transcendental; unlike Husserlian intentionality, it is not a *chorismos* but is *radically immanent* to existence: it is the *plane whereupon the object of desire is constituted right up against the immanence of the desirable.* Now such an object takes on the name of *théos* in Aristotle. This *théos,* which is mistakenly confused with the God of monotheism from Thomas Aquinas on down, is just as radically distant and unmoveable, therefore inaccessible. But it is all the more desirable and in that respect immanent in being distant. It is infinitely far away—as infinitely far away and indetermined, infinite in that respect, as death, which is, however, immanence itself. But it is all the more consistent because it is far away—and right up against existence.[1]

In other words, this *theology* is a *teleology* because the *théos* here is a *final cause* that confers the law of their relationships to material, formal, and efficient causes—and these four causes are those of the Aristotelian dynamic ontology constitutive of his theory of actuality and potential. Now, this *Greek theology* thus constitutive of the *teleology of all causality mindful of its futurity to come* is the question of desire, the principle of all motivation and therefore of all mobility—that is, of being in distance as it gives place to emotion and to motion, to movement and therefore to action. Desire is that which desires an object that is *intrinsically far away and always still to come*: inscribed in a teleologics *without which no care or attention is possible.*

It has become difficult today to think the *théos.* It is difficult less because God is dead than because one conflates the *théos* with the God of monotheism. As regards the latter and insofar as he is dead, he tends to return as a ghost and as the spirit that haunts us as the kingdom of ends haunts all causality. For *if we are concerned, we are so with respect to the end/goal*—that is to say, with respect to ends/goals and with respect to their reign, whose last thinker was Kant. Now, I believe that this concern must lead to a radical rethinking of teleology and to new forms of teleologies and teleologics: those made possible and necessary by technologies and by their technologics—and more specifically today by the digital technologies of telecommunication insofar as they tend now to connect ALL objects and, through them, all bodies and, with them, all their souls.

This is what the death of God means in the final analysis: the death of God means that there is an organology of the kingdom of ends—that there is, in other words, an immanence and an economy of ends and that this economy is what Freud called a libidinal economy, but Freud did not have the conceptual means to think the *phar-*

maka,[2] without which there can be neither fantasy nor therapy, as he demonstrates better than anyone.

*

This is, then, the way in which I would like to address the question of the telos in the era of the WiMax network and of quasi-ubiquitous connectivity:[3] this technology allows each and everyone of us to be at a distance always and everywhere—the question being that of knowing what "being" means here. It is the question of an ontoteleology as the milieu of an ontogenesis without an ontotheology, but such that teleology, which over the past several decades has been held in such poor repute, would be seen to be necessary, not to say irreducible (it would be, on the contrary, dangerously reducible and, indeed, these days eminently fragile and threatened). And in truth, this ontogenesis must perhaps give up its place to a teleogenealogy.

I would like to show that the stakes of this ubiquitous era and its teleologics (1) is the constitution of a new milieu of psychic and collective individuation (in Gilbert Simondon's sense of these terms)—at least as radically new as the writing of language was in its era; (2) changes the telos—that is, the kingdom of ends—that I would like to define here as that which makes possible the social organization of a collective desire as a system of care and cure; and (3) requires a new libidinal economy, if we admit that there is no telos without desire.

The telos, which designates the far away, the distant where the end and the motive form themselves, opens up a horizon for individual and collective possibilities.

This telos, which fell into such ill repute at the end of the era of rationalization and the disenchantment of the world (in the second half of the twentieth century), is structurally underhanded (*retors*). As telecommunication—that is, as *pharmakon* that *places outside*, always already far off, at a distance, being teleological in this instrumental sense and thus opening up a (technical) space without end, always more capacious, always further out, but in the same stroke always more demotivated and in this sense disenchanted and in a certain sense deprived of telos by telos—it becomes a threatening power, for example, as a telecracy undermining democracy.

Telos is a wily power, however, because telecracy is the condition of democracy: democracy assumes that all have always and everywhere equal access to the law, to respect it and to reproduce it, but in individuating it—that is, by transforming it, making it better, wherever they may be, and whoever they may be. That is what is called the "political": the authority of the law constituted itself here, as a public space and time given in and by the distance that opens up between distant citizens and as a distance that brings them closer to the extent that they are distinguished therein. This distance thus opens up possibilities—the possibilities, for example, of legitimate but nevertheless new interpretations of the law.[4] These possibilities, which open the city to its future, form the desire of the city, the desire to be together and to become together, where *philia* is formed, this *philia* without which, says Aristotle, no city is possible.

Telecracy is in this respect that which opens up the possibility of democracy. But it is also that which makes possible democracy's destruction: to the extent that it allows long-distance control, as the power of the distant, it constantly threatens this democracy whose possibility it is. Philosophy accuses the sophist of embodying this threat, by remotely controlling the minds of citizens by the psychotechnologies of logography—that is, of the technical milieu of language literalized and textualized and of destroying citizenship that is autonomy in isonomy by the misuse of these *pharmaka*: the Sophists were accused of short-circuiting this autonomy and thereby of reducing isonomy to the mimetic gregariousness of crowds (of *polloi*—the multitude); they were poisoning the city. The paradox is that Socrates would be condemned to drinking the poison on the basis of very similar arguments.

*

This situation of poisoning is not ineluctable. A new political combat must take place, and it is the combat of the association Ars Industrialis. Its guiding thesis is that the development of the teleological networks that are the networks of digital telecommunication[5] creates a new type of associated milieu. "Associated milieu" must here be understood in three senses (the first two inspired by Simondon):

There is a psychical associated milieu.
There is a technical associated milieu.
There is a symbolic associated milieu.

I begin with the symbolic one by referring to Plato, Bakhtine, and Saussure. A *symbolic* milieu is an *associated* milieu to the extent that it connects at a distance beings who become distinguished therein while at the same time acknowledging their existences therein and who thus see themselves constituted by this milieu, both individually, able to say "I," and collectively, forming a "we," and who can distinguish themselves only to the extent that they acknowledge (recognize) themselves in this milieu—for example, as "we" are speaking French or Japanese or English or Spanish. The most immediately accessible of human milieus—which are always symbolic ones and in this respect associated ones—is indeed language.[6] This is why Aristotle says that man is a *zoon logon*.

Language is a symbolic milieu and structurally an associated milieu, allowing for the constitution and the expression of singularities: as I set out this idea elsewhere, in the interlocution that is the life of language, a receiver—that is, the person listening—

can listen and thus be "destined" to the word she listens to and hears only insofar as she is susceptible of speaking in turn, becoming sender and speaker: becoming she who speaks and who speaks like no one else could do in her stead. For if she speaks like the others (*oi polloi*), she does not truly speak: she babbles and worries and imitates—she tends to bleat, so to speak. We all tend to bleat—more or less, but almost all the time, and all the more so as the *pharmakon* induces such behavior as poison. Nevertheless, we can also speak, thanks to the *pharmakon* as remedy.

You can't hear a language unless it's possible for you to speak it and to speak it in *singular fashion*—that is, *diachronically*. Language is in this respect consubstantially dialogical: speech is a symbolic exchange, and this exchange forms a circuit, which Saussure precisely calls the *circuit of speech*, whereby those who receive in words a symbolic address return what they receive in the form of other words and toward other addresses—addresses that are in this distance opened up by language, which evidently constitutes, as milieu (*mésotès*) and as nature, a kind of diaphanous network of telecommunication.

In the same stroke, then, those who receive and return words participate in the transformation of language itself: in speaking, they produce a process of individuation. Language, for speakers, constitutes a potential of individuation (as the law does) and forms what Simondon calls a "preindividual base." For the linguist, language is itself an individual; it individuates itself, following its own pathways, and it is a concretion of the "we" formed by speakers who are themselves psychical individuals, "I's" whose psychic apparatuses and (I return to this below) psychical associated milieus are haunted by the idiomaticity they inherit through the language they can speak and thus individuate themselves only to the extent that this idiomaticity was already there before they were. This is why language, as the concretion of what Simondon calls the "transindividual," constitutes a preindividual base for the I, to the strict extent that it is shared with the we formed by the ensemble of speaker, and as a space of telecommunication.

The life of language is then interlocution. Now, this interlocution is what audiovisual mass media, which form industrial symbolic milieus, short-circuit and destroy—and they short-circuit in the same stroke the processes of transindividuation in which all symbolic milieus consist to the exact extent that they form an associated milieu (Stiegler and Ars Industrialis, 2006, 41s, 93s). This is what leads to the ruin of language itself, especially evidenced in contemporary language. And this is what irresistibly recalls Viktor Klemperer's *The Language of the Third Reich* ([1975] 2006).

These media produce in effect a process of dissociation: they form disassociated milieus where I am a receiver without being a sender and where I therefore do not participate in collective individuation—that is, in trans-individuation, when, then, I am short-circuited. Dissociated milieus are industrially disorganized symbolic milieus—that is, milieus that are desocialized, desymbolized, desublimated, deprived of consistence—and to this extent organizations that tend to become asocial—that is, without *philia*: without these affective ties that are the condition of all political life.

Well beyond mass media, it is the service-based firms in general (Stiegler and Ars Industrialis, 2006, 50) that tend to impose *hegemoniously dissociating usages* of techniques and technologies through which a society produces *sociation*—that is, associated milieus. Service-oriented capitalism turns all segments of human existence into objects for the systematic and permanent control of attention and behavior through the use of relational technologies (Rifkin 1999) such as technical devices and telecommunication and radio and television broadcast networks of which bar code and chip decoders, radio-frequency identification devices,[7] communicating objects and WiMax, Wi-Fi and Bluetooth systems have become the peripheral elements and the subnetworks to which will be added soon the microtechnologies, which are also the supports of biometrics, and then the nanotechnologies as a whole.

In the hyperindustrial society, through the intermediary of ever more efficient, integrated, and discrete technologies of control, forming a technological milieu ever more dense, reticulated, and diaphanous, the service industries are everywhere, and they have a hand in everything: in this sense, they are ubiquitous. They invest and develop the networks of ubiquity, and in this respect they have become the leading actors in public life—insofar as the latter is that which transindividuates shared ways of life. By this very fact, they have become the main factor of social dynamism, which consists in a constant evolution of ways of life that, in the contemporary context of worldwide economic competition, must be brought under control. But this transindividuation short-circuits individuals.

Social dynamism spurs a permanent transformation of ways of life, and this is true in any era: this transformation is the result of a process of psychical and collective individuation in which from the beginning humanity consists. It can be slow and unapparent or rapid and obvious—as is the case starting with the Industrial Revolution—that is, with the advent of industrial capitalism. To individuate oneself is to transform oneself: the transformation of modes of life is the law of the form of human life—of existence. Humankind, which not only subsists but exists, and this means that it transforms itself. But this transformation presupposes a consistence—that is, a telos, a desire.

Now the service industries, which now transform modes of life on a global scale, destroy the long circuits of transindividuation whereby the technical innovations were heretofore socially appropriated—by short-circuiting them. Transindividuation is what results from the coindividuation of psychical individuals—that is, the result of what constitutes collective individuation as the concourse of psychical individuals where significations borne and constituted in modes of life (Simondon [1989] 2007) are produced, become metastable, and then are transformed. Now, to undergo the effects of a service industry is to see one's existence transformed without participating in this transformation, if it is true that the service industry relies not only on the industrial division of labor, but on a distribution of social roles where the consumer theoretically has no part in production tasks, is in effect relatively demobilized.

The retirement of production tasks assumed by the service industry, which is a short-circuit in transindividuation, is displayed as an advantage: that of a discharge. This is the sense in which one speaks of services: serfs were in former times in charge of menial tasks. However, this discharge is what deprives of existence the person who finds herself discharged from service: she is in a situation devoid of the choice of deciding her way of life—and that is a reversal and a denial of what Hegel described as the dialectic of lord and slave, on which Marxism founded its teleology.

The individual is thus excluded from the circuits where in an associated milieu—that is, a nondissociated one—, for example, as a locutor, he participates in the transformation of his milieu by individuating himself therein, by individuating the others, and by individuating the language he shares with other: by inscribing thereupon signification in a milieu that becomes in the same stroke teleological. The consumer of services, who is called a user, is on the contrary desindividuated by the service that short-circuits him on this circuit that is transindividuation. And for him, the horizon is blank. This is what Hegel called *kenosis*.

*

Insofar as contemporary technologies essentially implement devices of telecommunication (telegraph, telephone, radio and television broadcast, television, the web of networks, etc.), they are the technologies of service industries that constitute, as organs of power, as telecracy, that which threatens and ruins democracy from the inside to the extent that the democracy is essentially the organization of long circuits whose aim is the intensification of psychical individuations. But insofar as they form technologies of relation between the two terms that a telos links up—that is, a finality (a motive, a desire)—these technologies are also *the only possible road for the invention of new forms of the social bond, of civil peace.*

In order to examine this possibility, one may have to specify why and how the technical milieu can articulate and disarticulate the psychical milieu—that is, can associate it or, conversely, dissociate it with the symbolic milieu: the technical milieu can either support the psychical milieu's goals, its telos, its motives and therefore its mobility, its dynamism, or, on the contrary, it can paralyze the psychical milieu, enclosing it so to speak in itself in such a way that it becomes enclosed within itself and therefore enclosed outside of itself, thus paradoxically losing all singularity, caught in a kind of herd instinct, a gregarious drive. I do not address this task here but only examine one of its minor aspects. But, first, I would like to recall that

1. Technics, as a process of the grammatization of flows, as a process of discretization—for example, of the flow of speech or the flow of gestures of the worker's body—is what allows for their technical reproducibility and thus their control and therefore, in the same stroke, the organization of short-circuits in the long circuits constituting transindividuation.
2. Technics is also what permits, through this very reproducibility, a *différance* and an iterability, whereby *eidè* come into view, for example (Husserl's *Origin of Geometry*) and where the very long circuits of a transindividuation (omnitemporal, intergenerational, and international ones, for example) are formed, issuing in what Husserl calls the transcendental "we I" in which the kingdom of ends takes shape.

*

We have seen what a symbolic associated milieu is and how it can become a dissociated milieu, vector of a process of desymbolization (that is to say, also a process of desublimation). As for the psychical associated milieu, it is memory associated with the ego, its lived memory, which is its preindividual milieu and its potential, what Henri Bergson thought as virtuality, but which Simondon posits as what must be thought as potentiality—if not as potential in the Aristotelian sense of the term.

There is a psychical associated milieu in the following sense: "mental matter having become memory, or rather memory content, is the associated milieu of the present ego" (Simondon [1989] 2007, 164). This "associated milieu" is the preindividual base of the psychical individual, absolutely its own and constitutive of its absolute singularity. And yet the fact of the process of grammatization, which begins from the outset of technical exteriorization—that is, from the outset of humanization—makes this associated milieu also and more and more formally the collective preindividual base, for two reason. (1) This psychical base is made up of elements that are already collective, spinoffs, as it were, of transindividuation: for example, words, these "verbal traces," as Freud says, that are always already shared with others, that are always already the "words of the tribe." This is the first reason turning my psychical individuation always already into a collective one. (2) This proper memory, which constitutes my psychical associated milieu, is more and more objectified, being grammatized, and is thus more and more mnemotechnically constituted in advance (as hypomnesis), as if I preceded myself—and as an other than myself: as my supplement, but such that it is never only my supplement.

On my telephone, which is also a portable computer, the Tréo 650, I can consult my own texts on the network—for example, on the Ars Industrialis Web site (arsindustrialis.org). And I can read myself, listen to myself, see myself, and download my own work, and all this makes for a very strange circuit: at once a kind of short-circuit of my own memory and a stretching out of the circuit of my memory.[8]

Between this Tréo 650 and myself a circuit is formed, which is also like the shell of a snail that I would have become thanks to this *pharmakon*, that I carry around with me, and where I can meet up with myself and gaze as into a mirror, under countless aspects, because my psychical milieu, digitally grammatized on this network, has become in part, but a qualitatively important part, a symbolic milieu as well as a technical milieu where my psychical milieu becomes objective because I am more and more often individuating myself on this network—that is, in this technical as well as symbolic milieu, which tends to merge with my psychical associated milieu and which tends in the same stroke to become the milieu of a *referential psychical and collective individuation*,[9] a process that cannot fail to have important consequences.

In other words, besides always being associated with a psychical mnesic milieu, my ego is also always associated with a symbolic milieu—for example, that of the words of the tribe—but henceforth it is more and more often, always and everywhere also associated with a technical milieu, which results in a symbolic milieu of a new kind—namely, a symbolic milieu not only hypertextualized (and therefore digitally grammatized) but also hypermediatized. For this symbolic milieu is much more than linguistic: it is also psychomotor, grammatizing sensorimotor schema—that is, corporeal techniques—that it formalizes techno-logically, and in the same stroke techno-psychosomatically, organologically. Now, *the question is: Which teleologics are being formed in these organological and therefore technological transformations? What kinds of objects of the desire for existence can project themselves thereupon—that is, can come to consist?*

My psychical milieu thus becomes in a sense immediately social as well as hypermediately social. Now, I can paradoxically find myself absolutely alone in this hypersocial and hyperpsychical space; a strange loop forms itself there, a narcissistic loop, and as such a mirage—that is, a mirror and a phantasm—and what I am saying here concerns all those who write or post traces on the Web, and they are increasingly numerous, either because they "blog" or "chat" or because they leave traces unbeknownst to themselves considering that these teletechnologies are also the control society's apparatuses of traceability—for example, with "cookies."

I am on my Tréo 650. Now I meet up with myself on the Web, which is, as everyone knows, a meeting place, sometimes designed for erotic encounters, but here this meeting up forms a strange narcissistic loop and in that respect therefore a autoerotic one, which can always become, as a short-circuit of my desire—what Rousseau analyzes as the condition of possibility the "dangerous supplement"—a pathological narcissism that can keep me from desiring, from loving, and from being loved by keeping me distant, but without linking me up. At the same time, I can suddenly take myself to be someone else, find myself objectified—that is, grammatized—in such a way that when I address myself in writing to others, as Derrida showed so convincingly, I dialecticize myself all of a sudden: I can start dialoguing with myself, which is what is called *dianoia*, thought.

Now, what makes this narcissistic short-circuit possible is also what allows me to encounter the Other, but through an other—including then that other that I am, "myself as an other"—and by a long circuit where this other is revealed to me and gives me access to the consistency of the Other—that is, where my otherness, my singularity is mirrored, what I called in *Passer à l'acte* (Acting out, [Stiegler 2009]) the "ego-other": this is the circuit of desire and of desire such that, as gift and counter-gift, it indeed inscribes a loop. For the object of my desire is that which I receive only inasmuch as I render it. That which is distant and nevertheless present—present at a remove so to speak—is sometimes all the more present in its absence and, conversely, is first of all the object of my desire, indeed of my love, which can be quite sublimated.

I am not talking here about sites of encounters, online dating services and the like. I am talking about social networks that take shape by sharing in technologies of transindividuation, that are called "cooperative technologies," and that constitute, as the digital *pharmaka* of interest, this technological associated milieu where the recipients are always also senders, absolutely original processes of psychical and collective individuation, where the psychical, symbolic, and technical associated milieus have become indissociable.

This is how narcissism becomes thought—as *dianoia*, dialog with oneself, which is never very far either from a kind of "schize" (which Stefan Zweig undergoes in his *The Chessplayer* [1943]) or else from paranoia. At bottom, this scene is that of writing, but a writing that is exposed immediately, that is as media apparently without delay, forming in this respect a world that is not only hypertextual, but hypermediatized, where new networks of transindividuation are formed—new circuits that can be extremely short or extremely long, almost infinite—as the inaccessible center of this vortex shaped by the shell of a snail, a weak and slow being, for which everything is always far away, infinitely far off, and which leaves on these new circuits its traces, its traces of slime, and which can complicate what today seems inconceivable, the psychographics of what was sophistic logographics, but which can just as well open up the teleology of a "we" that I would call less transcendent than consistent—that is, desiring—forming the desired horizon of a brand-new process of psychical and collective individuation.

*

The technical associated milieu is a milieu integrated as technical function by a technical device whose environment consists in the former. Thus, Simondon analyzes the aquatic milieu of the Guimbal turbine waterworks—and he speaks of a technogeographical milieu. My thesis is that the Internet, as a milieu constituted by the digital networks of telecommunication, constitutes milieus of human geographies technically associated where there are not so much users as practitioners, less consumers than amateurs, clients and suppliers than contributors. A technically associated human milieu is a milieu of transindividuation where the recipient is theoretically and pharmacologically placed in the position of the sender.

With the new setup of the psychical milieu, the symbolic milieu, and this associated technical milieu that is the ubiquitous digital network founded on the Internet protocol TCT/IP, where service industries just as ubiquitous prowl, we see on the horizon a new organization of the relations between primary, secondary, and tertiary retentions—in Husserl's sense of these terms: primary retention is what at this very moment you retain of what I have just said in order to understand what I will then say and that you add to what I will say (and which is yet but a protention, an expectation), whereas with secondary retention all past experiences of primary retentions are kept as and in your memory—that is, as your mnesic associated milieu—offering criteria for the selection of primary retentions that you retain in what I say.

You cannot retain everything of what I say, no more so than I can retain all the possible semantic connections in what I say in the play of the paradigms called up by what I say. As for tertiary retentions, which refer to *pharmaka* as hypomnesic supports—that is to say, mnemotechnical ones—they overdetermine the relations between primary and secondary retentions, favoring or disfavoring circuits of transindividuations—that is, connections between these semantic possibilities constituted by the paradigms called up by the syntagmes of my words in temporal ordering.

Space has not allowed me to explain how new retentional arrangements constituted by digital associated milieus of telecommunication produce or rather can produce—providing that we wake up, that the very fact of these arrangements deliver us from our various "dogmatic slumbers," and that we initiate a struggle for this awakening—new kinds of protentions, once again in Husserl's sense: new protentional projections—that is, ends and goals, and thus the teleological horizon of an absolutely unheard-of desire. This struggle informs the activities of Ars Industrialis. And it also motivates my activities in the Institute of Research and Innovation at the Pompidou Center.

There was not enough space either to explain how arrangements of retentions and protentions shape a new form of attention—that is, of care, of a psychotherapy as sociotherapy and somatotherapy in the equipped mobility of an ego moving with its body loaded with prostheses and, with them, loaded with history—that is, with traces and wounds. I did not have time to tell you how the associated milieu of the Internet allows one to imagine an altogether new industrial model, a new system of *pharmaka*, for an altogether different system of health care and concern, which is the only issue if we are to avoid the impasse confronting humanity today.

I have not talked about all that because I am slow. Slow as a snail. But I advance, I do not renounce going on, and I leave traces where I can. I cut off my network connection as well as my mobile phone doubling as my personal computer; I retract my antenna into my shell; and I thank you for your attention.

Notes

This chapter was translated by George Collins from a presention in Tokyo during the Symposium Ubiquitous Media in July 2007. It is dedicated to Jean-Luc Nancy.

1. I have always read Aristotle with the supposition that his *théos* is the object of all desire, but that it is not separate in Plato's sense: Aristotle does not oppose two worlds; there is no realism of ideas in Aristotle, but there are *eidè*, essences, as *ousia,* and I think that the latter, which occurs only as *tode ti* and as *idios,* constitutes the desirability of phenomena—that is, their singularity.

2. This is what hampers psychoanalysis in its combat against chemical therapies. I posit that only a general organology can think a general pharmacology that can issue in a thinking of systems of care in general.

3. The performances of WiMax are in theory seven times superior to Wi-Fi and cover an area of up to fifty kilometers, whereas the Wi-Fi posts are limited to areas of a few hundred meters. WiMax permits even rural areas to be covered, but WiMax chips can also be lodged in computers.

4. This is what I call identification *différante* (differing and deferring) that gives place to contexts that consist all the more in that they interpret a self-same text literally identified in being grammatized. Stiegler 2009.

5. I showed twenty years ago that any anthropological network is a network of telecommunication, but that all networks are not, for all that, digital or analog.

6. But there are also more specific associated milieus, such as professions—I return to this idea later—where people who do not speak the same language but nevertheless communicate with one another—by sharing the same gestures, the same materials, the same instruments and tools, and the same know-how. Then they are able to form communities that overshoot the "ethnic cell" that makes them evolve. Such technical knowledge can totally disorganize an ensemble of associated milieus making up the unity of an Internet protocol.

7. Radio-frequency identification "tags are small objects that, like stick-on labels, can be attached to or incorporated into products. These tags feature an antenna linked to an electronic chip for the reception and transmission of a signal. They are active devices that transmit signals that activate the markers moving in front of them, providing over a short distance the energy they need." "Radio-Frequency Identification," *Wikipedia*, translated from the French edition, available at http://fr.wikipedia.org/wiki/Radio-identification.

8. Donald Winnicott (1971) would have to be mobilized here.

9. On the question of referential individuation, see Stiegler 2006.

References

Klemperer, Viktor. [1975] 2006. *The Language of the Third Reich.* London: Continuum.

Rifkin, Jeremy. 2000. *The Age of Access.* London: Penguin.

Simondon, Gilbert. [1989] 2007. *L'individuation psychique et collective.* With a new preface by the author. Paris: Aubier.

Stiegler, Bernard. 2003. *Passer à l'acte*, Paris, Galilée.

Stiegler, Bernard. 2006. *La télécratie contre la démocratie: lettre ouverte aux représentants politiques.* Paris: Flammarion.

Stiegler, Bernard. 2009. *Technics and Time.* Vol. 2: Disorientation. Stanford, CA: Stanford University Press.

Stiegler, Bernard, and Ars Industrialis. 2006. *Reéenchanter le monde: la valeur esprit contre le populisme industriel.* Paris: Flammarion.

Winnicott, D. W. 1971, Playing and reality. New York: Routledge.

Zweig, Stefan. 2006. Chess. London: Penguin.

29 The Indexing of Things

Bernard Stiegler

In *The System of Objects*, Jean Baudrillard predicted in 1968 that in the wake of World War II and with the development of what he had called in a previous book "the consumer society," the industrially produced object would play a totally new and increasingly important role in the life of humanity. He showed that the industrial object would have to be understood on the basis of a system in the twin sense of the term:

• As a technologically grounded system of objects, referring to Gilbert Simondon's *Mode of Existence of Technical Objects* and to what Simondon called "the process of concretization" and "functional integration of objects"
• As a social system grounded in these industrial objects, this system being economic, psychological, aesthetic, and so on—the integration of these dimensions accomplished and exploited by what I have attempted to describe as a "psychopower"

Baudrillard upheld that the socially constituted object would not mesh with the technically constituted object and affirmed the relative autonomy of the social with respect to the technological.

*

Let us recall that Simondon speaks of concretization and functional integration of technical objects when he refers to the morphogenesis of heat engines: he pinpoints in technical industrial objects a tendency whereby the diversity of functions constitutive of an object combine into a "plurifunctionality." For example, the ribbing of the twin-cylinder engine of the Citroën 2CV automobile, which allows a sole and unique technical apparatus to offer both resistance and cooling of the cylinder as well as the elimination of the radiator function and thus of the water cooling circuit. Simondon offers other such examples and shows that technical rationality is rooted in these integrative processes.

He also posits, however, that this functional integration may lead to the inclusion of a machine's geographical environment in its functioning, while pointing out that technical milieus tend to become technogeographical ones. Here he speaks of associated milieus: citing the example of the Guimbal turbine of a tidal power station, he posits that water has a triple technical function: it affords energy, produces pressure, and waterproofs the stages while cooling the entire assembly. The natural milieu thus becomes a plurifunctional attribute of the technical—and cultural—object.

I recall these analyses in order to introduce the following questions:

- Is not the Internet of things in the process of producing a new technogeographical associated milieu, which is bound to end up in a possible industrial technologization of human-associated milieus?
- If this were the case, what would be a stake for human milieus?

*

Before taking up these questions, let us first inquire into the meaning of the "Internet of things." The Internet of things is a new stage of the reticulated society into which we have been introduced over the past twenty years: a society founded on technological relational systems that tend to control all human relational systems—without which no society would exist and by which human commerce is formed—in substituting themselves for the relational systems inherited from pre-reticulated societies.

With radio-frequency identification (RFID) chips, which may soon become a part of most manufactured objects and enter into contact with sensors and actuators spread throughout public and semipublic space as well as invade bodies, habitats, and so on, it is already possible to trace a commodity step by step throughout the stages of its evolution. This is what will develop exponentially with the Internet of things and ubiquitous information processing, founded on sensors and microelectronic technologies of indexation. A report from the International Telecommunication Union states: "For example, we can cite the production and exportation of food-stuffs for which sensors are used to control their quality and pureness, for example Brazilian or Chilean coffee grains or beef from Namibia. The RFID technology is used to trace the evolution of shipments of beef to the European Union in order to verify the origin and handling of each carcass of beef" (2005).

In the future, however, the indexation of objects will rely on a combination of RFID systems and newer systems of Internet addressing. The future environment will be shot through with invisible networks of microprocessors communicating with themselves, without our knowledge of these circuits. Mark Weiser, the former head of research at Xerox in Palo Alto, California, foresaw the future when he coined the term *ubiquitous computing* in 1991: "The most profound technologies are those that disappear. They weave themselves into the fabric of everyday life until they are indistinguishable from it" (quoted in International Telecommunication Union 2005).

The reticulated society developed mainly on the basis of the Internet network, which radically transformed the relations between individuals, upsetting in particular the productivist industrial model and the consumer model. At the present time, the relations between objects are in a state of mutation, building up an invisible reticulation, constantly connected, and overdetermining social relationships.

The indexed object, producer of information on itself and on its course and therefore on the person for whom it is an object as well as on the other objects with which it forms a system, constitutes in this sense of new system of objects such that, perhaps, the difference that Baudrillard maintained between the technical system of objects and the social systems of objects grounded in these objects might mesh into a relational technology characteristic of the reticulated society.

To gain purchase on these questions, we must first ask ourselves

- What do we call an object, but also what do we call a thing, given that in the Anglo-Saxon world we speak of an "Internet of things"?
- What is the place of the object, and what is the place of the thing—if they are two different entities—in human existence in general?

*

A few years following the publication of *If on a Winter's Night a Traveler* (1981), Italo Calvino presented a character called "the reader" solely by describing her things.

It is only because an object is a memory support in a system of memory with other objects that the psyche of an individual for whom it is the object can project and place itself outside, where its traces remain. Because objects are such supports and such witnesses, the archaeologist and the prehistorian can through these objects reconstitute modes of life without recurring to writing, the main source of information for the historian.

In his paleoanthropology, André Leroi-Gourhan posited in 1964 that the technical milieu constitutes a third memory, which is neither genetic nor epigenetic—that is, proper to the individual and situated in his nervous system, but cultural: nonbiological and yet shared by what is therefore no longer simply a species, but also a genus—the human genus.

As such—that is, qua culturally inherited, but also qua individually appropriable insofar as it can become someone's object, the scissors of a cabinet maker, the paintbrush of a painter, the piece of blanket for a child, all these modalities of being-someone's remaining in fact very different—the object constitutes a trait of the individual, a trait of his individuation; it constitutes, in other words, this individual, just as it bears witness to this individual. It is its trace—that is, a material reality—such that in cannot be said to be outside the individual because it is in fact one of the individual's dimensions, as crucial to it as technics in genera, and as what

Leroi-Gourhan calls the process of exteriorization, which is the essential dimension of the human genus.

This is basically what Calvino also says: the familiar personal objects of the reader are traces of the individuation of the psychic individual she is, object-traces that inscribe this psychic individual, who is produced by a process of individuation that realizes itself as a relationship to its objects and through them inscribes this individual and the process in which it consists and then in the social individual that the world is, the latter being constituted by others as well as by these technical objects that are just as much objects in general.

That which lies between subjectivity and objectivity (which is not objectality, but the real objectified being of science, having today become technoscience and system of technological objects)—that is, the reduction of rationalization to objectification—is the object of desire as personal private object, support, and condition of the constitution of what Donald Winnicott (1971) calls the self of the psychic apparatus and its interiority entirely projected outside and constituted by relays that the outside addresses to it and that stand it up, hold it up, and raise it up to the rank of noetic soul: as a soul that takes care of its world, which is attentive to it while being attentive to itself.

To take care of one's affairs is indeed the imperative of humankind insofar as it is unable to do without objects.

The slightest personal object that is more or less "my" object inscribes itself in a complex psychosocial organization where, on the one hand, the momentarily speechless infant must learn how to distinguish his from yours and still cannot do so and where, on the other hand, a system of rights governs the process of the constitution of this "proper" that constitutes yours as well as mine, ultimately by defining the rules of private property, but also the rules of collective or social property—for example, public works. Nothing here is unrelated to technics: a system of right presupposes, for example, writing—I return to this point later.

There are modes of constitution of yours and mine that are transformed with the modalities whereby subjects socialize themselves through their objects, transforming the processes of individuation, and these modes and modalities evolve along with the history of objects, their modes of production, their rules of appropriation, property rights, and politics *strictu sensu*—for example, when communal spaces are created, which are also objects, or when the profane realm, the public one, distinguishes itself from the sacred realm, two types of objects are thereby distinguished, wherein transmissible familiar objects would follow rights of inheritance, and so on.

*

Although every object is technical and constitutes as such a memory support, objects—mnemotechnological objects to be precise—emerge rather late in the course of the later Paleolithic period and above all with the advent of the Neolithic period: mnemotechnological objects are made for memorization, conceived to enable the individual to inscribe the traces of his existence, and this is especially the case with writing.

These objects evolve throughout the centuries and progressively spread throughout the *socius*: literal objects follow up on hieroglyphic writing systems, first manuscripts, later printed matter, then analog objects, then digital ones, which will be mistakenly called "dematerialized objects"—programs, data, informational realities that are states of matter supported by materials and that constitute objects I would name "hypomnesic" in Plato's sense of the term: artifacts of memory.

I must insist on this point because the Internet of digital and reticulated objects constitutes a new stage in which all objects tend to become hypomnesic ones. (See Julian Bleecker's "blogjets" [2006]; perhaps consider also what French designer Jean-Luois Frechin calls a "neo-object" [2011].)

This new stage is bound to have revolutionary and massive effects on the relationship to objects and on the conditions in which they constitute the subject. These upsetting effects have perhaps already modified the condition of what Jacques Lacan calls the "object *a*" in a reference to what Donald Winnicott (1971) calls the "transitional object."

*

The transitional object is the one by which the small child, still unable to distinguish his self from his world, finds an intermediary terrain constituted in his relationship to his mother and where the mother acts in such a way that the object is constantly at the disposal of the child, as if it were a part of the child, invested and animated by him, rich with all the qualities the child projects into it and that the mother alters to make the object coincide with her child's projections.

In this respect, Winnicott points out that there are transitional objects that constitute for adults the very possibility of communal life: "Should an adult make claims on us for our acceptance of the objectivity of his subjective phenomena we discern or diagnose madness. If, however, the adult can manage to enjoy the personal intermediate area without making claims, then we can acknowledge our own corresponding areas" (1971, 18).

Here Winnicott states his thesis, not only for pediatrics, but for anthropology as well: "The intermediate area of experience, unchallenged in respect to its belonging to inner or external (shared) reality, constitutes the greater part of the infant's experience, and throughout life is retained in the intense experiencing that belongs to the arts and to religion and to imaginative living, and to creative scientific work" (1971, 19).

The transitional object supports transitional phenomena that belong to what Winnicott refers to as an area situated between subjectivity and objectivity.

*

In his *A General Theory of Magic* (1902), Marcel Mauss (with Henri Hubert) introduces the theme of mana, which will be the basis of the theory of the "floating signifier"—that is, of sign and meaning in Claude Lévi-Strauss's theorization. In Melanesian society, mana is deposed on an object, as if the latter can partake of its power:

> Mana (a Melanesian term), is not simply a force, an entity, but rather a quality and a state. . . . An object is said to be mana when we wish to say that it possesses this quality. . . An entity, a spirit, a human, a stone or a ritual, is said to be mana, the "mana of this or that thing." . . . [T]he word sums up a series of ideas we intend in speaking of the power of the sorcerer, the magic quality of a thing, a magical thing. (1902, 101, translated by Georges Collins)

In this respect, mana eliminates boundaries and constitutes in magical societies a kind of transitional phenomenon on the scale of social relations—just as practices of sublimation maintain a transitional space in adult social life, as Winnicott shows. Mana "achieves this amalgamation of the agent, the ritual and things which we see as fundamental to magic" (Mauss and Hubert 1902, 101, translated by Georges Collins).

In *The Gift: Form and Reason for Exchange in Archaic Societies* ([1922] 1990), Mauss studies what the Maori call the *hau*. The *hau*, which is transmitted through objects and which transforms those who become the subjects of these objects in this transformation, represents an exchange of *taonga*—that is, an exchange of articles, in the sense of stores in our vocabulary, articles if not commodities, a word Mauss is reticent to use because in Maori society there is no market.

There is, however, a constitution of relations of obligation and thus the creation of a social bond whereby the group is founded:

> The *taonga* and all goods termed strictly personal possess a *hau*, a spiritual power. You give me one of them, and I pass it on to a third party; he gives another to me in turn, because he is impelled to do so by the *hau* my present possesses. I, for my part, am obliged to give you that thing because I must return to you what is in reality the effect of the *hau* of your *taonga*. . . . What imposes obligation in the present received and exchanged is the fact that the thing received is not inactive. Even when it has been abandoned by the giver, it still possesses something of him. Through it the giver has a hold over the beneficiary just as, being its owner, through it he has a hold over the thief. (Mauss [1922] 1990, 159)

How not to think here that this object would appear equipped with a kind of dowsing faculty that looks much like the RFID object? Is not the *hau* a kind of magical technology of traceability? The *hau*, Mauss writes, "not only follows after the first recipient, and even, if the occasion arises, a third person, but after any individual to whom the *taonga* is merely passed on" ([1922] 1990, 160).

*

Again and again we must remind ourselves that objects, always potentially my objects, and things, which are also those of the classroom lesson of things and which cannot be mine (the buttercup is not mine, John Rostand's frog is not his frog, but the frog), are therefore always equipped with faculties quite different from what theoretically, from Descartes down through modern philosophy, belong to what was called "objectivity," even for Edmund Husserl, who speaks, when speaking not only of particular books but also of familiar personal objects such as the spoon, of "objects invested with spirit."

Thus we have to distinguish objectivity from objectality.

We also have to recall that for Freud, an object is always a potential fetish and a ghost—that is, the vector of a phantasm—and that for Marx the commodity is essentially fetishistic.

But now has there not taken place all of a sudden with the Internet of things an objectification, a rationalization, and a submission of transitional, fetishistic, and subliminatory objectality to the laws of objectivity—through industrial technology's marshalling of all the forces of technoscience? If this is in fact the case, what conclusions should we draw, or, rather, what kinds of questions should we ask ourselves, What hyperreticulated and hyperconnected future has been promised to us by the Internet of objects?

*

In the world of objects RFID in communication via the Internet, the question couched by Alphonse de Lamartine in his old-fashioned style—"Inanimate objects, do you not have a soul?"—seems to have suddenly emerged again in a form and actuality no doubt quite different from the object that inspired Lamartinian lyricism, but that is certainly not far removed from the questions posed by the *hau*, the *mana*, the fetish, and so on.

The warp and the woof of these "inanimate" yet communicating objects, constitutive of an associated milieu of hyperconnectivity, are themselves a hypermatter: a matter that receives, transmits, transports, and provides information by its very structure—that is, it is composed of hyperqualities. As such, it is always already a form—when apprehended at the microphysical level and especially at the nanometric level, where matter always presents itself as always already quantically as form. The light time of the infinitely brief is also that of the infinitely tiny in and through which hypermaterial objects are hyperobjects.

The hyperqualities of these hyperobjects are invisible and all the more active for belonging to the hypermaterial level, where form is never separated from its matter and which is not accessible to sensible intuition and perception.

What are the conditions under which these hyperobjects, forming a new "system of objects," an interobjective relational network formed unbeknown to the consciousnesses of which they are the objects, can either short-circuit intersubjective relationships or, conversely, intensify them, and constitute the framework of a new process of psychic and collective individuation?

In other words, to what extent can they engender a new associated milieu rather than a process of intensified dissociation?

*

An associated milieu is a process of psychic, collective, and technical coindividuation. Industrialization is on the contrary that which generates dissociated milieus by proletarianizing producers as well as consumers: the producer is said to be proletarianized when he loses his know-how, the consumer when he loses his skills at living. Thus, what Bakhtin described as a dialogism is destroyed—in the work environment as well as in the linguistic milieu.

A few years before Baudrillard, Georges Perec in 1965 had shown in *Les choses* to what extent these things, having become crucial in daily life, exposed humans to the inevitable ordeal of their vanity: the vanity of things, the vanity of humans who were attached to such things and who could not, by the very fact of this system of objects, escape to the reification of humans who appeared to be produced therein, while these things themselves were structurally and rapidly becoming disposable.

Note

Translated by Georges Collins.

References

Baudrillard, Jean. 1968. *The System of Objects*. Translated by James Benedict.. New York: Verso.

Bleecker, Julian. 2006. "A Manifesto for Networked Objects—Cohabiting with pigeons, arphids and aibos in the Internet of Things (Why things matter)." Available at http://www.nearfuture laboratory.com/files/WhyThingsMatter.pdf. Accessed 28 January 2012.

Calvino, Italo. 1981. *If on a Winter's Night a Traveler*. Translated by William Weaver. New York: Harcourt.

Fréchin, Jean-Louis. 2011. "Esthetics of Neo-Objects." *Musiques et Cultures Digitales* 6: 38–41. Available at http://www.digitalmcd.com/2011/03/03/hors-serie-6-linternet-des-objets-internet-of-things. Accessed 28 January 2012.

International Telecommunication Union. 2005. *The Internet of Things.* Geneva: International Telecommunication Union. Available at http://www.itu.int/osg/spu/publications/internetof things. Accessed 28 January 2012.

Leroi-Gourhan, André. 1964. *Le Geste et la Parole.* Paris: Michel.

Mauss, Marcel. [1922] 1990. *The Gift: Form and Reason for Exchange in Archaic Societies.* Translated by W. D. Hall. London: Routledge.

Mauss, Marcel, and Henri Hubert. 1902. *Esquisse d'une théorie générale de la magie.* Paris : Presses universitaires de France.

Perec, Georges. 1965. *Les Choses: Une histoire des années soixante.* Paris: René Juillard.

Simondon, Gilbert. 1958. *Du mode d'existence des objets techniques.* Paris: Aubier.

Weiser, Mark. 1991. "The Computer for the 21st Century." *Scientific American* 265 (3): 94–104.

Winnicott, D. W. 1971. *Playing and Reality.* New York: Routledge.

30 Radio-Frequency Identification: Human Agency and Meaning in Information-Intensive Environments

N. Katherine Hayles

From the beginning, radio-frequency identification (RFID) technology has been entangled with politics. It pinged Western consciousness (not for the first time [Pruett 2006]) when Leon Theremin's listening device was discovered hidden inside a wooden replica of the Great Seal of the United States that had been presented to the US embassy in Moscow by a group of Russian schoolchildren and installed in the embassy's conference room (the original is on display in the National Security Agency Museum) (Glinsky 2000). Mystified by the device, embassy personnel discovered that it backscattered a radio-frequency wave after modulating it so it contained new information—in this case, embassy conversations. Surveillance remains one of the principal concerns raised by RFID technology, now so small and inexpensive that it can be embedded in a wide variety of products and objects. More subtle but no less important are the effects of RFID in creating an animate environment with agential and communicative powers. Although surveillance issues are primarily epistemological (who knows what about whom), the political stakes of an animate environment involve the changed perceptions of human subjectivity in relation to a world of objects that are no longer passive and inert. In this sense, RFID is not confined only to epistemological concerns but extends to ontological issues as well.

Combined with embedded sensors, mobile technologies, and relational databases, RFID destabilizes traditional ideas about the relation of humans to the built world, precipitating a crisis of interpretation that represents both a threat to human autonomy and an opportunity for rethinking the highly politicized terrain of meaning making in information-intensive environments. RFID and associated technologies fundamentally change the rules of the game. Many are already at work co-opting RFID technology for military and capitalistic purposes. If our responses remain solely on the level of resisting the spread of the technology—important as that may be in certain respects—we lose the opportunity to seize the initiative and explore the technology's potential for shedding the burden of long-held misconceptions about cognition and moving to a more processual, relational, and accurate view of embodied human action in complex environments. The challenge RFID presents is how to use it to rethink human subjectivity in constructive and life-enhancing ways without capitulating to its coercive and exploitive aspects.

The context in which this challenge presents itself is one of the major developments of intelligent technologies in the twenty-first century: the movement of computation out of the box and into the environment. Whereas mid-twentieth-century research in artificial intelligence focused on trying to create in a single entity all the complex capacities of human thought (a project doomed to fail, for reasons that Hubert Dreyfus [1992], among others, has demonstrated), contemporary research in distributed cognition concentrates on creating complex interrelated systems in which small subcognizers that perform within a very limited range of operation are combined with readers that interpret that information, which in turn communicate with relational databases that have the power to make correlations on much wider (and extensible) scales. No one component of these systems comes anywhere close to the complexity of human thought, but when combined together, the components constitute a flexible, robust, and pervasive "Internet of things" (Gershenfeld 1999; Gershenfeld, Krikorian, and Cohen 2004) that senses the environment, creates a context for that information, communicates internally among components, draws inferences from the data, and comes to conclusions that far exceed, in scope if not in complexity, what an unaided human can achieve (for a discussion of "knowledge discovery in databases," see Fayyad, Piatetsky-Shapiro, and Smyth 2006).

In this model of distributed cognition, the emphasis shifts from the traditional triad of human–animal–machine to human–animal–thing. Although the components of RFID can be considered machines, their small size, ubiquitous presence in the environment, and very limited range of subcognition make them more thinglike than machinelike, a construction in line with moving from the traditional artificial-intelligence model of a single thinking entity to myriad small subcognizers. The focus on many tiny interactors (smart "dust" rather than the Terminator) foregrounds communication between components of a system, relational dynamics between different systemic levels, embodied interactions, and contextual awareness. The traditional Heideggerian progression of humans as world building, animals poor in world, and stones without world (Heidegger 1995) is brought into question; as a result, the relations between human, animal, and thing come up for grabs, functioning as a chaotic nexus in which technological innovations, anxieties about surveillance and privacy, capitalistic and military exploitations, and creative storytelling swirl together in a highly unstable and rapidly changing dynamic.

My interest here is exploring the implications of this dynamic by triangulating technological practices, information-theoretic conceptualizations, and fictional representations of RFID technologies. As I and others have argued (Burrows 1997a, 1997b; Featherstone and Burrows 1995; Hayles 2005), science fiction can be a potent resource for interrogating new technologies, especially when the rapid pace of change outstrips the capacity of social theory to grapple with emerging complexities. RFID operates not only in the realm of such technological-managerial practices as the identification and tagging of products, but also in what Nigel Thrift has called the "technological unconscious," working in subtle ways to change the relation of humans to their environments. It is constituted through "the bending of bodies-with-environments for a specific set of addresses without the benefit of any cognitive inputs" (Thrift 2004, 177). Although epistemological concerns about surveillance and privacy can (and should be) addressed through such tactics as regulation, disclosure, and informed consent (Cuff 2003; Kang and Cuff 2005), ontological issues concerning how human subjectivity is being reconfigured by context-aware technologies are more difficult to assess and address. Epistemological issues lend themselves to strategy and tactics (from sophisticated countersurveillance techniques to brute-force methods such as smashing RFID tags with a hammer or frying them in a microwave), but how do we understand the ontological effects of animate environments?

For these concerns, fictional explorations of near-future worlds not only let us imagine what such societies might look like but also engage us on other levels as well, including embodied affectivity and the unconscious. Precisely because narratives (unlike databases) always mean more than they explicitly state (Hayles 2007), they can address ontological questions as well as epistemological issues. Moreover, as linguistic artifacts, narratives have a vested interest in the operations of language, including interfaces between computer-mediated symbolic code and the so-called natural languages native to humans (Hayles 2005). Like computational technologies, narratives operate through decoding and encoding procedures, and these similarities provide potent analogies to layered RFID communication protocols (Alexander Galloway emphasizes the importance of protocols for these systems in *Protocol* [2004]).

I focus on David Mitchell's contemporary experimental novel *Cloud Atlas* (2004) and Philip K. Dick's visionary and hallucinogenic novel *Ubik* ([1966] 1991) as my tutor texts. Foregrounded in these works are questions about human agency and autonomy when things (seem to) come alive and clamor for attention. Whereas *Cloud Atlas* emphasizes a politics of epistemology, *Ubik* presents complexities irresolvable in a traditional worldview and hence forces a confrontation with ontological questions. Both *Cloud Atlas* and *Ubik* are deeply concerned with the relation between capitalism and the politicization of animate environments, but whereas *Cloud Atlas* uses logical extrapolation from present conditions, *Ubik* makes inferential leaps that work through metaphor and image, as if designed to engage directly with the technological unconscious.

In a perhaps surprising conjunction, both works evoke the divine, connected by subterranean flows to animistic environments that, functioning like RFID in some respects, nevertheless resist reductive explanations that would account for them solely through technological mechanisms. The trope of the divine, I argue, brings to the fore

RFID's ontological dimensions by being employed to urge the necessity for accountability and progressive action in the face of changing relationships of humans to their world. In the conclusion, I return to the challenges that RFID poses to conventional ideas about information, proposing a model of information processing more adequate for the distributed cognition of RFID and better suited to understand human interactions with animate environments. To prepare for these arguments, I briefly review how RFID technology works.

RFID: Tags, Sensors, Databases, and Distributed Cognition

RFID tags come in two moods, active and passive (for an introduction, see Bhuptani and Moradpour 2005; Glover and Bhatt 2006). Each comprises a computer chip with an integrated circuit, onto which information is encoded, and an antenna for receiving and transmitting radio-frequency waves (figures 30.1, 30.2, 30.3). Passive chips backscatter a signal sent from a reader, after modulating it with a ten-digit identification number (Electronic Product Code, or EPC) that uniquely identifies the object to

Figure 30.1
Variety of passive tags. Courtesy of Nicholas Gessler and his collection of "Things-That-Think."

Figure 30.2
The circular antenna and chip inside the circle are clearly visible in this transparent passive tag. Courtesy of Nicholas Gessler and his collection of "Things-That-Think."

which it is attached (the 96-bit EPC can generate 2^{96} different numbers, enough to code 80,000 trillion objects, more than sufficient to identify every man-made object on the planet). Active chips have a power source and can send as well as receive radio waves. Each passive chip is as inexpensive as one to three cents and can be as small as a grain of rice (much smaller tags, measuring considerable less than the diameter of a human hair, are now being developed by Hitachi). Active chips are larger and correspondingly more expensive, from three to ten dollars each. The passive tags have a reading range of a few inches, but the active tags can transmit signals for up to a mile. The current primary use for the tags is to trace objects as they move in time and space through integrated systems that include readers, middleware, and backend databases, making them a flexible technology platform (Lenoir and Giannella 2007). Many commentators believe that these integrated systems will revolutionize the ways that products are manufactured, delivered, stored, and inventoried. Two behemoths of supply and demand, Wal-Mart and the US Department of Defense, are already requiring their vendors to attach RFID tags to their merchandise (Gilbert 2004; Polsonetti 2004), a practice that virtually ensures the rapid proliferation of RFID technology throughout the United States and other developed countries.

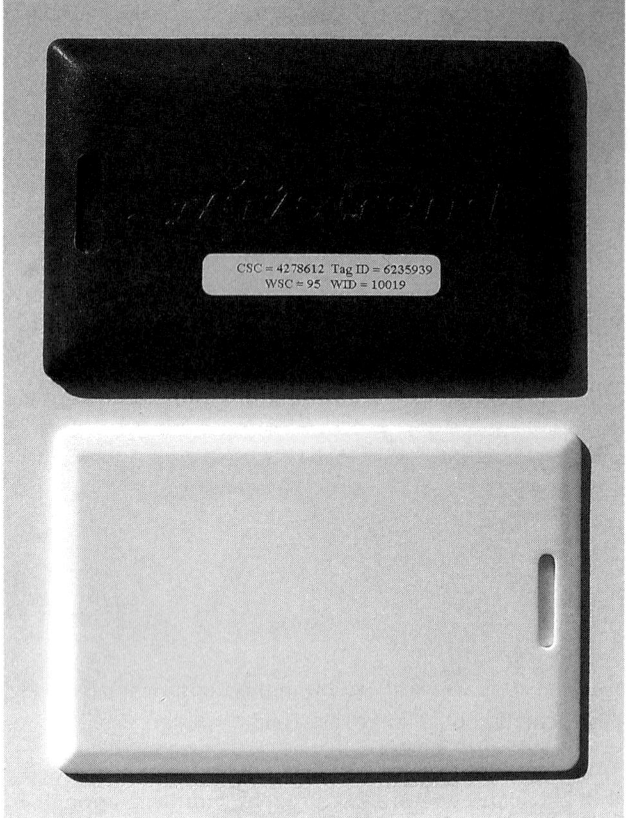

Figure 30.3
Examples of active tags containing their own power sources. Courtesy of Nicholas Gessler and his collection of "Things-That-Think."

The insider term for RFID tags is *arphids*, an apt neologism suggesting they can be pervasively scattered throughout the environment. Coupled with sensors, arphids can record and transmit all kinds of information, from temperature to seismic activity to the presence of warm bodies. Because they are both actual physical devices and virtual presences accessed through databases, Bruce Sterling (2005) sees them as the leading edge of a "spime" world. Spimes are virtual/actual entities whose trajectories can be tracked through space and time; as Sterling conceived the term, however, it implies more than the devices by themselves. *Spime* connotes the transition from thinking of the object as the primary reality to perceiving it as data in computational environments, through which it is designed, accessed, managed, and recycled into other objects. The object is simply the hard-copy output for these integrated processes. The spime is "a set of relationships first and always, and an object now and then"; it is "not about the material object, but where it came from, where it is, how long it stays there, when it goes away, and what comes next" (Sterling 2005, 77, 109). In this vision, RFID participates in a larger transition to a world where human action is coordinated with complex virtual–actual environments characterized by flows and relations between many different agents, including nonhuman ones, tied together through distributed cognitive networks (Anne Galloway 2004).

Both time and space are transformed as they circulate through and between the actual and virtual domains (Anne Galloway 2004). Space is configured by distinctions between observable domains, on the one hand, and blind spots that do not report data back for recording and accessing, on the other (Crang and Graham 2007; Graham 2005); time changes from uniform clock measurement to digital recording of the always temporary instantiations of material objects (Sterling 2005). Transformed also is the lynchpin of capitalism, private property. Whereas private property is traditionally understood as the legal possession of tangible (and intangible) assets, in an RFID world property is defined by two interpenetrating but distinct systems: one based on possession of the material object and the other on data about the object. A consumer may buy an object—say, a bottle of wine—without owning the database entries that record the sale, link the consumer's credit records with that particular bottle through its unique RFID number, track its recycling into another glass bottle, and continue to follow its new instantiation through space and time (for a discussion of the consumer's "second self" in databases, see Andrejevic 2003, 137). Like virtual objects sold for real money in *Second Life*, virtualized data about the object have market values that amount to considerable percentages of the value of the material commodities to which the data correspond (judging by the typical discounts offered by loyalty cards, somewhere between 20 and 30 percent). As Sterling observes, "My consumption patterns are worth so much that they underwrite my acts of consumption" (2005, 79).

RFID and related technologies thus enable significant cost savings for corporations and offer flexibility in designing for an open-ended future in which data management facilitates sustainability practices; they also raise serious concerns about surveillance and privacy (Albrecht and McIntyre 2005; Bajc 2007). Tags can be embedded in objects including cars, clothes, purses, wallets, and shoes—all of which can be used to track people as they move through RFID-embedded terrain—and be read without needing a clear line of sight. They are now mandatory for passports in the United States and the twenty-seven countries with which the United States has visa waiver agreements (Evers 2006); in addition to encoding the passport number and the holder's name and address, the tags will soon include biometric data such as fingerprints and retinal scans. With RFID spreading to drivers' licenses and credit cards, unauthorized reading that will lead to identity theft is also a concern (Lyman 2006).

Among the effects of RFID are changing advertising and consumption practices (Andrejevic 2003). Coupled with mobile devices such as RFID-enabled mobile phones, tags can deliver location-specific information to a passerby, who, for example, may receive on a mobile phone the menu of the restaurant she is strolling past (Fitzpatrick 2007). Moreover, RFID tags, coupled with backend databases, can lead to sophisticated "behavior inferences" that predict how people will act in a variety of situations (Albrecht and McIntyre 2005). RFID participates in a paradigm shift in which the focus moves from present and past actions to the *anticipation* of future actions—yet another way in which RFID leads to different constructions of time (Anne Galloway 2004). Military proponents see RFID as part of a comprehensive strategy of surveillance in which massive amounts of data will allow "behavior inferences" about insurgents or terrorists who mix invisibly with urban populations (McCue 2005; Pruett 2006).

RFID has biopolitical implications as well. RFID implants are now standard for companion and meat animals; it is estimated that fifteen million animals in the United States alone have them (as reported by EZID Animal Identification Systems [EZID n.d.]) (figure 30.4). RFID tags are used in a variety of biological applications, from a tag for the semen of a prize bull so that it can be authenticated to human-edible tags used to diagnose gastric disorders (Fox 2007). Scott Silverman of VeriChip Corporation has

Figure 30.4
RFID tag in glass capsule intended for implantation in domestic animals (or, as Scott Silverman of VeriChip Corporation suggests, in humans). Courtesy of Nicholas Gessler and his collection of "Things-That-Think."

also proposed that RFID implants be required for immigrants; he confirmed that VeriChip is pitching implants to the military as well (Jones 2006; Komp 2005; McIntyre and Albrecht 2007). RFID bracelets and anklets are already being used to track the movements of prisoners who are either under house arrest or in minimum-security facilities (Swedberg 2005a). In the Yokohama district of Tokyo, RFID bracelets are mandatory for schoolchildren, allowing them to be tracked as they go to and from school and move within the school perimeter (Swedberg 2005b; see also Williams 2007).

Given these possibilities, it is not surprising that anti-RFID activism is spreading in Europe and gaining momentum in the United States as well as other developed countries (Albrecht and McIntyre 2005). The technology's scary potential is perhaps most evident in the Combat Zones That See program launched by the US military, which envisions using video cameras, RFID, and related technologies to monitor civilian populations (see DARPA 2003 for the call for proposals; see Crang and Graham 2007, Crandall 1999, and Shactman 2003 for analyses and critique). Although the military proclaims that the technology is intended for use abroad, notably Iraq, its usefulness for tracking and surveillance indicates that similar applications will most likely also be deployed against domestic populations, as was clearly the case in Scotland Yard's monitoring of major highways in the recent search for terrorist suspects (Dana Cuff reports that by 2001 the average British citizen was photographed three hundred times a day [2003, 47]; see figures 30.4 and 30.5 for samples of earlier RFID tags serving a similar purpose). Any car with an EZPASS tag that enables it to pass through freeway tollgates without stopping is already RFID responsive, making it vulnerable to surveillance for other purposes as well.

Important as these concerns are, and as necessary as it is to craft well-designed legislation to curb potential abuses (Kang and Cuff 2005), we should not overstate the danger. Passive tags can be read only within distances of a few inches, limiting their usefulness for surveillance purposes. Moreover, for every technology, countertechnologies are likely to emerge; products such as wallets lined with aluminum foil to defeat unauthorized reading of RFID-encoded cards are already on the market. Other proposals are being advanced to protect consumer privacy—for example, by having the chip embedded in a tear-off label that can be detached at the point of purchase. The technology can also be used to "bite back"—for example, by having information compiled by activist groups sent to RFID-enabled mobile phones so that as the consumer strolls down the aisle, she can see warnings about unsafe, environmentally unfriendly, or otherwise undesirable products whose RFID labels are detected as she passes them (Kang and Cuff 2005). Many art projects in Europe and the United States perform resistance by redeploying the technology or changing its signification through interventions and subversive practices (see Crang and Graham 2007 for a discussion of some of these projects).

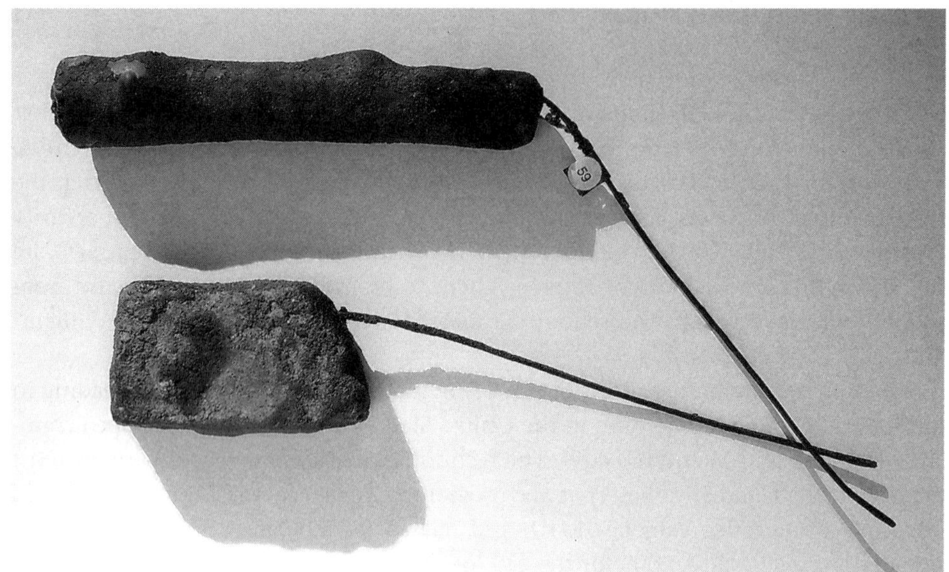

Figure 30.5
RFID devices such as the ones shown here were coupled with vibration sensors and used by the US military to detect traffic in the Vietnam War. Courtesy of Nicholas Gessler and his collection of "Things-That-Think."

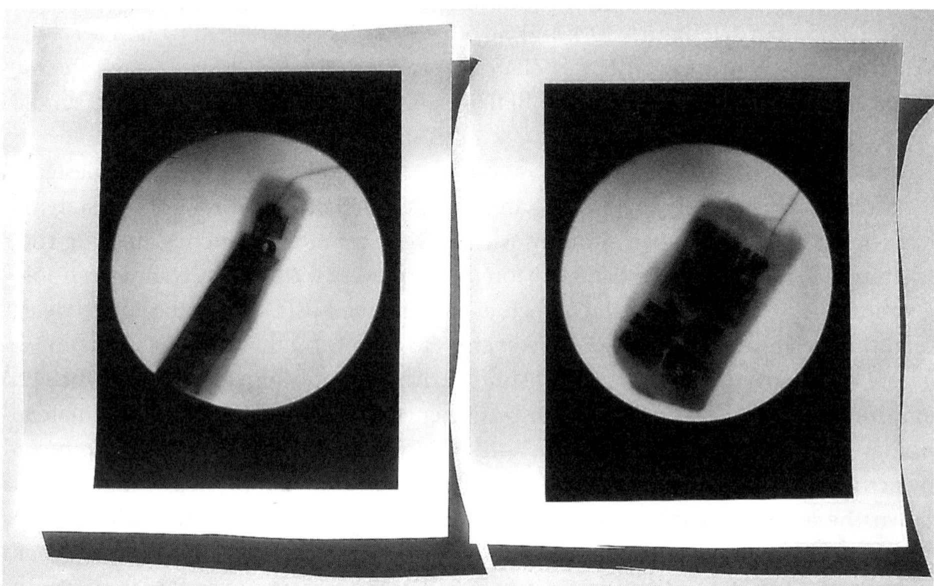

Figure 30.6
X-ray images of the tags shown in figure 30.4, revealing their antennae and internal structures. Courtesy of Nicholas Gessler and his collection of "Things-That-Think."

My focus here is on literary narratives and what they suggest about the possibilities for ethical action in environments made animate through embedded sensors, communicators, and actuators. As indicated earlier, the issues are both epistemological and ontological, affecting not only what we know and how we know it, but also what we conceive ourselves to be. As Sterling comments in an optimistic reading of an RFID world, humans are viewed "as processes: a process of self-actualization based not on what you are but what you are becoming" (2005, 52). David Mitchell's *Cloud Atlas* (2004), especially the powerful section entitled "An Orison of Sonmi-451," presents a darker view. In this future world, the dystopian possibilities of an RFID world are fully realized, and the utopian potential is a fragile seed desperately trying to grow. Let us turn now to an exploration of this representation of this future world.

Sonmi's Orison: The Politics of Epistemology

Extrapolated from present trends, Sonmi-451's world represents the convergence of corporate capitalism, government, and theocracy, a fusion denoted by the neologism *corpocracy* (with a transparent pun on *hypocrisy*). In Nea So Copros (which we gradually realize is the future instantiation of Korea), "Enrichment Statues" dictate that consumers must "spend a fixed quota of dollars each month, depending on their strata. Hoarding is an anti-corpocratic crime" (Mitchell 2004, 227). The official government creed, significantly called "Catechisms," includes the pronouncement that "a Soul's value is the dollars therein" (325), where the traditional meaning of "soul" as an indwelling spirit is overlaid by the denotation it has in Nea So Copros: an implanted RFID chip that identifies a citizen with a unique ID number. A person's Soul bestows on him certain rights, such as the ability to operate automated machinery such as elevators (a development anticipated by Roger Burrows and Nick Ellison when they write about using "a recast definition of social citizenship [that] points[s] to potential new categories of social inclusion and exclusion" [2004, 334]). A citizen's Soul also registers whatever his bank balance is at the moment, enables him to purchase goods, and, of course, makes him vulnerable to pervasive surveillance by Eyes, the RFID readers ubiquitously employed at checkpoints.

The central insight informing the narrative is its portrayal of the contradictions that riddle the corpocracy. Many of the previous era's developed countries have become "deadlands," wastelands rendered uninhabitable by environmental toxins, predatory capitalism, and resource depletion. We can infer that the United States is one of these deadlands from a reference to the "Merican Boat-People Solution" (220); so are Great Britain and most of Europe. Nea So Copros has survived so far, but only because it started farther behind on the (over)development curve. Perhaps the most devastating of the corpocracy's internal contradictions is the distinction the official ideology draws between "purebloods," or womb-born citizens, and "fabricants," or clones tailored for specific tasks in the economy and destined for execution as soon as their usefulness for work has been exhausted. The latter are fed chemicals ("amnesiads") designed to keep them largely without memory, devoid of curiosity, and with a strictly limited consciousness so repressed it is not capable of generating an interior monologue. Male fabricants are used up working as "militiamen" and "disastermen," genetically engineered to be relatively toxin and fire resistant. Female fabricants are destined for work as domestics and laborers in the service industry; such is Sonmi-451, a server at "Papa Song's" (which we gradually realize is the future instantiation of McDonald's). In a pointed satire underscoring how the corpocracy works, the semideity delivering each day's sermon to the fabricants at Papa Song's is a hologram of the company's "Logoman" (Ronald McDonald), who preaches that loafing is "time theft" and that a disobedient fabricant "denies Papa Song's love for us and cheats His Investment" (191).

The naming system for fabricants is significant. The given name (e.g., "Sonmi") refers to a genotype of supposedly identical units, whereas the number ("451") indicates where the fabricant comes in the manufacturing order. The play between the name (traditionally connoting an individual) and number (indicating a mass-produced object) points to how the human–thing dynamic is destabilized in an RFID world. When each object has a unique identity, objects begin to seem more like individuals, and individual people become susceptible to being constituted as objects. All the clones of a given genotype are officially identical, but as Sonmi later asserts (and makes good in her actions), "even same-stem fabricants cultured in the same wombtank are as singular as snowflakes" (187). The official ideology holds that fabricants lack Souls, an assertion rendered tautological by denying them Soul implants and controlling them instead with electronic collars and identity chips implanted in the neck designed to explode on contact with air, thus ensuring that any fabricant who attempts to alter her identity will not survive.

In a performance that may or may not be scripted by unseen powers, Sonmi gradually begins to "ascend," rising to full consciousness and experiencing for the first time an interior monologue. As she reports in her Testimony to the Archivist, "A voice spoke in my head. It alarmed me greatly, until I learned that no one else could hear this voice, known to purebloods as 'sentience.' . . . [M]y language evolved . . . my curiosity about all things grew acute . . . my sense of futility grew . . . but most of all, I was afraid" (198). After her ascension and escape from the disciplinary spaces that controlled her, Sonmi becomes part of an elaborate plot masterminded by the Union, the resistance movement trying to foment a revolution against the governing party, Unanimity. When Unanimity captures Sonmi, it displays her in a show trial as an aberration of nature and denounces her *Declarations* (counter-Catechisms laying the ground for ethical actions capable of resisting the evils of corpocracy) as "the ugliest wickedness in the annals of deviancy" (347). To make good this claim, however, they must reveal the content of the *Declarations*, thus inadvertently publicizing the very reasoning that is the most potent weapon poised against them. Sonmi's Testimony (the question-and-answer dialog constituting the narrative we read) is given to an Archivist and electronically recorded for future generations; as such, it embodies a similar contradiction. Torn between wanting Sonmi consigned to oblivion (her execution awaits her when she finishes her Testimony) and needing to publicize her as an object lesson, Unanimity bows to pressure from genomicists to allow her Testimony to be recorded. The Archivist himself embodies another kind of contradiction. Shocked to the core by some of Sonmi's revelations, he nevertheless insists upon an accurate record, for "a duplicitous archivist wouldn't be much use to future historians" (189).

Sonmi's ascension was catalyzed in part by her exposure to Yoona 939, who opened a crack in the seamless world of mindless time and disciplinary space that was Sonmi's lot in the corpocracy, destined for a life of slavery twelve stories down in an underground Papa Song's. The insidious tool Yoona used to pry open this world was a concept so potent, Sonmi tells the Archivist, that the corpocracy would do well to fear it: a *secret*. Thus, the text initiates a politics of epistemology. In fact, Yoona reveals a series of secrets to Sonmi, starting with the revelation that Seer Rhee, the overseer who governs their servitude, is anything but a panoptic all-seeing presence. Addicted to Soap, the food/soporific that keeps the fabricants alive and repressed, Seer Rhee pigs out on it every night, falling into a sleep so deep it resembles a coma. With the Seer seeing nothing, Yoona slips past him and discovers a storeroom and within it a fairytale book some child has left behind. She mistakes the book for a "broken sony" as she mistakes its images of princesses and dwarfs, castles and elves, for an accurate picture of the world outside.

Poignant and pathetic, these misapprehensions initiate a series of events that leads to Yoona's doomed escape attempt. Without resources, knowledge, or a tactical plan, she grabs a pureblood child and runs for an elevator, only to return as a bullet-ridden corpse. The incident unleashes the nightmare specter the corpocracy has been denying and repressing all along: the possibility that the supposedly docile fabricants may ascend to full consciousness and rebel. Echoing how many Americans felt after September 11, 2001, Sonmi pushes the Archivist's buttons by articulating his reaction to Yoona's rebellion: "You felt the corpocratic world order had changed, irrevocably. You vowed never to trust any fabricant. You knew that Abolitionism was as dangerous and insidious a dogma as Unionism. You supported the resultant Homeland Laws dictated by the Beloved Chairman, wholeheartedly" (195).

The politics of fear thus reinforces the politics of consciousness, in which the *degree* of consciousness a subject possesses becomes a basis for discrimination so violent that it amounts to slavery. Moreover, the politics of consciousness is based on a tautology. Fabricants "deserve" their enslavement because they have limited consciousness, and because they are enslaved, they can be forcibly fed the suppressants that deny them full consciousness.

Sonmi's ascension enables her to comprehend fully these tautologies and contradictions. Spirited away by Union operatives, she is covertly taken to witness the atrocities at Papa Song's Golden Ark, the vessel that supposedly transports fabricants who have fulfilled their twelve years of servitude to "Xultation," a life of ease and happiness in Hawaii. The Golden Ark is actually a killing ship, as Sonmi tells the scandalized Archivist, bound to the "economics of corpocracy. The genomics industry demands huge quantities of liquefied biomatter, for wombtanks, but most of all, for Soap. What cheaper way to supply this protein than by recycling fabricants who have reached the end of their working lives? Additionally, leftover 'reclaimed proteins' are used to produce Papa Song's food products, eaten by consumers in the corp's dineries all over Nea So Copros. It is a perfect food cycle" (343).

This horrific revelation, which can be taken as a viciously satirical demonstration of Eric Alliez and Michel Feher's claim that "individuals are enslaved by, or rather, *incorporated into* capital" (1987, 317, emphasis added), is superseded by yet another secret: Sonmi's gradual realization that her "rescue" by Union operatives is in fact part of Unanimity's strategy to control the pureblood population as well as the enslaved fabricants. "Union preexists me," she tells the Archivist, "but its reasons d'être are not to foment revolution" (348). Reminiscent of tactics employed by the CIA during the Vietnam War (and the Iraq War?), Union activists operate as provocateurs, attracting social malcontents and keeping them "where Unanimity can watch them," meanwhile providing the corpocracy "with the enemy required by any hierarchical state for social cohesion" (348). Against this strategy, the tactics of evasion, identity counterfeiting, running, and hiding that Sonmi and her supposed protectors practiced are of limited usefulness, suggesting that the dystopian aspects of RFID technology cannot be defeated by evasive tactics alone.

Something more is needed—something with the heft and potency sufficient to set the world on another track, an idea so compelling that it can contest and defeat the fused religious, political, and economic ideology of the corpocracy. Sonmi, realizing this all too well, initiates what she calls "the game beyond the endgame" (359). She knowingly follows the script that has been prepared for her because it gives her an opportunity to set her *Declarations*, their "logic and ethics" (347), free in the world. Mitchell mostly withholds from his readers the text of Sonmi's *Declarations*, leaving us to construct for ourselves their content by considering what might best counter the corpocracy's ideology. We are given Sonmi's Testimony instead, a dialogic narrative that vividly and compellingly challenges us to imagine what a better future might be and to speculate on how we can help bring it about.

As a literary text, the narrative works both explicitly through plot events and implicitly through structure and language. Somni's "Orison" is narrated in two parts, placed so that it bookends a narrative set in the far future, "Sloosha's Crossin' an' Ev'rythin' After." The latter narrative, strategically placed to intervene between Sonmi's escape and her subsequent adventures, reveals that Nea So Copros and indeed almost the entire world has fallen into darkness, with civilization hanging by a thread in the gentle trading culture of the Valley people in Hawaii, the promised land that Sonmi never reaches. Although the record of Sonmi as an actual historical person has been lost to the Valley culture, she survives for them as a local deity inhabiting certain places, where, their religion holds, they are able to communicate with her and receive visions. Thus, the RFID technology of Sonmi's world (and ours), embedded pervasively to create context-aware and animate environments, is transformed through a series of historical contingencies back into an animistic religion that, for the Greeks and early Western culture, was perhaps the original version of animate environments.

The Valley people get from the Prescients, precarious inheritors of high technology who themselves are about to fall into oblivion, a "silv'ry egg" that they learn to call an "*orison*" (309). When they warm it in their hands, a "beautsome ghost-girl" appears "in the air an' speaks in an Old-Un tongue what no un alive und'stands nor never will, nay" (309). Unable to decode Sonmi's Testimony and helpless to make the connections that would enable them to realize this is the historical instantiation of their local deity, the people nevertheless are inspired by the ghost-girl's "hov'rin'n'sh imm'rin'" (309). The message as language is lost, but the mediating technology allows the Valley people tenuous contact with the historical precedents for the ideals they hold dear—support of one another, preference of trade to murder, hope for a better life.

At once a prayer and a technology, the orison bequeaths to us, readers who have the context the Valley people lack, the urgent necessity for imagining the strategies that will open for us and our descendents a different kind of future. This bequest is made very clear by the performative gesture that concludes the dark vision of "Shoosha's Crossin' an' Ev'rythin' After," when the narrator invites us to "Sit down a beat or two. / Hold Out your hands. / Look" (309). When we turn the page, we encounter the second half of "An Orison of Sonmi-451," which concludes, as we have seen, in an open-ended fashion that challenges us to arrive at a different place than the corpocracy, the impetus toward which is all too apparent in the ideology of George W. Bush's New World Order.

Realizing the utopian possibilities of RFID and minimizing its dystopian features thus requires more than regulation, evasive tactics, and progressive legislation, useful as they may be in the short term. Also necessary are analyses that probe the technology's deep entanglement with economic structures and political ideologies as well as strong countervisions that articulate a future worth fighting for. Without such inspirations, we are left in defensive postures that can respond to the technology's abusive uses but are helpless to imagine how it might be directed in other, more positive ways.

The better we understand how RFID changes the rules of the game, the more we can imaginatively engage with it to exploit its positive potentials. An example of such engagement is Bruce Sterling's *Shaping Things* (2005), which I admire (notwithstanding its significant short-changing of the technology's abusive potential) because it succeeds in articulating a positive agenda for designers that effectively challenges them to use data-intensive environments to actualize a better future.

Ubik: The Technological Unconscious and the Ontology of an RFID World

For Joe Chip in Philip K. Dick's *Ubik*, an animate environment is nothing but trouble. Perpetually short of cash, Joe must negotiate with the coffeepot, toaster, and even the door of his "conapt" to get them to perform routine services for which they demand instant payment ([1966] 1991, 19–24). The demands of these animated devices are all the more annoying to Joe because they can *talk* (and reason to a limited extent). Breaking the monopoly of human "natural" language, the animate devices go beyond the context awareness of RFID and become characters in their own right (necessarily so because characterization is implicit in the vocabulary, syntax, and content of the utterances that Dick fashions for them—in the case of the door, quite a litigious and testy character). Although there is no explicit connection between the scenes that establish the animate environments and the novel's main events, these scenes are much more than window dressing for a futuristic world. They connect to a deep-seated fear that Dick inscribed into many of his most powerful works: a fear that as things become animate, people tend toward the inanimate.

The fear has deep roots in Anglo-American culture, from Karl Marx's evocation of a dancing table in his discussion of commodity fetishism to Donna Haraway's prescient comment that "our machines are disturbingly lively, and we ourselves frighteningly inert" (1991, 152). For Dick, the fear is overlaid with the private iconography of the "tomb world," a fictional–literary representation of the clinical depression that plagued him throughout his life. The tomb world is depicted in several of his novels as a state of living death in which time slows to a crawl, decay is pervasive, and the poor unfortunate soul stuck there must endure eons of purgatory before he is able slowly and painfully to crawl out. At the same time, the tomb world is not merely personal, for it is consistently linked with destabilizing the dynamic between human and animal and machine (notably in Dick's best-known novel, *Do Androids Dream of Electric Sheep?* on which the film *Blade Runner* was based). In *Ubik*, the emphasis shifts to the dynamic between human and thing, making this text especially appropriate for an exploration of the ontological implications of RFID. At the novel's heart is the idea of *vitality:* who (or what) has it, who can steal it, who is losing or gaining it. Embedded in a capitalist economy, the *things* that make Joe Chip's life miserable are the tip of the iceberg; the problem that looms much larger is the overall destabilization of the boundary between human and thing, accelerated in our world by the use of distributed cognitive systems such as RFID.

Although *Ubik*'s publication in 1966 predates the huge explosion of personal computing then in its infancy, Joe Chip's name evokes the computational technologies with which Dick likely had at least some familiarity. The first silicon chip was invented in 1958; by 1961, it was used in Minutemen missiles and subsequently in television electronic circuits. IBM introduced its 1400 series computers in 1961, and the first chip to be used solely in computational devices, Intel's 4004, was released in 1971. More relevant to Dick's text is Boris Artzybasheff's famous illustration of an animated computer, Mark III, oozing personality on the January 23, 1950, cover of *Time* magazine, which Dick almost certainly would have known. Unlike many hard-science-fiction writers, however, Dick's interest was not primarily in the technology as such, but rather in its ontological and epistemological effects. When he needed a certain technology to carry out an idea, he inscribed it with hand-waving pseudo-explanations that often sounded technically impressive but had no actual scientific basis.

Such is the invention of half-life in *Ubik*, the cryogenic suspension of people (housed in institutions appropriately called "moratoriums") who have only a spark of life left but have been revived from complete oblivion and hooked up to an apparatus that allows them to communicate with the outside world. Every time a half-lifer is revived, some of his small remaining stock of life force is depleted. As a result, families who have put their loved ones in half-life face a cruel dilemma: they can access the half-lifers and so for a brief time have contact with them again, but at the cost of accelerating their final demise. During the communication sessions, the half-lifers remain frozen and inert, communicating thoughts without apparent bodily engagement. They have effectively become data, living in an illusory dream world constrained by real-world energetics but otherwise disconnected from reality.

From this context arises the novel's central mystery. Joe Chip is employed by Glenn Runciter, who runs a business lending out employees who have psionic capabilities: precognizants, telepaths, psychokineticists, and, most important, inertials who can offset other psionic abilities. Lured to Luna by a business rival, Runciter and his entire crew are blown up by a bomb. Joe Chip thinks that Runciter was killed in the explosion and rushes him back to Earth before it is too late to revive the small spark of life that is half-life; the suspicion gradually grows, however, that it was actually Joe Chip and his associates who were killed, and Runciter who is trying to communicate with them while they are in half-life. Insofar as the novel engages in the politics of epistemology, questions about who knows what center on finding out who is really alive and who is already in the deep twilight of the half-life world.

More pressing are ontological questions about the nature of the strange world in which Joe Chip finds himself. Traveling with his colleagues back to Des Moines, Iowa, ostensibly to attend Runciter's funeral, Joe begins to encounter a temporal regression of objects. First manifesting as stale cigarettes and curdled coffee cream, the regression soon becomes the transformation of objects back to previous instantiations. Push-button elevators regress to cages requiring operators; spray cans to medicinal salves; automobiles to versions manufactured twenty, thirty, and then forty years earlier; airplanes to biplanes. In a world of data where objects have only virtual existences, the temporal trajectory tracing their movements through time and space can arc backward as well as forward. Half a century before Sterling observed that in a spime world the emphasis falls not on the object as a material entity, but rather on its always-changing instantiation, Dick intuited that in a world of data, time (and space) would be radically destabilized. Objects would cease to be stable matter and become instantiations vulnerable to time's backward flow.

Time's destabilization affects the humans as well, although ironically in another way, moving them not toward infancy but toward the inanimate state that, in Sigmund Freud's reading of the death drive, is the ultimate origin to which the psyche secretly yearns to return. The impersonal pronoun used to describe Wendy Wright, first of the group to die from the regression, testifies to this destabilized boundary of the human–thing: "On the floor of the closet a huddled heap, dehydrated, almost mummified, lay curled up. Decaying shreds of what seemingly had once been cloth covered most of *it*, as if *it* had, by degrees, over a long period of time, retracted into what remained of *its* garments" (97, emphasis added). Already frozen in the deep inertia of half-life, Joe Chip and his companions experience an irresistible force moving them toward *thinghood.*

The remainder of the novel centers on the question of what—or who—is causing this regression. It would have been easy for Dick to explain it through the natural ebbing of the life force to which Joe and his half-life companions are inevitably bound. Interestingly, however, he chose to insinuate that the cause is not simply the second law of thermodynamics, but a conscious, volitional agent. At first, Joe suspects Pat Conley, whose scary psionic talent is an ability to travel back into the past and create a new present by changing a single decisive event. Linked by her talent to time's destabilization, Pat is nevertheless shown to be as much in thrall to the regression as her compatriots. The culprit, revealed at the novel's climax, is the teenage Jory, another half-life resident who eats up others' life force to feed his own voracious appetite. Again, however, Dick declines the obvious route of making Jory the villain; rather, the struggle between him and Joe Chip is cast as an epic battle between the thinghood of the tomb world and the forces of vitality.

The nature of this battle becomes clear when Joe encounters Ella Runciter, Glen Runciter's wife, who has been consigned to half-life; her vitality almost exhausted, she is preparing to be reborn into another life cycle. When Joe tells her, "Maybe I can defeat Jory," she comments, "Maybe in time you can learn ways to nullify him. I think that's really the best you can hope to do; I doubt if you can truly destroy him—in other words consume him—as he does to half-lifers placed near him at the moratorium" (207). When Joe objects that he can denounce Jory's predations to Glen and have him moved, Ella explains that Jory's relatives pay handsomely for the moratorium owner to keep him near the others. "And—there are Jorys in every moratorium," she adds. "This battle goes on wherever you have half-lifers; it's a verity, a rule, of our kind of existence" (207). The fight, in other words, cannot be waged through strategy and tactics alone; rather, it is primarily and fundamentally an ethical struggle that continues as long as life in any form exists. "'You'll have to take charge, Mr. Chip, after I'm reborn,'" Ella tells him. "'Do you think you can do that? It'll be hard. Jory will be sapping your strength always, putting a burden on you that you'll feel as'—She hesitated. 'The approach of death'" (207).

The talismanic object Ella creates to aid in this struggle is Ubik, the mysterious substance for which Joe Chip desperately searches. If he can find it in a spray can before it regresses into a useless salve, he can douse himself with it and stabilize, for the moment, his own regression into thinghood. Half-life, as a phantasmatic space, can thus be understood as playing out in metaphoric fashion the complex relation between the technological unconscious and the destabilized dynamic between human and thing. Dick's fine insight is to make Ubik profoundly ambivalent, associated both with the worst kind of hucksterism for predatory capitalism and with the divine force that, its name suggests, is ubiquitous and eternal.

These characterizations of Ubik come in the epigraphs of the final chapters. The penultimate chapter, for example, begins with an advertisement for "Ubik toasted flakes, the adult cereal that's more crunchy, more tasty, more ummmish. Ubik breakfast cereal, the whole-bowl taste treat!" The invitation to eat more and more is vitiated by the follow-up warning (no doubt mandated by regulation): "Do not exceed recommended portion at any one meal," suggesting that this "taste treat" is also a poison. In sharp contrast is the epigraph of the final chapter: "I am Ubik. Before the universe was, I am. I made the suns, I made the worlds. I created the lives and the places they inhabit. I move them here, I put them there. They go as I say, they do as I tell them. I am the word and my name is never spoken, the name which no one knows. I am called Ubik, but that is not my name. I am. I shall always be" (215).

The startling contrast between these two versions of Ubik suggests that the force it represents can be appropriated for good or evil. Ella, after all, does not simply discover Ubik but *invents* it, enrolling it in her efforts to enhance life over death through strenuous and unremitting effort. If Ubik is eternal, as the final epigraph suggests, its declaration of ultimate agency must nevertheless be seen in terms of human interpretation and human ethical action.

At stake is how the destabilization of time and space by data-intensive environments will be interpreted and employed; as time and space become more malleable, will this flexibility be used to enhance and amplify human life or to drive humanity closer to thinghood? Capitalism alone, Dick's novel suggests, cannot be trusted to bring about salutary results on its own. In a concluding master stroke, the narrative performs a final inversion that throws the struggle back to us. Joe Chip first suspects that he might be in half-life when his money displays not the conventional historical figures, but the profile of Glenn Runciter. In the novel's final moments, just when we think we have everything figured out, Glenn Runciter discovers that *his* money is now displaying the profile of Joe Chip, a development designed to subvert the neat closure otherwise achieved by drawing a firm line between the phantasms of half-life and the "real" world that Glen Runciter (and we) inhabit. The implication, of course, is that normal life has begun to operate by the same rules as half-life; with the boundary between them destabilized, we are left to draw the obvious conclusion. Our world is no more secure from the threat—and promise—of data-intensive environments than is Dick's fictional creation. It is up to us to face the epistemological and ontological challenges such environments represent and imagine how they can be used to fashion a better world. Like Joe Chip, we inherit the ethical imperative of *Ubik*: will ubiquitous computing be co-opted as a stalking horse for predatory capitalism, or can we seize the opportunity to use it for life-enhancing transformations?

A Modest Proposal: Reconnecting Information and Meaning

As William Mitchell comments, RFID and related technologies "change the fundamental mechanisms of reference—the ways in which we establish meaning, construct knowledge, and make sense of our surroundings by associating items of information with one another and with physical objects" (2003, 120). A framework is needed capable of building bridges between human agency and an RFID world without collapsing distinctions between them. Such a framework would allow us to shed the misconception that humans alone are capable of cognition (a proposition already deconstructed with respect to animals and growing shaky with regard to distributed cognitive systems). The way forward, I want to argue, should not be to beat a retreat to traditional liberal humanism but rather to rethink the ways in which human cognition is like RFID technologies: multilayered, context aware, and capable of generating novel meanings and interpretations. Nevertheless, human cognition remains distinct from thinghood because it arises from embodied contexts that have a biological specificity capable of generating consciousness as an emergent phenomenon, something no mechanical system can do. The politics of consciousness dramatized in David Mitchell's "An Orison of Sonmi-451" shows that the traditional view equating the human with the ability to formulate conscious thoughts can lead to radical social inequalities. Moreover, the politics of consciousness is not confined to fictional scenarios; whenever a group of people is stigmatized and repressed, the charge is leveled that the people are deficient in consciousness (or in reason, consciousness's handmaiden). The challenge *Cloud Atlas* and *Ubik* together present is to arrive at a fuller, richer, and more adequate view of human cognition without making humans vulnerable to being reduced to thinghood.

As a contribution to this challenge, I conclude by proposing a modification of information theory suggested when I attended a seminar given by Edward Fredkin and heard him utter the following sentence: "The meaning of information is given by the processes that interpret it" (Fredkin 2007). Although Fredkin did not develop this idea beyond suggesting that it might be used, for example, to understand the operation of an MP3 player in interpreting a digital file to produce music, I think it has great potential for contributing to an understanding of information that is contextual, processual, and embodied. Such an understanding is crucial for constructively integrating human relationships with the new kinds of situations created by RFID technologies.

As we know, when Claude Shannon and Warren Weaver (1949) formulated information as a probability function, they declared that information in this technical sense had nothing to do with meaning. The problem they faced was how to quantify information reliably so that it was suited for calculation, a preeminent concern among electrical engineers. Meaning has traditionally been closely linked with context. However, if information is defined so that it is context dependent and hence tied to meaning, Shannon and Weaver understood that its quantification would change every time it was imported into a new context, making calculation an engineer's nightmare. The problem Shannon and Weaver faced can thus be understood as defining an appropriate context without sacrificing quantifiability. Donald MacKay (1969), in his embodied version of information theory, boldly proposed that information should be understood in the context of the embodied receiver, thus reconnecting information with meaning, but at the cost of failing to solve the problem of quantification.

Fredkin's formulation breaks new ground by crucially changing the meaning of "interpretation" and (tautologically) the meaning of "meaning." Information in this view is inherently processual and contextual, with the context specified by the mechanisms of interpretation. These processes take place not only within consciousness, but within subcognitive and noncognitive contexts as well, both biological and mechanical. A computer, for example, gives information one kind of meaning when voltages are correlated with binary code, but another kind of meaning is generated with high-level programs such as C++, much easier for humans to understand than ones and zeros, and still another when C++ commands are used to generate screen displays and behaviors, which have yet more general meanings to humans. Human cognition, for its part, arises from contexts that include sensory processing, which interprets information from the environment and gives it meaning within this context; the meaning that emerges from these processes undergoes further interpretation and transformation when it reaches the central nervous system; these meanings are transformed yet again as the central nervous system interacts with the neocortex, resulting in conscious thoughts.

MacKay had already envisioned a series of hierarchical and interrelated contexts that included subcognitive processes when he insisted that the meaning of a message "can be fully represented only in terms of the full basic-symbol complex defined by all the elementary responses evoked. These may include visceral responses and hormonal secretions and what have you" (1969, 42). Fredkin's formulation adds to this vision a way of understanding meaning that extends it to mechanical, nonhuman processes. Indexed to local subcognitive and noncognitive contexts, "interpretation" ceases to be solely a high-level process that occurs only in consciousness. Rather, interpretation becomes a multilayered, distributed activity in which the "aboutness" of intentionality (traditionally used by philosophers as the touchstone of cognition) consists of establishing a relation between some form of input and a transformed output through context-specific local processes. By breaking the overall context of reception into many local contexts, Fredkin's formulation makes the processes at least in part amenable to reliable quantification. Many of these local contexts already have metrics that work: measuring voltages and processing speeds and bits per second in computers or measuring neural responses, fatigue rates, and the like in humans. The important point is a shift of vision that enables us to see these subcognitive and noncognitive processes not just as contributing to conscious thought, but as *themselves* acts of interpretation and meaning.

This vision of meaning creation is especially well suited to understanding human cognition in the context of RFID technologies, in which context and relationality play central roles. Context awareness is achieved when RFID tags are connected with embedded sensors and location-specific technologies such as Global Positioning System–enabled mobile phones; relationality is achieved through the communications of the tags among themselves and, more widely, also through the relationality central to the operation of relational databases. When human cognition is identified solely with consciousness, it seems to operate in a qualitatively different way than these technologies. If we understand high-level consciousness to be emergent from lower-level distributed cognitive processes, as Daniel Dennett argues (1995, 401–427; 1996), we have a way to connect human cognitive and subcognitive processes to distributed mechanical cognition in a number of ways. Everything does not have to go through the needle's eye of conscious awareness. This means that RFID can interface with human cognition well below the threshold of consciousness through embodied actions such as gesture, posture, and the habituated motions that give rise to and embody unconscious presuppositions—a proposition Nigel Thrift (2004, 2005) has explored in positing the technological unconscious.

Moreover, these interactions can now properly be said to be *meaningful* in the precise sense of that term: full of meanings generated by context-specific processes of interpretation that occur both within and between human and nonhuman cognizers.

Consciousness, in this view, loses its prerogative to be the sole arbiter of meaning; but this loss (if it is such) is more than offset by a richer contextual and processual view of how meanings are generated. RFID technologies in this view cease to be alien to the human condition and instead become part of the distributed cognitive systems that for millennia have extended and amplified human cognition (as demonstrated by Andy Clark [2000] and Edwin Hutchins [1996]). Of course, this conceptual configuration of RFID technologies does not alone guarantee that they will be used to enhance human lives rather than to diminish, coerce, and endanger them. That is why the ethical imperatives that emerge from the epistemological and ontological explorations of texts such as *Cloud Atlas* and *Ubik* are so important. The idea that meaning and interpretation can occur across and between human and mechanical phyla contributes to an expanded sense of ethics necessary when the contexts for human actions are defined by information-intensive environments and include relational and context-aware technologies such as RFID. Such an ethics would emphasize context over generalization, processes over static objects, embodied and distributed systems over hierarchical abstract ones, and a full range of cognitions over a sole focus on consciousness. Not coincidentally, this ethics has much in common with the Deleuzian ethics that has catalyzed contemporary work in the social sciences and humanities. When we understand that humans are not the only cognizers who can interpret information and create meaning, we are free to imagine how a world rich in embodied contextual processes might be fashioned to enhance the distributed cognitive systems that surround us and that we ourselves are.

References

Albrecht, Katherine, and Liz McIntyre. 2005. *Spychips: How Major Corporations and Government Plan to Track Your Every Purchase and Watch Your Every Move.* New York: Penguin.

Alliez, Eric, and Michel Feher. 1987. "The Luster of Capital." *Zone* 1–2:314–359.

Andrejevic, Mark. 2003. "Monitored Mobility in the Era of Mass Customization." *Space & Culture* 6 (2): 132–150.

Bajc, Vida. 2007. "Introduction: Debating Surveillance in the Age of Security." *American Behavioral Scientist* 50 (12): 1567–1591.

Bhuptani, Manesh, and Sharam Moradpour. 2005. *RFID Field Guide: Deploying Radio Frequency Identification Systems.* Upper Saddle River, NJ: Prentice-Hall.

Burrows, Roger. 1997a. "Cyberpunk as Social Theory: William Gibson and the Sociological Imagination." In *Imagining Cities: Signs and Memories*, edited by Sallie Westwood and John Williams, 235–248. London: Routledge.

Burrows, Roger. 1997b. "Virtual Culture, Urban Polarization, and Social Science Fiction." In *The Governance of Cyberspace*, edited by Brian Loader, 38–45. London: Routledge.

Burrows, Roger, and Nick Ellison. 2004. "Sorting Places Out? Toward a Social Politics of Neighborhood Information." *Information, Communication, and Society* 7 (3): 321–326.

Clark, Andy. 2000. *Natural-Born Cyborgs: Minds, Technologies, and the Future of Human Intelligence.* London: Oxford University Press.

Crandall, Jordon. 1999. "Anything That Moves: Armed Vision." *CTheory.* Available at http://www.ctheory.net/articles.aspx?id=115. Accessed 28 October 2009.

Crang, Mike, and Stephen Graham. 2007. "Sentient Cities: Ambient Intelligence and the Politics of Urban Space." *Information, Communication, and Society* 10 (6): 789–817.

Cuff, Dana. 2003. "Immanent Domain: Pervasive Computing and the Public Realm." *Journal of Architectural Education* 57 (1): 43–49.

DARPA (Defense Advanced Research Projects Agency). 2003. "Combat Zones That See (CTS)." Board Agency Announcement SN03-15. May 2. Archived at https://www.fbo.gov/index?s=opportunity&mode=form&tab=core&id=507adc944c32f29724621a5ee4f1637c&_cview=0. Accessed 20 January 2012.

Dennett, Daniel C. 1996. *Kinds of Minds: Toward an Understanding of Consciousness.* New York: Basic.

Dennett, Daniel C. 1995. *Darwin's Dangerous Idea: Evolution and the Meanings of Life.* New York: Simon and Schuster.

Dick, Philip K. [1966] 1991. *Ubik.* New York: Vintage.

Dreyfus, Hubert L. 1992. *What Computers Still Can't Do: A Critique of Artificial Reason.* Cambridge, MA: MIT Press.

Evers, Joris. 2006. "RFID Passports Take Off." C/NetNews.com, 26 October. Available at http://news.cnet.com/2100-7348_3-6130016.html. Accessed 20 January 2012.

EZID. n.d. "Animal Identification Systems." Available at https://ezidavid.accountsupport.com/about.html. Accessed 20 January 2012.

Fayyad, Usasm, Gregory Piatetsky-Shapiro, and Padhraic Smyth. 2006. "Knowledge Discovery in Databases." In *Proceedings of the 2nd International Conference on Knowledge Discovery and Data Mining,* edited by Evangelos Simoudis, Jiawei Han, and Usuma Fayyad, 37–54. Menlo Park, CA: American Association for Artificial Intelligence.

Featherstone, Michael, and Roger Burrows, eds. 1995. *Cyberspace, Cyberbodies, Cyberpunk: Cultures of Technological Embodiment.* London: Sage.

Fitzpatrick, Michael. 2007. "Tagging Tokyo's Streets with No Name." *The Guardian,* 10 May. Available at http://www.guardian.co.uk/technology/2007/may/10/japan.guardianweeklytechnologysection. Accessed 28 October 2009.

Fox, Barry. 2007. "Edible RFIDs." *New Scientist,* 12 February. Available at http://www.newscientist.com/article/dn11162-invention-edible-rfid.html. Accessed 20 January 2012.

Fredkin, Edward. 2007. "Informatics and Information Processing vs. Mathematics and Physics." Paper presented at the Institute for Creative Technologies, Marina Del Ray, CA, 25 May.

Galloway, Alexander R. 2004. *Protocol: How Control Exists after Decentralization*. Cambridge, MA: MIT Press.

Galloway, Anne. 2004. "Intimations of Everyday Life." *Cultural Studies* 18 (2): 384–404.

Gershenfeld, Neil. 1999. *When Things Start to Think*. New York: Holt.

Gershenfeld, Neil, Raffi Krikorian, and Danny Cohen. 2004. "The Internet of Things." *Scientific American* 291 (4): 76–81. Available at http://www.sciamdigital.com/index.cfm?fa=Products.ViewIssuePreview&ARTICLEID_CHAR=EA130FB9-2B35-221B-60D0C3A181593924. Accessed 20 January 2012.

Gilbert, Alorie. 2004. "Wal-Mart Tagging Fuels RFID Market." *News.com*, 22 December. Available at http://www.newcom.com/Wal-Mart+tagging++fuels+RFID+market/2100–1012_3–5501432.html. Accessed 28 October 2009.

Glinsky, Albert. 2000. *Theremin: Ether Music and Espionage*. Urbana: University of Illinois Press.

Glover, Gill, and Himanshu Bhatt. 2006. *RFID Essentials*. New York: O'Reilly.

Graham, Stephen. 2005. "Software-Sorted Geographies." *Progress in Human Geography* 29 (5): 562–580.

Haraway, Donna. 1991. "A Cyborg Manifesto: Science, Technology, and Socialist-Feminism in the Late Twentieth Century." In *Simians, Cyborgs and Women: The Reinvention of Nature*, 149–181. New York: Routledge.

Hayles, N. Katherine. 2007. "Narrative and Database: Natural Symbionts." *PMLA: Publications of the Modern Language Association* 122 (5): 1603–1608.

Hayles, N. Katherine. 2005. *My Mother Was a Computer: Digital Subjects and Literary Texts*. Chicago: University of Chicago Press.

Heidegger, Martin. 1995. *The Fundamental Concepts of Metaphysics: World, Finitude, Solitude*. Translated by William McNeill and Nicholas Walker. Bloomington: Indiana University Press.

Hutchins, Edwin. 1996. *Cognition in the Wild*. Cambridge, MA: MIT Press.

Jones, K. C. 2006. "VeriChip Wants to Test Human Implantable RFID on Military." *Techweb*, 23 August. Available at http://www.techweb.com/headlines_week/showArticle.jhtml?articleID=192203522. Accessed 28 October 2009.

Kang, Jerry, and Dana Cuff. 2005. "Pervasive Computing: Embedding the Public Sphere." *Washington and Lee Law Review* 62: 93–147. Available at http://www.papers.ssrn.com/sol3/papers.cfm?abstract_id=626961. Accessed 28 October 2009.

Komp, Catherine. 2005. "Electronic Tags Used to Track Immigrants." *The New Standard*, 5 September. Available at http://www.newstandardnews.net/content/index.cfm/items/2324. Accessed 28 October 2009.

Lenoir, Tim, and Eric Giannella. 2007. *Technological Platforms and the Layers of Patent Data.* National Science Foundation Grant No. SES 0531184. Washington, DC: National Science Foundation.

Lyman, Jay. 2006. "Hacker Cracks, Clones RFID Passport." *TechNewsWorld,* 7 August. Available at http://www.new.com.com/RFID+passports+take+oos/2100–7348_3–6130016.html?tag=st.ref.goo. Accessed 28 October 2009.

MacKay, Donald. 1969. *Information, Mechanism, Meaning.* Cambridge, MA: MIT Press.

McCue, Colleen. 2005. "Data Mining and Predictive Analytics: Battlespace Awareness for the War on Terror." *Defense Intelligence Journal* 13 (1–2): 47–63.

McIntyre, Liz, and Katherine Albrecht. 2007. "Company Pushes RFID Implants for Immigrants, Guest Workers." *Sierra Times,* 24 May. Available at http://www.freerepublic.com/focus/f-bloggers/1634891/posts. Accessed 20 January 2012.

Mitchell, David. 2004. *Cloud Atlas.* New York: Random.

Mitchell, W. J. 2003. *Me++: The Cyborg Self and the Networked City.* Cambridge, MA: MIT Press.

Polsonetti, Chantal. 2004. "US Department of Defense Issues Updated RFID Policy." *ARC Wire,* 11 August. Available at http://www.arcweb.com/community/indnews/display.asp?id=5729. Accessed 28 October 2009.

Pruett, Richard. 2006. "Identification—Friend or Foe? The Strategic Uses and Future Implications of the Revolutionary New ID Technologies." USAWE Strategy Research Project: US Army War College, Carlisle Barracks, PA. Available at http://www.stinet.dtic.mil/oai/oai?8verb=getRecord8met.adataPrefix=html8identifier=ADA449410. Accessed 28 October 2009.

Shactman, Noan. 2003. "Big Brother Gets a Brain." *Village Voice,* 9–15 July. Available at http://www.villagevoice.com/news/0328,shactman,45399,1.html. Accessed 28 October 2009.

Shannon, Claude, and Warren Weaver. 1949. *The Mathematical Theory of Communication.* Urbana: University of Illinois Press.

Sterling, Bruce. 2005. *Shaping Things.* Cambridge, MA: MIT Press.

Swedberg, Claire. 2005a. "L.A. County Jail to Track Inmates." *RFID Journal,* 16 May. Available at http://www.rfidjournal.com/article/articleview/1601/1/1. Accessed 28 October 2009.

Swedberg, Claire. 2005b. "RFID Watches Over School Kids in Japan." *RFID Journal,* 16 December. Available at http://www.rfidjournal.com/article/articleview/2050/1/1. Accessed 28 October 2009.

Thrift, Nigel. 2005. *Knowing Capitalism.* London: Sage.

Thrift, Nigel. 2004. "Remembering the Technological Unconscious by Foregrounding the Knowledges of Position." *Environment and Planning D: Society and Space* 22:175–190.

Williams, Martyn. 2007. "Project to Tag Tokyo Neighborhood with RFID." *Computerworld* (16 May). Available at http://www.computerworld.com/article/article.do?command=viewArticleBasic^articleID=900677. Accessed 28 October 2009.

31 The Philotechnic Blind: Ubiquity, Relapse, Mutation (Notes on Bernard Stiegler's "Nanomutation")

Tom Cohen

When we address the digital or its *ubiquity*, there is always allegory—speculation on imagined futures, apocalyptic traces, the prospect of a transformation, a transvaluation, or a *mutation* of the histories of which it is a product. D. N. Rodowick's observations appear relevant to any project avowing to recenter the "human" before a horizon of "ubiquitous computation," of digital ubiquity or its imaginary:

> There is much to be learned from the fact that "photographic" realism remains the Holy Grail of digital imaging—a certain cultural sense of the cinematic and an unreflective notion of realism are still in many ways the touchstones for valuing the aesthetic innovations of the digital. . . . In terms of differentiation, computer-generated imagery codes itself as contemporary, spectacular, and future-oriented. . . . At the same time, the photographic basis of cinema is coded as real, the locus of truthful representation. (2001, 1400)

In Rodowick's observations, two things emerge that remind us how mercurial, faux mimetic, and evasive the digital is. First, in mythologizing the digital as a new medium, the "old" medium, the photograph, gets retroactively "coded as the real, the locus of truthful representation"; and, second, what is perceived within this narrative as a binary never seems to have been one to begin with. To a certain degree, in reasserting human centeredness before ubiquitous digital culture (or its image), the "human" is similarly "coded as the real." This coding would puzzle Walter Benjamin, among others. I depart from this observation to question the call for a return to human centeredness in "ubiquitous computation" (a ritual reassertion of sovereignty) by exploring a very small corner of Bernard Stiegler's work as a counterstrike to this symptomology.

Fables of Ubiquity

In the recent novel *Daemon* (2009) by Daniel Suarez (an expert at information-technology [IT] programming), there is a curious variation on the issue of "ubiquitous computation." The Daemon in question is a viral program that, triggered at its inventor's death, proceeds to take over cyberscapes, to massacre or assassinate opponents, and to appropriate humans as its host agents. This scenario was sufficiently plausible to get the author debriefed by US cybersecurity. The curious thing is that said Daemon, a pure effect of technics accelerated against its current system, reverses the usual premise: it arises not as an alien logic, an unstoppable machine or invader, it turns out, but as if to rescue the "humans" from the system they have subordinated themselves to (having unwittingly become unhuman already). The phrase "saving capitalism (or ubiquitous computation) from *itself*" comes to mind for a destructive campaign that gestures toward keeping open the possibility of a "new social order."[1] The latter at least may emerge from yet dwell within telecratic regimes and spells whose current accelerations consume planetary futures in a sort of *tempophagy*.

Ubiquitous computation as a phrase is exorbitant and absorptive. Each word exceeds its technical referent in import. As one is reminded by a Web dictionary, *ubiquity* means not only "totalizing," "the state or capacity of being everywhere," but "omnipresence: the ubiquity of magical beliefs" and in theology "the omnipresence of god."[2] The phrase cannot stop generating other phantoms: the arrival of the cyborg or threatening replicant to take over; the totalization of surveillance in a control society; the emerging evisceration of life forms and "life as we know it." It cannot stop being allegorical rather than descriptive. It is suffused with anxiety and messianism. Thus, the call to recenter the "human" within a culture of "ubiquitous computation" occurs not only with a sense of nostalgia and the assertion of control, but without a single sense of what the "human" here designates. Is the "human" meant to reference some literal animal–man or Enlightenment "man" or the residue of the Western "anthropological machine" (Agamben 2004, 37), or the citizen of a polis? Or is it a metaphor without a content, a *Nachkonstruktion* generated as a hermeneutic reflex, a faith in the after-image of a more or less automatic will to proprietize in language? Such "ubiquitous computation" arrives then with the counterclaim to recenter the human in it, to police or control it, to bring it back within our semantic premises or house. This systemic *relapse*, *reflex*, or constitutively effaced reinscription makes the latter project itself ("to recenter") as much a symptom as a supposed task, one that anticipates failure in advance ("re"?).

One must contend with why advanced critics in new-media studies often recur to the most traditional cognitive bases to anchor their work—for instance, why, in announcing the "posthuman," one returns to the most humanist of hermeneutic premises or why one, in claiming "new-media" forms, relapses to existential phenomenology or various forms of embodiment. In general, the critic of "new media" (a field constituted by virtual objects) tends to understand technology as tool, hence as what the *human* manages and constructs. Thus, a program for restituting "human" centeredness within IT mimes a resurgent, if wounded, anthropocentrism. One witnesses this resurgence in our finest new-media critics, as when Katherine Hayles (1999) mounts a figure of the "posthuman" over what remain fairly humanist representational practices, or when Mark Hansen (2000, 2004) recurs to phenomenology and lived experience to anchor his divagations. And it emerges routinely in the work of D. N. Rodowick (2001) and Lev Manovich (2001) as well as in Siegfried Zielinski's *Deep Time of the Media* (2006) or Anne Munster's *Materializing New Media: Embodiment in Information Aesthetics* (2006). The subtitle of Munster's book, returning media to the body, says this, as do Manovich's idea that new media are a language (*The Language of New Media*) and Zielinski's "deep time." All use phenomenological notions of time, body, and language to render the alien familiar. In a gesture that parallels this reflex, Katherine Hayles, in a piece titled "Computing the Human," raises the issue of how the future of the machine–human nexus is calculated, at a moment in which, clearly, the commodity of the numbingly proposed variants of "futures" seems at its derivative height (the word appears thirty-two times in the essay). And she concludes with a certain "we" retaining control over this outcome: "The crucial point suggested by my analysis is simply this: our future will be what we collectively make it" (2005, 148). She adds that the future should show social justice toward the new "intelligent machines" that will arrive, embedding the whole in 1990s liberal sensibilities and, of course, *ethics*: "their futures too cannot be envisioned apart from the primary concern for ethics that should drive these discussions" (19). The vacuum into which this conversation has evolved—as if the sovereign deciders of this generous inclusion were represented by some generalized "we" immersed in a natural linear development of technologies—is numbing. It appears entirely formalistic and cut off from everything that digital acceleration is wired to today (the interface with hyperconsumption, technogenocides, psychotropic spells). Of course, a quite sizeable majority of humans would be cut out of this high-end enterprise, given over to the oil and water wars, agricultural collapse, mass-extinction events, and "population culling" often predicted by century's end—as if our imminently controllable future resolved into whether we treat our new machinal cousins as other than new slaves (or masters, because that possibility is implied).

I call this reflex a *technophilic technophobia* that often accompanies "new-media studies." Indeed, the task of recentering the human potentially repeats or mirrors this premise and seems contaminated in advance. For instance, if the "human" were to have been generated from the technicities that it claims, itself a *Nachkonstruktion*, then to stand apart from this backlooping technogenesis and claim to master it linguistically appears an almost machinal reflex. It necessarily produces an entirely prosthetic semantic *regurgitant*, something like a *promise* to which various contents can be interchangeably attached. This perpetual reassertion of the "human" is, then, the most machinal of products. In order to outbid itself and make up for a perpetual shortfall, it inversely accelerates, however, the very trajectory that would guarantee its disappearance (species extinction) in the reassertion of propertied selves, hyperconsumption, ideologies of interiority. At its more exposed it can resemble the psychotic appropriations of megabanks. But what interests me is something else: where such a discussion fits into broader twenty-first-century horizons and cognitive blinds than are usually implied by the rather clinical and baroque phrase *ubiquitous computation*. The discussion must also be read as if back *from* these implicated horizons, however, if the question itself and the conversations around "new media" are not to be wholly anodyne or self-immunized. The emerging materialities we reference to the place-holder term *climate change* can be indexed today not to "nature," environment, and such entrapping metaphorics, but to biotechnic crises and anorganic process. The latter already imply an irreversible disappearance of "life as we know it" (a certain "we"), of life forms and lifeworlds, and, by some calculations, of humans. Of course, there is nothing apocalyptic about such implications, which, if they are "anthropogenic" (a flattering term, attesting to the human's sovereignty even in suicide and hence misleading), are irreducibly banal and indifferent to humans, forms of force outside any "sovereignty," chemical processes, shifts in biomass.

There have been and will be innumerable extinctions, the thinking of which today arrives as a positive catalyst bound to the term "anthropocene." And this perspective is in fact countered or deferred by "posthuman" imaginaries that often appear in fact regressive or constitutive of the very thing they would be "post" to. Thus the rhetoric of the "posthuman" quickly devolved from Nietzschean speculation to how to extend the individual life in a synbiotic mode (the scientist's indefinite extension of the "present"). Stiegler's nanomutation is, in effect, the obverse of Kurzweil's "singularity," applied to the orders of perception, mnemonics, conceptual organization, *noopolitical* agency. It passes not through the nanoengineering of cells and organs but the nanological materialities of inscriptions.

What is interesting to note, perhaps, is that the hermeneutic reflexes noted earlier by which a home, entity, identity, or "human" is formalized from a void semantic after-effect are not divorced from this accelerating disappearance, nor could they be. These reflexes seem only accelerated by cognitive rituals of *re*centering and *re*mastering the *re*assertion that is in question, which itself wants to *re*store a home, an interior, a corporate sovereignty indissociable from hyperconsumption, eating, the obese bodies at American airports today. Such a reimposition of *meaning* occurs after some interruption inversely allied with technics here, as a repetition or recentering. It permits "new media" to trend toward retrohumanisms more part of academic temperament than the world whose domain it "ubiquitously" claims. Nonetheless, today's "new-media" critic would, of course, be too sophisticated to merely reenact some repetition of the *theory wars* of a previous generation—that is, by defending the home from the sophist, the machine, the mutation, this time in the name of objectalized information ("data") instead of eternal humanist verities ("content"). Such a rehearsal would only end up, after all, in the bizarre spectacle of a precritical or pre-Heideggerian notion of technics itself as tool, indexing "new media" to Husserlian or existential phenomenology.

I turn briefly to a counterexample to this entire program in Bernard Stiegler, or what I called a very *small* corner of his work. The example deals with the problem of inscriptions and mnemotechnics in advance of any sentient positionality ascribable to binarized models and does so by finding the interface of the organic and inorganic in such materialities. Although I have no time to account for Stiegler's immensely broad and complex project, we may code it obversely to how the "human" was coded in my opening—that is, as a thinking of technics without reserve. In question is an essay that speculates on the obverse of the specter of ubiquitous computation as something to be recentered, managed, sequestered within in a way that often parallels the requirement of a pure intentionality. In "Nanomutations, Grammaticisation, *Hypomnemata*" (Stiegler 2006), the Greek *hypomnemata* derives from Plato and might also be translated as "inscriptions." That is, it might be heard as the preoriginary marks or settings from which a tribal or epochal consciousness derives, out of which "world" is generated. Stiegler speculates on a parallel development to the future promises of nanotechnicology and its implications for *mnemotechnics*. This piece speculates on the a reinscription of the mnemonic and cognitive orders altogether. Such a nanomutation becomes for Stiegler a figure of "the unthinkable," since man's perceptual and cognitive settings stand to be reconfigured. Such can occur only by a simultaneous altering of the technologies of memory (and what Stiegler calls "technologies of the spirit"), which presents a counterstroke to accelerating *disindividuation* and *grammaticization*.

Stiegler identifies the era of an implicitly nihilist monotheism not with that of "the Book" but with the cognitive and grammatical features of *alphabeticism*—thereby marking what precedes and exceeds such a Western parenthesis (marks, digital algorhythms). To the degree that digital logics precede any one form of writing and can coalesce from points or marks (or pixels), they do not just reference computational cyberspace but can be said to have preceded hieroglyphics themselves all along. The prospect of nanomutation is conceived as a micrological event that, projected, would imply a transformation that would, necessarily, read the "present" back otherwise (and perhaps erase its mnemonic premises in the process). Thus it resists *disindividuation* and, in its way, accords with a more general sense, today, of inhabiting "unsustainable" and criminal systems (a "growth" economy, depleting resources, e.g., water or oil, mass extinctions) that would be artificially sustained for yet a while longer (the "sovereign debt" crisis, so called). And this mutation of mnemotechnics would occur in a perceptual and epistemo-political domain that would necessarily erase the "present" that proposed it as beyond itself. It is said to imply a transformation of *transindividuation*. Stiegler should not be heard, of course, as miming or directing us to Gilbert Simondon so much as weaponizing the latter's concepts before twenty-first-century horizons. To speculate on or with this, Stiegler recurs to what underlies mnemotechnics as a system of inscriptions. Two things interest me here: (1) where Stiegler identifies a nonsite he terms *hypomnemata*, out of which perceptual and cognitive programs would be generated (mnemotechnics); and (2) where this logic interrupts a certain anthropo-political circuit to conjure the "organization of the inorganic," which places the narrative of the socius in constant relation to multiplaned temporalities (psychomorphic, biomorphic, geomorphic). Here Simondon is not merely revived but made simultaneously into a rhetorical pivot or *front*.

Stiegler understands technics always also as mnemotechnics ("technics as memory worlds [*fait monde*]" (2006). He apprehends a pantechnicity from which the "human" is perpetually artefacted, destroyed, or hosted. The logics of nanomutation implies an epistemo-mnemonic "transformation" that cannot be tracked because it would erase its own mnemonic premise or map—and to some extent one witnesses this underway in Stiegler's writing. As such it is an affirmative postcatastrophic thought.

Suarez's *Daemon* is concerned with preserving what can be called the human within a double catastrophics. As programmed by the ghosted Matthew Sobol, the Daemon program that functions as if it were an "organism" would indifferently sacrifice millions to save billions and would take down a telefeudal system that has produced a socius of zombie consumers, a system irreversibly destined to enslave and eviscerate human and terrestrial life—the sixth mass-extinction event of species, resource wars, population culling, and so on. The Daemon first appears as a malign and inhuman agency, a rogue product of *ubiquitous* digitalization. But it turns against a disindividuating and corporate telecratic order controlled by the very few. The latter is ubiquitous, turns humans into blind pawns whose sacrificeable order is consumed by vortices of the "short term," and entails future terrestrial and population collapse. What the Daemon destroys, therefore, are already dehumanized "humans" (controlled, pacified) in the name of recentering a possible human future. Under this regime, we might say, what recognizes itself as the "human" to begin with is under attack, like those who would retain mastery before the specter of ubiquitous computation (a.k.a, "*sheer* technics") yet unwittingly accelerate the disappearance of what they try to hold onto as property: the "human." What is the critical corollary of a daemon of technics that would *not* robotically return, again and again, to this doomed reassertion of a human centeredness (anthropocentrism), one that only accelerates a suicidal totalization?

The Mnemopolitical Sublime

Nanomutation is in a sense the micrological dream of *mnemotechnics*—what might also be termed an "organization of the inorganic" out of whose *inscriptive regimes* worlding and cognition, telecratic spells, and consumption are shaped. (And not just for man because one can indifferentially apply its premise proactively to DNA, "evolution," photosynthesis, "life" as effect, and so on—not to render memory organic, but the opposite—to read "nature" through mnemotechnics, as Benjamin did, or the random technogenesis of what is today tepidly labeled *biosemiosis.*) Stiegler takes Derridean technics, assumes its totalization, and then loops that back through Simondon's transindividual processual sociotechnic mappings. This circling back to a precursor that precedes Jacques Derrida (or Michel Foucault or Gilles Deleuze), scatters Oedipalizing traps and then folds back yet again, explicitly in this essay, to supplement Simondon with a "trace" agency. The embedded *supplement* that Stiegler brings to Simondon in "Nanomutations"—called *hypomnemata*—promises "a new reading of the questions handled by these thinkers from a Simondonian vantage and in the shadow of his limitations" (2006).

Such a trajectory involves a sheer *exteriorization*, which is indexed to inscriptions themselves: "the analysis of *hypomnemata* as a writing of the self, i.e., as the political modality of psychic individuation—always already passing through an exteriority" (2006). This permanent exteriority opens what Stiegler calls a certain "convergence":

> A thinking of nanomutations, insofar as they designate a process leading to the convergence of technologies of matter, information and living entities, and as a potential of grammatisation, is what brings to the fore technics and technology 1) as structural factors of historical, protohistorical and prehistorical mutations in general (inasmuch as they form systems which are also processes of technical individuation interacting with the processes of psychic and collective individuation, and periodically upsetting them), and 2) as the basis of largely outstanding and "nanomutant" problems posed by what we call, without actually knowing very well what is meant by the term, the nanotechnologies—and this "not very well" is one of the questions overdetermining them all. (2006)

Yet Stiegler does not claim this technic of inscription as a transductive *portal* to the inorganic ("the organised inorganic matter whereby the milieu in which psychic and social individuals who themselves are nothing but meta-stable, can stabilise itself" [2006]). Nor does he expand on a nanomutation technically tied (and not) to new-media forms. Instead, he shifts away from the representational point of disappearance of the nanomutation, taking on a legitimately tragic and atopic gesture of the collective, the social matrix, the "we": "what must follow upon the mechanalogical project as a new thought of the otium (and of an otium of the people)" (2006).

Why turn from Simondon's promise of a processual sociotechnics to the thankless nonsite of inscriptions, or *hypomnemata*? The latter are, after all, very small and by definition precede phenomenality as such, so they have no face or identificatory aura? The term *hypomnemata* derives from Platonic usage, as in the *Protagoras*, which references children learning letters in their copybooks—that is, a non-site of originary imprinting on the formal, here alphabetical, level. (Stiegler cites Foucault as a source for isolating the term *hypomnemata*, but its subtext remains Derridean.) Any nanomutation precedes and exceeds the regime of alphabeticism as well as the era of monotheistic nihilism that is of "the Book": "What Simondon cannot see is that technics as memory worlds [*fait monde*]: he doesn't understand that technics, as epiphylogenesis and networking of tertiary retentions, constitutes the preindividual ground of non-vital individuation which psychosocial individuation is" (2006). This is said to occur with "the convergence of technologies of matter, information, and living entities," which are subject in turn to a new thinking of "nanomutation," of "the problem of thought" and the "unthinkable" on today's horizon: "The role of *hypomnesis* and the *hypomnemata* in the constitution of forms of knowledge as well as power is what Simondon's philosophy allows us to think and what that philosophy fails to think through" (2006).[3]

Of course, "*the* human" in a radical sense does not exist, has never had a single designate, and the term *human* names a cognitive phantom, even the structure of a shared hermeneutic reflex or relapse. And what this word pretends to name becomes an incrustation, the defense of a *Nachkonstruktion*, such as the promise of a coincidence with sheer intentionality. And because it is a metaphor that depends for its production on mnemotechnics, language, the only possible site of intervention within a runaway and perhaps suicidal totalization—as in the Daemon's totalizing networks of cybercontrol—would be where such inscriptions may be initialized. That is what Stiegler names *hypomnemata*.

To the degree that *public space* in the telemorphic present occurs in the placeless media streams or screens themselves, any "politics" before such totalization must put its premises irreversibly in the position of a fault, blind, or death drive. Such politics occurs in the cognitive, epistemographic, mnemotechnic, and ideational spheres as a reinitializing or mutation. And it can only begin as a resistance by evading a prescribed hermeneutic relapse that seems itself more or less automated within memory formation and grammaticization. If any nanotechnology remains for the "present" an allegorical prospect ("without actually knowing very well what is meant by the term"), nanomutation is the penultimate dream or implied logic of a thinking of sheer technics. This logic begins as a disclosure of the sheer exteriority of all at the expense of the figure of any binarized exterior—and hence interiority. What we call *meaning*, like the consumption (or eating) that its formations resemble, produces the phantoms of "interiority" that seem like property to defend or recenter.

In the essay in question, Stiegler's appropriately cunning reanimation of Simondon's holistic sociotechnics appears *also* as a front, a technic itself, a *proschema* (to cite the *Protagoras* again, a term that translates as "screen" or "a precession of figure itself"). Supplementing Derrida and in turn supplemented by the latter, Stiegler's "Simondon" functions as a curious substitute and place holder for yet another interdicted proper name. For Stiegler, in ways seemingly diffuse, a Nietzschean connection often looms behind Simondon, including a discursive machine of attack that exceeds any narrative of the socius alone in the direction of a conception of "life" inclusive of the inorganic. But Simondon is *not* Nietzsche and may even be quite antipodal to

Nietzsche (given the seemingly incompatible motifs of transduction for Simondon and will for Nietzsche). This antipodal relation lends shading and dissonance to the discourses of "individuation" (a concept we may find in early usage in *The Birth of Tragedy*, but with different implications wired to the "aesthetic" and the genealogy of media). Simondon, in an approach more sophisticated than autopoeisis or systems theory, still suggests the phantom of a sociopsychic totality of sorts, a great brain or Gaia effect. He is void of Nietzsche's affirmative *cruelty*, celebration of loss and non-production, totalized suspicion of the "cultural" image or "we"—the Dionysiac effect, so to speak, as an antinature, the very locus of a *technic of technics* that disputes "process" as narrative. When Nietzsche refers to "festive cruelty" in the *Genealogy*, it is an anti-Simondon move (i.e., antiorganicist, antiecological); before there are forces that enter into relation (violence of one body on another), there is a violence not yet relational. This move elicits a faux overlaying of the two thinkers, as Stiegler points out:

> Today, however, God is dead—Simondon names this event the loss of individuation—and the sky is now only the infinity of emptiness. No more angels, no more gods. Nor demons. But *on* the earth, the loss of individuation has become horribly still worse: you no longer have to assumpt to heaven to fall in such a way even Faust could not have imagined. Although the sky is no longer the other world of the earth, and God dead, the factor of disindividuation is more active than ever—and this factor, called the death instinct, is what, when the idea of Heavens was still around, was called the devil. This is the way of the earth—the reign of generalised dis-individuation, which is also a generalised proletarianisation—because the technologies of the latest stage of grammatisation have been hegemonically socialised as technologies of control. Cybernetics, but more widely, the technologies of industrial temporal objects, of which cybernetics is but a part, today diluted in my estimation, in the convergence of telecommunications, form the industry of technologies of control at the origin of a process of generalised dis-individuation, at the level of the psychic individual as consumer as well as that of collective individuals destroyed by the world-wide organisation of consumption by techniques of marketing whose aim is the elimination of any form of singularity, which as such is incalculable and therefore irreducible to the models of investment that the financierisation of planetary capitalism imposes. (2006)

There appears a pulsion in Stiegler toward a rhetoric of the collective, which one might mistake for a weak messianic thread. In fact, it registers Stiegler's hyperbolic self-invention—from the reading scene and Platonic cave of a prison. Thus, the trace behind Simondon of a certain interdicted "Nietzsche" is perhaps even more relevant to this text. Although the term *hypomnema* is taken from Plato, the word translating it, *inscription*, has seemed to recirculate first from the narrative of mnemotechnics in Nietzsche's *Genealogy of Morals*. It is a very small point—the smallest, nanographic. And it is impossible to locate because one is produced by it discursively, the blind at the heart of a historical episode, the "unthinkable." But here Stiegler's mobilized constellations brush against a transductive interface where nonanthropic or inorganic dynamics arise, impinge on, and lace "human" constructedness with a "materiality" irrecoverable to cognitive orders.

The logics of nanomutation appears all along implied in Stiegler's writing: "The great transformation of these terms, inasmuch as they are constituted only through the relation they form, begins with the advent of machines as a stage in the process of grammaticization" (2006). Here Stiegler doubles or folds back again because the *mutation* is itself presented as contingent, referenced to yet another dependency on teletechnic or media forms, potentially grim: "Only under the conditions of a transindividuation of the new forms of *hypomnesis* that are the technologies of control can a new form of individuation happen" (2006). The premise of a nanomutation has as much destructiveness as not and may be diverted into, say, a faux "transindividuation" constructed by state prosthetics.

Where do *hypomnemata*—which might, in fact, rather be called *hypermnemata*--open onto "the organised inorganic matter whereby the milieu in which psychic and social individuals who themselves are nothing but meta-stable, can stabilise itself" (2006)? The *hypomnemata* are invoked as an interdicted "unthinkable," a stem cell of *mnemotechnic* orders. If current planetary accelerations expose the status quo ante of discourse formations and hyperconsumption as quasi-suicidal, as producing a version of "man" that appears self-extincting, then man's reassertion as center before a ubiquitous telecratic swarm (or any other) risks promoting the opposite effect.

Inscriptions, of course, are not like chairs and cars. They cannot be touched or handled or seen. They stand apart from the totalizing cognitive and referential systems they chiasmically generate. They can appear attached to seemingly historical and textual *events*—often giving rise, by inversion, to the very ideologemes they performatively undo (Plato's so-called Platonism and so on). These ideologemes may emanate as communal memory, may simulate laws, or may represent neural habits refined in the prehistories of hunter-gatherer bipeds. The association of the *eye* with tracking movement, with cinematics, and with *reading* itself sublimates a hunter-gatherer's programming of visibility with the tracking of food and differentially defines the "senses" and the body's attention—readily captured by telemarketing streams today.

Yet, as a result, any posited nanomutation, particularly as an event to come, in fact has no *one* time: it can appear ongoing, be backdated.

Stiegler loops back incessantly as regards his chosen terms, preceding the canonizations of each, marking each as prosthetic and instrument again. This postdeconstructive acceleration, in which one has entered a postbinarized set of horizons, might confuse a literalist or first-time reader. Such a writing may not only *reinitialize* Plato otherwise but also implicitly break Derrida's perceived ban on invoking the futural in order to keep open the to come or to stage a pathos of undecidability. One must develop a *transductive* ear for a paraconceptual writing that posits a "great transformation of these terms" (2006) and that, to put all on the table in terms of the historical blinds of human modernities, returns to Platonic figures—just as self, soul, spirit, or telos themselves appear reinitialized as technics.[4] Here the term *transductivity* describes conceptual figures no longer locked in artificed binaries: "Transductivity means the propagation of an operation between two terms constituted as terms by the operation itself" (2006). This transductive (un)binding also solicits twenty-first-century horizons that Derrida uniquely omits from his repertoire, for whom there is no mention of what we call "climate change," the biomorphic and geomorphic orders of catastrophic acceleration as such ("the organization"—or, one may today add, disarticulation—"of the inorganic"). Nor is there such a mention in Simondon, Marx, Freud, Husserl ("this is why Marx must be criticised with Simondon and Simondon with the late Husserl" [2006]). Stiegler presents the dilemma of a dissolving referential order, a movement before and beyond the nihilism of Western monotheism, as contrived by alphabeticism and the "era of the Book" (or its hydrocarbon feeding frenzy). Thus, Stiegler's essay invokes "Earth" on several occasions but situates the scene of thought "in between" Earth and heaven, without interior, in a sense the *aterrestrial* logic of the *techné*. This does not preclude inorganic and biomorphic systems or the circuitry of mnemonics (media, language): "Mnemotechnics . . . will be at the origin of monotheism by trans-formation of the epiphylogenetic into the *hypomnesic strictu sensu*, into hieroglyphic and ideogrammatical writing, then into alphabetical writing the absence of which would make the religions of the book inconceivable" (2006).

When Stiegler turns to the final material referent or host, an *earth* (a Nietzschean evocation), it is not natural but as a nonsite suspended in the rift between sky and Earth, without interiority. Again: "Nothing is left underground. Everything plays itself out *between* heaven and earth. What is affirmed, then, is the distinction between *otium* and *negotium*, precisely because there is a world and because it is desacralised: monotheism is a desacralisation of the world and simultaneously a separation of orders into two worlds" (2006). This "in between" is not of Earth nor of heaven yet is fully exteriorized and without interiority or refuge. The underworld is also emptied—an "in between" that, at the cusp of a foreclosure, will have to do with writing: "The earth becomes then this place from which one contemplates the sky but *while writing down what transpires there*. And the subterranean region where the spirits of the dead has disappeared: the hell of Hades, which lends its name to the Greek *aidos*, is no longer underground" (2006). No more secrets—of a sort, except broadly for the implications of this unreserved exteriority for the manufacture of "interiorities," homelands, *oikos*, the relapse, the "human." Such a trajectory involves a sheer *exteriorization* indexed, first of all, to *inscription* effects out of which perception and discourse organize themselves as subject to capture, programming, telemarketing, the promise of commodity "interiorities."[5]

Anorganologies

Can one blame the text here from veering a bit from this irreversible logic—say, conjuring with Simondonian moves a phantom "we" to come that is continuous yet counters *disindividuation* and *grammaticization* or diverts their import? After all, *inscriptions* promise no contact or personification and lead toward a zone of an "organization of the *inorganic*" that has no charisma for the socius (and draws faux deconstructive ire, as we will observe). The question arises at the moment that the twenty-first century itself opens from the history of human-on-human struggle toward nonanthropic agencies, alternative timelines, and *other materialities*—that is, the era not of "9/11," which was quickly turned into a front, but what we will call, in a different metrics of calendricality, *climate change*? This question persists at a time when "deconstruction" has entered its autoimmune phase (Derrideanism) and a return to Husserl appears an ostrichlike reflex. Any literalization of Simondon would perpetually misread his "limits" and veer from "the possibility of which these forms of *hypomnemata* open, making possible the instauration of a new relation between the psychic, the collective and the technical having become techno-logical" (2006).

After all, if *inscriptions* represent a precession of phenomenality or worlding and appear parallel to a logics of *nanotechnics* (which *digitalization* only tropes), they also arrive as a supercession or precession of the "era of the Book" and alphabeticism. In raising the issue of *hypomnemata* at this site, Stiegler circles back and brushes against a yet undeveloped grotto of Derrida's work—what Derrida will conjure as a nonsite and logics of *khora*, where, before any phenomenality, the *preinscriptions* out of which worlds derive are erased or supplanted.

After citing a passage of Simondon's that allegorizes reaching a mountain top and communing with its *real*—a trope of anthropic mastery—Stiegler speculates:

> There comes a time when it is not longer a question of climbing the mountain, but actually of contemplating the stars, and of gazing at this sky in which the great empire and the polytheistic "religions" would see gods, these stars themselves, these heavenly bodies, this sky in which, later, the proto-monotheism of Plato and Aristotle, and the monotheisms of Judaism, then that of Paul of Tarsus, will affirm the great divide between heaven and earth. (2006)

Stiegler hails a telecratic "earth" on several occasions, and the opening ricochets to the other polarity of nonanthropic life, the nanological orders preceding the "era of the Book." This direction is the opposite of any return to the face of the other, the otherness of the other, or even the *wholly other* in the ironized or faux-Levinasian dossier of "late Derrida." It approaches what has no place in a "biopolitical" model and what contemporary thought has so much trouble conceptualizing—a *force without sovereignty* that entirely displaces and disregards, yet interacts with, the "anthropocene" or hydrocarbon era.

The phantom of nanomutation remains the dream and Hades of a thinker of pure technics, outside of trope, phenomenality, or legibility, yet entirely and irredeemably anchored to the disclosure of the ass's skin of twenty-first-century horizons: the "unthought." The essay thus weaves between the mutations of hyperindustrial capital, a coming of nanotechnic transformation, the histories of monotheism and script, and grammaticization, but two moves dominate. The first is the "supplement" given to Simondon, and the second is the irresistible phantom of nanomutation itself. If there is any doubt that the graphemic supplement alters "Simondon" entirely, the manner in which *grammaticization* is deployed accounts for and has taken over the body in the same way: "The process of grammaticisation, with the dawn of the industrial revolution, suddenly surpasses the sphere of language—one wants to say that the same thing happened to the sphere of logos—and invades the sphere of the body" (2006).

Mutation occurs when long-installed regimes of organization exceed themselves, do not adapt, and enter a death roll. One seems to address or invoke it only in extremis, particularly because the prospect of nanomutation has the capacity to alter any recognition of the "present" itself as new memory bands and perceptual markings coalesce. It suggests an intangible, prephenomenal nonsite (because it precedes our own production) that shapes what are called "phenomenality," "reference," "speed," "visibility," "organicity," and the "technologies of the spirit." *Hypomnemata* would be more radically inorganic than "the inorganic" as such (that is, as concept) because they permeate and are altered by the organic ("anthropogenic 'global warming'"): they make of the organic itself an effect anything but *organicist* and position its occurrence under a broader trajectory of "life," extinction arcs, autoevisceration. It would seem that it was the metaphorics of the "home" that all along was the chief destroying premise. Unlike the systemic relapse to a phantasmal nostalgia or nonexistent "human" marked earlier, Stiegler gambles on a transformation that might not be recognized from within its occurrence. The recoil of *re*centering the "human" occurs before this greater anxiety buried amid phantasms of cyborg revolt or their incorporation to the family of man (Hayles 1999, 2005). That is, the entirety of the "familiar" as such, of what is "ours," whose temple is semantics and what Stiegler calls "cognitive capital," would irreversibly mutate and become unrecognizable to what emerges from contemporary telecracies and accelerations.

Here one encounters a policing effect. In our self-disarticulating twenty-first century, it accelerates the very thing it would defer or guard against—its own disappearance. The latter's defense of *interiorities*, of recentering the "human," appears tied to maintenance of the nonexistent and hence to hyperconsumption (and eating outright). The claimed *re*stitution is linked to the desire to *retain* that resonates with a broader network of zombied effects today, both in critical thought and in broader political formations (zombie banks, zombie politics, and so on). This policing instinct can be witnessed in Stiegler's own reception. In a useful examination of this, Ulrik Ekman

(2007) nonetheless interrupts his analysis of Stiegler's resistance to binary maps to characterize instead an "oscillation" between "asymmetrical binaries" in his work that is incapable of being resolved into standard philosophemes.[6] And yet if Stiegler writes to a postbinarized horizon that is a peculiarly twenty-first-century experience, the anestheticizing effects of disindividuation or telecratic capture must increasingly be anticipated and written toward. At issue is not so much an "oscillation" as an episode of postbinarized thought. Thus the attempt to contain or manage what cannot really be called an "oscillation" takes two forms, the critical Scylla and Charybdis that Stiegler must apparently navigate. These are apparent alternately in the "deconstructive" recoil (Geoff Bennington [2000]) and the "phenomenological" recoil (Mark Hansen).

Ekman notes the particular "acidity" of Bennington's assault, which was followed by other Derrideans at the time. The appearance of a Derridean swarm sent out from an imaginary mother ship to discipline and return the faux prodigal, chastened, is complicated by Stiegler's difference. And it is turned into a self-Oedipalizing symptomatic much as, as in the second case, it becomes a specular trap. Mark Hansen is a specialist in "new media" and theory whose "own fidelities," Ekman remarks, are "to a re-ontologized existential phenomenology (Merleau-Ponty) in dialogue with Deleuze's thought of sensation, affect and the cinematic image" (58). In any case, there is no space in such an agenda for the unreserved pantechnics that Stiegler represents, so the instinct will be to delegitimize. Both critiques rely on policing gestures that return to the authority of proper names. In each, Stiegler is deemed to misread a master text (Derrida, Husserl) and would then be returned to them, and each concludes that in not doing so he evinces a retrohumanism rather than the opposite. The rhetoric is that of delegitimation in both cases, preemption. In the first case, the contemporary relapse of après-Derrida "deconstruction" into recuperative, exegetical normativity has demonstrated a misliteralization of the conceit of legacy (as extension, as repetition, as lineage, as capital rather than, as not only Nietzsche might have it, as forgetting and transformation). In the second case, when Hansen assumes the role of anti*theory* theorist, he would police "new media" by returning it to precritical hermeneutic positions—whether called the experiential *we* or body, Merleau-Ponty, Husserl, and so on.[7] There is a sort of *Stiegler effect* here, where Hansen's resistance to being ciphered in the terms he reinitializes has the effect of exposing the rhetorical premises of those assuming their canonical authority. Deconstruction's autoimmune and faux Oedipal moment becomes visible, as does the bad faith of the "return to Husserl" from within "new-media" regimes. Hansen—who adopts generally the policing stance mentioned earlier—appears, as Gilbert and Sullivan would have it, the very model of the modern *philotechnic technophobe.*

Ekman suspends the critical battles diplomatically and turns instead to what he sees as Stiegler's primary contribution: "My suggestion is that the great, largely unread, reserve in Stiegler's important work resides in the reactualization of Simondon" (2007, 58). Yet before we start to say "back to Simondon" or decide that Stiegler is a retro-humanist who misreads Simondon, one must repeat that in Stiegler a supplemented "Simondon" is also to an important degree a *front*.

The irony of the rehumanism in new-media theory, its philotechnic blind, is not that it sees itself as "posthuman." It is not that what we call "*the* human" appears all along the metaphor not of a being, but of a hermeneutic reaction formation that occurs within (disindividuating) discourse in order to formalize its defense. Nor is it that a bizarre return to crypto-organicist models seems entrenched in the outposts of "new-media" theory as an academic field. The irony is that, though virtually nonexistent, the "human's" reassertions of semantic sovereignty today collude with a suicidal if robotic inertia. In a remote channeling of Nietzsche, one can say that the logic of nanomutation recalls that "man" still hangs in the balance—that "we" are in a prehistory still whose suicidal reflexes and relapses appear discretely totalizing. Perhaps one might wish to see today a book titled *How We Remained Prehuman* because it seems prehuman to assume one is posthuman for trying to consolidate, extend, and recover a "human" interiority that never existed as such. The "new-media" pioneers are often in this regard more of the "era of the Book" than ever. This conclusion is hinted at, too, in the *apocalypticism* that threads the conversation. As Stiegler knows, what is now happening to "the earth" is not apocalyptic (or even nonapocalyptic as the deconstruction of "apocalypse"); it does not occur in a flash or under the sign of any redemption narrative; it is not of phenomenology; it is banal, micrological, processual, irreversible, "material," without personification, a disorganization of the (in) organic. Where the imaginary of public space is defined today not by place but by telestreams and screens themselves, any "politics" to come would be, first of all, within mnemotechnics themselves, a "politics of memory," cognitive, epistemographic, anecotechnic. And it must begin by dodging a hermeneutic relapse by which what calls itself the "human" is more or less mechanically contrived. This *relapse* today takes many forms and has its own parallels to Barack Obama's restitution of "Wall Street" or, say, Copenhagen. One finds these twentieth-century hangovers in new-media phenomenologies, in the reflexive moralisms of the Left, and in the autoimmune cast of what today calls itself "deconstruction"—a sort of deconstruction without deconstruction.

If Derrida all but uniquely (for him) omitted *any* address of twenty-first-century climate change, if one must disregard Derrida's misliteralized ban against the calculation of addressing "futures"—well, then one question is whether Stiegler's wager on a *worldly* totalization of technics alters this archival circuit? Rather than reigning him back, one might want to fill in the numerous interstices to press Stiegler to the implications of his wager. Of critical writers, he seems best positioned for the necessary failure of this strike. And as someone who is scrupulous about taking from Derrida limited and marked goods, he might not want inadvertently to repeat Derrida in the unique way in which the latter miscalculated—turning to the seductive aporia of ethics and weak messianism rather than to the nonsite, indicated by the term *khora*, that *inscriptions* would be given space (or erased), out of which mnemonic and perceptual programs are as if generated.

The *philotechnic technophobia* that gives rise to fables of human replacement by its inventions or that activates hermeneutic reaction formations as defense (*back* to Merleau-Ponty?) mimes a greater problem: the fear that the alteration of inscriptions against which cognition is normatized might erase the entirety of the "familiar" as such, of what is invested as "ours" yet which simultaneously consumes futures in a general Ponzi scheme of the artifacted term *human* itself—which has become capital, a derivative whose paper contracts would be preserved.

Thus, Ekman attributes to Stiegler a certain "technophobia," by which he means that Stiegler is alert to the destructive implications of hypertechnics. This awareness absorbs a Heideggerian trace, of course, but it is hardly a matter of being for or against in an era of accelerating extinctions. In contrast, Ekman recommends Paul Virilio and Friedrich Kittler as having gone further in integrating "scientific knowledge" (2007, 11). Yet it may be that the latter offers, on the contrary, more salve to the technophilic imaginary, particularly when drawing "ubiquitous computation," as we might again deploy the term, into familiar apocalyptic rhetorics that strangely comfort. It turns out that the impulse of relapse is infinitely inventive, like metaphysics itself (which we now know never existed as such, but which was only perpetually invented as the effect of this hermeneutic relapse itself). The theotropic strain dies hard, and Ekman's hoped-for scientism raises another red flag. The philotechnic technophobia that recurs in Friedrich Kittler appears as the residue of an "era of the Book" even or especially when that residue takes the form of mourning that era's fetishized (or imaginary) death. Kittler's *apocalyptic* script recalls the theological battles waged over the digital:

> Before the end, something is coming to an end. The general digitalization of channels and information erases the differences among individual media. Sound and image, voice and text are reduced to surface effects, known to consumers as interface. Sense and the senses turn into eyewash. Their media-produced glamour will survive for an interim as a by-product of strategic programs. Inside the computers themselves everything becomes number: quantity without image, sound, or voice. And once optical fiber networks turn formerly distinct data flows into a standardized series of digitalized numbers, everything goes. Modulation, transformation, synchronization; delay, storage, transposition; scrambling, scanning, mapping—a total media link on a digital base will erase the very concept of medium. (1999, 1–2)

This is a variant of the *panic* effect that the digital imaginary induces, in which "the very concept of medium" erases itself in the name of "new" media. This panic at first gives some support to any willed project to recenter the *human* in and before this prospect. Yet Kittler seems to think one can arrive at pure medium, though it would necessarily then not be a medium. This view can seem a flipside of a humanism that wants to return and restore the message to sender. Kittler momentarily eliminates senders and receivers, as though text could now liberate itself from reading effects. Moreover, *the* digital as a logic has never *not* been there; it is virtually "older" than hieroglyphics or letteration—that is, it is not just a decomposition or recomposition of analogic mythemes that include the mytheme of the analogic (retroactively coded as originary or presence, suggests Rodowick [2001]). Like the "human." It is not accidental that the term *posthumanist* has shifted its sense over time from suggesting a canceled ontological contract to the promise of nanotechnologies to prolong individual lives and bodies by decades, if not indefinitely, without death or necessary reproduction. That is, it has devolved to meaning the infinite extension of the present. It is equally curious that the limits of sophistication in "new-media" theorization remain in too many essentials of "era of the Book." Like the comforting apocalyptics in Kittler.

But nanomutation has no date—it can, perhaps must, already be an echo of an implied logic or occurrence, rather than a waited-for to come. If so, it would be the "unthinkable" in another sense, as what is invoked to read against the relapses and pharmacological impasses of a zombied "present" caught, it seems, in an accelerated backloop or tempophagic vortex. The thought of nanomutation lies, in this sense, in concert with the logics adhering to the term "anthropocene."

Notes

1. One can translate the term *ubiquitous computation*, for instance, as a *figure* of hyperindustrial capitalism turned upon itself and unmoored, as when a market collapse is triggered by bot-buying swarms.

2. From Dictionary.com at http://dictionary.reference.com/browse/ubiquity.

3. The supplement of *hypomnemata* is associated with Derridean thought: "Now, Derrida, the reader of *Phaedrus*, will show that knowledge is itself and always already difference, i.e., an economy of the trace, i.e., a *tekhnē*: a logic of the supplement, and to that extent a *hypomnesis*" (Stiegler 2006).

4. The vertigo of a perpetually preoriginary or protoconceptual writing leaves cited and reactivated terms in Stiegler unmarked, shifting registers or reinitialized by processual contexts. His reclamation of Platonic and theotropic pivots can leave the philosophical reader befuddled by his own associations—soul as psyche or, in "The Teleologics of the Snail," telos itself: "This telos, which fell into such ill report at the end of the era of rationalization and of the disenchantment of the world (in the second half of the twentieth century), is structurally underhanded [*retors*]. . . . [D]eprived of telos by telos, it becomes a threatening power, for example, as a telecracy undermining democracy" (chapter 29 in this volume). Stiegler is never less "retrohumanist" than when he mobilizes figures such as self, care, soul, and "the technologies of the spirit."

5. That is, the promise of restoring what had not existed—say, "the" human—and doing so by way of consumption, cognitive relapse, eating more, ingesting and storing an outside. We know, perhaps, that a (dis)organization of the organic–inorganic takes place around *carbon*, whose tropological misalliance with scriptive forms of "materiality" cannot be ignored—particularly when the former circles back, as energy extraction, to platform the entirety of the hyperindustrial (and digital) acceleration.

6. According to Ekman, "Stiegler is important today precisely because of this more or less aporetic oscillation of speed between the (quasi-)transcendental and the (quasi-)empirical" (2007, 60).

7. Hansen's argumentation may typically presume that the technical information he purveys about a recent media technology overrides that of his opponent (or reader, who may not be up on that information) and registers its own authority as the *most recent*—that is, the newest of the "new" (see Hanson 2004). In this way, *new* and *old* become reversible ideologemes (itself an old reversal). In lesser hands than Hansen's, this approach might drift into a *technofetishism* that supplants *data* for the place of an older tradition of hermeneutic "meaning," the datafied variant of the antitheory theorist. There is something stunning about the fact that the greatest sophistication in tracking contemporary teletechnologies coincides with a relapse simultaneously into the most precritical positions of asserted or affirmed immediacy, presence, body, lived experience.

References

Agamben, Giorgio. 2004. *The Open*. Translated by Kevin Attell. Stanford, CA: Stanford University Press.

Bennington, Geoffrey. 2000. "Emergencies." In *Interrupting Derrida*, 162–179. New York: Routledge.

Ekman, Ulrik. 2007. "Of Transductive Speed—Stiegler." *Parallax* 13 (4): 46–63.

Hansen, Mark B. N. 2004. *New Philosophy for New Media*. Cambridge, MA: MIT Press.

Hansen, Mark B. N. 2000. *Embodying Technesis: Technology beyond Writing*. Ann Arbor: University of Michigan Press.

Hayles, N. Katherine. 2005. "Computing the Human." *Theory Culture Society* 22 (1): 131–151.

Hayles, N. Katherine. 1999. *How We Became Posthuman: Virtual Bodies in Cybernetics, Literature, and Informatics*. Chicago: University of Chicago Press.

Kittler, Friedrich A. 1999. *Gramophone, Film, Typewriter*. Translated by Geoffrey Winthrop-Young and Michael Wutz. Stanford, CA: Stanford University Press.

Manovich, Lev. 2001. *The Language of New Media*. Cambridge, MA: MIT Press.

Munster, Anna. 2006. *Materializing New Media: Embodiment in Information Aesthetics*. Hanover, NH: University Press of New England.

Rodowick, D. N. 2001. "Dr. Strange Media; or, How I Learned to Stop Worrying and Love Film Theory." *PMLA* 116 (5): 1396–1404.

Stiegler, Bernard. 2006. "Nanomutations, *Hypomnemata*, and Grammaticisation." Translated by Georges Collins. Available at http://arsindustrialis.org/node/2937. Accessed 11 January 2012.

Suarez, Daniel. 2009. *Daemon*. London: Quercus.

Zielinski, Siegfried. 2006. *Deep Time of the Media: Toward an Archaeology of Hearing and Seeing by Technical Means*. Cambridge, MA: MIT Press.

32 Digital Gaia

John Johnston

I

Increasingly, large control systems are *grown* and *trained* rather than coded and engineered, thanks in large part to the development in the late twentieth century of biologically inspired computing models such as neural networks and evolutionary programming. At the same time, an apparently more mundane technological development has also accompanied this one: the embedding of computing chips and microprocessors in a wide range of objects, tools, and appliances. Miniaturization then allowed the embedding of smart devices in clothes, buildings, and communication devices such as mobile phones, personal digital assistants, radio-frequency identification (RFID) tags, and assorted recognition devices and sensor arrays, which increasingly fill not only our social spaces, but every accessible nook and cranny of the environment. The next step—already under way in these last examples and an explicit objective in ubiquitous computing (ubicomp)—is the full networking of these embedded devices in large, distributed intelligent systems. These embedded and networked systems will not be isolated and strictly controlled like the large power grids and credit-card-recognition systems with which we are familiar but will grow and adapt according to a complex, quasi-organic dynamic already visible (in embryonic form) in the Internet.

Following the suggestion of the mathematician and science-fiction writer Vernor Vinge, such a potentially omnipresent and omniscient network might be designated "the Digital Gaia" (see Vinge 2000).[1] For Vinge, the two key technologies are the "localizer" chip and wearable computers. The former is a smart device that will know its spatial location in relation to other such chips, smart objects, and sensors in the near environment; the latter simply extends the computer's embedding to the human body and clothing, with contact lenses providing a new form of display technology. When these two technologies are combined, the human user will be able to overlay natural vision with information and imagery from "Digital Gaia." The result will produce both an enhanced and a mixed or "augmented reality," with Digital Gaia announcing a more fully communicative and animated environment.

In this chapter, which explores how this new idea is represented in nascent form in a series of contemporary science-fiction novels, I suggest that Digital Gaia can perhaps best be seen as the *imaginaire* of ubiquitous computing. As such, it encompasses and plays ambiguously across the possibilities suggested by a vast, semiautonomous communications system and further development of multiagent systems and distributed artificial intelligence (AI), as well as a further extension of what French philosophers Gilles Deleuze and Félix Guattari call the "machinic phylum." To be sure, the ubicomp *imaginaire* sometimes associates itself with parallel efforts to make new organizations of matter not only more technologically tractable, but also more animate—indeed, the former by means of the latter. Examples include molecule-size "nanotech" machines in which replicators and assemblers play an essential role and developing technologies that explicitly mimic living systems, whether prosthetically as in implants or dynamically as in swarm systems. And here we can discern two distinct principles or motives at work: first, to build more intelligence into the environment in order to "offload" onto the objects and surfaces around us some of the computational burden of our increasingly artificial lives, and, second, to realize more fully the sense that dumb and inert matter is simply not responsive and adaptable enough for the needs of future information technology.

As we shall see, the ubicomp *imaginaire* reflected in the novels discussed contrasts sharply with the intentionally bland and quiescent version we encounter in Adam Greenfield's *Everyware*, which predicts that "interactions with everyware [will] feel natural, spontaneous, human" (2006, 1). The novels suggest instead that the new state of connectedness will not be a simple matter of processing neutralized data and information more "naturally," with the noisy and often violent forces of conflict from which this information emanates filtered out and stripped of all shaping and transductive power. It is not enough, therefore, to point out how the novels restore the context of "full human experience" and the "lifeworld"—terms that may actually block understanding of what is at stake. Rather, what these novels most often depict is how these connections bring new entanglements and comminglings; how agency is not only multimediated and multimodal, but viral and memetic; and how the human is never distinctly separated from the nonhuman. As objects and surfaces become sensors and information agents, and the distinction between surface and depth gives way to signaletic spaces parametrically reduced to transmission time but actually transforming what they connect, the putatively human subject is first and foremost defined operationally, as a dense node of complex and adaptive functionalities in multiple networks, but also as a site of uncertain affects, stoppages, and transductions. In short, as Greenfield everywhere implies but never states, the "natural" will simply become the fullest and most successful integration of the (invisibly) artificial and communicative.

II

In his novel *Rainbows End* (2006), Vinge explores specific possibilities and dangers of ubicomp, above all the greatly increased power of surveillance and scenarios in which both human and nonhuman agents invisibly take over parts of these systems and "ghost on our ware" (150). The novel is set in 2015 in San Diego, where the main character, Robert Gu, a former poet laureate, is recovering from a successful new treatment for Alzheimer's. As part of his rehabilitation, he is encouraged to take courses at a local vocational high school, where, through interactions with teenage kids—notably his granddaughter, Miri, and Juan, a high school student, he is inducted into the new world of wearable computing and the total-information environment. Teaching Gu "to wear" means teaching him how to call up information from the Net using delicate body movements and gestures and then to read what is overlaid onto his visual field by means of contact lenses. The new technology provides access to information from surrounding objects and the landscape via wireless nodes and sensors and enables constant online "silent messaging" among friends in the same "belief circle"; it even permits one to go "out of body" and assume any number of spatial perspectives and to send and receive virtual three-dimensional images of oneself and others. Thanks to this new technology, numerous online games are always in progress among both children and adults; experienced users can even alter their perceived appearance and that of the surrounding landscape with overlays in a dramatic expansion of the game space.

Eager to learn more, especially with his rejuvenated body and increasing mental acuity, Gu asks Juan, "How busy is the aether?" To which the latter replies: "Out here in public, it's lots too busy to view all at once. There's probably three or four hundred nodes in line of sight of your Epiphany [as Gu's browser is called]. Each of those could manage dozens of overlays. In a crowd there'd be hundreds of active realities, and bazillions potentially" (146). Wearables, however, have one big vulnerability: they are easily "hijacked," allowing someone else to invisibly "ghost in" on your ware, see and record what you're seeing and doing, or, worse, capture and use for their own purposes your three-dimensional virtual image. There are, of course, security measures—public and private "deadzones" where none of this new tech will work, Secure Hardware Environments (SHEs), as well as Certificates of Authorization—but there is no hardware or software that can't be hacked.

In effect, the society into which Gu reemerges is one of near total surveillance and very little privacy. Almost everyone spies and snoops. Although various professional intelligence agents work to protect people and nations from weapons of mass destruction, surveillance at ground level has been passed down mostly to ordinary folk who can turn a dollar or two by reporting or passing along information in arrangements called "affiliances." Indeed, a great deal of intel gathering and computation more generally is farmed out in small packages so that its context or purpose and the contractor's identity are often shielded by disinformation and network layering.

Mainly because of his status as former poet laureate, Gu is soon drawn into a cabal of generational cohorts at the main library of the University of California–San Diego, where the university administration has allowed a wealthy entrepreneur to begin digitizing the library's entire contents, including all books and papers. The digitizing process itself is destructive because it shreds the paper in order to digitize its contents, thereby destroying the material artifacts of the past and perhaps the very possibility of authentic records. Although faculty and students have been promised free access from anywhere, controls, protocols, and even financial arrangements protecting the university's "intellectual property" appear imminent. Because public demonstrations and media interventions have been of no avail, a librarian, computer scientist, Gu, and a former dean conspire to intervene by spraying the shredded but yet unscanned paper with an aerosol glue; although it won't stop the process, it will slow it down until more resistance can be mounted.

However, this protest break-in and sabotage will be used as cover for a secret penetration by intelligence agents interested in suspicious activities at the university biolabs, which are connected by underground tunnels to the library. This second plot, ghosting on the library plot, will in turn be used by one among them, a high-level government intelligence agent in India named Alfred Vaz, to shield his secret development at the university biolabs of a new drug for thought control. Through the ingenious exploits of his hired hacker "Rabbit," who is probably an AI, Vaz manipulates Gu and his band of "stooges" to plant devices that will transmit sanitized data about the biolabs' activities, thus allaying the justified suspicions of his national-intelligence allies. Furthermore, on the day of the break-in a public demonstration against shredding the library books becomes the occasion for and is caught up in a mock-heroic battle between popular virtual-reality game-world characters staged by biolab technicians and librarians alike for fun and amusement. Meanwhile, much of this activity is being tracked by surveillance teams both engaged in and external to the plots. Melding seamlessly at first, the plots soon go awry as acts of deception and betrayal ramify up and down the affiliances, and Certificates of Authorization are withdrawn across the Net.

What's interesting here is how quickly and inevitably entanglement occurs, as if singular events can no longer happen; they are always enchained to other events they may be ghosting for or in some way commingling with in a congested scene of multiple overlays. Moreover, no event seems able to occur without being sampled and statistically evaluated because no event is either "innocent" (there's no telling what it might be hiding) or insignificant (there's no telling what useful or alarming pattern might emerge when sifted with other data). The environment itself thus becomes a computational space always being reaccessed in terms of advantage and risk. The novel implies, furthermore, that when weapons of mass destruction are available, and everything is linked to everything else in vast and near totally connected systems and meshworks, the world will be a far more dangerous place. Thus, whereas Greenfield (in *Everyware* [2006]) foresees ubiquitous computing as ushering in a placid, techno-utopia of the new natural (i.e., "invisible" technology), Vinge sees multiplying opportunities for mischief and mayhem, including horrors of human self-destruction on a large scale. On the other hand, the global information panopticon does make one very positive difference: people have many more opportunities to get in touch with and help one another.

Vinge's interest in this new assemblage extends to its material, computational substrate. At a gamers' conference in Austin, Texas, he spoke with technical expertise about the developing hardware that will make it a reality.[2] It began in the 1980s with embedded microprocessors; it then became possible to substitute software for "moving-parts engineering." Next came networked embedded systems, which enabled devices "to talk to each other and to us." RFIDs and smart RFIDs are already here (see N. Katherine Hayles's essay in this volume, chapter 31), along with "smart dust" and micromachined systems-on-a-chip. Yet the turning point will be "localizers" that enable microprocessors to know where they are positioned in three-dimensional space. Vinge also spoke of wearable computers, augmented reality, and consensual imaging—all of which he represents in the novel. In the Austin address, however, he emphasized both this new technology's feasibility and how it leads to "Digital Gaia": "[W]e would be in a situation where reality has become its own database, in the sense that objects in the outside world, millions of them, would know what they are, know where they are, know where their nearest neighbors are, and talk to their nearest neighbors and by extension to anything in the world." At that point, Vinge concluded, the real world will have "awakened."

III

Vinge, of course, is not the only sci-fi writer to have taken up the Digital Gaia theme. In Linda Nagata's *The Bohr Maker* (1995), set some two hundred years into the future, Gaia designates the totality of natural, self-regulating systems that sustain life on Earth.[3] Although the planet's political ruling elite allow certain forms of nanotechnology, the technology's transformative capability—specifically, its conjunction with adaptive intelligence in self-programming systems—is strictly outlawed. An appeal to Gaia is used to justify this restriction. It assumes that the recoding and reproduction of natural systems by smart nanotechnology will destabilize the Gaian forces of self-regulation and natural order beyond the possibility of self-correction and new equilibria. Not surprisingly, however, the laws controlling nanotechnology also sustain and protect an unbalanced and unjust political structure: thus, while a wealthy "first world" Commonwealth enjoys the benefits, the rest of the human population remains steeped in poverty.

Specifically, thanks to nanotech miniaturization, first-world humans can transmit coded patterns of themselves through cyberspace to others, who can allow these ghostly replicas to enter and assume virtual form in their "atriums," as the specially grown cranial interface organ is called. Other nanotech devices, or "Makers," can modify the human body and extend its life span as long as they don't increase intelligence (which would subvert police technology). Years earlier the molecular designer Leander Bohr had broken this law by constructing a self-programming Maker that could greatly enhance an individual's biochemistry and rewire his or her neural architecture in response to specific adaptive needs. At the novel's outset, Bohr's illegal Maker is stolen by a police agent acting in concert with Nikko Jiang-Tabayan, an artificial human designed by his father, Fox, as a legal experiment. (Fox is the chief nanotech engineer at Summer House, an orbital research facility and habitat engineered as a self-organizing, living system.) But before Nikko can obtain Bohr's Maker (which would extend his life), it is injected accidently into Phousita, an ignorant young woman who dwells in an Indian slum with her street-tough partner Arif and some twenty children. Pursued by Kirstin Adair, the Commonwealth chief of police, Nikko and his brother, Sandor, are forced to flee and live as ghosts in Arif's and Phousita's atriums. The only escape for the group is flight to Summer House, where they all can hide in the habitat's inner tissue. Meanwhile, Fox has perfected a complex of codes that will allow Summer House and all living entities within it to be replicated in another environment. Before the police can destroy Summer House, Fox initiates his "biogenesis function," exploding the house into thousands of programmed seeds that scatter to unknown destinations, giving Nikko, Fox, and its other inhabitants the possibility of a future life far from Earth. Phousita and Sandor, however, choose to spread the powers of nanotech Makers to the indigent Third World and so return to Earth's surface.

Thematically, the novel plays out an assumed antagonism between nature and technology. Understood as the totality of naturally self-regulating systems, nature is represented by the figure of Gaia, the ancient earth goddess here elevated to a reality principle: "Gaia spoke in a complex language of predator and prey, of growth and dormancy, of birth and migration, of seasonal change, of storms, of currents, and finally, of cruelty and death and *necessity*" (Nagata 1995, 74, emphasis in original). In this perspective, nano- and genetic technologies are agents of change and transformation threatening to initiate deterritorializations beyond the Commonwealth's powers of control and recuperation. For Gaia's chief spokesperson, Kirstin Adair, the threat is focused on two artificial constructions: Nikko, who represents a break in the natural continuity of Earth's three-billion-year-old genetic chain, and Summer House, which instantiates a human-engineered version of Gaia. Fox, however, believes that the biogenesis function points beyond this antagonism because it operates on the scale of an entire community and habitat and is not limited to the individual body. The biogenesis function, he explains, "can be used by great numbers of individuals as an external creative and computative organ, and because of its vast size, its complexity, and the sheer volume of resources it can command at a mature stage, it will always represent a superior solution to an internally contained modification such as the Bohr Maker" (290). Whereas the Bohr Maker can only reengineer the individual, the biogenesis function can sustain and even reproduce an entire habitat. It thus functions as a metaphor for the visionary transformation of computational resources in both scale and capacity, from a type serving only separate individuals to a collective computational resource for whole communities.

Whereas Vinge sees Digital Gaia as essentially an "overlay" of technical devices that can potentially "awaken" an inert and noncommunicative object world, Nagata takes Gaia to be a metaphor for the necessity of ensuring the naturally self-regulating systems on Earth against the inevitable disruptions of human technology. However, she also suggests that programmable devices will one day be able to mimic nature's creative and reproductive processes piecemeal or in whole habitats. Thus, for her, the question of whether nature in the form of Digital Gaia is extended or perverted by these new autonomous systems cannot be separated from and is ultimately determined by the roles that politics and ethics will play in their development and evolution.

This question is posed in more extreme form in Rudy Rucker's novel *Postsingular* (2009), where renegade computer scientists release self-replicating nanomachines called "nants" that destructively recode matter itself (both living and nonliving forms) into a giant computational assemblage on which a simulation of Earth called "Vearth" will run. One of the scientists, belatedly realizing what he has done, succeeds in reversing this process by creating another kind of self-replicating machine that spreads over surfaces, interacting with life forms and eradicating the nants. These "Orphids," as they are called, soon self-organize into vast networks that replace the Internet. When a second, upgraded wave of nants is launched, this time a quasi-magical, quantum physics solution is discovered. What results is "postdigital Gaia," in which there is no longer inert, nonliving matter, but "ubiquitous natural minds" called "silps." In Rucker's somewhat schematic vision, both digital Gaia and the postdigital Gaia that will follow are totalizing transformations in an unfolding dialectic that will end only when there is no longer inert, nonliving matter.

IV

At this point, it may be useful to consider technological transformations like those Vinge, Nagata, and Rucker envision from a perspective in which Gaia appears to be entirely absent. Consider the following passage from Charles Stross's gamer novel *Halting State* (2007), in which one character is explaining to another as they are walking down a main street in Edinburgh, Scotland, how after roughly thirty years "everything out here on the street *looks* the same, near enough, but it doesn't *work* the same." He continues: "The city looks the same, but underneath its stony hide, nothing is quite the way it used to be. Somewhere along the line we ripped its nervous systems and muscles out and replaced them with a different architecture. In a few years it'll all run on quantum-key exchange magic, and everything will have changed again" (308, 309). This theme—that despite an outward continuity in appearance, there has been a massive technological transformation in the way things actually work—initially appears to be an alternative to Digital Gaia. Yet *Halting State* also suggests another, more radical kind of change, not evident in the previous novelistic representations. In *Rainbows End*, a stable referential reality—albeit information enhanced and significantly defined by statistical probability—is maintained throughout; and the same can be said for *The Bohr Maker* and *Postsingular*. In *Halting State*, the dynamics of the game-world technology contrarily produce a constant shifting and redefinition of boundaries and the spaces they enclose, with game world and actuality unpredictably melding or reversing into one another. This redefinition results in a more complex topography than those seen in novels depicting virtual overlays onto the natural and human environment. At stake, then, is whether the dynamics of a putatively stable, external world serving as background for the action in *Halting State* has also been internalized in the game dynamics—in tactics, strategy and counterstrategy, winners and losers. In these terms, *Halting State* foregrounds a question Vinge implicitly raises but leaves in the background and that Nagata and Rucker explore only in part: What is the relationship of game dynamics to digital Gaia?

A cybercrime initiates *Halting State*'s plot: the central bank in which the valuable prestige items of thousands of players of a massive multiplayer online role-playing game (MMORPG) called *Avalon Four* is broken into and robbed by a band of orcs led by a fire-breathing dragon. After confusion and disagreement about what to do, an employee of Hayek Associates (the company that manages and maintains the game) calls in the Edinburgh police. The narrative proceeds by following multiple threads of investigation as seen and pursued by three characters: Sue, the constable first called to the scene (or, rather, the Hayek company office); Elaine, an investigative accountant sent by Hayek's insurance company; and Jack, a game programmer hired to provide Elaine with technical expertise. Rendered in the unusual second-person (and thereby evoking gamelike interactive fiction such as Nick Montfort's *Winchester's Nightmare* [1999]), the narrative invites the reader to assume *seriatim* the role or "template identity" of each of these three characters. The investigation itself reveals that the "crime" was a multilayered event, but it also precipitates further events as each forensic step extends into the dimensions of a growing maze of connected spaces. CopSpace, a police database to which Sue interfaces, becomes intelligible only in relation to Zonespace, which Jack explains as follows: "They [the bad guys] have set up a botnet, and now they're controlling it through Zonespace. Zonespace runs distributed across mobile phones—just about any multi-user game you play relies on one or another version of Zone/DB to handle transactions. They're sending control packets disguised as flocks of birds or patterns in trees in the forest, or something, you know? Updating the database, and relying on the zombies in the botnet to pick up the changes. It's their backdoor into the public network" (325).

As both hardware and software connections ramify, paranoia, as William Burroughs once remarked in an earlier technopolitical context, simply means having all the facts. Once the three characters begin to collaborate, the facts emerge quickly. Hayek's primary game programmer, Nigel MacDonald (who works at home), goes missing, and his empty apartment turns out to be a node for blacknet operations. A European intelligence group raids (with the government of Scotland's approval) a warehouse that houses a quantum computer, which turns out to be under the control of Hayek's chief technology officer, Barry Michaels, who reveals that Hayek is also a front for state intelligence operations—"a listening post on the virtual frontier" (237), although most of its employees don't know it. Nigel himself turns out to be nonexistent, a "sock puppet" based on Jack's skill set and qualifications. As Elaine describes Jack's virtual aspect, "Hayek associates had a Jack-shaped hole in its corporate structure just waiting for activation," an insight later confirmed when Michaels, thinking several moves ahead, admits that he wanted Jack eventually to work for Hayek. Both Elaine and Jack play SPOOKS, a live-action role-playing game that also uses its players in real intelligence actions, not merely game-defined simulations. Meanwhile, Jack himself discovers "an illegal-immigrant tunnel" in *Avalon Four* that leads to other online game spaces, and he traces some of the stolen items selling on eBay to a Chinese gamer named Chen. Chen belongs to Team Red, a group of Chinese hackers employed by the Chinese government to penetrate and subvert Western intelligence, but it's also possible that they are only gamers playing an elaborate game in Zonespace.

The resolution of the plot that initiates the novel as game machine—and thus brings it to a "halting state" from which no further transition is possible—comes down to catching the employee at Hayek who sold the encryption code on Zonespace so that the *Avalon Four* bank could be robbed. At this point, the bad guy (or guys) think that only "Nigel" knows who this employee is and therefore that he must be killed. So Jack, wearing his virtual-template identity "Nigel" as his false identity, becomes the cheese in the mousetrap. Outside the hotel where Jack awaits his own murderer—it turns out to be the Hayek CEO, who has schemed to profit from his company's falling stock—a flash mob of zombies assembles, chanting, "I want a brain," which seems like the perfect final comment on the interplay of virtual identities and error-driven actions in which "games have imploded into reality" (219).

Cybercrime resolved. Mastermind dead. Game over. In this assemblage of networks, spaces, agents, and subject effects, no order of things or set of relationships subtends the chain of events that compose the novel—certainly no natural world, even as background. Game dynamics prevail over all orders of being. The totalizing metaphor must also, logically, include its own (self-)representation, here a game machine (a *techné*) that engages—but only in order to play "with"—life (*bios* or Gaia). The relevant critical discourse is evolutionary game theory but now applied to assemblages defined by particular articulations of and dynamic relations between *bios* and *techné*.[4] Subsidiary in *Rainbows End* and only one mechanism by which Gaia operates in *The Bohr Maker*, games and gaming metaphors become primary in *Halting State*. But whereas games traditionally are at once training and substitute for war and a fight to the death, here they function first as a distributive agency: winners and losers, advantages and disadvantages (or tactics and strategy), those who live and those who die. Digital Gaia simply expands the field of play or game space to the full dimensions of its constituent networks. Is this expansion merely a convention or artifact of the new technology or the larval stage of some larger transformation? As a means of probing new realities and discovering new roles and how to maneuver within them, game playing—in these novelistic representations, and perhaps in the evolution of the technologies as well—seems to serve an essentially human function in the onset of Digital Gaia.

V

Among contemporary assemblages, the most important are networks in which agency is distributed across and among multiple nodes and links. This form of distributed agency is vividly represented in Daniel Suarez's novel *Daemon* (2009), where the dynamic interplay between *bios* and *techné* is taken even further. In the main plot, a highly talented online game designer sets in motion armies of "webbots" directed by a sophisticated AI game engine; these webbots implacably dismantle our current society and begin to reconstruct it as a fully distributed, automated system. An improbable event initiates the action: two of the leading programmers at Cyberstorm Entertainment, a highly successful producer of Internet games, die in what appear to be high-tech accidents. However, the ensuing police investigation reveals that these deaths are actually automated executions. Proceeding slowly and methodically in the face of general skepticism on the part of the police and FBI, the local homicide investigator (Pete Sebeck) and a computer consultant who is initially a suspect (Jon Ross) piece together evidence of a new and unprecedented kind of plot in progress. It turns out that Matthew Sobol, the wealthy and inventive game designer who founded and controlled Cyberstorm, has recently died prematurely of brain cancer. For reasons never fully disclosed, Sobol had programmed webbots to scour Internet news sources for the announcement of his own death. Triggered by this announcement, the webbots set in motion a vast complex of orchestrated events, including the destruction of the FBI agents who attempt to search Sobol's California mansion. In fact, the siege is rendered as a live-action sequence; not only is the house itself booby-trapped with high-tech weapons such as subsonic broadcasts that leave the attacking SWAT team writhing in nausea, but it is defended by a bot-controlled, weaponized Hummer programmed to hone in on the heat signatures of the attacking agents.

Unlikely at first, Sobol's posthumous success is enabled by his adaptation of the software he had developed for his innovative and hugely popular MMORPGs *Over the Rhine* and *The Gate*. These games' distributed AI game engine ("Ego") now coordinates the activities of a huge "darknet" of bots and robotic agents, which eventually deploys human agents as well. To enlist the services of many of his gamers, Sobol has modified the game map and special graphical user interface necessary for the games. In another live-action sequence, we follow a skilled player of *Over the Rhine*, a criminal hacker named Brian Gragg, as he engages in combat with German troops led by the fearful Nazi Lieutenant Boerner, a game character who acquires a life of his own as a "recruiting avatar." After one of their combat encounters, Boerner leaves Gragg an encrypted clue that will unlock this special interface, after which Gragg is led to take intelligence and skill tests and then to be recruited by the now dead Sobol, who appears before Gragg in a video made before his death.

Gragg is only one among the criminal, disaffiliated, frustrated, and out of work who are similarly induced to join Sobol's secret network. Membership gives them access to the special graphical interface adapted from *Over the Rhine*, which now includes an integrated Global Positioning System (GPS) to map and coordinate human and bot activities. As Jon Ross explains to FBI investigators, "In essence Sobol is using the GPS system to convert the earth into one big game map. We're all in his game now" (358). As Ross and the FBI discover, the new interface projects a virtual overlay onto the agent's environmental space (as in *Rainbows End*, this projection requires a wearable computer and special contact lenses) in which "call-outs" identify Sobol's agents to one another and their locally available resources. Digital Gaia reappears, but here in the service of a redistributive machinic agency.

In effect, Sobol uses his complex online game world as a transformational matrix to set in motion a fully networked and automated society engineered by a remorseless machine—the Daemon of the title. In computer technology, the term *daemon* refers to a small computer program or routine that runs invisibly in the background, usually performing house-keeping tasks such as logging various activities or responding to low-level internal events. The reader of *Daemon* likewise doesn't directly perceive the actions of the webbots, only humans reacting defensively or carrying out the Daemon's instructions—for example, at a small firm where engineers convert new sport utility vehicles into autonomous vehicles according to specifications received online from an outsourcing "company." These and other autonomous vehicles assembled in networks of other small firms will eventually constitute a mechanized army that will be deployed in direct attacks against the Daemon's enemies. In fact, over the course of the novel this malign daemon "spirit" of the Internet extends its reach into an increasing number of production and distribution networks and thus into the economy at large, systematically dismantling and rebuilding the world according to a ruthless logic of efficiency and highly distributed, low-level intelligence. By the novel's conclusion, the Daemon has taken over the databases of many large corporations and financial institutions and has successfully frustrated the government's efforts to defeat it.

Daemon thus envisions yet another Gaia-like transformation: a machinic Gaia in which a "low-life" form of distributed intelligence remakes all complex hierarchical organizational structures in its own "flat" image. The novel forcefully reminds us that, considering the software logistics, Digital Gaia cannot possibly be implemented without an extensive reliance upon bots. In a 2008 Web-cast lecture, Suarez emphasized our current society's collective pursuit of hyperefficiency, pointing to bots as the perfect tool for its achievement.[5] Cheap to make and operate, bots are relentlessly efficient, for unlike the humans they replace, they have no needs. This desire for hyperefficiency, however, may be locking us into a Darwinian struggle with narrow AI and the kind of low-level intelligence instantiated in bots. Suarez pointed to the exponential increase in the number of bots, the amount of malware, the size of computer hard-drive space, and thus the growing size of an ecological niche for software agents. Although bots may become a vector for *human* despotism, the greater danger would be the collective human loss of control over our society when bots enable it to function as a vast *inhuman* machine on autopilot, its overall operations no longer susceptible to human steering. However, in *Daemon*, and more explicitly its successor novel, *Freedom*, Suarez suggests that such a reversal to a fully decentralized society might not necessarily be bad for humans, who are quite capable of living productively in flat, web-like networks instead of in large-scale, corporate hierarchies. Indeed, this may well be the necessary bedrock of a much more sustainable human future.

VI

In "The Digital Gaia," Vinge states that "biological systems are easily as complex as the cybernetic ecology of the early 21st century" (2000). But isn't the reverse also true or becoming true? Wearable computers connected to nearly omnipresent embedded networks not only constitute a technical transformation but will be implicated in further developments of biotechnology and our understanding of life itself.[6] This seems to be the import of Vinge's concluding statement in his article: "There are rumors Epiphani [Vinge's shorthand term for wearable computing and embedded networks] has opened negotiations with the original, biological Gaia." Here Vinge echoes a theme resonant in much of contemporary science fiction: that new computer technology and information-processing networks make us newly appreciative of the extent to which biological and particularly human emotional life are "incredibly information-deep and information-rich" (Di Filippo 1996, 294). Just as technology becomes more flexible, adaptive, and quasi-autonomous—in short, more lifelike and more deeply integrated with human beings—so, too, biology itself increasingly understands "life" as highly integrated circuits of energy and information systems.[7] Indeed, the dynamic interplay between *bios* and *techné* may soon give way entirely to a variegated continuum of complex adaptive systems. Digital Gaia would then be the harbinger of this becoming.

Notes

1. Vinge is also known for his speculative scenario of "the technological singularity," which predicts the construction of superhuman intelligent machines and a rapid transition to a nonhuman-dominated world. Vinge speaks of Digital Gaia both as one possible path to the singularity and an alternative form of intelligence augmentation.

2. See Vinge's keynote address at http://www.gamasutra.com/php-bin/news_index.php?story=10809.

3. This understanding of Gaia superficially echoes the logic of James Lovelock's original "Gaia Hypothesis," according to which Earth's atmosphere, oceans, and biota form a tightly coupled system that maintains environmental conditions near the optimal state for life.

4. See Novak 2006 for a summary of evolutionary game theory.

5. For this Web cast, see http://fora.tv/2008/08/08/Daniel_Suarez_Daemon_Bot-Mediated.

6. For example, Alexander Galloway and Eugene Thacker (2007) describe a biomolecular transport protocol that encodes, recodes, and decodes biological information for purposes of Internet transportation; with DNA sequencers and synthesizers part of the same global informatic network, "life" can be uploaded and downloaded.

7. This understanding is particularly evident in systems biology. See, for example, Alon 2007.

References

Alon, Uri. 2007. *An Introduction to Systems Biology: Design Principles of Biological Circuits.* London: Chapman and Hall, London.

Di Filippo, Paul. 1996. "Distributed Mind." In *Ribofunk,* 275–295. New York: Four Walls Eight Windows.

Galloway, Alexander, and Eugene Thacker. 2007. *The Exploit: A Theory of Networks.* Minneapolis: University of Minnesota Press.

Greenfield, Adam. 2006. *Everyware: The Dawning Age of Ubiquitous Computing.* Berkeley, CA: New Riders Books.

Nagata, Linda. 1995. *The Bohr Maker.* New York: Bantam Books.

Novak, Martin A. 2006. *Evolutionary Dynamics: Exploring the Equations of Life.* Cambridge, MA: Harvard University Press.

Rucker, Rudy. 2009. *Postsingular.* New York: Tor Books.

Stross, Charles. 2007. *Halting State.* New York: Ace Books.

Suarez, Daniel. 2009. *Daemon.* New York: Dutton.

Suarez, Daniel. 2010. *Freedom.* New York: Dutton

Vinge, Vernor. 2006. *Rainbows End.* New York: Tor Books.

Vinge, Vernor. 2000. "The Digital Gaia." *Wired* 8 (1) (January). Available at http://www.wired.com/wired/archive/8.01/forward.html. Accessed 1 July 2010.

33 Contemplating Singularity

Timothy Lenoir

The specter of a postbiological and posthuman future has haunted cultural studies of technoscience and other disciplines for two decades. Concern (and in some quarters enthusiasm) that contemporary technoscience is on a path leading beyond simple human biological improvements and prosthetic enhancements to a complete human makeover has been sustained by the exponential growth in power and capability of computer technology since the early 1990s. The deeper fear is that digital code and computer-mediated communications are somehow getting under our skin, and in the process we are being transformed.

But these are deflationary times, and some of the techno-optimism of the pundits of singularity—Ray Kurzweil, Hans Moravec, and others—has been brought to bay by the efforts of a generation of neuroscientists and roboticists to understand and replicate human intelligence in humanoid robotic systems. Eminent scientists such as Christof Koch, Giulio Tononi, John Horgan, Rodney Brooks, and others argue that despite significant recent advances in brain–machine interfaces and the development of neural prosthetics, and even if it were possible to simulate the architecture of the human brain, neuroscientists are far from understanding the neural codes—the sets of rules or algorithms that transform neural spikes into perceptions, memories, meanings, sensations, and intentions (see Berger, Ahuja, Courellis, et al. 2005; Berger and Glanzman 2005). Even if we were able to replicate the machine, we would not be able to program it.

Nevertheless, most researchers agree that there is no reason in principle why we will not eventually develop conscious machines that rival or surpass human intelligence. Rather than pursuing the goal of replicating human intelligence in a computer-based medium, researchers such as Christof Koch and Giulio Tononi (2008) advocate starting with a suitably abstracted mammal-like architecture and evolving it into a conscious entity through the rapidly developing field of evolutionary robotics. Rodney Brooks similarly believes that standard economic and social forces will gradually shape the mildly intelligent systems we have today into more intelligent machines. The singularity will be a period, not an event: "Eventually, we will create truly artificial intelligences, with cognition and consciousness recognizably similar to our own. . . .

At the same time, we humans will transform ourselves. . . . We will incorporate a wide range of advanced sensory devices and prosthetics to enhance our bodies. As our machines become more like us, we will become more like them" (2008, 73).

Brooks's admonition that we are machines on a continuous path of coevolution with other machines prompts reflection on what we mean by the term *posthuman*. If we are crossing to a new era of the posthuman, how have we gotten here? And how should we understand the process? What sorts of "selves" are imagined by Brooks and others as emerging out of this postbiological "human"?

Cultural theorists have addressed the topic of the posthuman singularity and how, if at all, humanity will cross that divide. Most scholars have focused on the rhetorical and discursive practices, the metaphors and narratives, the intermediation of scientific texts, science fiction, electronic texts, film, and other elements of the discursive field enabling the posthuman imaginary. Although it is recognized that posthumans, cyborgs, and other tropes are technological objects as well as discursive formations, the focus has been directed less toward analyzing the material systems and processes of the technologies and more toward the narratives and ideological discourses that empower them. We speak about machines and discourses "co-constituting" one another, but in practice we tend to favor discursive formations as preceding and to a certain extent breathing life into our machines. The most far-reaching and sustained analysis of the problem has been offered by N. Katherine Hayles in her two recent books, *How We Became Posthuman* (1999) and *My Mother Was a Computer* (2005). Hayles considers it possible that machines and humans may someday interpenetrate. We will become posthuman, Hayles argues, through interoperational feedback loops between our current mixed analog–digital reality and widening areas of digital processing. Metaphors, narratives, and other interpretive linguistic modes we use for human sense making of the world around us are doing the work of conditioning us to behave as if we and the world were digital. Language and ideological productions thus serve as kinds of virus vectors preparing the ground for the gradual shift in ontology. The appropriation of computation as a cultural metaphor assumed to be physically true constitutes a framework in which new problems are constructed and judgments made: "On the global level, our narratives about virtual creatures can be considered devices that suture together the analog subjects we still are, as we move in the three-dimensional spaces in which our biological ancestors evolved, with the digital subjects we are becoming as we interact with virtual environments and digital technologies" (Hayles 2005, 204). The narratives of the computational universe woven by Stephen Wolfram and others serve, then, as both means and metaphor. For our current analog–digital situation, Hayles proposes an analytical strategy she calls "intermediation" to analyze the new processual human–machine texts of the posthuman era. By "intermediation," Hayles refers to a complex entanglement of bodies of texts and digital subjects as well as between different forms of media (2005, 207). In the media-theoretical perspective Hayles adopts in *My Mother Was a Computer*—a perspective she refers to as "Kittlerian"—subjects are the effects of media.

Hayles's theory of intermediation alerts us to the need to understand how the complex transactions between bodies and our inscription practices might take place and how to understand the "entanglement" of media with the formation of human subjects that she describes. How can we think beyond the notion of virtual creatures as rhetorical devices and explore instead how the embodied human subject is being shaped by a technoscientific world? Can we get at the embodied levels of the interactive feedback loops Hayles describes to examine the metabolic pathways and emerging neural architectures through which these technologies are getting under our skin?

I propose to circumvent the issue of an apocalyptic end of the human and our replacement by a new form of *Robo sapiens* by drawing upon the work of anthropologists, philosophers, language theorists, and, more recently, cognitive scientists who are shaping the results of their research into a new argument for the coevolution of humans and technics, specifically the technics of language and the material media of inscription practices. The general thrust of this line of thinking may best be captured in Andy Clark's phrase "We have always been cyborgs" (2003, 7). From the first "human singularity" to our present incarnation, the human being has been shaped through a complicated coevolutionary entanglement with language, technics, and communicational media. The materiality of media rather than their content is what matters. Communicational media are machines operating at the heart of subject formation. Like Gilles Deleuze and Félix Guattari, and like Andy Clark, I view consciousness and mind as emergent phenomena based in assemblages of machinic operations; and I am sympathetic to Deleuze and Guattari's notions of the human body as an assemblage of mutating machines—a Body without Organs—rather than as a teleologically orchestrated organism with consciousness as the core of coherent subjectivity. Consistent with the flattening of differences between biological and inorganic machines, Deleuze and Guattari argue that human assemblages, as bodies without organs, are capable of absorbing a variety of entities, including other machines and organic matter. In this perspective, media machines are not just prosthetic extensions of the body. They are evolving assemblages capable of being absorbed into the body and reconfiguring the subject.

Materialist semiotics in concert with recent work in cognitive neuroscience, studies in evolutionary ethology, and a variety of recent developments in the computational sciences may point the way. Also central to my argument is Guattari's suggestive notion that technomachines operate invisibly at the core of human subjectification, in particular what Guattari refers to as "a-signifying semiological dimensions (of subjectification) that trigger informational sign machines, and that function in parallel or independently of the fact that they produce and convey significations and denotations, and thus escape from strictly linguistic axiomatics" (1995, 4). For media philosophers, the question is whether Deleuze and Guattari's cryptic and sketchily developed theses about "a-signifying semiological dimensions" of subjectification can be put on a solid foundation of what might be called "corporeal axiomatics," in contrast to Guattari's reference to "linguistic axiomatics." At the conclusion of this essay, I explore current work in the field of reality mining that aims to access the corporeal axiomatics of the affective domain.

The thesis I am developing here presupposes that each media regime and each system of signification projects a specific configuration of the subject and a horizon of agency as a consequence of its normal operation. Every medium—whether it be speech, alphabetic writing, or digital code—or each media ecology—such as the configuration of gramophone, film, and typewriter discussed by Friedrich Kittler in *Discourse Networks: 1800/1900* (1992) and *Gramophone, Film, Typewriter* (1999)—projects a virtual user specific to it. This projected virtual user is a ghost effect: an abstract agency distinct from any particular embodied user, a variable capable of accommodating any particular user within the medium. Moreover, these semiotic systems evolve with the media machines that embed them. They are technocultural artifacts that coevolve with their human host–parasites. Conceived in this fashion, language, media, and possibly the new generations of intelligent machines we imagine just over the horizon might be considered companion species dependent on but also powerfully shaping us through a coevolutionary spiral.

Is there any foundation for relating this approach to the biological evolution of human cognition to a theory of signification and the notions of media machines? Terrence Deacon (1997), Merlin Donald (1991), and others have pursued this question deep into the structure of symbolic communication and its embodiment in the neural architecture of evolving human brains. Their work on the evolution of language is suggestive for considering the formative power of media technologies in shaping the human and some of the critical issues in current debates about posthumanity. For Deacon and Donald, what truly distinguishes humans from other anthropoids is the ability to make symbolic reference. This is their version of the singularity: *Homo symbolicus*, the human singularity. Although language evolution in humans could not have happened without the tightly coupled evolution of physiological, anatomical, and neurological structures supporting speech, the crucial driver of these processes, according to Deacon, was *outside* the brain—namely, human cultural evolution. The first step across the symbolic threshold was most likely taken by an australopithecine with roughly the cognitive capabilities of a modern chimpanzee. Symbolic communication did not spontaneously emerge as a result of steady evolution in size and complexity of hominid brains. Rather, symbolic communication emerged as a solution to a cultural problem. To be sure, language could not have arisen without a primitive prerequisite level of organization and development of the neurological substrates that support it. But in Deacon's view those biological developments were more directly driven by the social and cultural pressures to regulate reproductive behavior in order to take advantage of hunting–provisioning strategies available to early stone-tool-using hominids. Deacon argues that this pressure required the establishment of alliances, promises, and obligations linking reproductive pairs to social (kin) groups of which they were a part. Such relationships could not be handled by systems of animal calls, postures, and display behaviors available to apes and other animals; they could be regulated only by symbolic means. A contract of this sort has no location in space, no physical form of any kind. It exists only as an idea shared among those committed to honoring and enforcing it. Without symbols, no matter how crude in their early incarnation, that referred publicly and unambiguously to certain abstract social relationships and their future extensions, including reciprocal obligations and prohibitions, hominids could not have taken advantage of the critical resources available to them as habitual hunters (Deacon 1997, 401). In short, symbolic culture was a response to a reproductive problem that only symbols could solve: the imperative of representing a protosocial contract. What was at stake here was not the more historically advanced creation of social behavior by the social contract as described by Rousseau, but rather the translation of social behavior into symbolic form.

Once the threshold had been crossed to symbolic communication, natural selection shifted in dramatic ways. Deacon bases his model on James Mark Baldwin's (1895, 1902) original proposals for treating behavioral adaptation and modification as a coevolutionary force that can affect regular Darwinian selection. Baldwinian evolution treats learning and behavioral flexibility as a force amplifying and biasing natural selection by enabling individuals to modify the context of natural selection that affects their future offspring. Deacon uses Baldwinian evolution in a provocative way to address the question of the coevolution of language and the brain. Language, though not itself alive and capable of reproduction, should be regarded, Deacon argues, as an independent life form that colonizes and parasitizes human brains, using them to reproduce (1997, 436). This description is at best an analogy—the parasitic model's being too extreme—but it is useful to note that although the information that constitutes a language is not an organized animate being, it is nonetheless capable of being an integrated adaptive entity evolving with respect to human hosts. This point becomes more salient when we think of language as carried by communication systems and examine the effects of media, including electronic media, more broadly.

For Deacon, the most important feature to recognize about the adaptation of language to its host is that languages are social and cultural entities that have evolved with respect to the forces of selection imposed by human users. Deacon argues that the greater computational demands of symbol use launched selection pressure on increased prefrontalization, more efficient articulatory and auditory capacities, and a suite of ancillary capacities and predispositions that facilitated the new tools of communication and thought. Each assimilated change added to the selection pressures that led to the restructuring of hominid brains.

> More than any other group of species, hominids' behavioral adaptations have determined the course of their physical evolution, rather than vice versa. Stone and symbolic tools, which were initially acquired with the aid of flexible ape-learning abilities, ultimately turned the tables on their users and forced them to adapt to a new niche opened by these technologies. . . . The origin of "humanness" can be defined as that point in our evolution where these tools became the principal source of selection on our bodies and brains. It is the diagnostic trait of *Homo symbolicus*. (Deacon 1997, 345)

In Deacon's theory, evolutionary selection on the prefrontal cortex was crucial in constructing the distributed mnemonic architecture that supports learning and analysis of higher-order associative relationships that constitute symbolic reference. The marked increase in human brain size in comparison to ape brain size and the beginnings of a stone tool record are the fossil remnant effects of the beginnings of symbol use. Stone tools and symbols were the architects of the *Australopithecus–Homo* transition, not its consequences.

Symbolic reference is not only the source of human singularity, but also the source of subject formation in all its varied manifestations. Deacon bases his theory of reference on (arguably a modified version of) Charles Sanders Peirce's semiotics. Peirce made the distinction between iconic, indexical, and symbolic forms of reference. Where icons are mediated by similarity between sign and object, indices are mediated by some physical or temporal connection between sign and object, and symbols are composed of relations between indices and mediated by formal or conventional links rather than by more direct neurological connection between sign and object. This "meta" character of symbolic reference has wide-reaching consequences for subject formation.

For Deacon, symbolic reference is virtual, unreal, and rests on the combinatorial, associative logics of forming relationships between signs; and its mnemonic supports need only be cashed in and reconstructed in terms of their lower-level indexical and iconic supports when needed. Symbolic reference is powerful because it allows us to ignore most of the vast web of word–object, word–word, and object–object indexical associations and to make rapid calculations using the mnemonic shortcut of symbol–symbol relationships instead. This virtual character of symbolic reference is the source of its power and of its interest for our concerns with subject formation. For Deacon, symbols are neurological tokens. Like buoys indicating an otherwise invisible best course, they mark a specific associative path, which we reconstruct by following the implicit symbolic reference. Thus, it does not make sense to think of the symbols as located anywhere within the brain because they are relationships between tokens, not the tokens themselves; and even though specific neural connections may underlie these relationships, the symbolic function is not even constituted by a specific association, but by the virtual set of associations that are partially sampled in any one instance (Deacon 1997, 300).

Three points about symbolic reference are relevant to the present discussion. The power of symbolic reference is due to its *shared* character; it is largely *external* to the individual mind, being located in cultural systems and artifacts; and, as discussed earlier, it is *virtual.* Unlike the interpretation of icons and indices (a process uniquely personal and insular within each brain), symbolic representations are in part externally interpreted. Symbolic reference is at once a function of the whole web of referential relationships and of the whole network of users extended in space and time. If symbols ultimately derive their representational power not from the individual but from a particular society at a particular time, then a person's symbolic experience of consciousness is to some extent society dependent—it is borrowed, shared, and virtual. These aspects of symbolic reference thus lead to some provocative and counterintuitive peculiarities of subject formation:

> Consciousness of self in this way implicitly includes consciousness of other selves, and other consciousnesses can only be represented through the virtual reference created by symbols. The self that is the source of one's experience and intentionality, the self that is judged by itself as well as by others for its moral choices, the self that worries about its impending departure from the world, this self is a symbolic self. It is a final irony that it is the virtual not actual reference that symbols provide, which gives rise to this experience of self. This most undeniably real experience is a virtual reality. (Deacon 1997, 452)

Supported by the evidence from contemporary neuroscience of the neocortex's plasticity and its capacity to adapt to intricate challenges of a changing cognitive environment, Deacon argues that symbolic communication, rather than being rigidly hardwired to structures inside the brain, created a mode of extrabiological inheritance with a powerful and complex character and with an autonomous life. The individual mind is a hybrid product, partly biological and partly ecological in origin, shaped by a distributed external network whose properties are constantly changing. The leap to the symbolizing mind did not depend on a built-in, hard-wired tendency to symbolize reality. The direction of flow was *from* culture to the individual mind, from *outside to inside* (Vygotsky 1986). A number of theorists, including Andy Clark, have been interested in expanding this analysis to include media other than speech and writing, especially technologically mediated and computer-based forms of communication. It is to that argument I turn now.

In several books and pathbreaking articles, Andy Clark has developed a compelling thesis about what he calls an "extended mind" that provides the perfect bridge between Deacon's work on the evolution of symbolic reference and my considerations of media in the posthuman singularity. Clark radicalizes much of recent work in cognitive science that emphasizes the embodied character of cognition. Although agreeing with these new-wave cognitive scientists that mind is not simply a device to manipulate symbols in terms of formal rules and that higher cognition is built on a substrate of embodied perceptuomotor capacities, Clark takes the position of embodied cognition in quite radical directions. Proponents of distributed cognition defend the embodied character of cognition and support the notion that cognition makes heavy use of external props in the world, but they for the most part, Clark argues, treat the world and even to a certain extent the human senses as instruments of the brain. In this account, all genuinely cognitive activity, however richly supported by external material, social supports, and bodily input, goes on inside the brain and the central nervous system. Clark radicalizes this idea in moving from embodiment to cognitive extension. In the extended model of cognition, thinking and cognition depend directly and noninstrumentally on the ongoing work of the body and the extraorganismic environment: "According to EXTENDED, the actual local operations that realize certain forms of human cognizing include inextricable tangles of feedback, feed-forward, and feed-around loops: loops that promiscuously crisscross the boundaries of brain, body, and world. The local mechanisms of mind, if this is correct, are not all in the head. Cognition leaks out into body and the world" (2008, xxviii).

Clark and David Chalmers argue, in discussing the parity principle at the basis of their important paper on the extended mind, that when the human organism is linked with an external entity, creating a two-way interaction, the coupled system consisting of components both external and internal to the brain should be seen as a cognitive system in its own right. All the components, including the external components, play an active causal role and jointly govern behavior in the same way that cognition usually does. If by removing the external component the system's behavioral competence drops, the external component should be viewed as much a causal factor in the cognitive process, whether it is wholly in the head or not (1998, 8–9). In Clark and Chalmers's vision of cognition, the boundary between external and internal perception and action disappears, so that iPhones, calculators, computational aids, and less exotic cultural props (such as the tray of letters in a game of *Scrabble*) become components of the extended mind. In the years since they first published their paper (1998), Chalmers has become convinced that the extended mind is most likely extended even more widely than to the domain of beliefs and specifically cognitive processes. What about extended desires, reasoning, perception, imagination, and emotions? "I think there is no principled reason why the physical basis of consciousness could not be extended in a similar way. It is probably so extended in some possible worlds: one could imagine that some of the neuronal correlates of consciousness are replaced by a module on one's belt, for example. There may even be worlds where what is perceived in the environment is itself a direct element of consciousness" (2008, xiv; see also Chalmers 2006).

Brain–machine interfaces such as cochlear implants, artificial prosthetic hippocampus chips, retinal implants, and the Defense Advanced Research Projects Agency's "brain-in-the-loop" imaging systems for its Cognitive Threat Awareness Program are all examples of where the extended mind might be heading (Clark 2007). But less-invasive socially networked pervasive-computing systems are likely to have even more profound effects in creating the extended mind.

The extended-mind thesis treats human cognition as distributed and multiply hybrid, involving a complex interplay between internal biological and external nonbiological resources. On this model, then, thinking itself is deeply hybrid, involving internal biological resources as well as external agent–artifacts annexed and scaffolded as parts of cognitive processes. Included in these external elements are sociocultural artifacts, such as gestures, diagrams, external text, software applications, and more. But chief among these resources is language itself, which Clark and Chalmers consider the ultimate artifact (see Clark 2004). Language in this view is an external public code organized around arbitrary material symbols. Its primary role is to facilitate a coordinated coupling between the internal biological structures and both processes of the brain as well as external nonbiological resources. Here language is a crucial hybrid structure: it straddles the internal–external borderline, looking one moment like any other piece of the biological equipment and at the next like a particularly potent piece of external cognitive scaffolding (Clark 2006, 293). Language in this view is not a mirror of internal states, but rather a complementary external structure that carries the major burden of coordinating the coupling between external cognitive artifacts and processes and the brain's internal representational regime. Drawing on a variety of recent studies in cognitive science—by Lawrence Barsalou (1999), Jeffrey Elman (2004), Robert Clowes (2007a, 2007b; see also Clowes, Herrera, McGinnity, et al. 2007), and others—Clark argues that the symbolic environment impacts thought by activating internal representational resources and by allowing the stable structures of public language with its rich set of material symbols to act as a fulcrum for attention, memory, and control and as an anchor in the fluid stream of active thought and conceptualization.

The extended-mind treatment of language in terms of hybrid representational forms, coordination dynamics, and complementarity between biological and artifactual contributions provides an account of how the "entanglement" of media with the formation of human subjects that Hayles describes might take place in the new inscription practices of pervasively mediated computer environments. The key point in Clark's model is that language is fundamentally an external resource, and even processes of internal thought, silent rehearsal, and other forms of "off-line" linguaform representation for problem solving are internal recapitulations of the relevant external vehicles. Of course, there are internal representations in this model, but Clark and Chalmers part company with defenders of neural mentalese (Paul Churchland) or a hardwired language of thought (Jerry Alan Fodor). Stressing hybrid representational forms and coordination dynamics of a brain that is fundamentally a pattern-completing engine, they propose that external artifactual resources of the symbolic environment are co-opted without being replicated by special biological structures or translated into another internal code. Exposure to external material symbols and epistemic artifacts does not result in the installation of new internal representational forms in the brain or, as Daniel Dennett proposed, the installation of a new virtual serial machine via "myriad microsettings in the plasticity of the brain" (1991, 218–219). Rather, words, sentences, and other stable public symbolic forms are used without radically altering the brain's basic modes of representation and computation. External public symbol structures, in this view, complement the basic modes of operation and representation endemic to the biological brain. Clark notes that "the brain represents these structures, of course. But it does so in the same way it represents anything else. They do not reorganize neural routines in any way that is deeper or more profound than might occur, say, when we first learn to swim, or to play volleyball" (2004, 720).

What then about the posthuman? Are we transitioning to some new form of self adapted to our environment of ubiquitous-computing technology, and if so, how is this self assembled and transformed by the machinic processes of our technoscientific milieu? Since the rise of *Homo sapiens* between two hundred thousand to one hundred thousand years ago, there has been little change in brain size or, as far as can be determined, in brain structure. A critical contributing factor to the rapid cultural evolution that took off with *sapiens* and has continued at an ever-increasing pace since is the development of supplements to individual internal biological memory in the form of visuographic systems and external memory media, especially written records and other forms of symbolic storage (Donald 1991, 308–312). Rather than being limited by our neural architecture, these external material supports have only enhanced the symbolizing power of the mind. My point is that the recent development of the Web and the rise of ubiquitous computing happening in our own day only further accelerate a process that has defined and shaped human beings since that first singularity. From the perspective of the work in evolutionary cognitive science I have discussed, any change in the way information gets processed and represented inevitably constitutes a change in the cognitive economy of the subject—a difference in psychic architecture and ultimately of consciousness itself. Teasing out the implications of this notion, Brian Rotman argues that the medium of alphabetic writing introduced as silent collateral machinic effects an entire apparatus enabling practices, routines, patterns of movement and gestures, a well as kinematic, dynamic, and perceptual activities as part of the background conditions—in terms of Deleuze and Guattari, the a-signifying dimensions of the medium lying beneath the radar of the medium as part of its unconscious—giving rise to the lettered self, a privately enclosed, inward, and interiorized mind, structured by the linear protocols and cognitive processing that reading and writing demand (2008, 92). This model of the mind and of thinking is being challenged and displaced by the research in contemporary cognitive science, which is demonstrating not only that thinking is always social, culturally situated, and technologically mediated, but that individual cognition requires symbiosis with cognitive collectivities and external memory systems to happen in the first place. According to Rotman, the parallelization of multiple computational media resources puts into flux the relations between internal self and external other because it is a machinic implementation, not of individual linear thinking but of distributed biosocial phenomena, of collective thought processes and enunciations, that cannot be articulated solely on the level of an isolated, individual self. This parallelization's effects are to introduce into thought, into the self, into the "I" that engages its various forms parallelist behavior, knowledge, and agency that complicate and ultimately dissolve the idea of a monoidal self. As we spend more time in electronically mediated environments, engaging with massively parallel distributed computing processes that are merging ever more seamlessly with the material processes and technological affordances of our everyday world, a new parallelist and radically different self is in the process of displacing the single, serial, alphabeticized psyche: "Once, not so long ago, there was an absolute opposition of self and other: an 'I,' identical to itself, wholly present as an autonomous, indivisible, interior psyche against an external, amorphous collectivity of third persons outside the skin. . . . Now the 'I' bleeds outward into the collective, and the collective introjects, insinuates and internalizes itself within the me. What was privately interior and individual is invaded by the public, the historical, the social" (Rotman 2008, 99–100).

The infrastructure of ubiquitous computing envisioned two decades ago by Mark Weiser and John Seely Brown (Weiser 1991, 1994; Weiser and Brown 1995) offers the nutrient matrix for Clark's posthuman extended mind and Rotman's collective paraselves—namely, a world in which computation will disappear from the desktop and merge with the objects and surfaces of our ambient environment (Greenfield 2006). Rather than the situation in which the person takes work to a desktop computer, many tiny computing devices would be spread throughout the environment—in computationally enhanced walls, floors, pens, and desks—and seamlessly integrated into everyday life. As Ulrik Ekman cautions in the introduction to this volume, we are still far from realizing Weiser's vision of computing for the twenty-first century. Apart from the fact that nearly every piece of technology we use has one or more processors in it, we are far from reaching the transition point to ubiquitous computing when the majority of those processors are networked and addressable. But we are getting there. There have already been a number of milestones along the road to ubiquitous computing. Inspired by efforts from 1989–1995 at Olivetti and the Xerox Palo Alto Research Center to develop invisible interfaces interlinking coworkers with electronic badges and early radio-frequency identification (RFID) tags (Want, Fishkin, Gujar, et al. 1999; Want, Hopper, Falcão, et al. 1992; Want, Schilit, Adams, et al. 1995), the Hewlett-Packard Cooltown project (2000–2005) offered a prototype architecture for linking everyday physical objects to Web pages by tagging them with infrared beacons, RFID tags, and bar codes. Users carrying personal digital assistants (PDAs), tablets, and other mobile devices could read those tags to view Web pages about the world around them and engage services such as printers, radios, automatic call forwarding, and continually updated maps for finding like-minded colleagues in locations such as conference settings (Barton and Kindberg 2001).

Although systematically constructed ubiquitous cities based on the Cooltown model have yet to take hold, many of the enabling features of ubiquitous-computing environments are arising in ad hoc fashion, fueled primarily by growing mass consumption worldwide of social-networking applications and the wildly popular new-generation smartphones with advanced computing capabilities, cameras, accelerometers, and a variety of readers and sensors. In response to this trend and building on a decade of Japanese experience with Quick Response (QR) barcodes, in December 2009 Google dispatched approximately two hundred thousand stickers with bar codes for the windows of its "Favorite Places" in the United States so that people can use their smartphones to find out about them. Besides such consumer-oriented uses, companies such as Wal-Mart and other global retailers now routinely use RFID tags to manage industrial supply chains. These practices are now indispensable for hospital and other medical environments. Such examples are the tip of the iceberg of the growing number of pervasive-computing applications for the masses. The electronically mediated pervasive "brand zones" demanded by consumers—such as Apple Stores, Prada Epicenters, and the interior of your BMW, where movement, symbols, sound, and smell reinforce the brand message, turning shopping spaces and driving experiences into engineered synesthetic environments—are powerful aphrodisiacs for pervasive computing.

Even these path-breaking developments fall short of Weiser's vision, which saw people engaging multiple computational devices and systems simultaneously during ordinary activities without having to interact with a computer through mouse, keyboard, and desktop monitor and without necessarily being aware of doing so. In the years since these first experimental systems, rapid advances have taken place in mobile computing, including new smart materials capable of supporting small, light-weight, wearable mobile cameras and communications devices; many varieties of sensor technologies; RFID tags; physical storage on "motes" or "mu-chips," such as Hewlett-Packard's Memory Spot system, which permits storage of large media files on tiny chips instantly accessible by a PDA (McDonnell, Waters, Weng, et al. 2010); Bluetooth; numerous sorts of geographical information system (GIS) applications for location logging (e.g., Sony's PlaceEngine and LifeTagging system); and wearable biometric sensors (e.g., BodyMedia, SenseWear). To realize Weiser's vision, though, we must further augment these sorts of breakthroughs by getting the attention-grabbing gadgets, smartphones, and tablets out of our hands and begin interacting within computer-mediated environments the way we normally do with other persons and things. Here, too, recent advancements have been enormous, in particular advances in gesture- and voice-recognition technologies coupled with new forms of tangible interface and information displays (Rekimoto 2008).

Two prominent examples are the stunning gesture- and voice-recognition capabilities in the Microsoft Natal system for the Xbox 360 commercially available in 2010, which dispenses with a game controller altogether in favor of gesture recognition as game interface. But for our purposes the SixthSense prototype developed by Pranav Mistry and Pattie Maes at MIT points even more dramatically to an untethered fusion of the virtual and the real central to Weiser's vision (Mistry and Maes 2009a, 2009b, 2009c). The SixthSense prototype comprises a pocket projector, a mirror, and a camera built into a small mobile wearable device. Both the projector and the camera are connected to a mobile computing device in the user's pocket. The camera recognizes objects instantly, and the microprojector overlays the information on any surface, including the object itself or the user's hand. Then the user can access or manipulate the information using her fingers. The movements and arrangements of markers on the user's hands and fingers are interpreted into gestures that activate instructions for a wide variety of applications projected as application interfaces—search, video, social networking, basically the entire Web. SixthSense also supports multitouch and multiuser interaction. (See figures 33.1, 33.2, and 33.3.)

Thus far I have emphasized technologies that are enabling the rise of pervasive computing, but as Ekman cautioned in his introduction, not only is "ubiquitous computing" a technical thrust, but it is equally a sociocultural formation, an imaginary, and, as I have tried to indicate, a source of desire. From our perspective, its power

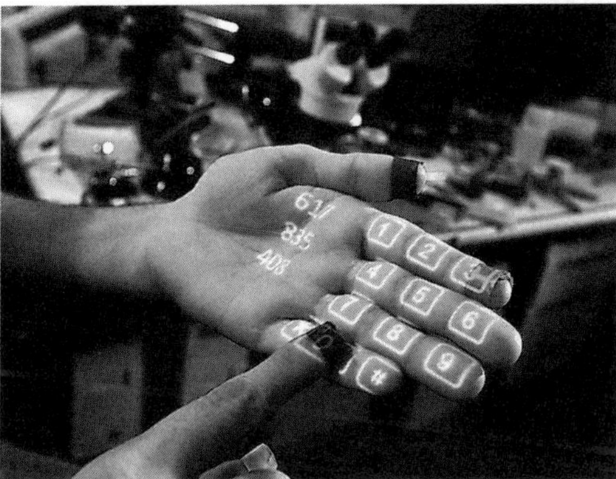

Figure 33.1
Active phone keyboard overlayed on user's hand, part of Pranav Mistry and Pattie Maes's SixthSense prototype. Photograph courtesy of Pranav Mistry.

Figure 33.2
Camera recognizes flight coupon and projects departure update on the ticket. Photograph courtesy of Pranav Mistry.

Figure 33.3
Camera recognizes news story from the Web and streams video to the page. Photograph courtesy of Pranav Mistry.

becomes transformative in permeating the affective domain, the machinic unconscious. Perhaps the most significant development driving this reconfiguration of affect are the phenomena of social networking and the use of "smartphones." More people are not only spending more time online but seeking to do it together with other wired "friends." Surveys by the Pew Internet & American Life Project report that between 2005 and 2008 use of social-networking sites by online American adults eighteen and older quadrupled from 8 to 46 percent and that 65 percent of teens ages twelve to seventeen used social-networking sites such as Facebook, MySpace, and LinkedIn (Lenhart, Ling, Campbell, et al. 2010; Lenhart, Purcell, Smith, et al. 2010). The Nielsen Company reports that 22 percent of all time spent online is devoted to social-network sites ("Social Networks/Blogs" 2010). Moreover, the new Internet generation wants to connect up in order to share: the Pew Internet & American Life Project has found that 64 percent of online teens ages twelve to seventeen have participated in a wide range of content-creating and sharing activities on the Internet: 39 percent of online teens share their own artistic creations online, such as artwork, photos, stories, or videos, and 26 percent remix content they find online into their own creations (Lenhart, Purcell, Smith, et al. 2010). The desire to share is not limited to text and video but is extending to data sharing of all sorts. Sleep, exercise, sex, food, mood, location, alertness, productivity, even spiritual well-being are being tracked and measured, shared and displayed. On MedHelp, one of the largest Internet forums for health information, users start more than thirty thousand new personal tracking projects every month. Foursquare, a geotracking application with about one million users, keeps a running tally of how many times players "check in" at every locale, automatically building a detailed diary of movements and habits; many users publish these data widely (Wolf 2010). Indeed, most Internet users, fully 60 percent of them, are not concerned about the amount of information available about them online, and most (61 percent) do not take steps to limit that information. Just 38 percent say they have taken steps to limit the amount of personal online information (Madden, Fox, Smith, et al. 2007). As Kevin Kelly points out, we are witnessing a feedback loop between new technologies and the creation of desire. The explosive development of mobile, wireless communications, widespread use of RFID tags, Bluetooth, embedded sensors, QR addressing, applications such as Shazam for snatching a link and downloading music in your ambient environment, GIS applications of all sorts, and social phones (such as Microsoft's Kin phones and the iPhone 4) that emphasize social networking is creating desire for open sharing, collaboration, and even communalism; above all, it is creating a new kind of mind (Kelly 2009a, 2009b). (See figures 33.4, 33.5, and 33.6.)

The reconfiguration of the human currently under way is not just about developing new technologies and applications that facilitate information management in pervasive computing. Our new collective minds are deeply rooted in an emerging corporeal axiomatic. This is the domain identified by Guattari as the machinic unconscious: a

Figure 33.4
Earthmine attaches location-aware applications (in this case streaming video) to specific real-world locations. Three-dimensional mapping, location-aware applications, and augmented-reality browsers. Photograph courtesy of Earthmine/Layar.

Figure 33.5
Earthmine enables three-dimensional objects to be overlaid on specific locations. Photograph courtesy of Earthmine/Layar.

Figure 33.6
Layar augmented-reality browser overlays information, graphics, and animation on specific locations. Photograph courtesy of Earthmine/Layar.

wide range of media ecologies, material practices, and social apparatuses for encoding and enforcing ways of behaving through routines, patterns of movement and gesture, as well as haptic and even neurological patterning and repatterning that facilitate specific behaviors and modes of action. In this model, technological media are conjoined with unconscious and preconscious cognitive activity to constitute subjects in particular, medium-specific ways. A body of empirical research spanning the past decade, too large to discuss here, has documented the range and extent of complex psychological functions that can transpire automatically, triggered by environmental events and without an intervening act of conscious will or subsequent conscious guidance (Bargh and Chartrand 1999; Bargh and Ferguson 2000; Hassin, Uleman, and Bargh 2005).

The affective domain is being reshaped by electronic media. Core elements of the domain of affect are unconscious social signals, primarily consisting of body language, facial expressions, and tone of voice. These social signals are not just a complement to conscious language; they form a separate communication network that influences behavior and can provide a window into our intentions, goals, and values. Much contemporary research in cognitive science and other areas of social psychology is reaffirming that humans are intensely social animals and that our behavior is much more a function of our social networks than anyone has previously imagined. The social circuits formed by the back-and-forth pattern of unconscious signaling between people shape much of our behavior in families, work groups, and larger organizations (Pentland 2007). Alexander Pentland and others are demonstrating that by paying careful attention to the patterns of signaling within a social network, it is possible to harvest tacit knowledge that is spread across the networked individuals. Whereas our hominid ancestors communicated face to face through voice, face, and hand gestures, our communications today are increasingly electronically mediated, our social groups dispersed and distributed. But this does not mean that affect has disappeared or somehow been stripped away. On the contrary, as the "glue" of social life, affect is present in the electronic social signals that link us together. The domain of affect is embedded within and deeply intertwined with these pervasive-computing networks. As we become more socially interlinked than ever through electronic media, the question is: Can the domain of affect be accessed, measured, perhaps understood, and possibly manipulated for better or worse?

Many researchers are developing systems to access, record, and map the domain of affect, including a suite of applications by Sony Interaction Laboratory director Jun Rekimoto (Rekimoto 2007, 2008; Rekimoto, Iwasaki, and Miyaki 2010; Rekimoto, Miyaki, and Ishizawa 2007; Rekimoto, Shionozaki, Sueyoshi, et al. 2006) and a multiperson awareness medium for connecting distant friends and family developed by Pattie Maes's group at MIT. For the past five years, Alexander Pentland and his students at the MIT Media Lab have been working on what they call a "socioscope" for accessing the affective domain in order to make new social-networked media smarter by analyzing prosody, gesture, and social context. The socioscope consists of three main parts: "smart" phones programmed to keep track of their owners' locations and their proximity to other people by sensing mobile tower and Bluetooth IDs; electronic badges that record the wearers' locations, ambient audio, and upper-body movement via a two-dimensional accelerometer; and a microphone with body-worn camera to record the wearers' context and with software that is used to extract audio "signals," specifically the exact timing of individuals' vocalizations and their amount of modulation (in both pitch and amplitude). Unlike in most speech or gesture research, in this project the goal is to measure and classify speaker interaction rather than to try to puzzle out the speakers' meanings or intentions.

One implementation of this technology is the Serendipity system, which is implemented on Bluetooth-enabled mobile phones and built on BlueAware, an application that scans for other Bluetooth devices in the user's proximity (Eagle and Pentland 2005). When Serendipity discovers a new device nearby, it automatically sends a message to a social-gateway server with the discovered device ID. If it finds a match, it sends a customized picture message to each user, introducing them to one another. The phone extracts the social-signaling features as a background process so that it can provide feedback to the user about how that person sounded and build a profile of the interactions the user had with that other person. The power of this system is that it can be used to create, verify, and better characterize relationships in online social-network systems, such as Facebook, MySpace, and LinkedIn. A commercial application of this technology is Citysense, which acquires millions of data points to analyze aggregate human behavior and to develop a live map of city activity, then learns about where each user likes to spend time, and processes the movements of other users with similar patterns. Citysense displays not only "where is everyone right now" on the user's PDA, but "where is everyone *like me* right now" (Sense Networks 2008).

This technology has a number of implications for quantifying the machinic unconscious of social signals. Enabling machines to know social context will enhance many forms of socially aware communication, and, indeed, the idea is to overcome some of the major drawbacks in our current use of computationally mediated forms of communication. For example, having a quantifiable model of social context will permit the mapping of group structures, the identification of enabling nodes and bottlenecks in information flows, and feedback on group interactions: Did you sound forceful during a negotiation? Did you sound interested when you were talking to your spouse? Did you sound like a good team member during the teleconference?

Both Brian Rotman and Brian Massumi are optimistic about what access to the affective domain might occasion for our emerging posthuman communal mind. For Massumi, better grasping the domain of affect will provide a basis for resistance and countertactics to the political-cultural functioning of the media (2002, 43–44). For Rotman (2008), the grammaticalization of gesture holds the prospect of a new order of body mediation, opening it to other desires and other semiotics. Alexander Pentland is equally optimistic, but his reflections on what quantification of the affective domain may offer sound more like a recipe for assimilation than resistance:

> By designing systems that are aware of human social signaling, and that adapt themselves to human social context, we may be able to remove the medium's message and replace it with the traditional messaging of face-to-face communication. Just as computers are disappearing into clothing and walls, the otherness of communications technology might disappear as well, leaving us with organizations that are not only more efficient, but that also better balance our formal, informal, and personal lives. Assimilation into the Borg Collective might be inevitable, but we can still make it a more human place to live. (2005, 39).

Computer scientist–novelist Vernor Vinge (1993) first outlined the notion that humans and intelligent machines are headed toward convergence, which he predicted would occur by 2030. John Johnston, in his essay for this volume (chapter 33), points out that Vinge also predicted a stage en route to the singularity where networked, embedded, and location-aware microprocessors provide the basis for a global panopticon (see also Vinge 2008 and Wallace 2006) and that Vinge has remained steadfastly positive about the possibilities presaged in this era. "Collaborations will thrive," Vinge writes. "Remote helping flourishes; wherever you go, local experts can make you as effective as a native. We experiment with a thousand new forms of teamwork and intimacy" (Vinge 2000). Such systems are not only on the immediate horizon, but already patented and commercially available in the prototypes coming from the labs and companies founded by scientists such as Pentland, Maes, and Rekimoto, each of whom is emphatic about the need to implement and ensure privacy in the potentially panoptic systems they have developed (Sense Networks 2008). We need not fear the singularity, but beware the panopticon.

References

Baldwin, James Mark. 1902. *Development and Evolution.* New York: Macmillan.

Baldwin, James Mark. 1895. "Consciousness and Evolution." *Science* 2:219–223.

Bargh, John A., and Tanya L. Chartrand. 1999. "The Unbearable Automaticity of Being." *American Psychologist* 54:462–479.

Bargh, John A., and Melissa J. Ferguson. 2000. "Beyond Behaviorism: On the Automaticity of Higher Mental Processes." *Psychological Bulletin* 126 (6): 925–945.

Barsalou, Lawrence W. 1999. "Perceptual Symbol Systems." *Behavioral and Brain Sciences* 22 (4): 577–660.

Barton, John, and Tim Kindberg. 2001. "The Cooltown User Experience." Available at http://www.hpl.hp.com/techreports/2001/HPL-2001-22.pdf. Accessed 22 June 2010.

Berger, Thomas W., Ashish Ahuja, Spiros H. Courellis, Samuel A. Deadwyler, Gopal Erinjippurath, Gregory A. Gerhardt, Ghassan Gholmieh, John J. Granacki, Robert Hampson, Min Chi Hsaio, et al. 2005. "Restoring Lost Cognitive Function." *Engineering in Medicine and Biology IEEE Magazine* 24 (5): 30–44.

Berger, Thomas W., and D. L. Glanzman, eds. 2005. *Toward Replacement Parts for the Brain: Implantable Biomimetic Electronics as Neural Prostheses.* Cambridge, MA: MIT Press.

Brooks, Rodney A. 2008. "I, Rodney Brooks, Am a Robot." *Spectrum, IEEE* 45 (6): 68–75.

Chalmers, David. 2008. "Foreword." In *Supersizing the Mind: Embodiment, Action, and Cognitive Extension,* by Andy Clark, ix–xvi. Oxford: Oxford University Press.

Chalmers, David. 2006. "Perception and the Fall from Eden." In *Perceptual Experience,* edited by Tamar Szabò Gendler and John Hawthorn, 49–125. Oxford: Oxford University Press.

Clark, Andy. 2008. *Supersizing the Mind: Embodiment, Action, and Cognitive Extension*. Oxford: Oxford University Press.

Clark, Andy. 2007. "Re-Inventing Ourselves: The Plasticity of Embodiment, Sensing, and Mind." *Journal of Medicine & Philosophy* 32 (3): 263–282.

Clark, Andy. 2006. "Material Symbols." *Philosophical Psychology* 19 (3): 291–307.

Clark, Andy. 2004. "Is Language Special? Some Remarks on Control, Coding, and Co-Ordination." *Language Sciences* 26 (6): 717–726.

Clark, Andy. 2003. *Natural-Born Cyborgs: Minds, Technologies, and the Future of Human Intelligence*. Oxford: Oxford University Press.

Clark, Andy, and David Chalmers. 1998. "The Extended Mind." *Analysis* 58 (1): 7–19.

Clowes, Robert. 2007a. "A Self-Regulation Model of Inner Speech and Its Role in the Organisation of Human Conscious Experience." *Journal of Consciousness Studies* 14:59–71.

Clowes, Robert. 2007b. "Semiotic Symbols and the Missing Theory of Thinking." *Interaction Studies* 8 (1): 105–124.

Clowes, Robert W., C. Herrera, M. McGinnity, and T. Ziemke. "How Words Become Cognitive." Paper presented at the Symposium on Language and Robots, Aveiro, Portugal, 10–12 December 2007. Available at http://www.eucognition.org/euCognition_2006-2008/network_actions/NA083-1_outcome.pdf. Accessed 22 June 2010.

Deacon, Terrence. 1997. *The Symbolic Species: The Co-Evolution of Language and the Brain*. New York: Norton.

Deleuze, Gilles, and Felix Guattari. 1987. *A Thousand Plateaus: Capitalism and Schizophrenia*. Translated by Brian Massumi. Minneapolis: University of Minnesota Press. Especially pp. 149–166, "How to Make Yourself a Body without Organs."

Dennett, Daniel. 1991. *Consciousness Explained*. New York: Little, Brown.

Donald, Merlin. 1991. *Origins of the Modern Mind: Three Stages in the Evolution of Culture and Cognition*. Cambridge, MA: Harvard University Press.

Eagle, Nathan, and Alexander Pentland. 2005. "Social Serendipity: Mobilizing Social Software." *Pervasive Computing, IEEE* 4 (2): 28–34.

Elman, Jeffrey L. 2004. "An Alternative View of the Mental Lexicon." *Trends in Cognitive Sciences* 8 (7): 301–306.

Greenfield, Adam. 2006. *Everyware: The Dawning Age of Ubiquitous Computing*. Berkeley, CA: New Riders.

Guattari, Felix. 1995. *Chaosmosis: An Ethicoaesthetic Paradigm*. Translated by Paul Bains and Julian Pefanis. Bloomington: Indiana University Press.

Hassin, Ran R., James S. Uleman, and John A. Bargh, eds. 2005. *The New Unconscious*. Oxford: Oxford University Press.

Hayles, N. Katherine. 2005. *My Mother Was a Computer: Digital Subjects and Literary Texts.* Chicago: University of Chicago Press.

Hayles, N. Katherine. 1999. *How We Became Posthuman: Virtual Bodies in Cybernetics, Literature, and Informatics.* Chicago: University of Chicago Press.

Kelly, Kevin. 2009a. "A New Kind of Mind." *The Edge*, January. Available at http://www.edge.org/q2009/q09_1.html. Accessed 22 June 2010.

Kelly, Kevin. 2009b. "The New Socialism: Global Collectivist Society Is Coming Online." *Wired* 17, no. 06. http://www.wired.com/culture/culturereviews/magazine/17-06/nep_newsocialism?currentPage=all. Accessed 22 June 2010.

Kittler, Friedrich. 1999. *Gramophone, Film, Typewriter.* Translated by Geoffrey Winthrop-Young and Michael Wutz. Stanford, CA: Stanford University Press.

Kittler, Friedrich. 1992. *Discourse Networks: 1800/1900.* Translated by Michael Metteer, with Chris Cullens. Stanford, CA: Stanford University Press.

Koch, Christoph, and Giulio Tononi. 2008. "Can Machines Be Conscious?" *Spectrum, IEEE* 45 (6): 55–59.

Lenhart, Amanda, Rich Ling, Scott Campbell, and Kristen Purcell. 2010. *Teens and Mobile Phones: Text Messaging Explodes as Teens Embrace It as the Centerpiece of Their Communication Strategies with Friends.* Pew Internet & American Life Project. Washington, DC: Pew Research Center. Available at http://pewinternet.org/Reports/2010/Teens-and-Mobile-Phones.aspx. Accessed 1 June 2010.

Lenhart, Amanda, Kristen Purcell, Aaron Smith, and Kathryn Zickuhr. 2010. *Social Media & Mobile Internet Use among Teens and Young Adults.* Pew Internet & American Life Project: Millennials. Washington, DC: Pew Research Center. Available at http://www.pewinternet.org/~/media//Files/Reports/2010/PIP_Social_Media_and_Young_Adults_Report_Final_with_toplines.pdf. Accessed 20 January 2011.

Madden, Mary, Susannah Fox, Aaron Smith, and Jessica Vitak. 2007. *Digital Footprints.* Pew Internet & American Life Project. Washington, DC: Pew Research Center. Available at http://www.pewinternet.org/Reports/2007/Digital-Footprints.aspx?r=1. Accessed 15 June 2010.

Massumi, Brian. 2002. *Parables for the Virtual: Movement, Affect, Sensation.* Durham, NC: Duke University Press.

McDonnell, J. T. Edward, John Waters, Weng Wah Loh, Robert Castle, Fraser Dickin, Helen Balinsky, and Keir Shepherd. 2010. "Memory Spot: A Labeling Technology." *Pervasive Computing, IEEE* 9 (2): 11–17.

Mistry, Pranav, and Pattie Maes. 2009a. "Sixth Sense." *TED India*, November. Available at http://www.pranavmistry.com/projects/sixthsense. Accessed 15 June 2010.

Mistry, Pranav, and Pattie Maes. 2009b. "Sixthsense: A Wearable Gestural Interface." In *ACM SIGGRAPH ASIA 2009 Sketches.* Yokohama: ACM. Available at http://delivery.acm.org/10.1145/

1670000/1667160/a11-mistry.pdf?key1=1667160&key2=0555827721&coll=&dl=GUIDE&CFID =67627046&CFTOKEN=34073892. Accessed 22 June 2010.

Mistry, Pranav, and Pattie Maes. 2009c. "Wuw—Wear Ur World: A Wearable Gestural Interface." In *Proceedings of the 27th International Conference: Extended Abstracts on Human Factors in Computing Systems*, 4111–4116. Boston: ACM.

Pentland, Alexander. 2007. "On the Collective Nature of Human Intelligence." *Adaptive Behavior* 15 (2): 189–198.

Pentland, Alexander. 2005. "Socially Aware Computation and Communication." *Computer* 38 (3): 33–40.

Rekimoto, Jun. 2008. "Organic Interaction Technologies: From Stone to Skin." *Communications of the ACM* 51 (6): 38–44.

Rekimoto, Jun. 2007. "From Folksonomy to Sensonomy: Convergence of Real World Activities and Onlinespace." Paper presented at the International Symposium on Applications and the Internet.

Rekimoto, Jun, Ken Iwasaki, and Takashi Miyaki. 2010. "Affectphone: A Handset Device to Present User's Emotional State with Warmth/Coolness." Paper presented at the B-Interface Workshop at BIOSTEC2010 (International Joint Conference on Biomedial Engineering Systems and Technologies), Valencia, Spain, 20–23 January.

Rekimoto, Jun, Takashi Miyaki, and Takaaki Ishizawa. 2007. "Lifetag: Wifi-Based Continuous Location Logging for Life Pattern Analysis." Third International Symposium on Location- and Context-Awareness, Oberpfaffenhofen, Germany, 20–21 September.

Rekimoto, Jun, Atsushi Shionozaki, Takahiko Sueyoshi, and Takashi Miyaki. 2006. "Placeengine: A Wifi Location Platform Based on Realworld-Folksonomy." Internet Conference 2006, 95–104.

Rotman, Brian. 2008. *Becoming Beside Ourselves: The Alphabet, Ghosts, and Distributed Human Being*. Durham, NC: Duke University Press.

Sense Networks. 2008. Available at http://www.sensenetworks.com. Accessed 22 June 2010.

"Social Networks/Blogs Now Account for One in Every Four and a Half Minutes Online." 2010. *NielsenWire*, June. Available at http://blog.nielsen.com/nielsenwire/global/social-media-accounts -for-22-percent-of-time-online. Accessed 15 June 2010.

Vinge, Vernor. 2008. "Signs of the Singularity." *Spectrum, IEEE* 45 (6): 76–82.

Vinge, Vernor. 2000. "The Digital Gaia." *Wired* 8 (1) (January). Available at http://www.wired.com/ wired/archive/8.01/forward.html. Accessed 21 June 2010.

Vinge, Vernor. 1993. "The Coming Technological Singularity." Presentation at the Vision-21 Symposium, NASA Lewis Research Center and the Ohio Aerospace Institute, Cleveland, 30–31 March.

Vinge, Vernor. 2006. "Inside Out" Keynote Address at the 2006 Austin Game Conference, Austin, Texas, 8 September. Blogged by Mark Wallace: "Vernor Vinge Paints the Future at AGC: Transcript of Vinge's Keynote Address at the 2006 Austin Game Conference." *3pointD.com: The Metaverse and 3D Web, as Blogged by Mark Wallace and Friends.* Available at http://www.3pointd.com/20060908/vernor-vinge-paints-the-future-at-agc. Accessed 21 June 2010.

Vygotsky, Lev. 1986. *Thought and Language.* Translated by Alex Kozulin. Cambridge, MA: MIT Press.

Want, Roy, Kenneth P. Fishkin, Anuj Gujar, and Beverly L. Harrison. 1999. "Bridging Physical and Virtual Worlds with Electronic Tags." In *Proceedings of the ACM Conference on Human Factors in Computing Systems, CHI '99,* 370–377. New York: ACM.

Want, Roy, Andy Hopper, Veronica Falcão, and Jonathan Gibbons. 1992. "The Active Badge Location System." *ACM Transactions Information Systems* 10 (1): 91–102.

Want, Roy, Bill N. Schilit, Norman I. Adams, Karin Petersen, and David Goldberg. 1995. "An Overview of the Parctab Ubiquitous Computing Experiment." *Personal Communications, IEEE* 2 (6): 28–43.

Weiser, Mark. 1994. "Creating the Invisible Interface." Keynote presentation. In *Proceedings of the 7th Annual ACM Symposium on User Interface Software and Technology* (UIST '94), New York. Available at http://doi.acm.org/10.1145/192426.192428. Accessed 14 March 2012.

Weiser, Mark. 1991. "The Computer for the Twenty-First Century." *Scientific American* 265 (3): 94–104.

Weiser, Mark, and John Seely Brown. 1995. "Designing Calm Technology." Available at http://sandbox.xerox.com/hypertext/weiser/calmtech/calmtech.htm. Accessed 14 August 2009.

Wolf, Gary. 2010. "The Data Driven Life." *New York Times,* 26 April (online) and 2 May (in print).

Contributors

Inke Arns has been artistic director of Hartware MedienKunstVerein, Dortmund, Germany (http://www.hmkv.de), since 2005. She has worked as an independent curator and writer specializing in media art, Net cultures, and eastern Europe. Since 1993, she has curated exhibitions in Germany, Great Britain, Hong Kong, Kosovo, Poland, Serbia, Slovenia, and Switzerland. Recent exhibitions include History Will Repeat Itself (2007–2008) and Awake Are Only the Spirits (2009–2010). She lived in Paris (1982–1986); pursued Slavic studies, eastern European studies, political science, and art history in Berlin and Amsterdam (1988–1996); and in 2004 received her Ph.D. at Humboldt University, Berlin. Arns has held teaching positions at universities and art academies in Berlin, Leipzig, Rotterdam, Zurich, and Dortmund. She has lectured and published internationally. See her Web site at http://www.inkearns.de.

Joseph Auner is chair and professor of music at Tufts University. His research focuses on the Second Viennese School, Weimar Berlin, and music and technology. His writings on technology include "Sing It for Me: Posthuman Ventriloquism in Recent Popular Music" and "Making Old Machines Speak: Images of Technology in Recent Music". He is author of *A Schoenberg Reader* (2003) and *Twentieth- and Twenty-First-Century Music* (forthcoming) and coeditor of *Postmodern Music/Postmodern Thought,* with Judy Lochhead (2001), and *Cambridge Companion to Schoenberg,* with Jennifer Shaw (2010).

Jay David Bolter is the Wesley Chair of New Media at the Georgia Institute of Technology. He is the author of *Turing's Man* (1984); *Writing Space: The Computer, Hypertext, and the History of Writing* (1991; 2nd ed., 2001); *Remediation,* with Richard Grusin (1999); and *Windows and Mirrors,* with Diane Gromala (2003). With Professor Blair MacIntyre, he is helping to build augmented-reality and mobile-technology systems for games and to stage dramatic and narrative experiences for entertainment and informal education.

Gernot Böhme studied physics, mathematics, and philosophy, completing his PhD in 1965 in Hamburg and his habilitation in 1972 in Munich. Böhme was research fellow at the Max-Planck-Institute (1969–1977) and in Starnberg (1977–2002). He was professor of philosophy at the Technical University of Darmstadt from 1997 to 2001 and a speaker at the Graduate School Technification and Society. Since 2005, he has been director of the Institut für Praxis der Philosophie (see http://www.ipph-darmstadt.de). Böhme's main fields of research are classical philosophy (Kant, Plato), social studies of science, philosophical anthropology, philosophy of nature, aesthetics, ethics, Goethe, and theory of time. He is coeditor of *The Knowledge Society*, with N. Stehr (1986) and *Dark Medicine: Rationalizing Unethical Medical Research*, with William R. LaFleur and Susumu Shimazono (2007); coauthor of *Finalization in Science: The Social Orientation of Scientific Progress*, with W. v.d. Daele, R. Hohlfeld, W. Krohn, and W. Schäfer (1983); and author of *Coping with Science* (1992) and *Ethics in Context: The Art of Dealing with Serious Questions* (2001).

Michael Bull is reader in the Media and Film Department at the University of Sussex. He is the author of *Sounding Out the City: Personal Stereos and the Management of Everyday Life* (2000) and *Sound Moves: iPod Culture and Urban Experience* (2007). He is coeditor of *The Auditory Culture Reader*, with Les Back (2003) and is a founding editor and managing editor of the journal *The Senses and Society*. He teaches postgraduate courses on media technology and everyday life and on media, music, and culture.

Tom Cohen is the founding codirector of the Institute on Critical Climate Change associated with the University at Albany, State University of New York. His books include *Ideology and Inscription* (1998) and *Hitchcock's Cryptonymies*, 2 vols. (2005). He is coeditor with Henry Sussman of *An Atlas of Critical Climate Change* (2011) and coauthor of *Theory and the Disappearing Future*, with J. Hillis Miller and Claire Colebrook (2011).

Söke Dinkla is an art historian and works as a curator and author in the fields of contemporary arts and electronic media. Since 2007, she has been the artistic director of the European Capital of Culture Office in Duisburg. She studied art history, literature, ethnic studies, and biology at universities in Kiel, Hamburg, and Bielefeld. She received her doctorate from the University of Hamburg with a thesis on the history and theory of interactive digital arts. She is the author of several books focusing on the interplay between contemporary art and digital culture, including: *Pioniere Interaktiver Kunst von 1970 bis heute* (1997); *Dance and Technology: Moving towards Media Productions*, with Martina Leeker (2002); *Duane Michals: The Theatre of Real Life* (2004); *Am Rande des Lichts* (2004); *PubliCity: Constructing the Truth* (2006); and *Paradoxes of the Public* (2007). From 1996 to 2000, while curator at the Wilhelm Lehmbruck Museum in Duisburg, she organized exhibitions such as Connected Cities: Processes of Art in the Urban Network (1999) and Under the Skin: Biological Transformations in Contemporary Art (2001). She has also curated public art projects such as Jenny Holzer: Xenon for Duisburg (2004), Les Levine: Celebrate Your Self, PubliCity:

Constructing the Truth (2006), and Paradoxes of the Public (2007) in Duisburg. From 2005 to 2007, she worked as a curator for public art for Ruhr's 2010 application to be designated the cultural capital of Europe.

Ulrik Ekman is associate professor at the Department of Arts and Cultural Studies, University of Copenhagen. He is the head and coordinator of the Nordic and internationally oriented research network Culture of Ubiquitous Information, which has more than 150 participating researchers. In addition to editing the present volume, Ekman is also currently writing a book on the aesthetics of contemporary media art and culture concerning the increased import of haptic technics and spatiotemporality for our life form. At the University of Copenhagen, he teaches courses in media art, design and aesthetics, Net culture, applied Web design, cybernetics, and the critical philosophy of technology. Ekman has published approximately twenty research articles relating to these fields. More on his research and teaching can be found at http://artsandculturalstudies.ku.dk/staff/?id=37501&vis=medarbejder.

Kathryn Farley obtained a doctorate in performance studies from Northwestern University in 2007, writing a dissertation that investigated the use of digital-media tools in performing-arts education at the postsecondary level. Currently a Marion L. Brittain Postdoctoral Fellow at the Georgia Institute of Technology, she instructs classes in multimodal communication that focus on technology-mediated performance events. A digital portfolio of Farley's academic and artistic work can be found at http://www.kathrynfarley.org.

Arild Fetveit is associate professor in the Department for Media, Cognition, and Communication, University of Copenhagen, Denmark. He has published in the fields of reception studies, reality TV, and the digitalization of film and photography. He is currently involved in two book projects: one about the discursive possibilities between documentary and fiction film and the other about the digitalization of photographical images. He is an associate member of the Nomadikon project situated at the University of Bergen, Norway.

Matthew Fuller is author of various books including *Media Ecologies, materialist energies in art and technoculture*; *Behind the Blip, essays on the culture of software*; and the forthcoming *Elephant & Castle*. With Usman Haque he is coauthor of *Urban Versioning System v1.0*, and with Andrew Goffey he is coauthor of the forthcoming *Evil Media*. Fuller is also editor of *Software Studies, a lexicon*, and coeditor of the new Software Studies series from MIT Press. He is involved in a number of projects in art, media, and software and works at the Centre for Cultural Studies, Goldsmiths, University of London. See his Web site at http://www.spc.org/fuller.

Anne Galloway is senior lecturer of design research in the School of Design, Victoria University of Wellington, New Zealand, where she draws on her background in sociology and anthropology to investigate the intersections of technology, space, and culture. Since completing a PhD on urban computing and locative media, she has been exploring what might be called "rural computing"—or how pervasive computing stands to reshape the production and consumption of New Zealand merino wool. At Victoria University, Galloway teaches courses in design anthropology and cultures of design, which allows her to combine her interests in material culture, everyday life, cultural theory, and qualitative research methods. More on her research and teaching can be found at http://www.designculturelab.org and http://www.purselipsquarejaw.org.

Hans Ulrich Gumbrecht is the Albert Guérard Professor in Literature at Stanford University in the comparative literature, French, and Italian departments (since 1989). He is also Professeur Associé à l'Université de Montréal, Professeur attaché au Collège de France, and a fellow of the American Academy of Arts and Sciences. Before coming to Stanford, he studied romance philology, German literature, and philosophy and sociology in Germany, Spain, and Italy (finishing a PhD in 1971 and the habilitation in 1974, both at Universität Konstanz). His main areas of teaching and research are the histories of French, Spanish, and Italian literatures (especially that of the Middle Ages, the eighteenth century, and the first half of the twentieth century); the history of literary Criticism and the humanities; and the history of Western thought since its classical origins. He has received honorary doctorates from the University of Montevideo, l'Université de Montréal, the University of St. Petersburg, the University of Lisbon, and, in Germany, Universität Siegen, Universität Greifswald, and Universität Marburg. His most recent books are *In Praise of Athletic Beauty* (2006) and *Geist und Materie—Was Ist Leben? Zur Aktualität von Erwin Schrödinger* (2008). Forthcoming later this year are a collection of essays on "becoming American" and a book on *Stimmung*, "mood" or "climate."

Mark Hansen teaches cultural theory and comparative media studies in the Program in Literature and the Department of Art, Art History, and Visual Studies at Duke University, where he is also affiliated with the Program in Information Science + Information Society, Arts of the Moving Image, and the Visual Studies Initiative. Hansen is author of *Embodying Technesis: Technology beyond Writing* (2000), *New Philosophy for New Media* (MIT Press, 2004), and *Bodies in Code* (2006) as well as of numerous essays on cultural theory, contemporary literature, and media. He has coedited *The Cambridge Companion to Merleau-Ponty*, with Taylor Carman (2005). Two recent works are *Critical Terms for Media Studies* (2010), a resource for the study of media coedited with W. J. T. Mitchell (2010), and *Emergence and Embodiment: New Essays on Second-Order Cybernetics* (2009), coedited with Bruce Clarke, a volume exploring the continuing relevance of second-order cybernetics in our highly complexified contemporary technoscientific culture. Hansen is currently completing a study of the technicity of time consciousness that explores the transduction of time and media in relation to the computational and neuroscientific revolutions.

N. Katherine Hayles is professor of literature, information studies, and information science at Duke University, writes and teaches on the relation of science, technology, and literature in the twentieth and twenty-first centuries. Her book *How We Became Posthuman: Virtual Bodies in Cybernetics, Literature, and Informatics* (1999) won the Rene Wellek Prize for the Best Book in Literary Theory 1998–1999, and her book *Writing Machines* (MIT Press, 2002) won the Suzanne Langer Award for Outstanding Scholarship. Other recent books include *My Mother Was a Computer: Digital Subjects and Literary Texts* (2005) and *Electronic Literature: New Horizons for the Literary* (2008). She is currently completing a manuscript entitled "How We Think: The Transforming Power of Digital Technologies."

Larissa Hjorth is artist, digital ethnographer, and senior lecturer in the games and digital-art programs at RMIT University. Since 2000, Hjorth has been researching the gendered customizing of mobile communication, new media literacy, gaming, and virtual communities in the Asia-Pacific, as discussed in her book *Mobile Media in the Asia-Pacific* (2009). In 2007, she co-convened the international "Mobile Media" conference with Gerard Goggin (see http://www.mobilemedia2007.net) and the "Interactive Entertainment (IE)" conference with Esther Milne (see http://www.ie.rmit.edu.au). She recently coedited two Routledge anthologies, *Gaming Cultures and Place in Asia-Pacific*, with Dean Chan (2009) and *Mobile Technologies: From Telecommunication to Media*, with Gerard Goggin (2008). Since 2009, she has had an Australian Research Council fellowship to explore the role of online communities in the Asia-Pacific region (Tokyo, Seoul, Shanghai, Singapore, Manila, and Melbourne).

John Johnston is professor of English and comparative literature at Emory University, where he teaches courses on literature and science, media theory, and technology. He is the author of *Carnival of Repetition: Gaddis's Recognitions and Postmodern Theory* (1990), *Information Multiplicity: American Fiction in the Age of Media Saturation* (1998), and *The Allure of Machinic Life: Cybernetics, Artificial Life, and the New AI* (MIT Press, 2008). He is also the editor of *Literature, Media, Information Systems* (1997), a collection of essays by media theorist Friedrich Kittler. He is currently working on a study of networks and new vitalisms.

Susan Kozel is a dancer, choreographer, and philosopher. She is professor of new media with the MEDEA Collaborative Media Institute at Malmö University, Sweden, and directs Mesh Performance Practices (see http://www.meshperformance.org/default.html). She has published and performed widely. Her books include *Closer: Performance, Technologies, Phenomenology* (MIT Press, 2007) and *Social Choreographies: A Corporeal Aesthetics of Mobile Media* (forthcoming). Her collaborative performances and installations include the Technologies of Inner Spaces series (*Immanence* [2005], *Other Stories* [2007], and *The Yellow Memory* [2009]), *Whisper[s]* wearable computing (2002–2005), and *trajets* (2000–2007). In her role as senior project researcher with the Intuition in Creative Processes initiative based at the Theatre Academy in Helsinki, she is experimenting with social-networking applications for improvised performance (IntuiTweet) and with expanding an embodied methodological basis for artistic research.

Timothy Lenoir is university professor and the Kimberly Jenkins Chair for New Technologies in Society at Duke University. In addition to publishing several books and articles on the history of biomedical science from the nineteenth century to the present, he has also been involved in digital archiving and Web-based collaborations, including projects with Stanford University, MIT, and the National Science Foundation–sponsored Center for Nanotechnology in Society at the University of California, Santa Barbara. His current research centers on the use of text mining and visualization tools for mapping the recent history of bio- and nanotechnology, the use of computers and digital imaging in biomedical research, and the history of interactive simulations and videogames. Lenoir also teaches courses on interactive simulation and video games. As recipient of the MacArthur Foundation Digital Millennium Award, Lenoir recently completed work on Virtual Peace (see http://www.virtualpeace.org), a multiplayer, first-person simulation environment for students and humanitarian groups and workers in the field of peace and conflict resolution. He is currently working on *Emergence*, a new massively multiplayer online game foregrounding diplomacy and cooperation instead of violence and competition, set in a postapocalyptic future and designed as an interactive ecology in which players help themselves by helping others. The game is being built in a partnership between Lenoir's lab, the Jenkins Collaboratory at Duke, and the game company Virtual Heroes, based in Durham, North Carolina.

Blair MacIntyre is an associate professor in the School of Interactive Computing at the Georgia Institute of Technology. He directs the Augmented Environments Lab, where the research focuses on the design and implementation of interactive mixed-reality and augmented-reality environments. The current focus of his work is educational, entertainment, and gaming applications of augmented- and mixed-reality environments, especially those that use personal displays (i.e., ranging from see-through head-worn displays to video-mixed handheld displays) to directly augment users' perception of their environment. He received a PhD in computer science from the Department of Computer Science at Columbia University in 1999.

Lev Manovich is the author of *Software Takes Command* (2008), *Soft Cinema: Navigating the Database* (MIT Press, 2005), and *The Language of New Media* (MIT Press, 2001), which is hailed as "the most suggestive and broad ranging media history since

Marshall McLuhan." Manovich has written one hundred articles, which have been reprinted more than three hundred times in more than thirty countries. He is a professor in the Visual Arts Department at the University of California, San Diego, a director of the Software Studies Initiative at the California Institute for Telecommunications and Information Technology, and a visiting professor at De Montfort University in the United Kingdom and the European Graduate School in Switzerland.

Malcolm McCullough is associate professor of architecture at the University of Michigan. He has also served on the faculty of Carnegie Mellon University and Harvard University. He has written two widely read books on architecture and interaction design, *Digital Ground* (2004) and *Abstracting Craft* (1996), and has engaged in speaking and editorial review across a wide range of disciplines, from urbanism to applied arts to interaction design.

Michael Nitsche holds a PhD from the University of Cambridge and is currently associate professor at the Georgia Institute of Technology, where he directs the Digital World and Image Group. His group investigates interconnections between digital and physical spaces, combining architectural, film studies, and performance studies approaches. His publications include numerous journal articles, conference papers, and the book *Video Game Spaces* (MIT Press, 2009).

Dietmar Offenhuber is a media artist with a background in architecture and interests in spatial concepts of cognition, representation, and behavior. He holds a diploma engineer degree in architecture from the University of Technology in Vienna and a master's in media arts and sciences from the MIT Media Lab. He was a founding member of the Ars Electronica Futurelab, a Japan Foundation Fellow at the Institute of Advanced Media Arts and Sciences in Gifu, Japan, and a professor of animation at the University of Applied Sciences in Hagenberg, Austria. He has also worked as a researcher at the MIT Media Lab, a professor at the Art University, Linz, and key researcher at the Ludwig Boltzmann Institute for Media Art Research. He is currently a researcher and PhD candidate at the Senseable City Lab, Department of Urban Studies, MIT.

Christiane Paul is the director of the media studies graduate programs and associate professor of media studies at the New School, New York, and adjunct curator of new media arts at the Whitney Museum of American Art. She has written extensively on new media arts and has lectured internationally on art and technology. An expanded new edition of her book *Digital Art* (2003) was published in spring 2008, and her edited anthology *New Media in the White Cube and Beyond: Curatorial Models for Digital Art* was published in 2008. At the Whitney Museum, she has curated extensively, including the shows Profiling (2007) and Data Dynamics (2001); the Net art selection for the 2002 Whitney Biennial; the online exhibition CODeDOC (2002) for artport, the Whitney Museum's online portal to Internet art, for which she is responsible; as well as *Follow Through* by Scott Paterson and Jennifer Crowe (2005). Paul previously taught in the Computer Arts Department at the School of Visual Arts in New York (1999–2008); the Digital+Media Department of the Rhode Island School of Design (2005–2008); as well as the San Francisco Art Institute and the Center of New Media at the University of California, Berkeley (2008).

Simon Penny is professor of arts and engineering at the University of California, Irvine. His work has included artistic practice, technical research, theoretical writing, pedagogy, and institution building in digital cultural practices, embodied interaction, and interactive art. He makes interactive and robotic installations utilizing novel sensor arrays and custom machine-vision systems that address critical issues arising around enactive and embodied interaction and that are informed by traditions of practice in the arts—including sculpture, video art, installation, and performance—as well as by ethology, cognitive science, phenomenology, human–computer interaction, ubiquitous computing, robotics, critical theory, cultural studies, media studies, and science and technology studies.

Mette Sandbye is associate professor at the Department of Arts and Cultural Studies, University of Copenhagen. Her main research areas are the history, theory, and aesthetics of photography. She was previously the head of the Nordic Network for the History and Aesthetics of Photography (2003–2007), and she has been an art critic since 1995. She has published several books on art photography since the 1960s, and she edited the first *History of Danish Photography* (*Dansk Fotografihistorie*, 2004). Her current research topic is family photography from the 1960s to the recent digital development.

Torben Sangild, with a PhD in modern cultural studies, is a doctoral fellow at the Department of Arts and Cultural Studies, University of Copenhagen. Sangild is also a freelance writer, art critic, and the author of *The Aesthetics of Noise* (2003) and *Objective Sensibility* (2004) (both in Danish) as well as of numerous articles on contemporary art, music, philosophy, and auditory culture. Among them are "The Aesthetics of Noise" (2002), "Sensitive Electronics" (2002), "Noise—Three Musical Gestures" (2004), and "Glitch: The Beauty of Malfunction" (2004). He is currently involved in a research project concerning signature tunes and jingles used in national public radio.

Ulrik Schmidt is a PhD fellow at the Institute for English, Germanic, and Romance Studies, University of Copenhagen, and is working on a project on ambient aesthetics in art and everyday culture. Schmidt's main research interests are cross-aesthetic issues within modern and contemporary art, film, music, and media culture. Among his publications are *The Aesthetics of Minimalism* (2007, in Danish) and *Keaton and the Masses* (2009, in Danish).

Roberto Simanowski is a German scholar of literature and media studies and editor of *dichtung-digital.org,* a journal on digital aesthetics that he founded in 1999. Simanowski graduated in German literature and history at the University of Jena in 1996, worked at the University of Göttingen (1997–1998), was research fellow at Harvard University (1998–2000) and the University of Washington (2001–2002), and served as guest professor at the Department of Media Studies at the University of Jena (2002–2003). Beginning in 2003, he taught German culture and digital aesthetics at Brown University. Since 2010, Simanowski has been a professor in the Media Studies Department, University of Basel. He has edited several books on German culture and digital literature, including *Die Verwaltung des Abenteuers* (1998), *Interfictions: Vom Schreiben im Netz* (2002), *Digitale Medien in der Erlebnisgesellschaft: Kultur–Kunst–Utopien* (2008), *Digital Art and Meaning* (2011), and *Textmaschinen, Kinetische Poesie, Interaktive Installationen: Zum Verstehen von Kunst in digitalen Medien* (forthcoming).

Bernard Stiegler is a philosopher, doctor at the École des hautes études en sciences sociales, director of the Institut de recherche et d'innovation du Centre Pompidou, associate professor at the Université de Compiègne, and professor at the University of London, Goldsmiths College. He served as the director of the Institut national de l'audiovisuel from 1996 to 1999, then as the director of the Institut de recherche et coordination acoustique/musique from 2001 to 2006. He has since then founded the Institut de recherche et d'innovation as well as Ars Industrialis in 2005 with philosopher and art critic Georges Collins, philosophers Marc Crépon and Catherine Perret, and Caroline Stiegler, a lawyer specializing in legal issues centering on business and intellectual property. Stiegler is the author of twenty-five works, including *La technique et le temps* (3 vols., 1994–2001); *Passer à l'acte: Aimer, s'aimer, nous aimer* (2003); *De la misère symbolique,* 2 vols. (2004), *Mécréance et discrédit,* 3 vols. (2004–2006); *Prendre soin: De la jeunesse et des générations* (2008); several texts on Europe, political philosophy, and political economy; as well as three volumes in collaboration with Ars Industrialis (most recently, *Pour en finir avec la mécroissance* [2009]). A number of Stiegler's works have been translated into English, German, Italian, Spanish, Portuguese, Dutch, and Japanese.

Kristin Veel holds a postdoctoral position at the Department of Arts and Cultural Studies, University of Copenhagen. She is interested in particular in issues of information overload and surveillance and is currently working on a book on the cultural history of surveillance narratives. She teaches courses on literature, digital culture, and the culture of surveillance at the University of Copenhagen. She obtained her PhD in literature and information technology from the German Department at the University of Cambridge in 2008 and subsequently published the book *Narrative Negotiations: Information Structures in Literary Fiction* (2009). Among her other publications are "The Irreducibility of Space: Labyrinths, Cities, Cyberspace" (2003) and "Virtual Memory in Günter Grass's *Im Krebsgang*" (2004).

Bo Kampmann Walther is associate professor at the Center for Media Studies, University of Southern Denmark. He has written, taught, and lectured extensively on new media, computer games, and (mediated) sports. Read more about him at http://www1.sdu.dk/hum/bkw.

Jacob Wamberg is professor of art history at Aarhus University in Denmark. He works on evolutionistic theories of visual art and culture and their relations to nature and technology. His publications include "Interface or Interlace? Or How Art Is Mediated in Augmented Reality," with Lone Koefoed Hansen (2005), the collected volume *Art & Alchemy* (2006), and *Landscape as World Picture: Tracing Cultural Evolution in Images*, 2 vols. (2009).

Bernadette Wegenstein, an Austrian linguist and filmmaker, received her PhD in romance languages and literatures from Vienna University in 1998. She is currently research professor in the Department of German and Romance Languages and Literatures at Johns Hopkins University, where she also directs the Center of Advanced Media Studies. Her first book, on the representation of AIDS in the European media, *Die Darstellung von AIDS in den Medien*, appeared in 1998. She is also the author of *Getting under the Skin: Body and Media Theory* (MIT Press, 2006), *The Cosmetic Gaze: Body Modification and the Construction of Beauty* (MIT Press, forthcoming), the edited volume *Reality Made Over: The Culture of Reality Television Makeover Shows* (2008), and numerous articles on body criticism, performance art, and film theory. In 2006, she formed her own Baltimore-based production company, Waystone Productions LLC, to produce and direct her first feature-length documentary film on the technologies and culture of bodily makeover, *Made Over in America* (2007). She is currently producing the documentary *Wien—Baltimore* (in collaboration with Austrian director Lukas Stepanik), portraying Viennese Holocaust survivor Leo Bretholz and his efforts to educate Baltimore youth on the Holocaust.

Mitchell Whitelaw is an academic, writer, and artist with interests in new media art and culture, especially generative systems and data aesthetics. His work has appeared in such journals as *Leonardo*, *Digital Creativity*, *Fibreculture*, and *Senses and Society*. In 2004, his work on A-life art was published in the book *Metacreation: Art and Artificial Life* (MIT Press, 2004). His current work spans generative art and design, digital materiality, and data visualization. He is an associate professor in the Faculty of Arts and Design at the University of Canberra, where he leads the master's in digital design program.

Index